For my friends in the culinary world,
an endless source of inspiration

Copyright © 1993 by Faye Levy
All rights reserved.

Warner Books, Inc., 1271 Avenue of the Americas, New York, NY 10020

 A Time Warner Company

Printed in the United States of America
First Printing: October 1993
10 9 8 7 6 5 4 3 2 1

Library of Congress Cataloging-in-Publication Data

Levy, Faye.
  Faye Levy's international vegetable cookbook : over 300
sensational recipes from Argentina to Zaire and artichokes to
zucchini [Faye Levy].
    p.   cm.
  Includes index.
  ISBN 0-446-51719-4
  1. Cookery (Vegetables)   2. Cookery, International.   3. Low-fat
diet—Recipes.   4. Quick and easy cookery.   I. Title.   II. Title:
International vegetable cookbook.
TX801.L484   1993
641.6′5—dc20   92-51034
                                                  CIP

Book design by Giorgetta Bell McRee

FAYE LEVY'S INTERNATIONAL VEGETABLE COOKBOOK

OTHER BOOKS BY FAYE LEVY

Faye Levy's International Chicken Cookbook
Faye Levy's International Jewish Cookbook
Fresh from France: Dessert Sensations
Fresh from France: Dinner Inspirations
Fresh from France: Vegetable Creations
Sensational Pasta
Sensational Chocolate
Classic Cooking Techniques
La Cuisine du Poisson (in French, with Fernand Chambrette)
Faye Levy's Favorite Recipes (in Hebrew)
French Cooking Without Meat (in Hebrew)
French Desserts (in Hebrew)
French Cakes, Pastries and Cookies (in Hebrew)
The La Varenne Tour Book

FAYE LEVY'S INTERNATIONAL VEGETABLE COOKBOOK

Over 300 Sensational Recipes from Argentina to Zaire and Artichokes to Zucchini

Faye Levy

WARNER BOOKS

A Time Warner Company

CONTENTS

ACKNOWLEDGMENTS *vii*

INTRODUCTION *ix*

1 · Why and How to Eat More Vegetables *1*

2 · Cooking Vegetables Around the World *3*

3 · Vegetable Cooking Techniques *11*

4 · Artichokes *19*

5 · Asparagus *31*

6 · Green Beans *45*

7 · Dried Beans and Shell Beans *59*

8 · Beets *81*

9 · Broccoli and Cauliflower *89*

10 · Brussels Sprouts *109*

11 · Cabbage *117*

12 · Carrots and Parsnips *131*

13 · Celery, Celery Root, and Fennel *143*

14 · Corn *153*

15 · Cucumbers *161*

16 · Eggplant *171*

17 · Greens   *193*

18 · Jersualem Artichokes, Kohlrabi, Jicama, and Radishes   *219*

19 · Mushrooms   *233*

20 · Okra   *249*

21 · Onions, Leeks, Shallots, and Garlic   *255*

22 · Peas   *267*

23 · Peppers   *277*

24 · Potatoes   *291*

25 · Sweet Potatoes   *307*

26 · Tomatoes   *313*

27 · Turnips and Rutabagas   *325*

28 · Winter Squash and Pumpkin   *335*

29 · Zucchini, Summer Squash, and Chayote   *347*

30 · Vegetable Medleys   *363*

31 · Sauces and Dressings   *379*

32 · Basic Recipes   *405*

33 · Menus   *415*

MAIL ORDER SOURCES   *437*

CONVERSION CHART   *439*

INDEX   *441*

ABOUT THE AUTHOR   *453*

ACKNOWLEDGMENTS

So many people from so many lands—home cooks, professional chefs, and food writers—have given me fresh ideas for cooking vegetables. I would especially like to thank my friends Fernand Chambrette, Claude Vauguet, Denis Ruffel, and Anne Willan of France; Sippy Levine of Holland, my mother Pauline Kahn Luria of Poland, Ruth Sirkis and Ronnie Venezia of Israel, Suzanne Elmaleh and Eva Angel of Lebanon, Paule Tourdjman of Morocco, Kusuma Cooray of Sri Lanka, my mother-in-law Rachel Levy and her sister Mazal Cohen of Yemen, Chinese cooking expert Nina Simonds, Somchit Singchalee of Thailand, Jorge Villanueva of Mexico, and Teri Appleton Villanueva of California.

I am grateful to Frieda and Karen Caplan and their staff at Frieda's Finest for being a constant source of useful facts about produce; to Jan DeLyser of the Fresh Produce Council for providing information on the seasons and on easy ways to add produce to menus; to George Martinez, the produce man at Pavilions, my local supermarket, for his advice on preparing new varieties of vegetables; and to the growers who bring fresh wonderful produce to the Santa Monica farmers' market for gladly discussing with me the best ways to savor their harvest.

A big thank-you to Liv Blumer, my editor, and to Harvey-Jane Kowal at Warner Books for helping to make every step of creating this book a pleasure. Thanks also to Carole Berglie for her fine recipe editing; Sally Boon and Kevin Craft for the lovely photographs; and to my husband Yakir, who helped cook the dishes and write this book.

INTRODUCTION

Most of us grew up with constant encouragement from our mothers to eat more vegetables. Recently this maternal advice has become official. The current recommendations of the U.S. Department of Agriculture, as shown on its Food Guide Pyramid, is to eat three to five servings of vegetables a day.

We are well aware of the healthful benefits of vegetables. Yet Americans lag behind other peoples in their consumption of vegetables. Europeans eat about twice as much produce as we do, and Asians eat even more. Indeed, throughout the world vegetables are prized for the variety they bring to daily menus. What other food comes to us in as many flavors, shapes, and colors?

Part of the reason for this higher consumption may be that, in many cultures, vegetables are loved for their taste and are not considered something you have to eat. In an old French movie of which I remember little, an escaped convict was captured and returned to prison. He described the good life on the outside, emphasizing all the fun he had and the parties he attended. But one old, longtime prisoner kept interrupting by asking him, "but was there green salad?" This was what he missed most. Although it's important to remember the nutritional advantages of vegetables, I prefer to think of the pleasure and beauty that produce brings to our meals.

I most enjoy meals that have a high proportion of vegetables. There is nothing better than a sumptuous feast of the aromatic stuffed vegetables of Mediterranean countries. I adore the spicy vegetable curries popular in India and much of Southeast Asia, as well as the lovely, crisp, colorful stir-fried vegetables of China. Simple vegetable dishes can also be a treat— the first asparagus of spring, or small fresh new potatoes sprinkled perhaps with a little tarragon vinaigrette.

My favorite kind of shopping is going to the produce market, whether I'm at home in California, visiting my other "home away from home" cities of Paris and Jerusalem, or traveling to new places. I find it a great pleasure to look at all the beautiful, fresh produce and imagine what local shoppers will make from it when they bring it home.

I'm delighted with the farmers' markets that are springing up in more and more areas of our country. I feel fortunate to have the largest certified farmers' market in California only a few minutes' walk from my home. If you have access to a farmers' market, go and enjoy the full flavor of locally grown produce and the friendly atmosphere there.

For most of us, the familiar supermarket is the most important source for vegetables. Here, things are looking better, too. The produce sections of many supermarkets are expanding, featuring more and more fresh produce of good quality. We are offered a growing selection of fresh native American vegetables as well as produce that orginates in foreign lands. Part of the excitement of cooking today is that going to the market can be a learning experience, with the discovery of new vegetables or exotic varieties of familiar ones. Next to the broccoli, carrots, and onions are Oriental snow peas, bean sprouts, and bok choy; Mexican chilies; French green beans, Belgian endive, Italian broccoli rabe; and Japanese and Chinese eggplants.

A brief glance at the products available in supermarkets today immediately reveals the taste for modern "new foods." There are "designer" lettuces and newer vegetables like purple potatoes, pear-shaped yellow tomatoes, and bright green sugar-snap peas. Americans' quest for healthful food, and a growing interest in pure, natural ingredients, are leading to more organic farming, more farmers' markets, and better quality in the common vegetables at the neighborhood supermarket.

The flavor of tired vegetables could sometimes be masked with plenty of butter or drenched in cheese sauce, but today when vegetables have to taste good on their own, people are demanding better and fresher produce, and the markets are responding. Unlike most parts of the market, the produce section offers a different selection from one week to the next. Even though the seasonal influence is much less than it used to be, the seasons still have an impact on what is available, at what quality, and at what price.

Home cooking around the world is essentially simple. For this book, as in the other volumes in my "international series," my goal is to present dishes that are delicious, enticing, and easy enough to be cooked often. I feel that recipes must be practical for cooking in the home kitchen. In choosing these recipes, I gave priority to those that are quick, mostly light and low in fat, and mainly meatless. I focused on developing delicious dishes for common fresh vegetables, but I have also included some recipes for exotic ones that are becoming easier to find.

The inspiration for these recipes comes from around the world. I explored the spicy cuisines for ideas on how to eat lighter food that is flavorful. But this doesn't mean I abandoned the European cuisines. There are plenty of useful recipes and techniques in the Western world's cuisines that do not require using fatty meats or large quantities of cream or butter.

Fresh healthful produce is more important to us than ever. With the following recipes I hope you will find vegetables delightful to cook and to eat.

1

Why and How to Eat More Vegetables

Nutritionists and doctors advise us to include more vegetables in our diet. Vegetables are not only rich in vitamins and minerals and a good source of fiber, they are also low in calories and contain no cholesterol, almost no fat, and very little sodium. Some vegetables provide protein and some contain complex carbohydrates, which give us energy. In addition, some vegetables like those in the crucifer, or cabbage, family contain compounds that are believed to help prevent certain types of cancer. If you eat more vegetables every day, it will naturally help you eat smaller amounts of less nutritious foods and those that contain fat.

For years home economists suggested we plan menus by deciding on a main course of meat, fish, or poultry and design the rest of the meal around it. Yet there can be good reasons to change this habit. If beautiful bunches of broccoli, snow-white mushrooms, shiny purple eggplants, or brilliant red bell peppers are featured in the market, why not start with them?

A flexible style of menu planning can result in more exciting meals as well as better nutrition. I have always liked the Chinese style of serving rice with a variety of accompanying dishes, rather than thinking in terms of a main course of meat and one or two side dishes.

To expand on this idea, you can prepare one, two, or three vegetable dishes and serve them with pasta, rice, or another grain. With this approach a meal is satisfying, colorful, and delicious. Often you may find you either don't need meat at all, or end up eating it in smaller amounts.

Vegetable dishes from around the globe can contribute to every part of the menu. For appetizers there are colorful Middle Eastern vegetable dips, zesty Italian vegetable antipasti, Greek filo pastries with vegetable fillings, delicate French salads with light, aromatic dressings, and much more. And almost any cooked vegetable—from Chilean "Succotash" (page 66) made with beans, corn, and winter squash and served with a spicy salsa, to Algerian Cauliflower with Tomato, Garlic, and Cilantro (page 96)—can become a main course if it is served with grains, pasta, or bread. (Some vegetables such as carrots, sweet potatoes, and squash are even made into desserts.)

For diversity in menus, try the exotic and newer vegetables—the many varieties of winter squash, the baby vegetables, the wild mushrooms, the Chinese greens. It's not unusual now to find vegetables that we didn't know several years ago, like broccoflower, sugar-snap peas, and sweet dumpling squash. This is true not only at farmers' markets but at regular produce markets and supermarkets as well.

To make it easier to include vegetables in menus, markets now provide many cut and cleaned vegetables for convenience. There are broccoli florets, sliced mushrooms, washed spinach, shredded cabbage, and other ready-to-cook vegetables from both the produce section and the salad bar section of the supermarket. Ready-washed salad greens make preparing salad a delight—you just put the greens you want in the bowl and sprinkle them lightly with a small amount of dressing.

Frozen vegetables are another convenience item that makes it easier to add more vegetables to menus. I prefer the frozen vegetables that do not contain any sauces or additional seasonings, so there is no added fat or extra salt. It's up to you to decide which frozen vegetables you like. I often use peas, corn kernels, spinach, lima beans and black-eyed peas, and occasionally okra and sugar-snap peas. I also like vegetable medleys, from the familiar one of lima beans, peas, corn, and carrots to some of the new ones containing water chestnuts or Chinese mushrooms. In the sauce chapter and throughout the book you will find many ideas you can use to dress up frozen vegetables.

One easy way to incorporate more vegetables in your diet is to cook enough for two meals at one time. Most vegetables can be cooked ahead; even green vegetables can be reheated easily (see Chapter 3, Vegetable Cooking Techniques). You can always heat the second portion of vegetables with a small amount of tomato sauce or sprinkle it with herb- or garlic-scented olive oil, vinaigrette, or a little salsa (see Chapter 31, Sauces and Dressings). You can add the vegetables to soups, meat or bean stews, or vegetable medleys. Or turn the extra vegetables into a new dish: make them into salads, soups, or purees, or toss them with rice pilaf, tortellini, or other types of pasta.

With so many possibilities, you can easily make vegetables into the most exciting part of the meal.

2

Cooking Vegetables Around the World

Although there are similarities in vegetable cooking between regions, each major area of the world has typical ways of preparing vegetables—often-used techniques, characteristic seasoning mixtures, sauces and condiments. In addition, some vegetables are confined to the cuisines of certain areas because of differences in climate and soil.

Many cuisines of the world are dynamic. We notice the changes in our own cuisine most easily, but in other regions culinary styles are also evolving, owing in part to newly available ingredients and to people's increasing awareness of the effect of food on health. The trend toward lighter cooking is evident in many cities around the globe.

3

EUROPE

Traditionally, Europeans often season vegetables lightly and cook them simply to highlight their natural flavors. The first tender vegetables of spring are just boiled, drained, and served with a touch of salt and freshly ground pepper, a pat of butter, and perhaps a sprinkling of fresh parsley. Old-fashioned recipes often specified long cooking times and produced mushy vegetables. Now more and more Europeans prefer their vegetables less cooked so that they remain bright colored and keep their texture.

Root vegetables and other winter vegetables tend to be braised in stock or served in creamy sauces. A favorite European way of preparing all sorts of vegetables is as a gratin—coated with a cheese, cream, or tomato sauce, sprinkled lightly with cheese or bread crumbs, and baked to brown the topping. The vegetable acquires a rich flavor and is a popular accompaniment to all sorts of meats and poultry. Sweet-and-sour vegetable dishes, especially of beets or red and white cabbage, are also well liked in Europe. Popular flavorings for vegetables are horseradish and fresh dill in northern and central Europe, fresh tarragon, thyme, shallots, and chives in France, and sautéed onions, mustard, bay leaves, and parsley in most areas. Garlic is used with a lighter hand in the north than in regions to the south. Sweet and hot paprika are loved in Hungary.

Salads have long held a place of honor on European menus. Most famous are the green salads of France, so esteemed that they are served in that country as a separate course, after the main course. Crisp cabbage and carrot salads, often accented by apples, raisins, or other fruit and seasoned with a light dressing of wine vinegar and oil, can be found as appetizers or accompaniments in most European homes.

Of the cooked vegetable salads, potato salads are king. They are loved across Europe, from Russia to the Atlantic and to the Mediterranean. There are creamy versions with mayonnaise, but also lighter, tangy potato salads moistened with vinaigrette. Almost any cooked vegetable, from asparagus to green beans to dried beans, is likely to appear in a salad.

Since the appearance of nouvelle cuisine in the 1970s, salads have become a staple of the appetizer selection in fine restaurants and a favorite first course at home as well. For these salads a noble vegetable like asparagus, artichoke hearts, or tiny green beans might be combined with a rich ingredient like toasted nuts, shrimp, or goat cheese. The salad ingredients are seasoned lightly with vinaigrette and often presented on a bed of baby greens.

THE MEDITERRANEAN AND THE MIDDLE EAST

The influence of this region's culinary heritage is widespread, extending to the Balkan countries in Europe and east to India. In this part of the world, boiled vegetables are frowned upon. Instead, a typical way to cook vegetables is to slowly braise them with tomatoes, onions, garlic, and olive oil and to season them with herbs, spices, or both. The vegetable is served in its cooking liquid. Whether a green vegetable remains bright green or crisp is not important; what people look for is the rich, tender texture the vegetable acquires from long, slow cooking.

The most festive of vegetable dishes, loved in the region for holidays and special occasions, is aromatic stuffed vegetables. Examples in this book from the eastern Mediterranean are Lebanese-style stuffed tomatoes filled with lamb and cilantro (page 317), and Turkish peppers with a rice stuffing accented with pine nuts, currants, and plenty of sautéed onions (page 284). From southern Europe there is eggplant stuffed in the Italian style with scamorza cheese and tomatoes (page 183), and Provençal Fennel with Mushroom Stuffing (page 151). The stuffings are spooned into the natural cavities of some vegetables, rolled up in leafy vegetables, or tucked into the hollowed-out centers of still others. Stuffings might be based on rice, bread crumbs, potatoes, meat, or simply the center of the vegetable that is cooked, chopped, and seasoned.

In Mediterranean and Middle Eastern countries salads are often made of cooked vegetables rather than raw leafy greens. In the eastern Mediterranean the way to begin a meal is with an assortment of salads. Selections might include a tangy potato salad, spicy zucchini salad, beet and yogurt salad, or hot and spicy tomato-pepper salad, served in small plates along with olives, pickles, and fresh bread.

Perhaps the most popular salads of all are those made of grilled vegetables, especially eggplant and peppers. They might be flavored with olive oil and lemon juice, or in the case of eggplant, with tahini. An important element of their appeal is that the vegetable acquires a smoky flavor during grilling.

Raw vegetables have their place in salads too, as in the ubiquitous Mediterranean diced salad of tomatoes, cucumbers, and onions (page 166)—a delicious appetizer or accompaniment.

AFRICA

Cooking in Africa is marked primarily by the continent's ingredients and native culinary styles, but also by interaction with foreign cultures. North African cuisine resembles Mediterranean and Middle Eastern cooking to a great extent, manifested in the preeminence of such flavorings as tomatoes, peppers, garlic, onions, cumin, cilantro, and lemon juice. Ethiopian cooking also has much in common with that of the Middle East because of its immigrants from Yemen and because of trade with Arab neighbors.

For several hundred years most of Africa was under European occupation, and this affected the selection of ingredients and the style of cooking. In South Africa there is a meeting of Dutch, French, English, Malay, and Indian cuisines. Favorite vegetables in Africa south of the Sahara are yams, squash, okra, eggplant, and greens.

Many Africans love food that is scorching hot. Throughout much of the continent chilies, which are thought to have been brought by the Portuguese from the New World, are used in generous amounts. This makes for a variety of fiery dishes such as hot West African vegetable stews thickened with ground peanuts, Ethiopian vegetable medleys flavored with a great variety of spices, and Indian-inspired vegetable curries in eastern and southern Africa. Moroccan vegetables poached in aromatic broth are served with a red-hot chili paste called *harissa*, to accompany their famous specialty, couscous.

In some vegetable dishes, North African cooks use a clarified butter similar to Indian *ghee* for sautéing vegetables. Ethiopian cooks take this recipe one step further by adding flavorings such as ginger, garlic, cardamom, turmeric, fenugreek, and cinnamon to the butter while clarifying it.

INDIA

Owing to the Moslem influence in northern India and Pakistan, there are some dishes that this region shares with the Middle East. One obvious example is pureed grilled eggplant. Yet even in similar dishes there are regional preferences. The grilled chopped eggplant is most often served cold as a salad or dip in the Middle East, while in India it is more highly spiced and is served as a hot vegetable dish.

The Buddhist meatless tradition has helped create an exceptional variety of Indian vegetarian dishes, which are usually served as a main course with rice. Indians love to braise vegetables in spicy sauces, as in Chickpeas with Spinach and Carrots (page 70). The dish is flavored with a zesty spice mixture of toasted coriander and cumin seeds along with chilies and garlic. Sautéed spicy vegetables like Okra with Hot Pepper and Garlic (page 252) are favorites in India as well.

In India vegetables also help calm the fires of spicy curries and appear in yogurt salads called *raitas*. These soothing salads most often contain cucumbers or tomatoes, but might also have cooked vegetables like potatoes or spinach. As in the Middle East and much of Southeast Asia, cilantro is an important flavoring for vegetables, both in *raitas* and sprinkled on hot cooked vegetable dishes.

THE ORIENT

Chinese cooking may be best known for its enticing vegetables—bright-colored, crisp-textured but not hard, and so enjoyable to eat. Stir-frying, the Chinese cooking technique responsible for these delicious vegetables, has become popular in Western countries as well. The major seasonings—fresh ginger, soy sauce, rice vinegar, oyster sauce, and sesame oil—are easy to find in most supermarkets, as are green onions and garlic. Now we can find a variety of fresh Chinese vegetables, from snow peas to bean sprouts to Chinese greens to shiitake mushrooms, and sometimes even fresh baby corn and water chestnuts. Contemporary Chinese vegetable dishes need not, therefore, contain a large amount of canned ingredients.

Japanese vegetable recipes use many of the same flavorings as Chinese, but some Japanese vegetable dishes bear a certain resemblance to those of Europe, in being simply boiled and sprinkled lightly with a few flavorings. In Japanese Sesame Spinach (page 200), for example, although the vegetable is cooked by a similar technique used for European spinach dishes and is seasoned delicately, it does not taste European. The reason is the different seasonings—soy sauce, sweet rice vinegar, and toasted sesame seeds. Sesame, in the form of both toasted seeds and aromatic sesame oil, is also a favorite flavoring for vegetables in Korea.

Thailand, Malaysia, and Indonesia combine characteristics of Indian and Chinese vegetable cookery and add their own seasonings. Stir-fried vegetables are common in these countries, but Thai versions might include mint or basil as well as chilies and fish sauce. Spicy vegetable curries are often cooked in coconut milk and seasoned generously with Indian-style spice mixtures as well as Southeast Asian flavorings like lemongrass and shrimp paste. Some Indonesian curries contain nuts and might be slightly sweet and sour as well as spicy. Peanuts are a popular accent for salads, both as toasted nuts and in the dressings.

NORTH AMERICA

Since the United States is largely a land of immigrants, much of its cooking is influenced by the countries of origin of its settlers. The main culinary legacy remains that of Europe, but there is a growing impact of Hispanic and Asian cuisines.

There are regional differences in what vegetables Americans eat and how they cook them. In the South, especially in Louisiana, eggplants, okra, cooked greens, sweet potatoes, and chayote squash appear frequently on the dinner table and are often seasoned with hot pepper, as in the Caribbean. Californians make great use of vegetables like Mexican jicama, Japanese eggplant, and Chinese snow peas as well as Mexican and Oriental flavorings. Italian vegetables like broccoli rabe and fennel are most widely used in East and West Coast cities with a large number of people of Italian origin. Cooks in the North and the Midwest have developed delicious ways to use potatoes, cabbage, parsnips, and beets. Winter squashes, especially butternut squash, are loved in New England and are used in a great variety of dishes.

As in Latin America, the North American fondness for corn and beans is largely due to the influence of the native Americans, from whom the settlers learned to use these foods. Which beans are most popular varies regionally: Great Northern or navy beans are the ones most used in the Northeast, pink beans or pinto beans in the Southwest, black beans are favorites in south Florida and in the Southwest, and black-eyed peas in the South.

European-style cheese sauces and cream sauces have long been favorite flavorings for hot vegetables in North America, and thick mayonnaise-based dressings were preferred for salads. Now with the interest in lighter cooking, tomato sauces, vinaigrettes, and Chinese sauces have become more popular; and sales of salsa have overtaken sales of ketchup!

In major American cities more and more ethnic products are available: Thai curry pastes, a variety of Mexican chilies and tortillas, Chinese and Japanese sauces, noodles, and vegetables. These items are found now not only in small shops in ethnic neighborhoods but also in mainstream supermarkets. At my local supermarket in southern California, I find it fascinating to see the selection of condiments and other staples sitting side by side on the shelf of the deli section: jars of horseradish next to containers of Korean *kimchi* (spicy pickles), Chinese won-ton wrappers, Mexican salsas, Italian pesto and pasta, Japanese noodles—the list goes on and on.

Of course, this wealth of ethnic ingredients makes cooking vegetables a pleasure and an adventure, and leads to creativity and experimentation. An Israeli friend of mine who lives in Los Angeles likes to flavor her Yemenite-style vegetable stews with store-bought Thai curry paste. Another uses Philippine won-ton wrappers to make Moroccan pastries called "cigars." A third finds hot Mexican salsa a good substitute for North African *harissa*.

Americans have developed a fondness for eating raw vegetables. Party snack trays and salad bars feature carrot and celery sticks, cauliflower and broccoli florets, mushrooms, radishes, and other raw vegetables served with all sorts of dips. We also like to expand on the European green salad and add a variety of other raw vegetables.

Cooked vegetables are boiled or steamed very briefly in the modern American kitchen so their color is bright and their texture is crisp—rather like the contemporary European style but less cooked than in Europe. This is a reaction to the previous way of cooking vegetables in water for a long time until they became mushy and tasteless.

LATIN AMERICA AND THE CARIBBEAN

Vegetable cooking styles in Latin America and the Caribbean share certain characteristics because of common influences: the mingling of European culinary styles with those of native cultures—the Aztecs and the Mayans in Mexico and the Incas in Peru. In the Caribbean, the Europeans—as well as the Africans they brought to the islands—left their mark on the local cooking. And in some South American countries, especially Brazil, the cooking is a mixture of all three influences—native Indian, African, and European.

The Spanish style is the predominant European influence on the region's cooking. Other nations whose cuisines had an impact are the Portuguese in Brazil and the French, British, and Dutch in the Caribbean islands and some parts of South America. The native Indian culinary contribution is most apparent in Mexico, Peru, Bolivia, and Ecuador, while the European style is more evident in Argentina, Uruguay, Chile, and the Spanish Caribbean islands.

Latin America is the source of many vegetables that have become central to the cuisines of much of the world: tomatoes, sweet and hot peppers, potatoes, sweet potatoes, corn, squash, and beans. These vegetables are widely used in their area of origin both as side dishes and in casseroles and soups with meat. In Brazil and the Caribbean, okra is also popular, a legacy of their African heritage.

Dried and fresh beans are frequently used throughout Latin America and in the Caribbean islands. Black beans are the basis for Brazil's national dish, *feijoada*, and for Cuba's famous black bean soup, but many other beans are popular, notably chickpeas (garbanzo beans) and pinto beans. Our familiar lima beans are named for Lima, Peru, where they have been on the menu for thousands of years. Other Latin American vegetables, such as tomatillos, nopales cactus, hearts of palm, taro, and plantains, are becoming known in our country. Once available exclusively at specialty grocers, they can now be purchased at many supermarkets.

Favorite flavorings for vegetable casseroles in much of Latin America include fresh and dried chilies both mild and hot, cilantro, cumin, tomatoes, onions, and garlic. Although chilies and hot salsas are popular in most of the region, the hottest cooking is that of Mexico and some Caribbean islands. Brazilian food is also hot and might be flavored with fresh ginger and coconut milk in addition to chilies. Peanuts, which originated in South America, are used to make sauces for vegetables in Peru, Ecuador, and Brazil.

—3—

Vegetable Cooking Techniques

egetables can be cooked by a variety of techniques. Once you are familiar with them, you can use these formulas to cook any vegetable, even those you've never seen before. Here are the most basic cooking methods.

BOILING AND SIMMERING

When I studied cooking at La Varenne Cooking School in Paris, I learned that the most important culinary distinction between vegetables is whether they are green vegetables or root vegetables. The group of green vegetables, which includes spinach and other leafy greens, green peas, snow peas, and broccoli, and such "nongreen" vegetables as cauliflower and summer squash, are cooked very much like pasta.

To cook green vegetables, you plunge them into a pot containing a generous amount of boiling salted water—enough so the vegetable pieces are completely surrounded by boiling water as they cook. Cook them uncovered over high heat at a full boil until they are crisp-tender; you can use specified cooking times as a guide, but you should check whether they're ready by tasting one. As soon as they are ready, pour them into a colander or large strainer to drain off all the water.

At this point you can serve the vegetable immediately or you can keep it for serving afterward. To save it for serving later, rinse the vegetable in the colander with cold running water, tossing it a few times, until it is completely cool. You can then refrigerate the vegetable. If you skip the step of rinsing, most green vegetables lose their bright green color and become too soft from the residual heat of cooking.

This cooking method is sometimes called *blanching* and is the most common way of cooking green vegetables in Europe. It is the beginning step for many dishes that are finished by other techniques such as stir-frying, braising, and baking.

The root vegetable category actually includes a mixture of roots and tubers, such as carrots, turnips, kohlrabi, and potatoes. These vegetables start cooking from cold water instead. You don't need as much water as for green vegetables, but just enough to cover the vegetables. The water is brought to a boil, then the vegetables are covered and cooked at a simmer. They are drained after cooking but do not require rinsing.

STEAMING

Most vegetables can be steamed. This technique requires a little more time than boiling, but preserves some nutrients like vitamin C, which are diminished by boiling. Like boiling and simmering, it is a favorite method for low-calorie cooking because no fat is added to the vegetables.

Steaming keeps in flavors and therefore is better suited to mild-tasting vegetables like summer squash, carrots, and beets rather than strong-flavored vegetables like cabbage or Brussels sprouts.

For steaming, the vegetables are placed on a rack above boiling water. The pan is covered tightly to keep in the steam. Several types of steamers are available. Pasta pots often come with steamer inserts that sit snugly in the pot above the water and are very convenient to use. Chinese bamboo or metal steamers also are useful because the steamer trays can be stacked. This enables you to steam a few different vegetables at the same time and to remove each when it is cooked. A couscous pot can also be used for steaming. French folding steamer racks can be set in any deep saucepan with a tight cover to turn the pan into a steamer.

When steaming vegetables, be sure they are at least one inch above the surface of the boiling water, so that when the water bubbles vigorously, it will not boil them. The water should be boiling before the vegetables are added. Steam vegetables over high heat so the water boils continuously and provides a constant flow of steam. Check occasionally and replenish the pot with boiling water if it boils out—for example, when steaming long-cooking vegetables.

When checking the vegetables to see if they are done, carefully and briefly uncover the pan. *Do be careful when uncovering the steamer, as the steam is very hot.* When uncovering the steamer, hold the cover away from you in order to avoid the steam.

Some water adheres to steamed vegetables, so they should be drained after cooking, especially if they will be served with a dressing or sauce, lest the water dilute it. If you are steaming green vegetables ahead and want them to keep their bright color, rinse them with cold water, as for boiled vegetables.

Steaming is most suitable for relatively small quantities of vegetables so that the steam can easily reach each piece and the pieces cook evenly. I love steamed baby beets, carrots, and new potatoes. Fresh steamed vegetables are delicious on their own but can be flavored with the same sauces that are used for boiled vegetables.

BRAISING

Braising is a method of slowly cooking vegetables with only a small amount of liquid, which might become a sauce for the vegetable. The braising liquid is either stock or water enhanced for added flavor with chopped tomatoes, onions, garlic, or herbs. The liquid can be thickened with flour or cornstarch or thickens naturally during the cooking. The best pans to use for braising are a deep sauté pan with a lid or a heavy wide casserole or Dutch oven.

Braising is best for long-cooking vegetables such as large pieces of carrots, turnips, or potatoes, but is also a good technique for cooking eggplant, celery, or mixtures of vegetables like Ratatouille (page 372). In Mediterranean and Balkan countries and in India, even quick-cooking vegetables like zucchini, cauliflower, or green beans are braised to give them a rich flavor from the braising sauce.

SAUTÉING AND STIR-FRYING

Sautéing means briefly cooking food in a small amount of oil over fairly high heat. You don't need much oil—just enough to coat the bottom of the pan.

Naturally tender vegetables like eggplant, mushrooms, peppers, and zucchini are best suited for sautéing. Other vegetables like cauliflower and asparagus are first briefly blanched so they soften slightly before being sautéed. Sautéing is an ideal method for heating leftover cooked vegetables because they heat quickly, keep their color, and do not dry out.

Butter can give a lovely flavor to sautéed vegetables, but it burns easily at high temperatures. To prevent it from burning, or simply to use a lower proportion of butter for reasons of nutrition, it can be combined with vegetable oil for sautéing, or the oil can be used on its own. Olive oil is another favorite oil for sautéing because of its characteristic flavor and its healthful properties.

A heavy skillet or frying pan of good quality is best for sautéing because it enables the oil to heat evenly and the vegetables to cook without scorching. It also makes it possible to sauté vegetables with a minimum amount of oil, whereas in a flimsy pan the vegetables would burn with so little oil.

Stir-frying is a Chinese technique similar to sautéing but even quicker. The heat is kept high and the cut vegetables are tossed continuously over the heat until they are crisp-tender. Vegetable oil is used for stir-frying because it can withstand the high temperature required. A wok is traditionally used for stir-frying, but a fine-quality skillet can be substituted; similarly, a wok can be used for sautéing.

A hot pan is essential for sautéing or stir-frying. If the pan is not hot enough, the food will absorb too much oil, will stick, and will begin to stew in its juices. In addition, when you add oil to a hot pan, you will need less oil to coat its base because hot oil is more fluid. During sautéing the food is not covered, so it will sauté and not steam.

The pan for sautéing should be large enough so the food is not crowded. If all the pieces do not fit easily, they should be cooked in batches. If they are spaced too closely together, the steam produced during sautéing cannot escape and the food does not sauté properly. When you sauté several batches of vegetables, add more oil to the pan between batches if the pan becomes dry, and heat the oil before adding the next portion of vegetables.

DEEP-FRYING

In most traditional cuisines deep-frying is a popular way to cook vegetables. However, deep-fried foods absorb a large amount of fat and most health-conscious people rarely deep-fry. Still, once in a while a crisp vegetable fritter is a welcome treat.

Deep-frying is a quick cooking method that is not complicated. Properly fried food is light and does not taste too greasy. The best oil to use is vegetable oil of a neutral flavor such as peanut oil, corn oil, soy bean oil, or safflower oil. You can save the oil used for deep-frying and use it again once or twice, but it should be carefully strained after use and kept in a cool place. If the oil smokes during frying, do not reuse it.

The easiest pan to use is a deep-fryer, but you can use a heavy, deep saucepan with a frying thermometer. The pan needs to be large enough so that it can hold enough oil to cover the food, but should not be more than half full of oil. It is important to use a pan that is very stable so that there is no danger of its tipping over. A wire skimmer or slotted spoon is best for removing the food from the pan.

Correct temperature is essential for successful deep-frying. If the oil is too hot, the coating or outer surface of the food may burn before the interior is cooked. But if it is not hot enough, the vegetables will absorb too much oil. Using a deep-frying thermometer is the most efficient way to ensure that the oil remains at the proper temperature.

After deep-frying any food, be sure to drain it on paper towels and pat the food's surface with paper towels as well to remove excess oil. For the same purpose, deep-fried foods are often served on a platter lined with a doily or napkin. Do not coat the fried vegetables with a sauce, as it would make them soggy. You can serve a sauce separately for dipping.

HINTS ON DEEP-FRYING

It's important to follow a few simple rules so that deep-frying is a pleasant and safe experience:

✗ Don't fill the pan more than half full of oil.

✗ Hold ingredients near the surface of the oil and slide them in gently. Don't drop ingredients from high above the oil because they'll splash hot oil.

✗ When food is added to the oil, it bubbles vigorously. Don't crowd the pan because the oil can bubble up to the top and even overflow.

✗ Regulate the heat if necessary to keep the oil at the right temperature.

✗ Give your full attention to the frying; don't leave in the middle to do something else.

BAKING

Baking or roasting is a favorite method for cooking winter squash, potatoes, sweet potatoes, and the "Mediterranean vegetables"—eggplant, peppers, and tomatoes. The dry heat preserves their flavor better than boiling or steaming, especially in the case of eggplant. But other vegetables can be prepared by this technique—carrots, beets, turnips, and even asparagus can be roasted and produce delicious results.

The vegetable to be roasted is sometimes moistened with a little oil and baked in a hot oven until tender. The vegetable can also be placed around a chicken so it gains flavor from the chicken's juices as it roasts.

Vegetables can also be baked as part of casseroles, as in the Balkan vegetable stew called Givetch (page 370), for which baking is simply a form of braising done in the oven.

Baking is a favorite method for cooking stuffed vegetables. Some vegetables like winter squash and eggplant are prebaked before the stuffing is added, while others like peppers and tomatoes can bake along with their stuffing. Most stuffings designed for poultry also taste good baked in vegetables, as in Stuffed Acorn Squash with Apples and Pecans (page 343).

The technique of baking is the finishing step for preparing a vegetable gratin. The vegetable is first boiled, steamed, or prebaked. Then it is coated with tomato sauce, cream sauce, or cheese sauce or is sprinkled with oil. Last it is sprinkled with cheese, bread crumbs, or nuts and baked to reheat the vegetable.

For lower-fat cooking, many vegetable recipes that call for frying can instead be baked in the oven at high temperature.

GRILLING AND BROILING

Grilling and broiling are suitable techniques for cooking certain vegetables. Sweet peppers, chilies, tomatoes, large mushrooms, small halved onions, potatoes, sweet potatoes, and corn on the cob are delicious grilled. Eggplants are wonderful grilled, but the manner by which this is done varies from place to place. In the United States and much of Europe, it is usually grilled in slices, but in the Middle East the vegetable is most often grilled whole for making salads and spreads.

Unlike meats, vegetables are not usually marinated before being grilled, as their cooking time is quick and they are naturally tender. They are simply brushed with a little oil to prevent drying. Marinades are optional, but if used they will impart more flavor if sprinkled on the vegetable after it is cooked, as in Grilled Eggplant Antipasto (page 188), for which the grilled slices are sprinkled with olive oil, fresh mint, and basil.

MICROWAVING

I prefer to use the microwave when it presents a significant savings in time—mainly for vegetables that take long to cook by other methods, such as winter squash and sweet potatoes.

Microwaving is most suitable for cooking relatively small quantities of vegetables because the greater the amount of vegetables being microwaved, the longer it takes to cook them. Vegetables are usually microwaved on high power.

4

Artichokes

Artichokes are a symbol of elegant cooking. They frequently appear in luxurious chefs' creations with such ingredients as *foie gras*, sweetbreads, and shellfish. In spite of this aristocratic image, artichokes have been a part of home cooking in Mediterranean areas for centuries. In this sunny region they are often combined with humble ingredients like beans and rice.

Artichokes are considered to have originated in North Africa; the word *artichoke* comes from Arabic. In its native land artichokes are cooked with olive oil, garlic, herbs, and spices, or are stuffed with a savory mixture of lamb, rice, and cilantro. These artichoke recipes are now popular in much of the Middle East.

Greeks and Turks cook artichokes with lemon juice, olive oil, and dill, and sometimes pair them with fava beans. The vegetable is a great favorite in Italy, where it is prepared with piquant stuffings flavored with garlic and mint or with capers and olives. Italians also cook artichokes with rice for a risotto or with eggs for a frittata. In France artichokes have long been an important ingredient in haute cuisine, and are stuffed with peas, mushrooms, or other vegetables as an accompaniment for meat, or filled with seafood as a first course.

19

Spanish cooks prefer artichoke stuffings flavored with ham, tuna, or anchovies. Some South American cooks, influenced by the European style, use artichokes in salads or stews.

Nearly all commercially grown artichokes in the United States are cultivated in California. Castroville, California, calls itself the artichoke capital of the world. The most popular way to serve artichokes in California is cold—either marinated or in salads. The meaty texture of artichokes makes them a satisfying element in vegetarian dishes.

The most common way of preparing *whole artichokes* is the simplest—boiled or steamed, and accompanied by a tangy vinaigrette. Other popular sauces for artichokes are garlic- or mustard-accented mayonnaise, or melted butter for dipping the leaves and heart.

The leaves can be removed from artichokes to form cup-shaped *artichoke bottoms*. Prepared this way, artichokes have a great many uses—in salads, stuffed, marinated, or braised on their own or with other vegetables. They are wonderful cut in pieces and added to stews, rice dishes, or pasta sauces.

Artichoke hearts resemble artichoke bottoms, but technically are slightly different. For hearts, parts of the small tender leaves and stem are left attached to the artichoke bottom. Hearts are used for marinating or stewing with other vegetables. To prepare them, see Greek Marinated Artichokes (page 27).

In Mediterranean countries artichokes are sometimes eaten raw, either plain or in salads, but they must be tiny and very tender to be enjoyed this way; it's rare to find them at this stage in our markets.

ARTICHOKE BASICS

Season: Artichokes are available during most of the year, but their price is significantly lower during spring, their peak season. There is also a substantial artichoke crop in the fall.

Choosing: Artichokes should be compact and plump with an even green color and tightly packed leaves. They should feel heavy for their size and the leaves should not be bruised. In fall and winter, the leaves might have brown spots caused by frost, but these do not affect the quality.

Artichoke hearts are available frozen but sometimes they have not been trimmed adequately and may contain inedible parts. Try several brands to find the best ones. Marinated artichoke hearts also come in jars and can be a savory addition to salads or cold vegetable dishes.

Storing: When handling artichokes, grasp them by their stems so you don't prick your finger on the sharp tips of the leaves. Occasionally artichokes are sold with the thorny tips removed.

Keep artichokes unwashed in a plastic bag or tightly covered container in the refrigerator up to 1 week.

Serving Size: Allow 1 medium or 2 or 3 baby artichokes per appetizer or side-dish serving.

Nutrients: Artichokes are a good source of vitamins A and C and potassium. One medium artichoke contains 45 calories.

Preparing Artichokes for Cooking Whole

Rinse artichokes. Cut off the tip of each large leaf with a scissors, so you won't be pricked by the sharp tips when you're eating the leaves. Then with a knife, cut off the top inch or so of the artichoke. Cut off stems if you want; you can pare them and cook them in the pot alongside the artichoke.

Baby artichokes, of 1½-inch diameter or less, do not need trimming.

Cook immediately after trimming to avoid discoloration.

After trimming artichokes wash your hands well; they tend to give your fingers a bitter taste and will affect the next food you pick up and eat.

Preparing Artichoke Bottoms

This is the preferred way to prepare artichoke bottoms, as their cooking time is shortest. But you can instead prepare artichoke bottoms by simply cooking whole artichokes and pulling the leaves off, then scraping off the choke.

Squeeze the juice of ½ lemon into a medium bowl of cold water. Break off stem of 1 artichoke and largest leaves at bottom. Put artichoke on its side on board. Holding a very sharp knife or small serrated knife against side of artichoke (parallel to leaves), cut lower circle of leaves off, up to edge of artichoke heart; turn artichoke slightly after each cut. Rub cut edges of artichoke with cut lemon. Cut off leaves under base. Trim base, removing all dark green areas. Rub again with lemon. Cut off central cone of leaves just above heart. Put artichoke in bowl of lemon water. Repeat with remaining artichokes. Keep artichokes in lemon water until ready to cook them.

To cook artichoke bottoms, squeeze any juice remaining in lemon into a medium saucepan of boiling salted water. Add artichoke pieces. Cover and simmer over low heat until tender when pierced with knife, 15 to 20 minutes. Cool to lukewarm in liquid. Using a teaspoon, scoop out hairlike "choke" from center of each artichoke.

Eating Whole Artichokes

A whole artichoke is not the kind of food you would serve for a meal in a hurry, but rather for a slow, relaxed one.

At the base of each leaf there is a small amount of tasty "meat." To eat it, pull off a leaf, dip its base in sauce if you like, then bite into the base of the leaf and pull it out of your mouth, scraping off the meat from the leaf with your teeth. You discard the upper part of the leaf. After you have eaten all the leaves, you have a purple-tipped cone of small leaves, which you pull off. Underneath it is the fuzzy "choke." Remove it with a spoon. The remaining bottom, or heart, is the best part and can be eaten with a fork.

ARTICHOKE HEARTS WITH LIMA BEANS AND DILL

A favorite in Turkey and in Greece, this dish makes a lovely side dish or vegetarian main course, in which case it might be accompanied by yogurt. Traditional versions of the recipe call for fresh fava beans, which you can use if you find them (see cooking instructions in Note on page 68), but I substitute our more common lima beans.

4 medium artichokes
1 lemon, cut in half
2 tablespoons olive oil
1 medium onion, chopped
¾ cup water
1 tablespoon lemon juice, or more to taste

½ teaspoon sugar
3 tablespoons chopped fresh dill
Salt and freshly ground pepper
1 10-ounce package frozen baby lima beans
Lemon wedges (optional)

Prepare the artichoke hearts. Squeeze juice of ½ lemon into a bowl of cold water. Leave stems on artichokes. Pull off bottom leaves of an artichoke. Snap back side leaves to remove tough parts. Pare stem with paring knife. Halve artichokes and trim top leaves so they are only ½ inch long. Halve each piece again. Using a spoon, scrape out hairlike choke from each quarter and pull out small, central purple-tipped leaves. Rub each piece with cut lemon; put in lemon water. Continue with remaining artichokes.

Heat oil in sauté pan over medium heat. Add onion and sauté about 5 minutes or until softened. Add artichoke quarters and sauté 1 or 2 minutes. Add water, 1 tablespoon lemon juice, sugar, 1 tablespoon dill, salt, and pepper. Bring to a boil. Cover and cook over low heat about 10 minutes. Add lima beans, stir, and bring to a boil. Cover and cook over low heat for 10 to 12 minutes or until artichokes and beans are tender, adding a few tablespoons water if pan becomes dry. If too much liquid remains, boil uncovered for 2 or 3 minutes, stirring gently. Add remaining dill. Taste and adjust seasoning; season generously; add a squeeze of lemon juice if desired. Serve hot or cold, with lemon wedges. (*Artichokes can be kept, covered, 2 days in refrigerator.*)

Makes 2 or 3 main-course servings with rice or other grains; or 4 or 5 first-course or side-dish servings

WHOLE ARTICHOKES WITH DIPPING SAUCE

In Spain, France, and most Mediterranean countries, this is a popular way to serve artichokes, as they are fun to eat with a sauce for dipping. Melted butter is a traditional accompaniment, but today lighter sauces are more popular, such as Classic Vinaigrette, Provençal Herb Dressing, Walnut Oil Vinaigrette, or Sun-Dried Tomato Dipping Sauce (see pages 383–387). For a richer sauce, you can serve Chipotle Chili Dip (page 373), Garlic Mayonnaise (page 402), or Tartar Sauce (page 403). For a party, you might like to serve a selection of several sauces.

4 medium or 8 small artichokes
About ½ cup dipping sauce (any of the
   above)

To trim artichokes, cut off top 1 inch of large artichokes or ½ inch of small ones. Trim spikes from tips of leaves with scissors. Put artichokes in a large saucepan of boiling salted water and cover with a lid of slightly smaller diameter than that of pan to keep them submerged. Cook over medium heat until a leaf can be easily pulled out; large artichokes will require about 45 to 50 minutes and small ones about 15 to 20 minutes. Using tongs, remove artichokes from water, turn them upside down, and drain thoroughly.

   Either cover to keep warm, or let cool and serve at room temperature or chilled. (*For serving cold, artichokes can be cooked 2 days ahead.*) Accompany with dipping sauce.

Makes 4 appetizer servings

NOTE: To serve the sauce inside the artichoke, first remove the central cone of leaves: Grasp it, twist it, and lift it out in one piece. Reserve the cone. Scoop out the choke from inside the artichoke with a teaspoon and discard it. Put the cone of leaves upside down in the artichoke. It forms a cup, which you can fill with sauce.

MOROCCAN STUFFED ARTICHOKES

These artichokes filled with an aromatic stuffing of rice, beef, herbs, and spices, then braised with tomatoes and garlic, make an elegant appetizer.

2 tablespoons white rice
6 large artichoke bottoms (page 22), uncooked
2 tablespoons olive oil
⅓ cup minced onion
¼ pound lean ground beef (about ½ cup)
1 medium garlic clove, minced
¼ cup chopped cilantro
¼ teaspoon sweet paprika

¼ teaspoon ground cumin
⅛ teaspoon ground cinnamon
⅛ teaspoon ground ginger
¼ teaspoon salt
¼ teaspoon freshly ground pepper
4 fresh or canned plum tomatoes, chopped
2 garlic cloves, sliced
⅛ teaspoon turmeric

Boil rice uncovered in a small saucepan of 1 cup of boiling salted water for 10 minutes. Rinse with cold water and drain well. Transfer to a medium bowl.

Using a melon ball cutter, remove chokes and small purple leaves from centers of artichoke hearts. Rub with a cut lemon and put in a bowl of water.

Heat 1 tablespoon oil in a small skillet, add onion and cook over medium-low heat 4 or 5 minutes. Add beef and sauté, stirring to crumble meat, about 4 minutes or until meat changes color. Remove from heat. Add minced garlic, cilantro, paprika, cumin, cinnamon, ginger, salt, and pepper; mix well. Add to rice; mix well.

Sprinkle artichoke bottoms with additional salt and pepper. Spoon stuffing into artichoke bottoms. Spoon remaining tablespoon oil into a Dutch oven or wide casserole and add artichokes. Add tomatoes, sliced garlic, turmeric, a pinch of salt and pepper and 1 cup water to pan. Bring to a simmer. Cover and cook over low heat about 30 minutes or until artichokes are tender. Serve hot, with a little tomato from pan spooned over each artichoke.

Makes 6 appetizer servings

BRETON ARTICHOKE OMELET

The farmers of the northwestern French region of Brittany are proud of their large artichokes, and farmers in the southern region of Provence of their tiny ones. In both places, they know artichokes and they like to use them as a filling for omelets.

2 large cooked artichoke bottoms (page 22)
4 large eggs
Salt and freshly ground pepper

1 tablespoon chopped fresh chives
3 tablespoons butter, or half oil and half butter

Dice the artichoke bottoms. Thoroughly beat the eggs with salt, pepper, and chives.

Heat 1 tablespoon butter in a frying pan. Add the artichokes and sprinkle with salt and pepper. Stir to coat the artichokes with the butter. Heat gently. Keep hot over low heat.

Heat the remaining butter in a 9- or 10-inch omelet pan or heavy frying pan over medium heat until foaming. Tip the pan so the butter coats its sides also. When the butter foam subsides, pour the egg mixture into the pan. Heat, stirring quickly with a fork or a pancake turner held flat, until the eggs begin to thicken. Carefully lift the egg at the sides of the pan, tipping the pan so the uncooked egg runs to the sides. Let cook about 15 seconds to slightly brown the bottom.

Spread the artichokes over the center of the omelet. Using the fork or pancake turner, carefully fold the side of the omelet nearest you over the filling. Slide the omelet to the edge of the pan. Hold the pan's handle in your left hand and a large plate at the pan's edge. Quickly turn the omelet pan over so the omelet lands on the plate. If necessary, neaten the edges of the omelet with a fork. Serve immediately.

Makes 2 main-course servings

ARTICHOKES AND MUSHROOMS WITH FETA STUFFING

This recipe is from Eva Angel, who began her career as a cooking teacher at the age of seventy. It is from her native country of Lebanon, which she says used to be ''the Switzerland of the Middle East.'' When she lived there, Lebanon had wonderful vegetables that were used in many creative ways.

She also uses the feta stuffing to fill halved zucchini, small eggplants, and tomatoes. She fries the vegetables and then braises them, but I have simplified and lightened the recipe by baking them instead.

1 pound potatoes, cooked
1½ cups finely crumbled feta cheese, preferably of ewes' milk
2 large eggs, beaten
¼ teaspoon ground allspice

Salt and freshly ground pepper
6 large artichoke bottoms, cooked (page 22)
12 large mushrooms (about 1 pound)
1 tablespoon vegetable oil

Peel and mash potatoes. Measure 2 cups. Mix well with feta cheese, egg, allspice, and salt and pepper to taste. Mash well with fork to combine.

Preheat oven to 400°F. Remove chokes from artichoke bottoms with a spoon. Remove stems from mushrooms. (Stems can be frozen and reserved for making vegetable stock.) Fill mushrooms and artichoke bottoms with a teaspoon, mounding generously.

Put vegetables in an oiled baking dish. Brush oil on sides of mushrooms and artichokes. Sprinkle filling with remaining oil. Bake 20 to 30 minutes or until tender. Then put in broiler very briefly to brown filling. Let cool slightly before serving.

Makes 6 main-course servings

GREEK MARINATED ARTICHOKES

Artichokes gain a new dimension of flavor from cooking directly in this marinade of olive oil, white wine, garlic, and coriander seeds. They make a delicious appetizer, for which they can be garnished with tomato wedges and black olives, or can be served as an accompaniment for sandwiches.

This Greek specialty has become popular in France and other parts of Europe. Other favorite vegetables for marinating this way are mushrooms, pearl onions, and cauliflower. When we prepared Greek marinated vegetables at La Varenne Cooking School in Paris, the chefs frequently added a tablespoon of tomato paste to the marinade to give it a pretty color. This is a light version of the marinade, with less oil than in classic recipes. There is no need to remove the coriander seeds; they add a pleasing crunch.

1 cup dry white wine
1½ cups water
2 medium garlic cloves, chopped
1 celery stalk, halved
¼ teaspoon fennel seeds
½ teaspoon dried thyme
½ teaspoon coriander seeds
Pinch of salt and freshly ground
    pepper

2 tablespoons lemon juice
¼ cup olive oil
4 to 5 medium artichokes (see Note)
1 lemon, cut in half
1 tablespoon extra-virgin olive oil
1 tablespoon chopped fresh parsley
    (optional)

In a sauté pan combine wine, water, garlic, celery, fennel seeds, thyme, coriander seeds, salt, pepper, 1 tablespoon lemon juice, and olive oil. Bring to a boil and simmer uncovered over medium heat for 10 minutes. Remove from heat.

Prepare artichoke hearts. Squeeze juice of ½ lemon into a bowl of cold water. Leave stems on artichokes. Pull off bottom leaves of an artichoke. Snap back side leaves to remove tough parts. Pare peel from stem with paring knife. Halve artichokes and trim top leaves so they are only ½ inch long. Halve each piece again. Using a spoon, scrape out hairlike choke from each quarter and pull out small, central purple-tipped leaves. Rub each piece with cut lemon; put in lemon water. Continue with remaining artichokes.

Rinse artichokes and add to hot marinade. Cover and bring to a boil. Cook over medium heat, gently stirring from time to time, for about 20 to 25 minutes or until tender. Remove to a shallow dish with slotted spoon. Boil marinade to reduce it for 2 or 3 minutes. Discard celery. Add extra-virgin oil, remaining lemon juice, and parsley. Taste and adjust seasoning. Pour over artichokes and let cool. (*Artichokes can be kept, covered, 5 days in refrigerator.*) Serve cold or at room temperature.

Makes 4 or 5 appetizer servings

NOTE: If you have large artichokes, prepare them as artichoke bottoms without leaves, instead of as artichoke hearts. See page 22. Quarter them before cooking them in the marinade.

ARTICHOKE SALAD WITH OLIVES AND CAPERS

In much of the Mediterranean region, the tangy flavor of olives and capers makes them popular partners for artichokes. I tasted a hot dish of artichokes braised with garlic, then accented with olives and capers in Naples; this is a salad version of that dish. A colorful variation I enjoyed recently in Jerusalem had strips of roasted red pepper tossed with the artichoke pieces. For a spicy variation in the Algerian style, flavor the dressing with a little Harissa (page 393) or other hot pepper sauce to taste.

4 large artichokes, or 1 9-ounce package frozen artichoke heart pieces
1 medium garlic clove, very finely minced
1½ tablespoons strained fresh lemon juice
3 tablespoons extra-virgin olive oil

1 tablespoon capers, drained and coarsely chopped
1½ tablespoons chopped fresh parsley
Salt and freshly ground pepper
12 Kalamata olives
2 large hard-boiled eggs, quartered (optional)

If using fresh artichokes, prepare and cook artichoke bottoms (page 22). If using frozen artichokes, cook them according to package directions. Drain artichokes well. Quarter fresh artichokes.

Mix garlic, lemon juice, oil, capers, parsley, and salt and pepper to taste. Toss with artichokes. (*Salad can be kept, covered, 1 day in refrigerator.*) Serve garnished with olives and hard-boiled eggs.

Makes 4 appetizer servings

MOROCCAN ARTICHOKE AND ORANGE SALAD

Oranges add a refreshing touch to this unusual, easy-to-make salad. For this recipe some people cook oranges directly in the dressing, but I prefer to leave them raw for a fresher taste and to flavor the light, garlic-scented dressing with orange juice and grated orange zest. Serve this salad as part of a buffet or as a light appetizer before a chicken or couscous dinner. If you like, serve the salad on a bed of mixed greens.

6 medium artichokes, or 1 9-ounce
    package frozen artichoke hearts
2 cups water
2 medium garlic cloves, peeled
1 lemon, cut in half
1 teaspoon sugar
Salt and freshly ground pepper

1 tablespoon olive oil
2 tablespoons strained fresh orange
    juice
½ teaspoon grated orange rind
2 oranges, peeled and divided in
    segments
1 tablespoon chopped fresh parsley

If using fresh artichokes, shape them in bottoms (page 22). Bring water to boil with garlic cloves, juice of ½ lemon, sugar, and salt. Add artichokes, reduce heat, and cook, covered, for 20 minutes for fresh or 6 minutes for frozen, or until just tender.

Remove artichokes and garlic. Drain artichokes well and let cool. Remove chokes from fresh artichokes with spoon. Quarter fresh artichokes.

Chop garlic. Mix it with the oil, orange juice, grated orange rind, and 2 teaspoons lemon juice. Season to taste with salt and pepper.

Combine artichokes and orange segments in a serving dish. Pour dressing over them. (*Salad can be kept, covered, 4 hours in refrigerator.*) Serve cold, sprinkled with parsley.

Makes 4 appetizer servings

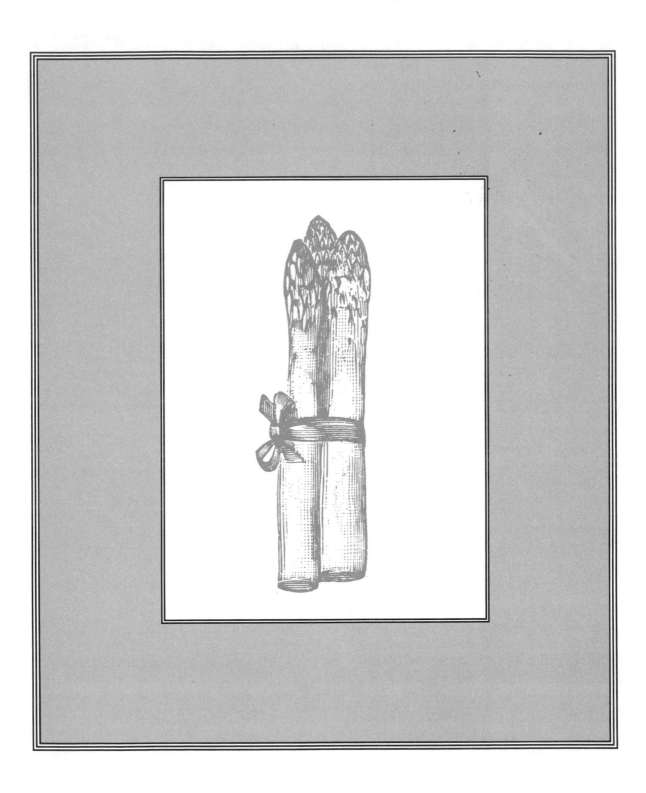

5

Asparagus

Native to southern Europe, asparagus was already cultivated in the time of the ancient Romans, but only the wealthy could afford it; the poor had to make do with the wild version of the vegetable. Now asparagus is popular throughout Europe and North America, and in recent years has become a favorite in Chinese and Vietnamese cooking as well.

I have encountered various ways to prepare asparagus. "You should use a special steamer so the spears stand up," advise gadget-loving cooks. Another method favored by professional chefs is to tie each portion of asparagus spears in a neat bundle, cook the bundles in lots of boiling water, remove the string, and drain the asparagus on towels. Some purists insist that you peel the asparagus and serve the stalks whole; and woe to you if you break one while peeling it!

There are sound reasons behind these techniques, but I prefer a much simpler approach, which is the most practical in home kitchens. I cut the spears in three or four pieces and cook them in an uncovered saucepan of boiling salted water until they are tender but retain a little bite and remain a vivid green. This takes only a few minutes. Asparagus should never be overcooked; it's important to remember that after being boiled, it continues to cook from the heat of the water.

Students in my cooking classes often ask me why I peel asparagus. Peeled asparagus is much more pleasant to eat. I find it worthwhile to take the time to peel them, because this helps ensure cooked asparagus of a perfect texture. If you do not peel asparagus, the peel remains tough and fibrous, while the center of the vegetable becomes crisp-tender. Of course, pencil-thin asparagus stalks don't need peeling; you could hardly peel them if you wanted to. Another exception is asparagus that will be roasted, which doesn't need peeling either (see page 39).

The first spring asparagus is best savored on its own as an appetizer, delicately flavored with a light dressing such as Sun-Dried Tomato Vinaigrette (page 36) or Tarragon Vinaigrette (page 103). I like it the French way, served warm rather than chilled. As a side dish or a component of other dishes, the asparagus can be simply cooked, drained, and seasoned; for a special treat, the cooked asparagus can be briefly sautéed in a little olive oil or fresh butter.

In Europe asparagus is clearly the king of spring vegetables. When it appears, restaurants in Germany and Austria proudly announce its arrival on menus and even display banners outside their establishments proclaiming "We have asparagus!" Several years ago I was very impressed by the menu at a small restaurant in Salzburg, Austria, where I happened to be during the asparagus season. There was a seasonal section on the menu devoted to this noble vegetable, with such dishes as veal chops with hollandaise sauce topped with asparagus, cream of asparagus soup, asparagus vinaigrette, asparagus tips with scrambled eggs, and asparagus and carrots in parsley cream sauce. Europeans love asparagus with seafood, either as a side dish or in a seafood sauce such as the Polish dish Asparagus with Shrimp and Dill Sauce (page 38).

At one of my favorite Los Angeles Chinese restaurants, Panda Inn, asparagus might be added in springtime to almost any dish you choose, whether it is rice-wine–flavored shrimp or stir-fried chicken strips with brown sauce. Asparagus cooks so quickly and marries so beautifully with most ingredients that it can enhance many home-cooked dishes with almost no effort. Try it as a partner for grilled salmon, or toss it with scrambled eggs, fettuccine, or rice pilaf.

A favorite Italian way of preparing asparagus is to sprinkle it with melted butter and grated Parmesan cheese and top it with a fried egg. In Spain, Italy, and southern France asparagus is also loved seasoned with oil and lemon juice, and is added to omelets and frittatas.

ASPARAGUS BASICS

✗ Season: Although asparagus is available during most of the year, spring is its peak season.

✗ Choosing: Asparagus should be firm, with compact, closed tips; the green variety should be bright green. Most asparagus in the United States is green, but occasionally you can find white asparagus, the type that is more common in France and Germany. Their flavors are quite similar, though some people have a strong preference for one or the other. They are interchangeable in recipes and make a difference mainly in the color of the dish.

✗ Storing: Remove any rubber bands. Store unwashed in a plastic bag or closed container in the refrigerator for up to 3 days. You can wrap the bases in damp paper towels or set asparagus upright in a container with their bases in water to prolong freshness, as is done in some supermarkets.

✗ Serving Size: 4 to 8 ounces per person as an appetizer or side dish, or 5 to 8 medium or 10 to 12 thin spears.

✗ Nutrients: Asparagus is a good source of vitamins A and C, and contains some calcium and iron. Eight medium spears contain about 30 calories.

✗ Basic Preparation: If asparagus is more than ¼ inch thick, peel it if you like. Snap or trim off tough asparagus bases—usually the bottom inch or two—and discard them. Rinse asparagus.

How to Peel Asparagus

Asparagus is peeled like carrots, but is held flat on a surface rather than in the air. You put a stalk on a cutting board or counter lined with paper towels, grasp the base, and use a swivel-type peeler to peel downward from below the tip. At about an inch from the bottom, you stop peeling, as you'll trim this tough part later. Next you turn the asparagus stalk slightly and remove another strip of peel. When all the stalks are peeled, cut off the bases and rinse the asparagus.

Notes on Asparagus

✗ Tying asparagus in bundles is practical for restaurant use or when preparing very large quantities, because it's easier to remove the asparagus from the water. This is not necessary for average home portions.

✗ Asparagus cookers are tall saucepans that enable you to cook asparagus standing up, so the stalks boil and the delicate tips are steamed. This is a good method, but in kitchens that lack room for a pot that is good for cooking only one vegetable, using a sauté pan or skillet for cooking asparagus works fine.

BASIC SAUTÉED ASPARAGUS

Serve this as a simple side dish, or use this method for preparing asparagus to add to other dishes such as sautéed chicken strips, scrambled eggs, or cooked fettuccine.

1 pound medium asparagus spears, peeled if over ¼ inch thick
1 to 2 tablespoons butter, olive oil, or vegetable oil

Salt and freshly ground pepper

Cut asparagus tips from stems. Cut stems into 2 or 3 pieces, discarding tough ends (about ½ inch from end). Put all the asparagus in a medium saucepan containing enough boiling salted water to cover it generously. Boil uncovered until asparagus is just tender when pierced with a small sharp knife, about 2 to 3 minutes. Drain, rinse with cold running water until cool, and drain thoroughly.

Melt butter in a medium skillet over medium heat. Add asparagus, salt, and pepper and sauté about 1 minute. Serve hot.

Makes 4 side-dish servings

CHINESE ASPARAGUS IN GINGER-SCENTED BROWN SAUCE

Chinese cooks excel in cooking asparagus so that it is well seasoned but the natural flavor shines through. This is an easy, delicious example. The asparagus is briefly braised in a tasty mixture of fresh ginger, green onion, soy sauce, and rice wine, then the liquid is lightly thickened to coat the vegetable. Serve it as an accompaniment to roast chicken or grilled fish, or on its own with white rice.

1 pound medium or thick asparagus
½ cup Chicken or Vegetable Stock
   (pages 407, 406) or canned broth
1 tablespoon plus 1 teaspoon soy sauce
½ teaspoon sugar
1 tablespoon rice wine or dry sherry

1½ teaspoons cornstarch
1 tablespoon water
1 tablespoon vegetable oil
1 teaspoon minced peeled fresh ginger
1 green onion, minced (2 tablespoons)

Peel asparagus and trim ends. Cut stalks diagonally into 2-inch pieces. In a bowl mix stock, soy sauce, sugar, and wine. In a small cup, mix cornstarch and water.

Heat oil in wok or skillet over high heat. Add ginger and green onion, and stir-fry for 15 seconds. Add asparagus and stir-fry a few seconds more. Add broth mixture and bring to a boil. Cover and simmer over medium heat about 3 minutes or until asparagus is crisp-tender. Push asparagus to side of pan. Stir cornstarch mixture, stir it into simmering liquid, and cook 1 to 2 minutes or until thickened. Toss with asparagus. Serve immediately.

Makes 2 main-course servings with rice, or 4 side-dish servings

NOTE: For a more substantial main course, add 1 small can straw mushrooms, drained, or 8 ears of cooked fresh or drained canned baby corn.

ASPARAGUS WITH SUN-DRIED TOMATO VINAIGRETTE

Asparagus with vinaigrette is a favorite appetizer throughout Europe. This vinaigrette is flavored with chopped sun-dried tomatoes, a southern Italian staple that became the symbol of trendy restaurants on both sides of the Atlantic in the eighties. Now that sun-dried tomatoes are widely available for home cooking and are produced in America as well, trend-happy chefs have moved on to other items. But the time-honored Italian tomatoes have their merits and are a tasty, colorful addition to the dressing.

1 teaspoon herb or white wine vinegar
Salt and freshly ground pepper
1 tablespoon extra-virgin olive oil
1 teaspoon chopped oil-packed sun-
    dried tomatoes

1 teaspoon minced fresh parsley
8 to 12 ounces medium asparagus,
    peeled and ends trimmed

Whisk vinegar with salt and pepper. Whisk in oil. Stir in tomatoes and parsley. Taste and adjust seasoning.

In a sauté pan of boiling salted water to generously cover, cook asparagus uncovered for 3 to 5 minutes or until just tender. Drain thoroughly; rinse if not serving immediately.

Transfer asparagus briefly to a plate covered with a cloth or with paper towels, then to a serving platter or plates. Arrange so spears point in same direction.

Stir dressing and spoon over center of asparagus spears. Serve warm or at room temperature.

Makes 2 appetizer servings

ASPARAGUS WITH COLD MUSTARD-SHALLOT SAUCE

Asparagus and artichokes are considered noble vegetables in the European and North American kitchens, and so they are sometimes served like expensive seafood—with butter or sauces for dipping, as in this recipe and its variations.

When I worked in the kitchen of the elegant Parisian restaurant Maxim's, I noticed that asparagus was served on a white cloth napkin. I assumed this was done just for a fancy presentation, but in fact it had another purpose. Steamed asparagus is best when well drained, and the napkin absorbs any water clinging to the vegetable. At home, too, whole asparagus should be set briefly on a cloth or paper towel before being served.

The zesty mustard-shallot sauce in this recipe is also a fine accompaniment for green beans.

1 pound medium asparagus
3 tablespoons mayonnaise, regular or
  reduced-calorie
1 teaspoon Dijon mustard

1½ teaspoons minced shallot
1 teaspoon chopped fresh parsley
A few drops warm water
Salt and freshly ground pepper

Peel asparagus stems and cut off about ½ inch of bases. Rinse well.

Mix mayonnaise with mustard, shallot, and parsley. If sauce is too thick, stir in a little water. Season to taste with salt and pepper.

Pour enough water to easily cover asparagus into a sauté pan, add salt, and bring to a boil. Add asparagus and boil about 3 minutes, or until just tender when pierced with a sharp knife. With a slotted spatula, transfer asparagus carefully to a plate lined with paper towels. Serve asparagus hot or cold, with mustard sauce for dipping.

Makes 2 or 3 side-dish servings

VARIATIONS:

Quick Italian Asparagus with Lemon and Anchovy
Cook asparagus as above. Serve hot, with the following dipping sauce: Mix 2 tablespoons extra-virgin olive oil or melted butter with 1 finely chopped anchovy fillet, 1 tablespoon chopped parsley, 1 tablespoon strained fresh lemon juice, and freshly ground pepper to taste.

Asparagus with Herb-Lemon Butter
Prepare Herb-Lemon Butter (page 391). Melt it in a small saucepan over low heat. Cook asparagus as above. Serve hot, with Herb-Lemon Butter for dipping.

ASPARAGUS WITH
SHRIMP AND DILL SAUCE

This luxurious recipe from the Polish kitchen pairs asparagus with a creamy crawfish sauce, as this freshwater crustacean is plentiful in that country. In our markets it's easier to find shrimp, so I have substituted them. The sauce is made from the shrimp cooking liquid and is finished with fresh dill. For special occasions enrich it with sour cream, but for casual meals you can use the light variety of sour cream, and the dish will still make a savory appetizer.

½ cup dry white wine
½ cup fish stock, homemade or frozen; or 6 tablespoons bottled clam juice plus 2 tablespoons water
2 small dill sprigs
¼ pound small or medium shrimp, in shell, rinsed
2 tablespoons (¼ stick) butter

1 tablespoon plus 1 teaspoon all-purpose flour
Salt and freshly ground pepper
1½ pounds asparagus
⅓ cup sour cream or light sour cream
1 tablespoon plus 1 teaspoon chopped fresh dill

Bring wine, stock, and dill to a boil in a small saucepan. Add shrimp, cover, and cook 3 minutes over low heat or until just cooked; meat should be white. Remove and shell shrimp, return shells to pan, and simmer covered for 10 minutes. Strain cooking liquid into a bowl, pressing. Discard shells and dill sprigs.

Melt butter in same saucepan over low heat. Whisk in flour and cook for 1 or 2 minutes or until foaming but not browned. Whisk in shrimp cooking liquid. Bring to a boil, whisking. Add salt and pepper, and simmer uncovered for 2 minutes, whisking occasionally. (*Sauce can be kept, covered, up to 1 day in refrigerator; refrigerate shrimp in separate container.*)

Peel asparagus stems and cut off about ½ inch of bases. Rinse well. Cut shrimp in half.

Reheat sauce in small saucepan over low heat, whisking. In a small bowl, stir sour cream until smooth, then whisk in about ⅓ cup sauce. Return to pan of sauce and bring just to a simmer, stirring. Add shrimp and chopped dill, and heat gently. Taste and adjust seasoning. Cover to keep warm.

Bring at least 1 inch of water to boil in base of steamer. Put asparagus in steamer above boiling water. Sprinkle with salt, cover, and steam about 5 minutes, or until just tender when pierced with a sharp knife. With a slotted spatula, transfer asparagus carefully to a plate lined with paper towels. Arrange spears on a platter or on plates, pointing in same direction. Spoon warm sauce with shrimp across center of spears.

Makes 4 appetizer servings

✗ROASTED ASPARAGUS

Consider this a basic recipe for preparing asparagus. For people like me, who used to believe that asparagus must be peeled to be enjoyed, this method is a discovery. Just rinse the asparagus, cut off the bases, and roast. The result is excellent. Unlike boiled or steamed asparagus, the peel doesn't get tough or stringy when you roast the vegetable; the asparagus acquires a good texture and an intense flavor.

When I began to see roasted asparagus on modern menus, I thought it was a new method for preparing the vegetable, but this is actually an old technique. There are seventeenth-century records from Italy that describe moistening asparagus with olive oil, sprinkling it with salt and pepper, and roasting it, then squeezing a little orange juice over it.

2 pounds medium-width or thick
    asparagus
2 tablespoons olive oil

Salt and freshly ground pepper
Lemon and orange wedges, for serving
    (optional)

Preheat the oven to 500°F. Rinse asparagus and cut off tough bases, about 1 to 1½ inches. Put asparagus in a roasting pan or large shallow baking dish so it makes 1 or 2 layers. Sprinkle evenly with oil, salt, and pepper and toss. Roast uncovered, shaking dish often to turn spears, about 8 to 10 minutes, or until crisp-tender. Serve with lemon and orange wedges.

Makes 4 appetizer servings

ROASTED ASPARAGUS, RED PEPPER, AND PASTA SALAD

The deep flavor of roasted vegetables adds excitement to this summery salad. You can roast the pepper and asparagus at the same time. Or if you already have cooked asparagus on hand, you can use roasted peppers from a jar. This might seem to be an Italian recipe, but it is actually an American one. Salads of vegetables and pasta, which often feature Italian seasonings like this one, are much more widespread in the United States than in Italy.

Lemon, orange, or herb-accented pasta is perfect in this salad, and so is plain pasta of good quality. SEE PHOTOGRAPH.

1 pound medium-width or thick
    asparagus, bases trimmed
3 tablespoons extra-virgin olive oil
Salt and freshly ground pepper to taste
1 red bell pepper
8 ounces linguine or tagliarini

½ teaspoon dried oregano
1 green onion, chopped
3 tablespoons chopped fresh parsley
2 teaspoons strained fresh lemon juice
Hot pepper sauce to taste

Preheat the oven to 500°F. Put asparagus in a roasting pan or shallow baking dish large enough to hold them in 1 or 2 layers. Sprinkle evenly with 1 tablespoon oil, salt, and pepper and toss.

Halve the pepper, core, and put on a small foil-lined baking dish, cut side down.

Roast both vegetables uncovered in oven, shaking asparagus dish often to turn spears; asparagus should roast about 8 to 10 minutes or until crisp-tender, peppers 10 to 15 minutes or until tender. As soon as asparagus is tender, transfer to a plate. Cover pepper with towel or enclose in its foil and let stand about 10 minutes. Remove peel from pepper with aid of a paring knife.

Cook pasta in a large pot of boiling salted water until *al dente*, about 3 minutes. Drain well. Rinse lightly to cool. Transfer to a bowl. Add remaining oil, oregano, and green onion and toss. Let cool.

Cut off asparagus tips. Cut stalks into ½- to 1-inch lengths, and peppers into 2-inch strips. Reserve some asparagus tips and pepper strips for garnish. Add remaining asparagus and pepper pieces to bowl of pasta. Add parsley, salt and pepper, lemon juice, and hot sauce. Toss well. Taste and adjust seasoning. (*Can be kept, covered, 1 day in refrigerator.*) Serve garnished with asparagus tips and pepper strips.

Makes 4 appetizer or 2 or 3 main-course servings

BAKED EGGS WITH ASPARAGUS

Visitors to France return with memories of wonderful baked eggs. In elegant restaurants eggs baked on a bed of asparagus and sometimes served with a ribbon of truffle sauce make a lovely first course. A favorite light main course for a casual café lunch or supper is the simple but delicious oeufs à la crème, or eggs baked in plenty of crème fraîche. This is a combination of both, with the eggs baked on a bed of creamed asparagus.

For a variation popular in Italy, sprinkle the eggs with freshly grated Parmesan cheese before baking.

½ pound tiny asparagus (about ½ bunch; see Note), ends trimmed, rinsed

Salt and freshly ground pepper
6 to 7 tablespoons heavy cream
4 large eggs

Position rack in center of oven and preheat to 425°F. Cut off asparagus tips so that they are about 2½ inches long and reserve for garnish. Cut stems into ½-inch pieces. Cook asparagus pieces (but not tips) in medium saucepan of boiling salted water until just tender, about 2 minutes. Drain thoroughly.

Combine cooked asparagus pieces with 2 or 3 tablespoons cream in heavy, medium skillet and bring to boil, stirring. Simmer over medium-low heat until cream coats asparagus, about 1 minute. Season well with salt and pepper; seasoning should also be enough for eggs. (*Can be prepared 1 day ahead. Cover and refrigerate.*)

Reheat asparagus mixture if necessary in heavy, medium skillet over low heat. Butter 4 individual 6-inch shallow baking dishes or one 5-cup shallow dish of about 8½-inch diameter. Divide hot mixture among individual dishes or spread in large dish. Break eggs on top. Spoon 1 tablespoon cream over each egg. Bake until egg whites are just set and yolks are still soft, about 6 minutes for individual dishes or 8 minutes for large dish, or until done to your taste.

Meanwhile, cook asparagus tips in medium saucepan of boiling salted water until just tender, about 2 minutes. Drain well and keep warm.

When eggs are done, arrange asparagus tips around edges of eggs in small dishes. Set tips between eggs and around edges of whites in large dish, letting yolks show. Set individual baking dishes on plates and serve immediately.

Makes 4 first-course or 2 main-course servings

NOTE: Three-fourths pound large asparagus can be substituted. Peel stems. Cook stems about 4 minutes, tips about 3 minutes.

SUMMERTIME ANGEL-HAIR PASTA

This delicate, colorful pasta dish is a lovely way to showcase asparagus. It is based on a pasta dish I tasted in Salerno in southern Italy, but unlike many other pasta dishes from that region, it doesn't have a thick, heavy tomato sauce.

For this quick, easy dish, the sauce consists of cut tomatoes marinated in olive oil and herbs. It requires no cooking and could be more accurately called a dressing or salsa rather than a sauce. You simply let the tomatoes stand with the seasonings while the water for cooking the vegetables and pasta is coming to a boil.

For a quick dish I season the sauce with dried thyme, but this light, Italian-style salsa can also be flavored with cilantro, Italian parsley, basil, or oregano for delicious variations. Naturally, the better the olive oil you use, the better the dish will taste.

Since this dish is so versatile, I think of it as a basic formula. I love it on its own, or with a sprinkling of freshly grated Parmesan. Sometimes I toss in strips of roast chicken, smoked turkey, or additional cooked green vegetables like spinach or broccoli. For a tangy touch, I scatter a few capers on top. When I want a hot taste, I add a chopped fresh jalapeño pepper to the oil when marinating the tomatoes, or a few shakes of cayenne pepper.

Flexible for serving, the pasta is good at room temperature as a salad or hot as an appetizer or a main course. It's simple enough to be a convenient accompaniment for roast chicken or grilled fish as well. And it's excellent for those warm days when you feel like dining on the patio or having a picnic in the park.

You can substitute dried angel-hair pasta, which is sometimes called cappellini, for the fresh version. Either way, this tricolored dish is elegant and easy.

4 ripe plum tomatoes, diced
2 to 3 tablespoons extra-virgin olive oil
½ teaspoon dried thyme, crumbled
1 to 2 tablespoons chopped fresh
    parsley (optional)
Salt and freshly ground pepper

½ pound medium-width asparagus,
    peeled
1 8-ounce package fresh angel-hair
    pasta
Freshly grated Parmesan cheese
    (optional)

In a large bowl combine tomatoes, 2 tablespoons oil, thyme, parsley, salt, and pepper.

Bring a large pot of water to a boil. Add salt. Cut each asparagus stalk in 3 pieces, discarding tough bases (about ½ inch from end). Cook asparagus in boiling water uncovered until crisp-tender, about 4 minutes. Remove with slotted spoon. Add pasta and cook until *al dente*, about 1 minute. Drain well. Reserve asparagus tips for garnish. Transfer pasta and asparagus stem pieces to bowl of tomatoes and toss quickly. Taste and adjust seasoning; add remaining oil if desired. Serve pasta topped with remaining asparagus. Accompany with cheese.

Makes 4 appetizer or 2 main-course servings

ASPARAGUS FEUILLETES WITH DRIED MUSHROOM SAUCE

This is a rich, super-elegant appetizer like those served at the best French restaurants. It makes use of asparagus in its traditional role as a noble vegetable. The asparagus tips are given a regal presentation by being served in feuilletes, *or diamond or square puff pastry cases.*

For this recipe you can make the sauce and bake the pastries in advance. Purchase puff pastry dough from a bakery rather than using prerolled sheets for these pastries, so they will puff high.

1 pound good-quality puff pastry
   dough, well chilled
1 egg, beaten with a pinch of salt
   (for glaze)

18 medium asparagus spears
Dried Mushroom Sauce (page 398)
1 tablespoon butter
Salt and freshly ground pepper

Before shaping the pastries, sprinkle a large baking sheet lightly with water. Roll pastry on a cold, lightly floured surface until ¼ inch thick. Work as quickly as possible. Keep edges of dough as straight as possible and flour often. Cut it into six 4-inch squares or diamonds. Turn each one over and transfer to prepared baking sheet. Refrigerate 30 minutes or freeze 15 minutes, or until pastry is firm. (*Cases can be kept, covered, 1 day in refrigerator.*)

Position rack in center of oven and preheat to 450°F. Brush pastries with egg glaze. Using the point of a sharp knife, mark a crisscross design on top, cutting through only top few layers of pastry.

Bake pastries 5 minutes. Reduce oven temperature to 400°F. and bake about 15 minutes or until pastries are puffed and browned. Transfer to racks. (*Baked cases can be kept 1 day in an airtight container or can be frozen.*)

Cut off asparagus tips about 3 inches long. (Rest of asparagus can be used in soups or salads.) Add asparagus to a saucepan of boiling salted water and boil uncovered over high heat about 2 minutes or until crisp-tender. Drain in a colander, rinse with cold water, and drain well.

Reheat pastry cases, if necessary, in a 300°F. oven. Reheat sauce over medium heat, stirring. Melt butter in a skillet, add asparagus tips, salt, and pepper and sauté over medium heat for 1 minute or until hot.

Carefully cut each pastry case in half horizontally, using a serrated knife. Put bottom half of each case on a plate. Top with 3 asparagus tips and a little sauce. Set top pastry half on at an angle, allowing asparagus to show. Spoon a little more sauce on plates near pastry. Serve immediately.

Makes 6 appetizer servings

6

Green Beans

When I lived in France I learned to treasure green beans. *Haricots verts*, the thin French green beans, are equally at home in salads for Bastille Day picnics and at elegant dinners where they are paired with seafood, *foie gras*, and other luxurious ingredients.

French cooks treat beans with care. My chef/teacher at La Varenne Cooking School in Paris chided me for pinching off too much of the precious beans when removing the ends. He instructed me to cook the beans precisely. The way to judge whether they were done, I was told, is simple—you taste one. It should be tender yet slightly crisp, not hard and raw-tasting but not mushy, either.

When my students ask me how to ensure that green beans cook to a beautiful color and a perfect texture, I recommend the French method. I tell them to cook fresh beans like pasta, in plenty of boiling salted water in an uncovered pot, and to drain them immediately. The beans taste good even plain, and in these diet-conscious days they make a fine accompaniment for roast chicken or grilled fish.

This cooking technique makes it easy to prepare green beans ahead at home, as chefs do in many fine restaurants. When the beans are barely crisp-tender, you pour them with their cooking water into a colander and rinse them with cold water until they are completely cool. You then drain them, refrigerate them, and they are ready for reheating, for salads, or as a healthful snack.

Of course, the French are not the only people to enjoy green beans. The beans are popular in most of Europe. In Austria and Germany they are loved in cream sauce, and in tangy salads with onions. Czech and Slovak cooks serve green beans in sour cream sauce, and so do Hungarians, who season the beans with paprika and garlic.

In Mediterranean countries green beans are made into appetizer salads, flavored with an olive oil and lemon juice dressing. But the favorite way to prepare the beans is in stews. The Italians stew them with zucchini, potatoes, and garlic, or simmer them in a sage tomato sauce. The Lebanese stew green beans in a garlicky tomato sauce. A similar dish is prepared in the Balkan countries, but the sauce is flavored with green peppers, hot paprika, and dill.

Green beans are loved in the Far East also. The Chinese braise them with ginger, garlic, and sometimes black mushrooms. In Indonesia and Malaysia green beans are cooked in curries with coconut milk or in tangy sauces seasoned with chilies and lemongrass. Curried beans are frequently prepared in India as well, on their own or combined with other vegetables and seasoned with chilies, ginger, garlic, and turmeric.

Latin American cooks serve green beans cold in salads flavored with cilantro dressing or hot and seasoned with cumin and hot red pepper. In North America they're also popular in salads, such as sweet-and-sour three-bean salad, or are served hot with butter, salt, and pepper.

If you plan to serve the beans in tomato sauce, a recipe that is popular from Provence to Lebanon, or in Indonesian-style curry sauce, it might seem a good idea to cook them directly in the sauce. However, their cooking time is much shorter if they are cooked in water, rinsed, then heated briefly in the sauce. Besides, this way their color remains an appealing green.

You also can reheat cooked beans in a skillet in a little butter or olive oil with garlic, or by dipping them quickly in boiling water and draining them.

To preserve the beans' green color in salads, add any vinegar or lemon juice at the last minute. If beans remain in contact with these acidic ingredients for long, they acquire an unattractive grayish tinge.

The French have traditionally used very thin green beans called *haricots verts*, which are occasionally available in American markets. The U.S. varieties of green beans are also available in France. Like my Parisian teachers, I don't bother to "French" my beans, or cut them in thin pieces to imitate *haricots verts*. American beans taste delicious as they are.

Green beans used to be called string beans, but today's varieties rarely have strings. French beans, Chinese foot-long beans, flat Romano beans, and yellow beans (wax beans) are available in some markets and can be cooked like green beans. If you find purple beans, don't expect to serve purple food—they turn green in cooking.

GREEN BEAN BASICS

✗ **Season:** Green beans are available all year. Wax beans are available mainly in the summer, which is also the peak of the green bean season.

✗ **Choosing:** Beans should be crisp, firm, smooth, and free of brown spots. Choose slender beans of approximately equal size for even cooking.

✗ **Storing:** Keep beans unwashed in a plastic bag in the refrigerator for up to 3 or 4 days.

✗ **Serving Size:** Allow about ¼ pound beans per person as a side dish.

✗ **Nutrients:** Beans are a good source of vitamin A and have some vitamin C and potassium. One cup of cooked beans has 30 to 40 calories.

✗ **Basic Preparation:** Rinse beans and pinch or cut off ends. Cook them whole or break or cut each bean into 2 or 3 pieces.

GREEN BEANS BASQUAISE

Sometimes the simplest recipes are the best, and not many green bean preparations top this one of simply heating the briefly cooked beans with olive oil and garlic. It is a favorite in the Basque regions of northern Spain and southern France, and is popular in Italy as well. And it's also a terrific way to reheat leftover cooked beans.

1 pound green beans, ends removed
Salt and freshly ground pepper
2 tablespoons olive oil

2 large garlic cloves, minced
Cayenne pepper (optional)

Add beans to a large saucepan of boiling salted water and boil about 6 minutes or until crisp-tender. Drain in a colander or strainer, rinse under cold running water until cool, and drain thoroughly.

In a large skillet heat oil over medium heat, add garlic and sauté 10 seconds. Add beans and sauté over low heat, stirring often, for 2 minutes or until heated through. Season to taste with salt, pepper, and cayenne pepper.

Makes 3 or 4 side-dish servings

LEBANESE GREEN BEANS WITH TOMATOES AND GARLIC

I first tasted this traditional Middle Eastern dish in Israel, where it is one of the most popular ways of cooking beans. The fresh, natural flavors of the dish make it appeal to everyone. The beans simmer gently with fresh tomatoes, onions, and garlic, which form a sauce. Serve these savory beans as a side dish or sprinkle them with a little extra-virgin olive oil and lemon juice for a tasty salad.

You can use the same water used to scald the tomatoes before peeling them to also cook the beans.

1½ pounds green beans, ends
    removed, halved
2 tablespoons olive oil
1 medium onion, halved and sliced
6 large garlic cloves, minced
1½ pounds ripe tomatoes, peeled,
    seeded, and chopped; or 1 28-
    ounce and 1 14-ounce can plum
    tomatoes, drained and chopped

Salt and freshly ground pepper
1 to 2 tablespoons extra-virgin olive oil
    (optional; for serving cold)
A few drops of lemon juice (optional;
    for serving cold)

Add beans to a large saucepan of boiling salted water and boil about 5 minutes or until crisp-tender. Drain in a colander or strainer, rinse under cold running water until cool, and drain thoroughly.

Heat 2 tablespoons oil in a large sauté pan over medium heat. Add onion and sauté for 5 minutes. Add garlic and sauté for 1 minute. Add beans and toss over low heat. Add tomatoes, salt, and pepper. Bring to a boil, cover, and cook for 10 minutes over low heat. Uncover and cook over high heat for 1 or 2 minutes to thicken slightly. Taste and adjust seasoning.

Serve hot, cold, or at room temperature. If serving cold, add extra-virgin olive oil and lemon juice to taste.

Makes 4 side-dish servings

SPANISH GREEN BEAN AND RED PEPPER STEW

In this quick, beautiful vegetable stew the vegetables retain their vibrant color because each is separately precooked—the peppers are grilled and the beans are boiled. They finish cooking together briefly with garlic. This is a perfect summertime partner for grilled chicken or steak, or a good accompaniment for rice or pasta.

1 pound green beans, ends trimmed, halved
Salt and freshly ground pepper
2 red bell peppers, grilled and peeled (page 281)

1 to 2 tablespoons olive oil
2 large garlic cloves, chopped
2 tablespoons water
2 tablespoons chopped fresh parsley

Add beans to a sauté pan of boiling salted water, return to a boil, and boil 4 minutes to partly cook. Drain in a colander or strainer, rinse under cold water, and drain thoroughly.

Cut grilled peppers in strips.

Heat oil in the same pan over medium heat. Add garlic and sauté, stirring, about 15 seconds. Add beans, salt, and pepper and sauté 2 minutes. Add peppers and the water. Cover and cook over medium-low heat, stirring often, about 2 to 3 minutes or until beans are crisp-tender. Stir in parsley. Taste and adjust seasoning. Serve hot.

Makes 3 or 4 side-dish servings

ETHIOPIAN SPICED GREEN BEANS AND CARROTS

The idea for this dish came from a vegetarian entree I enjoyed at a casual Ethiopian restaurant in my neighborhood. It is typical of the stews made in Ethiopia with all sorts of vegetables. Instead of green beans and carrots, it might be a mixture of eggplant, carrots, zucchini, and tomatoes; other versions include potatoes or cauliflower.

Usually the vegetables are sautéed in clarified spiced butter, but they also taste very good sautéed in oil. It's the spices—chilies, fresh ginger, cayenne, turmeric, cinnamon, and others—that give the stew its lively character.

Serve the vegetables as a main course with rice and with yogurt to balance the spiciness; in Ethiopia it's likely to also be served with injera—*sourdough pancakes made with a special flour called* teff.

1 pound green beans, ends removed,
    cut into 2- or 3-inch pieces
2 to 3 tablespoons vegetable oil, or half
    oil and half butter
1 large onion, chopped
2 medium garlic cloves, chopped
2 teaspoons minced peeled fresh
    ginger
1 or 2 jalapeño peppers or other hot
    chilies, chopped; or 1 to 2
    teaspoons canned diced roasted
    jalapeño (optional)
Salt to taste

1 teaspoon paprika
⅛ to ¼ teaspoon cayenne pepper, or
    more to taste
¼ teaspoon ground cinnamon
⅛ teaspoon ground cloves
¼ teaspoon turmeric
Pinch of freshly grated nutmeg
1¼ cups plus 1 tablespoon water
1 pound carrots, quartered lengthwise,
    cut into 2-inch sticks
1 tablespoon tomato paste
1 green onion, chopped

Add beans to a large saucepan of boiling salted water and boil uncovered over high heat for 6 minutes or until crisp-tender. Drain in a colander, rinse with cold water, and drain well.

In large casserole or sauté pan, heat oil, add onion, and sauté over medium heat until golden brown, about 10 minutes, stirring often. Add garlic, ginger, chilies, and spices and cook over low heat, stirring, for 1 minute. Stir in 1¼ cups water and bring to a simmer. Add carrots and pinch of salt. Cover and cook over low heat about 15 minutes or until carrots are tender, stirring occasionally.

Mix tomato paste with 1 tablespoon water and add to casserole. Heat gently. Sauce should be fairly thick. Uncover and simmer 1 or 2 minutes if sauce is too thin. Add beans to sauce; heat through. Taste and adjust seasoning. (*Stew can be kept, covered, 2 days in refrigerator.*) Serve hot, sprinkled with green onion.

Makes 4 main-course servings with rice

GREEN BEANS WITH SAUTÉED ONIONS

In France this dish is known as green beans Lyonnaise, since sautéed onions are the hallmark of the cooking of Lyons. But in fact this way of serving green beans, both the thin haricots verts *and the larger beans, is also popular in Brittany, Normandy, and other regions of France.*

A classic variation of this recipe, known as haricots verts bonne femme, *or "good woman's green beans," includes sautéed bacon sprinkled over the beans. But today many "good women" would omit the bacon.*

1 pound green beans or *haricots verts* (thin French beans)	2 medium onions, halved and thinly sliced
Salt and freshly ground pepper	2 tablespoons chopped fresh parsley
2 tablespoons (¼ stick) butter, vegetable oil, or a mixture of both	

Add beans to a large saucepan of boiling salted water and boil uncovered about 4 minutes or until crisp-tender. Drain in a colander or strainer, rinse under cold running water until cool, and drain thoroughly. (*Cooked beans can be kept, covered, 1 day in refrigerator.*)

In a large skillet or sauté pan, heat butter or oil over medium heat. Add onions and sauté about 10 minutes or until light brown. Add beans and sauté over low heat, stirring often, for 2 minutes or until heated through. Add parsley and toss. Season to taste with salt and pepper. Serve hot.

Makes 4 side-dish servings

GREEN BEANS "MIMOSA" WITH FETA CHEESE AND WALNUTS

The classic French green beans "mimosa" dish calls for moistening the vegetable with vinaigrette and sprinkling it with chopped hard-boiled eggs. In this version feta cheese and toasted walnuts add flavor and texture to the topping and make this a beautiful buffet dish. You can serve asparagus, leeks, cauliflower, or broccoli the same way.

⅓ cup walnut halves or pieces, toasted
    (page 413)
4 teaspoons white wine vinegar
Salt and freshly ground pepper
¼ cup walnut or vegetable oil
1 tablespoon minced shallot or green
    onion

1½ pounds green beans, ends removed
½ cup crumbled feta cheese (about 2½
    ounces)
2 large hard-boiled eggs, whites and
    yolks chopped separately

Cool nuts. Chop them fine but not to a powder.

    For dressing, whisk vinegar, salt, and pepper in a small bowl. Whisk in oil, then shallot. Taste and adjust seasoning.

    Add beans to a large pan of boiling salted water and boil until crisp-tender, about 4 minutes. Rinse under cold running water until cool and drain thoroughly. Gently pat dry.

    Transfer beans to a large round platter, with all beans pointing to center. Whisk vinaigrette and spoon it evenly over beans. Sprinkle feta cheese over center, covering part where ends of beans meet. Sprinkle walnuts in a circle around feta. Sprinkle chopped egg yolks around walnuts. Last, sprinkle chopped egg whites around yolks. Allow ends of green beans to show. Serve at room temperature.

Makes 4 first-course servings

INDONESIAN GREEN BEANS

For this zesty dish, the beans are seasoned with coriander, garlic, cumin, and hot pepper flakes. Traditionally this recipe calls for coconut milk, but I have omitted it to keep the dish light. The beans are delicious with Thai jasmine rice or Indian Basmati rice.

¾ pound green beans, ends removed,
    broken into 3 pieces
⅓ cup coarsely chopped onion
2 large garlic cloves, peeled
½ teaspoon ground cumin
1 teaspoon ground coriander
½ teaspoon turmeric
¼ to ½ teaspoon hot red pepper flakes,
    or more to taste

1 tablespoon vegetable oil
¾ cup Chicken or Vegetable Stock
    (pages 407, 406) or canned broth
2-inch piece fresh lemongrass
    (optional)
1 plum tomato, halved, seeded, and
    chopped
Salt
Hot sauce to taste (optional)

Add beans to a large saucepan of boiling salted water and boil uncovered over high heat for 5 minutes or until crisp-tender. Drain in a colander, rinse with cold water, and drain well.

Grind onion, garlic, cumin, coriander, turmeric, and pepper flakes to a paste in a blender or mini food processor.

Heat oil in saucepan, add spice mixture, and sauté over low heat for 1 minute. Add stock and lemongrass and bring to a boil. Cover and simmer 5 minutes. Add tomato and boil 2 minutes or until sauce thickens to taste. Remove lemongrass.

Add beans, sprinkle with salt, and cook uncovered over medium heat until crisp-tender, about 2 minutes. Taste and adjust seasoning; add more pepper flakes or hot sauce if desired. (*Can be kept, covered, 1 day in refrigerator.*) Serve hot.

Makes 2 main-course servings with rice

GREEN BEAN AND CHICKPEA SALAD WITH TOMATOES AND OLIVES

This Provençal salad tastes best with oil-cured Niçoise black olives, but is also delicious when made with Greek Kalamata olives; it is quickest to prepare using canned pitted olives. Serve this colorful salad warm or cold, as an appetizer or main course.

¾ pound green beans, ends removed, halved
Salt and freshly ground pepper
5 to 6 tablespoons olive oil
1 large onion, cut into thin slices
1 15- or 16-ounce can chickpeas (garbanzo beans); or 2 cups cooked chickpeas, drained

½ pound ripe tomatoes, diced
⅓ to ½ cup oil-cured black olives, halved and pitted
3 tablespoons coarsely chopped fresh basil; or 2 to 3 teaspoons dried thyme, crumbled
1 tablespoon strained fresh lemon juice

Add beans to a large saucepan of boiling salted water and boil uncovered over high heat for 6 minutes or until crisp-tender. Drain in a colander, rinse with cold water, and drain well.

Heat 3 tablespoons olive oil in medium skillet over low heat. Add onion and cook, stirring often, until soft but not brown, about 12 minutes.

Combine chickpeas, green beans, cooked onion with its oil, tomatoes, olives, and basil in a glass bowl and toss lightly.

Whisk lemon juice with remaining 2 tablespoons olive oil and salt and pepper to taste; salt lightly because olives are salty. Add to bowl and toss until ingredients are coated. Taste and adjust seasoning. Add more oil if desired. Serve at room temperature.

Makes 4 appetizer or 2 main-course servings

GREEN BEAN, SHRIMP, AND TOMATO SALAD

In my cooking classes on light summer dinners, my students love this easy but elegant French salad flavored with a fresh herb vinaigrette. Serve the salad as an appetizer or main course. To turn it into a side-dish salad, omit the shrimp.

1½ pounds green beans, halved
Salt and freshly ground pepper
1 pound raw medium shrimp, unshelled
1 tablespoon tarragon or herb vinegar
½ teaspoon Dijon mustard (optional)
3 tablespoons extra-virgin olive oil or vegetable oil

2 teaspoons chopped fresh tarragon or thyme, or ½ teaspoon dried
1 teaspoon chopped fresh parsley (optional)
2 ripe medium tomatoes, diced small

Add beans to a large saucepan of boiling salted water and boil about 6 minutes or until crisp-tender. Drain in a colander or strainer, rinse under cold running water until cool, and drain thoroughly.

To cook the shrimp, heat 1 quart water in a sauté pan until simmering. Add a pinch of salt. Add shrimp and simmer over medium heat about 2 minutes or until pink. Drain immediately. Let cool; shell shrimp.

Combine vinegar, mustard, salt, and pepper in a small bowl. Whisk until blended, then whisk in oil. Stir in tarragon and parsley. Taste for seasoning. (*Beans, shrimp, and dressing can be kept in covered containers 1 day in refrigerator.*)

Arrange the green beans on a platter and top with shrimp. Spoon the diced tomatoes in the center of platter. Spoon vinaigrette evenly over shrimp, tomatoes, and beans. Serve at room temperature.

Makes 4 or 5 appetizer, or 2 or 3 main-course servings

*Corn adds flavor and texture to the popular Mexican appetizer, **Tomato and Corn Tortilla Soup** (page 320), in two ways—as kernels and as crisp fried tortilla strips.*

Stuffed Peppers with Rice, Pine Nuts, and Currants (page 284), *a specialty of Turkey, are served hot or cold as an appetizer or main course. The peppers can be presented as the centerpiece of a Mediterranean vegetable feast, along with **Italian Eggplant Stuffed with Scamorze Cheese** (page 183) or **Lebanese Stuffed Tomatoes** (page 317).*

For a fresh, lively North African salad buffet, serve **Moroccan Carrot Salad with Garlic, Cumin, and Parsley** *(page 139),* **Tangy North African Sweet Potato Salad** *(page 311) flavored with olives, saffron, and cilantro, and* **Moroccan Tomato Salad with Red Onions and Parsley** *(page 316). Accompany the salads with fresh pita bread and oil-cured black olives.*

Cuban Black Beans with Peppers and Rice (page 75), flavored with garlic, tomatoes, and cilantro, makes a light and colorful main course, side dish, or salad.

*An easy Indian vegetarian dinner menu features aromatic **Cauliflower with Fresh Ginger and Cumin** (page 98), zesty **Sri Lankan Eggplant Relish** (page 185) flavored with curry and mustard, and cooling **Cucumber Salad with Yogurt and Cumin Seeds** (page 167). Fragrant Basmati rice is the perfect accompaniment.*

Greek Spinach Pastries (page 204) are made of filo dough wrapped around a savory filling of fresh spinach and feta cheese. Whether you serve them hot or at room temperature, these flaky, melt-in-your-mouth pastries are an irresistible party treat.

Roasting highlights the taste of asparagus and peppers. Together they make a delicious **Roasted Asparagus, Red Pepper, and Pasta Salad** *(page 40), seasoned with an herb-lemon-olive oil dressing. For a light, California-style lunch, serve this main-course salad with* **Sauteed Wild Mushrooms with Herbs** *(page 245) or* **Mediterranean Diced Salad, California Style** *(page 376).*

Vegetables are beautifully complemented by flavors of the Orient in Broccoli with Chinese Mushrooms and Oyster Sauce (page 93) and in spicy Thai Vegetable Medley with Mint and Chilies (page 365). Either makes a tasty partner for poultry, meat, or fish or a light main course if served with steamed rice.

GERMAN GREEN BEAN SALAD WITH RED ONIONS

For this light salad the vegetables are seasoned with equal amounts of vinegar and oil rather than the classic French amounts of 3 oil to 1 vinegar. In the summer, when you can find tender, flavorful beans, use these smaller amounts of oil and vinegar to highlight but not mask the beans' delicate flavor.

1½ pounds green beans, ends removed
1 small red onion, sliced thin
½ cup chopped fresh parsley
4 to 6 teaspoons vegetable oil

4 to 6 teaspoons distilled white
   vinegar (5% acidity)
Salt and freshly ground pepper

Add beans to a large saucepan of boiling salted water and boil uncovered over high heat for 7 minutes or until crisp-tender. Drain in a colander, rinse with cold water, and drain well.

   Mix beans with remaining ingredients. Taste and adjust seasoning. Serve within a short time so beans keep their color.

Makes 4 appetizer or side-dish servings

WAX BEANS WITH CÈPES AND GARLIC

In cèpes à la bordelaise, *the sautéed cèpes are flavored with shallots, garlic, and plenty of parsley. They make a delicious ''sauce'' or seasoning mixture for other vegetables like wax beans. These beans are a great accompaniment for shrimp, scallops, or fish.*

¾ to 1 ounce dried cèpes or porcini
   mushrooms
1¼ pounds wax beans or green beans,
   ends removed
Salt and freshly ground pepper

2 tablespoons extra-virgin olive oil
1 medium shallot, minced
2 large garlic cloves, minced
¾ teaspoon dried thyme, crumbled
3 tablespoons chopped fresh parsley

Soak dried cèpes in hot water to cover about 30 minutes or until swollen. Lift into a strainer, rinse, and drain well. Cut into bite-size pieces.

Add beans to a large sauté pan of boiling salted water and boil about 6 minutes or until crisp-tender. Drain in a colander or strainer, rinse under cold running water until cool, and drain thoroughly. (*Cèpes and beans can be kept separately, covered, 2 days in refrigerator.*)

In same sauté pan, heat 1 tablespoon oil over medium-low heat; add shallot, garlic, and cèpes and sauté 1 minute, stirring. Cover and reserve until a short time before serving. Heat cèpe mixture until sizzling. Add remaining oil and heat briefly. Add beans, thyme, salt, and pepper and sauté over medium heat, tossing often, 2 minutes or until heated through. Taste and adjust seasoning. Add parsley, toss, and serve.

Makes 4 side-dish servings

CHINESE LONG BEANS WITH BLACK MUSHROOM SAUCE

This tasty dish is a favorite of mine at Chinese restaurants, but I also enjoy preparing it at home because it is very simple. Its zesty flavor comes from ginger, garlic, and hoisin sauce, and of course, the aromatic dried Chinese black mushrooms.

Chinese long beans are more and more available in U.S. markets. In addition to Oriental markets, some farmers' markets carry them; I've even bought them a few times at my local supermarket. But this recipe is also delicious with ordinary green beans. Serve it with rice, or as an accompaniment for grilled salmon or roast duck.

4 large Chinese dried black
    mushrooms
¾ to 1 pound Chinese long beans or
    green beans, rinsed, ends
    trimmed, cut into 2-inch lengths
1 tablespoon soy sauce

1 tablespoon hoisin sauce
1 to 2 tablespoons vegetable oil
1 tablespoon minced fresh ginger
2 large garlic cloves, minced
Salt and ground white pepper
    (optional)

Soak mushrooms in 1 cup hot water for 30 minutes. Remove mushrooms, reserving liquid. Squeeze out excess liquid from mushrooms. Cut off stems. Cut mushrooms in thin strips and set aside. Measure 6 tablespoons mushroom liquid; add soy sauce and hoisin sauce.

Heat oil in a large skillet, sauté pan, or wok over high heat. Add ginger and garlic, and stir-fry about 15 seconds. Add mushrooms and beans; mix well. Reduce heat to medium-low and add soy sauce mixture. Stir well, cover, and cook, stirring often, for 4 to 5 minutes or until beans are crisp-tender. Uncover and boil 1 minute to evaporate excess liquid. Taste and adjust seasoning, adding salt and pepper if needed. Serve immediately; if allowed to stand, the beans lose their bright color.

Makes 3 side-dish servings or 2 main-course servings with rice

HARICOTS VERTS MAÎTRE D'HÔTEL

Thin French haricots verts *are quite expensive in our country, and therefore they are reserved for special occasions. In France the delicate beans are most often boiled until crisp-tender, and then sautéed lightly in butter, and seasoned only with salt, pepper, and perhaps a little chopped fresh parsley.*

Haricots verts are a better choice for a menu for a romantic dinner for two than for a large party, since removing the ends of a sizable quantity of the tiny beans takes some time. This recipe works for ordinary green beans or wax beans as well.

½ **pound** *haricots verts* **(thin French beans)**
Salt and freshly ground pepper

1 tablespoon butter
1 tablespoon chopped fresh parsley

Add beans to a large saucepan of boiling salted water and boil about 4 minutes or until crisp-tender. Drain in a colander or strainer, rinse under cold running water until cool, and drain thoroughly.

In a medium skillet melt butter over medium heat. Add beans and sauté over low heat, stirring often, for 2 minutes or until heated through. Add parsley and toss. Season to taste with salt and pepper.

Makes 2 side-dish servings

Dried Beans and Shell Beans

⚹ DRIED BEANS

Dried beans, peas, and lentils have gained much interest in recent years because they have turned out to be nutritionally desirable. They are the best plant source of protein and, because they are low in fat, are an excellent substitute for meat. From their previous role mainly as humble, peasant food, legumes have become glamorous. At fine restaurants chefs are now pairing all sorts of beans and lentils with "fancy" ingredients like scallops and duck.

Beans and dried peas are particularly popular in North and South America, Europe, and the Middle East. Many favorite bean dishes in North and South America have their roots in the cooking of the native Indians. The best known example is succotash (page 66), our familiar stew of corn and beans. It is made in many variations, including some South American versions that contain squash, another traditional Indian crop. Mexican refried beans also is a dish of Indian origin.

Hearty, winter soups like Tuscan Bean Soup (page 73) and casseroles like French *cassoulet* and American baked beans come to mind when we think of beans, but they are wonderful in light dishes too, such as a zesty Provençal Chickpea Salad with Fennel, Pistou, and

Tomatoes (page 377), or Turkish-style Artichoke Hearts with Lima Beans and Dill (page 23). In Iran and India split peas are often cooked with a variety of herbs and spices. In the southern U.S., black-eyed peas cooked with rice are a traditional dish for New Year's Day.

Beans can be interchanged in many recipes for interesting, colorful results. They don't taste the same and yet different kinds of beans can take similar seasonings.

Several types of beans are available at the supermarket, but there are more varieties in ethnic grocery stores and specialty shops. For example, you can find meaty, tasty black (turtle) beans at Latin American and gourmet shops or delicate, pale green French *flageolets* at stores specializing in European foods. Chickpeas (garbanzo beans) are sold in some supermarkets and are available in many types of specialty stores; my local Iranian grocery store carries them in a few different sizes, and they're easy to find in other Middle Eastern and Latin American shops. Black beans, *flageolets*, and chickpeas are beautiful in salads and bean casseroles.

Cooking dried beans might seem like a lot of work because it requires soaking and fairly long simmering, but during the soaking and cooking beans demand almost no attention. Also, there is a quicker method to soak beans instead of leaving them overnight; you simply bring them to a boil and then let them stand for an hour. It's practical to cook a generous amount of legumes, as they reheat well. Now some types of beans can be purchased already soaked or frozen, which makes them easier to use. Canned beans don't have quite the same texture as freshly cooked dried ones, but usually canned chickpeas (garbanzo beans) are pretty good.

Another time-saver is dried bean-soup mixes. These contain several kinds of legumes and often dried vegetables as well, and are convenient to keep in the pantry, making it easy to have a pot of soup ready with little effort. I like the mixes best as a soup base; I usually add onions, carrots, potatoes, and zucchini to the soup as it simmers, and dill, cilantro, or parsley at the last moment.

LENTILS

Lentil stew may be one of the most ancient recipes; the Bible tells us that Esau sold his birthright to his brother Jacob in exchange for this dish. The Holy Bible doesn't give the recipe, but the French "culinary bible," Escoffier's *Le Guide Culinaire*, provides us with a formula for "Esau's soup": lentils are cooked with beef consommé and diced bacon and the soup is finished with butter, rice, and chervil sprigs. Somehow I doubt that Jacob made it that way.

Lentils have remained popular in the Middle East to this day. A Lebanese friend of mine told me that when she lived in Beirut fifty years ago, the regional specialty called *majadrah*, or lentils with rice, was a dish for the servants and the poor. The only time that it appeared on the tables of the bourgeoisie was on laundry day when there was little time to cook. Now, she tells me, the dish is popular among people of all classes because of the recognized nutritional merit of lentils. It is served as a main course, accompanied by a cucumber and yogurt salad, or as a side dish with meat, chicken, or even fish. Pairing lentils and rice is so widespread in the Middle East that you can even buy packaged *majadrah* mix at the market.

Actually, this dish is known by different names in a broad area that stretches from India to Armenia. In its simplest form, as prepared by the Armenians and the Lebanese, the lentils and rice are flavored with deeply browned sautéed onions, salt, and pepper, and that's all. As you travel east, spices are added. There's an Iraqi version with cumin and tomato paste, and an Indian recipe called *kitcheree* that includes fresh ginger, garlic, turmeric, cardamom, and cloves.

Lentil-with-rice preparations are only part of the extensive repertoire of lentil dishes. They are made into an impressive variety of dishes, from sauces to pancakes to salads.

In spite of the memorable role of lentils in the Bible and their prominence in the cuisines of the region where the famous biblical bargain took place, we Americans used to overlook them. Here lentils were considered modest fare for sustenance when the food budget is low. But in the last few years lentils, like dried beans, have become fashionable and appear on menus of trendy eateries.

From a nutritional standpoint, lentils have many reasons to be valued. They contain no cholesterol and practically no fat but can play the role of meat in a menu. Lentils are high in complex carbohydrates and fiber and rich in iron and potassium.

Lentils have an advantage over other legumes: they do not require soaking. And they cook quickly, taking only about 20 or 30 minutes to become tender, whereas other legumes usually take over an hour. This makes them the most useful legume for people with busy schedules.

✗ SHELL BEANS

In most countries in which dried beans are widely used, shell beans—their fresh version—are popular too. Shell beans like fresh lima beans and fava beans can be found at our farmers' markets and some supermarkets in the summer. The beans need to be removed from their pods like fresh peas, and this takes some time but it's worth it; for us these beans are a rare treat, with a more delicate texture and flavor than dried beans. When fresh shell beans are not in season, frozen lima beans make an easy, always available, substitute.

BEAN SPROUTS

In the Orient mung beans are allowed to sprout, resulting in the familiar delicate white bean sprouts with light green tails. Bean sprouts are available in Chinese grocery stores and many supermarkets, and are a delightful addition to salads, such as Arugula Salad with Bean Sprouts and Enoki Mushrooms (page 217). They can also be added at the last minute to hot vegetable, rice, or noodle dishes for a delicately crunchy texture. Choose them crisp and white, and use them within a few days.

A variety of other sprouts are becoming available at many markets, such as spicy radish sprouts, mild alfalfa sprouts, and lentil sprouts. Thin, grasslike sprouts are best in salads or sandwiches. More substantial sprouts with beans attached are also good heated.

DRIED BEAN AND SHELL BEAN BASICS

✂ **Season:** Shell beans, especially fava beans and lima beans, are available in summer in some markets. Occasionally you will find other types of shell beans at farmers' markets. Dried beans and frozen lima beans are available throughout the year.

✂ **Choosing:** Shell beans should be heavy and firm, and the pods tightly closed. When buying dried beans, pay attention to the "sell by" date; if a year has passed since this date, the beans might never become tender.

✂ **Storing:** Store shell beans in a plastic bag in the refrigerator; they will keep about 3 days. Dried beans should be kept in a closed container in the pantry.

✂ **Serving Size:** Allow about ¾ pound shell beans in pods, or about 3 ounces dried beans per serving.

✂ **Nutrients:** Shell beans and dried beans are good sources of protein, potassium, and iron. Shell beans contain vitamin C. One cup of cooked lima beans has 190 to 200 calories. One cup cooked navy beans has 258 calories.

Basic Preparation

Shell beans should be removed from their pods and rinsed.

To prepare dried beans, lentils, and split peas, first sort them. Put enough beans on a plate to make one layer. Pick over beans, discarding pebbles and broken or discolored beans. Continue with remaining beans. Rinse beans.

To soak dried beans, put them in a bowl, cover generously with cold water, and let stand 8 hours or overnight. To quick-soak, put beans in a medium saucepan, cover generously with water (about 4 or 5 cups water for 1½ cups beans), bring to a boil, and boil uncovered for 2 minutes. Remove from heat, cover, and let stand 1 hour. Drain beans and rinse. Use fresh water for cooking.

Lentils and split peas do not require soaking; just rinse them before cooking.

DRIED BEANS

TYPE	DESCRIPTION	USES	CUISINE
adzuki beans	small red, slightly sweet; available dried	side dishes, Oriental desserts	Chinese, Japanese
black (turtle)	pea-sized, deep black earthy flavor; available dried and canned	stews, salads	Caribbean, Latin American
black-eyed peas (cowpeas)	black dot on inner rim, kidney-shaped, cream color; available dried, frozen, and soaked	stews, with rice	South U.S.
chickpeas (garbanzo beans, ceci beans)	tan, round, nutty flavor, firm texture; available dried and canned	hummus, casseroles, salads, soups	Middle Eastern, Indian, Latin American
cranberry	beige, dotted with pink; available dried	casseroles	North and South American
flageolet	pale green, kidney-shaped; available dried and canned	stews	French
Great Northern	large, white, kidney-shaped; mild flavor; available dried	casseroles	U.S.
kidney	white or red; available dried and canned; Italian cannelini beans are available canned	chili, stews	European, Middle Eastern, U.S.
lentil	green, red, brown; available dried; need no soaking	soups, with rice, salads	Middle Eastern, Indian, African, European, North and South American

DRIED BEANS

TYPE	DESCRIPTION	USES	CUISINE
lima	white when dried; green when frozen or canned; large and small; large also called butter beans	side dishes, salads, casseroles	North and South American
pinto	reddish-tan with brown dots; available dried or canned	side dishes, chili, refried beans	Mexican, U.S.
red	oval, medium-sized; rich flavor; available dried or canned	with rice, soups, chili	South U.S.
split pea	yellow or green; available dried; need no soaking	soup, purees	Northern European, U.S., Iranian

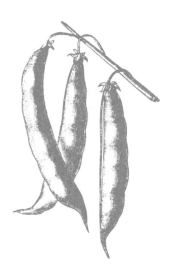

CHILEAN "SUCCOTASH"

Beans and corn are popular in much of America, both North and South. We have succotash; Argentina has puchero, *which also contains meat, potatoes, and peppers; and Chile has this vegetarian version of the corn and bean stew. Like American succotash, this dish is of Indian origin, but the Chilean version also includes winter squash or pumpkin and tomato sauce. It is accompanied by hot sauce to liven it up.*

Chileans use fresh cranberry beans in this stew. To turn it into a quicker dish, I use frozen lima beans, which also make it colorful and besides are easy to find. If you already have 2 cups cooked dried white beans, you can substitute them. Or cook 2 cups fresh lima beans or other shell beans (page 68).

Serve this colorful bean casserole with Chilean Hot Cilantro Salsa (page 388) or your favorite fresh salsa or bottled hot sauce.

1 10-ounce package frozen baby lima
    beans (about 2 cups)
2 tablespoons vegetable oil
1 large onion, chopped
1 tablespoon paprika
1 pound ripe tomatoes, peeled, seeded,
    and chopped; or 1 28-ounce can
    plum tomatoes, drained and
    chopped

1½ teaspoons dried oregano
Salt and freshly ground pepper
1-pound piece winter squash such as
    butternut or banana squash,
    peeled and cut into 1-inch cubes
    (2 to 2½ cups cubes)
1¼ to 1½ cups fresh or frozen corn
    kernels (see Note)

Cook lima beans until barely tender, about 5 minutes or according to instructions on package. Drain, reserving liquid.

Heat oil in a large sauté pan, add onion, and sauté over medium heat for 5 minutes. Add paprika and sauté for 2 minutes over low heat, stirring. Add tomatoes, oregano, salt, and pepper. Stir and cook over medium heat for 5 minutes or until thickened. Add squash and ¾ cup bean liquid. Bring to a simmer. Cover and cook over low heat for 15 minutes, occasionally stirring gently. Add corn and cook 7 minutes or until corn and squash are tender. Add beans, salt, and pepper. Cover and heat over low heat about 2 minutes. Taste and adjust seasoning. Serve with hot sauce.

Makes 4 or 5 side-dish or 3 main-course servings

NOTE: If using fresh corn, use 2 ears of corn weighing a total of 1¼ pounds.

TWO-BEAN SALAD WITH FENNEL

Fresh fennel complements shell beans beautifully. In Cyprus it is matched with fresh fava beans to produce a refreshing yet satisfying salad. I have substituted our more common lima beans so that this becomes a quick and easy salad.

To make the salad lighter, I like to add green beans, wax beans, or some of each. Be sure to add green beans to the salad at the last moment; otherwise the vinegar in the dressing gives them a grayish tinge.

1 medium or large fennel bulb with
    tops
2 to 3 tablespoons extra-virgin olive oil
1 tablespoon white wine vinegar
Salt and freshly ground pepper
2 pounds fresh fava or other shell
    beans; or 1 10-ounce package
    frozen lima beans, cooked
    (see Note)

½ pound green beans or wax beans, or
    some of each
10 to 12 Kalamata olives

Remove outer layer from fennel bulb. Chop 1 tablespoon of the fennel fronds. Cut off stalks and reserve for soups and stews. Halve the fennel bulb, put it cut side down, and cut each half in thin slices. Separate slices into half rings. Soak fennel in cold water to cover for 15 minutes, then drain well and put in a bowl.

Sprinkle fennel with 2 tablespoons oil, vinegar, salt, pepper, and chopped fronds. Marinate 15 minutes. Add cooked fava or lima beans.

Add green beans to a large saucepan of boiling salted water and boil uncovered over high heat for 5 minutes or until crisp-tender. Drain in a colander, rinse with cold water, and drain well. Cook wax beans the same way; they may need 7 minutes. Cut green and wax beans in half. (*Salad can be kept, covered, 2 days in refrigerator; keep green beans separate.*)

Just before serving, add green beans to salad. Taste and adjust seasoning. Add 1 tablespoon oil if desired. Serve at room temperature or cold in a shallow bowl, garnished with olives.

Makes 4 to 6 appetizer or side-dish servings

NOTE: To cook fava beans, see Note on page 68. Cook lima beans according to package directions.

EGYPTIAN BEANS WITH GREENS

Beans cooked with greens of different types—spinach, Swiss chard, and many others—are a popular dish in Egypt. In fact, they are well liked in several other countries too, such as India (see Chickpeas with Spinach and Carrots, page 70) and Italy (see Tuscan Bean Soup, page 73).

For this recipe, the beans are flavored with a pestolike green sauce of sautéed Swiss chard, garlic, and mint. The generous amount of garlic adds a pleasing flavor that is not aggressive. In some homes, ground or diced beef is cooked with the beans, but I prefer this light vegetarian version. It makes a good main course accompanied by yogurt, or a side dish with lamb or chicken. Instead of mint, this dish is sometimes accented with dill, cilantro, or a combination of both.

2 tablespoons olive or vegetable oil	6 large garlic cloves, chopped
1 small or medium onion, chopped	1½ cups coarsely chopped Swiss chard
⅓ cup long-grain rice	leaves
1¾ cups chicken, beef, or vegetable	1 tablespoon chopped mint;
stock	or 1 teaspoon dried mint,
1 10-ounce package lima beans,	crumbled
or 2 pounds fava beans (see Note)	Salt and freshly ground pepper

Heat 1 tablespoon oil in a heavy saucepan, add onion, and sauté over medium heat for 7 minutes or until golden. Add rice, then 1½ cups stock and bring to simmer. Cover and cook over low heat for 10 minutes. Add beans and remaining ¼ cup stock, shake pan, and bring to boil. Cover and cook 5 minutes or until rice and beans are barely tender.

Heat the remaining oil in a heavy, medium skillet. Add garlic and sauté 15 seconds. Add chard and sauté over medium heat, stirring, for 3 minutes. Stir in mint, then puree mixture in food processor.

Add garlic-chard mixture to beans and stir gently. Add salt and pepper to taste. Cook uncovered over medium heat for 2 minutes or until vegetables and rice are tender. (*Can be kept, covered, 2 days in refrigerator, although rice will soften.*) Serve hot, in bowls.

Makes 2 main-course or 4 side-dish servings

NOTE: If fresh fava beans are available, use 2 pounds. Remove beans from pods. Put beans in large saucepan of boiling salted water and cook uncovered over high heat for 5 minutes or until tender. Drain well; peel off thick skin if desired. Add to recipe above after adding chard mixture.

PORTUGUESE LIMA BEANS
WITH CILANTRO

Bacon and chorizo sausage are often cooked with the beans in this dish, but I usually omit them to make the recipe leaner. If you like, you can heat a few slices of lean smoked turkey sausage with the cooked beans for a light smoky flavor. Serve the beans as a side dish with roast or braised chicken or as a main course with rice.

1 tablespoon olive oil
1 large onion, halved and cut in thin
  slices
2 large garlic cloves, minced
½ cup chopped cilantro (fresh
  coriander)
1 small carrot, thinly sliced

¾ cup Chicken or Vegetable Stock
  (pages 407, 406), beef stock, or
  canned broth
1 10-ounce package frozen baby lima
  beans or 2 pounds fava beans,
  shelled and cooked (see Note,
  page 68)
Salt and freshly ground pepper

Heat oil in a medium saucepan, add onion, and sauté over medium heat for about 5 minutes or until soft. Add garlic and half the cilantro, and sauté ½ minute. Add carrot and ½ cup stock, and bring to a boil. Cover and cook over low heat for 8 minutes.

   Add remaining ¼ cup stock and lima beans and bring to a boil. Cover and cook over low heat for about 5 minutes or until vegetables are tender. Add remaining cilantro. Taste and adjust seasoning. Serve hot.

Makes 3 or 4 side-dish or 2 main-course servings

CHICKPEAS WITH
SPINACH AND CARROTS

This colorful, tasty, hot dish is inspired by an Indian recipe for which the chickpeas, spinach, and carrots cook together for about two hours. I add the carrots and spinach at the end so they keep their texture. To save time, I sometimes use canned chickpeas.

Otherwise this recipe is traditional. The spices—cumin, coriander, and poppy seeds—are toasted whole, then ground and blended with fresh chilies and garlic. The spice paste is sautéed with onions and blended with the vegetables to give them a wonderful flavor. Fortunately, all the spices can be found in well-stocked supermarkets. Serve this spicy dish with Indian breads such as naans or chapattis, *or substitute Iranian flat bread or pita. It's also delicious with Basmati rice.*

½ pound dried chickpeas (garbanzo
    beans) (1¼ cups); or 2 15- or
    16-ounce cans, drained
6 cups water
½ pound carrots, sliced ¼ inch thick
½ teaspoon turmeric
Salt to taste
1 10-ounce package frozen spinach,
    thawed and rinsed; or 1 pound
    spinach, leaves and small stems
    only, rinsed and cut or torn into
    bite-size pieces

1 teaspoon cumin seeds
1 teaspoon coriander seeds
½ teaspoon poppy seeds
2 green or red jalapeño or other
    chilies, seeds discarded if desired
    (see page 280)
1 large garlic clove, peeled
1 tablespoon vegetable oil or *ghee*
    (Indian clarified butter)
1 medium onion, halved and sliced
½ cup coarsely chopped cilantro (fresh
    coriander)

Pick over and soak dried chickpeas (page 63). Put peas in a saucepan with 5 cups water. Bring to a simmer, cover, and cook over low heat 2 hours or until tender. Drain well.

In a saucepan combine carrots with remaining 1 cup water, turmeric, and pinch of salt. Bring to a boil, cover, and cook over low heat for 7 minutes. With pan on low heat, add spinach in 3 batches, covering briefly after each addition so spinach wilts. After adding all spinach, simmer uncovered about 3 minutes or until tender.

In a small skillet toast the cumin, coriander, and poppy seeds over medium heat, shaking skillet constantly, for 2 to 3 minutes or until fragrant. Transfer to a shallow bowl and cool. Grind in a spice grinder to a fine powder. Transfer to a mini food processor or blender. Add chilies and garlic, and grind to a paste.

In a medium sauté pan or deep skillet, heat the oil, add onion, and sauté over medium heat for 7 minutes. Add the spice paste and stir over low heat for 3 minutes. With a slotted spoon, add carrot-spinach mixture, then pour in ½ cup of the cooking liquid. Add chickpeas and bring to a boil. If desired, simmer uncovered for 2 to 3 minutes to thicken slightly. Taste and adjust seasoning. (*Dish can be kept, covered, 2 days in refrigerator. Reheat before serving.*) Serve sprinkled generously with cilantro.

Makes 4 or 5 main-course servings with rice

HEALTHY HOPPIN' JOHN

Hoppin' John is a southern dish of black-eyed peas and rice served on New Year's Day to bring good luck during the year. Traditional versions call for adding salt pork or ham, but this light, healthy version calls for colorful vegetables instead—the popular southern seasoning trio of onions, celery, and bell peppers. It also makes use of brown rice, which is richer in fiber and nutrients than white rice and contributes a pleasing, nutty flavor.

Beans and rice are a favorite combination in the South and in many Caribbean countries. Red beans and rice are popular in Louisiana, black beans and rice are loved in Cuba and Puerto Rico, and pigeon peas or pink beans in other Caribbean islands. For this dish you can use frozen, dried, or packaged soaked black-eyed peas.

1 tablespoon vegetable oil	Salt and freshly ground pepper
1 medium onion, chopped	¼ cup water
1 green bell pepper, diced fine	2 cups cooked black-eyed peas
1 red bell pepper, diced fine	2 cups cooked brown rice
2 celery stalks, diced fine	¼ teaspoon Tabasco or other bottled
1 teaspoon dried thyme	hot sauce, or more to taste
½ teaspoon Creole seasoning, or more to taste	⅓ cup chopped fresh parsley

Heat oil in sauté pan, add onion and sauté 1 minute over medium heat. Add bell peppers, celery, thyme, ¼ teaspoon Creole seasoning, salt and pepper, and sauté, stirring often, 5 minutes. Cover and sauté, stirring occasionally, 5 minutes or until tender to taste.

Add water and black-eyed peas and mix with vegetables. Spoon rice on top, sprinkle with more salt and ¼ teaspoon Creole seasoning, cover, and heat through, about 5 minutes. Season to taste with Tabasco. Lightly stir in parsley. Serve hot.

Makes 3 main-course servings

WHITE BEANS, MIDDLE EASTERN STYLE

This bean dish is flavorful but not hot, warming and hearty but not heavy. I learned the recipe from a Lebanese woman, Suzanne Elmaleh, who seasons it in the classic way with coriander and cumin; her daughter, Ronnie Venezia, likes it even better with a good dash of cayenne pepper. You can add more water at the end and serve it as a tasty bean soup as well. Although it's not authentic, I sometimes add ½ pound of "light" kielbasa sausage in slices and heat them in the beans.

1 pound dried white beans, such as
    Great Northern (2¼ to 2½ cups),
    sorted and soaked (page 63)
2 tablespoons tomato paste
1 to 1½ teaspoons ground cumin

1 to 1½ teaspoons ground coriander
Salt and freshly ground pepper
Cayenne pepper to taste (optional)
3 to 4 tablespoons olive oil
2 large onions, chopped

Bring about 7 cups water to a boil in a large pot. Add beans, cover, and cook over low heat for about 1 to 1½ hours or until beans are tender. Drain beans, reserving liquid.

Return beans to pot. Mix tomato paste with ½ cup bean cooking liquid and add to pot. Add cumin, coriander, salt, pepper, and cayenne pepper. Bring to a simmer.

In a heavy skillet, heat oil, add onions, and sauté over medium heat, stirring often, about 15 minutes or until deeply browned. Add to pot of beans. Cover and heat gently for 5 minutes. Taste and adjust seasoning. Serve hot. (*Beans can be kept, covered, 2 days in refrigerator. When reheating, add a few tablespoons cooking liquid. Stir very gently to avoid breaking up beans.*)

Makes 6 to 8 side-dish or 3 or 4 main-dish servings

VARIATION: Add ½ pound light kielbasa or turkey sausage, sliced ¼ inch thick, to cooked beans. Heat through for about 5 minutes. Serve sprinkled with fresh parsley.

TUSCAN BEAN SOUP

Trust the Italians to find a way to make a tasty dish out of two bland, starchy ingredients. I'm not referring to their famous pasta e fagioli, *or pasta with beans, but rather to this soup made of beans and rice. Rosemary and chopped vegetables add a fresh touch to the hearty soup, which is thickened with pureed beans and rice. The beans are cooked with escarole, a lettuce with curly leaves that tastes bitter when raw but becomes mild when blanched. If you like, serve the soup with a sprinkling of Parmesan cheese.*

¾ pound white beans (1¾ to 2 cups),
    sorted and soaked (page 63)
1 bay leaf
¾ pound escarole, rinsed well
2 to 3 tablespoons olive oil
1 large onion, chopped
2 celery stalks with leaves, chopped
5 ripe plum tomatoes, peeled, seeded,
    and coarsely chopped; or 1 14-
    ounce can plum tomatoes, drained
    and chopped

½ teaspoon dried rosemary
Salt and freshly ground pepper
¼ cup long-grain white rice
⅓ cup chopped fresh parsley

Bring about 6 cups water to a boil in a large pot. Add beans and bay leaf. Cover and cook over low heat about 1 to 1½ hours or until beans are tender.

Add escarole to a large saucepan of boiling salted water and boil uncovered over high heat for 3 minutes. Drain in a colander, rinse with cold water, and drain well. Squeeze lightly to remove excess water and chop.

Puree 1½ cups beans in a food processor. Measure cooking liquid; add enough water to obtain 5 cups. Discard bay leaf.

Heat oil in pot from beans, add onion and celery, and sauté about 7 minutes over medium heat. Add tomatoes and rosemary, and cook 5 minutes. Stir in escarole and add the measured water. Add salt and pepper and simmer a few minutes. (*Beans, bean puree, and soup can be kept in separate containers 1 day in refrigerator.*)

Just before serving, bring soup to a boil. Add rice, cover, and cook over low heat for 12 minutes. Stir in pureed and whole beans, and bring to a simmer. Cook 3 minutes or until rice is tender. Add parsley, let stand a minute, then taste and adjust seasoning and serve.

Makes 6 appetizer servings

CUBAN BLACK BEAN SOUP
WITH CUMIN AND GARLIC

This dark aromatic soup is what I look forward to when I go to a Cuban restaurant. Usually it is served in a bowl accompanied by white rice, so you can spoon the soupy beans over the rice on your plate, or add rice to the bowl and eat it as soup. Either way it's wonderful. Cubans call black beans and rice Moros y Cristianos, *or "Moors and Christians."*

1½ cups black beans (about ½ pound)
1 whole small onion, peeled
1 bay leaf
4 cups water
Salt and freshly ground pepper

3 to 4 tablespoons olive oil
2 large onions, chopped
4 large garlic cloves, chopped
2 teaspoons ground cumin

Rinse and sort beans. Soak in about 4 cups water overnight, or quick-soak (page 63). Drain, rinse, and put in a saucepan with the whole onion, bay leaf, and 4 cups water. Bring to a boil, cover, and cook over low heat for 1 to 1½ hours or until tender, adding salt after about 45 minutes. Discard onion and bay leaf.

With a slotted spoon remove 1 cup beans and mash them. Return to soup and mix well.

Heat oil in a large, heavy skillet over medium heat. Add onions and sauté for 10 minutes or until light brown. Add garlic and cumin, and sauté 1 minute. Add 2 or 3 tablespoons water if pan becomes dry.

Add onion mixture to beans, mix well, and bring to a boil. Simmer 5 minutes or until soup is well flavored and thickened to your taste. Season to taste with salt and pepper. (*Beans can be kept, covered, 2 days in refrigerator.*) Serve hot, with white rice.

Makes 4 side-dish or 2 main-course servings

CUBAN BLACK BEANS WITH PEPPERS AND RICE

Beans and rice are popular in much of the Caribbean and the American South—black beans and rice in Cuba, red beans and rice in Louisiana, black-eyed peas and rice in the American Southeast.

My husband loves Spanish Caribbean dishes like this one because the flavors—cumin, garlic, and cilantro—remind him of his mother's Middle Eastern cooking. Actually the connection is not so surprising. These flavorings were probably brought to the Caribbean by the Spanish, who had learned them from the Moors when they ruled Spain. Cumin and cilantro somehow became more popular in their new homeland than in Spain. Both are wonderful seasonings for beans and rice. Together with the colorful combination of red and green peppers and tomatoes, they make this dish very versatile—as a main course, side dish, or, with a dash of lime or lemon juice or herb vinegar, as a satisfying salad. SEE PHOTOGRAPH.

2 tablespoons olive oil
1 medium onion, sliced
2 green or red bell peppers or 1 of
  each, cut into strips
4 medium garlic cloves, chopped
1 teaspoon ground cumin (optional)
1 large ripe tomato or 2 canned plum
  tomatoes, diced
1½ to 2 cups cooked or canned black
  beans

½ cup black bean cooking liquid (from
  freshly cooked beans) or water
Salt and freshly ground pepper
3 cups cooked white rice
2 to 3 tablespoons chopped cilantro
  (fresh coriander), green onion, or
  parsley
Hot sauce to taste

Heat the oil in a large sauté pan over medium heat. Add onion and peppers, and sauté about 7 minutes. Add garlic and cumin, and stir over low heat 1 minute. Add tomato, beans, ¼ cup liquid, salt, and pepper. Stir and bring to boil. Cover and simmer 5 minutes or until peppers are tender.

Sprinkle rice into pan. Cover and cook over low heat, stirring as little as possible, until heated through. Add more bean liquid if mixture is dry. Add half the cilantro and mix gently with a fork. Cover and let stand 1 or 2 minutes. Taste and adjust seasoning, adding hot sauce to taste. Serve sprinkled with remaining chopped cilantro. Accompany with hot sauce.

Makes 4 or 5 side-dish or 2 or 3 main-course servings

VARIATIONS
1. Black Bean, Pepper, and Rice Salad: Cool mixture and fold in 3 diced ripe plum tomatoes. Sprinkle with cilantro, green onion, or parsley as above. Serve cool or at room temperature, with lime wedges and hot sauce.
2. Substitute cooked or canned chickpeas or red beans for the black beans.

CORSICAN RED BEANS WITH LEEKS

What's special about this recipe is that it is flavored with a generous amount of herbs and with red wine. Cooking red beans with red wine is also popular in Burgundy; the wine contributes a delicately tangy flavor. The beans cook with plenty of leeks—I add some at the beginning so they flavor the beans' cooking liquid, and the rest at the end so they keep their character. You can follow tradition and cook sausage slices in the beans, as in the variation made with turkey sausage, or you can omit them for a leaner dish. Whichever version you make, these beans are at their best when served over rice.

2 pounds leeks (4 large), white and
   light green parts, cleaned (page
   258)
2 tablespoons olive oil
3 large garlic cloves, coarsely chopped
1 pound small red beans (2½ cups),
   sorted and soaked (page 63)
1 bay leaf
1 cup dry red wine
1 cup Chicken or Vegetable Stock
   (pages 407, 406) or canned broth

1 quart water
1 tablespoon tomato paste
Salt and freshly ground pepper
1 tablespoon fresh thyme leaves, or 1
   teaspoon dried
1 tablespoon chopped fresh oregano,
   or 1 teaspoon dried
4 to 6 tablespoons chopped fresh basil
   or Italian parsley

Slice leeks ¼ inch thick. Heat oil in a large, heavy casserole over medium heat, add leeks and garlic, and sauté, stirring often, for 5 minutes. Remove 3 cups of leek mixture and reserve. Add the beans to pan and stir. Add bay leaf, wine, stock, and water. Bring to a boil, cover, and cook over low heat about 1 hour or until beans are just tender.

Dissolve the tomato paste in ¼ cup bean cooking liquid and add to the pot. Add salt and pepper, and simmer uncovered for 15 minutes. Discard bay leaf. Add reserved leek mixture, thyme, and oregano. Cover pan if mixture is thick enough. Simmer 15 minutes or until added leeks are just tender. Taste and adjust seasoning; season generously. Serve each portion sprinkled with parsley or basil.

Makes 4 to 6 main-course servings over rice

VARIATION: Add ½ pound sliced smoked turkey sausage to casserole for last 5 minutes of cooking. Heat with beans, covered.

COLOMBIAN LENTIL SOUP

The tomato-onion sauce that is stirred into this thick, satisfying soup at the last moment contributes a bright, fresh flavor and appealing color. Some versions of the soup contain salt pork, but for this lighter rendition I omit it and use chicken or vegetable stock as part of the cooking liquid for added flavor. The soup is easy to make, as lentils cook more quickly than other pulses and don't require soaking.

1½ cups lentils
3 large garlic cloves, chopped
1 quart water
1 cup Chicken or Vegetable Stock
    (pages 407, 406) or canned broth
Salt and freshly ground pepper
1 cup Colombian Tomato-Onion Sauce
    (page 395)

2 tablespoons chopped cilantro (fresh
    coriander) or parsley
2 teaspoons strained fresh lemon juice,
    or to taste
2 large hard-boiled eggs, sliced

Spread lentils in batches on a plate, pick through them carefully, rinse, and drain them.

In a medium saucepan, combine lentils, garlic, water, and stock and bring to a boil. Cover and simmer over low heat about 40 minutes or until lentils are tender. (*Soup can be kept, covered, 2 days in refrigerator.*)

Reheat soup if necessary. Add salt, pepper, and tomato sauce. Return to a boil. Remove from heat and add 1 tablespoon cilantro, salt, and lemon juice to taste. Serve garnished with slices of hard-boiled egg and sprinkled with remaining cilantro.

Makes 4 appetizer servings

MIDDLE EASTERN LENTILS WITH RICE

The most popular accompaniment for this hearty dish is a refreshing cucumber salad. A good choice is Afghan Cucumber Salad with Yogurt, Walnuts, and Raisins (page 164), Algerian Cucumber and Pepper Salad (page 165), or Sri Lankan Tomato and Watercress Salad with Cucumber-Yogurt Dressing (page 322).

1 cup lentils, sorted (page 63)
4 to 5 tablespoons vegetable oil
2 large onions, chopped
4 large garlic cloves, chopped
1 teaspoon ground cumin
Salt

1½ cups long-grain white rice
Freshly ground pepper
Cayenne pepper to taste
2 tablespoons coarsely chopped
    cilantro (fresh coriander) or fresh
    parsley (optional)

Combine lentils and 2 cups water in a medium saucepan. Bring to a boil. Cover and cook over medium heat about 20 minutes or until lentils are just tender. Drain liquid into a measuring cup and add enough water to make 3 cups; reserve.

In a heavy skillet heat oil over medium heat. Add onions and sauté, stirring occasionally, until they are well browned, about 15 minutes. Add garlic and cumin and sauté 1 minute. Add onion mixture to pan of lentils. Add measured liquid and bring to a boil. Add salt and rice and return to a boil. Cover, reduce heat to low, and cook, without stirring, until rice is tender, about 20 minutes. Taste and adjust seasoning, adding pepper and cayenne to taste. Serve hot, sprinkled with cilantro or parsley.

Makes 4 or 5 main-course servings

DUTCH SPLIT PEA SOUP

I learned the recipe for this main-course soup from a Dutch friend, Sippy Levine. She flavors the soup with leeks and carrots, but adds them toward the end of the cooking time so they retain their flavor. The soup cooks with a whole celery root and is finished with chopped celery leaves from stalk celery.

Traditional recipes for this soup call for cooking the split peas with a smoked ham hock or other meats and with sausages, but you can cook it instead with chicken stock for flavor and finish the soup with a small amount of ''light'' kielbasa sausage.

1 pound split peas, sorted and rinsed
2 quarts water, or half water and half
    stock
1 celery root, peeled and halved
1 large onion, sliced
2 large leeks, white and light green
    parts, cleaned (page 258) and
    sliced

2 large carrots, diced small
½ pound smoked sausage such as
    kielbasa
2 tablespoons chopped celery leaves or
    chopped fresh parsley
Salt to taste

Combine the peas, water, celery root, and onion in a large saucepan and bring to a boil. Cover and cook over low heat for 1 to 1½ hours, or until split peas are very soft. Add leeks, carrots, and sausage and simmer 15 to 20 minutes or until vegetables are just tender.

Discard celery root. Remove sausage, slice it, and return slices to soup. Add celery or parsley leaves. Taste, and add salt if needed. (*Soup can be kept, covered, 2 days in refrigerator.*) Serve hot.

Makes 4 to 6 main-course servings

8

Beets

There are several types of beets newly arrived in our markets. At the famous Chino Farms near San Diego, which supplies California's best-known restaurants with baby vegetables, I bought baby beets that were only about an inch in diameter. Some were called "white beets," as they were white inside, though their peel was red. There also were golden beets and striped red-and-white beets. They were delicious, and their color didn't run even after they were peeled. You can find these at farmers' markets and some supermarkets, alongside the familiar large red beets.

In the markets of France and England beets are sold cooked. Their most popular use is in salads, either combined with sturdy greens like Belgian endive, or on their own with vinaigrette. They also are a wonderful addition to potato salads. In Scandinavia they are marinated and served with assorted appetizers. In Iran and much of the Middle East, beets are dressed with yogurt.

Europeans also serve beets hot. They are the basis for the famous Polish soup borscht, which has both hot and cold versions. In central Europe, hot cooked beets are popular in cream sauce, seasoned with a pinch of sugar and a squeeze of lemon juice; for this dish you

BEET BASICS

✖ **S**eason: Beets are available year-round. The height of their season is summer and early fall.

✖ **C**hoosing: Select smooth, firm round beets that are not too large. If the leaves are attached, they should be fresh-looking and dark green.

✖ **S**toring: Cut off leaves and stems and reserve for cooking separately; leave about 1 inch of stem attached to beets. Do not cut off roots. Beets can be kept unwashed in a plastic bag in the refrigerator for up to 1 week; greens can be kept in a plastic bag for 1 or 2 days.

✖ **S**erving **S**ize: Allow 5 to 8 ounces per serving as a side dish.

✖ **N**utrients: Beets are a fair source of vitamin C. One-half cup of diced cooked beets has 26 calories.

✖ **B**asic **P**reparation: Beets are easiest to peel after cooking. Scrub well under cold running water; leave roots and short stem attached. After cooking, rinse beets with cool water and slip off their peels. Trim the roots and stems.

can use either the rich or the leaner version of Cream Sauce (pages 400, 401). Hot sliced beets or small whole beets are good with Orange Vinaigrette (page 385) or Mint Butter (page 391). Beets can also be made into rosy-hued, tasty timbales.

You can cook the stems of baby beets, too; they have a pleasant beet flavor. Beet greens also taste good and can be cooked like spinach—see Chapter 17.

STEAMED BEETS WITH MINT BUTTER

This French-style dish is a tasty accompaniment for roasted or poached chicken or braised turkey.

1 bunch or 5 small beets (about 1½ inches in diameter)
1 to 2 tablespoons Mint Butter (page 391), at room temperature

Salt and freshly ground pepper

Rinse the beets, taking care not to pierce the skin.

Put 1 inch of water in a steamer and bring to a boil. Place the beets on a steamer rack above the boiling water. Cover tightly and steam 50 to 60 minutes or until tender, adding boiling water occasionally if the water evaporates. Run them under cold water briefly and slip off the skins. (*Steamed beets can be kept, covered, 2 days in refrigerator. Reheat in steamer or in microwave, covered.*)

Dice or slice beets and toss with Mint Butter and salt and pepper to taste. Serve hot.

Makes 4 side-dish servings

ROASTED BEETS WITH DILL DRESSING

In much of Europe roasting is a popular way to cook beets, and this is how they are cooked for sale in French markets.

These beets are served with a light dill dressing, which gives them a Scandinavian accent. They are good hot or cold.

8 small beets, about 1½ inches in
    diameter
1 tablespoon wine vinegar
Salt and freshly ground pepper

Pinch of sugar
2 tablespoons vegetable oil
1 to 2 teaspoons chopped fresh dill
Small dill sprigs, for garnish

Preheat the oven to 325°F. Rinse beets and trim roots and tops, leaving bulbs whole and skin intact. Put beets in a gratin dish or other heavy, shallow baking dish, cover tightly with foil, and bake 1½ hours, or until beets are tender when pierced with a knife.

For dressing, in a small bowl whisk the vinegar with salt, pepper, and sugar. Whisk in oil and dill. Taste and adjust seasoning. (*Beets and dressing can be kept separately, covered, 2 days in refrigerator.*)

To serve, peel beets and quarter them. Spoon a little dressing over each. Serve garnished with dill sprigs.

Makes 4 side-dish servings

SWEDISH BEET SALAD WITH HORSERADISH DRESSING

The sharp flavors of the spicy dressing really wake up your taste buds, yet provide the perfect balance for the delicately sweet flavor of the beets. This salad makes a colorful addition to a buffet table, or you can serve it as a first course, Swedish style, followed by split pea soup.

Horseradish and beets are matched not only in Scandinavian kitchens but in central European cuisines as well. From as far back as I can remember, my Polish-born mother always had in the refrigerator a small jar of a sharp horseradish-beet condiment she served with fish and meat.

4 medium beets, about 1½ to 2 inches
    in diameter
4 teaspoons distilled white vinegar
1 teaspoon sugar
Salt
Pinch of ground cloves

2 teaspoons vegetable oil
4 teaspoons prepared hot white
    horseradish, or 2 to 4 teaspoons
    peeled finely grated fresh
    horseradish
1 to 2 teaspoons chopped fresh parsley

Rinse beets, taking care not to pierce their skins. Put in a pan, cover with water, and bring to a boil. Cover and simmer over low heat 35 to 40 minutes or until tender. Let cool. Run beets under cold water and slip off the skins. Slice beets.

In small bowl, whisk vinegar with sugar, salt, cloves, and oil. Stir in horseradish. Put beets in a shallow serving dish, pour dressing over beet slices, and turn each over to coat well. (*Salad can be kept, covered, 2 days in refrigerator.*) Sprinkle with parsley and serve.

Makes 4 appetizer or side-dish servings

BEET SALAD WITH WALNUTS AND GREENS

I learned to make this simple salad, a specialty of northern France, from a great Parisian chef, Fernand Chambrette. He seasoned the beets with a mustardy vinaigrette, spooned them onto a bed of mixed greens, and topped them with walnuts. The salad is at its best when some of the greens are bitter ones. Belgian endive is a favorite green in northern France, usually mixed with tender delicate greens like mâche *or butter lettuce. If you don't have endive, use a mixture of small watercress sprigs and romaine lettuce. Another tasty alternative is to use mixed baby lettuces, which are showing up in many markets.*

The endive is marinated briefly in the dressing to soften it slightly, but the other greens are not, as they would wilt.

5 small beets, about 1½ inches in
    diameter
½ pound Belgian endive
6 to 8 tablespoons Mustard Vinaigrette
    (page 382)
3 cups bite-size pieces of butter lettuce
    or romaine lettuce

1 cup *mâche* (lamb's lettuce) (optional),
    rinsed very well and patted dry
Salt and freshly ground pepper
½ cup walnut pieces

Bring at least 1 inch of water to a boil in the base of steamer. Boiling water should not reach holes in top part of steamer. Rinse beets, taking care not to pierce the skin. Place beets on steamer top above boiling water. Cover tightly and steam over high heat about 50 minutes or until beets are tender, adding boiling water occasionally if water evaporates. Remove beets and let cool. Peel beets while holding them under cold running water. (*Beets can be kept, covered, 3 days in refrigerator.*)

Wipe endive and trim bases. Cut leaves in fairly thin slices crosswise. In a medium bowl, combine endive with 2 tablespoons vinaigrette and toss. Let stand 5 minutes.

Just before serving, dice the beets. Add remaining greens to endive mixture and toss gently. Add beets and toss. Add 4 to 6 tablespoons vinaigrette. Taste and adjust seasoning. Sprinkle with walnuts and serve.

Makes 6 appetizer servings

PERSIAN BEET SALAD WITH YOGURT AND MINT

I love this light, easy, pretty salad because the tang of yogurt goes beautifully with the sweetness of the beets. Similar beet salads are made in other countries where yogurt is popular. In Bulgaria, the salad is seasoned with fresh dill instead of mint, and in Turkey, it is flavored with garlic.

If you find yellow beets at a farmers' market, you can make this with equal quantities red and yellow beets for a colorful variation.

4 medium beets, about 1½ to 2 inches
    in diameter
2 cups plain nonfat or low-fat yogurt
3 tablespoons chopped fresh mint, or 2
    to 3 teaspoons dried

Salt and freshly ground pepper
Mint sprigs, for garnish (optional)

Rinse beets, taking care not to pierce their skins. Put 1 inch of water in a steamer and bring to a boil. Place beets on steamer rack above boiling water. Cover tightly and steam 50 to 60 minutes or until tender, adding boiling water occasionally if the water evaporates. Let cool. Run beets under cold water and slip off the skins. Cut beets in ¾-inch dice. (*Cooked beets can be kept, covered, 3 days in refrigerator.*)

Mix yogurt with 2 tablespoons fresh or all of dried mint and with salt and pepper to taste.

Fold beets partly into yogurt, so that yogurt remains white with some pink streaks and beets still show. Spoon into a shallow serving bowl and sprinkle with remaining fresh mint. Garnish with mint sprigs.

Makes 4 side-dish servings

9

Broccoli and Cauliflower

These beautiful, inexpensive, easy-to-prepare vegetables are used widely in many cuisines. Cauliflower is most frequently used in European, Middle Eastern, Indian, and Latin American cuisines, while broccoli is a favorite in North American, Italian, and Chinese dishes. In most countries the vegetables are preferred cooked; presenting them raw is an American way of serving them.

Cauliflower and *broccoli* may be the most popular members of the health-promoting cruciferous, or cabbage, family (see also Chapters 10, 11, 17, and 18). We are most familiar with dishes that call for covering cauliflower and broccoli in rich cheesy sauces, but there are many lighter, more healthful methods to prepare these vegetables.

When cooked, the florets of cauliflower and broccoli are delicate in flavor and taste good plain or with a variety of sauces, from a simple vinaigrette to tomato sauces, curries, Chinese mushroom sauces, and guacamole. You can sprinkle cooked florets lightly with cheese, bread crumbs, or nuts and brown them in the oven for a quick gratin. Cooked or raw cauliflower and broccoli florets can be added to salads. In North Africa, cauliflower is braised with tomatoes, garlic, and cilantro. When cooked this way, it is satisfying enough to be served as a main course with rice or couscous. For special occasions these vegetables can be made into elegant creations, like Cauliflower Flan with Roasted Red Pepper Sauce (page 100).

Both vegetables are at their best when cooked briefly in boiling salted water, then heated in a sauce. Cauliflower is more suitable than broccoli for slow braising, as in Indian Cauliflower with Fresh Ginger and Cumin (page 98), because broccoli loses its color if cooked for long.

A new relative of these vegetables in our markets is *broccoflower*, which looks like a light green cauliflower. It can be substituted for either vegetable, but begins to lose its green color if even slightly overcooked. Like cauliflower, it goes well with spicy Mediterranean seasonings and Mexican salsas, as in Broccoflower and Rice Pilaf with Chipotle Salsa (page 104). Purple cauliflower is available is some markets in the fall. It is very pretty raw and turns green when cooked.

Broccoli rabe, or broccoli di rape, sometimes called broccoletti or rapini, is a slightly bitter type of leafy flowering broccoli used almost exclusively in Italian cuisine. It is delicious sautéed with garlic and tossed with pasta, as in Pasta Shells with Broccoli Rabe (page 107). *Chinese broccoli* is quite similar and the two vegetables can be interchanged in recipes.

BROCCOLI AND CAULIFLOWER BASICS

Season: Both vegetables are available all year. Their peak season is late fall through spring.

Choosing: In both vegetables, florets should be compact. Broccoli florets should be dark green and not yellowish, while cauliflower should be creamy white without dark spots. Be especially careful to choose them very fresh if you are serving them raw. Broccoli rabe should be firm, with small stems.

Storing: Refrigerate unwashed in a plastic bag. Broccoli and cauliflower keep up to 5 days; broccoli rabe keeps up to 3 days.

Serving Size: Allow about 5 or 6 ounces per person. One large cauliflower head makes about 4 servings.

Nutrients: Broccoli and cauliflower are good sources of vitamin C and potassium, while broccoli and broccoli rabe also contain vitamin A, iron, and calcium. One cup of cooked cauliflower contains 28 calories; a cup of cooked broccoli or broccoli rabe has about 40 calories. One half cup raw broccoli or cauliflower has 12 calories. Broccoli and cauliflower are members of the cruciferous family, considered helpful in preventing some types of cancer.

Basic Preparation: Rinse vegetable. For cauliflower, cut off the green leaves. Both cauliflower's core and broccoli's large stalk can be cooked along with the florets; peel first with a knife, then slice the stem. Cut off ends of stalks of broccoli rabe. Cut vegetable in 1- or 2-inch pieces.

GARLIC-SCENTED BROCCOLI

In this old-fashioned Italian recipe, broccoli florets are slowly stewed with garlic. The broccoli is not as bright green as when boiled in water, but there is a trade-off in taste; it gains great flavor as it slowly cooks with the olive oil and garlic.

This easy dish is ideal for small-quantity cooking. For even cooking, use a heavy, large sauté pan so that all of the broccoli is in contact with the pan's base.

1¼ pounds broccoli
1 tablespoon olive oil
2 large garlic cloves, chopped

Salt and freshly ground pepper
About 2 tablespoons water

Divide broccoli into small florets. Peel stalk and cut diagonally in ½-inch pieces.

Heat oil in a heavy sauté pan over medium heat. Add garlic, stir for about 10 seconds, and add broccoli. Sprinkle with salt and sauté 3 minutes. Cover and cook over medium-low heat, stirring often and adding water as necessary to prevent burning, about 12 minutes or until done to taste. Sprinkle with salt and pepper and serve.

Makes 2 or 3 side-dish servings

BROCCOLI WITH CHINESE MUSHROOMS AND OYSTER SAUCE

This popular, delicious Chinese restaurant standard is simple to make at home. Oyster sauce is a favorite flavoring in the Cantonese kitchen for broccoli, mushrooms, bok choy, and other vegetables. Like Vietnamese fish sauce, to the American taste it's better as part of a sauce than if used alone. It might seem somewhat aggressive if you taste it on its own, but it's an excellent seasoning for vegetable sauces, providing a rich color and a flavor that is slightly sweet and slightly salty. Now it's popular in the West too, and is available in many American supermarkets, in the "Oriental products" section; however, it has not yet attained the popularity of another sauce of similar consistency that also has an Oriental origin—ketchup.

For convenience you can use broccoli florets, often sold separately. If using a broccoli bunch, allow 1¼ pounds; use the stalks for another recipe.

6 dried Chinese black mushrooms	1 pound broccoli florets
1 cup hot water	Salt
1 tablespoon dry sherry	1 tablespoon vegetable oil
1½ tablespoons oyster sauce	1 garlic clove, minced
2 teaspoons soy sauce	1 teaspoon minced peeled fresh ginger
1 teaspoon sugar	1 teaspoon cornstarch mixed with 2
1 6-ounce can straw mushrooms	teaspoons water

Rinse mushrooms, then soak in hot water for 30 minutes or until soft. Remove mushrooms and rinse them. Cut off stems and discard; quarter caps. Reserve soaking liquid. Strain it through cheesecloth if it's sandy; pour liquid into another bowl. Measure ½ cup. Mix with sherry, oyster sauce, soy sauce, and sugar. Whisk to blend. Rinse straw mushrooms with warm water; drain well.

Add broccoli to a large saucepan of boiling salted water and boil uncovered over high heat about 4 minutes or until crisp-tender. Drain in a colander, rinse with cold water, and drain well.

Heat oil in a heavy skillet or wok over medium-high heat. Add garlic and ginger, and stir-fry about 10 seconds. Add black mushrooms and oyster sauce mixture. Bring to a boil, cover, and simmer over low heat for 5 minutes.

Stir cornstarch mixture, then blend into sauce and cook 1 minute, stirring. Add straw mushrooms and broccoli, and heat through.

Makes 3 appetizer servings or 2 main-course servings with rice

QUICK BROCCOLI GRATIN WITH PECANS AND CHEDDAR

This is a very easy American-style broccoli gratin. The cooked vegetable is simply sprinkled with a little oil so that the crunchy topping of nuts and cheese sticks to the vegetable, then it is quickly browned in the oven.

If you prefer a richer broccoli gratin, prepare Cream Sauce (page 400) or Cheese Sauce (page 399), and pour the sauce over the broccoli before adding the topping. Either version is a good accompaniment for roast turkey, chicken, or beef.

1½ pounds broccoli
Salt
2 to 4 tablespoons olive or vegetable
    oil or melted butter
½ cup coarsely grated sharp cheddar
    cheese (about 2 ounces)

¼ cup coarsely chopped pecans
2 tablespoons unseasoned bread
    crumbs

Preheat the oven to 425°F. Divide broccoli into medium florets, discarding stalks and leaves. Put florets into a large saucepan containing enough boiling salted water to cover them generously. Return to a boil and boil uncovered until just tender, about 4 minutes. Drain broccoli gently, rinse with cold running water until cool, and drain thoroughly.

Butter a shallow 5-cup gratin dish or other heavy baking dish. Arrange broccoli in one layer in prepared dish, stems pointing inward. Sprinkle with half the oil. Mix cheese, pecans, and bread crumbs and sprinkle evenly on top. Sprinkle with remaining oil.

Bake until cheese melts, about 8 minutes. If topping is not brown, broil just until lightly browned, about 1 minute, checking often and turning dish if necessary so topping browns evenly. Serve hot, from baking dish.

Makes 4 side-dish servings

COUSCOUS PILAF WITH BROCCOLI AND GARLIC BUTTER

This tasty recipe was a favorite in classes I taught on quick cooking. The presentation and flavors are French—the couscous is mixed with garlic butter and with briefly blanched, bright green broccoli florets. Unlike the traditional Moroccan way of steaming couscous in a special pot, this dish makes use of a fast technique, somewhat like that of making rice pilaf.

3 large garlic cloves, peeled
Salt and freshly ground pepper
1 bunch broccoli (about 1½ pounds),
    cut into florets
¼ cup (½ stick) butter, at room
    temperature

2 tablespoons extra-virgin olive oil
1¼ cups couscous
1¼ cups boiling water, Chicken Stock
    (page 407), or Vegetable Stock
    (page 406)

Mince the garlic cloves in a food processor. Add butter and process until blended.

In a large saucepan of boiling salted water, cook broccoli uncovered over high heat for 5 minutes, or until just tender. Drain broccoli well, return it to saucepan, and keep it warm, covered. Set aside about ½ cup small florets for stirring into couscous.

Heat garlic butter and 1 tablespoon oil in a heavy, medium saucepan until melted. Stir in couscous, using a fork. Shake pan to spread couscous in an even layer and sprinkle it with salt and pepper. Pour the boiling water evenly over the couscous, immediately cover saucepan tightly, and let mixture stand for 5 minutes. Add remaining oil and reserved small broccoli florets, cover, and let stand for 1 minute.

Fluff the mixture with a fork to break up any lumps in couscous, tossing until mixture is blended. Taste it for seasoning.

To serve, mound couscous mixture on a large platter and encircle it with a ring of remaining broccoli florets.

Makes 4 main-course servings

ALGERIAN CAULIFLOWER WITH TOMATOES, GARLIC, AND CILANTRO

Generous quantities of garlic, cilantro, and the North African hot pepper sauce called harissa *are a lively Algerian flavoring combination for cauliflower and other vegetables. Here the seasoning mixture simmers briefly with cauliflower and tomatoes, for a delicious side dish or salad. I also like it as a light main course with rice or couscous.*

1 medium or large cauliflower, divided
    into medium florets
Salt and freshly ground pepper
2 tablespoons olive oil
3 large garlic cloves, chopped
1 pound ripe tomatoes, peeled, seeded,
    and diced small; or 1 28-ounce can
    plum tomatoes, drained and diced

½ teaspoon paprika
½ teaspoon Harissa (page 393) or hot
    pepper sauce to taste
3 tablespoons chopped cilantro (fresh
    coriander)

Add cauliflower to a large saucepan of boiling salted water and boil uncovered over high heat for 6 to 7 minutes or until crisp-tender. Drain in a colander, rinse with cold water, and drain well.

Heat oil in a large sauté pan, add garlic, and sauté over medium heat for 10 seconds. Add tomatoes, paprika, salt, and pepper and simmer 5 minutes. Stir in Harissa and all but 1 teaspoon of the cilantro.

Add the cauliflower and stir gently. Heat to simmer. Cover and cook over low heat for 5 minutes, stirring occasionally. Taste and adjust seasoning. Sprinkle with remaining cilantro and serve hot or at room temperature.

Makes 4 side-dish or 2 main-course servings

CZECH CAULIFLOWER WITH ONIONS AND EGGS

I learned to make this simple tasty dish from an Israeli friend, who recommended it as a way to use cooked cauliflower stalks when you've used the florets for another dish. For a long time I thought it was a thrifty Israeli dish. Later I found out that the recipe is Czech, and must have arrived in Israel with eastern European immigrants.

In fact, this a general eastern European technique for making use of other leftover cooked vegetables such as cabbage, kale, or green beans: heat them with a sautéed onion, add eggs, and scramble them. It makes a good supper dish with rye bread, and a cucumber or tomato salad.

2 tablespoons vegetable oil or butter
1 medium onion, chopped
About 3 cups cooked small cauliflower
   florets or diced stalks (half a 2-
   pound cauliflower)

Salt and freshly ground pepper
2 or 3 large eggs, beaten
2 tablespoons milk
1 tablespoon chopped green onion or
   parsley (optional)

Heat oil or butter in a nonstick skillet over medium heat, add onion, and sauté until golden, about 3 minutes. Add cauliflower, sprinkle with salt and pepper, and heat through. Add eggs and milk and cook over low heat, stirring, until set to your taste. Stir in half the green onion. Serve sprinkled with remaining green onion.

Makes 2 main-course servings

CAULIFLOWER WITH FRESH GINGER AND CUMIN

Cauliflower stewed slowly with Indian spices and a minimum of water has a deep golden color and an appetizing aroma. Serve it with roasted, broiled, or sautéed meats. Use a large, heavy skillet with a tight cover so the cauliflower cooks evenly with the spices without burning. SEE PHOTOGRAPH.

1 medium cauliflower (about 2¼ pounds), divided into small florets
Salt and freshly ground pepper
2 to 3 tablespoons vegetable oil
1 tablespoon minced peeled fresh ginger

1½ teaspoons ground cumin
½ teaspoon turmeric
About 6 to 8 tablespoons water, more if needed

Add cauliflower pieces to a large saucepan of boiling salted water and boil uncovered for 3 minutes. Drain thoroughly.

Heat oil in a large, heavy skillet over low heat. Stir in the ginger and sauté over medium heat for ½ minute. Reduce heat to low and stir in cumin and turmeric. Add cauliflower and stir well until florets begin to turn yellow.

Add 2 tablespoons water, a generous pinch of salt, and a small pinch of pepper; stir. When the water evaporates, pour in ¼ cup more water. Cover tightly and cook over low heat, stirring occasionally, for 30 minutes or until cauliflower is very tender when pierced with a knife; if necessary add more water, 1 tablespoon at a time, so spices don't burn. Taste and adjust seasoning. (*Can be kept, covered, 2 days in refrigerator. Reheat in covered pan with 1 or 2 tablespoons water, or in covered dish in microwave.*) Serve hot.

Makes 4 side-dish servings

BEER BATTER CAULIFLOWER FRITTERS

For these fritters, cauliflower florets are dipped in a beer batter and fried until crisp and golden brown. In France and much of northern Europe, fritter batters may contain water, milk, or white wine but beer is popular among chefs because it gives lightness to the batter.

The cauliflower is precooked in water so it will not remain in the oil for too long and will not absorb too much fat. Other vegetables, such as broccoli and sliced carrots, can also be prepared this way. Tender vegetables such as zucchini and mushrooms can be dipped in batter and fried without preliminary boiling. Serve the fritters as a first course or a side dish. If you like, serve Spinach Watercress Dip (page 403), Tartar Sauce (page 403), Garlic Mayonnaise (page 402), or Chipotle Chili Salsa (page 389) for dipping.

Fritter Batter

1 cup all-purpose flour
¼ teaspoon salt
Pinch of pepper
1 tablespoon vegetable oil

⅔ cup beer (measured after foam
    dissipates)
2 large eggs, separated

1 large cauliflower (about 2 pounds),
    divided into medium florets
Salt

At least 6 cups vegetable oil, for deep-
    frying

[Note: Read deep-frying hints page 15 before beginning.]

To make fritter batter, sift flour into a medium bowl. Add salt, pepper, and oil. Add beer gradually, stirring with a whisk just until blended. Gently whisk in yolks. Cover batter and refrigerate 1 hour. Just before using, beat egg whites until stiff, then fold gently into batter.

In a large saucepan, boil enough water to generously cover cauliflower and add a pinch of salt. Add cauliflower and boil uncovered until crisp-tender, about 5 minutes. Drain cauliflower, rinse with cold water, and drain thoroughly. Line ovenproof trays with 2 layers of paper towels.

Heat the oil in a deep-fryer or deep, heavy saucepan to about 375°F. on a frying thermometer. If a thermometer is not available, test by adding a 1-inch cube of bread to oil; when oil is hot enough, bread should turn golden brown in about 50 seconds.

Dip a floret into the batter so that it is well coated, then add to oil. Repeat with 5 or 6 more florets. Fry until golden brown, about 4 minutes. Remove carefully with a slotted spoon to prepared trays. Sprinkle with salt. Keep warm in a low oven (about 275°F.) with the door slightly open while frying remaining florets.

Reheat oil if necessary. Continue dipping and frying remaining cauliflower in batches. Serve hot.

Makes 4 side-dish servings

SPICY CAULIFLOWER PUREE

If you think of vegetable purees as bland baby food, this one should change your mind. It is spiced with the favorite Yemenite duo of cumin and turmeric, which gives it a delicious flavor. Serve this bright yellow-orange puree with poached or hard-boiled eggs or grilled chicken or meat. You can also make this out of leftover cooked cauliflower.

3 pounds cauliflower (2 small or 1 large head)
Salt and freshly ground pepper
2 tablespoons vegetable oil

2 medium onions, finely chopped
1 teaspoon ground cumin
1 teaspoon turmeric

Divide cauliflower into medium florets. Add to a large saucepan of boiling salted water and boil uncovered over high heat for 9 to 10 minutes, or until stems are very tender when pierced with a sharp knife. Drain thoroughly.

In a large skillet, heat oil over medium-low heat. Add onions and cook, stirring often, about 10 minutes or until very light brown and very soft. Stir in cumin and turmeric, and cook 2 minutes, stirring.

Puree the cooked cauliflower in batches in a food processor or a food mill. If desired, leave a few chunks. Stir puree into onion mixture. Heat until very hot and season to taste with salt and pepper. Transfer to a deep serving dish and serve hot. (*Puree can be kept, covered, 2 days in refrigerator.*)

Makes 6 side-dish servings

CAULIFLOWER FLAN WITH ROASTED RED PEPPER SAUCE

Creamy white cauliflower flan, accented with nutmeg and served with a bright red pepper sauce, makes a stunning appetizer. I learned to make these mini flans in France, where they are also popular as an accompaniment for meat and poultry. Instead of the pepper sauce, you can serve this with Ten-Minute Tomato Sauce (page 394).

Roasted Red Pepper Sauce (page 397)
4 tablespoons (½ stick) butter, cut into
    4 pieces
1 2-pound head of cauliflower, divided
    into medium florets
Salt and white pepper

⅔ cup heavy cream, at room
    temperature
3 large eggs
Freshly grated nutmeg

Prepare sauce. Preheat the oven to 375°F. Generously butter four 5-ounce ramekins or five 4- or 4½-ounce timbale molds, being careful to thoroughly butter bases of molds. Butter a sheet of foil to cover the ramekins.

Add cauliflower florets to a large saucepan of boiling salted water and boil uncovered over high heat for 8 minutes or until very tender. Drain, rinse with cold water, and drain thoroughly. Puree in a food processor until very smooth. Measure 2 cups puree.

Cook puree in a medium, heavy, wide saucepan over low heat, stirring often, for 5 minutes to evaporate excess moisture. Stir cream into puree. Raise heat to high, and bring to boil. Reduce heat to medium and cook, stirring often, until cream is absorbed and mixture is reduced to 2 cups. Transfer to a bowl and cool 7 minutes.

In a medium bowl, whisk the eggs until blended. Gradually whisk in the cauliflower puree. Season to taste with salt, pepper, and nutmeg; season well so timbales will not be bland.

Divide mixture among ramekins. Tap each on counter to pack down. Smooth tops, set ramekins in roasting pan, and transfer to oven. Add enough boiling water to roasting pan to come halfway up sides of ramekins. Set sheet of buttered foil atop ramekins.

Bake about 40 minutes, or until timbales are firm to touch and a cake tester inserted into center comes out dry. If necessary, add hot water occasionally to roasting pan so that it does not become dry. If water comes close to a boil, add a few tablespoons cold water.

Remove molds from water bath. Cool on rack 5 minutes. Carefully run a thin-bladed flexible knife around the edge of a ramekin or mold. Set a small plate atop ramekin and invert. Holding them together, tap on towel-covered working surface. Gently lift off ramekin. Repeat with remaining ramekins. Cover each timbale gently with a ramekin while finishing sauce.

Just before serving, bring sauce to a simmer. Reduce heat to low. Stir in butter, 1 piece at a time. Remove from heat as soon as butter is absorbed.

Spoon a little sauce around base of timbales. Serve any remaining sauce separately.

Makes 4 or 5 appetizer or side-dish servings

BROCCOLI SALAD WITH CHIMICHURRI

The tangy Argentine garlic-herb dipping sauce called chimichurri *makes a good dressing for cooked vegetables. Serve this simple salad of broccoli, tomatoes, parsley, and olives as a light appetizer.*

2 pounds broccoli, divided into
    medium florets
Salt and freshly ground pepper
5 to 6 tablespoons Chimichurri (page
    388)

2 ripe plum tomatoes
1 tablespoon chopped fresh parsley
8 to 12 black or green olive halves

Add broccoli to a large saucepan of boiling salted water and boil uncovered over high heat for 4 to 5 minutes or until florets are crisp-tender. Drain in a colander, rinse with cold water, and drain well. Transfer to a bowl.

   Toss broccoli florets with Chimichurri. Season to taste with salt and pepper. Cut tomatoes in lengthwise slices, and each slice into 4 strips. Add to salad and toss gently. Sprinkle with parsley and garnish with olives.

Makes 4 to 6 appetizer servings

VARIATION: Substitute 1 large cauliflower (about 2 pounds) for the broccoli. Cook about 6 or 7 minutes.

BROCCOLI SALAD WITH CARIBBEAN LIME JUICE DRESSING

This easy, refreshing salad is a good appetizer to have ready for a barbecue lunch or supper, or a fine accompaniment for grilled meats or fish. The dressing gains its flavor from lime juice and cumin, but has only a touch of heat; for those who want it hotter, serve hot sauce on the side.

1½ pounds broccoli, divided into
    florets
Salt
½ red onion, sliced thin, slices cut into
    slivers

2 tablespoons chopped cilantro (fresh
    coriander) or parsley
Caribbean Lime Juice Dressing (page
    382)

Add broccoli to a large saucepan of boiling salted water and boil uncovered over high heat for 4 to 5 minutes or until florets are crisp-tender. Drain in a colander, rinse with cold water, and drain well. Transfer to a bowl.

   Add onion and cilantro to broccoli. Add dressing and toss. Taste and adjust seasoning. Serve at room temperature.

Makes 4 appetizer or side-dish servings

VARIATION: Substitute 1 medium cauliflower for the broccoli. Cook it about 6 or 7 minutes.

CAULIFLOWER WITH
TARRAGON VINAIGRETTE

Fresh tarragon and shallots—the flavors of traditional Béarnaise sauce—are used here in a much lighter, more healthful dressing, perfect for hot or cold cooked cauliflower. It also is delicious with asparagus and artichokes and is a great dressing for potato salad.

1 medium cauliflower, divided into
    medium florets
Salt and freshly ground pepper
1 tablespoon tarragon vinegar

3 tablespoons vegetable oil
1 tablespoon minced shallot
1 tablespoon chopped fresh tarragon

Add cauliflower to a large saucepan of boiling salted water and boil uncovered over high heat for 7 minutes or until florets are crisp-tender. Drain in a colander, rinse with cold water, and drain well. Transfer to a bowl.

   Whisk vinegar with salt and pepper. Whisk in oil. Stir in shallot and tarragon. Taste and adjust seasoning. Toss with cauliflower. Taste again for seasoning. Serve hot or cold.

Makes 3 or 4 appetizer or side-dish servings

BROCCOFLOWER AND RICE PILAF
WITH CHIPOTLE SALSA

A generous dose of salsa stirred into this colorful rice and broccoflower medley lends a Mexican flair. Homemade chipotle salsa is best here, but you can use your favorite bottled salsa or taco sauce. This makes a perfect supper main course or a fine accompaniment for grilled chicken or steak.

1 medium broccoflower (¾ to 1
    pound), divided into medium
    florets
Salt and freshly ground pepper
1½ to 2 tablespoons vegetable oil
1 small or medium onion, minced
2 medium garlic cloves, minced
1½ cups long-grain white rice

3 cups hot water
½ teaspoon ground cumin
½ teaspoon dried oregano
2 ripe plum tomatoes, diced
½ cup Chipotle Chili Salsa (page 389),
    plus additional salsa for serving
    separately

Add broccoflower to a medium saucepan of boiling salted water and boil uncovered over high heat for 5 to 7 minutes or until crisp-tender. Drain in a colander, rinse with cold water, and drain well. Divide in small florets.

Heat oil in a large saucepan, add onion, and sauté until soft but not brown, about 5 to 7 minutes. Add garlic, stir about 15 seconds, then add rice and stir over low heat for 2 minutes. Add water, cumin, and oregano and bring to a boil. Cover and cook over low heat for 15 minutes. Put broccoflower and tomatoes on top and sprinkle with salt and pepper; do not stir. Cover and cook 3 minutes or until rice is tender and vegetables are hot. Stir gently with a fork. Cover and let stand 10 minutes. Lightly stir in salsa. Taste and adjust seasoning. Serve hot, with more salsa.

Makes 3 main-course or 4 or 5 side-dish servings

BROCCOFLOWER AND TOMATO SALAD

Broccoflower reminds me of the Italian broccoli romanesco, a pale green, conical broccoli that piqued my curiosity at Roman outdoor markets. Its taste goes well with Italian seasonings, as in this colorful, easy, and light salad flavored with olive oil, Balsamic vinegar, garlic, oregano, and fresh basil. Take care not to overcook the broccoflower, or its color may fade. You can also make this salad with cauliflower.

1 tablespoon extra-virgin olive oil
1 teaspoon Balsamic vinegar
1 small garlic clove, minced
Salt and freshly ground pepper
¼ teaspoon dried oregano, crumbled

1 broccoflower (about 1 pound),
    divided into medium florets
1 ripe medium tomato
2 tablespoons coarsely chopped fresh
    basil

In a large bowl, mix oil, vinegar, garlic, salt, pepper, and oregano. Set aside.

Add the broccoflower to a large saucepan of boiling salted water and boil uncovered over high heat about 7 minutes or until crisp-tender. Drain in a colander, rinse with cold water, and drain well. Add to dressing and mix gently.

Fold in tomato and half the basil. Season to taste with salt and pepper. Serve sprinkled with remaining basil.

Makes 3 appetizer or side-dish servings

BROCCOLI RABE WITH GARLIC

Broccoli rabe, an Italian flowering variety of broccoli, has a pleasant, slightly bitter taste. Once available only in Italian specialty markets, it can now be found in many supermarkets. For this simple, time-honored Italian way to cook the vegetable, the broccoli rabe is briefly cooked in boiling water, then sautéed with garlic and hot pepper flakes. Serve it as a contorno, or side dish, with grilled or roasted chicken or veal, toss it with pasta, or simply accompany it with rice. Broccoli rabe can also be cooked directly in the pan, without being blanched in water, as in Garlic-Scented Broccoli (page 92).

1 pound broccoli rabe
Salt and freshly ground pepper
1 tablespoon extra-virgin olive oil

2 medium garlic cloves, chopped
⅛ teaspoon hot pepper flakes

Cut tough stems off broccoli rabe. Cut stems into 1- to 2-inch pieces. Add to a large saucepan of boiling salted water and boil uncovered over high heat for 4 to 5 minutes or until crisp-tender. Drain in a colander, rinse with cold water, and drain well.

Heat oil in a large, heavy skillet over medium heat. Add garlic and pepper flakes, and sauté 10 seconds. Add rabe, salt, and pepper, and sauté until heated through, tossing gently.

Serve hot.

Makes 4 side-dish or 2 main-course servings, with pasta or rice

PASTA SHELLS WITH BROCCOLI RABE

Greens and pasta shells are a favorite combination in southern Italy, as in this simple recipe. If broccoli rabe is not available, the recipe is also good with ordinary broccoli. Orecchiette, or "little ears," are the traditional pasta shape for this dish, but any shell-type pasta works well. Serve this zesty dish with freshly grated Parmesan cheese.

½ pound broccoli rabe
Salt and freshly ground pepper
1 large tomato, diced
1 teaspoon dried oregano, crumbled
1½ to 2 tablespoons extra-virgin olive
    oil

8 ounces pasta shells
1 large garlic clove, finely chopped
⅛ teaspoon hot red pepper flakes

Cut tough stalks off broccoli rabe. Cut stalks into 1- to 2-inch pieces. Add to a large saucepan of boiling salted water and boil uncovered over high heat for 4 to 5 minutes or until crisp-tender. Drain in a colander, rinse with cold water, and drain well. Coarsely chop.

   In a large bowl mix tomato, oregano, 1 tablespoon oil, salt, and pepper.

   Add pasta to a large saucepan of boiling salted water and boil uncovered over high heat for 8 minutes or until tender but still firm to the bite. Drain well. Toss with tomato mixture.

   Heat remaining oil in a heavy, medium skillet over low heat. Add garlic and pepper flakes, and sauté a few seconds. Add rabe, salt, and pepper, and sauté until heated through, tossing gently. Add to pasta and toss. Taste and adjust seasoning. Serve hot.

Makes 4 side-dish or 2 or 3 main-course servings

10

Brussels Sprouts

The first time I cooked Brussels sprouts was twenty years ago in my kitchen in Tel Aviv. They were new in Israel and were available at the market only frozen. A young cousin of mine watched me cook the foreign-looking buds and asked whether they would expand into full-size cabbages!

Years later I moved to Europe, where Brussels sprouts originated and are a familiar autumn vegetable. I tasted this popular vegetable prepared in a multitude of ways—in Belgium it was sautéed with bacon, in France it was braised with chestnuts, and in England it was baked in cheese sauce. Often the Brussels sprouts were cooked with lavish amounts of butter, sour cream, or creamy sauces, which softened the vegetable's assertive flavor and turned it into a delightful accompaniment.

For everyday cooking, however, I looked for leaner ways to prepare the vegetable. Brussels sprouts are in the health-protecting cruciferous family, whose vegetables nutritionists recommend we eat several times a week. But if they are served in an overly rich sauce, their nutritional benefits are diluted. Even for the holidays, if the Brussels sprouts are to accompany a rich main course, I prefer a recipe that is fairly low in saturated fat.

Over the years I have learned easy, tasty ways to serve Brussels sprouts with little fat. Of primary importance, no matter what seasonings or sauces you use, is making sure the sprouts are fresh. In farmers' markets and some supermarkets, you can buy them on the stalk; in this form they are likely to be freshest. Choose heads that are small, compact, and bright green, without brown spots or yellow leaves. Occasionally you can find purple baby Brussels sprouts at specialty markets. Keep Brussels sprouts unwashed in a bag with a few holes in it. Try not to store them longer than three days.

Before cooking Brussels sprouts, some people recommend cutting an *X* into the base of each one to shorten the cooking time, but I do not find this extra step makes any difference.

For good flavor and a vivid color, cook Brussels sprouts uncovered in plenty of boiling salted water and check by piercing the base of one with a small sharp knife. They taste best when they are just tender—not hard and undercooked, but not overcooked and mushy, either. Drain them well before adding them to a sauce.

As for sauce recipes, I find that replacing part of the butter with oil or chicken stock works well, as in French-style buttered Brussels Sprouts with Shallots (page 114) or the Hungarian-style Brussels sprouts in a lightened, cream-free but delicious mushroom sauce (page 113). Although Brussels sprouts are not available in the Far East, Oriental seasonings like fresh ginger, garlic, and soy sauce complement them perfectly.

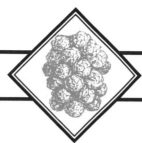

BRUSSELS SPROUTS BASICS

✂ **Season:** Brussels sprouts are available all year; their peak season is fall and winter.

✂ **Choosing:** Small, firm, compact, bright green Brussels sprouts are best. They should feel heavy for their size. Avoid those with yellow spots or wilted outer leaves and those that have holes.

✂ **Storing:** Keep sprouts unwashed in a plastic bag in the refrigerator up to 3 days.

✂ **Serving Size:** Allow about 4 or 5 ounces per person as a side dish.

✂ **Nutrients:** Brussels sprouts are a very good source of vitamin C, and contain significant amounts of vitamins A, B_6, and E and some protein. They are in the cruciferous family, and have a potential to inhibit some types of cancer. One cup of cooked Brussels sprouts has 50 to 60 calories.

✂ **Basic Preparation:** Rinse well. Trim dried bases of sprouts; do not remove so much of base that leaves come off.

BASIC BOILED
BRUSSELS SPROUTS

1 pound Brussels sprouts
Salt

Put sprouts in a large saucepan containing enough boiling salted water to cover them generously. Return to boil and cook uncovered for 8 to 10 minutes or until they are just tender; check by removing one with slotted spoon and piercing its base with a small sharp knife. Drain gently in a colander or large strainer, rinse with cold running water until cool, and drain well. (*Sprouts can be refrigerated overnight, covered. If they were refrigerated, reheat them before adding to a sauce. Put sprouts in a saucepan of boiling salted water, boil 1 minute, then drain well. If sprouts were at room temperature, they can be reheated directly in desired sauce.*)

Makes 4 side-dish servings

PURPLE BABY
BRUSSELS SPROUTS

These tiny Brussels sprouts keep some of their purple color when cooked but turn partly green, so they end up a two-colored vegetable. Cook them briefly and they will be delicious. Because they are a new vegetable, I prefer to serve them plain or with just a touch of butter.

1 pound baby purple Brussels sprouts   **1 to 2 tablespoons (¼ stick) butter**
Salt and freshly ground pepper   **(optional)**

Trim bases of Brussels sprouts only if necessary, cutting off a very thin slice. Cook uncovered in a saucepan of boiling salted water for 6 or 7 minutes or until crisp-tender. Drain well. Melt butter in saucepan, add Brussels sprouts, and toss lightly over low heat. Sprinkle lightly with salt and pepper and serve immediately.

Makes 4 side-dish servings

BRUSSELS SPROUTS IN HUNGARIAN MUSHROOM SAUCE

This easy-to-make mushroom sauce is a wonderful complement to Brussels sprouts. The sauce gains flavor from sautéed onion, paprika, and chicken stock and does not require any cream or butter.

2 tablespoons vegetable oil
1 medium onion, minced
½ pound medium or small
   mushrooms, quartered
Salt and freshly ground pepper
1 teaspoon sweet paprika

2 teaspoons all-purpose flour
1 cup Chicken Stock (page 407) or
   broth
Hot paprika or cayenne pepper to taste
1 pound Brussels sprouts, cooked
   (page 112)

Heat oil in a medium sauté pan or skillet, add onion, and sauté over medium heat for 5 minutes. Add mushrooms, salt, and pepper, and sauté together over medium heat for about 3 minutes, then over medium-high heat for about 2 minutes, or until mushrooms and onions are light brown. Over low heat, add sweet paprika and flour, and sauté 1 minute. Off the heat stir in ¾ cup stock. Bring to a boil, then simmer 5 minutes. Add hot paprika. (*Sauce can be kept, covered, 2 days in refrigerator. Reheat before continuing.*)

   Add cooked sprouts to sauce. Heat about 5 to 7 minutes, uncovered, turning them occasionally and adding stock by tablespoons if sauce becomes too thick. Taste and adjust seasoning.

Makes 3 or 4 side-dish servings

BRUSSELS SPROUTS WITH WATER CHESTNUTS AND GINGER

Chestnuts are traditional partners for Brussels sprouts, but preparing them is time-consuming. For quick cooking, pair the sprouts with water chestnuts instead. Season the dish with a flavorful mixture of soy sauce, ginger, garlic, and mirin, *a Japanese sweet rice wine found in the Oriental foods section of many supermarkets.*

2 teaspoons vegetable oil
1 medium garlic clove, minced
1½ teaspoons minced peeled fresh
   ginger
¼ cup Chicken Stock (page 407) or
   broth
¾ cup canned whole water chestnuts,
   rinsed and drained

1 pound Brussels sprouts, cooked
   (page 112)
1 tablespoon *mirin* (Japanese sweet
   rice wine)
1 tablespoon soy sauce

Heat the oil in a medium sauté pan, add garlic and ginger, and sauté for 10 seconds over medium-high heat. Add stock and water chestnuts, and bring to a boil. Add cooked sprouts and heat 2 minutes over medium heat, shaking pan or stirring gently. Add *mirin* and soy sauce, then cook over medium-high heat for 2 to 3 minutes or until most of liquid has evaporated. Serve hot.

Makes 3 or 4 side-dish servings

BRUSSELS SPROUTS WITH SHALLOTS

In this simple variation on a French classic, the sprouts are moistened with chicken stock and with a little butter and oil, rather than with butter alone.

1 tablespoon vegetable oil
1 tablespoon butter
1 large or 2 medium shallots, minced
1 pound Brussels sprouts, cooked
   (page 112)

¼ cup Chicken Stock (page 407) or
   broth
Salt and freshly ground pepper

Heat the oil and butter in a sauté pan, add shallot, and sauté 1 minute over low heat. Add cooked sprouts, cover, and heat gently 2 minutes. Add chicken stock, sprinkle sprouts with salt and pepper, and heat uncovered over high heat, shaking pan or stirring sprouts gently, until most of liquid is absorbed. Serve hot.

Makes 3 or 4 side-dish servings

BRUSSELS SPROUTS BAKED IN CREAM SAUCE

In much of northern Europe, this is a time-honored way to prepare Brussels sprouts, as the creamy sauce balances the vegetable's assertive flavor. You can use either the rich version with cream or the leaner version made with nonfat milk.

¾ pound Brussels sprouts
Salt
1 cup Cream Sauce (page 400) or
    Lighter Cream Sauce (page 401)

2 tablespoons freshly grated Parmesan
    cheese

Preheat the oven to 425°F. Trim sprouts, removing tough bases and any yellow leaves. Put sprouts into a large saucepan containing enough boiling salted water to cover them generously. Return water to a boil, then cook sprouts uncovered for about 10 minutes, or until they are just tender when pierced with a small sharp knife. Drain, rinse with cold water until cool, and drain thoroughly.

Butter a heavy 5-cup gratin dish or other shallow baking dish. Arrange sprouts in one layer in dish. Spoon sauce carefully over them to coat completely. Sprinkle evenly with cheese. (*Dish can be kept, covered, 1 day in refrigerator; bring to room temperature before continuing.*)

Bake until sauce begins to bubble, about 7 to 10 minutes. If desired, brown lightly in broiler, about 1 minute, checking often and turning dish if necessary so cheese browns evenly. Serve hot, from baking dish.

Makes 4 side-dish servings

11

Cabbage

Cabbage is not at the top of most people's list of best-loved foods. It doesn't have the status appeal of being costly, rare, or seasonal. It is considered a winter vegetable—not because it is available mainly in winter but because many other vegetables are not. Some people have the impression that its flavor and odor are too strong, and that cabbage dishes are heavy.

Nutritionists, however, give us good reasons to put cabbage at the head of our shopping list. They recommend all members of the cabbage family as rich in nutrients and useful in fortifying our bodies against disease, and they urge us to serve these vegetables frequently.

And cabbage can be great tasting. Indeed, the French are so fond of it that they even call loved ones *mon petit chou*, or "my little cabbage." Cabbage has been used in the European Mediterranean area since prehistoric times and was already highly regarded by the ancient Greeks and Romans. Today cabbage is popular throughout most of Europe, the Middle East, and much of Asia, Africa, the Caribbean, and Latin America and appears in salads, soups, pastry fillings, main courses, and, of course, as an accompaniment.

Cooks around the world have developed many tricks for tempering *green* and *red cabbage* in order to create dishes that are delicate and light. These techniques are also useful for the curly *Savoy green cabbage*. They are not required for the cooking of the milder Chinese *napa cabbage* or *bok choy*, which are good stir-fried, cooked in soups, and shredded for salads.

One of the best methods for softening the taste and texture of green cabbage also is the quickest—blanching, or cooking briefly in boiling salted water. This technique also keeps the vegetable bright green. A few minutes are sufficient to make the vegetable tender, if it is shredded or chopped. It can then be served as is, or quickly sautéed or gently braised in order to absorb other aromas. If cabbage is boiled for a long time, it develops a strong smell and a dull color.

Salting is an alternative technique used mainly in eastern Europe for green and red cabbage. As with eggplant and cucumber, sprinkling shredded cabbage with salt, leaving it for almost an hour, then drying it removes strong-tasting juices. Salted cabbage becomes softened, although not as much as blanched cabbage, and has the added advantage that it does not absorb extra water. The salted cabbage is then sautéed or braised. Making sauerkraut is an extension of this procedure.

Whether it is blanched or salted, cabbage that is afterward cooked gently, even for a long time, will not be aggressive in flavor or odor.

Balancing the character of cabbage with other assertive ingredients is a good way to moderate its nature. In almost every cuisine, fried onions are paired with cabbage. A sweet-and-sour combination of vinegar with fruit, especially apples and raisins, is preferred in much of Europe. Mustard is another popular European seasoning for cabbage. Smoked meats also provide a pleasing accent, as do Parmesan, gruyère, and other cheeses. The exuberant Provençal flavors of garlic and olive oil produce cabbage dishes entirely different from those of colder climates. Spices such as ginger, cumin, and hot pepper complement cabbage in Middle Eastern and Indian dishes.

A different approach is to combine cabbage with mild ingredients such as butter or cream to make the vegetable taste rich and delicate. In eastern Europe, sour cream is a popular partner for cabbage.

In order to match cabbage with other ingredients, turn it into a main course, and give it an attractive shape, many cooks like to stuff it. A cabbage can be stuffed whole and then sliced, or each leaf can be used to encase a few tablespoons of a savory mixture. The filling can contain a variety of meats and vegetables, according to the cook's imagination. Some chefs give cabbage leaves the supreme honor by rolling them around a small amount of *foie gras*.

The cooking method chosen greatly affects the color of cabbage. Cooking red cabbage with an acid ingredient such as vinegar gives it a bright color. In contrast, green cabbage becomes discolored when simmered for some time with vinegar or wine. Although brief cooking of green cabbage in boiling salted water is the best way to keep it a vibrant green, long slow simmering is desired in some country dishes and color is sacrificed in order to obtain a harmony of tastes. Decorative serving platters or plates, or a sprinkling of chopped parsley, can then compensate for the lost color.

CABBAGE BASICS

✗ **Season:** Green and red cabbage and Chinese bok choy and napa cabbage are available all year.

✗ **Choosing:** Cabbage heads should be firm and feel heavy. Outer leaves of green cabbage should be light green, and those of red cabbage should be purple. Leaves should not be blemished.

✗ **Storing:** Keep unwashed in a plastic bag in the refrigerator up to 1 week.

✗ **Serving Size:** About ¼ to ½ pound per person.

✗ **Nutrients:** Cabbage is a cruciferous vegetable believed to help protect the body from certain cancers. It is also a good source of vitamin C. Bok choy is rich in vitamins A and C and calcium. One cup of shredded raw cabbage has only 20 calories; 1 cup cooked cabbage has about 32 calories. For bok choy, the same amounts have about 10 calories raw or 20 calories cooked.

✗ **Basic Preparation:** Discard any wilted outer leaves. Rinse cabbage. When shredding cabbage with a knife, it's easiest to cut out the core last, so you can hold the core end while shredding the leaves.

One reason given for not using cabbage often is that cutting it in small pieces takes long. In fact, it's easy to shred cabbage for four to six servings with a knife in a few minutes, or with a food processor in seconds. And if this is not easy enough, you can now buy fresh shredded cabbage in packages in many supermarkets.

SIMPLE SAUTÉED CABBAGE

This bright green, slightly crisp cabbage can be served with meat, poultry, and even seafood. This version is flavored with garlic, thyme, and a touch of hot pepper in the style of the Pyrenees region on the border between France and Spain. For this small amount of cabbage it is easiest to use a deep sauté pan both for blanching and for sautéing; for larger quantities, you can blanch the cabbage in a large saucepan and sauté it in a skillet.

1 small head green cabbage (about 1 pound), cored, rinsed, and shredded
Salt and freshly ground pepper
2 tablespoons vegetable or olive oil

2 medium garlic cloves, minced
⅛ to ¼ teaspoon hot red pepper flakes, or cayenne pepper to taste
½ teaspoon dried thyme, crumbled

In a deep sauté pan, boil enough water to cover cabbage. Add a pinch of salt and the cabbage, and boil it for 5 minutes or until just tender. Drain in a colander, rinse under running cold water, and drain thoroughly. Gently squeeze cabbage by handfuls to remove excess water. Heat oil in the same pan, add garlic and pepper flakes, and sauté about 15 seconds. Quickly stir in cabbage and sprinkle with salt, pepper, and thyme. Sauté over medium heat, stirring, for 3 minutes, or until hot. Taste for seasoning.

Makes 2 or 3 side-dish servings

"UNSTUFFED" CABBAGE

My Yemen-born mother-in-law, Rachel Levy, taught me to make this easy, aromatic dish. She said that this is a dish to make when you're feeling too lazy to prepare stuffed cabbage. Instead you cook the ingredients together, and the result is delicious. The cabbage braises quickly with rice and is flavored with the popular Yemenite "soup seasoning" mixture—cumin, turmeric, and pepper— along with garlic and onions. I love this as a supper main course or as an accompaniment for roasted or braised chicken, beef, or lamb.

For an even quicker dish, use packaged shredded cabbage or cole slaw mix (without the dressing, of course!).

2 tablespoons vegetable oil
2 medium onions, sliced
1 small head cabbage (1 to 1¼
    pounds), shredded; or 8 to 10
    cups packaged shredded cabbage
Salt and freshly ground pepper
4 large garlic cloves, chopped

2 teaspoons ground cumin
½ teaspoon turmeric
2 cups long-grain white rice
1 quart Chicken or Vegetable Stock
    (pages 407, 406) or water
4 plum tomatoes, diced (optional)

Heat oil in a large casserole or Dutch oven. Add onions and sauté over medium heat for 5 minutes or until softened. Add cabbage and salt, cover, and cook over low heat, stirring often, for 5 minutes to wilt. Add garlic, cumin, turmeric, and rice and sauté about 2 minutes. Add broth, salt, and pepper. Stir and bring to boil, cover, and cook over low heat for 15 minutes. Sprinkle tomato on top, cover, and cook 5 minutes or until rice is tender. Taste and adjust seasoning.

Makes 4 main-course or 6 to 8 side-dish servings

ROMANIAN BRAISED CABBAGE WITH TOMATOES AND PEPPERS

Cabbage cooked in a light onion-tomato sauce has the old-fashioned taste of grandmothers' cooking (if Grandma came from central Europe). Although Romanians usually do not blanch the cabbage, this simple step makes the vegetable cook much more quickly. The braised cabbage is good with chicken, beef, or rice or with its traditional accompaniment of mamaliga, *the Romanian polenta.*

1 medium head green cabbage (about 2 pounds), cored, rinsed, and shredded
Salt and freshly ground pepper
2 tablespoons vegetable oil
1 large onion, chopped

1 green bell pepper, cut into thin strips
2 tablespoons tomato paste
½ cup water
2 ripe medium tomatoes, sliced

In a Dutch oven or heavy large pot, boil enough water to cover cabbage. Add a pinch of salt and the cabbage, and boil it for 3 to 5 minutes or until just tender. Drain in a colander, rinse under running cold water, and drain thoroughly. Gently squeeze cabbage by handfuls to remove excess water.

Heat oil in the same pan, add onion and pepper, and sauté about 5 minutes over medium heat. Add cabbage and sauté lightly for 5 minutes. Sprinkle with salt and pepper. Mix tomato paste with ¼ cup water and add to the pan. Add remaining water and sliced tomatoes. Cover and cook over low heat, stirring often, about 15 minutes or until cabbage and peppers are tender. Taste and adjust seasoning. (*Cabbage can be kept, covered, 2 days in refrigerator.*) Serve hot.

Makes 4 side-dish servings or 2 or 3 main-course servings, with rice or polenta

CABBAGE AND PROSCIUTTO CREPES

Cabbage is a popular filling for crepes and other filled pancakes in Hungary and Russia. I find that prosciutto gives these fillings a tasty accent, even if it is from a different country; it is available in Italian markets and some supermarkets. For a less expensive alternative, you can substitute smoked turkey; and for a vegetarian variation, omit the meat entirely. The filling of cabbage with sautéed onions and sour cream will still have plenty of flavor.

Buckwheat crepes are particularly tasty wrappings for cabbage filling, but you can use white or whole wheat flour crepes if you prefer; to save time, use packaged crepes.

½ large head green cabbage (about 1¼ pounds), cored and rinsed
4 ounces prosciutto
½ cup (1 stick) unsalted butter, or half butter and half vegetable oil
2 large onions, minced

Salt and freshly ground pepper
¾ cup sour cream, at room temperature
8 Buckwheat Crepes (page 410), at room temperature
½ to 1 cup sour cream or yogurt, at room temperature, for serving

Shred cabbage finely, using food processor fitted with shredding disc. Cut 24 strips of prosciutto of about 1½ × ⅛ inch, cover, and reserve for garnish. Cut remaining prosciutto in ½-inch squares. Cover prosciutto tightly to prevent drying.

Preheat the oven to 425°F. if planning to serve crepes as soon as they are ready. Melt 4 tablespoons of butter in a large skillet over low heat. Add onions and cook, stirring occasionally, until very soft but not browned, about 15 minutes. Add prosciutto squares and stir over low heat just until moistened evenly, about ½ minute. Remove mixture to large bowl.

Wipe skillet clean. Melt 3 tablespoons butter in skillet over medium heat. Stir in cabbage and a pinch of salt and pepper. Cook over medium heat, stirring often, until very tender, about 15 minutes. Mix cabbage with onion-prosciutto mixture. Cool to room temperature. Stir in ¾ cup sour cream and a pinch of pepper. Taste and adjust seasoning.

Butter a 14 × 8-inch oval baking dish or other shallow baking dish. Spoon 3 tablespoons filling onto the less attractive side of each crepe, across lower third of crepe. Roll up in cigar shape, beginning at edge with filling. Arrange crepes seam side down in a single layer in buttered dish. Melt remaining tablespoon butter and brush crepes with melted butter. (*Crepes can be prepared up to this point and kept, covered, up to 1 day in refrigerator. Bring crepes to room temperature and preheat oven before continuing.*)

Bake in preheated oven until hot, about 10 minutes. Transfer crepes to plates. Spoon a dollop of sour cream or yogurt onto center of each crepe. Sprinkle sour cream with 3 prosciutto strips.

Makes 4 appetizer servings

BRETON CABBAGE SALAD WITH SHRIMP AND WALNUTS

Brittany, in western France, is famous for its seafood, which chefs use to add a special touch to appetizers like this festive cabbage salad garnished with freshly cooked shrimp. The cabbage is flavored with a simple Dijon mustard vinaigrette, a popular flavoring for cabbage salad throughout France. If you would like an even more colorful salad, you can use equal parts green and red cabbage. To save time, you can purchase packaged shredded cabbage.

2 tablespoons white wine vinegar
2 teaspoons Dijon mustard
Salt and freshly ground pepper
6 tablespoons vegetable oil
4 to 5 cups finely shredded green
     cabbage (½ a medium head of 1 to
     1¼ pounds), cored, rinsed, and
     shredded fine

¼ pound raw medium shrimp,
     unshelled
¾ cup walnut halves, toasted (page
     413)

In a bowl combine vinegar, mustard, and salt and pepper to taste. Whisk in oil. Toss with the cabbage and taste for seasoning.

In a medium saucepan of simmering salted water, cook the shrimp, covered, over low heat for 1 minute. Drain in a colander and rinse under running cold water. Shell and devein shrimp. Cut half the shrimp in half crosswise. Break two-thirds of the walnuts in pieces.

Add shrimp halves and walnut pieces to cabbage mixture and toss. Transfer salad to a platter or serving bowl. Decorate with walnut halves and whole shrimp.

Makes 4 appetizer servings

MALAYSIAN CABBAGE SALAD WITH SPICY PEANUT DRESSING

This recipe is inspired by a salad I tasted at Kuala Lumpur, a Malaysian restaurant in Pasadena, California. Generally the vegetables are cooked, but I find this zesty dressing of peanut butter accented with chilies, garlic, ginger, and lime juice is perfect with raw vegetables as well.

4 cups shredded red cabbage
4 cups shredded green cabbage
1 cup shredded carrot
Malaysian Peanut Dressing (page 386),
    cooled

1 medium cucumber, cut in thin sticks
2 or 3 large hard-boiled eggs,
    quartered
1 cup bean sprouts
Lime wedges

Mix both types of cabbage with the carrot in a bowl. Add enough dressing to coat them lightly, about ¾ cup. Taste and adjust seasoning. Serve each portion topped with cucumber sticks, hard-boiled egg quarters, bean sprouts, and lime wedges. Serve remaining dressing separately.

Makes 4 to 6 appetizer servings

RED AND GREEN CABBAGE SALAD WITH CITRUS FRUIT

Cabbage salads with fruit are popular throughout Europe. In Germany and Poland there are cabbage salads with apples. On rue Cler, my local market street when I lived in Paris, cabbage salad with raisins was available from several charcuteries, or French-style delis.

This salad is adapted from one I learned to make when I worked at the restaurant La Ciboulette in Paris. It's colorful, tasty, and extremely easy to prepare. At the restaurant they garnished each portion of this appetizer salad with a pinch of chives.

¼ cup dried currants or raisins
1 quart shredded red cabbage
1 quart shredded green cabbage or cole
    slaw mix
2 tablespoons plus 2 teaspoons red
    wine vinegar

3 tablespoons plus 1 teaspoon
    vegetable oil
Salt and freshly ground pepper
1 orange, divided in sections
1 grapefruit, divided in sections
¼ cup pecan pieces

Rinse currants with warm water; drain well. In a large bowl mix red and green cabbage. Mix in currants.

In a small bowl whisk vinegar with oil, salt, and pepper. Add to cabbage mixture and mix well until cabbage is evenly moistened. Taste and adjust seasoning. Divide among plates. Top each serving with orange and grapefruit sections and sprinkle with pecans.

Makes 4 or 5 appetizer servings

SALVADORAN COLE SLAW

This salad might appear tame at first bite, but after a few forkfuls you'll see that it's quite hot, from the red pepper flakes in the dressing. It is a standard item on the table in Salvadoran restaurants called pupuserias, *which are named for their star item,* pupusas, *savory griddle cakes made of tortilla dough with meat or vegetable fillings. Salvadorans tell me their country's cooking is less hot than that of Mexico, but after you taste this dish you might find that hard to imagine.*

Serve this cole slaw as an accompaniment for meat or burritos, or as a tasty relish with sandwiches of smoked fish, smoked turkey, or other meats.

Half a 1¼-pound cabbage (about 5
    cups shredded)
1 medium carrot (about 1 cup coarsely
    grated)
½ teaspoon dried oregano, crumbled

¾ teaspoon hot red pepper flakes
Salt to taste
2 tablespoons distilled white vinegar
1 tablespoon vegetable oil
1 tablespoon water

To shred cabbage, cut in half through the core and put on board cut side down. Cut in thin slices with a large knife (like slicing an onion in half-rings); separate into shreds. Grate carrot using large holes of grater; hold carrot almost parallel to grater so it forms long shreds.

Combine oregano, pepper flakes, and salt in a bowl. Add vinegar and whisk to blend. Whisk in oil and water. Let stand 10 minutes for flavors to blend.

Toss cabbage with carrot in a bowl. Add dressing and toss. Taste and adjust seasoning. (*This salad tastes best fresh, when the vegetables are crunchy; you can make it 1 or 2 days ahead, but the vegetables soften the longer it stands.*)

Makes 5 or 6 side-dish servings

DUTCH RED CABBAGE
WITH APPLES

I learned this recipe from my friend Sippy Levine, who was born in Holland. The red cabbage cooks with vinegar, which keeps its color bright. Most recipes call for balancing the vinegar with sugar, but Sippy uses strawberry preserves as part of the sweetening for a slight fruit flavor. She serves the cabbage with hachee, a traditional Dutch onion beef stew, and with boiled potatoes, or with meatballs and mashed potatoes. I like it with roast chicken or duck too, or cold as a salad. The cabbage braises just until it is tender but retains a pleasant texture.

Sweet-and-sour red cabbage is also a favorite in Germany and throughout central Europe. Some people cook the cabbage with raisins; a French variation includes red wine as part of the cooking liquid.

1 large red cabbage (about 1¾ pounds)
3 tablespoons margarine or butter
1 medium onion, chopped
2 tart green apples, halved, cored, and
    cut thin wedges
Salt to taste

½ cup red wine vinegar
¼ cup water
2 tablespoons sugar
1 bay leaf
3 tablespoons strawberry preserves

Quarter cabbage, then slice each piece in thin shreds; discard core.

Melt margarine in a large casserole, add onion, and sauté over medium heat, stirring occasionally, for 5 minutes. Add apples and sauté, stirring often, for 3 minutes or until onion is lightly browned.

Add cabbage, sprinkle with salt, and mix well over low heat. Add vinegar, water, sugar, and bay leaf; mix well. Bring to a boil, stirring. Cover and cook over low heat, stirring occasionally, about 30 minutes, or until cabbage is tender. Discard bay leaf.

Uncover and cook cabbage over medium heat, stirring often, for 2 or 3 minutes or until excess liquid evaporates. Add preserves; heat briefly over low heat, stirring, to blend. Taste and add more salt, sugar, or preserves if desired. (*Cabbage can be kept, covered, 3 days in refrigerator.*) Serve hot.

Makes 6 to 8 side-dish servings

BABY BOK CHOY WITH CHINESE MUSHROOMS

A few years ago you had to go to Chinatown or to a Chinese specialty shop to find baby bok choy. Fortunately, they and other Chinese greens are becoming available in supermarkets. This delicate vegetable dish is based on a recipe I learned in Hong Kong from cooking teacher Lucy Lo, who prefers subtle flavors that enhance the natural taste of the vegetables—in this case just Chinese mushrooms and a little soy sauce.

For an easy and tasty light meal, serve the bok choy and mushrooms with grilled or poached shrimp and with rice or rice noodles.

6 large dried Chinese black mushrooms	2 teaspoons water
1½ cups hot water	1 tablespoon vegetable oil
4 baby bok choy (total about 1 pound)	1 tablespoon soy sauce
1 teaspoon cornstarch	Salt and pepper (optional)

Soak mushrooms in hot water for 20 minutes or until tender. Cut off stems. Pour soaking liquid carefully into another bowl, leaving any sand at bottom of first bowl. Measure ½ cup of liquid.

Soak bok choy in a bowl of cold water about 10 minutes to remove any sand. Mix cornstarch with 2 teaspoons water.

Heat oil in a medium sauté pan over medium heat. Add bok choy; stand back to avoid splatters as wet vegetable comes in contact with oil. Sauté about 1 minute, turning the vegetable until it is coated.

Add ½ cup mushroom soaking liquid. Add mushrooms and soy sauce. Cover and cook over medium heat, turning bok choy occasionally, for 8 to 10 minutes or until just crisp-tender when base is pierced with a sharp knife. If pan becomes nearly dry during cooking, add 2 tablespoons water. Remove vegetables from pan with a slotted spoon and arrange on a platter.

Measure cooking liquid; add enough water to obtain ⅓ cup. Bring liquid to a simmer over medium heat. Stir cornstarch mixture and pour into liquid, stirring. Return to simmer to thicken, stirring. Taste and adjust seasoning. Pour sauce over vegetables and serve.

Makes 2 to 4 side-dish servings

STIR-FRIED BOK CHOY WITH BLACK BEAN SAUCE

Black bean sauce, a thick paste that comes in a jar and is often flavored with garlic, is a good, simple way to add zest to leafy Chinese vegetables, such as bok choy and Chinese mustard greens. It's also good with eggplant—see Chinese Eggplant and Peppers with Black Bean Sauce (page 177). Do not be tempted to increase the quantity of black bean sauce before tasting first—a little bit of this pungent paste goes a long way. Serve this easy vegetable stir-fry with chicken, turkey, or beef and with rice or rice noodles.

¾ to 1 pound bok choy or baby bok choy
1 medium carrot, peeled and cut into diagonal slices ¼ inch thick
1 tablespoon vegetable oil

2 teaspoons minced peeled fresh ginger
2 medium garlic cloves, minced
1 teaspoon bottled garlic-flavored black bean sauce

Rinse bok choy. Chop leaves into 1-inch pieces. Cut stems into ¼-inch-thick diagonal slices.

Put carrot in a medium saucepan, cover generously with water, and bring to a boil. Simmer 5 minutes or until crisp-tender. Add bok choy, cover, and bring to a boil. Uncover and boil 1 minute. Drain and rinse.

Heat oil in a heavy, medium skillet over medium-high heat, add ginger and garlic, and sauté 10 seconds. Add bok choy and carrot, and stir-fry 1 minute. Add sauce and cook over low heat until heated through.

Makes 2 or 3 side-dish servings

12

Carrots and Parsnips

We rely on carrots to provide color in our winter menus, but they are one of the most versatile vegetables for using year-round. Prominent in practically every cuisine, from Oriental to Indian to Middle Eastern to African to European to American, they are popular both raw and cooked, as a colorful side dish and as a delicately sweet flavoring for sauces, soups, and stews.

Americans associate carrot salad with a rich, thick mixture of grated carrots, sweet mayonnaise, and raisins. But around the globe there are plenty of lighter, zesty, delicious carrot salads, such as French Crudités (page 374), Danish Carrot and Apple Salad (page 138), flavored with horseradish, and Moroccan salad of cooked carrots with garlic, cumin, and parsley (page 139). The sweetness of carrots is a wonderful complement for spicy radishes (as in Daikon Radish and Carrot Salad, page 230) and celery root, in a Polish salad made with that vegetable (page 149).

Cooked carrots can be quickly flavored with *gremolata*, a lemony Italian seasoning mixture with a hint of garlic (page 134). For a holiday dish, toss lightly cooked carrots with fresh

131

tarragon, sautéed mushrooms, and wild rice (page 137); or make them into festive timbales (page 138).

Carrots star in all sorts of vegetable medleys, from Ukrainian Carrot and Potato Stew with Dried Mushrooms (page 136) to Indian Chickpeas with Spinach and Carrots (page 70). They're good with yogurt dill sauce (page 141), with Vinaigrette (page 383), and Turkish style with Yogurt-Garlic Sauce (page 380).

CARROT BASICS

✗ **Season:** Available all year.

✗ **Choosing:** Carrots should be firm, smooth, and bright orange. Carrots with leaves attached are usually freshest; these leaves should be bright green. Avoid carrots that are pale, greenish near the top, or cracked.

✗ **Storing:** Cut off green leaves. Store carrots unwashed in a plastic bag or closed container in refrigerator. They keep about 2 weeks.

✗ **Serving Size:** About ¼ pound per person.

✗ **Nutrients:** Carrots are an excellent source of beta carotene and vitamin A. One medium raw carrot has 30 calories; ½ cup cooked carrot slices has 35 calories.

✗ **Basic Preparation:** Cut off top and root ends. Rinse and scrub well; peel if you like.

Parsnips look like white carrots, and indeed are related to them. They can be used in many carrot recipes and are delicious when glazed together with carrots, as on page 140. In central Europe they are a popular addition to vegetable soups.

PARSNIP BASICS

✕ **Season:** Available in late fall and winter.

✕ **Choosing:** They should be firm, plump, and not too large. Avoid those that are soft or shriveled.

✕ **Storing:** Store parsnips unwashed in a plastic bag; they keep for about a week.

✕ **Serving Size:** About ¼ pound per person.

✕ **Nutrients:** Parsnips contain vitamin C and potassium. One cup diced cooked parsnips has about 100 calories.

✕ **Basic Preparation:** Cut off top and root ends. Rinse and scrub well; peel with a vegetable peeler.

CARROTS WITH GREMOLATA

Gremolata is a popular Italian flavoring mixture of grated lemon zest, garlic, and parsley that is most famous as a finishing touch on osso buco. *It also does wonders for plain cooked carrots, turning them into an exciting dish in no time.*

Gremolata

½ teaspoon finely grated or finely
    chopped lemon zest
1 small garlic clove, very finely minced
    (¼ teaspoon)

2 tablespoons minced fresh parsley

4 cups sliced carrots, sliced ⅛ inch
    thick
2 teaspoons vegetable oil

Salt and freshly ground pepper

Combine ingredients for *gremolata* in a small bowl and mix thoroughly with a fork. Cover and reserve at room temperature.

Put carrots in a saucepan, cover with water, and bring to a simmer. Cook 7 to 10 minutes or until just tender. Drain, reserving 1 tablespoon cooking liquid. Return carrots to pan.

Just before serving, add oil to carrots, sprinkle them with salt and pepper, and toss briefly over low heat until hot. Add reserved liquid, sprinkle with *gremolata*, cover, and heat over low heat 1 minute. Serve hot.

Makes 4 side-dish servings

SAUTÉED CARROTS WITH YOGURT

For this Turkish recipe, the carrots are precooked whole, then are sautéed in olive oil. They make an easy and savory side dish. For an appetizer, they are usually served with a cool yogurt-garlic sauce, which tastes great with the hot carrots. Some people simply sprinkle the hot carrots with cinnamon and spoon plain yogurt over them.

The Turks love all sorts of vegetables with yogurt, and naturally sweet carrots are particularly well complemented by its tangy flavor. They also like salads of grated carrots with raisins, similar to our American version but dressed with yogurt rather than mayonnaise.

1 pound medium carrots, peeled
Salt and freshly ground pepper
Turkish Yogurt-Garlic Sauce (page
    380)

2 tablespoons olive oil
Mint or Italian parsley sprigs, for
    garnish (optional)

Cut each carrot in 3 chunks. Cook carrots in water to cover with a pinch of salt in a covered pan over medium-low heat about 10 minutes or until nearly tender. Drain thoroughly. Cut in diagonal slices about ¼ inch thick. Prepare sauce.

Heat oil in a large skillet over medium-high heat. Add carrots, sprinkle with salt and pepper, and sauté about 5 minutes, stirring often, until very lightly brown; color changes just a little. Drain on paper towels, if desired. Serve carrots hot, garnished with herbs; serve yogurt sauce separately.

Makes 4 appetizer servings

KOREAN CARROTS WITH ZUCCHINI

A simple dressing flavored with toasted sesame seeds and sesame oil lends zest to this quick vegetable sauté. Serve it hot as a side dish or cold as a salad, on a bed of salad greens.

1 pound carrots, cut in thin sticks
2 tablespoons plus 2 teaspoons soy
    sauce
2 teaspoons Oriental sesame oil
2 tablespoons rice wine or dry sherry
½ to 1 teaspoon chili oil or hot sauce,
    or to taste
2 medium garlic cloves, minced

2 tablespoons vegetable oil
1 pound zucchini, cut in thin sticks
Salt
1 tablespoon finely chopped green
    onion
1 tablespoon sesame seeds, toasted
    (page 413)

Put carrots in a saucepan with water to cover, bring to a boil, and cook 3 minutes. Drain carrots.

In a small bowl combine soy sauce, sesame oil, rice wine, chili oil, and garlic. Mix well.

Heat vegetable oil in a large skillet over medium heat. Add zucchini and sauté 2 minutes. Add carrots and sprinkle with salt. Toss briefly over heat until vegetables are just tender. Add sauce and toss well. Taste and adjust seasoning. Serve sprinkled with green onion and toasted sesame seeds.

Makes 4 side-dish servings, or 2 main-course servings with rice

UKRAINIAN CARROT AND POTATO STEW WITH DRIED MUSHROOMS

Dried mushrooms turn ordinary vegetable stews, like this one of carrots and potatoes, into a festive dish. Polish mushrooms are the most authentic, but in fact any dried mushrooms will give a good flavor to the sauce; I often use shiitake. I find dried mushrooms a useful item to keep in the pantry; they enable me to prepare delicious dishes like this at any time.

You can prepare other vegetable stews the same way by substituting turnips, celery root, kohlrabi, or parsnips for the potatoes or the carrots.

1 ounce dried mushrooms
1 pound carrots, peeled
1 tablespoon vegetable oil
1 small onion, chopped
¾ pound potatoes, peeled and diced
1½ cups water

1 bay leaf
Salt and freshly ground pepper
1 tablespoon butter
4 teaspoons flour
3 tablespoons chopped fresh parsley

Soak mushrooms in hot water to cover 30 minutes. Drain well. If using shiitake mushrooms, discard tough stems. Slice mushrooms.

Halve carrots lengthwise if they are large. Cut in ½-inch slices.

Heat oil in a saucepan, add onion, and sauté 5 minutes over medium heat. Add mushrooms, carrots, potatoes, water, bay leaf, salt, and pepper. Bring to a boil. Cover and cook 20 minutes or until vegetables are tender. With a slotted spoon, remove vegetables to a bowl. Discard bay leaf. Measure 1 cup liquid. Reserve remaining liquid.

Melt butter in pan, add flour, and cook, stirring constantly, until lightly browned. Whisk in measured vegetable cooking liquid. Bring to a boil, whisking. Return vegetables to pan, stir gently, and bring to a simmer. Stir in a tablespoon of reserved liquid if sauce is too thick. Taste and adjust seasoning. Stir in half the parsley. Serve sprinkled with remaining parsley.

Makes 4 or 5 side-dish or 3 main-course servings

CARROTS WITH WILD RICE, MUSHROOMS, AND TARRAGON

Wild rice, a product of Canada and the northern United States, is loved in both countries. For this French Canadian dish I like to add carrots and mushrooms as well as a generous amount of fresh tarragon.

This colorful dish is a perfect partner for a holiday turkey. It also makes a delicious vegetarian main course.

¾ pound slim carrots, peeled
½ pound mushrooms
5 cups water
Salt and freshly ground pepper
1 cup wild rice, rinsed and drained

2 tablespoons vegetable oil or butter
1 large onion, halved and sliced thin
¾ cup thinly sliced celery
3 tablespoons chopped fresh tarragon
⅓ cup chopped fresh parsley

Cut carrots into 2-inch lengths; quarter each piece lengthwise. Quarter small mushrooms; cut larger ones into 6 pieces.

Bring 4 cups water to a boil and add a pinch of salt. Add carrots and boil for 5 minutes or until crisp-tender. Remove with a slotted spoon. Add 1 cup water to pot and bring to boil. Add rice, return to boil, cover, and cook over low heat 50 to 60 minutes or until kernels begin to puff open.

Meanwhile, heat oil in a large sauté pan over medium-low heat. Add onion and sauté for 5 minutes. Add celery and sauté for 2 minutes. Add mushrooms, salt, and pepper and sauté over medium heat for 7 minutes or until tender. Remove from heat, add carrots, and reserve.

Reheat vegetables. Drain rice and add to pan of vegetables. Heat together briefly. Add tarragon and all but 1 tablespoon parsley. Taste and adjust seasoning. Serve hot, sprinkled with remaining parsley.

Makes 4 main-course or 6 side-dish servings

CARROT TIMBALES

These rich, festive, bright orange carrot molds from the French repertoire make a beautiful appetizer for a festive occasion. For a really lavish dish, accompany them with Madeira Cream (page 398) and garnish them with cooked baby carrots, asparagus tips, or a few of each.

1½ pounds carrots, peeled
Salt and ground white pepper
⅔ cup heavy cream, at room
temperature

3 large eggs
Pinch of sugar

Preheat the oven to 375°F. Generously butter four ⅔-cup ramekins or five ½-cup timbale molds. Cut carrots into ½-inch slices. Put in saucepan, cover with water, add a pinch of salt, and bring to a boil. Cover and cook over medium-low heat until very tender, about 20 minutes. Drain well. Puree in a food processor until very smooth.

Measure 2 cups puree. Cook puree in a heavy, wide, medium saucepan over low heat, stirring often, about 5 minutes. Stir in cream and bring to a boil. Cook over medium heat, stirring often, until mixture is reduced to 2 cups, about 5 minutes. Transfer to bowl and cool 7 minutes.

Lightly whisk eggs in a medium bowl. Gradually whisk in vegetable mixture. Season well with salt, pepper, and a pinch of sugar. Divide mixture among buttered molds. Tap each on counter to pack down mixture. Smooth tops. Set molds in roasting pan and put in oven. Add enough boiling water to pan to come halfway up sides of molds. Set a sheet of buttered foil atop molds; do not fold it over sides of pan.

Bake until timbales are firm and a cake tester inserted into mixture comes out dry, about 40 to 50 minutes; add hot water to pan during baking if most of it evaporates. Carefully remove molds from water. Cool 5 minutes.

Run a thin-bladed flexible knife around edge of one mold. Set small serving plate atop mold and invert both. Holding them together, tap them on towel-lined counter. Gently lift up mold. Repeat with remaining timbales. Serve hot or warm.

Makes 4 or 5 appetizer servings

DANISH CARROT AND APPLE SALAD

We tend to think of horseradish primarily as a seasoning for meat, but in Scandinavia and much of northern Europe it is popular with vegetables as well, as in this easy carrot salad. Polish versions of the salad are enriched with sour cream.

2 tablespoons strained fresh lemon
 juice
1 teaspoon bottled white horseradish
 or grated fresh horseradish
1 tablespoon sugar
Salt

2 tart medium apples, such as Granny
 Smith
2 large carrots, coarsely shredded (2⅓
 cups)
1½ to 2 tablespoons mayonnaise,
 regular or reduced-calorie

Mix lemon juice with horseradish, sugar, and a pinch of salt. Peel apples and coarsely grate them. Add to dressing. Add carrots and mix. Stir in mayonnaise. Taste and adjust seasoning. Serve cold.

Makes 2 or 3 side-dish servings

MOROCCAN CARROT SALAD WITH GARLIC, CUMIN, AND PARSLEY

This is my favorite way to prepare carrot salad—the carrots are cooked and tossed with a light and zesty cumin dressing and a generous amount of fresh Italian parsley. It turns carrot salad into a truly enticing dish. For Moroccan meals, whether at home or in a restaurant, the salad is often put on the table as part of an assortment of appetizers before the dinner begins. The recipe is inspired by a salad I've enjoyed many times at Timgad, the best Moroccan restaurant in Paris, where it is served with salted toasted hazelnuts, olives, and pickled vegetables.

The sweetness of the carrots enables the use of a lighter dressing, with equal amounts of vinegar and oil, than in most salads.

1 pound carrots, peeled and sliced into
 ¼-inch-thick rounds
3 small garlic cloves, peeled
Tangy Moroccan Dressing (page 381)

¼ cup chopped fresh parsley,
 preferably Italian
Parsley sprigs, preferably Italian, for
 garnish

In a saucepan, cover carrots with water, add salt, and bring to a boil. Add garlic and simmer about 7 minutes or until carrots are just tender. Drain carrots, reserving garlic.
 Chop garlic and add to dressing. Add dressing to carrots and mix gently. Fold in parsley. Taste and adjust seasoning, adding more salt and cayenne pepper if needed. Serve cool in a shallow bowl or dish. Garnish with a few small parsley sprigs.

Makes 4 appetizer servings

GLAZED PARSNIPS AND CARROTS

I learned to make glazed carrots in France, but this method of cooking carrots is popular in most European countries. A friend of mine from Holland speaks fondly of the glazed carrots she grew up with, cooked with a pinch of cinnamon; this was a treat for both children and adults.

I like to glaze carrots and parsnips together because of the color contrast and because they are so delicious prepared this way that it's hard to decide which of them tastes better. Of course, you can double the amount of either vegetable and glaze it on its own.

A classic way to prepare the vegetables in restaurants is to trim them to an oval shape with a paring knife, rounding off the corners of each piece so they look like little footballs. It makes for an attractive presentation but it's time-consuming.

¾ pound long, thin, straight carrots
¾ pound parsnips
Salt and freshly ground pepper

1 teaspoon sugar
2 tablespoons vegetable oil or butter

Cut carrots into 2-inch lengths. Quarter any wide pieces (over ¾ inch in diameter) lengthwise. Cut parsnips the same way; trim any woody centers from vegetables.

Put carrots and parsnips in a medium sauté pan (about 10-inch diameter) and add enough water to cover, about 2½ cups. Add salt, pepper, sugar, and oil. Bring to a boil. Reduce heat to medium and simmer uncovered until the largest carrot pieces are very tender, about 30 minutes; stir once or twice during first 5 minutes, but afterward shake pan to stir.

When vegetables are tender, if too much liquid remains in pan, cook over medium-low heat, shaking pan often, until liquid evaporates and vegetables become coated with a light glaze, about 1 or 2 more minutes.

Makes 4 side-dish servings

PARSNIPS WITH BULGARIAN YOGURT-DILL SAUCE

Bulgaria is known for the quality of its yogurt, and Bulgarian cooks use it to make sauces for vegetables. This sauce has a warm orange hue from the paprika and is also good with carrots and potatoes. You can make it with nonfat, low-fat, or regular yogurt.

1 pound parsnips
½ cup **Chicken** or **Vegetable Stock** or
    broth
1½ tablespoons butter, margarine, or
    vegetable oil
2 tablespoons flour
1 teaspoon sweet paprika

1 medium garlic clove, minced
    (optional)
½ cup plain yogurt, at room
    temperature
1 tablespoon chopped fresh dill or 1
    teaspoon dried
Salt and freshly ground pepper

Peel parsnips and cut into 2-inch lengths. Quarter any wide pieces (over ¾ inch in diameter) lengthwise. Trim any woody centers.

Put parsnips in a medium saucepan and add enough water to cover, about 2 cups, and a pinch of salt. Bring to a boil. Cover and simmer until tender, about 15 to 20 minutes. Drain, reserving ½ cup of the cooking liquid. Combine with the stock.

Heat butter in medium saucepan, add flour and paprika, and cook over low heat, whisking, about 1 minute. Off heat, whisk in stock mixture. Bring to boil, whisking. Add garlic. Cook over low heat, whisking often, 2 minutes. In a bowl stir yogurt until smooth. Gradually stir sauce into yogurt. Return to pan and whisk until smooth. Gently heat through; do not boil. Stir in dill. Add parsnips and heat through without boiling. (*Parsnips can be kept, covered, 2 days in refrigerator. Reheat carefully in uncovered pan over medium heat, stirring often; do not boil.*) Taste and adjust seasoning. Serve hot.

Makes 4 servings

13

Celery, Celery Root, and Fennel

These three vegetables are prepared in similar ways. All are served either raw in salads or cooked as side dishes, and each can help add variety to our winter vegetable selection.

Both celery and celery root are available in North America and in Europe, but stalk celery is much more widely used by Americans, while Europeans prefer celery root. In the United States and Canada, *celery* is popular as a snack vegetable, a salad ingredient, an appetizer with dip (see Raw Vegetables with Chipotle Chili Dip, page 373), and a container for rich salads like chicken salad with mayonnaise. Europeans and North Africans braise celery with stock and onions, and serve it as a side dish. On both sides of the North Atlantic celery stalks and leaves are used to flavor soups, stews, and sauces. Celery cut in diagonal slices can be added to Chinese stir-fried vegetable or meat-and-vegetable dishes.

Celery root, or celeriac, a relative of celery, is a bulbous root vegetable best loved as a salad ingredient in Europe, from France through eastern Europe. The beloved *celeris rémoulade*, a part of most *crudité* plates served in bistros in France, is made of grated celery root mixed

143

with a mustard and mayonnaise dressing (page 150). In central Europe celery root is also made into salads, often with a light sweet-and-sour dressing like the one in Polish Celery Root and Carrot Salad with Apples and Walnuts (page 149). Celery root makes delicious soup (page 148), and along with carrots and onions is a common flavoring in winter vegetable and meat soups.

Fennel originated in southern Europe and has long been a favorite in Mediterranean and Balkan cuisines. In more recent times it has gained popularity in northern European countries

✕ CELERY BASICS

✕ **Season:** Available all year-round.

✕ **Choosing:** Celery should look firm and crisp and be free of bruises, and its leaves should be green and not wilted.

✕ **Storing:** Keeps up to 2 weeks in a plastic bag in the refrigerator.

✕ **Serving Size:** Allow 1 or 2 stalks raw celery or 4 to 5 ounces cooked per serving.

✕ **Nutrients:** Celery contains some vitamin C and is very low in calories—about 10 calories for ½ cup diced raw celery and 13 calories for ½ cup cooked celery.

✕ **Basic Preparation:** Rinse celery well. If celery is stringy, you can peel it with a vegetable peeler for a more delicate texture.

as well. Because of its crisp texture, it can be substituted for celery in salads, but the flavor it contributes is aniselike and does not resemble that of celery. It adds zest to bean salads, such as the Cypriot Two-Bean Salad with Fennel (page 67).

Fennel bulbs are also delicious as a cooked vegetable. They can be stuffed with mushrooms in the French manner (page 151), or baked with fontina cheese in the Italian style (page 150). Like celery, fennel stalks and fronds are used to season soups, salads, and stews.

CELERY ROOT BASICS

✂ **Season:** Most easily found in fall and winter.

✂ **Choosing:** Celery roots should be heavy for their size and fairly clean and smooth. If the stem is attached, it should look fresh and green.

✂ **Storing:** Keeps about 1 week in a plastic bag in the refrigerator.

✂ **Serving Size:** Allow 5 to 6 ounces per serving.

✂ **Nutrients:** Celery root contains vitamin C and potassium. One half cup contains about 25 to 30 calories.

✂ **Basic Preparation:** Rinse celery root thoroughly. Cut off tops and brown root ends. Peel root well with a knife.

FENNEL BASICS

✕ **Season:** Available in fall, winter, and early spring.

✕ **Choosing:** Choose fennel that is crisp and clean, with fresh green leaves, firm stalks, and no brown spots on the white bulbs.

✕ **Storing:** Store fennel in a plastic bag in the refrigerator; it keeps up to 1 week.

✕ **Serving Size:** Allow ½ to 1 cup raw or half a cooked fennel bulb per serving.

✕ **Nutrients:** Fennel is an excellent source of vitamin C and a good source of vitamin A, iron, and potassium. It also contains calcium. One cup chopped raw fennel has 23 calories.

✕ **Basic Preparation:** Cut off and reserve stalks and leaves for seasoning. Rinse the fennel bulb. It can be cooked whole or in pieces.

BRAISED CELERY WITH BLACK-EYED PEAS

Braised celery with beans or chickpeas in a sauce flavored with onions and cinnamon is popular in Tunisia and Algeria. Europeans braise celery too, but do not add beans, and they flavor the braising juices with sautéed onions and carrots. In both areas the celery is often braised with meat, but for a lighter dish you can simply use chicken stock as part of the braising liquid.

I find it convenient to use black-eyed peas in this dish because there are several quick-cooking versions—frozen or presoaked. You can also soak and cook dried black-eyed peas for this dish or substitute chickpeas.

9 or 10 celery stalks (about 1 pound)
2 tablespoons olive or vegetable oil
1 large onion, chopped
2 large garlic cloves, minced
4 teaspoons tomato paste
1½ cups Chicken or Vegetable Stock
    (pages 407, 406) or broth

Salt and freshly ground pepper
Pinch of ground cinnamon
1½ cups cooked black-eyed peas
2 tablespoons chopped fresh parsley

Peel celery to remove strings; cut into 3-inch lengths.

   Heat oil in a large, deep skillet over medium heat. Add onion and sauté 7 minutes until beginning to brown. Add garlic and sauté a few seconds. Whisk tomato paste with stock and add. Add a little salt and pepper and a pinch of cinnamon. Bring to a boil, add celery, cover, and cook over low heat about 30 minutes, or until celery is very tender; add a little water occasionally if sauce becomes too thick. Add black-eyed peas and heat through. Stir in 1 tablespoon parsley, taste sauce, and adjust seasoning; season generously with black pepper. Serve hot, sprinkled with remaining parsley.

Makes 4 side-dish servings

CELERY WITH TURKEY STUFFING

Celery sticks don't necessarily have to be stuffed with cream cheese. For this light and tasty recipe, they are filled with an eastern Mediterranean stuffing made of ground turkey, rice, cilantro, and garlic.

⅓ cup rice
10 celery stalks, patted dry
3 tablespoons olive oil
1 cup minced onion
¾ pound ground turkey (about 1½
    cups)
2 large garlic cloves, minced
½ cup chopped cilantro (fresh
    coriander) or parsley
¾ teaspoon sweet paprika

1 teaspoon ground cumin
½ teaspoon ground cinnamon
½ teaspoon ground ginger
¾ teaspoon salt
¾ teaspoon freshly ground black
    pepper
1 large egg
4 fresh or canned plum tomatoes,
    chopped
2 garlic cloves, sliced (for cooking)

Boil rice uncovered in a saucepan of 2 cups of boiling salted water for 10 minutes. Rinse with cold water and drain well. Transfer to a large bowl. Peel celery and cut into 3-inch lengths.

Heat 2 tablespoons oil in a large skillet, add onion, and cook over medium-low heat 5 minutes. Add turkey and sauté, stirring to crumble meat, about 5 minutes or until meat changes color. Remove from heat. Add minced garlic, cilantro, paprika, cumin, cinnamon, ginger, salt, and pepper; mix well. Add to rice; mix well. Add egg. Mix well.

Spoon stuffing into celery stalks. Spoon remaining oil into one large or 2 medium sauté pans and add celery. Add tomatoes, sliced garlic, a pinch of salt and pepper, and 1 cup water to pan. Bring to a simmer. Cover and cook over low heat about 25 minutes or until celery is tender. Serve hot, with a little tomato from pan spooned over celery.

Makes 3 or 4 main-course servings

CELERY ROOT SOUP

Anyone who thinks cream soups are bland should try this eastern European soup. It has an assertive celery flavor and creamy texture even when made with low-fat milk. Serve it with rye or pumpernickel bread, or with crusty French bread or croutons.

1½-pound celery root
1½ pounds boiling potatoes
2 tablespoons vegetable oil or butter
1 large onion, chopped
1 quart Chicken Stock (page 407), or 2
    14½-ounce cans chicken or
    vegetable broth with water to
    make 1 quart

Salt and ground white pepper
3 cups 2% low-fat or whole milk

Trim base of celery root with knife, then finish peeling it with a vegetable peeler. Rinse celery root, quarter it, and slice it ⅛ inch thick. Peel and quarter potatoes; slice ¼ inch thick.

In a large saucepan heat oil, add onion, and sauté for 5 minutes over medium-low heat or until soft but not brown. Add celery root and stock. Bring to boil, cover, and simmer 5 minutes. Add potatoes, salt, and white pepper. Cover and simmer 25 minutes or until vegetables are very tender.

Puree the vegetables with liquid in batches in food processor or blender. Return to cleaned pan and heat over medium heat. Gradually stir in milk. Heat but do not boil. Taste and adjust seasoning. Serve in heated bowls.

Makes 6 appetizer servings

POLISH CELERY ROOT AND CARROT SALAD WITH APPLES AND WALNUTS

Thin strips of carrots and celery root make a pretty mixture; both are easily shredded with a food processor. With apples, nuts, and a light sweet-and-sour dressing, this is a delightful winter appetizer and a good accompaniment for sandwiches or cold cuts. Serve it whenever you would serve cole slaw.

2 tablespoons vegetable oil
2 teaspoons sugar
2 tablespoons strained fresh lemon
    juice
Salt and freshly ground pepper

2 large carrots (about ¾ pound)
¾-pound celery root
1 tart medium apple
¼ cup diced walnuts
8 walnut halves, for garnish

In a small bowl mix oil, sugar, lemon juice, salt, and pepper.

Shred carrots using the coarse grating blade of a food processor, or grate by hand on large holes of grater. Cut off gnarled parts of celery root. Peel root and rinse. Shred like carrots. You will need about 2½ to 3 cups of each shredded vegetable.

Mix shredded celery root and carrots in a large bowl. Add dressing and toss. Peel apple and cut into ¼-inch dice. Add to salad and toss. Taste and adjust seasoning. Mix in diced walnuts. Serve garnished with walnut halves.

Makes 4 appetizer servings

CELERY ROOT RÉMOULADE

This is the most popular recipe in France for using celery root—tossed with a zesty mustard dressing. This version is lighter than traditional recipes but is still creamy, even if you use reduced-fat mayonnaise.

When I studied cooking at La Varenne, we made this often, and served it as part of crudités *(see recipe, page 374), as is traditional in France. As students, we painstakingly cut the celery into very thin julienne strips with a knife. Our strips were never thin enough to satisfy the chef! If the strips are too thick, the texture of the vegetable, which is used raw, is too firm. Fortunately, there's a simpler way to do it. The food processor makes doing this practically effortless. You simply use the large-hole grater and push the vegetable through quickly.*

1 tablespoon Dijon mustard	1 teaspoon herb vinegar
¼ cup mayonnaise, regular or reduced-calorie	Salt and freshly ground pepper
2 tablespoons vegetable oil	1 medium celery root (about ¾ pound)

In a bowl, mix mustard with mayonnaise. Gradually stir in oil and vinegar. Season with salt and pepper.

Thoroughly peel the celery root. Grate it in food processor; you will need 2½ cups grated celery. Add to dressing and mix well. Taste and adjust seasoning. (*Salad can be kept, covered, ½ day in refrigerator.*) Serve cold or at room temperature.

Makes 4 appetizer servings

FENNEL WITH FONTINA

In the beautiful Italian valley known as Valle d'Aosta, near Mont Blanc, the cooking is rich and hearty. I tasted vegetable, polenta, and pasta dishes in the region flavored with the area's famous cheese, fontina. Here is an easy way to use it to enliven cooked fennel.

2 large fennel bulbs (total about 1¾ pounds)	Freshly grated nutmeg to taste
Salt and freshly ground pepper	½ cup coarsely grated Italian fontina cheese

Preheat the oven to 425°F. Rinse fennel and discard any bruised leaves. Cut off stalks. (Reserve for salads or soups.) Cut bulbs in half downward through the base of the stalk to the base of the bulb to make 2 thin halves.

Add fennel to a large saucepan of boiling salted water, return to a boil, and simmer uncovered over medium heat about 30 minutes or until just tender. Drain well.

Lightly oil or butter a 9-inch square shallow baking dish and arrange fennel in it cut side up. Sprinkle with salt, pepper, and nutmeg. Sprinkle cheese on fennel, not on dish. Bake 15 minutes or until light brown. Serve hot.

Makes 4 side-dish servings

FENNEL WITH MUSHROOM STUFFING

In this recipe of Provençal inspiration, a light shallot-accented mushroom stuffing bakes between the fennel layers and gives the vegetable a wonderful flavor. Serve it as a festive accompaniment for roast chicken, turkey, or veal, or as a vegetarian main course along with other stuffed vegetables and crusty bread or rice.

3 large fennel bulbs (total 2½ pounds)
Salt and freshly ground pepper
8 ounces fresh mushrooms, halved

1 tablespoon plus 2 teaspoons olive oil
1 medium shallot, minced
About 2 teaspoons bread crumbs

Preheat the oven to 425°F. Rinse fennel and discard any bruised leaves. Cut off stalks. (Reserve them for salads or soups.) With fennel on board and base facing you, cut each bulb in half through base to form thick halves.

Add fennel to a large saucepan of boiling salted water and simmer uncovered over medium heat for about 30 minutes or until just tender.

Meanwhile, chop the mushrooms in a food processor with pulsing motion so they are chopped in fine pieces but are not pureed. In a medium skillet, heat 1 tablespoon oil over low heat, add the shallot, and sauté about ½ minute or until soft but not brown. Add mushrooms and sprinkle with salt and pepper. Cook over high heat, stirring, for 3 to 5 minutes or until mixture is dry. Transfer to a bowl. Taste and adjust seasoning.

When fennel bulbs are tender, drain them well. Cut a thin slice from the curved uncut end of each fennel half so they can stand straight. Spread the fennel layers apart and put a little stuffing into each, between layers. Lightly oil a shallow baking dish and arrange fennel in it stuffing side up. Sprinkle with salt and pepper, then with bread crumbs, and finally with 2 teaspoons oil. Bake about 15 minutes or until heated through.

Makes 6 side-dish servings

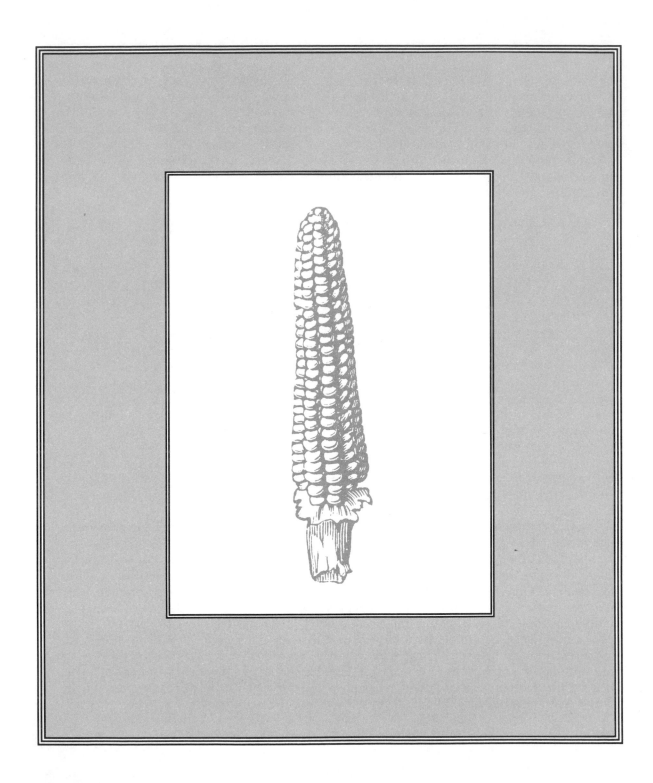

14

Corn

Like many Americans, I grew up eating corn one way—cooked on the cob, then smeared generously with butter and sprinkled with lots of salt. It was only when I moved to Israel that I tasted corn sold by street vendors. To my surprise, the corn was delicious even though it was served without butter. Since then, I always buy excellent quality corn, and I thoroughly enjoy eating it on the cob with just a sprinkling of salt.

In the Middle East I was also introduced to grilled corn on the cob. Grilling is also a familiar and well-liked technique for cooking corn in the United States. A relatively new, quick, and convenient way to cook corn on the cob is in the microwave.

Native Americans introduced the colonists to corn, and since then it has become one of the best-loved vegetables in the United States. From the Indians we learned to cook it with beans to make succotash, and this dish remains an American favorite. Corn is also popular made into fritters and relishes.

One of my favorite corn dishes, Corn Maquechou (page 156), comes from Louisiana. For this Creole specialty the kernels are briefly cooked with tomatoes, bell peppers, and onions.

153

But the best-known corn dish in this country is corn chowder, which often is quite rich but can be made in a tasty, lighter manner (page 157).

Corn originated in Latin America and still is a staple in the diet of its people. There are many traditional ways to prepare corn in this part of the world. It is used in tamales, as a filling for the Argentine turnovers called empanadas, and as a topping for chicken or meat pies. The kernels are cooked with other vegetables to make stews like Chilean "Succotash" (page 66), made with beans, tomatoes, and winter squash. South American cooks make corn into soups and even sauces. In Caribbean countries corn is often prepared as chowder and as spicy fritters.

Mexicans sprinkle corn on the cob with chili powder. Corn kernels are a frequent addition to Mexican vegetable soups, like Tomato and Corn Tortilla Soup (page 320), or are made into chowders flavored with green chilies. Corn is stewed with other vegetables, especially peppers and chayote squash.

Corn soups are prepared in China, Vietnam, and Indonesia. In India and in eastern Africa, which is influenced by Indian cuisine, corn is cooked as a curry with garlic, ginger, onions, and cumin.

Which variety of corn is best is a matter of personal preference: some like it white, some like it yellow, and some favor bicolor corn, which has some white and some yellow kernels. But everyone agrees that corn should be eaten as fresh as possible.

Hominy, which is made from dried corn kernels and is available canned, is a staple of native Americans, who use it in stews and make it into puddings. It remains popular in the United States in the South, both whole and in its ground form, as hominy grits. Mexican cooks simmer hominy in spicy meat soups flavored with chilies.

Baby corn, for which you eat the kernels with the cob, is a frequent addition to Chinese vegetable dishes. Occasionally you can find fresh baby corn in the exotic section of the supermarket. It can be cooked in water like regular corn, but its cooking time is shorter.

Popcorn is a type of nonsweet dried corn. When it is heated, steam is caught inside, which causes the corn to pop. Popcorn is high in complex carbohydrates and fiber and is a healthful snack if not sprinkled with too much butter, oil, or salt.

Corn is also used to make desserts. Corn puddings are favorites in the Caribbean. A popular Brazilian dessert is made with hominy and coconut milk. Thai chefs even add corn kernels to ice cream.

CORN BASICS

- **Season:** Available year-round; its peak season is in summer.
- **Choosing:** Corn husks should be fresh and tight, not dry; the kernels should be plump and tightly packed. Whether white or yellow corn is better is a matter of taste.
- **Storing:** Corn tastes best if used as soon as possible. If you're not cooking it the day you bought it, refrigerate it in its husk in a plastic bag for up to 2 days.
- **Serving Size:** Allow 1 ear of corn per person.
- **Nutrients:** Corn is a good source of vitamin C; yellow varieties also contain vitamin A. One small ear of corn has 70 calories.
- **Basic Preparation:** Unless you're grilling corn in the husk, remove the husk and silks. To cut kernels from the cob, either hold the stem end and cut straight down, or place cob on board and cut off a few rows of kernels at a time.

To Cook Corn on the Cob

To boil: Add prepared cobs to a large pan of boiling water without adding salt. Cover and boil about 5 minutes or until kernels are tender when pierced.

To grill: Remove all husks and silk. Grill 5 to 10 minutes, turning often, until corn is dotted with brown.

To microwave: Either leave corn in husks, or remove husks and silk and wrap ears in microwave plastic wrap. Put 1 or 2 ears in center of oven. Microwave on high; 1 ear takes about 2 or 3 minutes, 2 ears about 5 minutes in a full-power oven. If you cooked corn in husks, remove husks and silk after cooking.

CORN MAQUECHOU

It's easy to love this creamy, delicately sweet dish of fresh corn, onion, pepper, and tomato. I first tasted the Cajun specialty several years ago, in Lafayette, Louisiana. Unlike other local dishes, it was not fiery hot, only lightly seasoned with black pepper and cayenne. Of course, you can make it as hot as you like by increasing the amounts of these two spices to your taste.

6 ears corn
2 tablespoons vegetable oil or butter
1 medium onion, chopped
½ green bell pepper, chopped
1 large ripe tomato, peeled, seeded,
    and chopped

1 teaspoon sugar
Salt and black pepper to taste
Cayenne pepper to taste

Remove corn husks and silk. Place cob on board and cut off kernels, a few rows at a time. Then lightly scrape cobs with knife to remove any remaining parts of kernel and "milk" attached to cob, and add this to corn. You should have 4 to 4½ cups.

In a sauté pan heat oil over medium heat, add onion and pepper, and sauté 5 minutes. Add corn, tomato, sugar, black pepper, and cayenne. Cook 3 minutes, stirring. Cover and cook over low heat, stirring often, for 20 minutes or until corn is tender to your taste. Taste and adjust seasoning, adding salt to taste. If desired, cook uncovered 2 or 3 minutes to evaporate excess liquid. (*The corn can be kept, covered, 2 days in refrigerator.*) Serve hot.

Makes 4 side-dish servings

MEXICAN CORN, ZUCCHINI, AND PEPPER STEW

This colorful summer dish features the popular Latin American combination of corn, peppers, and squash. It is very quick and easy to cook. Green onions and garlic are the main flavorings; if you would like a hot vegetable stew, add 1 or 2 chopped jalapeño peppers along with the vegetables.

Many versions of this dish call for liberal quantities of bacon, cheese, or cream, but in fact the dish is appealing, tasty, and of course more healthful without them. I find this vegetable medley a great accompaniment for just about anything, from grilled shrimp to poached or grilled chicken, sausages, or eggs.

1½ pounds zucchini (4 medium)
2 tablespoons vegetable oil
1 green bell pepper, cut into ½-inch dice
1 red bell pepper, cut into ½-inch dice
Kernels cut from 3 ears of corn, or 2
    cups frozen corn kernels

2 medium garlic cloves, minced
2 green onions, chopped
Salt and freshly ground pepper
Pure chili powder or cayenne pepper
    to taste

Quarter the zucchini lengthwise and slice ½ inch thick; the zucchini will be diced.

    Heat oil in a large sauté pan over medium heat. Add bell peppers and sauté 5 minutes. Add zucchini, corn, and garlic and mix well. Cover and cook over medium-low heat, stirring often, about 10 minutes or until zucchini are crisp-tender. Add green onions. Season to taste with salt, pepper, and chili powder. Serve hot.

Makes 4 or 5 side-dish servings

LIGHT CORN CHOWDER

This American classic often has bacon or salt pork, and is enriched with cream or whole milk. I find that fresh corn gives the soup a delicately sweet flavor and that it is still delicious when made with nonfat milk. For a meaty flavor and pretty color, I often add lean smoked turkey breast instead of fatty meats.

3 large ears corn (total 2¼ pounds), or
    2⅓ cups frozen kernels
1 to 2 tablespoons vegetable oil or
    butter
1 large onion, chopped
2 large baking potatoes (1 pound),
    peeled and diced

1 to 1¼ cups water
2 cups nonfat or low-fat milk
Salt and freshly ground pepper
Cayenne pepper to taste
1 cup finely diced smoked turkey
2 tablespoons chopped fresh parsley

Remove corn husks and silks. Place cobs on board and cut off kernels a few rows at a time. Then lightly scrape cobs with knife to remove any remaining parts of kernel and "milk," and add to corn.

    Heat oil in heavy, large saucepan, add onion, and sauté until light brown, about 7 minutes. Add potatoes and 1 cup water, cover, and simmer 10 to 15 minutes or until tender. Add corn; add ¼ cup water if pan is dry. Simmer 5 minutes or until corn is cooked to taste. Stir in milk and season to taste with salt, pepper, and cayenne. Heat over medium heat, stirring often, until very hot; do not boil. Stir in turkey and heat gently. Serve sprinkled with parsley.

Makes 4 appetizer servings

AMERICAN SUCCOTASH

Succotash, which has its roots in native American cooking, is a favorite dish in the United States; indeed, the word succotash *comes from an Indian word for corn. The favorite version of the dish is made with corn and lima beans, as in this easy recipe, but succotash is also made with dried cranberry beans or kidney beans. Corn is always included, but some older versions call for hominy, or dried corn. Succotash can be a stew with beef, venison, or chicken, or a side dish flavored with salt pork or bacon. The dish is especially popular in the Midwest, where it is sometimes made into a salad, with a tangy dressing added instead of the milk.*

Serve this dish as a side dish for meat or poultry, or as a main course with cottage cheese or yogurt and a green salad or tomato salad.

1 tablespoon vegetable oil or butter
⅓ cup minced onion
⅓ cup minced celery
1 10-ounce package frozen corn or 2 cups fresh kernels
¼ cup water
1 10-ounce package lima beans, cooked, or 2 cups cooked fresh or dried lima beans or cranberry beans

1 tablespoon fresh thyme or savory or 1 teaspoon dried
Salt and freshly ground pepper
Pinch of pure chili powder or cayenne pepper (optional)
¼ cup low-fat or whole milk
1 tablespoon chopped green onion or fresh parsley

Heat oil in a medium saucepan over medium heat, add onion and celery, and sauté about 5 minutes. Add corn and water, cover, and bring to a boil over high heat. Reduce heat to low and cook, stirring occasionally, about 5 minutes or until corn is just tender.

Add beans, thyme, salt, pepper, and chili powder and heat through. Stir in milk and heat, uncovered, over medium-high heat, stirring often, about 2 minutes or until it is absorbed. (*Succotash can be kept, covered, 2 days in refrigerator.*) Serve hot, sprinkled with green onion or parsley.

Makes 4 side-dish or 2 main-course servings

BABY CORN AND CHINESE LONG BEAN SALAD

At a cooking class in Taipei, Taiwan, I learned to briefly blanch canned baby corn, and indeed any canned Chinese vegetable, to avoid a ''canned'' taste. Of course, if you find fresh baby corn, you can prepare it like ordinary corn but reduce the cooking time to 3 to 4 minutes.

This easy salad—with a dressing flavored with rice vinegar, soy sauce, and a hint of fresh ginger— is perfect for summer, when beans are at the height of their season. When long beans are not available, you can use ordinary green beans or haricots verts.

1½ pounds Chinese long beans, ends removed
Salt and freshly ground pepper
12 ears canned baby corn, cut in half
½ teaspoon finely grated peeled fresh ginger

1 tablespoon soy sauce
4 teaspoons rice vinegar
Pinch of sugar
2 tablespoons vegetable oil
2 tablespoons chopped green onion

Cut beans into 2-inch lengths. Add beans to a large saucepan of boiling salted water and boil uncovered over high heat for 5 minutes or until crisp-tender. Add the corn and boil a few seconds. Drain both in a colander, rinse with cold water, and drain well.

For the dressing, mix the ginger, soy sauce, vinegar, sugar, and oil. Toss with bean mixture. Add salt and pepper if needed. Sprinkle with green onion just before serving.

Makes 4 or 5 appetizer/side-dish or 2 or 3 main-course servings

15

Cucumbers

Since I am always experimenting with new recipes, there are only a few dishes I make often. But there is one salad I prepare almost every day. It is made of three basic ingredients—cucumbers, tomatoes, and onion, seasoned with salt and pepper (page 166). If tomatoes are not available, there might be shredded red cabbage or a little grated carrot instead. But there are always cucumbers. No separate dressing is needed, just a dash of olive oil and a squeeze of fresh lemon juice.

Popular in Turkey, Lebanon, Egypt, and throughout the eastern Mediterranean as well as Iran, this salad is known simply as "vegetable salad." I first became familiar with it as "Israeli salad" when I lived in that country where no dinner, from a casual supper to a wedding reception, is complete without it. If you've eaten falafel, you'll recognize it as the salad that's added to the pita bread along with the falafel balls.

The salad's character derives from the way the vegetables are cut. The cucumbers and tomatoes are diced in small cubes and the onion is chopped fine. Many call it "chopped salad," though this is somewhat misleading: its texture would be mushy if you chopped the vegetables instead of cutting them into even dice.

161

There are many seasonal variations of the salad. The onion used can be green, yellow, or red. In spring diced radishes might be added. Diced bell peppers of all colors make a beautiful and tasty summertime accent. Some people stir in strips of romaine lettuce, spinach, or arugula. Although not traditional, I find that diced celery, jicama, or even the white stalks of bok choy contribute a pleasant crunch.

As for herbs, the favorite in the region is Italian parsley, and next comes cilantro. Some of my Israeli relatives add minced jalapeño-type peppers or a dash of hot sauce. One of my husband's aunts, who was born in Yemen, adds homemade hot green salsa (see Green Zehug, page 392). Stirring in cubes of feta cheese and garnishing the salad with a few black olives makes it more substantial and turns it into a cousin of Greek salad.

Changing the dressing gives the salad a completely different character. A richer eastern Mediterranean version of the salad calls for adding tahini, the popular sesame sauce. If you substitute yogurt for the dressing ingredients, you have a salad resembling Indian *raita*.

Unlike green salad, a diced vegetable salad does not need to be tossed at the last moment and can be completely made several hours ahead. Somehow cutting the vegetables small helps them absorb the seasonings better and makes them more flavorful than if they were simply sliced, as in a typical American dinner salad. Mediterranean vegetable salads add a fresh, colorful touch to any menu and can entice your family members, even the children, to eat more vegetables.

Of course, cucumbers are used in many other salads as well. Austrians and Germans like them in a tangy dressing with plenty of vinegar (page 166). In India, where cucumbers originated, they are used in many ways—in salads with chickpeas or tossed with yogurt and toasted cumin seeds to make a version of *raita*, a dish designed to cool the fires of hot curries. Afghan cooks mix cucumbers with yogurt, walnuts, and raisins for an intriguing appetizer salad (page 164). In central Europe cucumber slices are sometimes briefly sautéed like zucchini and sprinkled with chopped dill or parsley.

CUCUMBER BASICS

⚔️ **Season:** Cucumbers are available year-round. They are at the height of their season in early summer.

⚔️ **Choosing:** Cucumbers should have smooth skin and should be firm and fairly slender. I find that small pickling cucumbers and the "gourmet" or "European" cucumbers that come wrapped in plastic are usually tastier than the common cucumbers.

⚔️ **Storing:** Cucumbers keep in the refrigerator for up to 1 week. They should be kept in a plastic bag.

⚔️ **Serving Size:** Allow about half a medium cucumber per person.

⚔️ **Nutrients:** Half a medium cucumber has about 22 calories.

⚔️ **Basic Preparation:** Rinse cucumbers and cut off the ends. If they have been waxed, peel them.

AFGHAN CUCUMBER SALAD WITH YOGURT, WALNUTS, AND RAISINS

This festive salad was inspired by a first course I had at an Afghan restaurant in Paris. A similar salad is made in Iran and is flavored with dill rather than dried mint. Usually it is made with a very rich yogurt resembling sour cream that you can buy at Iranian specialty shops, but it's also delicious with low-fat and even nonfat yogurt.

2 medium cucumbers, coarsely grated
1½ cups plain yogurt
4 tablespoons dark raisins
4 tablespoons coarsely chopped
  walnuts
6 tablespoons chopped fresh parsley

2 green onions, chopped
1 to 2 teaspoon dried mint, crumbled;
  or 2 to 4 teaspoons chopped fresh
  dill
Salt and freshly ground pepper

Drain grated cucumber in a strainer. If there is water in the yogurt, pour it out. If raisins are very dry, soak in hot water until softened, then drain. Reserve 2 tablespoons raisins, 2 tablespoons walnuts, and 2 tablespoons parsley for garnish.

Mix yogurt with cucumber, green onions, mint, and remaining raisins, walnuts, and parsley. Season to taste with salt and pepper. Serve cold in a bowl, with garnishing ingredients sprinkled on top.

Makes 4 appetizer servings

ALGERIAN CUCUMBER AND PEPPER SALAD

With this zesty salad, cucumbers will never seem boring again. An olive oil and mint dressing is a favorite match for cucumbers in North Africa. This Algerian version contains cilantro as well, but if you prefer you can omit it and double the mint. You can also prepare this salad in the Moroccan style by adding a finely minced garlic clove to the dressing.

1 large European cucumber
1 red or green bell pepper, cut in
    strips 2 × ¼ inch thick
⅓ cup pitted black or green olives,
    halved
2 tablespoons olive oil
1 tablespoon distilled white vinegar, or
    more if needed

Salt to taste
Cayenne pepper to taste
1 tablespoon plus 1 teaspoon chopped
    cilantro (fresh coriander)
1 tablespoon plus 1 teaspoon chopped
    fresh mint

Peel cucumber if desired. Halve cucumber and cut into thin slices. Mix in a shallow serving bowl with pepper and olives.

In a small bowl whisk oil with vinegar, salt, and cayenne. Add to salad and mix. Add cilantro and mint, and toss lightly. Taste and adjust seasoning, adding more vinegar if you like.

Makes 4 appetizer servings

MEDITERRANEAN "CHOPPED" SALAD

Be sure to use ripe tomatoes—plum tomatoes or medium or large tomatoes—that are not too soft. When small cucumbers sold as "Iranian" cucumbers are available at our local farmers' market, I grab them for this salad. Otherwise I choose the long European type or small pickling cucumbers over the common cucumbers, although they too can be used. A dash of extra-virgin olive oil gives a nice touch; and because it is so flavorful, a little goes a long way. Another delicious twist is to add 2 or 3 teaspoons of capers, as I had at my favorite Moroccan restaurant in Los Angeles, Koutoubiya.

½ long European cucumber, 3 pickling
    cucumbers, or 1 medium common
    cucumber
8 plum tomatoes, or 4 medium
    tomatoes, cut into small dice
2 green onions, chopped
3 to 4 tablespoons chopped fresh
    Italian parsley

1 to 2 tablespoons olive oil, preferably
    extra-virgin
1 to 2 teaspoons strained fresh lemon
    juice
Salt and freshly ground pepper
Hot sauce to taste (optional)

Peel cucumbers if desired and cut into small dice no larger than ½ inch. Mix the diced tomatoes, cucumber, green onions, and parsley. Add oil, lemon juice, salt, pepper, and hot sauce to taste. Serve at cool room temperature.

Makes 4 side-dish servings

AUSTRIAN CUCUMBER SALAD

I sampled this simple salad at Demel's, the most famous pastry shop in Vienna, before I got to my main course—tasting as many chocolate desserts as I could!

Usually this Austrian salad consists of cucumbers with a refreshing vinegar and parsley dressing, but Demel's added sweet peppers to make it more colorful. Serve it as a light appetizer or accompaniment in summer. Even if you're having a supper of cold cuts or sandwiches, you can quickly throw together this salad to add a fresh touch to the meal.

1 European cucumber, cut in 2 × ½ ×
    ¼-inch strips
½ green, red, or yellow pepper, cut
    into thin strips

1 tablespoon vegetable oil
2 to 3 teaspoons herb vinegar
Salt and freshly ground pepper
2 tablespoons chopped fresh parsley

Mix cucumber and pepper strips with oil, 2 teaspoons vinegar, salt, and pepper. Taste and adjust seasoning, adding more vinegar if desired. Add parsley and toss lightly.

Makes 4 appetizer or side-dish servings

CUCUMBER SALAD WITH YOGURT AND CUMIN SEEDS

Toasted cumin seeds give a tangy flavor to this salad from India. Serve it as a first course or as an accompaniment to spicy chicken or meat dishes. Diced tomato can replace or be mixed with the cucumber. The dressing can also be used for cooked potatoes or eggplant, for a refreshing low-calorie salad.

1 cup plain yogurt
¼ teaspoon paprika
¼ teaspoon ground cumin
Pinch of cayenne pepper (optional)
1 teaspoon chopped cilantro (fresh
    coriander)
1 small green onion, green and white
    parts, chopped

Pinch of salt
1 medium common cucumber (about
    ½ pound), peeled and cut into
    small dice
1 teaspoon cumin seeds

Mix yogurt with paprika, ground cumin, cayenne pepper, coriander, green onion, and salt. Stir in cucumber and taste for seasoning. Cover and refrigerate for 1 to 3 hours.

    Toast cumin seeds in a small, heavy skillet over medium heat for 2 minutes, stirring often; be careful not to let them burn.

    Just before serving, sprinkle cumin seeds over salad. Serve cold.

Makes 4 appetizer or side-dish servings

CUCUMBER SALAD WITH SMOKED SALMON AND CHIVES

Cucumber is a classic accompaniment for smoked salmon, and the two make perfect partners in this easy, light, Norwegian-inspired appetizer.

2 or 3 pickling cucumbers (about ¾ to 1 pound)
2 tablespoons vegetable oil
2 teaspoons mixed herb or tarragon vinegar

Salt and freshly ground pepper
Pinch of sugar
1 tablespoon chopped fresh chives
3 tablespoons diced smoked salmon

Slice cucumbers; you will need 3 or 4 cups of slices. Whisk oil with vinegar, salt, pepper, sugar, and 2 teaspoons chives. Mix with cucumbers. (*Salad can be kept, covered, 8 hours in refrigerator.*) Just before serving, add chopped smoked salmon. Sprinkle with remaining chives and serve.

Makes 4 appetizer servings

SICHUAN CUCUMBER SALAD

This salad always reminds me of Chinese breakfast! When I was on a culinary study tour of Taiwan led by Chinese cooking expert Nina Simonds, this was on the breakfast menu. Breakfast basically was a soft, hot rice dish called congee, *accompanied by green vegetables and often this salad. Other selections were shredded meat with a soy-flavored sauce; napa cabbage with dried shrimp, fried fish, deep-fried peanuts, and flat omelets.*

During our cooking classes on the tour, the Sichuan chef showed us the classic way of preparing this salad. He heated sesame oil with dried chilies until there was lots of smoke and everyone ran out of the room coughing. But he also taught us this easier method and I find it much more practical in home kitchens.

1 European cucumber
1 small carrot, coarsely grated
1 celery stalk, cut into thin sticks
2 tablespoons Oriental sesame oil
½ teaspoon Oriental chili oil, or to taste

¼ teaspoon ground Sichuan peppercorns
Salt to taste
1 tablespoon rice vinegar
1 teaspoon sugar
½ teaspoon grated peeled fresh ginger

Cut cucumber into thin sticks about ¼ inch wide. Mix with carrot and celery.

In a bowl, whisk remaining ingredients to make dressing. Mix with vegetables. Taste and adjust seasoning. (*Salad can be kept, covered, 1 day in refrigerator.*) Serve cold.

Makes 4 side-dish servings

16

Eggplant

Moving to the Middle East made me aware of the versatility of eggplant. In this part of the world eggplant is perhaps the favorite vegetable, and local cooks have developed an endless variety of exciting dishes with it.

I discovered an array of particularly intriguing eggplant salads I had never tasted before. They were usually flavored with garlic, sometimes with diced vegetables, with creamy mayonnaise, or with the exotic-tasting sesame tahini. Some were chunky while others were smooth, almost like spreads or dips.

Although eggplant calls to mind images of Mediterranean lands, it actually originated in India. It was introduced to Europe with the Saracen invasion. The French word for eggplant, *aubergine*, which is used also by the English, is derived from Arabic and Persian words and ultimately from Sanskrit, and demonstrates the path the vegetable traveled on its way west. In the other direction, eggplant spread through the Far East and is important in the cuisines of the Orient, notably those of China and Japan.

Eggplant can be fried, grilled, stewed, or baked. Eggplant slices sautéed in olive oil are often served as a side dish or are lightly marinated with lemon juice and garlic or with a spicy vinegar marinade to make a zesty appetizer. Grilling eggplant slices, a traditional southern Italian technique, has become a favorite in modern cooking because the eggplant absorbs less oil than when it is fried. Stewing is also a popular method for cooking eggplant, and produces the familiar French Ratatouille (page 372) and Italian Caponata (page 179), and numerous Indian eggplant curries.

Unfortunately, traditional recipes can create the impression that eggplant is complicated to cook and needs lots of fat. Some cooks advise salting the slices and even drying them in the sun for several hours to remove bitter juices. And this is even before you begin cooking! Other recipes demand that you dip the slices in egg and bread crumbs, fry them in plenty of oil, then bake them with copious quantities of cheese.

For most meals I want the eggplant to be ready in a short time and with a minimal amount of fat. Boiling the eggplant was not a good solution, I found, as it absorbed too much water and lost its flavor.

My favorite technique for eggplant-in-a-hurry is a combination of sautéing and steaming. I cut the eggplant in cubes, sauté them lightly, cover the pan, and let them steam until fork-tender (page 175). The eggplant is done in minutes and does not require standing over a hot pan for a prolonged frying session. I use just enough oil for good flavor, and sprinkle the cubes with thyme or oregano and a dash of cayenne pepper. If the eggplant is fresh, there is no need to salt it first to remove the juices.

Prepared this way, eggplant is as simple to use as zucchini or broccoli. It can be cooked ahead and reheated easily, and can be served hot as a side dish or cool as a salad.

Quick-sautéed eggplant is delicious mixed with cooked rice, pasta, or couscous for an accompaniment or vegetarian main course. You can add diced tomatoes, garlic, and herbs at the steaming stage for a quick version of the famous Provençal eggplant stew, Ratatouille (page 355). Or follow the example of Mediterranean cooks: add the cooked eggplant cubes to meat or chicken stews a few minutes before serving so they gain flavor from the sauce.

Another way I like to cook eggplant may be the easiest of all, and is definitely one of the tastiest. It requires no advance preparation and can be virtually fat-free. This method is grilling. I'm not talking about grilling eggplant slices, which you can also do, but rather a technique that is much more basic. You simply put the whole eggplant on the grill after you have finished grilling meat or fish. The vegetable acquires an intriguing smoky flavor and aroma, and needs just a little seasoning to become a delectable appetizer.

Grilling eggplant is an ancient method that has long been a favorite in the Middle East. Once the eggplant is tender and cool, it is peeled, chopped, and flavored with garlic, lemon juice, and a little olive oil, tahini sauce, or mayonnaise. Other classic additions are chopped onion, cilantro, parsley, tomatoes, and even diced cucumbers. These appetizers are called salads, but they really are more like spreads, and are perfect for scooping up with pieces of pita bread.

The timing for grilling eggplant is exceedingly flexible. The eggplant has to be soft inside but doesn't seem to mind overcooking. Once, after my husband and I had a barbecue dinner, we put an eggplant on the grill and forgot it overnight. The next day it was very small because much of its water had evaporated, but it tasted absolutely delicious.

Two alternatives to grilling over charcoal are broiling or baking the eggplant. The first eggplant dish I ever made involved baking, and turned out to be a disaster. At the time I lived in a suburb of Tel Aviv. My neighbor gave me a recipe for eggplant salad. When she instructed me to put the whole eggplant directly on a rack in a hot oven, that's exactly what I did. I was not prepared for what happened minutes later—a loud boom came from my oven, and when I opened the door, there was almost nothing left of my eggplant. It had exploded into many tiny pieces!

What I didn't know was that you have to prick the eggplant a few times with a fork before putting it in the oven, to let the accumulating steam escape. I have never forgotten to do this since!

When I plan to cook dinner on the barbecue, I find it convenient to have several eggplants on hand. After the other food is cooked, I put them on the grill. This way I have the makings of a savory vegetarian sandwich spread, a snack, or the beginning of the next day's lunch or supper ready in the refrigerator.

One of the best-loved ways of preparing eggplant is stuffing and baking it. Stuffings generally include the flesh of the eggplant, which can be simply seasoned, chopped, and returned to the eggplant skin or can be combined with meat, rice, cheese, eggs, onions, other vegetables, and a great variety of flavorings. In traditional recipes for stuffed eggplant, often the halved eggplant is fried first. Because this procedure requires a generous amount of oil, now the eggplant is usually baked instead. Besides being stuffed, eggplant itself can be a filling for crepes, blintzes, or burritos.

Steaming and boiling are rarely used for cooking eggplant because it absorbs water. These techniques are good only if the eggplant is highly seasoned, to offset the loss of flavor.

Eggplant can be the basis of more complex dishes. Sautéed eggplant slices make a savory topping for pizza, long popular in Rome and now in vogue in California. A widespread use of sautéed eggplant slices is in preparing layered dishes, the most famous of which are the Greek specialty *moussaka* and the Italian eggplant Parmesan. The French make sautéed eggplant slices into gratins by pouring tomato or béchamel sauce over them, sprinkling bread crumbs or grated cheese on top, and browning the topping in the oven. Sautéed eggplant cubes are often added to meat or poultry stews a few minutes before serving, so they absorb flavor from the sauce but still keep their shape and texture.

Cooks love to take advantage of the eggplant's chameleon personality by turning it into mock versions of other foods. It is made into "schnitzel" by being coated in layers of flour, egg, and bread crumbs and fried, just like the well-known Viennese veal dish. There are Italian recipes for eggplant sautéed with garlic so it will taste like mushrooms, Israeli recipes for eggplant made to taste like chopped liver, and even sweet Moroccan eggplant preserves with sugar and spices.

If you find the slim, zucchini-size Japanese or Chinese eggplants, or smaller versions of Italian eggplants, be sure to try these. They have a slightly more delicate flavor and take only about half as long to cook. You can also use the egg-shaped white eggplants, which illustrate how this vegetable got its name.

EGGPLANT BASICS

✖ **Season:** Eggplants are available year-round; their peak season is in late summer and early fall.

✖ **Choosing:** Select eggplants that feel heavy and have glossy, firm skin with no brown spots; small or medium eggplants are usually better than very large ones.

✖ **Storing:** Eggplant can be kept about 3 days in the refrigerator; although its appearance may not alter, it becomes bitter when stored too long.

✖ **Serving Size:** Allow 4 to 6 ounces per person.

✖ **Nutrients:** Eggplant contains some folic acid but is not high in any single vitamin or mineral. Still it is a favorite choice for vegetarian entrees because it has a satisfying texture, is low in calories, and contains practically no fat. One cup cooked eggplant has about 30 to 40 calories.

✖ **Basic Preparation:** For grilling whole, nothing is removed from the eggplant. For other recipes, when eggplants are fresh, there is no need to peel them, but if the peel feels tough or if you don't like the peel, cut it off with a thin-bladed knife. The peel of white eggplants is usually tough.

✖ **Cooking Tips:** Eggplant is best when thoroughly cooked. Unlike many vegetables, it should not be cooked just until *al dente*.

Salting Eggplant

For some recipes for sautéed or grilled eggplant slices, the eggplant is first sprinkled with salt so its juices leach out. This technique eases the eggplant's bitterness but is not necessary if you have a fresh eggplant. Salting also can reduce the amount of oil absorbed by the eggplant during cooking.

To salt eggplant, sprinkle the slices lightly but evenly with salt on both sides and put in a colander. Put a bowl with a weight on top and leave to drain 1 hour, turning slices over after 30 minutes. Pat dry with paper towels.

QUICK SAUTÉED EGGPLANT

Because sautéed eggplant tends to absorb large amounts of oil, I prefer to cook it this easy way, which is a combination of sautéing and steaming, and uses relatively little oil. I often season the eggplant with thyme and fresh parsley in the style of Provence, but you can substitute oregano or savory for the thyme or, for a popular eastern Mediterranean version, use cilantro instead of the parsley. Serve this basic eggplant as a side dish with sautéed, roasted, or broiled chicken or beef, or with rice for a vegetarian meal. If you have roasted red peppers in a jar, cut a few of them in strips and mix them with the cooked eggplant for a colorful dish. A chopped green onion or sautéed sliced mushrooms also make tasty additions.

1 medium eggplant (about 1 pound)
2 to 3 tablespoons olive oil
Salt and freshly ground pepper
½ teaspoon dried thyme

Cayenne pepper to taste
2 tablespoons chopped fresh parsley or cilantro (fresh coriander)

Cut eggplant into ¾-inch dice. Heat 2 tablespoons oil in a large, heavy skillet or sauté pan over medium heat. Add eggplant cubes, salt, and pepper and sauté, stirring, about 3 or 4 minutes. Sprinkle with thyme and cayenne. Cover and cook over medium-low heat, stirring often, for 7 to 10 minutes or until eggplant is tender. Taste and adjust seasoning; sprinkle with a bit more oil if desired. Gently stir in parsley before serving.

Makes 3 or 4 side-dish servings

VARIATION: **Quick Sautéed Eggplant with Mushrooms**
Cut 8 ounces fresh mushrooms into thick slices. Sauté in 1 tablespoon oil in a skillet for about 3 minutes. Remove to a plate. Sauté eggplant as above. Before covering pan of eggplant, add sautéed mushrooms. Cover and cook together until tender.

BROILED EGGPLANT SLICES

Many recipes call for frying eggplant slices. Here is a tasty, low-fat way to prepare them in the broiler instead. Substitute them for fried eggplant in casseroles, or serve them as an appetizer with Moroccan Garlic Dressing (page 381), Provençal Pistou (page 387), or Argentinean Chimichurri (page 388).

1 medium eggplant (1 to 1¼ pounds), cut in ¼-inch-thick slices
2 to 3 teaspoons olive oil

Salt and freshly ground pepper

Arrange the eggplant on a foil-lined baking sheet or broiler pan. Brush lightly with oil and sprinkle with salt and pepper. Broil about 8 minutes. Turn over and broil about 7 minutes or until tender. Serve hot, warm, or at room temperature.

Makes 2 appetizer servings

EASY EGGPLANT WITH GINGER

This very simple, tasty Vietnamese recipe is flavored with fresh ginger, soy sauce, and sautéed onion. It is sometimes made with garlic instead of ginger, and fish sauce instead of soy sauce. Long, slim Chinese or Japanese eggplants are ideal for the dish as they make small rounds that are easy to sauté. If you wish to prepare large eggplants this way, quarter them lengthwise before slicing them. Serve the eggplant with rice.

1 pound Chinese or Japanese eggplants, unpeeled (see Note)
2 tablespoons vegetable oil
1 large onion, chopped
1 tablespoon minced peeled fresh ginger
2 tablespoons soy sauce

1 to 2 tablespoons water
Few drops Vietnamese hot sauce (optional)
1 to 2 tablespoons chopped green onion or cilantro (fresh coriander), for garnish

Cut eggplants into ¼-inch crosswise slices. In a sauté pan that has a cover, heat 1 tablespoon oil over medium-high heat. Add onion and sauté 5 minutes or until beginning to brown. Add ginger and remaining oil, and heat until sizzling. Add eggplant and sauté ½ minute, tossing. Reduce heat to medium-low. Add 1 tablespoon soy sauce and 1 tablespoon water. Cover and cook, stirring often but gently, until eggplant is very tender, about 10 minutes, adding another tablespoon water if pan becomes dry. Add remaining soy sauce and hot sauce and toss gently. Serve sprinkled with green onion or cilantro.

Makes 2 to 4 main-course servings with rice

NOTE: If Chinese or Japanese eggplant is not available, substitute 1 Italian eggplant and cut it into ¾-inch dice. Cooking time will be about 15 minutes.

CHINESE EGGPLANT AND PEPPERS WITH BLACK BEAN SAUCE

Ginger, garlic, and black bean sauce give this colorful dish its zip. It makes a great accompaniment for chicken, beef, or lamb, or a delicious vegetarian main course with rice.

Unlike many Chinese vegetable dishes, this one involves little preparation; there aren't many ingredients to chop and there's no cornstarch sauce to make. You can use Chinese, Japanese, or Italian eggplant. The dish is prettiest with three colors of peppers—red, green, and yellow—but you can make it with a large pepper of one color.

¾ to 1 pound Chinese or Japanese
    eggplants
3 tablespoons plus 1 teaspoon
    vegetable oil
1½ cups diced bell peppers, preferably
    mixed red, green, and yellow; or 1
    large pepper, diced
2 teaspoons minced fresh ginger

1 garlic clove, minced
1 teaspoon garlic-flavored black bean
    sauce
2 teaspoons soy sauce
Oriental hot pepper sauce to taste
    (optional)
1 green onion, chopped

Halve eggplants lengthwise and slice thin. Heat 1 tablespoon oil in a large skillet, add peppers, and sauté over medium-high heat for 5 minutes or until crisp-tender. Remove to a plate. Add 2 tablespoons oil to skillet and heat over medium-high heat. Add eggplant and sauté 1 minute. Cover and cook over medium heat, stirring often, about 5 minutes or until eggplant is tender. Transfer to a plate.

Heat 1 teaspoon oil in skillet over medium heat, add ginger and garlic, and sauté 10 seconds. Return vegetables to skillet, add bean sauce and soy sauce, and toss thoroughly but gently. Season to taste with hot sauce. Serve sprinkled with green onion.

Makes 2 main-course servings with rice or 4 side-dish servings

SAUTÉED EGGPLANT WITH FRESH TOMATO TOPPING

This is a popular way to serve eggplant in the Middle East. I've had it as an appetizer at weddings in Israel. The eggplant is sautéed and topped with a fresh, colorful mixture of tomatoes, garlic, and parsley.

In the Middle East the eggplant is usually salted for this recipe, but you can skip this step if you're using Japanese eggplants or if the eggplant is very fresh. To counteract eggplant's tendency to absorb oil like a sponge, it is best to begin sautéing it in a small amount of oil and to add more only as needed.

1 large eggplant (about 1¼ pounds), unpeeled
Salt and freshly ground pepper
About 7 tablespoons olive oil
2 to 3 medium garlic cloves, minced

2 tablespoons chopped fresh parsley, preferably Italian
2 ripe medium tomatoes (about 1 pound), diced

Cut eggplant into ⅜-inch slices crosswise, discarding ends. Salt eggplant (see page 174).

Heat 2 tablespoons olive oil in a large, heavy skillet over medium heat. Quickly add enough eggplant slices to make 1 layer; if slices are added too slowly, the first ones soak up all the oil. Sauté 2 or 3 minutes per side or until tender when pierced with a fork. Transfer to a plate with a slotted spatula.

Add 2 tablespoons oil to pan, heat oil, and sauté second batch of eggplant in same way. Repeat with another 2 tablespoons oil and remaining eggplant.

Heat 1 tablespoon oil in pan over medium-high heat. Add garlic and sauté ½ minute. Add parsley and toss over heat a few seconds. Remove from heat and stir in tomatoes. Season to taste with salt and pepper. Spoon tomato mixture over center of each eggplant slice. Serve hot or at room temperature.

Makes 4 to 6 appetizer servings

CAPONATA
(SICILIAN EGGPLANT SALAD
WITH CAPERS AND GREEN OLIVES)

A favorite at Italian delis, this tangy, colorful salad is easy to make at home and keeps well. Basically it's eggplant cooked in a tomato sauce accented with onions, celery, wine vinegar, and a touch of sugar. What makes caponata *unique are the pine nuts, capers, and olives that cook with the eggplant.*

Traditionally, the eggplant is first deep-fried in generous amounts of oil, but I use a combination of sautéing and steaming so less oil is needed. On the other end of the scale, some new versions skip the sautéing step entirely, but that results in a far less tasty caponata. *I like a middle-of-the-road approach.*

1 large eggplant (1¼ to 1½ pounds),
    unpeeled
4 tablespoons olive oil
1 medium onion, halved and sliced
3 celery stalks, thinly sliced
1 pound ripe tomatoes, peeled, seeded,
    and chopped; or 1 28-ounce can
    plum tomatoes, drained and
    chopped

Salt and freshly ground pepper
2 teaspoons sugar
2 tablespoons red wine vinegar
⅔ cup pitted green olives, halved
2 tablespoons capers, rinsed
1 tablespoon pine nuts (optional)

Cut eggplant into 1-inch dice. Heat 3 tablespoons oil in a large, heavy skillet or sauté pan. Add eggplant and sauté over medium-high heat, stirring, for 2 minutes. Cover and cook over medium heat, stirring a few times, for 3 minutes. Remove eggplant from skillet.

Heat remaining tablespoon oil in same skillet. Add onion and celery, and sauté over medium heat for 5 minutes. Add tomatoes and cook uncovered for 5 minutes. Return eggplant to pan and sprinkle with salt and pepper. Cover and cook over low heat for 10 minutes. Sprinkle with sugar, then vinegar. Add olives, capers, and pine nuts. Cover and simmer over low heat, stirring often, for 10 minutes, or until eggplant is tender. Taste and adjust seasoning. Serve cold or at room temperature. (*Caponata can be kept, covered, 4 to 5 days in refrigerator.*)

Makes 5 or 6 appetizer servings

EAST AFRICAN EGGPLANT CURRY
WITH CHICKPEAS

If this recipe appears Indian to you, your impression is right. There is a great Indian influence on the cooking of Tanzania, Kenya, and Mozambique, as well as that of South Africa, because historically Arab traders brought spices from India to Africa and because people from India settled in eastern and southern Africa. Serve this hearty, spicy stew over rice.

1 medium eggplant (1 pound 2
    ounces), unpeeled
3 tablespoons vegetable oil
1 medium onion, chopped
4 large garlic cloves, minced
1 or 2 jalapeño peppers, minced; or 2
    to 3 teaspoons diced canned
    roasted jalapeño peppers
1 tablespoon minced peeled fresh
    ginger
2 teaspoons ground coriander
2 teaspoons ground cumin
½ teaspoon turmeric
¼ to ½ teaspoon dried hot red pepper
    flakes, or to taste

2 cardamom pods (optional)
Salt to taste
1 pound ripe tomatoes, peeled, seeded,
    and coarsely chopped; or 1 28-
    ounce can plum tomatoes, drained
    and chopped
1 tablespoon tomato paste
½ cup water
1½ to 2 cups cooked chickpeas
    (garbanzo beans), or 1 15-ounce
    can chickpeas, drained
Cayenne pepper to taste

Cut eggplant into ¾-inch dice. In a heavy, wide casserole, heat oil, add onion, and cook over low heat for 7 minutes, or until soft but not brown. Add garlic, jalapeño peppers, ginger, coriander, cumin, turmeric, pepper flakes, and cardamom. Cook mixture, stirring, for 1 minute.

Add eggplant and salt, and mix well over low heat until eggplant is coated with spices. Add tomatoes and bring to a boil over high heat. Mix tomato paste with water, and stir into mixture. Cover and simmer over low heat, stirring often, for 20 minutes. Add chickpeas and simmer 10 to 20 more minutes or until eggplant is very tender and mixture is thick. Taste and adjust seasoning, adding cayenne pepper if desired. Remove cardamom. (*Stew can be kept, covered, 3 days in refrigerator.*) Serve hot.

Makes 4 main-course servings over rice

EGGPLANT AND TOFU CASSEROLE WITH TOMATOES AND GARLIC

This is an example of cross-cultural cuisine, or the blending of ingredients or techniques from different styles of cooking. I find that tofu is a good addition to Mediterranean-style vegetable dishes like this light, easy-to-prepare garlic-scented eggplant, pepper, and tomato stew. With the tofu, the dish becomes more substantial and makes a satisfying main course. Sometimes, I finish the stew with a dash of Mexican salsa verde or a sprinkling of grated Parmesan cheese. Serve it with rice or pasta, and with a green salad or a salad of diced cucumbers, radishes, tomatoes, and red onion.

1 medium eggplant (1 to 1¼ pounds), unpeeled
2 tablespoons olive oil
4 large garlic cloves, chopped
1 small red bell pepper, diced
Salt and freshly ground pepper
1 28-ounce can plum tomatoes, drained (juice reserved) and coarsely chopped

¼ teaspoon hot red pepper flakes
1½ teaspoons dried thyme, crumbled
1 14-ounce package tofu, preferably firm
2 tablespoons chopped green onion, cilantro (fresh coriander), or Italian parsley

Cut eggplant into ¾-inch cubes. In a heavy, wide casserole, heat oil over medium heat. Stir in garlic and immediately add eggplant, red pepper, salt, and pepper. Sauté, stirring, for about 3 minutes. Add tomatoes, pepper flakes, and 1 teaspoon thyme and bring to a boil. Cover and simmer over low heat, stirring often, about 20 minutes or until eggplant is tender. If stew is too thick, add 1 tablespoon reserved tomato juice.

Thoroughly drain liquid from tofu. Cut tofu into ¾-inch cubes. Add to casserole, spoon a little of sauce over tofu cubes, and sprinkle with salt, pepper, and remaining thyme. Cover and heat gently, without stirring, about 3 minutes. Taste and adjust seasoning. Serve sprinkled with chopped green onion.

Makes 4 main-course servings with rice or pasta

ROASTED EGGPLANT
WITH BASIL AND GARLIC

For this Sardinian specialty, cuts are made in each eggplant to introduce a mixture of garlic, basil, and parsley, which flavors the eggplant as it bakes, rather like the technique of putting garlic slivers into meat. The eggplant is flexible and it's easy to slip in the fresh herb mixture. Serve this as an appetizer, as part of a vegetable and pasta buffet, or as an accompaniment for roast or grilled chicken.

6 Japanese eggplants, or 2 large Italian
    eggplants
Salt and freshly ground pepper
2 large garlic cloves, peeled
½ cup fresh Italian parsley leaves

½ cup fresh basil leaves, medium
    packed
¼ cup tomato paste
¾ cup water
2 tablespoons olive oil

Preheat the oven to 400°F. Halve the eggplants lengthwise and sprinkle with salt; set aside. Mince garlic in a food processor. Add parsley and basil, and mince together.

Pat eggplants dry. With sharp knife make 4 lengthwise slits in large eggplant or 2 in each Japanese eggplant; make cuts deep but not to bottom of eggplant so you don't pierce the skin. Insert some of herb mixture in each slit. Sprinkle eggplants with pepper. Put them in an oiled baking dish.

Mix tomato paste with all but 2 tablespoons of the water and spoon over eggplants. Sprinkle with oil. Add remaining water to pan.

Bake small eggplants uncovered for about 30 minutes or until tender. Cover large eggplants and bake 30 minutes, then uncover and bake 10 minutes or until tender. Serve hot or at room temperature.

Makes 4 side-dish servings

EGGPLANT STUFFED WITH SCAMORZA CHEESE

This dish from central Italy is a distant cousin of the famous Turkish stuffed eggplant dish imam bayıldı, *but it includes no garlic and adds cheese and egg to the basic flavorings of olive oil, tomato, and onion. If scamorza cheese is not available, substitute provolone.*

6 Japanese or small Italian eggplants (total about 1½ pounds), unpeeled
5 tablespoons olive oil
1 medium onion, finely chopped
Salt and freshly ground pepper
¾ pound ripe tomatoes, peeled, seeded, and finely chopped
2 tablespoons chopped fresh parsley

5 ounces scamorza cheese (available at Italian markets or specialty cheese shops), trimmed of rind
2 ripe plum tomatoes, peeled and each cut in 6 slices
3 large hard-boiled large eggs, ends trimmed and each cut crosswise in 4 slices

Cut off green eggplant caps and halve eggplants lengthwise. Using a sharp knife, cut around each eggplant half about ¼ inch from its edge, outlining a ¼-inch-thick shell. Scoop out center pulp with a teaspoon without piercing skin, leaving a ¼-inch-thick shell. Chop pulp fine.

Preheat the oven to 350°F. Heat 3 tablespoons oil in a large skillet. Add onion and sauté over low heat, stirring often, for 10 minutes or until soft but not brown. Stir in eggplant pulp and a pinch of salt and pepper, followed by the chopped tomatoes. Bring to a boil over high heat. Cook over low heat for 25 minutes, or until eggplant is very tender. Stir in parsley. Taste and adjust seasoning. Remove from heat; let cool.

Cut cheese into 12 sticks about ½ inch thick, 1 inch wide, and 3 inches long. Cut plum tomatoes into thin crosswise slices; gently poke out their seeds.

Lightly oil a large, shallow baking dish. Arrange eggplant shells in dish in 1 layer with cut side up. Brush them with 1 tablespoon oil. Bake 15 minutes or until tender when pierced with point of a knife.

Spoon about 1 tablespoon filling into each eggplant shell. Put 1 stick of cheese in each shell. Place an egg slice on top of cheese. Divide remaining filling among shells, spreading it to cover cheese and egg. Top each stuffed eggplant with a plum tomato slice. Sprinkle tomatoes with remaining tablespoon oil. (*Eggplant can be kept, covered, 1 day in refrigerator.*) Bake eggplants for 10 to 15 minutes to melt the cheese. Serve hot.

Makes 6 appetizer or 2 or 3 main-course servings

EGGPLANT WITH MUSHROOM STUFFING

For this simple Provençal stuffed eggplant, the French mushroom stuffing called duxelles *is mixed with the baked eggplant pulp, garlic, and parsley to make a savory filling. Serve the eggplant halves as an appetizer or as a vegetarian main course with tomato sauce (page 394) and rice, or as an accompaniment for roast chicken or lamb.*

2 to 2½ pounds small or medium
    eggplants, unpeeled
Salt
Duxelles (page 408)
2 medium garlic cloves, minced

2 tablespoons chopped fresh parsley
Cayenne pepper or bottled hot pepper
    sauce to taste
3 tablespoons fresh bread crumbs
2 tablespoons olive or vegetable oil

Preheat the oven to 450°F. Halve the eggplants lengthwise. With a sharp knife, score the flesh of each half lightly to make a border about ⅜ inch from skin. Score center of each half lightly 3 times (so heat penetrates more evenly). Sprinkle cut surface with salt. Place eggplants in a lightly oiled roasting pan or shallow baking dish, cut side up. Bake about 20 to 25 minutes, or until flesh is tender when pierced with a knife. Let cool slightly.

Cut each eggplant gently along scored border and remove pulp carefully with a spoon without piercing skin. Put eggplant shells in an oiled gratin dish. Chop eggplant flesh. Mix with *duxelles* and stir in garlic, parsley, and cayenne pepper. Taste and adjust seasoning.

Spoon stuffing into eggplant shells. Sprinkle with bread crumbs, then with oil. Bake 10 to 15 minutes, or until eggplant is hot. If bread crumbs have not browned in that time, brown for a few seconds in broiler. Serve hot.

Makes 4 servings as appetizer, side dish, or light main course

SRI LANKAN EGGPLANT RELISH

*H*ot, spicy, sour, and slightly sweet, this dish flavored with mustard, curry powder, cayenne pepper, and vinegar will surely wake up your taste buds. My friend Kusuma Cooray, a chef born in Sri Lanka who studied French cooking with me in Paris, taught me how to prepare it. She noted that deep-frying is the traditional way to cook the eggplant, but today many people bake the eggplant instead with just a little oil for a lighter dish; this is the method I have used in this recipe.

Serve the zesty eggplant slices as an appetizer, or accompany them with rice and Sri Lankan Tomato and Watercress Salad with Cucumber-Yogurt Dressing (page 322). SEE PHOTOGRAPH.

1 medium eggplant (1 to 1¼ pounds)
3½ tablespoons vegetable oil
Salt to taste
1 medium onion, halved and sliced
⅓ cup distilled white vinegar
2 teaspoons Dijon mustard

1 teaspoon curry powder, preferably
  imported
¼ teaspoon pure chili powder or
  cayenne pepper, or more to taste
1 tablespoon sugar
2 tablespoons water

Preheat the oven to 450°F. Leave eggplant unpeeled; cut in crosswise slices ⅜ inch thick. Put slices on a large lightly oiled baking sheet in 1 layer. Sprinkle with 1½ tablespoons oil, then sprinkle lightly with salt. Bake 10 minutes; turn slices over, sprinkle with salt, and bake about 10 more minutes or until tender. Transfer to a plate.

Heat remaining 2 tablespoons oil in a heavy, large skillet. Add sliced onion and sauté over medium heat, stirring often, about 12 minutes or until brown. Remove onion to plate.

Add vinegar, mustard, curry powder, chili powder, sugar, water, and a pinch of salt. Stir over low heat until smooth. Return eggplant slices to pan, and toss quickly but gently over low heat to coat each slice with the seasonings. Taste; sprinkle with salt and chili powder if desired. Put eggplant slices on a serving plate, overlapping. Top with sautéed onion slices. (*Can be kept, covered, 3 days in refrigerator.*) Serve at room temperature.

Makes 3 or 4 appetizer servings

THREE-WAY EGGPLANT SALAD

This is one of my favorite ways to prepare eggplant, as it's so tasty, versatile, and easy. It's a popular appetizer in much of the eastern Mediterranean and Balkan areas, and in parts of Russia as well. It starts the same way: with an eggplant grilled whole. For the Russian version, mix in mayonnaise; for the Lebanese, add tahini (sesame paste); and for other Mediterranean countries like Greece and Turkey, add olive oil and lemon juice. When I lived in Israel I became familiar with all three kinds of salad; they are as common at Israeli delis and supermarkets as cole slaw is here, and are often made at home.

You can add garlic to any of these salads, as well as minced white, yellow, or green onions. Some renditions have diced roasted bell peppers or hot peppers as well. A version I enjoyed recently in Israel, which is also popular in neighboring Jordan, had finely diced tomato and cucumber added, as in the first variation below.

Serve the salad with fresh pita or other bread. It's also good spread in a thin layer on a warm flour tortilla.

2 medium eggplants (total 2 to 2½ pounds)
2 or 3 medium garlic cloves, finely minced
⅓ cup mayonnaise, ½ to ¾ cup Tahini Sauce (page 401), or 2 to 4 tablespoons extra-virgin olive oil

1 to 3 tablespoons strained fresh lemon juice (optional)
Salt and freshly ground pepper
Cayenne pepper or hot pepper sauce to taste
2 tablespoons chopped fresh parsley, for garnish (optional)

Prick eggplants a few times with fork. Grill above medium-hot coals for about 1 hour; broil for about 40 minutes, turning often; or bake at 400°F. for about 1 hour. When done, eggplant's flesh should be tender and eggplant should look collapsed. Remove eggplant peel, cut off stem, and drain off any liquid from inside eggplant. Chop flesh fine with a knife.

Transfer eggplant to a bowl. Add garlic and mix well. Stir in mayonnaise, tahini sauce, or olive oil. If adding mayonnaise or oil, add lemon juice to taste. (There is already lemon juice in the tahini sauce, so probably no more will be needed.) Season to taste with salt, pepper, and cayenne pepper; season generously. (*Salad can be kept, covered, 2 days in refrigerator.*)

To serve, spread on a plate and sprinkle with parsley.

Makes 6 to 8 appetizer servings

VARIATIONS: **Eggplant Salad with Tomatoes and Cucumbers**
Prepare the version seasoned with olive oil. Stir in 1 finely diced large tomato and 1 finely diced pickling cucumber.

Turkish Eggplant Salad with Garlic and Yogurt
Use 2 tablespoons extra-virgin olive oil and 2 teaspoons lemon juice to season the chopped eggplant. Stir in 5 to 6 tablespoons plain yogurt. Flavor with garlic, salt, pepper, and cayenne as above.

CATALAN ROASTED EGGPLANT AND PEPPER SALAD

For this simple dish the eggplants and peppers are roasted whole, then cut in pieces and served sprinkled with a little olive oil or a mixture of olive oil and fresh garlic. They make a tasty first course accompanied by fresh or toasted country bread, or a side dish for roast chicken. Restaurant chefs sometimes arrange the vegetables around a small mound of baby lettuces dressed with sherry vinaigrette, for an elegant appetizer. For the best flavor, use extra-virgin olive oil.

6 Japanese or 2 small Italian eggplants (total 1¼ to 1½ pounds)	1 or 2 small garlic cloves, minced (optional)
2 large green bell peppers	3 to 4 tablespoons virgin olive oil
2 large red bell peppers	Salt and freshly ground pepper

Preheat the oven to 400°F. Rinse vegetables and pat dry. Prick each eggplant a few times with a fork and put in a roasting pan. Bake peppers 45 to 50 minutes, eggplants 50 to 60 minutes or until tender; turn vegetables once during roasting. Mix garlic with oil, salt, and pepper.

When pepper is done, transfer to a bowl and cover tightly; or wrap in a plastic bag. Let stand 10 minutes, then peel with aid of a paring knife. Halve and drain liquid from inside peppers. Remove core and quarter lengthwise. Peel eggplant with aid of paring knife. Quarter each eggplant lengthwise.

Alternate eggplant and pepper pieces on plates. Sprinkle with oil-garlic mixture, then with salt and pepper. Serve at room temperature.

Makes 4 to 6 appetizer or side-dish servings

GRILLED EGGPLANT ANTIPASTO

For this specialty of southern Italy, the eggplant can be grilled on a ridged stovetop grill, in the broiler, or on a charcoal barbecue. The grilled slices are then marinated with garlic-herb oil and leaves of fresh basil and mint.

1 medium eggplant (about 1¼ pounds), unpeeled
1½ teaspoons salt
About ¼ cup olive oil, for brushing
Garlic-Herb Oil (page 390)
2 tablespoons minced fresh parsley
1 tablespoon coarsely chopped basil leaves

1 tablespoon minced fresh mint leaves
Freshly ground pepper
Fresh mint leaves, for garnish
Sliced French or Italian bread, as accompaniment

Cut eggplant into ⅜-inch slices crosswise, discarding ends. Arrange slices in 1 layer on a rack set over a tray. Sprinkle them evenly with about ¾ teaspoon salt, turn them over, and sprinkle second side evenly with about ¾ teaspoon salt. Let slices drain for 1 hour, turning them over after 30 minutes. Pat them dry very thoroughly with several changes of paper towels.

   Brush olive oil on one side of 6 eggplant slices or enough to make a layer in broiler. Put slices oiled side down on rack of preheated broiler about 2 inches from heat source (or see Note to use grill pan). Brush the other side of the slices lightly with oil. Broil for 3 minutes on each side, lightly oiling the top after turning, or until eggplant is tender when pierced with a fork.

   Transfer eggplant slices to a shallow dish, such as a round 8½-inch gratin dish, 1½ to 2 inches deep, so that eggplant makes 3 layers. Stir Garlic-Herb Oil. Mix chopped herbs. Sprinkle each layer of eggplant evenly with oil, then with herbs, last with pepper. Refrigerate slices, covered, at least 4 hours or overnight, turning them over once. (*The slices can be kept 2 days in refrigerator.*)

   Serve eggplant cool or at room temperature; garnish with mint leaves and accompany with fresh bread.

Makes 4 appetizer servings

NOTE: To grill eggplant on a ridged stovetop grill pan, lightly oil one side of the eggplant slices and put them oiled side down in one layer on the preheated pan over medium-high heat. Grill them for 3 minutes on each side, lightly oiling the top of each slice before turning it, or until it is tender.

EGGPLANT PUREE WITH GARLIC AND CORIANDER

This Egyptian specialty takes the celebrated Middle Eastern eggplant salad one step further: The grilled chopped eggplant is sautéed with garlic, coriander, and cumin, which contribute a wonderful flavor. The eggplant makes a delicious hot or cold appetizer with fresh pita bread. You can also serve it as a main course with rice and a Mediterranean chopped salad of tomato and cucumber, or with other cooked vegetables like grilled tomatoes, peppers, or mushrooms.

2 medium eggplants (2½ pounds)
¼ cup olive oil
6 large garlic cloves, finely chopped
1½ teaspoons ground coriander

1 teaspoon ground cumin
Salt and freshly ground pepper
Italian parsley sprigs, for garnish

Prick eggplants a few times with a fork. Grill above medium-hot coals about 1 hour; broil it about 40 minutes, turning often; or bake at 400°F. about 1 hour. When done, the flesh should be tender and eggplant should look collapsed. Remove eggplant peel and cut off stem. Drain off any liquid from inside eggplant. Chop flesh fine with knife.

   Heat oil in a heavy, large skillet over low heat. Add garlic and cook, stirring, for 1 minute. Stir in coriander and cumin. Add eggplant and mix well. Cook over low heat for 4 to 5 minutes to thicken. Season to taste with salt and pepper. (*Puree can be kept, covered, 2 days in refrigerator.*) Serve hot or cold, garnished with parsley.

Makes 4 appetizer servings

EGGPLANT BHARTA

This specialty of Pakistan and northern India is one of my favorite eggplant dishes. Like many dishes in this area, it shows an Arab influence; it begins like many Middle Eastern eggplant salads, with grilling or baking of the eggplant. Next the chopped eggplant simmers with sautéed onions, fresh ginger, garlic, hot pepper, and spices, so it absorbs their flavors.

At Pakistani and Indian restaurants, eggplant bharta *is served hot with rice, but I find it's also delicious cold with bread or pita as an appetizer. Often it's rich in cream or in oil, but I prefer this lighter version. This dish is easy to make and keeps well.*

2¼ pounds eggplant (2 medium
    eggplants)
2 tablespoons vegetable oil
1 medium onion, chopped
1 or 2 jalapeño peppers or other hot
    peppers, seeded, minced
2 teaspoons minced peeled ginger
2 large garlic cloves, minced
1 teaspoon ground cumin
1 teaspoon ground coriander

½ teaspoon turmeric
½ pound ripe tomatoes, peeled,
    seeded, and chopped, or 1 14-
    ounce can plum tomatoes, drained
    and chopped
Salt to taste
Cayenne pepper (optional)
2 tablespoons chopped cilantro (fresh
    coriander)

Prick eggplant a few times with fork. Grill eggplant above medium-hot coals about 1 hour, broil about 40 minutes, turning often, or bake at 400°F. about 1 hour. When done, eggplant's flesh should be tender and eggplant should look collapsed. Remove eggplant peel. Cut off stem. Drain off any liquid from inside eggplant. Chop flesh fine with knife, or puree in food processor.

Heat oil in a large sauté pan over medium heat. Add onion and sauté 7 minutes or until beginning to brown. Add hot pepper, ginger, garlic, cumin, coriander, turmeric, and tomatoes. Bring to a boil. Cook 10 minutes over medium heat. Add eggplant and salt and cayenne pepper to taste and cook 5 to 10 minutes or until mixture is thick, stirring often. (*Eggplant can be kept, covered, 4 days in refrigerator.*) Serve hot, cold, or room temperature, from a shallow bowl. Sprinkle with cilantro just before serving.

Makes 4 to 6 appetizer or side-dish servings

EGGPLANT AND FETA CREPES

In Turkey and Greece, vegetables and feta are a popular filling for savory pastries. The same type of filling is also good in crepes, when the sautéed eggplant and feta are combined with garlic, oregano, and green onions. You can fill the crepes ahead and keep them in the refrigerator, ready to be heated. Moroccan Tomato Salad with Red Onions and Parsley (page 316) is a fresh, light accompaniment.

2 medium eggplants (total about 2 pounds) or white eggplants
Salt and freshly ground pepper
¾ cup plus 2 teaspoons olive oil, approximately
4 medium garlic cloves, minced
½ cup ricotta cheese
1¼ cups finely crumbled feta cheese (about 3¾ ounces)

¾ teaspoon dried oregano, crumbled (optional)
6 tablespoons minced green onions
12 Crepes or Whole Wheat Crepes (pages 409–410), at room temperature
1 to 2 tablespoons melted butter or vegetable oil
1 tablespoon plus 2 teaspoons grated Parmesan cheese

Peel eggplant and cut in ⅜-inch-thick slices. Salt the eggplant (see page 174). Pat slices dry with several changes of paper towels.

Preheat the oven to 425°F. if planning to serve crepes as soon as they are ready.

Heat 3 tablespoons oil in large, heavy skillet. Quickly add enough eggplant slices to make 1 layer. (If slices are added too slowly, first ones soak up all of oil.) Sauté until tender when pierced with a fork, about 2½ minutes on each side. Remove to a plate. Add 3 tablespoons oil to skillet, heat oil, and sauté second batch of eggplant in same way. Repeat with remaining eggplant, adding oil as needed.

Add 2 teaspoons oil to skillet and reduce heat to low. Add garlic and cook, stirring, for 5 seconds. Immediately pour garlic mixture into a small bowl.

Chop the eggplant with a knife and transfer to a large bowl. Add ricotta cheese, feta cheese, garlic, oregano, green onions, and pepper and mix very well. Taste and adjust seasoning.

Oil a large, shallow baking dish or 2 medium baking dishes. Spoon 3 tablespoons filling onto the less attractive side of each crepe, across the lower third. Roll up in cigar shape, beginning at edge with filling. Arrange crepes seam side down in one layer in the buttered dish or dishes. Brush crepes with melted butter and sprinkle with Parmesan cheese. (*Crepes can be kept, covered, 1 day in refrigerator. Bring crepes to room temperature and preheat oven before continuing.*)

Bake crepes until filling is hot and cheese melts and browns very lightly, about 10 minutes. Serve immediately.

Makes 6 main-course servings

17

Greens

An incredible variety of greens is available to us today in our markets. Some, like the common romaine, iceberg, and Boston lettuces and the less familiar arugula (also called rocket) and mixed baby lettuces, are primarily eaten raw. Others are usually eaten cooked, like Swiss chard, kale, and collard and mustard greens. Many, like spinach, Belgian endive, and escarole, are equally popular raw or cooked. And the selection of greens keeps getting better. Belgian endive now comes with red-tipped leaves in addition to the usual white leaves. Some supermarkets now carry Chinese cooking greens, like gai choy.

Green salads are traditional mostly in Europe and America. In much of Africa, Asia, the Far East, and Central America, greens are usually cooked. But whether cooked or raw, greens form an important part of people's diets in most parts of the world.

There are more ways than ever to vary the basic green salad. The lettuces in the market change with the seasons, so salad can always be interesting. You can choose the greens that appeal to you—robust, hearty bitter greens like chicory, dandelion greens, or radicchio; tender Boston lettuce or looseleaf lettuce; crisp leaves of romaine or iceberg lettuce; or spicy watercress or arugula leaves. The ability to serve an elegant salad of beautiful baby greens is no longer the exclusive privilege of chefs of expensive restaurants. Now it's easy to prepare salads like this at home (page 215). Rinse and dry the greens well, then toss them with Classic Vinaigrette or Walnut Oil Vinaigrette (page 383), or just sprinkle them very lightly with wine vinegar, salt, pepper, and oil.

For cooking, there are mild greens like spinach and chard and more spicy greens like kale, mustard greens, turnip greens, and collard greens. You can also cook the greens attached to beets and kohlrabi. Greens are cooked in boiling water like spinach, though Belgian endive is best braised gently in the oven. Tender greens can be cooked directly in a sauce, as in Zairian Spinach in Tomato Sauce (page 201).

The cooked greens can then be heated with oil, garlic, and coriander, as in Kale with Egyptian Garlic Sauce (page 207), sprinkled with vinaigrette, or baked in cheese sauce as a gratin. They also make good soups, like Portuguese Green Soup (page 208) or Watercress Soup with Leeks and Potatoes (page 212). In many cuisines greens are popular cooked with other vegetables, as in the Indian Chickpeas with Spinach and Carrots (page 70), Egyptian Beans with Greens (page 68), and the African Peppery Okra with Greens (page 251).

Cooking greens with seafood is traditional in many African countries. An acquaintance of mine from Ghana often cooks leafy vegetables with shrimp and crab. In central Africa, smoked fish is often cooked with spinach and other greens.

Meats are also a favorite flavoring for greens. Sausage is added to Portuguese Green Soup (page 208), and smoked meats are a traditional flavoring for cooked greens in the American South.

It's simple to include nutrient-rich greens in everyday menus. The markets have made it easy by providing cleaned spinach leaves, rinsed and dried baby lettuces, and other convenient greens. With these greens you can have a tasty salad or cooked vegetable ready in minutes.

SALAD GREENS BASICS

✗ **Season:** Raw salad greens are available all year, but the availability of specific greens varies with the season.

✗ **Choosing:** Raw salad greens should be crisp and fresh looking, with good color and no brown spots or yellow leaves.

✗ **Storing:** Keep greens in a plastic bag in the refrigerator. They keep 2 to 5 days. Some greens, like watercress, arugula, and mâche, are very perishable and should be used within a day or two.

✗ **Serving Size:** For raw salads, allow about 1½ to 2 cups greens per serving.

✗ **Nutrients:** Most raw salad greens are good sources of fiber and vitamin A. One cup of shredded romaine lettuce has about 8 calories.

✗ **Basic Preparation:** If salad greens have not already been rinsed and packaged, they should be rinsed to remove any sand, then dried well in a salad spinner or towel. You can rinse and dry the greens ahead, wrap them in paper towels, put them in a plastic bag, and keep them for a few hours in the refrigerator.

SPINACH BASICS

✂ **Season:** Available all year.

✂ **Choosing:** Spinach should have deep green leaves without blemishes or yellowing leaves.

✂ **Storing:** Spinach can be kept in a plastic bag 3 or 4 days in the refrigerator.

✂ **Serving Size:** Allow about ¼ pound spinach for salads, about 5 to 8 ounces for cooking.

✂ **Nutrients:** Spinach is an excellent source of vitamin A. It also contains vitamins C and E, iron, calcium, potassium, and folic acid. One cup of chopped fresh spinach has 12 calories; 1 cup of cooked spinach has 21 calories.

✂ **Basic Preparation:** Remove thick stems from spinach. Rinse spinach by putting it in a large bowl of cold water. Lift spinach leaves from water, drain off water, and if it is sandy, replace with new water and rinse spinach leaves again. If using the spinach for salad, pat it dry.

To Substitute Frozen Spinach for Fresh

Frozen spinach can be substituted for fresh in recipes calling for cooked pureed spinach, although the flavor and texture will not be quite as good because frozen spinach usually contains stems. Because frozen spinach is already blanched, it does not require cooking in water, but simply thawing; to save time, it can be cooked in boiling water until it thaws, then drained and squeezed according to the recipes.

Both fresh and frozen spinach vary in the amounts of actual cooked spinach obtainable from a certain weight. One and a half pounds of fresh spinach (weight including stems) or a 10-ounce package of cleaned spinach leaves yields ½ to ¾ cup puree. A 10-ounce package of frozen spinach also yields between ½ and ¾ cup puree.

GREENS

TYPE	DESCRIPTION	USES	CUISINE
arugula (rocket)	small, flat, bright green, serrated leaves; peppery taste, tender	in salads	Italy, U.S.
baby lettuces (European salad mix)	mixture of lettuces; usually includes radicchio and a variety of other small, tender lettuces; available in bulk or packaged	in salads	France, U.S.
beet greens	large leaves, red stems; mild flavor; sold in bunches or attached to beets	boiled, braised, sautéd	Europe, Middle East
Belgian endive	small, smooth, slender, pointy heads, leaves almost white, tips light green or occasionally red; flavor pleasantly bitter, texture crisp	salads, braised, gratins	Belgium, France
butter lettuce (Bibb, Boston)	bright green, tender leaves; delicate flavor	in salads, braised, stewed with peas	Europe, North America
chicory	very curly leaves, outer ones dark green, inner ones pale; bitter flavor	in salads, braised	Europe
collard greens	smooth, flat, large dark green leaves; sold in bunches, also sold frozen	braised, boiled	South U.S., Africa, Brazil

GREENS

TYPE	DESCRIPTION	USES	CUISINE
dandelion greens	dark green, long, slender; bitter taste, tough if not young; sold in bunches	salads with hot dressings to wilt the leaves; boiled	France, U.S.
escarole	sturdy, wavy leaves; bitter flavor	in salads (often wilted), soups	Europe
iceberg lettuce	light green, crisp leaves; mild flavor	salads, sandwiches	U.S.
kale	deep green, curly leaves; crisp texture even when cooked; pleasantly sharp flavor	braised, sautéed, boiled	Portugal, Brazil, South U.S.
leaf lettuce (green leaf, red leaf)	ruffled, deep green or green-and-red leaves; tender texture, delicate flavor	in salads	U.S., Europe
mache (lamb's lettuce)	small, tender oval leaves; delicate taste; available at specialty grocers	in salads	France
mustard greens	bright green, ruffled leaves; spicy when raw; also sold frozen; Asian varieties have large stalks and are milder	braised, boiled	South U.S., China
radicchio	mostly red and white, heads round or long; bitter flavor	in salads, with other greens; braised	Italy, U.S.
Romaine lettuce	long, crisp leaves; hearty lettuce flavor	in salads	U.S., Europe

GREENS

TYPE	DESCRIPTION	USES	CUISINE
sorrel	smooth, bright green; tart flavor	salads, soups, pureed	France, Eastern Europe
spinach	smooth, deep green leaves; mild flavor, tender; sold in bunches, packaged cleaned leaves, and frozen	salads, soups, side dishes, in casseroles, gratins, creamed	Europe, Middle East, India, North and South America
Swiss chard	large, deep green leaves, white or red ribs; mild flavor	braised, gratins, cooked for salads, sautéed, creamed	Europe, Middle East, Mexico
turnip greens	somewhat curly, deep green leaves; sharp flavor; also sold frozen	boiled, braised	South U.S.
watercress	small, dark green, round leaves; tender texture, spicy flavor	salads, soups; garnish	France, England, China

JAPANESE SESAME SPINACH

This is one of the best ways to prepare spinach, and is a great example of how a few ingredients can turn a vegetable into a delicious treat. You simply pour a dressing flavored with soy sauce and mirin *(Japanese rice wine) over cooked spinach, then sprinkle it with toasted sesame seeds.*

The recipe is inspired by a delicate, tasty spinach dish I enjoyed at a luncheon highlighting the specialties of Tokushima prefecture, a region of Japan. The area is especially known for its soba *and* udon *noodles, so fittingly this spinach dish makes a light, delicious appetizer before a pasta main course. Since the spinach is served at room temperature, it is a convenient item for a buffet and makes a good accompaniment for shrimp, fish, or chicken.*

3 pounds fresh spinach, stems
    removed; or 2 10-ounce bags
    cleaned spinach leaves
Salt
2 tablespoons soy sauce
4 teaspoons *mirin* (Japanese sweet rice
    wine)

2 teaspoons vegetable oil
2 teaspoons sugar
2 tablespoons sesame seeds, toasted
    (page 413)

Add spinach to a saucepan of boiling salted water and boil uncovered over high heat for 2 minutes or until just tender. Drain in a colander, rinse with cold water, and drain well. Gently squeeze dry by handfuls. Separate the squeezed balls of spinach and spread on a serving plate in a fairly thin layer.

In a small bowl, whisk soy sauce, *mirin*, vegetable oil, and sugar. Pour over spinach. Just before serving, sprinkle with sesame seeds. Serve at room temperature.

Makes 4 appetizer or side-dish servings

ZAIRIAN SPINACH IN TOMATO SAUCE

Spinach cooked with smoked fish is a favorite dish in Zaire. For this dish Zairians generally use the type of smoked fish that requires cooking, such as smoked haddock, which is sometimes called finnan haddie. Ready-to-eat smoked fish is more widely available in most markets and delis, and also makes this dish quicker and easier to prepare; I like to use smoked whitefish. The fish can be omitted for a vegetarian version of the dish.

This recipe was given to me by Mrs. Monzili, the wife of a colonel in the Zairian army. She serves the spinach accompanied by rice, plantains, or boiled or steamed potatoes.

2 10-ounce packages fresh spinach
    leaves
1 pound ripe tomatoes, peeled and
    seeded, or 1 28-ounce can plum
    tomatoes, drained
3 to 4 tablespoons vegetable oil

2 large onions, sliced
Salt and freshly ground pepper
½ teaspoon hot red pepper flakes, or
    more to taste
½ pound smoked whitefish, free of
    skin and bones (optional)

Rinse spinach; coarsely chop it. Puree tomatoes in food processor or blender.

Heat oil in a large saucepan or Dutch oven, add onions, and sauté over medium heat 10 to 15 minutes or until golden. Add tomato puree, salt, pepper, and hot pepper flakes. Bring to a boil. Cook 10 minutes over low heat or until thickened. Add chopped spinach and cook over medium-low heat about 7 minutes or until tender.

Flake whitefish into about ½-inch pieces. Add to spinach mixture. Heat 1 or 2 minutes over low heat. (*Spinach can be kept, covered, 2 days in refrigerator.*) Reheat before serving. Serve hot.

Makes 3 or 4 main-course servings, with rice

SPINACH WITH PINE NUTS

A favorite in Italy, this easy dish often includes raisins in addition to the pine nuts. Similar dishes of spinach or Swiss chard with a hint of sweetness are popular in southern France, where they even make a sweet Swiss chard tart with raisins and pine nuts.

1½ pounds fresh spinach (weight with stems), or 1 10-ounce package spinach leaves
1 tablespoon vegetable oil

Salt and freshly ground pepper
1 tablespoon dark raisins (optional)
1 to 1½ tablespoons pine nuts

Rinse spinach well; discard large stems. Add spinach to a sauté pan with the water clinging to its leaves. Cover and cook over medium-high heat for 2 minutes. Uncover and cook, stirring often, for 1 or 2 minutes or until wilted. Drain in a colander, rinse with cold water, and drain well. Squeeze gently to remove excess water.

Heat oil in same pan over medium heat. Add spinach, salt, pepper, raisins, and pine nuts. Stir 2 or 3 minutes over medium heat and serve.

Makes 2 or 3 side-dish servings

NUTMEG-SCENTED SPINACH

This is an easy and absolutely delicious way to prepare spinach; it is the spinach recipe I love most. This classic dish is served frequently in French homes as an accompaniment for delicate fish, chicken, or veal dishes.

2 pounds fresh spinach
Salt and freshly ground pepper
1 to 2 tablespoons butter

2 to 3 tablespoons heavy cream
Freshly grated nutmeg to taste

Discard spinach stems and rinse leaves thoroughly in a bowl of water. Remove leaves to a colander; if water is sandy, rinse spinach again and drain.

Add spinach to a large saucepan of boiling salted water and boil uncovered over high heat for 3 minutes or until wilted and just tender. Drain in a colander, rinse with cold water, and drain well.

Squeeze spinach by handfuls to remove as much liquid as possible. Chop spinach coarsely with a knife.

Melt butter in a saucepan over medium heat. Add spinach and cook, stirring, for 2 minutes. Stir in cream, salt, pepper, and nutmeg and cook, stirring, until cream is absorbed. Taste and adjust seasoning. Serve hot.

Makes 4 side-dish servings

SPINACH FLANS

Vegetable flans are festive accompaniments beloved of chefs of elegant restaurants, but they are also easy to make at home. Flans are molds of chopped vegetables mixed with milk and eggs and baked in a water bath.

At La Varenne Cooking School in Paris, where I learned to make spinach flans, our chefs lined the molds with blanched spinach leaves before adding the spinach flan mixture, but this was time-consuming, so I have omitted this step. The French accompaniment has become a favorite at classes that I teach on quick dinners. It's a lovely partner for grilled or baked salmon steaks, veal chops, or roast chicken.

1½ pounds spinach, or 1 10-ounce
   package cleaned leaves
Salt and freshly ground pepper
3 slices French bread (½ inch thick
   and 3 to 4 inches in diameter)

1½ cups whole milk
2 tablespoons (¼ stick) butter
2 large eggs
1 large egg yolk
Pinch of freshly grated nutmeg

Preheat the oven to 400°F. Clean spinach. Cook uncovered in a large saucepan of boiling salted water over high heat, pushing leaves down into water often, until tender, about 3 minutes. Rinse with cold water and squeeze by handfuls until dry. Chop with a knife.

Butter five ⅔-cup ramekins. Discard the bread crusts, tear the bread into pieces, and put them in a large bowl. Heat the milk to a simmer and pour 1 cup of it over the bread. Let soak for 5 minutes. Squeeze the bread. Then whisk the mixture until bread is fairly well mixed into the milk.

Melt butter in saucepan used to cook spinach. Add chopped spinach and cook 3 minutes or until all moisture evaporates. Add to soaked bread. Whisk in remaining milk, eggs, yolk, salt, pepper, and nutmeg. Taste and adjust seasoning. Spoon into the ramekins, set in a roasting pan, and add enough boiling water to come halfway up their sides. Bake 18 to 20 minutes or until flans are firm.

Using a slotted metal pancake turner, remove molds from water bath. Let cool 1 to 2 minutes. Unmold onto plates.

Makes 5 side-dish servings

GREEK SPINACH PASTRIES

These individual pastries turnovers, called spanakopitas, *are made with filo dough and a savory filling of spinach and feta cheese accented with green onions and nutmeg. They make a terrific party dish. I find the filling tastes best with creamy ewes' milk feta cheese imported from Greece, France, or Bulgaria.* SEE PHOTOGRAPH.

¾ pound filo sheets (about 15 sheets)

Spinach-Feta Filling

1 10-ounce package spinach leaves, stems discarded, rinsed
½ cup water
2 tablespoons olive oil
¾ cup finely chopped green onions

Salt and freshly ground pepper
4 ounces feta cheese, crumbled (about 1 cup)
1 large egg

⅔ cup melted butter or olive oil, for brushing dough

About 2 teaspoons sesame seeds, for sprinkling (optional)

If filo sheets are frozen, defrost them in refrigerator 8 hours or overnight. Remove sheets from refrigerator 2 hours before using; leave them in their package.

Place spinach leaves in a large sauté pan with water. Cover and bring to a boil over high heat. Cook over medium-high heat, stirring occasionally, about 3 to 4 minutes or until wilted. Drain, rinse with cold water, and squeeze to remove as much liquid as possible. Chop spinach finely with a knife.

Heat oil in a skillet, add green onions, and cook over low heat, stirring, about 2 minutes or until tender. Add spinach, salt, and pepper and sauté 2 minutes. Remove from heat, transfer to a bowl, and let cool. Mix with cheese, egg, and salt and pepper to taste.

Remove filo sheets from their package and spread them on a dry towel. Using a sharp knife, cut stack in half lengthwise, to form 2 stacks of sheets of about 16 × 7 inches. Cover filo immediately with wax paper, then with a damp towel. Work with only 1 filo sheet at a time; keep remaining sheets covered with paper and towel, so they don't dry out.

Remove 1 pastry sheet from pile. Brush it lightly with butter and fold it in half lengthwise so its dimensions are about 16 × 3½ inches. Dab it lightly with butter. Place about 2 teaspoons filling at one end of strip. Fold end of strip diagonally over filling to form a triangle and dab it lightly with butter. Continue folding it over and over, keeping it in a neat triangular shape after each fold, until you reach end of strip. Set pastry on a lightly oiled baking sheet. Brush top lightly with butter. Shape more triangles with remaining dough and filling. (*Pastries can be shaped 1 day ahead and refrigerated on baking sheets or on plates. Cover them tightly with plastic wrap.)*

Preheat the oven to 350°F. Brush pastries again with butter. Sprinkle with sesame seeds. Bake 15 to 18 minutes or until golden brown. Serve warm (not hot) or at room temperature.

Makes about 25 to 28 pastries, or 8 to 10 appetizer servings

SPINACH SALAD WITH FETA CHEESE AND TOMATOES

This easy-to-make Greek salad was a popular beginning to several of my "sixty-minute Mediterranean menu" classes. With cleaned spinach readily available in the supermarket, the salad is a snap to make.

¾ pound fresh spinach (1 medium bunch)

Greek Salad Dressing

¼ cup extra-virgin olive oil
1 tablespoon red wine vinegar
1 tablespoon strained fresh lemon juice

½ teaspoon dried oregano, crumbled
Salt and pepper

2 hard-boiled eggs, quartered
2 medium tomatoes, cut into eighths

2 ounces feta cheese, crumbled (about ½ cup)

Remove stems from spinach and any wilted leaves and wash remaining leaves thoroughly. Dry spinach well in salad spinner or towel. Tear any large leaves in 2 or 3 pieces.

Whisk together the olive oil, vinegar, lemon juice, and oregano. Season lightly with salt and add pepper to taste.

Toss ¼ cup dressing with the spinach in a large bowl and taste for seasoning. Arrange spinach on a platter. Set the eggs in center of bed of spinach and tomatoes around the edge. Scatter feta cheese over tomatoes. Sprinkle remaining dressing over salad. *(The salad can be served immediately or kept for 2 hours in the refrigerator.)*

Makes 4 appetizer or 2 main-course servings

IRANIAN SPINACH BORANI

*F*or this light appetizer, sautéed onions and spinach are mixed with garlic-scented yogurt. Iranians also make borani out of eggplant and beets. Borani is also popular in neighboring regions of what used to be the Soviet Union.

Borani bears a certain resemblance to Indian raita, but Iranians serve it as part of an appetizer buffet rather than as an accompaniment. On the table there will also be fresh bread and a vegetable and cheese platter of radishes, green onions, watercress, parsley, mint, other herbs, and a fresh white cheese resembling Indian panir. For festive occasions there might be other appetizers as well—a bowl of walnuts and raisins, a cucumber-tomato salad, a plate of diced beets, sliced melon, pickled vegetables, and containers of olive oil, vinegar, lemon juice, and yogurt for seasoning.

Serve this borani with fresh bread, either Iranian flat bread or pita.

4 cups tightly packed spinach leaves,
   rinsed and chopped
1 medium onion, halved and sliced
2 medium garlic cloves, chopped

2 tablespoons vegetable oil
1 cup nonfat or low-fat plain yogurt
Salt and freshly ground pepper

Add spinach to a medium sauté pan with the water clinging to its leaves. Cover and cook over medium heat, stirring often, for 5 minutes or until wilted. Drain in a colander, rinse with cold water, and drain well. Squeeze gently to remove excess water.

In a large skillet, heat oil over medium heat, add onion and sauté about 5 minutes; continue sautéing over low heat 3 minutes or until golden. Add garlic and sauté 1 minute. Stir in spinach and sauté 2 minutes. Transfer mixture to a bowl and cool.

In a bowl, stir yogurt until smooth. Stir into spinach mixture. Season to taste with salt and pepper. Serve cold. (*Borani can be kept, covered, 2 days in refrigerator.*)

Makes 4 appetizer servings

KALE WITH EGYPTIAN GARLIC SAUCE

Kale is a tasty green and deserves to be better known. Its ruffled leaves cook to a deep green, appealing accompaniment for rice, meat, or poultry.

Kale is delicious with an Egyptian sauce of browned garlic and ground coriander. It's not exactly a ''sauce,'' but a seasoning mixture—a way to add a quick burst of flavor to a hot cooked vegetable. The mixture is the most popular Egyptian flavoring for cooked greens and soups made with greens, and is also loved with okra, baked eggplant, and tomato sauce. I also like to mix it with cooked white or brown rice and zucchini.

To turn the kale into a quick and tasty main dish, toss it with cooked pasta and diced plum tomatoes.

1 pound kale	2 teaspoons ground coriander
2 tablespoons vegetable oil	Salt and cayenne pepper to taste
4 medium garlic cloves, minced	

Rinse kale and remove stems, including tough stem running through each leaf. Pile leaves and cut in thin strips. Add kale strips to a large saucepan of boiling salted water and boil uncovered over high heat for 5 minutes or until crisp-tender. Drain well and transfer to a bowl.

Heat oil in a small skillet or saucepan, add garlic, and cook over low heat until light brown, about 1 minute. Add coriander, salt, and cayenne and stir over low heat for 15 seconds to blend. Immediately toss with kale, in pan or in a bowl. Taste and adjust seasoning. Serve hot.

Makes 2 or 3 side-dish servings

PORTUGUESE GREEN SOUP

In our latest visit to Paris, my husband and I talked with a produce man of our old neighborhood's open-air market. We discussed what was new on the vegetable stands in the past ten years. He said one important change was that he carried many more greens for cooking. "The Portuguese people like them for soup," he said, alluding to the large number of immigrants from Portugal living in France. This caldo verde, *or "green soup," is the type he was referring to.*

The soup is very simple, consisting basically of greens, potatoes, onion, a little olive oil, and often garlic sausage, as in the variation. All sorts of greens can be used. I especially like kale in this soup.

As in French bouillabaisse, *the soup is boiled to emulsify the olive oil with the liquid, giving it a rich flavor throughout.*

1¼ pounds boiling potatoes, scrubbed and quartered	¾ pound kale, stalks discarded, leaves rinsed well
5 cups water	1 medium onion, finely chopped
Salt and freshly ground pepper	2 tablespoons extra-virgin olive oil

In a medium saucepan, combine potatoes with water and a pinch of salt. Cover and bring to a boil. Cook over low heat for about 25 minutes or until very tender.

Meanwhile, pile kale leaves on a cutting board, halve lengthwise, and use sharp knife to shred in crosswise strips as thin as possible.

With a slotted spoon, transfer potatoes to a bowl. Remove peel and mash potatoes. Return to pan of their cooking liquid.

Just before serving, bring soup to a boil, stirring. Add onion, kale, and oil. Boil uncovered over medium-high heat about 5 minutes or until kale and onion are crisp-tender. Taste and adjust seasoning. Serve immediately.

Makes 3 or 4 appetizer servings

VARIATION: **Portuguese Green Soup with Sausage**
Cut 4 ounces garlic sausage or turkey garlic sausage into ¼-inch slices. Sauté in a skillet about 3 to 5 minutes or until most of the fat is rendered. Drain on paper towels if necessary. Add to soup after cooking kale and simmer 2 to 3 minutes.

SWISS CHARD GRATIN WITH CHEESE SAUCE

This rich, warming dish is a staple of French home cooking. It's well liked in casual bistros as well. At a Parisian restaurant where I trained, a favorite side dish was two-layered gratin, with Swiss chard on the bottom and cauliflower florets on top, coated with cheese sauce and browned in the oven.

If the Swiss chard in your market has wide ribs, these can be peeled like celery, cooked until tender, and combined with the leaves in the gratin.

You can prepare this gratin with other greens as well, such as kale or spinach. If you prefer, substitute Cream Sauce (page 400) or Ten-Minute Tomato Sauce (page 394) for the cheese sauce.

1½ to 2 pounds Swiss chard
1⅓ cups hot Cheese Sauce (page 399)

2 tablespoons freshly grated Parmesan cheese

Preheat the oven to 425°F. Cut chard leaves from ribs, discarding ribs. Pile chard leaves, halve them lengthwise, and cut them crosswise into strips ½ inch wide. Cook uncovered in a medium saucepan of boiling salted water until just tender, about 3 minutes. Drain, rinse with cold water, and drain well. Squeeze by handfuls to remove excess moisture.

Butter a heavy 5-cup gratin dish or other shallow baking dish. Arrange chard in one layer in dish. Spoon sauce carefully over it to coat completely. Sprinkle evenly with cheese. (*Dish can be kept, covered, 1 day in refrigerator; bring to room temperature before continuing.*)

Bake until sauce begins to bubble, about 7 to 10 minutes. If desired, brown lightly in broiler, about 1 minute, checking often and turning dish if necessary so cheese browns evenly. Serve hot from baking dish.

Makes 4 side-dish servings

RED SWISS CHARD WITH OIL AND LEMON

Red Swiss chard has green leaves and brilliant red stems that have a taste slightly reminiscent of beets. It looks beautiful served very simply, as you have a pretty red and green vegetable. This recipe is an Italian way of cooking and seasoning greens. Serve the chard to accompany fish, chicken, turkey, or veal, or alongside a pasta or couscous main course.

1 pound red Swiss chard	Salt and freshly ground pepper
1 to 2 tablespoons extra-virgin olive oil	1 lemon, cut in wedges

Rinse chard well to remove any sand. Separate stems from leaves. Peel stems lightly to remove strings, but do not peel too much, or the chard will lose its red color. Cut peeled stems diagonally into 2- or 3-inch pieces. Cut leaves in strips, about 1 inch wide.

Add stems and leaves to a medium saucepan of boiling salted water and boil, uncovered, over high heat 2 or 3 minutes or until stems are crisp-tender. Drain in a colander.

Transfer to a serving dish and toss lightly with oil, salt, and pepper. Serve with lemon wedges.

Makes 2 or 3 side-dish servings

GREENS WITH ONIONS AND MUSHROOMS

Greens are popular in the American South. Traditional recipes call for bacon or salt pork and for about two hours of simmering, but I like to cook the greens briefly and to use sautéed onions, garlic, mushrooms, and stock for a flavorful, lighter dish. Serve these greens as a side dish. I like them with turkey burgers or eggs, and with boiled potatoes or cornbread as additional accompaniments. The red pepper variation is good spooned over rice or pasta. Have a bottle of hot sauce or hot pepper vinegar on the table for sprinkling on the greens.

1 bunch (¾ to 1 pound) collard or
    mustard greens
Salt and freshly ground pepper
2 tablespoons olive oil or vegetable oil
1 medium onion, chopped

2 garlic cloves, chopped
1 cup sliced mushrooms
½ cup Chicken or Vegetable Stock
    (pages 407, 406)

Wash greens thoroughly in several changes of water. Discard stems, and coarsely chop the leaves.

Add greens to a medium saucepan of boiling salted water and boil, uncovered, over high heat about 3 minutes for collard greens or about 5 minutes for mustard greens or until nearly tender. Drain in a colander, rinse with cold water, and drain well. Squeeze lightly to remove excess water.

Heat oil in sauté pan over medium heat, add onion, and sauté 7 minutes or until light golden. Add garlic and mushrooms and sauté 2 minutes. Add greens, sprinkle with salt and pepper, and mix well. Add stock and bring to a boil, stirring. Cover and cook over low heat 5 minutes or until tender. Taste and adjust seasoning. (*Greens can be kept, covered, 2 days in refrigerator.*)

Serve hot.

Makes 2 or 3 side-dish servings

VARIATION: **Greens with Red Pepper**
Substitute 1 red bell pepper for mushrooms. Cut pepper into ½-inch dice. After adding stock to mixture in sauté pan, cook about 10 minutes or until greens and pepper are tender.

WATERCRESS SOUP WITH LEEKS AND POTATOES

A favorite in the British Isles as well as in France, this pale green soup is lightly thickened with potato and can be served hot or cold. Crusty fresh bread, whether French, Italian, or sourdough, is the best accompaniment.

A food mill is useful for pureeing the watercress, so that its strings do not go through into the soup. Another way to eliminate strings is to puree the soup in a blender or food processor and then strain it.

2 medium leeks, cleaned (page 258)
2 bunches watercress (total 8 to 10 ounces)
2 tablespoons (¼ stick) butter or vegetable oil
1 medium onion, sliced
1 medium potato

1½ cups Chicken or Vegetable Stock (pages 407, 406) or canned broth
Salt and white pepper
1½ to 1¾ cups milk
¼ cup heavy cream (optional)
Freshly grated nutmeg

Cut white and light green parts of leeks into thin slices; reserve dark green for other uses.

Thoroughly rinse watercress, discard large stems, and reserve only the upper, leafy third of each bunch. Reserve 8 to 12 attractive watercress leaves for garnish. Plunge bunches of remaining watercress into a large saucepan of boiling water. Bring back to boil, drain, and rinse under cold running water. Drain thoroughly and squeeze dry.

Melt butter in a heavy saucepan over low heat. Add onion and leeks and cook, stirring often, until soft but not brown, about 10 minutes. Add watercress bunches and cook, stirring, for 2 minutes. Peel potato, cut it into thin slices, and add to pan. Add stock and a pinch of salt and white pepper, and bring to boil. Cover and simmer over low heat, stirring occasionally, about 20 minutes or until potato is tender.

Puree the soup through a food mill; or puree it in a blender or food processor, then strain to remove stringy parts of watercress.

Return soup to saucepan and add 1½ cups milk. Bring to boil. Add cream and bring again to boil. If soup is too thick, stir in ¼ cup milk. Add nutmeg. Taste and adjust seasoning.

If you would like to garnish soup, put reserved watercress leaves in a small strainer and dip in a small saucepan of boiling water for ½ minute. Rinse and drain.

Serve soup hot or cold, garnished with blanched watercress leaves.

Makes 4 appetizer servings

BRAISED BELGIAN ENDIVE

Braising is the best way to cook Belgian endive. This technique accentuates its natural flavor rather than making it mild-tasting, as when it is boiled. The vegetable does have a slightly bitter flavor, but once you become familiar with it and expect it, the taste is delightful. Serve braised endive with roast poultry or meat.

I learned to make this dish in Paris, but a Belgian acquaintance noted that this method of cooking endive is at least as popular in her country as in its neighbor to the south. When I asked whether oil is sometimes substituted for the butter, she expressed her disapproval: "The French cook vegetables with oil but we in Belgium prefer butter!"

1 pound Belgian endive
2 to 3 tablespoons butter, or half butter
   and half vegetable oil
Salt and freshly ground pepper

A few drops lemon juice
Pinch of sugar (optional)
1 tablespoon chopped fresh parsley

Preheat the oven to 400°F. Trim any brown spots from endive. Spread butter in a heavy ovenproof saucepan just large enough to contain endive in one layer. Set endive in saucepan and sprinkle with salt and pepper.

Cover tightly and cook over medium heat until butter begins to sizzle. Transfer to oven and bake 30 minutes. Turn endive over, cover tightly, and continue baking 20 to 30 minutes more, or until endive are very tender when pierced with a small sharp knife near base; cooking time varies with size. Check occasionally to be sure they do not burn. Sprinkle with lemon juice and sugar, and return to oven for 1 minute. Serve hot, sprinkled with parsley.

Makes 3 or 4 side-dish servings

BEET GREENS WITH RICE

This is an Armenian recipe, but this way of cooking greens is in fact popular in eastern Mediterranean countries as well. The rice absorbs the flavor of the greens as they cook together. It's a convenient dish, as the greens and rice cook in one pot. Instead of beet greens, you can use green or red Swiss chard or spinach.

¾ to 1 pound beet greens
2 tablespoons olive oil
1 medium onion, chopped
2 large garlic cloves, chopped
1 cup long-grain white rice

Salt and freshly ground pepper
2 cups boiling water
3 tablespoons slivered almonds,
    toasted (page 413)

Rinse greens thoroughly, and cut stems into ½-inch pieces. Chop leaves.

Heat oil in a heavy sauté pan over medium heat. Add onion and sauté for 5 minutes, stirring often. Add beet stems and sauté 2 minutes. Add leaves, cover, and cook over low heat, stirring occasionally, for 5 minutes or until wilted. Add garlic and rice, sprinkle with salt and pepper, and mix with greens. Add water, cover, and cook over low heat, without stirring, about 18 minutes or until rice is tender. Taste and adjust seasoning. Serve sprinkled with toasted almonds.

Makes 4 side-dish or 2 or 3 main-course servings

SALAD OF BABY GREENS

A great innovation in the produce section of supermarkets is rinsed dried baby greens. Now it's easy to have a delicious green salad, like those served in French restaurants, even on the busiest days. All you do is put the greens in a bowl, toss with a little vinegar and olive oil or your favorite vinaigrette (such as Tarragon Vinaigrette, page 103, or Walnut Oil Vinaigrette, page 383), and enjoy the salad.

Only a small amount of dressing is needed—just enough to barely coat the leaves; there should never be a puddle of dressing at the bottom of the bowl.

This is the type of salad served in France after the main course, or as an accompaniment for grilled chicken or duck. It's also great served with cheese and bread.

3 cups mixed baby greens, such as
    escarole, endive, and radicchio
1 teaspoon herb or white wine vinegar

2 to 3 teaspoons extra-virgin olive oil
Salt and freshly ground pepper

If greens are not already rinsed, rinse and dry thoroughly. Transfer to a bowl. Add vinegar, 2 teaspoons oil, and salt and pepper to taste. Toss thoroughly. Taste, and add more oil if desired.

Makes 2 side-dish servings

DINNER SALAD, AMERICAN STYLE

This is basically a green salad with a few topping elements—slices of very fresh white mushrooms, tomato wedges, a little shredded cheese or diced hard-boiled egg, or perhaps a few toasted nuts. Other good additions are grated carrot, a few thin slivers of red onion or any sweet onion, or thin slices of radish. You can use any dressing you like, but I find vinaigrette is best because it coats the lettuce leaves lightly and seasons them well so they are delicious. Serve the salad as a light appetizer.

6 cups bite-size leaves of butter lettuce
 (Boston lettuce), romaine lettuce,
 or mixed lettuces
4 to 6 fresh white mushrooms
2 to 4 tablespoons Classic Vinaigrette
 (page 383)

Salt and freshly ground pepper
2 small tomatoes, cut into wedges
2 to 3 tablespoons toasted walnuts or
 pecans, diced
1 large hard-boiled egg, diced
 (optional)

Rinse lettuce leaves and dry thoroughly. Slice mushrooms and sprinkle with 1 or 2 teaspoons vinaigrette to keep them white.

 Just before serving, toss lettuce with enough vinaigrette to just moisten the leaves. Season to taste with salt and pepper. Transfer to a serving bowl or plates and top with mushrooms and tomato wedges, sprinkling tomato with vinaigrette if you like. Sprinkle with nuts and egg and serve.

Makes 4 appetizer servings

ARUGULA SALAD WITH BEAN SPROUTS AND ENOKI MUSHROOMS

Arugula is a slightly spicy Italian salad green that makes a delicious addition to green salads or can be the basis of a salad on its own. It's also a tasty addition to hot dishes like pasta or pizza. Recently I had a pizza spread with mascarpone cheese and baked, then sprinkled while very hot with fresh arugula leaves. Here arugula is used in a warm California-style salad with Chinese seasonings.

2 tablespoons vegetable oil
½ teaspoon Oriental sesame oil
1½ teaspoons rice vinegar
1 teaspoon soy sauce
A few drops chili oil or bottled hot pepper sauce
2½ to 3 cups arugula leaves, rinsed and patted dry

¼ pound button mushrooms, sliced
1 ounce (⅓ package) enoki mushrooms, bases trimmed, rinsed
Salt and freshly ground pepper
½ cup bean sprouts, rinsed, ends removed
2 teaspoons chopped green onions

For dressing, whisk together 1 tablespoon vegetable oil, sesame oil, vinegar, soy sauce, and chili oil.

Mix arugula leaves with 2 teaspoons dressing. Divide between two plates.

In a medium skillet, heat remaining 1 tablespoon oil over medium-high heat. Add button mushrooms, salt, and pepper and sauté about 3 minutes. Add enoki mushrooms and sauté 1 minute or until slightly wilted.

Spoon mushroom mixture over arugula. Sprinkle salad with bean sprouts, remaining dressing, and green onions, and serve.

Makes 2 servings as appetizer or green salad course

18

Jerusalem Artichokes, Kohlrabi, Jicama, and Radishes

JERUSALEM ARTICHOKES

The Jerusalem artichoke—sometimes called sunchoke—is a vegetable with an identity problem. It does not come from Jerusalem, nor is it related to the familiar globe artichoke. Even though some people find its taste similar to that of an artichoke heart, this is true only of cooked Jerusalem artichokes, and even then requires a bit of imagination. On the other hand, many people find that Jerusalem artichokes resemble other vegetables. When raw, they recall kohlrabi, jicama, and celery root. When cooked, they bear a certain similarity to turnips, potatoes, and even water chestnuts. They look like knobby small potatoes.

Jerusalem artichokes originated in North America and were used by the Indians in soups, relishes, and as a cooked vegetable. Although Jerusalem artichokes are part of our culinary heritage from the days of the pioneers, for many of us they are a new and exotic vegetable.

219

How Jerusalem came into their name is unclear. Some say it was a mispronunciation of *girasole*, the Italian word for the sunflower, to which they are related. Others explain that in seventeenth-century Europe, when the tubers were introduced, giving plants names of exotic places was in vogue. In some parts of Europe they were called Canada potatoes or American potatoes, while their French name *topinambour* is derived from the name of a Brazilian Indian tribe, some members of which were paying a visit to France when the vegetable was first brought there. The names of certain classic recipes were inspired by the English term, and a soup of Jerusalem artichokes, for example, became known as *potage palestine*.

The vegetable has had its ups and downs in popularity. When the explorers brought them back to Europe, they were fashionable for a while. Since they grow easily, they became so abundant that people tired of them. In France they were a wartime food during the Second World War and still remind some people of that period when there was little else to eat. Yet as those memories fade, cooks are rediscovering this versatile vegetable. It is good braised in aromatic sauces, sautéed, deep-fried, and baked. It can also be turned into pickles, gratins, purees, and soufflés. To emphasize their resemblance to artichokes, some chefs serve Jerusalem artichokes with hollandaise sauce, while others choose a cream sauce or tomato sauce. In Morocco they are braised with meat and spices to make aromatic stews called *tajines*.

Recipes for other vegetables that Jerusalem artichokes resemble can be used as a guide for cooking them. Many European cooks like to treat them like potatoes, and a favorite way is to shape them into balls or dice and gently cook them in butter. Unlike potatoes, Jerusalem artichokes are also good partly cooked so they retain their crunchy texture. They are pleasant when served raw and can be made into salads, much like celery root, or can be used as a vegetable for dipping. Like turnips, they can be glazed with butter and sugar.

Jerusalem artichokes are a delightful addition to meat or poultry stews, from the creamy ones of France to the spicy stews of the Middle East and India, as their crispness and lightness provide a refreshing contrast to the texture of the meat and the richness of the sauce.

Because the crunchiness of Jerusalem artichokes is a desired feature, it is best not to overcook them. Often they will still seem firm during cooking and then suddenly become soft and mushy if not watched carefully.

JERUSALEM ARTICHOKE BASICS

✗ **Season:** At the market, Jerusalem artichokes can easily be found from the fall through the spring. They are sometimes displayed in the specialty produce section of the supermarket, and are sometimes sold as sunchokes.

✗ **Choosing:** Jerusalem artichokes should be purchased when firm, which indicates that they are crisp and fresh. They are often sold in packages. When they're sold in bulk, select the smoothest ones that resemble potatoes rather than the knobby ones that resemble fresh ginger, to make peeling easier.

✗ **Storing:** They can be stored unwashed in their package or in a perforated plastic bag in the refrigerator for 4 or 5 days.

✗ **Serving Size:** Allow 4 to 5 ounces per person as a side dish.

✗ **Nutrients:** Jerusalem artichokes contain iron and vitamin B. One-half cup of raw sliced Jerusalem artichokes has 55 to 60 calories. Some people have trouble digesting Jerusalem artichokes; it's best to eat a modest amount if you've never had them before.

Basic Preparation

Rinse Jerusalem artichokes and scrub well with a stiff brush, which is helpful in getting into the crevices between the knobs. Cut away any small knobs or blemishes. If they are very knobby, they can be cut in pieces and each one peeled separately.

Like potatoes, Jerusalem artichokes darken quickly once peeled or cut, and should be put immediately into water. For some recipes, they can be cooked in the skin and then peeled or the skin can be left on.

KOHLRABI

Kohlrabi is a delicately flavored bulbous vegetable popular in Germany and central Europe. It has green or purple skin and tasty white meat. Both the bulbs and the leaves can be used. Its name is derived from a German word meaning ''cabbage turnip'' because it's a relative of cabbage, although it doesn't taste like one. Kohlrabi cooks quickly and is wonderful cooked simply and served as a side dish, as in Eastern European Stewed Kohlrabi (page 228), or added to soups or stews a short time before they are served. In central Europe kohlrabi is also grated and made into salads, just like celery root.

KOHLRABI BASICS

✂ **Season:** Available in summer and early fall.

✂ **Choosing:** Small kohlrabi are best. They should have smooth, unblemished skin. If leaves are attached, they should be fresh.

✂ **Storing:** Kohlrabi bulbs keep about 1 week in a plastic bag in the refrigerator; leaves keep a few days.

✂ **Serving Size:** Allow 1 medium bulb per serving.

✂ **Nutrients:** Kohlrabi contains vitamin C, calcium, and potassium. One cup raw kohlrabi has about 40 calories. One cup cooked kohlrabi has 48 calories.

✂ **Basic Preparation:** Scrub well and peel with a paring knife.

JICAMA

Jicama looks like a large brown turnip, with an uninspiring outer appearance that hides white flesh of a wonderful crisp texture and a delicate sweet flavor. This Mexican vegetable is traditionally served raw on its own, seasoned with lime juice and hot chili powder, or mixed with cilantro, or with diced oranges or other fruit. It is also great cut in sticks and served with dip. I love it in chopped salads, such as Mediterranean Diced Salad, California Style (page 376). Sliced jicama can be sautéed with other vegetables or substituted for water chestnuts in Chinese vegetable stir-fries.

JICAMA BASICS

✂ **Season:** Jicama is available all year but is less plentiful in late summer.

✂ **Choosing:** Select jicama that is firm and blemish-free. Choose small ones, so they won't be woody inside.

✂ **Storing:** Wrap cut jicama in plastic wrap or keep in a plastic bag in the refrigerator; it will keep up to a week.

✂ **Serving Size:** Allow about 4 ounces per person.

✂ **Nutrients:** Jicama is a good source of vitamin C and contains iron, calcium, and potassium. A cup of shredded raw jicama has about 50 calories.

✂ **Basic Preparation:** Rinse, scrub well, and cut off peel with a knife.

RADISH BASICS

✂ **Season:** Available all year.

✂ **Choosing:** All radishes should be firm, smooth, and crisp. If the leaves are attached, they should be green and not wilted.

✂ **Storing:** Keep radishes unwashed in a plastic bag in the refrigerator. They keep about 1 week. If they came with greens attached, remove the greens and store separately; they keep for 2 or 3 days.

✂ **Serving Size:** Allow 2 or 3 small radishes per person.

✂ **Nutrients:** Radishes are a good source of vitamin C. A medium radish has only 1 calorie.

✂ **Basic Preparation:** Rinse radishes well and cut off root ends. Daikon should be peeled. Rinse greens several times, like spinach.

RADISHES

We are most familiar with the small, round red radishes, but now a variety of radishes is available in our markets, from small, oval, pink delicate-tasting French breakfast radishes to large, long white Japanese daikon radishes. Radishes are popular in Europe, the Middle East, and the Far East. They are generally used raw but can also be cooked.

Whole small radishes make pretty garnishes for all sorts of cold foods, from pâtés to platters of raw vegetables for dipping. Sliced or diced radishes are a good addition to mixed salads like Mediterranean "Chopped" Salad (page 166), or can be the basis of salads, as in Moroccan Radish Salad with Orange (page 231). Large radishes are often grated to make salads like Daikon Radish and Carrot Salad (page 230). Small radishes can be braised whole, and then their taste is mild.

The Chinese eat radish greens, and so do the French, who like to use them, like watercress, in soups. Radish sprouts are delicate in appearance but have a hot, peppery taste and add zest to sandwiches and salads.

SAUTÉED JERUSALEM ARTICHOKES WITH PEPPERS

Red peppers, jalapeño peppers, and cilantro give this North African recipe its zest. Serve it as an accompaniment for sautéed turkey or chicken breasts.

1 pound Jerusalem artichokes
    (sunchokes), scrubbed
¼ cup olive oil
Salt
1 medium red bell pepper, cored,
    seeded, and cut in about ¾-inch
    dice

1 fresh jalapeño pepper, cored, seeded,
    and minced (wear rubber gloves)
2 tablespoons minced shallot
2 tablespoons minced cilantro (fresh
    coriander) leaves

Peel Jerusalem artichokes with a paring knife. Put each as it is peeled into a bowl of water. Cut in slices ¼ inch thick, then return to the water until ready to cook them. Drain well and pat dry with paper towels.

Heat 3 tablespoons oil in a large, heavy skillet, add the Jerusalem artichokes, and sprinkle them with salt. Cook over medium-high heat, turning them often and shaking the skillet occasionally, for 5 minutes, or until they are just tender when checked with a knife and are lightly browned at the edges. Transfer to a plate with a slotted spoon.

Add remaining tablespoon oil to skillet and heat it. Add the bell pepper and sauté over medium heat, stirring often, for 1 minute. Add jalapeño pepper and sauté for 1 minute. Stir in shallot and sauté mixture for 1 minute, or until bell pepper is crisp-tender. Stir in cilantro and remove from heat. Return Jerusalem artichokes to skillet and toss to combine them with pepper mixture. Add salt to taste. Serve immediately.

Makes 4 side-dish servings

JERUSALEM ARTICHOKE GRATIN WITH WALNUTS

This is really two recipes in one. The Jerusalem artichokes can be simply cooked in butter, as in the first two paragraphs, as an accompaniment for roast chicken or broiled meat. For a richer dish that is prepared both in Europe and South America, continue with the recipe and prepare the gratin. For even cooking, choose smooth Jerusalem artichokes.

1 pound Jerusalem artichokes
   (sunchokes)
3 tablespoons butter
Salt and freshly ground pepper

Cream Sauce (page 400)
¼ cup coarsely chopped walnuts
2 tablespoons freshly grated Parmesan
   cheese

Peel Jerusalem artichokes with a paring knife. Put each as it is peeled into a bowl of water. Cut large ones into 1-inch chunks, leaving whole those that are 1 inch in diameter or smaller. Return them to the water until ready to cook them. Drain them well, and pat dry with paper towels.

Melt butter in a heavy, medium sauté pan. Add Jerusalem artichokes and a pinch of salt and pepper. Sauté Jerusalem artichokes over medium heat for 3 minutes, tossing them with a slotted spatula. Cook them over low heat, covered, shaking pan often and turning them over occasionally, for 15 minutes, or until largest pieces are just tender when pierced with a thin-bladed knife.

Butter a heavy 4- or 5-cup gratin dish or other shallow baking dish. Remove Jerusalem artichokes with a slotted spoon, reserving butter in pan, and arrange them in one layer in prepared dish. Spoon sauce carefully over Jerusalem artichokes to coat them completely. Sprinkle evenly with walnuts, then with Parmesan, and last with 1 tablespoon of the reserved cooking butter. (*Dish can be kept, covered, 1 day in refrigerator. Bring it to room temperature before continuing with the recipe.*)

Preheat the oven to 425°F. Bake the coated Jerusalem artichokes for 7 minutes if the sauce was hot or for 10 minutes if the ingredients were at room temperature, or until sauce begins to bubble. If the top is not brown, transfer the dish to a broiler and broil for 1 minute, or just until the topping is lightly browned, turning dish if necessary so the topping browns evenly. Serve immediately.

Makes 4 side-dish or 2 or 3 main-course servings

JERUSALEM ARTICHOKE STEW À LA PROVENÇALE

Stewed with onions, fresh thyme, and rosemary, then finished with a zesty persillade *of sautéed garlic and parsley, these Jerusalem artichokes make a fine accompaniment for roast chicken, lamb, or beef; or serve them simply with a bowl of rice and a serving of French carrot salad (see Crudités, page 214).*

1 pound Jerusalem artichokes
    (sunchokes)
3 tablespoons olive oil
1 medium onion, chopped
2 fresh thyme sprigs
1 fresh rosemary sprig
1 cup Chicken or Vegetable Stock
    (pages 407, 406) or low-salt
    canned broth

Pinch of cayenne pepper
1 teaspoon sweet paprika
2 medium garlic cloves, minced
2 tablespoons minced fresh parsley

Peel Jerusalem artichokes with a paring knife. Put each as it is peeled into a bowl of water. Cut large ones into 1 × 1 × ½-inch chunks, leaving whole those that are 1 inch in diameter or smaller. Return them to the water until ready to cook them.

Heat olive oil in a heavy, medium saucepan over low heat. Add onion and sauté for 7 minutes, or until it is very soft but not brown. Meanwhile drain Jerusalem artichokes well. Tie thyme and rosemary in a piece of cheesecloth.

Into saucepan stir stock, cayenne, paprika, and salt to taste, then add the cheesecloth bag. Bring to a boil. Add Jerusalem artichokes, return to a boil, cover, and cook over low heat, stirring occasionally, for 15 minutes, or until Jerusalem artichokes are tender when pierced with a knife but still have a touch of crunchiness.

Remove artichokes and onion carefully with a slotted spoon; a few onion pieces may remain in cooking liquid. Boil liquid until it is reduced to ⅓ cup. Discard cheesecloth bag. Return artichokes to reduced liquid and bring to a boil, stirring so artichokes are coated with the liquid. Add garlic, toss quickly, and remove the pan from the heat. Add parsley and toss until it is evenly distributed. Taste for seasoning, adding freshly ground pepper to taste, and serve.

Makes 4 side-dish servings

EASTERN EUROPEAN STEWED KOHLRABI

If you have not yet tried the round green- or purple-skinned kohlrabi, a tasty discovery awaits you. The most common ways to use it are grated in salad rather like cole slaw, boiled in water, or braised. Kohlrabi cooks quickly and is easy to prepare; it's hard to understand why many of us have ignored such a delicious vegetable.

Kohlrabi is a favorite in Germany, Poland, Ukraine, and Hungary. I first encountered it when I lived in Israel, as it is popular among Israelis of central European origin.

Often kohlrabi is prepared in cream sauce, but it's even more delicious stewed as in this recipe. Here it is sautéed in a little oil, then cooked gently in chicken or vegetable broth flavored simply with salt, pepper, and a pinch of sugar. The cooking liquid is thickened to become a light sauce for the vegetable. The greens are cooked like spinach.

2 pounds kohlrabi (4 medium),
    including greens
Salt and freshly ground pepper
2 tablespoons plus 2 teaspoons
    vegetable oil

1 teaspoon sugar
2 tablespoons flour
2 cups Chicken or Vegetable Stock
    (pages 407, 406) or canned broth
¼ cup chopped fresh parsley

Rinse kohlrabi greens and discard stalks. Add leaves to a large saucepan of boiling salted water and boil uncovered over high heat for about 15 minutes or until crisp-tender. Drain in a colander, rinse with cold water, and drain well. Chop fine.

Peel kohlrabi bulbs. Cut into ½- to ¾-inch cubes.

Heat 2 tablespoons vegetable oil in a large, heavy saucepan. Add kohlrabi cubes, salt, and pepper. Cook over medium heat for 5 minutes, then sprinkle with sugar and sauté ½ minute. Sprinkle with flour and sauté another ½ minute. Off the heat, slowly stir in the broth. Bring to a boil, stirring. Cover and cook over low heat, stirring often, for 15 minutes or until the kohlrabi is tender. If desired, uncover and simmer 1 to 2 minutes, stirring, to thicken sauce. Remove from heat. Add chopped parsley; season to taste with salt and plenty of black pepper.

In a small skillet, reheat kohlrabi leaves in 2 teaspoons oil. Season with salt and pepper. Serve as a separate vegetable or stir into kohlrabi stew.

Makes 4 side-dish servings

JICAMA SALAD WITH ORANGE AND LIME JUICE

Jicama is served as a refreshing snack in Mexico, sprinkled simply with a little ground chili, salt, and a squeeze of lime juice. Sometimes it is tossed with orange segments and fresh cilantro and made into a cooling appetizer salad, as in this recipe.

2 small jicamas (total about 1½ pounds)
2 tablespoons strained fresh lime juice
Salt to taste
Pure chili powder or cayenne pepper to taste

2 medium Navel oranges
2 to 3 tablespoons chopped cilantro (fresh coriander) or parsley (optional)
Lime wedges (for serving)

Peel jicama and cut into ½-inch dice; you will need 4½ to 5 cups dice. Sprinkle jicama with lime juice and toss. Sprinkle lightly with salt and chili powder and toss again. Let stand 5 minutes.

Peel oranges, divide them in segments, and cut each into 2 or 3 bite-size pieces. Add cilantro and orange pieces to jicama and mix lightly. Serve cold, in a shallow bowl or serving dish. Serve with lime wedges and containers of salt and chili powder.

Makes 6 appetizer servings

GLAZED RADISHES

Cooking radishes might seem unusual, but in fact they taste good when glazed in the French style; they acquire a light pink hue and a turniplike flavor, and make a good accompaniment for braised or sautéed meats.

28 to 32 small red radishes (3 bunches, 1½ pounds total)
2 tablespoons (¼ stick) butter or vegetable oil

¼ teaspoon sugar
Salt and freshly ground pepper
½ cup water

Rinse radishes; scrape clean if necessary. Trim tops. Heat butter in a medium saucepan, add radishes, sugar, salt, pepper, and water. Cook uncovered over low heat about 15 minutes, or until tender when pierced with a knife. Remove radishes. Boil liquid until it coats bottom of pan. Add radishes and cook over low heat, shaking pan often, until they are coated and shiny. Be careful not to brown. Sprinkle lightly with salt and pepper. Serve hot.

Makes 4 side-dish servings

DAIKON RADISH AND CARROT SALAD

This simple salad is a sort of Japanese version of French crudités. It's a quick way to add a fresh touch to a meal and is low in fat. I like to serve the two vegetables as side-by-side salads, one snow-white and the other bright orange.

1½ cups coarsely grated peeled daikon radish
1½ cups coarsely grated peeled carrots
4 teaspoons vegetable oil
6 teaspoons *mirin* (Japanese sweet rice wine)

Pinch of salt
1 teaspoon toasted sesame seeds (optional)

When grating radish and carrots, hold each vegetable almost parallel to the grater to get attractive long shreds.

With a fork, lightly mix grated radish with 2 teaspoons oil, 4 teaspoons *mirin*, and a pinch of salt. Lightly mix carrot with remaining oil, remaining *mirin*, and a pinch of salt. Spoon salads on a plate side by side. Sprinkle the radish salad with sesame seeds if desired.

Makes 4 appetizer or side-dish servings

MOROCCAN RADISH SALAD WITH ORANGE

This salad is tasty, light, colorful, refreshing, and easy to make—and it contains no fat! The seasoning is a mixture of lemon juice and sugar. Be sure to cut the radishes into very thin slices. Serve this salad as an appetizer or, better yet, as part of a selection of salad appetizers.

2 bunches red-skinned radishes	**1 orange, peeled and diced**
1 tablespoon sugar	**Pinch of salt**
1 tablespoon strained fresh lemon juice	

Halve the radishes and place on a board cut side down. Cut in thin slices; use 1½ to 2 cups slices for this salad.

Mix radish half-slices with sugar, lemon juice, and salt. Lightly mix in diced orange. Serve immediately in a shallow serving dish.

Makes 4 appetizer servings

19

Mushrooms

A camping trip is not my idea of a culinary adventure. But when the location is Italy in the fall, the unexpected treasure can come your way. While exploring the area near Florence, my husband and I couldn't resist buying fresh porcini mushrooms at the market. We sautéed them in a little oil over our van's burner, tossed them with pasta, and we had a delightful picnic we will never forget.

Mushrooms stand out in my recollections of dinners in countless settings—buttery wild mushrooms with a hint of mint presented in puff pastry cases at the celebrated Michel Guérard restaurant in southwest France; aromatic chanterelles and morels tossed with chicken strips and wine sauce at the elegant La Réserve restaurant near Bordeaux; an omelet filled with garlic-scented cèpes at a little café in Provence; and many other inspiring creations served in grand and modest surroundings. I have also enjoyed them in Thai and Indian curries and Chinese stir-fried vegetable dishes.

Ten years ago I had to go to a specialty grocer to find fresh exotic mushrooms. I am thrilled that now chanterelles, shiitake mushrooms, oyster mushrooms, morels, porcini, and sometimes other "wild" mushrooms can be found at many fine supermarkets and grocery stores. Today many are wild in name only; most are cultivated. Some are also available dried; in this form, they are a wonderful flavoring for sauces and soups.

Whether wild or domestic, mushrooms are easy to prepare even in a camper. The technique favored by a majority of leading chefs for cooking mushrooms, both the exotic and the familiar, also happens to be the quickest. They are simply sautéed in a little oil or a mixture of butter and oil over fairly high heat. They acquire a wonderful "toasted" flavor and a pleasant, almost crunchy texture, and are done in less than five minutes. In contrast, if cooked over low heat, they often exude moisture and end up with a softer texture resembling that of boiled mushrooms.

Mushrooms should be cleaned just before they are cooked. There's no mystery to cleaning them—the chefs I studied with in Paris simply rinsed each mushroom carefully and rubbed it gently to remove any sand. Delicate exotic mushrooms can be rubbed gently with a damp paper towel instead so they don't lose flavor.

Exotic mushrooms vary greatly in size. At our local farmers' market in Santa Monica, I've purchased cèpes that were big enough for two portions. For even cooking, large mushrooms should be sliced or cut into bite-size chunks. Small ones can be left whole to show their attractive shape. Regular button mushrooms are best quartered or sliced. In recipes you can freely exchange one type of wild mushroom for another, or substitute regular mushrooms.

Members of the onion family are the mushroom's natural companions. Onions should be sautéed first, while chopped shallots and garlic can be added to the skillet with the mushrooms a minute or two before they're done. In the French kitchen, a favorite flavor enhancer for mushrooms is a *persillade*, a finely minced mixture of parsley and either shallots or garlic. Hungarian cooks love to use mushrooms sautéed with onions and paprika to accent a variety of foods, from noodles to beef stew. For a Mexican flavor, you can sauté mushrooms with jalapeño peppers and add a sprinkling of cilantro. The popular Middle Eastern and Indian spices of ground coriander, cumin, and turmeric marry well with mushrooms, and so do the Chinese flavorings of ginger, garlic, soy sauce, and sesame oil.

Sautéed mushrooms are perfect partners for meat, seafood, poultry, and grains. And they are wonderful on their own as a first course. The packaged sliced mushrooms available today at many markets make using mushrooms most convenient. It's so easy to slip them into a pan. The sautéed mushrooms add a lovely accent to all sorts of vegetables, from peas to broccoli to zucchini, as well as to rice and pasta.

A classic French mushroom preparation is *duxelles*, or sautéed chopped mushrooms with shallots (see recipe, page 408). Like stock, *duxelles* is a basic mixture that is not served on its own but is treasured in the kitchen as a filling, flavoring, or sauce base. But *duxelles* has a great advantage over stock—it is ready in no time.

Mushrooms are good cooked by other techniques too. Add them to vegetable stews, cook large ones briefly on the grill, or remove the stems, stuff the caps, and bake them. Fresh button mushrooms are also good raw. In Europe wild mushrooms have a traditional place of honor on autumn menus. With their increased availability in our markets, this may soon become an American custom as well.

MUSHROOM BASICS

✕ **Season:** Button mushrooms are available all year. Availability of exotic mushrooms varies, mostly spring or fall.

✕ **Choosing:** Mushrooms should be free of blemishes or bruises and should not be slimy.

✕ **Storing:** Button mushrooms keep unwashed in a paper bag or in their package about 4 or 5 days in the refrigerator. Exotic mushrooms should be kept the same way and used within 2 or 3 days.

✕ **Serving Size:** Allow about 4 or 5 ounces mushrooms per serving.

✕ **Nutrients:** Button mushrooms are a good source of potassium, folic acid, and vitamins B_2 and B_3. One cup raw mushrooms contains about 20 calories; 1 cup cooked button mushrooms has about 40 calories. One cup cooked shiitake mushrooms has 80 calories.

Basic Preparation

Rinse button mushrooms one by one and rub each to remove any sand. Fresh morel mushrooms should also be rinsed carefully but thoroughly. Rub other exotic mushrooms gently with a damp paper towel. Do not soak fresh mushrooms in water. Dry mushrooms upside down on paper towels.

The stems of shiitake mushrooms, whether fresh or dried, are tough and should be discarded.

Dried mushrooms should be soaked in hot water about 30 minutes to soften them before being cooked. They should be rinsed after soaking to be sure they are not sandy.

To Slice Button Mushrooms

If base of stem is dark brown, cut it off. Cut mushrooms in half, set each mushroom, cut side down, on board, and thinly slice.

EXOTIC MUSHROOMS

TYPE	DESCRIPTION	USES	CUISINE
black trumpet	black, flower-shaped; available fresh or dried; mild flavor, delicate texture	sauté, use in sauces and stuffings	French
cèpe or porcini	large, brown; available fresh or dried; rich flavor, meaty texture	fresh—sauté, can grill large ones; dried—good in sauces and soups	French, Italian, Polish, German
chanterelle	flower or trumpetlike shape, golden or yellow-orange; fresh or dried rich flavor; meaty texture	sauté, add to omelets or pasta, serve with chicken	French, Russian, Central European
enoki	white, long stems, tiny caps, joined at bases; available fresh, in packages; very delicate flavor; soft texture	raw in salads; add to mixed vegetables and cook very briefly	Japanese
morel	dark brown, oval, spongy-looking; available fresh or dried; intense, distinct flavor and aroma; springy texture	must be cooked; braise, use in creamy sauces, stuffings, toss with pasta, serve with eggs, chicken, seafood	French, Central European, North American
oyster	gray or yellow large caps; grow in clumps; available fresh; mild flavor; smaller ones are most tender	sauté or stir-fry; mix with other vegetables, pasta, or rice	French, North American

EXOTIC MUSHROOMS

TYPE	DESCRIPTION	USES	CUISINE
shiitake (Oriental black)	dark brown, large cap, thin stem; available fresh or dried; rich flavor	braise, add to stews, vegetable medleys, pasta; dried shiitakes make flavorful broth	Oriental
straw	light brown, oval cap; available canned; mild flavor, springy texture	add to stir-fries, soups, stews, rice	Oriental
wood ear	dark brown, flower-shaped, no stem; available fresh or dried; mild flavor, crunchy texture	add to stir-fries, mixed vegetables, pasta sauces	Oriental

NOTE: Dried mushrooms should be soaked before using. See page 137.

237

MEXICAN MUSHROOMS

*F*or a quick, zesty variation of sautéed mushrooms, flavor them Mexican style with fresh jalapeño pepper and cilantro. Use red jalapeño peppers when they are available for a color contrast. Sautéed mushrooms are good with just about anything! They are delicious served on their own with rice, or as an accompaniment for chicken, meat, eggs, or fish.

3 to 4 tablespoons vegetable oil
1 medium onion, chopped
1 pound fresh mushrooms, quartered
Salt to taste

2 jalapeño peppers, preferably red,
   seeded and minced
6 to 8 tablespoons chopped cilantro
   (fresh coriander)

Heat the oil in a large skillet, add onion, and sauté over medium heat for 5 minutes. Add mushrooms, sprinkle with salt, and sauté 5 minutes. Add jalapeño and sauté 2 minutes more or until mushrooms are tender. Remove from heat, add cilantro, and toss. Taste and adjust seasoning. Serve hot.

Makes 4 side-dish servings

MUSHROOMS WITH RED PEPPERS, CUMIN, AND THYME

This quick dish is one of my favorite ways to prepare mushrooms. The flavorings of cumin, paprika, and cayenne pepper give the mushrooms a Middle Eastern accent. It's so quick to prepare that it's easy to fit it into everyday menus. The recipe is based on the way I have often enjoyed mushrooms in Israel, both at homes of relatives and in restaurants, but I add red bell pepper, parsley, and thyme for a touch of freshness and color. Serve these delicious mushrooms as an appetizer with pita or Italian sesame bread, as a main course with rice or couscous, or as a side dish with any main course, from sautéed shrimp to grilled lamb chops to roast turkey.

¼ cup olive oil
1 medium onion, chopped
1 red bell pepper, diced
1 pound fresh mushrooms, quartered
1 teaspoon ground cumin
1 teaspoon dried thyme, crumbled

½ teaspoon paprika
¼ teaspoon cayenne pepper, or to taste
Salt and freshly ground pepper
2 tablespoons chopped fresh Italian
    parsley

Heat the oil in a large, heavy skillet. Add onion and red pepper, and sauté about 7 minutes over medium heat. Add mushrooms, cumin, thyme, paprika, cayenne, salt, and pepper and sauté over medium heat, stirring often, about 10 minutes or until all vegetables are tender. (*Mushrooms can be kept, covered, 2 days in refrigerator. Reheat in a skillet.*) Add parsley and remove from heat. Taste and adjust seasoning. Serve hot.

Makes 4 side-dish servings

THAI MUSHROOM AND RED CHILI CURRY

My friend Somchit Singchalee, a Thai chef in Paris, taught me how to make this dish. She used this as a basic Thai red curry recipe for all sorts of vegetables—squash, eggplant, even potatoes. For this dish we sometimes bought tiny Thai green eggplants that looked like large peas. But our common large eggplants work just fine, too.

Most of the ingredients for this dish are available in good supermarkets. My local market in Santa Monica often has the Thai chili paste, canned coconut milk, and even the fish sauce, which is occasionally labeled ''Thai seasoning sauce.'' You can also buy them in Asian specialty shops; or see the mail order sources, page 437.

This curry is very rich, and so I like to serve it in small portions with Thai jasmine rice and another simple dish such as grilled chicken breasts or a quick spinach salad.

2 tablespoons vegetable oil
½ pound fresh large mushrooms,
    halved
Salt and freshly ground pepper
1 medium shallot, chopped
2 medium garlic cloves, chopped
1 tablespoon Thai red chili paste
1 14-ounce can coconut milk
2 teaspoons sugar
2 tablespoons plus 1 teaspoon Thai
    fish sauce (*nam pla*)

1 small eggplant (1 pound), cut into 1-
    inch cubes
1 red bell pepper, cut into strips
½ cup shelled fresh or frozen peas
1 15-ounce can baby corn, rinsed and
    halved
½ cup small Thai or Italian basil leaves
    (optional)
Basil sprigs, for garnish

Heat 1 tablespoon oil in sauté pan over medium-high heat. Add mushrooms, salt, and pepper and sauté 4 minutes or until lightly browned. Remove. Add 1 tablespoon oil and heat over low heat. Add shallot and garlic, and sauté 1 minute. Stir in chili paste, then 1¼ cups coconut milk and bring to boil. Simmer over low heat 5 minutes, stirring often. Add sugar and 2 tablespoons fish sauce.

Add cubed eggplant and pepper strips, and bring to a boil. Cover and simmer, stirring often, about 15 minutes or until tender. Add remaining coconut milk and bring to a boil. Add mushrooms, peas, and corn. Cover and simmer 5 minutes or until vegetables are tender. (*Curry can be kept, covered, 2 days in refrigerator. Reheat in covered pan.*) If sauce is too thick, gradually stir in 1 or 2 tablespoons water. Add remaining teaspoon fish sauce, or more to taste. Off the heat, add basil. Taste and adjust seasoning. Serve garnished with basil sprigs.

Makes 4 or 5 main-course servings

MUSHROOM PIZZA

*W*henever I travel in Italy I am impressed by the purity in flavor of many pizzas. Often they do not have layers of sauce, cheese, and several different topping ingredients, but rather concentrate on a single ingredient. For this pizza the mushrooms are sautéed with a little garlic. There is no need for tomato sauce or cheese.

This was always a popular pizza in my pizza workshop classes because it's very simple and you really taste the mushrooms. Besides, many students are happy to have a tasty pizza recipe that does not use cheese.

Thick Crust Pizza Dough (page 411)
5 tablespoons good-quality olive oil
1 medium garlic clove, finely chopped
10 ounces fresh mushrooms, halved
    and cut in thin slices

Salt and pepper
2 tablespoons chopped fresh parsley

Prepare dough and let rise.

Heat 3 tablespoons oil in a skillet, add garlic, and sauté briefly over medium heat for ½ minute. Add mushrooms, salt, and pepper and sauté over medium-high heat, stirring often, for about 5 minutes or until mushrooms are light brown and the liquid that is released during sautéing has evaporated. Stir in parsley and taste for seasoning.

Oil a baking sheet. Knead dough again briefly and put it on the baking sheet. With oiled hands, pat dough out to a 10- to 11-inch circle, with a rim slightly higher than the center.

Spread topping over dough. Let pizza rise for about 15 minutes. Sprinkle topping and dough with remaining oil. Set oven at 400°F. Let pizza rise for about 15 more minutes.

Bake pizza for about 30 minutes, or until dough is golden brown and firm but not hard. Serve hot.

Makes 3 or 4 main-course servings

SESAME MUSHROOM CREPES

This is an ''East meets West'' recipe uniting French and Chinese flavors. The filling is fresh and flavorful, marrying white and shiitake mushrooms with butter-sautéed leeks, fresh ginger, garlic, and Oriental sesame oil. A sprinkling of toasted sesame seeds on the rolled crepes completes the festive dish. To turn this into a quicker recipe, you can substitute packaged crepes or even steamed flour tortillas, which contribute a third culinary influence, and change this to Sesame Mushroom Burritos. Whatever you call them, these festive treats can be prepared ahead and make a delicious party dish, appetizer, or main course.

Shiitake mushrooms are available in Chinese markets and many supermarkets.

1 ounce dried shiitake mushrooms
    (about 8 mushrooms)
1½ pounds leeks (white and light
    green parts only)
2 tablespoons (¼ stick) butter
Salt and freshly ground pepper
2 tablespoons vegetable oil
½ pound fresh white mushrooms,
    halved and cut into ⅛-inch slices
2 tablespoons plus 1 teaspoon Oriental
    sesame oil

1 tablespoon minced garlic
1 tablespoon minced peeled fresh
    ginger
¼ cup dry white wine
2 tablespoons sesame seeds, toasted
    (page 413)
12 Basic Crepes (page 409) or Whole
    Wheat Crepes (page 410), at room
    temperature

Soak shiitake mushrooms in hot water to cover for 30 minutes. Drain mushrooms, discarding liquid. Cut off and discard stems. Halve caps lengthwise and cut them crosswise into thin strips about ⅛ inch wide. Halve the leeks lengthwise, rinse well, and cut into ¼-inch slices.

Melt the butter in a heavy, medium skillet over medium heat. Add leeks, salt, and pepper. Cook uncovered, stirring very often, until leeks are very soft but not brown, about 10 minutes. If liquid remains in pan, cook leeks over medium-high heat, stirring, until liquid evaporates. Transfer leek mixture to a large bowl.

Wipe skillet clean. Add vegetable oil and heat over medium-high heat. Add white mushrooms, salt, and pepper and sauté, stirring often, until they begin to brown, about 6 minutes. Add shiitake mushrooms and sauté until any liquid released evaporates. Add 1 teaspoon sesame oil, quickly stir in garlic and ginger, and sauté ½ minute. Add white wine and bring to a boil, stirring. Boil over high heat until wine is completely absorbed by mushroom mixture.

Transfer mushroom mixture to bowl with leeks. Mix well. Stir in 1 tablespoon sesame oil and a pinch of pepper. Taste and adjust seasoning.

Lightly oil a large, shallow baking dish. Spoon 3 tablespoons filling onto the less attractive side of each crepe, across lower third. Roll up in cigar shape, beginning at edge with filling.

Arrange crepes seam side down in one layer in dish. Brush crepes with 1 tablespoon sesame oil and sprinkle with sesame seeds. (*Crepes can be kept, covered, 1 day in refrigerator. Bring to room temperature before continuing.*)

Preheat oven to 400°F. Bake crepes until filling is hot, about 12 minutes. Serve immediately.

Makes 6 main-course servings

MUSHROOM TOSTADAS

Tostadas are usually made from deep-fried corn tortillas, but for this lighter version, the tortillas are toasted instead. I got the idea for this dish after eating a delicious vegetarian tostada in a little Mexican restaurant in Santa Barbara where they also make their own corn tortillas. At the restaurant they used cooked beans on the tostadas, but I love them with spicy mushrooms instead, along with fresh tomatoes, lettuce, and a sprinkling of Monterey Jack cheese. Serve these with your favorite salsa.

6 corn tortillas
½ recipe Mexican Mushrooms (page 238)
1½ cups mixed baby lettuces or shredded iceberg or romaine lettuce
1½ cups diced fresh tomatoes
¾ to 1½ cups grated Monterey Jack cheese

Sour cream (optional)
Guacamole (optional, page 392)
Mexican Fresh Tomato Salsa (page 390), Chipotle Chili Salsa (page 389), or your favorite red or green salsa

Toast each tortilla in a dry frying pan over medium heat on both sides until hot and a little puffy. Put on a plate, cover, and keep warm in 250°F. oven while toasting the remaining tortillas.

Heat mushrooms in a skillet.

To serve, spoon hot mushrooms onto center of each tortilla and sprinkle with lettuce, tomato, and cheese. Top with a little sour cream or guacamole if you like. Accompany with salsa.

Makes 6 appetizer or 2 or 3 main-course servings

MUSHROOM-MACADAMIA TART

Macadamias are the richest of nuts and the most subtle in flavor. These buttery, crisp, creamy-beige nuts add an elegant touch to salads and to cooked vegetables.

The nuts were discovered in the mid-nineteenth century in their native Australia by a scientist, John Macadam, and were named for him. It was only about seventy years later that they were grown commercially in Hawaii, which now produces most of the world's macadamia nuts and most of the world's macadamia nut recipes!

This recipe uses the nuts in a French-style mushroom tart, both in the creamy duxelles *filling and as a crunchy garnish on top; the whole nuts become toasted as the tart bakes. Serve this luscious tart as a party buffet dish, or as a festive main course with a simple green salad.*

French Pie Dough (page 411)
2 tablespoons (¼ stick) butter
2 tablespoons chopped shallot
6 ounces fresh mushrooms, chopped fine
Salt and freshly ground pepper
¾ cup heavy cream
1 large egg
2 large egg yolks

3 tablespoons minced fresh parsley
1¼ cups (about 6½ ounces) salted roasted macadamia nuts, ground fine in a food processor
Freshly grated nutmeg
12 to 15 salted roasted macadamia nuts
1 large egg, beaten with a pinch of salt, for glaze

Prepare dough and refrigerate. To make filling, melt butter in a deep skillet, add shallot, and sauté over low heat, stirring occasionally, until softened. Add mushrooms, salt, and pepper and cook over medium-high heat, stirring often, for 3 minutes or until mixture is dry. Transfer to a bowl; let cool to room temperature. Whisk cream with egg and yolks until blended. Add mushroom mixture and parsley, and mix well. Gently stir in ground nuts. Season to taste with salt, pepper, and nutmeg.

Butter an 8-inch round fluted tart pan with a removable rim. Let dough soften 1 minute before rolling it. Roll about two-thirds of dough on a lightly floured surface to a round about ⅛ inch thick and about 10 inches in diameter. Roll dough loosely around rolling pin and unroll it over tart pan. Gently ease dough into pan. Using your thumb, push dough down slightly at top edge of pan, making top edge of dough thicker than remaining dough. Roll rolling pin across pan to cut off excess dough. With your finger and thumb, press dough gently against pan so that it rises ¼ inch above the rim.

Prick bottom of shell lightly with a fork. Refrigerate shell for 30 minutes. Roll remaining dough to a thin sheet and cut in strips about ⅜ inch wide and 8½ inches long. Refrigerate strips side by side on a lightly floured plate. If they become stiff, let them soften about 5 minutes at room temperature before using them.

Put a baking sheet in lower third of oven and preheat oven to 425°F. Spoon cool filling into tart shell. Brush rim of shell lightly with egg glaze. Arrange 4 pastry strips parallel to each other at equal intervals above filling. Press to stick ends of each strip to glazed rim. Arrange 4 more parallel strips crossing first group of strips in a diamond pattern. Stick these strips to rim. Remove excess dough by pressing edges of strips against rim of pan.

Set tart carefully on hot baking sheet and bake it for 10 minutes. Pull out oven shelf, leaving tart on baking sheet in oven. Set macadamia nuts on filling between pastry strips; brush nuts and strips quickly with egg glaze. Reduce oven temperature to 400°F. and bake tart for 25 minutes, or until pastry browns and filling sets. Transfer tart to a rack and let it cool for 10 minutes. Remove sides of pan. (*Tart can be kept, covered, overnight in refrigerator.*) Serve it hot, warm, or at room temperature.

Makes 8 appetizer or 6 main-course servings

SAUTÉED WILD MUSHROOMS WITH HERBS

Wild mushrooms are usually cooked simply to keep their wonderful flavor. Using high heat keeps their good texture; some mushrooms become mushy if cooked for a long time over low heat. Chanterelles are the most beautiful to use because of their lovely golden-orange color.

½ pound wild mushrooms, such as
    chanterelles, porcinis, cèpes, or
    shiitakes
1 tablespoon vegetable oil
2 tablespoons (¼ stick) butter
Salt and freshly ground pepper

1 shallot, finely chopped
1 to 2 tablespoons chopped fresh
    parsley
1 tablespoon chopped fresh tarragon or
    chives

Clean mushrooms very gently with a damp paper towel. If using shiitake mushrooms, cut off stems, which are tough. If mushrooms are large, cut into bite-size pieces, following the mushroom's shape.

Heat oil and butter in a heavy skillet over medium-high heat. Add mushrooms, salt, and pepper. Sauté about 3 minutes. When liquid is released, raise heat to high and sauté, tossing often, for 2 minutes. When liquid has nearly evaporated, add shallot and sauté 1 to 2 more minutes or until mushrooms are lightly browned and tender. Add parsley and tarragon or chives. Taste and adjust seasoning. Serve hot.

Makes 4 appetizer servings

BLACK MUSHROOMS WITH SESAME SEEDS

When I was on a culinary tour of Taiwan led by Nina Simonds, we had a wonderful vegetarian banquet at the Kuan-Do Buddhist Temple, near Taipei. One intricate delicacy followed another: There was mock goose made from bean curd skin stuffed with bean threads and black mushrooms, mock sweet-and-sour fish made from taro root and garnished with white wood ear mushrooms, and fried nori seaweed with bean curd filling on a bed of Chinese broccoli. All were impressively garnished with sculptured vegetables—birds made of carrots, roses made of turnips, and fans made of cucumbers.

My favorite dish of all was a simple delicious dish of black mushrooms with sesame seeds. This is a re-creation of that dish. The dried black mushrooms are braised with a little soy sauce, rice wine, and fresh ginger, then flavored with sesame oil and sprinkled with toasted sesame seeds. They are delicious hot or cold, as an appetizer or as accompaniment for roast chicken, sautéed turkey breast, or grilled steak.

20 dried Chinese black mushrooms
   (about 2 ounces) or shiitake
   mushrooms
4 teaspoons vegetable oil
2 teaspoons minced peeled fresh
   ginger
⅔ cup Vegetable or Chicken Stock
   (pages 406, 407) or canned broth

2 tablespoons soy sauce
2 tablespoons rice wine or sherry
2 teaspoons sugar
1 teaspoon Oriental sesame oil
1½ teaspoons sesame seeds, toasted
   (page 413)

Rinse mushrooms, then soak them in hot water for ½ hour. Remove mushrooms, reserving liquid. Rinse again. Cut off stems.

Heat vegetable oil in a heavy, medium saucepan over medium heat. Add ginger, and stir 15 seconds. Add mushrooms, stock, soy sauce, wine, and sugar. Bring to a boil. Cover and cook over low heat, stirring occasionally, about 5 minutes or until mushrooms are tender; add 2 or 3 tablespoons water if pan becomes dry. Off the heat, add sesame oil and toss. Serve hot or cold, sprinkled with sesame seeds.

Makes 4 appetizer or side-dish servings

OYSTER MUSHROOMS WITH FRESH DILL

This simple Russian dish makes a savory appetizer on its own when served on toast. Cultivated oyster mushrooms are now widely available in our markets, generally the least expensive of the exotic mushrooms. For this dish, cèpes, chanterelles, or other wild mushrooms are most likely to be used in Russia, but this is a good way to use oyster mushrooms as well. Classically, the mushrooms are enriched with large amounts of sour cream, but I like to add just a little so they have a pleasant creamy taste and the dish stays light.

8 ounces oyster mushrooms, rinsed
    gently
2 tablespoons vegetable oil or butter
1 medium onion, halved and cut into
    thin slices
Salt and freshly ground pepper

1 teaspoon flour
¼ cup sour cream, regular or reduced-
    calorie
4 teaspoons chopped fresh dill
A few drops lemon juice, or to taste

Cut mushrooms into bite-size pieces, keeping their shape. Slice stems.

In a medium skillet, heat 1 tablespoon oil, add onion, and sauté over medium heat until lightly browned, about 7 minutes. Add remaining oil and heat it. Add oyster mushrooms, salt, and pepper and sauté over medium-high heat for about 5 minutes or until tender. Sprinkle with flour and cook 1 minute over low heat. Off the heat, stir in sour cream. Heat over low heat, stirring, for 1 minute, then remove from heat and stir in dill. Taste and adjust seasoning, adding lemon juice to taste. Serve hot.

Makes 3 or 4 appetizer servings

20

Okra

Okra is loved in places where there is a fondness for spicy food—Africa, India, the Middle East, the Caribbean, and parts of the American South. Believed to have originated in North Africa, okra was brought to America and the Caribbean by slaves. Ever since, it has been one of the star ingredients of the cooking of the American South and the Caribbean.

The vegetable has a satisfying, somewhat meaty texture. When cooked with tomatoes and peppers in the Egyptian style (page 251), or sautéed with chilies and garlic (page 252) as is popular in India, it can be served with rice as a main course. It also tastes good sautéed and sprinkled just with a little salt and pepper, or with a spicy vinaigrette as in Caribbean Okra Salad (page 253). Okra is also terrific pickled.

One reason that some people do not like okra is because it can be sticky. I find this is true of boiled okra, especially if it is sliced. If you cook okra whole and either sauté or stew it rather than boil it, the okra tastes delicious and does not have that undesirable slippery quality.

OKRA BASICS

✕ **Season:** Okra is easiest to find in summer. During other times of the year, it is available frozen.

✕ **Choosing:** Select firm, deep green, small pods, not more than 3 inches long. Large ones are often stringy and tough. Okra is also available frozen. I prefer whole frozen pods, as diced okra becomes sticky.

✕ **Storing:** Keep okra unwashed in a plastic bag in the refrigerator. It will keep up to 3 days.

✕ **Serving Size:** Allow 4 ounces per person.

✕ **Nutrients:** Okra is a good source of vitamin C and contains vitamins A, B_1, B_6, calcium, and potassium. Eight cooked pods have about 27 calories.

✕ **Basic Preparation:** Rinse lightly and quickly just before cooking. Prolonged contact with water makes okra sticky. Trim the stems carefully, without piercing the pods.

Okra's stickiness is appreciated in some regions. For Creole gumbo, okra is sliced and simmered for a long time so that its juices help thicken the soup. When I lived in Israel and I asked a friend of mine from India how to cook okra so it would not be sticky, her answer was, "Why do you want to do that? Okra's stickiness is the secret of its charm."

OKRA, EGYPTIAN STYLE

Okra is believed to have originated in Egypt, and the people of this country have developed many delicious ways of making use of it. In this easy recipe, the okra stews gently with garlic, coriander, bell peppers, and tomatoes and is seasoned with a little lemon juice. In a variation from Syria, the okra cooks in a sweet-and-sour tomato sauce with sautéed onion, lemon juice, and sugar.

The secret to tasty okra dishes is to choose small, young tender okra pods and not to overcook them. In this dish yellow bell peppers give the prettiest result, but green or red are traditional.

1 pound okra
2 tablespoons olive or vegetable oil
1 yellow, red, or green bell pepper, cut
    in 3 × ¼-inch strips
4 medium garlic cloves, minced
1 pound ripe tomatoes, peeled, seeded,
    and chopped; or 1 28-ounce can
    plum tomatoes, drained and
    chopped

Salt and freshly ground pepper
1 teaspoon ground coriander
¼ cup water
1 tablespoon strained fresh lemon juice

Rinse okra and pat dry. Trim off okra stems without cutting into pods. In a deep skillet or medium sauté pan, heat oil over medium heat and add pepper strips. Sauté, stirring often, 5 minutes. Add garlic and okra, and sauté over low heat, stirring gently, 1 minute.

Add tomatoes and stir gently. Add salt, pepper, coriander, and water. Bring to a boil. Cover and cook over medium-low heat, stirring gently from time to time, about 25 minutes or until okra is tender. Uncover and cook 5 minutes if sauce is too thin. Add lemon juice. Taste and adjust seasoning; season generously with pepper. Serve hot, lukewarm, or cold.

Makes 2 or 3 main-course servings with rice, or 4 or 5 side-dish servings

PEPPERY OKRA WITH GREENS

Soups and stews of greens with okra are popular in Africa and the Caribbean. We're familiar with preparations of greens from the southern United States, in which they are cooked with fatty meats, but this meatless version from West Africa has lots of flavor from chilies, sautéed onions, and peanuts. Serve with rice.

¾ to 1 pound mustard greens, collard
    greens, kale, Swiss chard, or
    spinach, rinsed well
¼ to ½ pound okra
2 tablespoons vegetable oil
1 large onion, chopped
2 red or green jalapeños or other
    chilies, finely chopped (optional)

½ cup water
Salt to taste
Cayenne pepper to taste
¼ cup toasted peanuts, coarsely
    chopped

Remove stems from greens. Cut leaves crosswise into thin strips less than ¼ inch wide. Lightly rinse okra. Trim caps.

    In a large, heavy skillet or sauté pan, heat oil over medium heat. Add onion and sauté about 7 minutes or until golden brown. Add hot peppers and okra, and sauté 2 minutes. Add greens and water, sprinkle with salt, and cover. Cook over low heat until okra and greens are tender, about 15 minutes, adding a few tablespoons water during cooking if pan becomes dry. Taste and adjust seasoning, adding cayenne if desired. Serve sprinkled with toasted peanuts.

Makes 3 or 4 side-dish or 2 main-course servings

OKRA WITH HOT PEPPER AND GARLIC

When my husband and I ordered this dish at our favorite Indian restaurant, the okra came out so hot and spicy that I couldn't eat it; it was too hot for him too, but he ate it with lips burning and tears streaming down his cheeks. And he kept saying, ''This is so hot but so good!''

    At home you can flavor the okra to the hotness you like. This delicious recipe has garlic, onion, and cumin as additional flavors, and the okra cooks very quickly. Indian cooks use different hot red or green peppers, but jalapeños are the easiest to find in our markets.

3 tablespoons vegetable oil
⅔ cup minced onion
3 medium garlic cloves, minced
1 large fresh red or green jalapeño or
    other hot pepper, seeded if
    desired, chopped
½ teaspoon turmeric

1 teaspoon ground cumin
1 pound small okra, rinsed lightly,
    caps trimmed
Salt to taste
¼ cup water
Cayenne pepper to taste

Heat oil in a sauté pan. Add onion and sauté over medium heat for 5 minutes or until golden brown. Add garlic and hot pepper, and sauté over medium heat for ½ minute. Stir in turmeric and cumin, then add okra, stir lightly, and sprinkle with salt. Cover and cook over low heat, shaking pan occasionally, for 5 minutes. Add water and cook about 10 more minutes or until okra is tender. Taste and add salt and cayenne pepper if desired.

Makes 4 side-dish servings

CARIBBEAN OKRA SALAD

Some versions of this okra salad suggest boiling the okra in water, but the okra becomes too sticky that way. I prefer it sautéed, then stewed gently with a little water. It tastes so good that you could serve it as a simple accompaniment, even without the dressing. The okra also makes a delicious salad with this light dressing of garlic, lime juice, hot sauce, and cilantro, seasoned with a touch of allspice. Serve extra hot sauce on the side.

½ pound fresh, small tender okra,
    rinsed and patted dry
2 tablespoons vegetable oil
Salt and freshly ground pepper
¼ cup water
1 tablespoon strained fresh lime juice
1 small garlic clove, very finely minced

Pinch of ground allspice
¼ teaspoon bottled Caribbean or other
    hot pepper sauce, or to taste
1 tablespoon chopped cilantro (fresh
    coriander) or parsley
1 small ripe tomato, diced

Trim okra caps. In a medium sauté pan, heat 1 tablespoon oil. Add okra and sauté 2 minutes over medium heat, stirring lightly. Sprinkle with salt and pepper. Add water, cover, and cook over low heat, shaking pan occasionally and adding water only if needed, for about 7 minutes or until just tender. Transfer okra gently to a serving plate.

In a bowl, combine remaining tablespoon oil, lime juice, garlic, allspice, hot pepper sauce, and salt and pepper. Pour dressing over okra. Sprinkle with cilantro and diced tomato. Serve at room temperature or cold.

Makes 2 side-dish servings

21

Onions, Leeks, Shallots, and Garlic

Onions may be the most universal flavoring. In every cuisine some member of the onion family—whether it is yellow or brown, white, red, or green onions, leeks, shallots, or garlic—is used to add sweetness and pungency to soups, stews, and casseroles of all sorts, from vegetables to grains to meats.

But onions, leeks, shallots, and garlic are not just flavorings. They are served as vegetables in their own right. Europeans love glazed baby onions as a side dish, while Americans serve creamed onions on Thanksgiving, grilled onions on the Fourth of July, and fried onion rings as a popular snack at any time. In homes around the Mediterranean onions are baked with all sorts of savory stuffings. Algerian onion compote makes a delicious side dish or a tasty topping for pizza.

Sautéed onions and leeks lend their taste to a great variety of dishes. But they cook most easily if you use a generous amount of butter or oil. If you wish to sauté onions in a minimum of oil, be sure to heat the pan and the oil well before adding the onions. Using a heavy pan helps too, so the onions cook evenly without burning. However, if you drastically reduce the amount of oil, the onions never really soften and will retain their raw texture and taste.

If the pan becomes dry when you're sautéing onions and you do not wish to add more oil, add stock or water one tablespoon at a time until the onions cook enough.

Which onion you use has a great influence on the flavor of the dish. Yellow and white onions have a sharper flavor than sweet onions and are better for most cooking, while sweet onions and red onions are better for serving raw or cooking very lightly. If you find the taste of raw onions too strong, rinse or soak them briefly in cold water, then drain them before adding them to salads.

Sweet onions have become much more popular in recent years. The best known sweet onions are Vidalia onions from Georgia, Maui onions from Hawaii, and Walla Walla onions from Washington. Recent additions to this group are the Sweet Imperials from California and the Texas 1015 Supersweet, named for its planting date.

Sweet onions are usually large, mild, juicy, and much sweeter than other onions. Their season is quite short and they do not keep well. Sweet onions are best in salads and sandwiches and in recipes where the onions stand on their own, such as onion rings, grilled onions, onion soup, and onion tarts.

Green onions are an essential flavoring in Chinese stir-fries. But they are also grilled whole in Mexico and in the American southwest and served as an accompaniment for grilled meats.

Leeks look like large green onions and have a delicate onion flavor. Europeans love to use leeks in soups and to serve poached whole leeks in vinaigrette as an appetizer. French leek compote is a good accompaniment for meat or fish or a tasty filling for tarts.

Shallots, which look like small, oval, brown-skinned onions, are used most often to flavor European-style sauces and are also a popular flavoring in Thai cuisine. They also taste delicious glazed and served whole like pearl onions and make a luscious puree.

Garlic cloves are wonderful roasted and served plain, spread on bread or made into a rich-tasting puree. Milder-flavored large elephant garlic can be used in the same ways as garlic for a more subtle taste.

ONION, LEEK, AND GARLIC BASICS

✗ **Season:** Available year-round.

✗ **Choosing:** Onions, shallots, and garlic should be dry and firm, with no soft spots. Leeks should be smooth and white at the bottom, with fresh-looking green tops without any wilted or yellow parts.

✗ **Storing:** Keep onions and garlic in a cool, dry, dark area; they will keep a few weeks if the weather is not humid. Sweet onions keep 1 to 2 weeks in netting or wrapped and refrigerated. Green onions should be free of rubber bands and stored in a plastic bag in the refrigerator; they keep for only 3 days. Pearl onions keep at least 1 week in a dry area at room temperature or about 2 weeks in the refrigerator. Leeks should be stored loosely wrapped and will keep in the refrigerator for up to a week. Shallots can be kept like onions or stored in the refrigerator for a few weeks.

✗ **Serving Size:** Allow about 4 ounces per serving.

✗ **Nutrients:** Onions and leeks contain vitamin C. Leeks and green onions also contain iron. One half cup of chopped raw onions has 38 calories; one half cup of chopped cooked onions has 47 calories. One half cup chopped cooked leeks has 16 calories. One tablespoon chopped shallots has 7 calories.

✗ **Basic Preparations:** Peel onions and shallots (see below). Rinse green onions. Clean leeks (see below).

Peeling Onions or Shallots

Cut off the root; do not cut off too much of the root end or the onion will begin to fall apart. Pull off the peel with the aid of a paring knife. Cut off the onion top.

257

Peeling Pearl Onions

Put pearl onions in a saucepan, cover with water, and bring to a boil. Cook 1 minute, rinse under cold water, drain well, and peel.

Peeling Garlic

To use all the cloves on a head of garlic, pound or press on the head to break the cloves off. Otherwise, pull off the number of cloves you need.

Put the garlic cloves on a cutting board and tap each with a large knife held flat. The peel will be released and can be pulled off. If it remains partially attached at one end of the clove, cut it off at that end.

Cleaning Leeks

Discard very dark green parts of leeks. Split leeks lengthwise twice by cutting with a sharp knife beginning about 1 inch from root end and cutting toward green end, leaving root end attached. Dip leeks repeatedly in a sinkful of cold water. Check the layers to be sure no sand is left. If dirt remains, soak the leeks in cold water for several minutes. Then separate the leaves under running water to rinse away any clinging dirt, and drain. Cut off root ends.

Slicing and Chopping Onions and Shallots

To avoid tears while chopping onions, you can turn on a fan to blow the onions' vapors away from you. If you chop them in a food processor, avert your face when you open the processor container.

For sautéing, it is most practical to cut onions in half from stem to root end. Put the onion on a cutting board cut side down. Cut onion in half-slices, holding the knife against the curved fingers of your left hand and moving your left hand gradually back to guide the knife in cutting slices of an even thickness.

To chop onions or shallots, halve the onion or shallot from top to bottom and place cut side down. With a slicing knife, cut each onion half into vertical slices, starting nearly at root end and slicing toward the stem end, but leaving the onion joined at its root end. Then cut the onion half into several horizontal slices, leaving it attached at root end. Slice onion crosswise from the stem end, forming tiny cubes. With a chopping knife, chop onion cubes smaller.

Onions and shallots can also be sliced or chopped in a food processor, according to the machine's instruction manual. If using a food processor, drain the chopped onion on paper towels before cooking so it will not be watery.

To chop green onions, cut each onion in three crosswise pieces. Cut the lower third (the wider piece) in four pieces lengthwise. Line up the onion pieces and cut them into thin slices. Chop further if desired.

ALGERIAN ONION COMPOTE
WITH TOMATOES

This zesty, useful vegetable dish is made of slow-cooked onions stewed with jalapeño peppers and tomatoes, and brightened with parsley. Serve it as a side dish with meat or poultry, mix it with pasta or rice, wrap it in a hot tortilla, spoon it inside a pita bread, or use it as a pizza topping. I like to double the recipe because it keeps well and has so many uses.

2 to 2¼ pounds onions (4 large),
   peeled
¼ cup olive oil
Salt and freshly ground pepper
2 jalapeño peppers, seeded if desired,
   minced
1 pound ripe tomatoes, peeled, seeded,
   and chopped; or 1 28-ounce can
   plum tomatoes, drained and
   chopped

1½ teaspoons paprika
3 to 4 tablespoons chopped fresh
   parsley
Cayenne pepper (optional)

Halve the onions and cut into thin slices lengthwise. Heat oil in a heavy Dutch oven, add onions and salt, and sauté over medium heat for 10 minutes. Cover and cook over low heat, stirring often, for 20 minutes or until tender and beginning to brown. Stir in jalapeño peppers, then tomatoes, paprika, salt, and pepper. Cook uncovered over medium heat about 15 minutes or until mixture is thick. (*Compote can be kept, covered, 3 days in refrigerator. Reheat in covered pan.*) Stir in parsley. Taste and adjust seasoning; add cayenne pepper if desired. Serve hot.

Makes 4 side-dish servings (about 4 cups)

VARIATION: **Pizza with Algerian Onion Compote**
   Cook 2 cups compote from recipe above in a skillet over medium heat until thick and no liquid is left in pan. Prepare Pizza Dough (page 410) and let rise. Divide in 2 pieces. Pat each on a lightly oiled baking sheet to a 10-inch circle, with rim higher than center. Spread compote on dough, leaving a ½-inch border. Brush dough edges lightly with olive oil. Sprinkle topping lightly with olive oil and, if desired, with 6 tablespoons of grated Parmesan cheese. Let rise 15 minutes. Bake in a preheated 425°F. oven 18 minutes or until dough is golden brown and firm. Makes 2 pizzas, total 6 to 8 main-course servings.

FRENCH ONION COMPOTE

In France, sliced onions, leeks, or shallots that are cooked slowly until very tender are often called compotes. They are served warm as a side dish for poultry or meat. Today some restaurants in France and in California are serving these savory mixtures along with the bread as a replacement for butter.

3 to 4 tablespoons butter, olive oil, or
    vegetable oil
1½ pounds white or yellow onions,
    halved and thinly sliced

Salt and freshly ground pepper
1 to 2 teaspoons white wine vinegar
    (optional)
¼ teaspoon sugar (optional)

In a heavy casserole, heat butter over low heat and add onions, a pinch of salt, and pepper. Cover and cook, stirring often, for 30 minutes. Uncover and cook, stirring very often, about 20 minutes longer, or until onions are tender enough to crush easily with a wooden spoon and are golden; be careful not to let them burn. (*Compote can be kept, covered, 1 day in refrigerator; reheat in saucepan over low heat.*) Stir in vinegar and sugar, if desired, and heat until absorbed. Taste and adjust seasoning.

Makes 4 to 6 side-dish servings

VARIATION: **Leek Compote**
   Omit vinegar and sugar. Substitute 2 pounds leeks for onions. Use white and light green parts of leeks only. Clean leeks (see page 258) and cut them in thin slices. Add ¼ cup chicken or vegetable stock to pan with leeks. Cook for a total of about 20 minutes. If any liquid remains, uncover and simmer until it evaporates.

SWEET ONION RINGS

A delectable way to make use of sweet onions is to turn them into an all-American favorite, crunchy onion rings. Read the Hints on Deep-Frying (page 15) before frying the onions.

4 large sweet onions, peeled
2 cups cornmeal
½ teaspoon salt
½ teaspoon ground cumin

¼ teaspoon freshly ground pepper
Pinch of cayenne pepper
About 6 cups oil (for deep-frying)
½ cup milk

Place each onion on its side and slice onions into rounds ¼ inch thick. Separate slices into rings. (Save onion centers for soup or compote.)

Mix cornmeal with salt, cumin, pepper, and cayenne pepper.

Line trays with two layers of paper towels. Heat oil in a deep-fryer or deep heavy saucepan to about 375°F. on a frying thermometer.

Dip several onion rings in milk, then in cornmeal mixture. Drop into deep oil, adding only enough to make one layer. Fry until golden, about 2 minutes. Drain on paper towels. Skim any coating bits from oil. Keep onion rings warm in a single layer in a low oven while frying remaining onions. Serve as soon as possible.

Makes 4 to 6 servings

BABY ONIONS AND CARROTS WITH RAISINS

Stews of vegetables and dried fruit are popular in eastern Europe, especially Poland and Russia. My mother, who was born in Poland, cooks carrots with prunes as a tasty accompaniment for roast or boiled chicken, duck, or beef. This is a delicate variation of the dish, made with raisins and white wine so the stew is slightly sweet and sour. You can cook parsnips the same way.

2 to 3 tablespoons butter, margarine, or vegetable oil
1 to 1¼ pounds carrots, quartered and cut into 2-inch pieces
½ pound pearl onions, peeled (page 258)
½ cup dark raisins

⅓ cup Chicken or Vegetable Stock (pages 407, 406), broth, or water
⅓ cup dry white wine or additional broth
Salt and freshly ground pepper
1 bay leaf
Lemon juice to taste (optional)

Melt butter in a large skillet over medium heat. Add carrots and onions, and sauté until lightly browned. Add raisins, broth, wine, salt, pepper, and bay leaf and bring to a boil. Cover and cook over low heat, stirring occasionally, about 30 minutes or until vegetables are tender. Discard bay leaf.

Raise heat to medium, uncover, and cook until liquid forms a syrupy glaze, about 10 minutes. If mixture is still too watery, remove vegetables carefully with a slotted spoon and boil the liquid until it thickens; return vegetables to liquid and heat gently. (*Stew can be kept, covered, up to 2 days in refrigerator; reheat in covered skillet over low heat.*) Taste and adjust seasoning; add lemon juice if desired. Serve hot.

Makes 4 side-dish servings

SWISS ONION TART

*T*his is actually a Swiss version of quiche. I learned to make it in Paris, from Master Chef Albert Jorant. He explained that the gruyère cheese not only adds flavor but also helps prevent the egg and milk custard mixture from overflowing during baking.

9- or 10-inch Tart Shell (page 412)
3 tablespoons butter, or half butter and
    half vegetable oil
3 large onions, halved and thinly
    sliced
Salt and freshly ground pepper

3 large eggs
¾ cup milk
¾ cup heavy cream or additional milk
Freshly grated nutmeg
1 cup grated gruyère cheese

Prepare tart shell. Line with paper and beans and prebake crust, as in Leek Tart (page 263). Reduce oven temperature to 350°F.

In a large skillet, melt butter over low heat. Add onions and a pinch of salt and pepper, and cook, stirring often, about 10 minutes, or until soft but not brown.

In a bowl, whisk eggs with milk, cream, and salt, pepper, and nutmeg to taste.

Spoon onions into cooled pastry shell. Sprinkle with ½ cup grated cheese.

Return shell to baking sheet in oven. Ladle egg and cream mixture slowly into tart shell and sprinkle with remaining cheese. Bake tart for 30 minutes, or until it is puffed, golden, and set; when you touch filling gently, it should not stick to your finger. Do not overbake or filling may separate. Let cool on a rack for 10 minutes. Set tart on an upside-down flat-bottomed bowl and remove tart pan rim. (*The tart can be kept, covered, 1 day in refrigerator. Warm it in a 300°F. oven before serving.*) Serve warm or at room temperature.

Makes 4 or 5 main-course or 6 appetizer servings

LEEK AND BUTTERNUT SQUASH SOUP

*T*his light orange soup is an American adaptation of a French pumpkin soup. Creamy without containing cream, it's easy to make and very flavorful because of the generous amount of leeks. Toasted pecans and chives provide an elegant finishing touch to the soup, which makes a perfect beginning for a Thanksgiving dinner.

3 large leeks (total weight of leeks 2¾
    pounds), white and light green
    parts
1 tablespoon vegetable oil
1½-pound butternut squash
2 cups Chicken Stock (page 407), or 1
    14½-ounce can low-salt canned
    chicken broth with enough water
    to make 2 cups

1½ cups whole milk
Salt and freshly ground pepper
Freshly grated nutmeg to taste
1 tablespoon thinly sliced fresh chives
¼ cup toasted pecans, coarsely
    chopped

Split leeks in quarters, beginning ½ inch from root end and cutting upward. Thoroughly rinse and slice leeks; you will need 2 quarts of slices. Heat oil in large saucepan or small Dutch oven over low heat. Add leeks, stir, cover, and cook over low heat, stirring often, for 10 minutes.

Cut squash into pieces and cut off peel. Remove seeds and any stringy flesh. Cut flesh into 1-inch cubes; you will need 1 quart cubes.

Add squash and stock to pan of leeks and bring to a boil. Cover, reduce heat to low, and simmer, stirring occasionally, about 30 minutes or until squash is very tender.

With a slotted spoon, transfer vegetables to a food processor and add a few tablespoons of their cooking liquid; puree until smooth and return to saucepan containing remaining cooking liquid. If using a blender, puree vegetables with all their liquid.

Bring soup to a simmer. Gradually stir in milk, reduce heat to low, and cook uncovered 5 minutes or until hot, not boiling. Season to taste with salt, pepper, and nutmeg. (*Soup can be kept, covered, 1 day in refrigerator.*)

Reheat soup over low heat if necessary. Sprinkle each serving with chives and pecans.

Makes 4 appetizer servings

LEEK TART

This recipe from the French region of Champagne does not make use of the region's world-famous bubbly wine, but it certainly can be accompanied by it! For this delicious tart, sliced leeks are stewed in butter, then mixed with a creamy batter and baked in a shell of pâte brisée, *the wonderful buttery French pie pastry. It makes a fabulous dish for late-night or afternoon parties, or a main course for brunch.*

Tart Shell (page 412)
2 to 2¼ pounds leeks, white and light
    green parts only, rinsed well and
    sliced
3 tablespoons butter
Salt and freshly ground pepper
2 large eggs

1 large egg yolk
¼ cup sour cream
½ teaspoon salt
⅛ teaspoon pepper
¾ cup heavy cream
Freshly grated nutmeg

Prepare tart shell. Briefly soak sliced leeks in a bowl of cold water for a few minutes to be sure they're not sandy. Lift into a colander and drain well. Melt butter in a large skillet. Add leeks and a pinch of salt and pepper. Cover with buttered parchment paper or foil and with a lid, and cook over low heat, stirring often, for 20 to 25 minutes or until very soft but not brown. If any liquid remains in pan, uncover and cook over medium heat until it evaporates. Transfer leeks to a bowl and let cool to room temperature.

Preheat the oven to 425°F. Line tart shell with parchment paper or foil, fill paper with dried beans or pie weights, and bake shell on a baking sheet in lower third of oven for 10 minutes. Remove beans and paper carefully and bake shell for about 8 minutes, or until it is golden. Transfer tart pan to a rack and let shell cool. Leave baking sheet in oven.

Reduce oven temperature to 350°F. In a bowl whisk eggs with yolk, sour cream, salt, and pepper. Whisk in heavy cream. Mix with leeks, add nutmeg, and taste for seasoning.

Return tart shell to baking sheet in oven. Ladle leek mixture carefully into shell. Bake tart for 30 to 35 minutes, or until center is set. Broil for a few seconds to lightly brown top surface. Let cool on a rack for 10 minutes and remove tart pan rim. Serve tart warm or at room temperature.

Makes 6 first-course or 4 light main-course servings

SHALLOT PUREE

Serve this wonderful, richly flavored, smooth puree as a spread for bread, a filling for tiny puff pastry cases, or a stuffing for baked mushrooms, tomatoes, or pattypan squash.

For the puree, the shallots are first braised gently in butter. In this form they also make a delicious accompaniment.

½ pound shallots, peeled and cut in
    half
2 to 3 tablespoons butter, vegetable oil,
    or a mixture of both
Salt and freshly ground pepper

2 to 3 tablespoons Chicken or
    Vegetable Stock (pages 407, 406)
    (optional)
2 to 4 tablespoons heavy cream
About 1 teaspoon thinly sliced fresh
    chives, for garnish

In a medium saucepan, cover shallots with water, bring to a boil, and cook 2 minutes. Drain thoroughly.

In a heavy, medium sauté pan, heat butter over low heat, add shallots, a pinch of salt, and some pepper, and cover. Cook, stirring often, about 20 minutes, or until shallots are very tender; be careful not to let them burn. If pan becomes too dry, add a few tablespoons stock.

Puree the shallots in a food processor. Put puree into a small, heavy saucepan and stir over low heat. Add cream and heat, stirring until absorbed. Taste and adjust seasoning. Serve puree hot or warm, garnished with chives.

Makes 4 side-dish servings

FORTY ROASTED CLOVES OF GARLIC

Many of us love the Provençal specialty, chicken with forty cloves of garlic, because of the tasty garlic cloves that come with the chicken. The long, slow cooking mellows the garlic so that it acquires a delightful flavor. Here is the garlic without the chicken.

Serve the garlic with thin slices of crusty baguette or toast, and squeeze out the tender garlic from each clove onto the bread. Or serve a few garlic cloves with almost any food, from eggs to meat to vegetables to grains, to add a burst of sweet garlic flavor. A few mashed cloves of garlic also make a wonderful addition to many sauces.

40 medium garlic cloves, unpeeled
(about 3 heads)
½ cup Chicken or Vegetable Stock
(pages 407, 406), more if needed

1 tablespoon olive oil
Salt and freshly ground pepper

Preheat oven to 350°F. Separate garlic cloves from heads and remove any loose skin. Put garlic cloves, stock, oil, salt, and pepper in a small, heavy ovenproof saucepan or casserole with a tight cover. Cover tightly. Bake 30 minutes; check pan and add a few more tablespoons stock if it is dry. Bake 30 minutes more or until largest garlic clove is tender.

Serve hot. To eat, press each clove between your fingers to remove the pulp.

Makes 6 to 8 servings

22

Peas

Fresh peas are a sign of spring in much of Europe and North America, but they don't seem to be one in southern California. Most American sources specify the peak season for peas as late spring and early summer but this is not true for warm areas of the country. At my local supermarket, the produce manager considers them a winter vegetable because in California they grow in winter. But in some parts of the country fresh peas have become rare in any season.

While so-called exotic snow peas and sugar-snap peas are available year-round in many supermarkets in my area, to find ordinary *green peas* I now have to go to the farmers' market or to a gourmet supermarket. Apparently there is less demand for fresh peas because people use frozen ones, which are much easier to prepare and to store. I love the taste of fresh peas, however. When I find them, I consider them a real treat.

In Europe, green peas are usually seasoned lightly, often with just a little salt, a pinch of sugar, and a pat of butter to highlight their flavor. Because they are colorful and cook quickly, they are a favorite addition to mixed vegetable stews and to Chinese vegetable medleys. Peas are often highly seasoned in the Middle East and India; an example of this style is the Yemenite Peas in Spicy Tomato Sauce (page 271).

PEA BASICS

✂ **Season:** Green peas are available in summer and occasionally in winter. Snow peas are sold year-round in Asian markets and some supermarkets, and are most widely available in summer. Sugar-snap peas are most plentiful in summer, but can be found during most of the year in some areas of the country.

✂ **Choosing:** Pea pods should be bright green and firm. Green peas and sugar-snaps should be fairly plump. Snow peas should be firm, not limp.

✂ **Storing:** Peas are best if cooked as soon as possible but can be kept in a plastic bag in the refrigerator for up to 3 days.

✂ **Serving Size:** Allow about ½ pound unshelled or ½ cup shelled peas per serving, or about ¼ pound snow peas or sugar-snap peas.

✂ **Nutrients:** Green peas contain vitamins A, B_1, B_3, B_6, and C and iron. One-half cup cooked green peas has 67 calories; 1 cup cooked snow peas or sugar-snap peas has 68 calories.

✂ **Basic Preparation:** Remove green peas from pods; rinse them. Rinse snow peas and sugar-snap peas; break off ends, pulling off strings from each side of peas.

Snow peas are a symbol of Chinese cuisine, lending their color and crispness to many stir-fried dishes of vegetables, fish, or meat. They are also used in Japanese, Indonesian, and Philippine dishes. Usually they are cooked whole, but they also make a beautiful, tasty side dish when cut in strips and sautéed with carrots and yellow squash.

Sugar-snap peas are the newest variety and may be the best of all. A cross between green peas and snow peas, they combine the best of both—the sweetness of green peas and the crisp texture and ease of preparation of snow peas. They taste best briefly cooked so they are still crisp; they can also be eaten raw.

ENGLISH PEAS

The French laugh at the English when it comes to culinary matters, and call all boiled vegetables à l'anglaise, or "in the English style." But the French prepare English Peas often. In fact, this is the most frequent way to cook green vegetables in France.

To keep the color bright and texture crisp-tender, green peas are boiled in a large pan of salted water rather like pasta, and then drained in a strainer. If the peas will not be served immediately, they are rinsed with cold water to stop further cooking. Before serving, the peas are heated in a small amount of butter and sprinkled with salt and pepper. Peas are also seasoned with a small pinch of sugar. When fresh peas are prepared this way, they are absolutely delicious.

**2 pounds fresh peas (2 cups shelled),
  or 2 cups frozen
1 to 2 tablespoons butter**

**Salt and freshly ground pepper
¼ teaspoon sugar (optional)**

Add peas to a saucepan of boiling salted water and boil uncovered over high heat for 5 minutes for fresh or 1 to 2 minutes for frozen, or until just tender. Drain well. (*If cooking the peas ahead, rinse with cold water until cool and drain well.*)

Melt butter in a saucepan. Add peas and heat gently over low heat. Season to taste with salt, pepper, and sugar.

Makes 4 side-dish servings

PEAS WITH PEPPERS

This Hungarian-inspired dish of green peas with red peppers is colorful and slightly spicy from hot paprika, which Hungarian cooks often use in generous amounts. It makes a lovely accompaniment for noodles, roast chicken, duck, turkey, or lamb and is very quick and easy to prepare.

2 tablespoons vegetable oil, butter, or a mixture
1 large onion, chopped
1 teaspoon sweet paprika, preferably Hungarian
Pinch of hot paprika or cayenne pepper

2 red bell peppers, cored and cut into ¼-inch rings or strips
⅓ cup water, approximately
2 pounds peas in pods, shelled; or 2 cups frozen
Salt and freshly ground pepper
2 tablespoons chopped fresh parsley

Heat oil in a sauté pan, add onion, and sauté over medium heat for 5 minutes or until tender but not brown. Over low heat, stir in sweet and hot paprikas. Add bell peppers and ⅓ cup water, and bring to a simmer. Cover and cook over low heat for 10 minutes. Add peas, salt, and pepper and bring to a simmer. Cover and cook over low heat until peas are just tender, about 5 minutes for frozen or 7 to 10 minutes for fresh, adding 2 or 3 tablespoons water if pan becomes dry. Taste and adjust seasoning. Sprinkle with parsley and serve.

Makes 4 side-dish servings

GREEN PEAS WITH MUSHROOMS

For this recipe my sister-in-law Michal Levi makes use of an eastern European technique of flavoring the peas with sautéed onions and mushrooms, but then adds a Middle Eastern spice mixture loved in Israel. The result is a deliciously different way to prepare peas that is also quick and easy. If you buy fresh sliced mushrooms and frozen peas, you have a practically instant vegetable dish. I love them with white or brown rice, or with roast chicken or grilled lamb chops.

2 tablespoons vegetable oil
1 medium onion, sliced
8 ounces fresh mushrooms, sliced ¼ inch thick
Salt and freshly ground pepper
½ teaspoon sweet paprika

½ teaspoon ground cumin
¼ teaspoon turmeric
⅓ cup water
2 to 3 pounds peas in pods, shelled and rinsed; or 3 cups frozen

Heat oil in a sauté pan over medium heat, add onion, and sauté about 5 minutes or until soft but not brown. Add mushrooms and sauté over medium-high heat for 3 or 4 minutes or until lightly browned. Sprinkle with salt, pepper, paprika, cumin, and turmeric and sauté over low heat about ½ minute. Stir in water and peas, and bring to a simmer. Cover and cook peas until tender, about 10 minutes for fresh or about 5 minutes for frozen. (*Peas can be kept, covered, 2 days in refrigerator.*) Taste and adjust seasoning. Serve hot.

Makes 4 side-dish servings

PEAS IN SPICY TOMATO SAUCE

*W*e tend to pair peas with sweet flavors, but in other countries it's not necessarily so. My husband's aunt, Mazal Cohen, who was born in Yemen, taught me how to prepare peas in the Middle Eastern style. In that region of the world vegetables are liked thoroughly cooked and very tender. If you prefer lightly cooked peas that remain bright green, cook them in water as in English Peas (page 269), and add them to the sauce just long enough to reheat them.

Peas are prepared in a similar sauce in India, often combined with another vegetable such as cauliflower, potatoes, or mushrooms. For the Indian version, a chopped fresh hot pepper and some cilantro might be added to the dish, but Mazal Cohen serves these condiments on the side, in a fiery chutney called Green Zehug (page 392). Serve the peas as a vegetarian main dish with rice, or as an accompaniment for braised chicken or turkey.

2 tablespoons vegetable oil	Salt and freshly ground pepper
1 medium onion, minced	1 tablespoon tomato paste
1 teaspoon ground cumin	2 to 4 tablespoons water
½ teaspoon turmeric	2 medium garlic cloves, minced
1 pound ripe tomatoes, coarsely grated or pureed in food processor; or 1 28-ounce can plum tomatoes, drained and pureed	About 2 pounds fresh peas, shelled and rinsed; or 2 cups frozen

Heat oil in large saucepan or sauté pan. Add onion and sauté over medium-low heat for about 7 minutes or until soft and light brown. Add cumin, turmeric, tomatoes, salt, and pepper. Bring to boil, cover, and cook over low heat for 10 minutes, stirring occasionally. Add tomato paste, water, garlic, and peas. Cover and cook 10 to 20 minutes or until peas are tender. Taste and adjust seasoning. (*Peas in sauce can be kept, covered, 2 days in refrigerator.*)

Makes 2 main-course or 4 side-dish servings

SNOW PEAS WITH BABY ONIONS AND GINGER

Here is a fresh, light, and colorful California-style alternative to the usual holiday creamed onions.

¾ pound snow peas, rinsed, stemmed, ends removed
¾ pound pearl onions, unpeeled
1½ to 2 tablespoons vegetable oil or butter

¾ teaspoon sugar
1 tablespoon finely grated peeled fresh ginger
Salt and freshly ground pepper

Add snow peas to a large saucepan of boiling salted water and boil uncovered over high heat for 1 minute or until crisp-tender. Drain in a colander, rinse with cold water, and drain well.

Add pearl onions to a pan of boiling salted water and boil about 8 to 10 minutes or until just tender. Drain, rinse with cold water, and drain well. Peel onions with a paring knife.

Heat oil in a heavy, medium skillet over low heat. Add pearl onions and sauté over low heat for 1 minute. Sprinkle onions with sugar and sauté 1 minute, shaking pan often. Stir in ginger, then peas, and sprinkle with salt and pepper. Cook over low heat about 30 seconds or until peas are heated through. Serve immediately.

Makes 4 side-dish servings

STIR-FRIED SNOW PEAS, CARROTS, AND YELLOW SQUASH

The Chinese technique of stir-frying has become popular in the United States for cooking vegetables because they keep their bright color and crisp texture and cook quickly. Serve this multicolored vegetable medley with white or brown rice, orzo or couscous, or as an accompaniment to any meat or fish.

1 large carrot	4 ounces snow peas
2 small yellow crookneck squash or	2 tablespoons vegetable oil or olive oil
yellow summer squash	Salt and freshly ground pepper

Peel carrot and cut into thin strips about 2 × ¼ × ⅛ inch. Cut squash into strips of about the same size as carrots. Remove ends from snow peas, pull off strings, and cut diagonally in strips about ¼ inch wide.

In a large skillet, heat oil over medium-high heat. Add carrot and sauté, stirring, for 2 minutes. Add squash and snow peas, and sauté 2 minutes or until crisp-tender. Season to taste with salt and pepper. Serve hot.

Makes 2 side-dish servings

SUGAR-SNAP PEAS WITH SAUTÉED MUSHROOMS

Sugar-snap peas are the best new vegetable to come to markets in recent years. They are easy to find in California supermarkets and are becoming better known in some other parts of the country.

This is a California adaptation of a French recipe, for which the cooked sugar-snaps are tossed briefly with shallot-scented mushrooms. In France the mushrooms are more likely to be sautéed in butter, but in California olive oil is fashionable. If you use a heavy skillet, you can keep the amount of oil to a minimum, for a dish that is low in fat.

This is an elegant dish for a special occasion. I like to serve the sugar-snap peas as an accompaniment for wild rice and soft-shell crabs.

½ pound sugar-snap peas, rinsed, strings and ends removed
Salt and freshly ground pepper
1 tablespoon olive oil

½ pound large mushrooms, halved and cut into thick slices
1 small shallot, chopped

Add peas to a large saucepan of boiling salted water and boil uncovered over high heat for 3 minutes or until crisp-tender. Drain in a colander, rinse with cold water, and drain well.

Heat oil in a heavy, medium skillet over medium-high heat. Add mushrooms, salt, and pepper and sauté about 5 minutes or until tender. Add shallot and sauté about 30 seconds.

Just before serving, reheat mushrooms, add peas, sprinkle with salt and pepper, and sauté over medium heat until heated through.

Makes 2 to 4 side-dish servings

SUGAR-SNAP PEA, CARROT, AND BLACK MUSHROOM SALAD

Hong Kong impressed me as a center for creative Chinese cooking where new ingredients and techniques are incorporated into traditional recipes. This beautiful, easy-to-make salad is typical of this style, combining dried Chinese mushrooms, carrots, and sugar-snap peas. The tasty dressing is flavored with hoisin sauce and a touch of sesame oil.

8 large dried Chinese black
    mushrooms
2 large carrots (about 8 ounces), peeled
Salt and freshly ground pepper
8 ounces sugar-snap peas, rinsed,
    strings and ends removed

2 teaspoons soy sauce
2 teaspoons hoisin sauce
2 teaspoons rice vinegar
2 teaspoons vegetable oil
½ teaspoon Oriental sesame oil

Rinse mushrooms. Soak them in hot water to cover for 30 minutes or until soft. Remove mushrooms and rinse them. Cut off stems and discard; halve caps.

Cut carrots into chunks of about same length as sugar-snap peas. Cut each chunk in lengthwise slices about ¼ inch thick. Cut any wide slices in half lengthwise to form sticks.

In a medium saucepan, combine carrot sticks with black mushrooms. Add a pinch of salt and water to cover. Bring to a boil, cover, and simmer 5 minutes or until just tender; drain well.

Add sugar-snap peas to a medium saucepan of boiling salted water and boil uncovered over high heat for 3 minutes or until crisp-tender. Drain in a colander, rinse with cold water, and drain well.

Whisk soy sauce, hoisin sauce, and vinegar until combined. Whisk in vegetable and sesame oils. Add salt and pepper to taste. Toss dressing with carrots and mushrooms. Add sugar-snap peas just before serving. Taste and adjust seasoning.

Makes 4 appetizer servings

23
Peppers

I n late summer our local farmers' market is a pepper lover's heaven. There is an incredible variety of these kitchen gems, both hot and sweet. Besides the familiar sweet red and green bell peppers, there are slightly sweeter fresh, red heart-shaped pimientos and long, pale green Hungarian peppers. Attracting the most attention are the small, tapered, bright red "lipstick" peppers, touted as the sweetest.

Plenty of chilies of many types and colors are out in force—round, red-hot cherry peppers, yellow chilies, small serrano chilies, and larger red and green jalapeños. Sellers offer samples, and adventurous shoppers taste the hot chilies raw. The slim, tiny Thai hot peppers remind me of what a friend from Bangkok told me: The Thai way of saying "good things come in small packages" is "the smaller the pepper, the hotter the taste." There are mild chilies too—long, pointed, light green Anaheim chilies, also known as California chilies or sometimes just "green chilies," and dark green pasilla chilies.

This bounty of peppers is not limited to farmers' markets. Supermarkets are featuring more types of peppers and chilies than ever. There are orange, purple, yellow, and even chocolate bell peppers. No, they don't taste a bit like chocolate; their skin is a chocolate-brown color and inside they're the familiar green bell pepper.

A tasty and easy way to cook peppers and chilies of all types is to roast, broil, or grill them. The first time I saw this done was when I lived in Jerusalem. I was visiting my neighbor and was surprised to see her placing a red pepper on the burner of her stove. She showed me how she roasted the pepper over the burner's flame until its skin turned black, and after a few minutes she peeled the skin off easily. The pepper's flesh was bright red and tender, and it had a wonderful aroma and a more intense flavor than when raw. It was a fascinating trick that is frequently used in the Middle East. A friend from Mexico told me the technique is popular there too.

After experimenting with this method I found that, for even cooking, it's easier to use the broiler, or the grill if you happen to be barbecuing. Whichever method you use, you need to turn the pepper frequently with tongs. Once the pepper's skin has blackened, the pepper is put in a bowl and covered or placed in a closed bag, so the steam can force the skin away from the flesh.

Whether hot or sweet, grilled peppers are treasures in the kitchen, adding flavor, color, and a fresh touch to food. Cut grilled bell peppers in wide strips, sprinkle them with olive oil and lemon juice, garnish them with olives, and you have a fine appetizer in the Mediterranean style. Mix diced grilled sweet peppers or chilies with cooked rice or pasta, or add them to vinaigrette, for spooning over grilled chicken breasts or fish fillets. Or use grilled red or green peppers in salads of all types; they'll give even a standard chicken or tuna salad a lively new look.

Green peppers seem to have been ignored lately in favor of their more colorful relatives. It's true that the sweetness of red, yellow, and orange bell peppers makes them the first choice for serving raw or plainly grilled. Yet there are many ways to turn economical green peppers into delectable side dishes and appetizers. One of the best is pepper stews, which are popular in many European and Mediterranean countries.

Wonderful green pepper stews have been developed in Hungary, Morocco, and the Basque regions of France and Spain. Slow cooking gives the green peppers an enticing rich taste and a tender texture that makes them appeal even to people who do not enjoy eating raw green peppers.

In these stews the peppers cook with tomatoes, which provide moisture, an attractive color, and a tangy-sweet flavor that complements the peppers. The Hungarian Pepper Stew (page 282), or *lecso*, also contains sautéed onions; the Moroccan stew, which can be used as a dip, as on page 321, is accented with garlic; and the Basque stew (page 283)—*pipérade* or *piperrada*—includes both.

Moroccan pepper stew tends to be the hottest, with fresh hot peppers added with a liberal hand. But Hungarian and Basque stews might be highly seasoned too—*pipérade* with dried hot peppers or pepper flakes, and *lecso* with hot paprika. A sister-in-law of mine of Moroccan origin often makes her pepper stew without hot peppers so it will appeal to the whole family, including the children.

Pepper stews are delicious meatless, but they can be enhanced by smoked meats. Classic recipes for Hungarian *lecso* call for cooking the peppers with bacon and lard, while Basque *pipérade* might include Bayonne ham.

Pepper stews are simple to make and have a multitude of uses. All make a light, tasty appetizer or salad when served cold or at room temperature with fresh bread or toast. Hot or cold, pepper stews are fine accompaniments for meats and fish, and can play a double role as vegetable and sauce.

Another time-honored use of pepper stews is as a cooking base, especially for putting together quick meals. All these stews are loved as a flavoring for scrambled eggs. Moroccan pepper stew might have eggs poached in it, while *pipérade* often becomes a filling for omelets. In Hungary, sliced sausages are cooked in *lecso* for a hearty, satisfying supper.

So central are these pepper stews to Hungarian and Basque cooking that they are available canned, for use when peppers are not in season. Throughout the year the stews are used as a flavorful base to cook with chicken or meat, or to add zip to rice or potatoes.

Use pepper stews as terrific new toppings for pizza or as flavorful sauces for pasta. In fact, these pepper stews can replace tomato sauce in many of its traditional roles, for a peppery change of pace.

Stuffed peppers are another favorite way to prepare the vegetable in European, Balkan, Mediterranean, Middle Eastern, and Latin American countries. Stuffings can be made of rice and vegetables, as in Stuffed Peppers with Rice, Pine Nuts, and Currants (page 284), a specialty of Turkey; or can be based on meat, bread crumbs, bulgur wheat, or corn.

Mild or medium-hot chilies can also be stuffed, but the most common use for fresh and dried chilies is to flavor salsas, such as Chipotle Chili Salsa (page 389) and Mexican Fresh Tomato Salsa (page 390). Chilies can form the main body of salsas and sauces, such as Green Zehug (page 392) from Yemen, the North African hot sauce known as Harissa (page 393), and Indian fresh chutneys.

Peppers and fresh and dried chilies are popular additions to meat and vegetable stews in Africa, the Caribbean, and South America, and to Indian, Thai, and Indonesian curries. In many of these countries sweet and hot peppers provide a quick way to add flavor to sautés, such as Thai Vegetable Medley with Mint and Chilies (page 365).

In China bell peppers are used in stir-fried dishes. Chilies are used primarily in Sichuan and Hunan cuisines to flavor sauces as well as stir-fried dishes. Dried chilies are also used to make chili oil, a favorite Sichuan flavoring.

PEPPER BASICS

✗ **Season:** Peppers are available all year; the peak of the season is late summer, and at this time their price usually comes down.

✗ **Choosing:** Sweet and hot peppers should be firm, with smooth glossy skin and no soft areas.

✗ **Storing:** Keep bell peppers and chilies in plastic bags in the refrigerator. They will keep up to 1 week.

✗ **Serving Size:** Allow about 1 bell pepper per serving.

✗ **Nutrients:** Bell peppers and chilies are good sources of vitamins C and B_6. Red peppers are also a good source of vitamin A. One medium-size raw bell pepper has 20 to 35 calories.

✗ **Basic Preparation:** Rinse peppers. Remove stem, core, and seeds. You can cut around the core and usually it will come out in one piece with the seeds. The seeds and membranes of chilies make them even hotter. Remove them if you wish, or leave some in for a hotter effect.

Handling Hot Peppers

Be careful when handling hot chilies. Wear gloves if your skin is sensitive. Wash the knife or other utensils used and the cutting board with hot soapy water after cutting chilies. If you didn't wear gloves, be sure to wash your hands thoroughly with soap and warm water after handling chilies. Do not touch your eyes or any part of your face when your hands have just touched chilies.

Grilling Peppers

Bell peppers: Put peppers on a broiler rack about 4 inches from heat. Broil peppers turning every 4 or 5 minutes with tongs, until pepper skin is blistered and charred, 15 to 20 minutes. Transfer to a bowl and cover tightly, or put in a bag and close bag. Let stand 10 minutes. Peel using a paring knife. Discard top, seeds, and ribs. Be careful; there may be hot liquid inside pepper. Drain well and pat dry.

Anaheim chilies (long, mild green chilies) and poblano chilies: Put broiler rack 2 inches from heat. Roast chilies, turning often, until skin is blackened on all sides, about 7 to 10 minutes. Continue as for bell peppers.

Jalapeño peppers: Roast as for mild chilies, for a total of about 5 minutes.

SAUTÉED TRICOLOR PEPPERS WITH HERBS

One of the most delightful and easiest ways to enjoy peppers of any color is to sauté them briefly in olive oil and add a sprinkling of aromatic fresh basil or thyme. This Mediterranean-style dish is good with everything, from white or brown rice to baked eggs to grilled steak.

2 red bell peppers
1 green bell pepper
1 yellow bell pepper
2 to 3 tablespoons olive oil

Salt and freshly ground pepper
2 to 4 tablespoons slivered fresh basil,
  or 1½ teaspoons dried thyme,
  crumbled

Halve peppers lengthwise, core, and remove ribs. Cut into strips ¼ inch thick.

Heat oil in a large skillet over medium-low heat. Add peppers, salt, and pepper and cook, stirring often, until tender but not brown, about 10 minutes. Taste and adjust seasoning. (*Peppers can be kept, covered, 1 day in refrigerator.*) Add basil or thyme. Serve hot, warm, or at room temperature.

Makes 4 side-dish servings or 2 or 3 main-course servings with rice

HUNGARIAN PEPPER STEW

The savory stew called lecso *is traditionally made with pale green peppers, sometimes called frying peppers or Hungarian peppers. Although they cook a little faster than bell peppers, I find that green bell peppers give an equally delicious result. The stew can be served with rice or pasta, or makes a tasty side dish for poultry, meat, or fish. For a quick Hungarian-style supper, either serve the stew with potatoes, stir in eggs, and scramble them; or heat slices of Polish kielbasa sausage in the stew and serve it with crusty bread.*

2 pounds green bell or Hungarian
   peppers
3 to 4 tablespoons vegetable oil
2 medium onions, halved and sliced
   thin
4 teaspoons paprika

1½ pounds ripe tomatoes, peeled,
   seeded, and diced
Salt and freshly ground pepper
Pinch of hot paprika or cayenne
   (optional)

Core the peppers and cut into lengthwise strips about ½ inch wide and 2 to 3 inches long.

Heat oil in a large sauté pan or skillet. Add onions and sauté over medium-low heat for 8 minutes or until beginning to turn golden. Add peppers and sauté, stirring occasionally, 10 minutes for Hungarian peppers or 15 minutes for bell peppers. Add paprika and sauté 1 minute, stirring.

Add tomatoes, salt, and pepper. Cover and simmer, stirring occasionally, for 25 to 30 minutes or until peppers are tender and mixture is thick. If there is too much liquid in the pan, uncover and boil mixture 1 or 2 minutes, stirring often. Taste and adjust seasoning, adding hot paprika if desired. (*Stew can be kept, covered, 2 days in refrigerator.*)

Makes 4 main-course servings with rice or 6 side-dish servings

VARIATION: **Noodles with Lecso and Chicken**

Cook 8 ounces wide egg noodles and drain. Toss with *lecso* and 1½ cups strips of cooked chicken or turkey and season to taste with salt, pepper, and hot paprika. Serve sprinkled with chopped green onions.

BASQUE PEPPER STEW

This is an easy version of pipérade *or* piperrada, *the garlic-accented pepper-tomato mixture from the Basque region of southern France and northern Spain. More elaborate renditions call for roasting and peeling the peppers before sautéing them; if you happen to have peeled grilled peppers (page 281), you can cook them in the* pipérade *for a slightly smoky flavor. This stew makes a delicious accompaniment for eggs, a side dish for grilled or broiled chicken or lamb, or a sauce with pasta.* Pipérade *is welcome in both rustic and elegant settings; in my latest trip to Paris I found it in* tarte pipérade *in the city's most celebrated food emporium, Fauchon.*

3 to 4 tablespoons vegetable oil
2 large onions, chopped
4 to 6 large green or red bell peppers (about 1½ to 2 pounds), cored and diced small (¼- to ½-inch dice)
4 large garlic cloves, chopped

3 pounds ripe tomatoes, peeled, seeded, and chopped; or 3 28-ounce cans plum tomatoes, drained and chopped
½ teaspoon dried hot red pepper flakes, or to taste
Salt and freshly ground pepper

Heat oil in a large, wide casserole over low heat. Add onions and cook, stirring often, about 5 minutes or until soft but not brown. Add peppers and garlic and cook, stirring often, about 10 minutes or until peppers soften.

Add tomatoes, pepper flakes, and a pinch of salt and pepper. Cook uncovered over medium heat, stirring often, about 30 to 40 minutes or until stew is thick. Taste and adjust seasoning.

Makes 4 to 6 side-dish servings

STUFFED PEPPERS WITH RICE, PINE NUTS, AND CURRANTS

Rice with pine nuts and dried fruit is loved in the Middle East and North Africa for weddings and other special occasions. The combination is also a favorite stuffing for vegetables, as in this recipe.

In traditional versions of this Turkish recipe a very generous amount of oil is used, and the dish is called ''stuffed peppers in oil.'' This is a lighter and easier rendition, with the oil amount considerably reduced, yet it is still rich in flavor. The stuffing can also be baked in eggplants.

Choose peppers that can stand up easily; these are baked upright. SEE PHOTOGRAPH.

Stuffing

5 tablespoons olive oil, preferably
    extra-virgin
3 medium onions, finely chopped
¾ cup long-grain white rice
¼ cup pine nuts
2 tablespoons currants or raisins

6 or 7 fairly small red, green, or yellow
    bell peppers (total weight about
    2¼ to 2½ pounds)

2 fresh plum tomatoes, chopped
2 teaspoons dried mint
¼ teaspoon ground allspice
½ teaspoon sugar
Salt and freshly ground pepper
1¼ cups water

Lemon wedges, for serving (optional)

Stuffing: Heat 3 tablespoons oil in a sauté pan, add onions, and sauté over medium heat for 10 minutes. Add rice and pine nuts, and stir 5 minutes over low heat. Add currants or raisins, tomatoes, mint, allspice, sugar, salt, and pepper; cook 2 minutes. Add water and bring to a boil. Cover and cook over low heat about 12 minutes or until liquid is absorbed. Taste and adjust seasoning; rice will not be cooked yet.

Preheat the oven to 350°F. Cut a slice off stem end of peppers. Reserve slice, leaving stem on; remove core and seeds from inside pepper. Spoon stuffing into peppers and cover with reserved slices. Stand them in a baking dish in which they just fit. Add 1½ cups hot water to dish. Sprinkle peppers with remaining oil. Cover and bake about 1 hour or until peppers are tender. Serve hot or cold, with lemon wedges.

Makes 6 or 7 main-course servings

ARMENIAN PEPPER, PARSLEY, AND WHEAT SALAD

This is a colorful salad I enjoyed at the Armenian Cultural Festival in Los Angeles. It is a cousin of tabbouleh, *the Lebanese bulgur wheat and parsley salad, but this Armenian rendition is spicier and includes both cooked and raw vegetables—sautéed peppers and onions, and plenty of fresh green onions and parsley. The Lebanese version has only raw vegetables, usually cucumbers and tomatoes.*

If you can find sumac, a purple spice available in Middle Eastern specialty shops and by mail order (see page 437), use it here; it is a traditional addition to this recipe and imparts a wonderful tangy flavor.

For a lovely summer menu, I like to serve this salad with cold salmon and with Sri Lankan Tomato and Watercress salad with Cucumber-Yogurt Dressing (page 322); for an everyday menu, it makes a fine vegetarian main course on its own, accompanied by plain yogurt.

2 cups boiling water
1 cup bulgur wheat, fine or medium
5 to 6 tablespoons extra-virgin olive oil
1 medium onion, chopped
1 red bell pepper, finely diced (about ⅜-inch dice)
1 green bell pepper, finely diced
1 tablespoon tomato paste
¼ cup strained fresh lemon juice, or more to taste

Salt and freshly ground pepper
½ teaspoon paprika
Cayenne pepper to taste
½ teaspoon crushed sumac (optional)
1½ cups finely chopped fresh parsley
½ to ⅔ cup thinly sliced green onions (3 green onions)
Lettuce leaves (optional)
Tomato wedges (optional)

Pour boiling water over bulgur wheat in a large bowl, and soak it until it is completely cool and tender, 45 to 60 minutes; stir a few times. Transfer wheat to a colander and drain off excess water. Gently squeeze wheat dry and transfer to a large bowl.

Heat 3 tablespoons oil in a large skillet. Add chopped onion and diced bell peppers, and sauté over medium heat, stirring often, about 10 minutes or until tender but not brown.

Mix tomato paste with 2 tablespoons oil, lemon juice, salt, pepper, paprika, cayenne pepper, and sumac. Add to wheat. Fold in sautéed vegetables with their oil, parsley, and green onions. Taste and adjust seasoning; add more lemon juice or oil if desired. Serve at room temperature. If desired, spoon onto a platter lined with lettuce leaves and garnish with tomato wedges.

Makes 5 or 6 main-course servings

ROASTED PEPPER SALAD WITH CAPER DRESSING

This simple salad is a favorite in many Mediterranean countries and can be made with red, green, or orange bell peppers or any combination of these. In Tunisia the peppers are sometimes garnished with tuna in olive oil, to make a light main course. In Algeria they might be embellished with oil-cured black olives instead of the capers. In some homes the pepper pieces are alternated on the platter with ripe tomato slices.

2 green bell peppers, roasted and
    peeled (page 281)
2 red or orange bell peppers, roasted
    and peeled (page 281)
2 teaspoons lemon juice or vinegar

2 tablespoons extra-virgin olive oil
Salt and freshly ground pepper
2 tablespoons chopped green onion or
    fresh parsley
2 teaspoons capers, rinsed and drained

Cut each pepper into 4 to 6 pieces lengthwise, each about ¾ to 1 inch wide. Halve pieces if pepper is long. Arrange peppers on a platter, pieces radiating outward like spokes of a wheel.

    Combine vinegar, oil, salt, and pepper in a small bowl. Whisk to combine. Spoon over peppers. Sprinkle with green onion and capers. Serve at room temperature.

Makes 4 to 6 appetizer servings

VINEGAR-SCENTED PEPPERS

For this Algerian recipe, the peppers are usually fried whole and peeled, but to make the salad lighter and easier, I prefer to broil them. The peppers are then heated briefly with a little olive oil and vinegar, which act as a light, tangy dressing.

2 bell peppers, 1 red and 1 green,
    roasted and peeled (page 281)
1 tablespoon extra-virgin olive oil

1 tablespoon distilled white vinegar
Salt and freshly ground pepper

Cut roasted peeled peppers in quarters, discarding core and seeds. Heat oil in a medium sauté pan over low heat. Add peppers and cook gently 1 minute per side. Add vinegar, sprinkle peppers with salt and pepper, and cook 1 more minute per side. Transfer mixture to a plate and cool. (*Peppers can be kept, covered, 2 days in refrigerator.*) Serve at room temperature.

Makes 2 or 3 appetizer or side-dish servings

PEPPER AND GOAT CHEESE TARTLETS

For this festive appetizer, the pepper-tomato stew is topped with cubes of creamy goat cheese to make a luscious filling for individual pastry shells.

Tartlet Shells (page 412)
About ¾ cup Basque Pepper Stew
   (page 283)
3 ounces creamy goat cheese, such as
   Montrachet

1½ teaspoons fresh thyme leaves, or ½
   teaspoon dried, crumbled
1 large egg
¼ cup heavy cream
Salt and freshly ground pepper

Position rack in lower third of oven and preheat to 400°F. Prepare tartlet shells. Cook stew until thick and liquid has evaporated. If goat cheese has a dark rind, remove it. Cut cheese into ¼-inch dice.

   Set tartlets on a baking sheet. Spoon 1 tablespoon pepper mixture into each tartlet pan. Spread smooth. Put 4 cheese cubes in center. Sprinkle with a few thyme leaves.

   Whisk egg with cream and salt and pepper to taste until blended. Ladle 1½ to 2 teaspoons egg and cream mixture over pepper mixture, using enough to just cover it without running over side of tartlet.

   Bake 15 minutes. Reduce oven temperature to 350°F. and bake about 18 minutes longer, or until filling sets and puffs and pastry is golden brown. Serve warm or at room temperature. (*The tartlets can be kept, covered, up to 1 day in refrigerator. Warm them in a 300°F. oven before serving.*)

Makes 12 small tartlets

NOTE: For small hors d'oeuvre, the pastry and filling can be baked in 2-inch tartlet pans; for a more substantial first course, large tartlet pans of 4 inches in diameter can be used.

POBLANO CHILI STRIPS WITH ONIONS

Roasted chili strips are a popular accompaniment for a variety of foods in Mexico and the American southwest and are known as ''rajas.'' Dark green, heart-shaped poblano chilies, which are mild to medium-hot, are the favorite chili for making these. In fact, they are the most widely used chilies in Mexico. In California they are sometimes labeled pasilla chilies.

The roasted peeled chili strips are sautéed with browned onions and sometimes with garlic. Often the mixture is finished with cream or Monterey Jack cheese but for a lighter dish, tomatoes or chicken broth are added instead. Sometimes other vegetables, especially corn kernels or diced squash, are cooked with the mixture.

If poblano chilies are not available, you can make this dish with Anaheim or mild, long green chilies, or even with bell peppers. Serve this chili sauté as a peppery-hot accompaniment for eggs, steak, rice, or beans. Because it's hot, most people will prefer to eat only a small amount; it's a good idea to provide another vegetable dish for the meal.

4 fresh poblano chilies
2 tablespoons vegetable oil
1 medium onion, chopped
1 large garlic clove, chopped
3 ripe fresh or canned plum tomatoes,
    peeled, seeded, and diced

⅓ cup chicken or vegetable broth
½ teaspoon dried oregano
Salt to taste

Roast and peel the chilies (page 281). Cut them into thin strips (about ¼ inch thick).

Heat oil in a skillet. Add onion and sauté over medium heat about 10 minutes or until beginning to brown. Add chilies and garlic and sauté about 2 minutes. Add tomatoes, broth, oregano, and salt, and cook over medium heat about 3 to 5 minutes or until mixture thickens to taste. Taste and adjust salt amount. Serve hot.

Makes 4 to 6 servings

GRILLED JALAPEÑO PEPPERS

I had these peppers recently at a party given by Moroccan friends. I mistook them for grilled green peppers and they literally took my breath away! They do make a zesty addition to a buffet, as a hot relish to accompany relatively bland dishes like potato or rice salad. But they do need little flags warning guests that they are hot!

4 jalapeño peppers
2 to 3 teaspoons extra-virgin olive oil

Salt to taste

See note on handling hot chilies (page 280).

Put peppers on a broiler rack about 2 inches from heat. Broil peppers, turning every minute with tongs, until pepper skin is blistered and charred, about 4 or 5 minutes total. Transfer to a bowl and cover, or put in a bag and close bag. Let stand 10 minutes. Peel using paring knife. Discard top, seeds, and ribs. Be careful; there may be hot liquid inside pepper. Drain well and pat dry.

Quarter chilies lengthwise to form strips. Transfer to a platter. Sprinkle lightly with oil and salt.

Makes 4 condiment servings

24

Potatoes

otatoes are America's favorite vegetable. Most of the rest of the world loves them too. It's hard to imagine the cooking of Ireland, Russia, or for that matter, France, without the potato.

We are so fond of potatoes that it seems odd to us that the Europeans had to be persuaded to eat them. Native to Peru, potatoes were discovered by Spanish explorers and brought back to Europe. At first they were admired as an ornamental plant, but people would not eat them because they considered them poisonous. An eighteenth-century agronomist in France named Antoine Parmentier resorted to a trick to convince his countrymen to eat potatoes. He had potatoes planted in the king's garden and had guards stand outside making sure nobody would steal them. People realized, of course, that if potatoes were worth guarding, they must be good. Soon chefs began to create all sorts of potato dishes, many of them named for Parmentier, like potato soup called *potage parmentier*. The French are grateful to him to this day; a recent French cookbook devoted to the potato is called *Merci, Monsieur Parmentier*.

291

Potatoes can be baked, boiled, steamed, and stewed. One of the world's most universal dishes is French fries. In the Middle East, potatoes are stuffed and made into cakes. Cooks in northern and southern Africa add potatoes to aromatic stews of meats and vegetables. Potatoes are a typical filling for the Indian pastries known as *samosas*, and the main element of *latkes* for the Jewish holiday of Hanukkah. And how would we celebrate the Fourth of July without potato salad?

For many people mashed potatoes are the ultimate comfort food. When a friend of mine needs cheering up, she makes a big bowl of mashed potatoes just for herself. Most people appreciate the soothing quality of mashed potatoes, but not everyone realizes how simple they are to prepare.

With homey mashed potatoes now holding a place of honor on fine restaurant menus and accompanying luxurious entrees like scallops, lobster, and squab, some chefs make them sound like a big production. In fact nothing could be easier. You simply cook the potatoes until tender, drain them, mash them while they are still hot, and beat in milk and a little butter.

Recipes from celebrity chefs, whether French or American, often require so much butter that few people would want to make mashed potatoes at home. Yet the great chef I studied with in Paris proved to me that fabulous, silky-smooth potato puree can be made with only a modest pat of butter, a generous amount of milk, and a touch of freshly grated nutmeg. Even when I use low-fat milk and only about a teaspoon of butter per person, the mashed potatoes are still excellent.

Not all mashed potatoes are soft, creamy, and delicate. There is another basic type that is hearty and robust. The potatoes are mashed coarsely and are fairly stiff. They are moistened with only a small amount of liquid, which might be the potato cooking liquid or chicken stock instead of milk. Butter is not necessarily added. In the Périgord region of central France, the potatoes might be enhanced with chicken roasting juices and flavored with chopped shallots. Spicy Calabrian mashed potatoes from southern Italy gain their zest from hot and sweet peppers and garlic. Onions sautéed in oil flavor an Israeli version. In India the potatoes might be spiced with chilies.

At La Varenne Cooking School in Paris we always mashed our potatoes restaurant style, by pushing them through a large drum sieve. This took some effort, not to mention the labor of cleaning the sieve afterward. Pressing the potatoes through a ricer or a food mill is easier and produces a light fluffy puree. I don't like to use the food processor—it tends to make the potatoes gluey. Actually, I find the easiest tool for small quantities (eight servings or fewer) is the old-fashioned potato masher because you can mash the potatoes right in the saucepan. If you don't have a masher, you can crush the drained potatoes in the pot with a wooden spoon, the way our chef's wife did at home.

You can steam or bake the potatoes, but cutting them in pieces and cooking them in water is the quickest way. I peel the potatoes before I mash them, but to save time you can skip this step.

The starch of mature potatoes is needed for fluffy-textured mashed potatoes. Russets, or Idaho, potatoes are favorites for mashing as well as for baking. You can also make good mashed potatoes from large red- or white-skinned potatoes, which are also known as boiling or all-purpose potatoes.

Another delectable potato dish that is very simple to prepare is steamed new potatoes. Occasionally I come across really fresh small new potatoes, and they taste wonderful served plain. Potatoes are also delicious baked whole, sliced and baked in cream, broth, or a flavorful sauce, and, of course, as French fries.

Many people think of potatoes as fattening. But it's the butter and sour cream that are slathered on baked or boiled potatoes that can make them high in fat, not the potato itself. If you wish to serve boiled or baked potatoes with a low-calorie sauce, they are good with Turkish Yogurt-Garlic Sauce (page 380), a light sprinkling of Classic Vinaigrette (page 383), or South American style with Colombian Tomato-Onion Sauce (page 395).

Potato salads can also be light if you sprinkle them with oil and lemon juice dressing instead of mayonnaise. Much more mayonnaise than vinaigrette is needed to coat a given quantity of potatoes because of its thickness. Try a low-fat but satisfying Lebanese Potato Salad with Tomatoes and Mint (page 302), for example.

Another way to enjoy potatoes without adding fat is to make use of Yukon gold potatoes, which already taste buttery.

Purple or blue potatoes were recently introduced to this country and contribute a surprising color to potato salads and other potato recipes.

POTATO BASICS

✂ **Season:** Available year-round.

✂ **Choosing:** Select smooth-skinned, firm potatoes with no bruises, sprouts, or green spots.

✂ **Storing:** Potatoes keep for months in a storage cellar but in most home kitchens will keep 1 or 2 weeks. Store them in a cool, dark place. You can store them in a paper or burlap bag but not in a plastic bag. Do not store in the refrigerator.

✂ **Serving Size:** Allow about 6 ounces, or 1 medium or large potato per serving.

✂ **Nutrients:** Potatoes are a good source of potassium and contain vitamin C, B_3, B_6, and iron. One medium potato has 110 to 150 calories.

✂ **Basic Preparation:** Rinse potatoes with cold water and scrub gently with a vegetable brush. Cut out any sprouts or bruised or green areas.

POTATOES WITH PEANUT SAUCE AND CHEESE

This is a specialty of Peru, the birthplace of the potato. These potatoes are served with a flavorful, easy-to-make sauce of peanuts ground with milk and accented with chilies and raw onion. Often the sauce contains cream and a substantial amount of oil, but this leaner version still tastes plenty rich.

Ecuadorians also like potatoes with peanut sauce. They add ground roasted peanuts and sautéed green peppers to a sauce similar to Colombian Tomato-Onion Sauce (page 395).

⅓ cup roasted unsalted peanuts
⅓ cup plus 2 tablespoons nonfat or low-fat milk
Salt and freshly ground pepper
Pure chili powder or cayenne pepper to taste (optional)
1 teaspoon roasted jalapeño pepper (page 281) or canned diced roasted jalapeños
⅓ cup diced onion

1½ pounds medium-small white or red potatoes
⅓ cup finely grated munster cheese
1 large hard-boiled egg, diced, for garnish (optional)
3 tablespoons chopped fresh parsley, preferably Italian
8 pitted olives, halved, for garnish (optional)

Grind peanuts in a food processor. Add ⅓ cup milk, salt, pepper, jalapeños, and onion. Puree until quite smooth. Transfer to a bowl and stir in 2 tablespoons milk. Taste and adjust seasoning; add chili powder if desired. Sauce should be spicy.

Peel potatoes and cut in half. Put in a saucepan, cover with water, and cook until tender, about 35 minutes. Drain. Put potatoes with rounded side up on a platter and pour sauce over. Sprinkle potatoes with cheese, then with egg and parsley. Garnish with olives.

Makes 4 side-dish or 2 main-course servings

STEAMED NEW POTATOES WITH HERB-LEMON BUTTER

Even a small pat of this herb butter will add a wonderful flavor to steamed potatoes. But if you prefer a lighter topping, substitute Yogurt-Garlic sauce (page 380), Garlic-Herb Oil (page 390), or a sprinkling of Classic Vinaigrette (page 383). In Europe steamed potatoes are traditional partners for poached fish.

Potatoes may be steamed peeled or unpeeled, but be sure to cook them until fully tender, not crisp-tender.

1½ pounds new potatoes, scrubbed	2 to 3 tablespoons Herb-Lemon Butter
Salt and freshly ground pepper	(page 391), at room temperature

Peel potatoes if desired. Bring at least 1 inch of water to a boil in base of steamer. Boiling water should not reach holes in top part of steamer.

Set potatoes in steamer top and sprinkle with salt. Cover tightly and steam over high heat for about 20 minutes or until tender when pierced with a sharp knife. Remove potatoes, drain briefly on paper towels, and transfer to a serving bowl.

Add herb butter in small spoonfuls and toss lightly with potatoes. Serve hot.

Makes 4 side-dish servings

CALABRIAN MASHED POTATOES WITH PEPPERS

In contrast to smooth, creamy American-style mashed potatoes, these spicy mashed potatoes from southern Italy are robust. They gain their zest from hot and sweet peppers and from garlic. Serve the potatoes with chicken, turkey, sausages, or grilled fish. Or serve them on their own, accompanied by a green salad and by yogurt, cottage cheese, or a warm hard-boiled egg.

1 pound large potatoes, scrubbed
Salt and freshly ground pepper
1 red or green bell pepper, or ½ of
    each
1 dried hot red pepper, halved
    crosswise
2 tablespoons olive oil

1 medium garlic clove, minced
1 tablespoon chopped fresh parsley
    (optional)
2 to 3 tablespoons grated pecorino or
    Parmesan cheese, plus more for
    serving separately (optional)

Cut each potato into 2 or 3 pieces. Put in a non-corrosive saucepan and add enough water to just cover and a pinch of salt. Cover, bring to a boil, and simmer over medium heat for about 20 minutes or until potatoes are very tender.

Meanwhile, cut peppers into strips and halve crosswise. Heat oil in a skillet, add hot and sweet peppers, and sauté for 7 minutes over medium heat, stirring often. Reduce heat and sauté for 2 minutes or until cooked to taste. Add garlic and sauté over low heat for 15 to 20 seconds. Transfer mixture, including oil, to a bowl. Discard hot pepper pieces.

Drain potatoes thoroughly, reserving liquid. Peel potatoes if you like. Mash them in a saucepan, leaving some pieces. Beat in 2 or 3 tablespoons potato liquid. Reserve a few pepper strips for garnish and stir remaining pepper-garlic mixture into potatoes. Add parsley and cheese if desired, and freshly ground pepper. Taste and adjust seasoning. Garnish with pepper strips and serve, if you like, with more cheese.

Makes 2 or 3 side-dish servings

IRISH MASHED POTATOES
WITH GREEN ONIONS

Traditional versions of this recipe call for beating generous amounts of butter into the potatoes or topping each serving with a pat of butter. I find that it tastes very good without butter, even when made with nonfat milk.

1 pound boiling potatoes, unpeeled
Salt and freshly ground pepper
About ¾ cup nonfat or low-fat milk

1 cup chopped green onions, both
white and green parts

Cut potatoes into 2 or 3 pieces each and cook in water with salt. Drain and peel. Return peeled cooked potatoes to saucepan and mash with a potato masher.

In a small saucepan, bring ½ cup milk to a simmer. Add chopped green onions and simmer uncovered over medium heat, stirring often, for 3 or 4 minutes.

Put pan of mashed potatoes over low heat. Gradually stir in green onions in their milk. Gradually beat in enough milk to give a soft, creamy texture, about ¼ cup more. Taste and adjust seasoning. Serve hot.

Makes 2 side-dish servings

CREAMY MASHED POTATOES

Mashed potatoes prepared the French way are light, smooth, soft, and rich tasting. Chefs usually heat the milk in a separate saucepan, but you can skip this step if you add the milk gradually to the hot puree over low heat.

2 pounds Russet or white boiling potatoes, scrubbed	**2 to 4 tablespoons (¼ –½ stick) butter**
	About ¾ cup milk
Salt and white pepper	**Freshly grated nutmeg**

Cut each potato into 2 or 3 pieces. Put in a non-corrosive saucepan and add enough water to just cover and a pinch of salt. Cover, bring to a boil, and simmer over medium heat about 20 minutes or until potatoes are very tender. Drain thoroughly and peel. Mash with a potato masher in saucepan; or puree potatoes in a food mill or potato ricer and return to saucepan.

Add butter and a little milk to the potatoes and season with salt, pepper, and nutmeg. Heat over low heat, stirring vigorously with a wooden spoon, until puree is light and smooth. Add remaining milk gradually, still stirring vigorously over low heat. The potatoes should be soft but not soupy; if mixture is too stiff, beat in a few tablespoons milk. Taste and add more salt, pepper, and nutmeg, if desired.

(*The mashed potatoes can be prepared 30 minutes ahead. To keep them hot, pour a few tablespoons cold milk over the top without stirring it in to prevent a skin from forming on surface; set saucepan of potatoes in a pan of hot water over low heat. Before serving, stir in milk.*) Serve hot.

Makes 6 side-dish servings

AUSTRIAN POTATO SOUP WITH CHIVES

Besides chocolate, one thing I really enjoyed eating in Austria was potatoes. They were of very good quality and were tasty even plain or simply prepared.

Austrians excel in making potato soup. There are many versions; some contain marjoram, others celery root or tomatoes, hearty ones have ground beef. Some soups are pureed; this one is creamy and chunky, with cubes of potato and carrot and a generous amount of chives.

2 tablespoons vegetable oil or butter
1 large onion, chopped
2 teaspoons paprika
3 pounds boiling potatoes, peeled and
    cut into ¾- to 1-inch dice
2 small carrots, peeled, halved
    lengthwise, and sliced

5 cups Chicken Stock (page 407), or
    stock mixed with water
½ cup sour cream, light or regular
Salt and freshly ground pepper
3 to 4 tablespoons finely sliced fresh
    chives

Heat the oil in a large saucepan. Add the onion and sauté over medium heat for 5 minutes or until softened. Add the paprika and sauté 1 minute. Add potatoes, carrots, and stock. Bring to a boil, cover, and simmer about 30 minutes or until vegetables are tender.

Stir sour cream in a bowl. Gradually stir 1 cup soup into the sour cream, then stir sour cream soup mixture gently into remaining soup. Heat gently; do not boil. Season to taste with salt and pepper. Serve hot, sprinkled with chives.

Makes 6 appetizer servings

POTATOES DAUPHINE

In the interest of eating low-fat meals, I rarely deep-fry my vegetables. However, these classic French potato puffs are so delicious that occasionally I indulge in them. They are made of mashed potatoes mixed with choux pastry dough—the pastry used for cream puffs—which makes them puff in the oil. These potatoes are traditionally served as accompaniments but I like them as an appetizer.

1½ pounds boiling potatoes
⅓ cup milk
6 tablespoons (¾ stick) butter
Salt and white pepper
Freshly grated nutmeg
½ cup plus 1 tablespoon all-purpose
   flour

½ cup water
¼ teaspoon salt
2 large eggs
At least 6 cups vegetable oil, for deep-
   frying

Read the Hints on Deep-Frying (page 15) before beginning.

Peel potatoes and cut each into 2 or 3 pieces. Put in a saucepan and add enough water to just cover and a pinch of salt. Cover, bring to a boil, and simmer over medium heat for 20 to 25 minutes, or until potatoes are very tender. Drain thoroughly. Puree the potatoes in a food mill and return to saucepan. Add milk and 2 tablespoons butter, and season with salt, pepper, and nutmeg to taste. Over low heat, stir vigorously with a wooden spoon until milk and butter are absorbed. Remove from heat and let cool.

Sift the flour onto a piece of wax paper. Heat the water, ¼ teaspoon salt, and remaining 4 tablespoons butter in a medium saucepan until butter melts. Raise heat to medium-high and bring to a boil. Remove from heat, add flour immediately, and stir quickly with a wooden spoon until mixture is smooth. Set pan over low heat and beat mixture for about 30 seconds. Remove and let cool for a few minutes. Add 1 egg and beat it thoroughly into mixture. Beat in second egg until absorbed. Add potato puree, then taste and adjust seasoning.

Preheat the oven to 300°F. Heat the oil in a deep-fryer or deep, heavy saucepan to about 370°F. Do not fill pan more than halfway with oil. If a thermometer is not available, test by putting a drop of potato mixture into oil; when oil is hot enough, it should bubble energetically.

Take a rounded teaspoonful of batter and use a second teaspoon to slide it gently into the oil, forming a rounded fritter. Do not crowd pan because fritters need room to puff. While frying, turn them over occasionally until they are golden brown on all sides. Remove to ovenproof trays lined with paper towels. Keep in oven with door slightly open while frying remaining fritters. Serve as soon as possible.

Makes 6 to 8 side-dish servings

LEBANESE POTATO SALAD WITH TOMATOES AND MINT

Some potato salads are bland, white, and heavy, but this one is refreshing and colorful. Fresh mint and green onions give it a lively flavor, and it needs only a small amount of zesty lemon juice and olive oil dressing.

2 pounds red potatoes, scrubbed but
    not peeled
Salt and freshly ground pepper
2 tablespoons strained fresh lemon
    juice
Cayenne pepper to taste

1 tablespoon water
2 to 3 tablespoons extra-virgin olive oil
¼ cup chopped fresh mint
⅓ cup chopped green onions
3 or 4 ripe plum tomatoes, cut in small
    dice

Put potatoes in a large saucepan, cover with water by about ½ inch, and add salt. Bring to a boil, cover, and simmer over low heat about 25 minutes, or until a knife can pierce center of largest potato easily and potato falls from knife when lifted.

Meanwhile, in a bowl large enough to contain potatoes, whisk lemon juice with a pinch of salt, pepper, cayenne pepper, and water. Add 2 tablespoons olive oil and whisk again.

Drain potatoes and leave just until cool enough to handle. Peel and cut in 1-inch dice, then add to bowl. Fold gently but thoroughly with dressing. Let cool.

Fold in mint and green onions. Taste and adjust seasoning; add another tablespoon oil if desired. Gently fold in tomatoes. Serve at room temperature.

Makes 4 side-dish servings

PÉRIGORD POTATO SALAD

Périgord in southwest France is best known for its black truffles, but potatoes, sometimes known as poor man's truffles, are also popular there, especially in salads seasoned with the region's delicious walnut oil.

2 tablespoons dry white wine
1 tablespoon mild white wine vinegar
   (5% acidity)
1 tablespoon vegetable or olive oil
Salt and freshly ground pepper
2 pounds red potatoes of uniform size,
   scrubbed but not peeled

2 tablespoons minced red onion
6 to 8 tablespoons Walnut Oil
   Vinaigrette (page 383)
2 tablespoons chopped fresh parsley,
   preferably Italian
2 tablespoons chopped fresh tarragon
   or chives, or 1 tablespoon each

Combine wine, vinegar, oil, salt, and pepper in small bowl and whisk until blended.

Put potatoes in a large saucepan, cover with water by about ½ inch, and add salt. Bring to a boil, cover, reduce heat to low, and simmer until tender enough so that a knife pierces center of largest potato easily and potato falls from knife when lifted, about 25 minutes. Do not overcook or potatoes will fall apart when cut.

Drain potatoes in a colander and peel while hot. Using a thin-bladed knife, halve potatoes lengthwise, put them cut side downward, halve again lengthwise, and quickly cut them in ⅜-inch crosswise slices; they will be of medium dice.

Put potatoes in a large bowl. Rewhisk wine mixture until blended and pour it over potatoes. Toss or fold gently to mix thoroughly, separating any potato pieces that are stuck together. Cool to room temperature. Fold in red onion and enough vinaigrette to moisten. (*Mixture can be prepared 1 day ahead, covered, and refrigerated.*)

Just before serving, fold in parsley and tarragon or chives. Taste and adjust seasoning. Serve salad at room temperature.

Makes 4 side-dish servings

POTATO SALAD WITH AVOCADO AND CILANTRO

South of the border flavors—cilantro, chili, and avocado—lend zest to this new potato salad. Use either mayonnaise or vinaigrette for a richer or lighter salad. Colorful Russian potato salad, in the variation, is flavored with dill and contains carrots, peas, and sometimes beets. For an elegant presentation, you can sprinkle it with diced pecans and chopped hard-boiled eggs.

2 tablespoons dry white wine
1 tablespoon mild white wine vinegar
    (5% acidity)
1 tablespoon vegetable or olive oil
Salt and freshly ground pepper
2 pounds red potatoes of uniform size,
    scrubbed but not peeled
2 tablespoons minced green onion
2 hot pickled chilies in vinegar, each 1
    to 1¼ inches long, or more to taste

3 tablespoons chopped cilantro (fresh
    coriander), or more to taste
1¼ cups mayonnaise or ½ cup Classic
    Vinaigrette (page 383)
1 ripe medium avocado, preferably
    Haas (7 ounces)
1 large ripe tomato (8 ounces), cut into
    ¾-inch dice

Combine wine, vinegar, oil, salt, and pepper in a small bowl and whisk until blended.

Put potatoes in a large saucepan, cover with water by about ½ inch, and add salt. Bring to boil, cover, reduce heat to low, and simmer until tender enough so that knife pierces center of largest potato easily and potato falls from knife when lifted, about 25 minutes. Do not overcook or potatoes will fall apart when cut.

Drain potatoes in a colander and peel while hot. Using a thin-bladed knife, halve the potatoes lengthwise, put them cut side downward, halve again lengthwise, and quickly cut them into ⅜-inch crosswise slices; they will be of medium dice.

Put potatoes in a large bowl. Rewhisk wine mixture until blended and pour it over potatoes. Toss or fold gently to mix thoroughly, separating any potato pieces that are stuck together. Fold in green onion. Cool to room temperature.

Drain chilies, pat dry, and remove seeds. Mince them as finely as possible. Stir minced chilies and 2 tablespoons of cilantro into the mayonnaise. Taste and add more chilies or cilantro if desired. Fold mayonnaise into salad. (*Mixture can be prepared 1 day ahead, covered, and refrigerated.*)

Just before serving, halve, pit, and peel the avocado. Cut one-fourth of it into thin crosswise slices and reserve for garnish. Cut rest of avocado into ½-inch dice. Fold avocado dice and tomato dice into salad. Taste and adjust seasoning. Transfer salad to a serving dish. Sprinkle with remaining cilantro and garnish with avocado slices. Serve salad at room temperature.

Makes 6 side-dish servings

VARIATION: **Russian Potato Salad**
  Omit chilies, cilantro, avocado, and tomato.
  Add 1½ cups diced cooked carrots, 1 cup cooked peas, and 2 tablespoons minced fresh parsley or dill. Just before serving, fold in 1⅓ cups diced cooked beets.

25

Sweet Potatoes

As I child I thought I didn't like sweet potatoes. Later I realized this might have been because they always appeared in casseroles topped with marshmallows. Sweet flavorings are not necessarily the best ones for sweet potatoes (unless you're making sweet potato pie). In many cases, tangy or spicy flavors are better choices.

Like potatoes, sweet potatoes are easy to bake whole. When you bake them, consider other toppings instead of butter. For example, they're good with Turkish Yogurt-Garlic Sauce (page 380) or Moroccan orange dressing (page 309). These tangy dressings complement the potato's sweetness.

Sweet potatoes are native to South America where they are widely used as side dishes and in soups, stews, and desserts. What is sold in our markets as yams is actually a moist variety of sweet potato, usually with sweet orange flesh. (True yams are very large starchy roots grown in tropical areas and are rarely available in the United States.) The drier sweet potatoes have yellow or cream-colored flesh. In most recipes these two types of sweet potatoes are interchangeable.

SWEET POTATO BASICS

✕ **Season:** Available year-round. Peak season is in fall and winter.

✕ **Choosing:** Choose firm, evenly shaped sweet potatoes.

✕ **Storing:** Sweet potatoes keep in a dry place at room temperature for 1 week; or in a cool, dark storage cellar for 1 or 2 months.

✕ **Serving Size:** Allow 1 medium or large sweet potato per person.

✕ **Nutrients:** Sweet potatoes are an excellent source of vitamin A and also contain vitamin C and B_6. One medium sweet potato has about 120 calories.

✕ **Basic Preparation:** Scrub sweet potatoes well. If you will be cutting them in pieces, peel them first.

Sweet potatoes are available in most parts of the world. Baking them whole or frying them in slices are the most popular ways to prepare them. Caribbean cooks make them into fritters and use them in desserts. In Africa sweet potatoes are added to stews of meat or poultry with vegetables. In India they are made into spiced purees, similar to Eggplant Bharta (page 190). Japanese restaurants use them as an element of vegetable tempura. Vietnamese cooks make them into nests and use them in soups and stews.

Sweet potatoes can be substituted for ordinary potatoes in many recipes and give good results. For example, I tried making my favorite potato pancakes using orange-fleshed sweet potatoes, and they came out even better than the classic dish. You can also make tasty potato salads from sweet potatoes, such as North African sweet potato salad with a tangy lemon juice dressing flavored with cumin and ginger.

BAKED SWEET POTATOES WITH ORANGE DRESSING

A light Moroccan-style citrus dressing makes a simple tasty seasoning for hot baked sweet potatoes.

3 pounds sweet potatoes, rinsed
2 tablespoons vegetable oil
3 to 4 tablespoons strained fresh
    orange juice

1 teaspoon grated orange rind
4 to 5 teaspoons strained fresh lemon
    juice
Salt and freshly ground pepper

Preheat the oven to 400°F. Put sweet potatoes in a foil-lined roasting pan or baking dish. Bake about 1 hour to 1 hour and 10 minutes, or until tender when tested with a fork.

Meanwhile, whisk oil with 3 tablespoons orange juice, grated orange rind, and 4 teaspoons lemon juice. Season to taste with salt and pepper. Whisk in remaining orange juice or lemon juice if desired.

Cut potatoes in half. Serve hot, spooning a little dressing over each half. Serve any remaining dressing separately.

Makes 4 side-dish servings

OVEN-FRIED SWEET POTATOES

Sweet potatoes are popular deep-fried in Brazil, Peru, and the Caribbean islands. This is a lighter alternative. These potatoes make a good accompaniment for grilled or roasted chicken, beef, or lamb.

¼ cup vegetable oil
2 pounds sweet potatoes, peeled and
    cut into sticks 2½ × ½ × ½ inch

½ teaspoon salt, or to taste
Freshly ground pepper

Preheat the oven to 325°F. Pour oil in a baking dish that can hold potatoes in 1 layer. Heat oil in oven for 5 minutes, then add the sweet potatoes, taking care not to splatter oil, and toss with slotted spatula to coat them with oil. Sprinkle them evenly with salt and toss again.

Bake potatoes uncovered, turning them over 2 or 3 times, about 1 hour or until tender. Raise heat to 400°F. Sprinkle potatoes with salt, toss, and bake 10 minutes. Sprinkle with pepper, toss, and serve.

Makes 4 side-dish servings

SWEET POTATO LATKES

This is a delicious new twist on potato pancakes, the favorite Hanukkah treat in Polish and Russian Jewish cooking. These pancakes need no toppings if served as an accompaniment, but for a separate course or a party dish, serve them with yogurt, sour cream, applesauce, or sugar.

You can make the pancakes ahead and reheat them on a cookie sheet in a 450°F. oven for about 5 minutes, but watch them carefully as their edges burn easily.

1½ pounds orange-fleshed sweet
   potatoes, peeled
1 medium onion
2 large eggs

¾ teaspoon salt
¼ teaspoon ground white pepper
5 tablespoons all-purpose flour
About ½ cup vegetable oil, for frying

Grate sweet potatoes and onion, using grating disc of a food processor or large holes of a grater. Transfer to a large bowl. Beat eggs with salt and pepper, and add to potato mixture. Add flour and mix well.

Heat ¼ cup oil in a heavy 10- to 12-inch skillet, preferably nonstick. Fill a ¼-cup measure with mixture, pressing to compact it, and turn it out in a mound into skillet. Quickly form 3 more mounds. Flatten each with back of a spoon so each cake is about 2½ to 3 inches in diameter, pressing to compact it. Fry over medium heat for 3 minutes; turn carefully with 2 slotted spatulas and fry second side about 2½ minutes or until golden brown and crisp. Drain on paper towels. Stir potato mixture before frying each new batch and add a little more oil to pan. Serve pancakes hot.

Makes about 4 side-dish servings

TANGY NORTH AFRICAN SWEET POTATO SALAD

You will see sweet potatoes in a new light after tasting them in a savory, light dressing flavored with saffron, ginger, and lemon juice. The sweet potatoes cook directly in the dressing. SEE PHOTOGRAPH.

1 pound orange-fleshed sweet potatoes
2 tablespoons vegetable oil
1 large onion, chopped
Salt
⅛ teaspoon saffron threads
½ teaspoon ground ginger
½ cup water
¼ teaspoon ground cumin

1 teaspoon paprika
6 pitted black olives, halved
2 tablespoons strained fresh lemon juice
2 tablespoons chopped cilantro (fresh coriander) or fresh parsley
Cayenne pepper

Peel sweet potatoes and cut into ¾-inch dice. Heat oil in a heavy, medium sauté pan, add onion, and sauté over medium-low heat for 5 minutes. Add salt, saffron, ginger, and water. Add sweet potatoes and bring to a boil. Cover and cook 10 minutes or until nearly tender. Add cumin, paprika, and olives. Simmer uncovered about 2 minutes or until most of liquid evaporates and potatoes are tender. Off the heat, stir in lemon juice and 1 tablespoon cilantro. Season to taste with salt and cayenne pepper. Serve at room temperature, sprinkled with remaining cilantro.

Makes 4 appetizer servings

26

Tomatoes

A friend of mine who is a very good cook recently told me she simmers her tomato sauces for three days.

I was amazed. After spending six years studying cooking in France, with frequent culinary study trips to Italy, I learned that freshness and brief cooking are the key features of fine tomato sauces. The chefs I worked with at La Varenne Cooking School in Paris proved that a luscious tomato sauce demands only ten or fifteen minutes of simmering. The short cooking retains the tomato's natural taste and bright color. And the cooking technique is foolproof.

Which tomatoes to use is easy—just pick the ripe ones. Those that are a bit too soft for salad are perfect for sauce. I prefer plum tomatoes, as their meaty texture produces a richer sauce. There is a trade-off, however. It takes longer to peel 2 pounds of small tomatoes than a few large ones.

Quick tomato sauce consists basically of cooked chopped tomatoes. They are first peeled and seeded so that the skin and seeds won't interfere with the sauce's texture. Still, cooks in a hurry who know their families don't mind the skins sometimes puree the whole tomatoes

313

in a food processor. Another shortcut, especially useful when ripe tomatoes are scarce, is to use canned ones. For every pound of ripe tomatoes, substitute a drained 28-ounce can of plum tomatoes.

The sauce is cooked over fairly high heat in a skillet or sauté pan rather than a saucepan. The idea is to evaporate the tomato juice as quickly as possible, so the sauce thickens and the flavor remains fresh.

Tomato sauce is convenient to prepare ahead as it keeps well and reheats easily. I often cook it in large quantities when tomatoes are at their peak and freeze it in small containers. Of course, the more you make, the longer the sauce takes to cook because there is more liquid to evaporate. Yet even 8 pounds of tomatoes require only about 45 minutes of simmering.

There is no end to the possible uses of this simple, low-calorie sauce. Its pure, robust flavor makes it a natural for pasta and rice and a wonderful topping for pizza. It's great with Mediterranean vegetables like sautéed eggplant and zucchini. In elegant restaurants a little fresh tomato sauce is spooned onto plates, and then grilled or sautéed fish, poultry, or meat is set on top.

Of course, there are many more good dishes to make out of tomatoes besides sauce, pizza, and pasta. Tomatoes contribute flavor, color, and moistness to numerous vegetable casseroles, from Provençal Ratatouille (page 372) to Napoli Zucchini Casserole (page 355) to Romanian Givetch (page 370). Salads made of ripe tomatoes, such as Moroccan Tomato Salad with Red Onions and Parsley (page 316), are one of the delights of summer. You can stuff tomatoes with lamb and rice in the Lebanese style (page 315) or cook them as delicious soups. Red and yellow cherry tomatoes and tiny pear tomatoes make beautiful garnishes.

Tomatoes are also available sun-dried, both dry packed and bottled in olive oil. The dry ones can be simmered in water or stock and make a tasty addition to sauces. Oil-packed tomatoes are ready-to-eat and can be added to salads, vegetable casseroles, and pasta and rice dishes or used for garnish.

Another common tomato product is tomato paste, which comes in cans or in tubes, and is used in sauces as a substitute for tomatoes or to impart a stronger tomato flavor or color when fresh tomatoes are too pale.

Mediterranean cooking is identified with the tomato, but in fact tomatoes, like potatoes, originated in the New World and their use in the Old World is relatively recent. Today they are used in almost all regions of the world. In North and South America tomatoes are loved in salads, sauces, and soups. Mexican cooks use tomatoes in fresh salsas as well as cooked sauces, often in combination with chilies. Tomatoes are a common ingredient in meat and vegetable stews and casseroles throughout the New World and in Africa, the Middle East, India, Indonesia, and the Philippines. Middle Eastern cooks also use tomatoes raw in salads, often mixed with cucumbers and onions, and Indian cooks use them in chutneys. Tomatoes are less popular in the Far East, but in China and Thailand they are occasionally used in stews.

Tomatillos look like small green tomatoes covered with a papery husk. They are available at Hispanic markets and some supermarkets. Tomatillos can be eaten raw but most often they are cooked briefly and made into green salsas.

TOMATO BASICS

✕ **Season:** Tomatoes are available all year but are at their peak in summer and early fall. Still, ripe tomatoes can be found during other seasons, either shipped from other areas of the United States, imported from other countries, or grown in hothouses.

✕ **Choosing:** Tomatoes should have smooth skins and should be plump, heavy, and aromatic. If they are not yet ripe, they should be firm but not rock-hard. You can buy them ripe and soft if you plan to use them immediately. Plum tomatoes are meaty and good for sauces and stews.

✕ **Storing:** Keep tomatoes unwrapped and unwashed at room temperature away from sunlight rather than in the refrigerator. If tomatoes are ripe, they will keep a day or two at room temperature. If you need to keep them longer, refrigerate them up to 4 days.

✕ **Serving Size:** Serve 1 medium tomato per person.

✕ **Nutrients:** Tomatoes contain vitamins A, C, and E. One large tomato has about 40 calories.

✕ **Basic Preparation:** Rinse tomatoes. For salads, cut them just before serving so they don't lose their juices.

To Peel and Seed Tomatoes

To peel, cut cores from tomatoes. Turn tomatoes over and slit skin in an *X*-shaped cut. Fill a large bowl with cold water. Put tomatoes in a saucepan of enough boiling water to cover them generously and boil 10 to 15 seconds or until the skins begin to pull away from flesh. Remove tomatoes with a slotted spoon and put them in the bowl of cold water. Leave for a few seconds. Remove tomatoes and pull off skins.

To seed, cut tomatoes in half horizontally. Hold each half over a bowl, cut side down, and squeeze to remove the seeds and juice. You can strain the juice and refrigerate it for drinking.

MOROCCAN TOMATO SALAD WITH RED ONIONS AND PARSLEY

Make the garlic-cumin dressing ahead if you like, but prepare the salad at the last moment so the tomatoes won't become watery. SEE PHOTOGRAPH.

1 large or 2 medium tomatoes (total ½ pound) cut in wedges
⅓ to ½ cup quarter-slices red onion, separated in slivers

Moroccan Garlic Dressing (page 381)
¼ cup chopped fresh parsley, preferably Italian

In a bowl, combine tomatoes and red onion slivers. Toss gently with dressing. Transfer to plate or platter and sprinkle with parsley.

Makes 3 side-dish servings

LEBANESE STUFFED TOMATOES

A luscious filling in the best eastern Mediterranean tradition, this is accented with pine nuts, garlic, cilantro, and allspice to turn these tomatoes into a festive entree.

½ cup long-grain rice
3 cups water
Salt
2 tablespoons plus 1 teaspoon olive oil
1 medium onion, finely chopped
½ pound lean ground lamb, beef, or
    chicken
2 tablespoons pine nuts (optional)

2 large garlic cloves, minced
4 tablespoons chopped cilantro (fresh
    coriander) or fresh parsley
¾ teaspoon salt
¾ teaspoon ground black pepper
½ teaspoon ground allspice
6 or 7 medium to large tomatoes (2¼
    to 2½ pounds), ripe but firm

Preheat the oven to 400°F. Boil the rice uncovered in boiling salted water for 10 minutes. Rinse with cold water and drain well. Transfer to a bowl.

Heat 2 tablespoons oil in a skillet, add onion, and cook over medium-low heat until soft but not brown, about 5 minutes. Add the lamb and pine nuts and sauté, stirring to crumble meat, about 5 minutes or until meat changes color. Add to rice. Stir in garlic, cilantro or parsley, salt, pepper, and allspice.

Cut off a slice from the bottom (smooth) end of each tomato, cutting about one-fourth of the tomato, reserve the slice as a "hat." Remove the pulp and seeds with spoon, then sprinkle the interior of and cut side of hats lightly with salt. (Removed pulp can be added to soups.)

Put tomato shells in an oiled baking dish. Fill with stuffing, mounding slightly, and cover with hats. Sprinkle with remaining oil. Bake uncovered for 30 to 40 minutes or until tomatoes are tender. Serve hot.

Makes 6 or 7 main-course servings

EASY STUFFED TOMATOES, ROMAN STYLE

This garlic-scented stuffed tomato with mint, rice, and olive oil is a traditional Roman specialty that I came to know by accident. My husband and I were in the Trastevere, an old section of Rome known for its restaurants and taverns. We were looking for a particular restaurant recommended by the Espresso Guida d'Italia when we were caught in a downpour. An Italian passerby suggested we instead try the nearby birreria, *or "beer house," that he said was the most popular eatery in the area. What interested us most was the great selection of vegetables that were served buffet style. We had the Italian tomato and bread salad called* panzanella, *peppery fava beans, stuffed eggplant with cheese, and stuffed yellow bell peppers. When we tasted these aromatic stuffed tomatoes made with the luscious, ripe tomatoes for which Italy is famous, we were glad we hadn't found the restaurant we had been looking for.*

These tomatoes are usually served on their own, but Turkish Yogurt-Garlic Sauce (page 380) makes a tasty accompaniment; double the amount of sauce so you'll have enough.

⅔ cup long-grain white rice

3 cups water

Salt

8 medium tomatoes (2½ pounds), ripe but firm

2 medium garlic cloves, minced

3 tablespoons chopped fresh mint

3 tablespoons olive oil

Salt and freshly ground pepper

1 tablespoon tomato paste diluted with ½ cup water

Mint sprigs, for garnish (optional)

Preheat the oven to 400°F. Boil the rice in a saucepan of boiling salted water for 10 minutes. Rinse with cold water and drain well.

Cut off a slice from the bottom (smooth) end of each tomato, cutting about one-fourth of the tomato; reserve slice as a "hat." Remove pulp and seeds with a spoon. Finely chop removed pulp; reserve. Sprinkle interior of tomatoes and cut side of hats lightly with salt.

Mix garlic with mint. Mix rice, garlic mixture, 2½ tablespoons oil, 4 tablespoons chopped tomato puree, and salt and pepper to taste. Mix well.

Put tomato shells in an oiled baking dish. Fill with stuffing, mounding slightly, and cover with hats. Pour diluted tomato paste around tomatoes; sprinkle them with remaining oil. Cover and bake 20 minutes. Uncover and bake, adding a few tablespoons water to pan if it becomes dry, for 10 to 20 more minutes or until tomatoes are tender. Serve hot or cold, garnished with mint sprigs.

Makes 8 side-dish or 4 main-course servings

LIGURIAN TOMATO, OLIVE, AND CAPER PIZZA

Pesto is the most famous recipe from the Italian Riviera province of Liguria, but cooks from this area have created other delectable dishes. Tomatoes and onion accented with garlic slivers, black olives, and capers make a tasty topping for this cheeseless, thick-crust pizza. This is a popular recipe in my all-day pizza workshop classes.

Thick Crust Pizza Dough (page 411)
7 tablespoons good-quality olive oil
½ small onion, cut into thin slices
¾ pound ripe tomatoes, peeled, seeded, and chopped
4 anchovy fillets, rinsed and chopped

1 teaspoon tomato paste (optional)
3 medium garlic cloves, cut into thin slivers
1 tablespoon capers, drained
⅓ cup pitted black olives
1 teaspoon dried oregano

Prepare the dough and let rise. Heat 6 tablespoons oil in a skillet over medium heat. Stir in onion and cook until soft but not brown, about 5 minutes. Stir in tomatoes and anchovies. Cook over high heat, stirring constantly, for 5 to 6 minutes or until anchovies blend into mixture and mixture becomes dry. There will be some oil that is not absorbed. Add tomato paste for deeper color and flavor; mix well over low heat.

Oil a baking sheet. Knead dough again briefly and put on baking sheet. With oiled hands, pat dough out to a 9- or 10-inch circle, with a rim slightly higher than center.

Arrange garlic slivers and capers over dough. Cover with tomato mixture, including oil remaining in pan, and arrange olives on top. Crumble oregano in your fingers and sprinkle it over pizza. Sprinkle topping and dough with remaining tablespoon oil.

Set oven at 400°F. Let pizza rise for about 15 minutes. Bake pizza for about 30 minutes or until dough is golden brown and firm but not hard. Serve hot.

Makes 3 or 4 main-course servings

TOMATO AND CORN TORTILLA SOUP

I first tasted this soup cooked by a friend's teenage guest from Mexico City, who knew how to cook only one thing—tortilla soup. We thought it sounded like a strange dish, but it turned out to be delicious!

The soup is made in different ways throughout Mexico. It might contain only tomatoes and onion, or might have zucchini, carrots, chilies, or sweet peppers. I like to add corn for its taste and texture, and because it complements the corn tortillas. I also stir raw tomatoes and cilantro into the finished soup for a fresh touch.

Many versions of this soup call for cheese, such as crumbled Mexican queso fresco *or grated Monterey Jack. You can serve cheese separately if you like, but I prefer the soup without it; it's lighter and still flavorful. You can also accompany the soup with avocado slices.*

In the interest of lightness I have tried making the soup with toasted tortillas instead of fried ones, but the results were disappointing. If you don't wish to fry the tortillas, use 2 or 3 cups packaged tortilla strips instead; some are now available made without oil or without salt. SEE PHOTOGRAPH.

Corn tortillas and mild green chilies are available at many supermarkets and at Mexican grocery stores.

6 corn tortillas, preferably stale
5 tablespoons vegetable oil
1¼ pounds ripe tomatoes, peeled, seeded, and chopped or 1 28-ounce can plum tomatoes, drained and chopped
1 medium onion, chopped
2 long mild green chilies, diced small (see Note)
2 large garlic cloves, minced

4 cups Chicken or Vegetable Stock (pages 407, 406), or mixed broth and water
1 ear of corn, kernels removed; or 1 cup frozen kernels
⅓ cup plus 1 teaspoon coarsely chopped cilantro (fresh coriander)
Salt and freshly ground pepper
Pure chili powder or cayenne pepper to taste

If tortillas are not stale, let stand about 30 minutes unwrapped in 1 layer until dry. Cut tortillas in half, then each half in strips about ¼ inch wide.

Heat 4 tablespoons oil in heavy, medium sauté pan over medium-high heat; test with 1 tortilla strip—when oil is hot enough, it should bubble around strip. Add half the strips to pan and fry 2 to 3 minutes or until slightly darker and firmer but not crisp; do not brown. Do not stir too often or strips will break up. Turn off heat and quickly transfer tortilla strips with a slotted spoon to paper towels. Reheat oil slightly, add remaining strips, and fry them; remove to towels.

Set aside ¾ cup chopped tomatoes for finishing soup. In a large saucepan heat remaining 1 tablespoon oil. Add onion and chilies, and sauté over medium heat for 5 minutes or until light brown. Add garlic and sauté ½ minute. Add broth and remaining tomatoes and bring to a boil. Cover and simmer 10 minutes. Add corn and simmer 5 to 10 minutes or until corn is tender.

Just before serving, reheat soup if necessary. Add reserved tomatoes, ⅓ cup cilantro, salt, and chili powder to taste. Serve soup sprinkled with tortilla strips and remaining cilantro.

Makes 4 appetizer servings

NOTE: If fresh green chilies are not available, substitute 1 cup diced green bell peppers or canned mild green chilies.

MOROCCAN TOMATO-PEPPER DIP

This is a ''cooked salad'' of grilled peppers simmered with tomatoes, garlic, and spices. It's a Moroccan specialty now popular in much of North Africa and the Middle East. I like it with one jalapeño pepper, but if you like a fiery-hot dip, use two. Serve it cold as an appetizer with pita or other fresh bread, or as an accompaniment for grilled chicken or meat. I also like it hot as a sauce for cooked vegetables, such as green beans, corn, or carrots, served with rice.

1 red bell pepper
1 green bell pepper
1 jalapeño pepper
2 pounds ripe tomatoes, peeled and
    diced
4 to 6 medium garlic cloves, diced
    small

1 teaspoon paprika
½ teaspoon ground cumin
Salt and pepper
1 tablespoon vegetable oil

Broil all the peppers according to instructions on page 281 and then peel. Drain well and pat dry. Dice bell peppers and mince jalapeño pepper.

In a medium saucepan, combine peppers with tomatoes, garlic, paprika, cumin, salt, pepper, and oil. Bring to a boil. Cook uncovered over medium-low heat, stirring occasionally, about 1 hour or until thick. Taste and adjust seasoning. Serve cold or at room temperature.

Makes 4 appetizer or side-dish servings

SRI LANKAN TOMATO AND WATERCRESS SALAD WITH CUCUMBER-YOGURT DRESSING

This is a two-way salad. You serve it as given here, or as watercress and cucumber slices with a tomato-yogurt dressing (see Variation). The dressing resembles Indian raita, *and the salad fulfills the same function in Sri Lankan as in Indian dinners—to calm the fires of the hot curries. But it has other uses. I love it with bean, lentil, and rice dishes, whether they are spicy or not, and with Armenian Pepper, Parsley, and Wheat Salad (page 285).*

Try to buy watercress not more than 1 day ahead; it quickly turns yellow. SEE PHOTOGRAPH.

2 cups plain yogurt
Salt and freshly ground pepper
1 teaspoon sugar
2 teaspoons lemon juice
2 tablespoons plus 1 teaspoon chopped
 cilantro (fresh coriander)

1 cup finely diced cucumber (¼-inch
 dice)
1 bunch watercress, leafy parts only
2 large ripe tomatoes, sliced
1 small ripe tomato, cut into half-
 slices, for garnish (optional)

Stir yogurt until smooth. Stir in salt, pepper, sugar, and lemon juice. Lightly stir in 2 tablespoons cilantro and diced cucumber. Taste and adjust seasoning. Refrigerate until ready to serve. Spoon yogurt mixture into a serving bowl and sprinkle with remaining cilantro. Set bowl of dressing in center of a round platter.

Arrange watercress sprigs on platter around yogurt dressing. Arrange tomato slices over-lapping around watercress.

If you like, garnish by alternating small watercress sprigs with half-slices of small tomato against rim of bowl of dressing.

Makes 4 to 6 side-dish servings

VARIATION: **Watercress and Cucumber Salad with Tomato-Yogurt Dressing**
Substitute 1 European cucumber or 2 to 3 pickling cucumbers for the sliced tomato. Cut cucumbers into thin slices and arrange on a platter with the watercress. In the dressing, substitute finely diced tomato for the diced cucumber, and chopped fresh mint for the cilantro.

GREEK COUNTRY SALAD

Like the common Middle Eastern chopped salad, the ingredients for Greek salad change with the seasons. Tomatoes, feta cheese, and black olives are standard, but the salad often contains onions, cucumbers, or green bell peppers and sometimes also thin slices of fennel or salad greens. The favorite seasoning for the dressing is the Greek herb rigano, *which is available at Greek grocery stores, but you can use its more widely available relative, oregano. Serve the salad in summer when tomatoes are at their peak, as a first course with crusty bread.*

½ medium onion
2 large ripe tomatoes, cut into wedges
1 green or yellow pepper, cut into thin
　　strips or rings
½ European cucumber, cut into thin
　　half-slices
2 tablespoons extra-virgin olive oil

2 teaspoons wine vinegar or lemon
　　juice
2 teaspoons dried oregano, crumbled
Salt and freshly ground pepper
8 to 12 Kalamata or other black olives
4 ounces feta cheese, preferably
　　imported, cut into cubes

Halve the onion half, and thinly slice each quarter. Separate slices into slivers; if desired, rinse pieces with cold water so onion is milder; pat dry.

Toss tomato, onion, pepper, and cucumber in a large salad bowl or arrange on platter. Mix oil, lemon juice, oregano, salt, and pepper and sprinkle over vegetables. Top with olives and feta and serve.

Makes 4 generous first-course servings

27

Turnips and Rutabagas

When a Frenchman describes a machine that turns out to be what we would call a lemon, he says *c'était un navet*, or "it was a turnip." I'm not sure how this expression came to be, as the French are actually very fond of turnips. The vegetable is a standard addition to the popular Sunday dinner *pot au feu*, or poached beef with winter vegetables, and to spring lamb stews.

Rutabagas are a different story. "This vegetable is used as fodder for cattle," said French chefs I studied with, "and as food for humans only in wartime."

We Americans tend to skip over both rutabagas and turnips in the supermarket. But it's time to give these root vegetables another look, as they are inexpensive and readily available, and can add variety to our menus. Both of these humble vegetables can make tasty side dishes and contribute good flavor to beef, lamb, and chicken stews or vegetable soups. Besides, they are good sources of vitamin C and potassium, and are fairly low in calories; ½ cup of rutabaga has about 30 calories or about the same as carrots; turnips have even fewer calories.

Rutabagas are usually sold in the market alongside turnips and resemble them quite a bit. On the outside, rutabagas look like slightly darker yellowish turnips, but once you peel them, you'll see that their meat is pale orange, while that of turnips is white. The best turnips and rutabagas are those that are small, firm, and heavy for their size.

The less-familiar rutabagas have a slight advantage over turnips because they're more colorful. Their flavor is similar to that of turnips though a little more pronounced, their texture is more substantial, and they don't tend to fall apart in soups or stews. Turnips are a better choice when you prefer a more delicate flavor; they also cook more quickly.

These vegetables are usually associated with northern Europe, especially Scandinavia. The word *rutabaga* comes from Swedish. The vegetable is sometimes called the Swedish turnip, and the British simply called them "swedes." In Europe the vegetables are usually sliced or diced and cooked in chicken or beef broth as a side dish or made into a puree. They might be seasoned with a pinch of allspice or a sprinkling of sugar and finished with a pat of butter.

For a change of pace, I like to turn to the southern Mediterranean for lively flavorings for these vegetables. We don't think of North Africa as a treasure trove of cold-weather recipes, but in fact cooks in that region have developed delicious ways to prepare turnips and rutabagas. Who can resist a colorful Moroccan stew of turnips, potatoes, carrots, and onions flavored with garlic, cumin, olive oil, and plenty of Italian parsley (page 329)?

Turnips are also used in China. Cooks braise them with leeks or stew them with beef and soy sauce.

Serve these hearty vegetables as an accompaniment for meat or poultry, or as the basis for a winter vegetarian meal, with a steaming bowl of rice or couscous or simply good crusty bread.

TURNIP AND RUTABAGA BASICS

✕ **Season:** Turnips and rutabagas are available all year. The peak of their season is fall and winter, although turnips also appear in spring.

✕ **Choosing:** Choose firm, smooth, fairly small turnips and rutabagas. They should feel heavy for their size.

✕ **Storing:** Turnips should be kept unwashed in a plastic bag in the refrigerator. They will keep 1 week. If turnips have greens, these will keep 2 or 3 days. Rutabagas keep about 1 week at room temperature or about 2 weeks in the refrigerator.

✕ **Serving Size:** About 5 or 6 ounces per person as a side dish.

✕ **Nutrients:** Both vegetables have significant amounts of vitamin C. Rutabaga is also a good source of potassium and iron. One cup of cooked turnip has 30 to 35 calories; 1 cup of cooked rutabaga has about 60 calories.

✕ **Basic Preparation:** Rinse vegetable, cut off ends, and peel with a vegetable peeler.

ALGERIAN TURNIPS WITH PEAS, GARLIC, AND CILANTRO

This spicy, delicious dish shows turnips in a completely new light. Garlic, olive oil, cilantro, and cayenne contribute a wonderful zesty flavor to the turnips. Serve these turnips with beef, lamb, or chicken or as a light main-course supper dish.

2 pounds turnips, peeled and cut into
⅜- to 1-inch dice
4 large garlic cloves, chopped
2 tablespoons olive oil
1 tablespoon paprika
Salt and freshly ground pepper
¼ teaspoon cayenne pepper, or more
to taste

1½ cups water
½ cup long-grain white rice
½ cup chopped cilantro (fresh
coriander)
2 pounds green peas in pod, or 2 cups
shelled or frozen

In a large saucepan, combine turnips, garlic, oil, paprika, salt, pepper, cayenne, and water. Stir and bring to a boil. Cover and cook over low heat for 10 minutes, stirring occasionally. Stir in rice and ¼ cup cilantro. Cover and cook 10 minutes. Add peas without stirring. Cover and cook 10 more minutes, or until rice is tender. Gently stir in 3 tablespoons cilantro. Taste and adjust seasoning. Serve sprinkled with remaining cilantro.

Makes 2 or 3 main-course or 4 or 5 side-dish servings

MOROCCAN WINTER VEGETABLE STEW

Our image of Mediterranean countries is of never-ending summer, but cool weather arrives in this region and, with it, winter cooking. The Moroccan way with winter vegetables is zesty and full of exciting tastes, as in this colorful stew of turnips, potatoes, carrots, and onions flavored with garlic, cumin, olive oil, and plenty of Italian parsley.

2 tablespoons olive oil
2 large onions, halved and sliced thin
2 large garlic cloves, chopped
1 pound turnips, peeled and cut into
    ¾- to 1-inch dice
1 pound boiling potatoes, peeled and
    cut into ¾- to 1-inch dice
2 medium or large carrots, halved and
    sliced ¼ inch thick

1 cup water
1 teaspoon paprika
½ teaspoon ground cumin
Salt and freshly ground pepper
Pinch of cayenne pepper
¼ cup chopped fresh Italian parsley

Heat oil in a large, heavy sauté pan over medium heat. Add onions and sauté over medium heat about 5 minutes. Add garlic and sauté 15 seconds. Add turnips, potatoes, carrots, water, paprika, cumin, salt, pepper, and cayenne. Bring to a boil, stirring. Cover and cook over low heat, occasionally stirring gently, about 35 minutes or until all vegetables are tender. Uncover and cook 2 or 3 minutes to evaporate excess liquid, stirring as little as possible. Lightly stir in 3 tablespoons parsley. Serve sprinkled with remaining parsley.

Makes 2 main-course or 4 or 5 side-dish servings

TURNIP TIMBALES ON A BED OF GREENS

You can use this as a master recipe for all sorts of vegetable timbales—beet, parsnip, winter squash, and spinach, for example. Start with 2 cups puree of the cooked vegetable and heat until thick and dry. Serve the timbales on a salad of baby greens as a rich, elegant appetizer.

1½ to 1¾ pounds small turnips, peeled
    and quartered
Salt and ground white pepper
⅔ cup heavy cream, at room
    temperature
3 eggs
Freshly grated nutmeg

1 quart mixed baby lettuces, rinsed
    and dried
1 to 1½ teaspoons olive or vegetable
    oil
½ teaspoon wine vinegar
Freshly ground black pepper

Preheat the oven to 375°F. Generously butter four ⅔-cup ramekins or five ½-cup timbale molds.

Put turnips in a saucepan, cover with water, add a pinch of salt, and bring to a boil. Cover and cook over medium-low heat until very tender, about 12 minutes. Drain well. Puree in food processor until very smooth.

Measure 2 cups puree. Cook puree in a heavy, wide, medium saucepan over low heat, stirring often, about 5 minutes. Stir in cream and bring to boil. Cook over medium heat, stirring often, until mixture is reduced to 2 cups, about 5 minutes. Transfer to a bowl and cool 7 minutes.

Lightly whisk eggs in a medium bowl. Gradually whisk in turnip puree. Season well with salt, pepper, and nutmeg. Divide mixture among buttered molds. Tap each on counter to pack down mixture. Smooth tops. Set molds in roasting pan and put in oven. Add enough boiling water to pan to come halfway up sides of molds. Set a sheet of buttered foil atop molds; do not fold it over sides of pan.

Bake until timbales are firm and a cake tester inserted into the mixture comes out dry, about 40 to 50 minutes; add hot water to pan during baking if most of it evaporates.

Using a metal pancake turner, remove molds from water. Cool 5 minutes. Run a thin-bladed flexible knife around edge of one mold. Set small plate atop mold and invert both. Holding them together, tap them on towel-lined counter. Gently lift up mold. Repeat with remaining timbales. Serve hot or warm.

Toss lettuce with oil and vinegar. Season with salt and pepper to taste. Put on serving plates and top with timbales.

Makes 4 or 5 appetizer servings

CREAMY TURNIP SOUP

*O*ne *of the best New Year's parties I ever attended took place in Paris fifteen years ago. All of us at the party were Americans who came to France to study the culinary arts. We all lived in small apartments with tiny kitchens, so the party food had to be quick and easy. Much of it was purchased; we each brought slices of pâté from nearby charcuteries or a terrific French cheese from the neighborhood fromagerie. And of course there was Champagne.*

The star of the party turned out to be a soup. Not a complicated shellfish bisque, but a vegetable soup made from a humble, unglamorous ingredient—the turnip. The soup was smooth, creamy in texture, and delicate in flavor. Served hot in deep, heavy bowls and accompanied by slices of crisp-crusted baguette, it was a winner.

Although classic French recipes for turnip soup call for cream, butter, or egg yolks for enrichment, I find that low-fat milk also gives this soup a creamy taste and color. Naturally the milk-enriched version of the soup is much more healthful.

1 tablespoon vegetable oil or butter
1 small or medium onion, chopped
4 medium turnips (1½ pounds),
    peeled, quartered, and sliced about
    ¼ inch thick
2 medium boiling potatoes (½ pound),
    peeled, quartered, and sliced about
    ¼ inch thick

2 cups Chicken Stock (page 407) or
    canned chicken or vegetable broth
    (see Note)
Salt and ground white pepper
1½ cups low-fat (2%) or whole milk

Heat oil in a medium saucepan. Add onion and sauté over medium-low heat for about 5 minutes or until soft but not brown. Add turnip and potato slices, stock, salt, and pepper. Stir and bring to a boil. Cover and simmer about 25 minutes or until vegetables are very tender. Puree soup in batches in a blender or food processor.

Return soup to cleaned pan and heat soup gently. Gradually stir in milk. Heat but do not boil. Taste and adjust seasoning, then serve in heated bowls.

Makes 4 or 5 appetizer servings

NOTE: For canned broth, use a 14½-ounce can with enough water to make 2 cups.

RUTABAGA WITH GARLIC AND GREENS

Egyptian cooks love to stew vegetables with greens, sautéed onions, and garlic. These flavors do wonders for rutabaga, turning it into a tasty accompaniment for braised beef, or as a main course with white or brown rice.

¾ pound rutabaga, peeled
2 tablespoons plus 1 teaspoon olive or
    vegetable oil
4 medium garlic cloves, chopped
½ cup finely chopped Swiss chard or
    spinach leaves

1 medium onion, chopped
1¼ cups chicken, beef, or vegetable
    broth
Salt and freshly ground pepper
A few drops lemon juice (optional)

Cut ends off rutabaga and cut in ¾-inch dice. Heat 1 tablespoon oil in a deep skillet or sauté pan. Add rutabaga and sauté over medium heat for 3 minutes. Remove with a slotted spoon. Add 1 teaspoon oil to pan and heat briefly. Add garlic and sauté 15 seconds. Add chard and sauté until dry, about 30 seconds. Remove chard mixture.

   Add remaining tablespoon oil to pan. Add onion and sauté over medium heat about 5 minutes or until beginning to brown. Add broth and bring to a boil. Add rutabaga, cover, and simmer over low heat for 25 minutes. Add chard mixture and cook 10 minutes or until rutabaga is tender, adding a few tablespoons water if pan becomes dry. Add lemon juice. Taste and adjust seasoning. Serve hot.

Makes 2 or 3 side-dish servings

RUTABAGA WITH RAISINS

The sweetness of sautéed onions and raisins is a good complement for the earthy taste of rutabaga. For this simple North African recipe a little cayenne pepper and paprika accent the vegetable. Serve the rutabaga with roasted or braised lamb, or for a simple supper, serve it with couscous prepared the quick way and accompany with yogurt. The same recipe is also good with turnips, as in the variation.

1 tablespoon vegetable oil
1 large onion, sliced
1½ pounds rutabaga, peeled and cut
    into 1-inch dice
Salt and freshly ground pepper

1 teaspoon paprika
1¼ cups water
¼ cup dark raisins
Cayenne pepper to taste

Heat oil in a large saucepan, add onion, and sauté over medium heat about 5 minutes or until wilted. Add rutabagas, salt, pepper, paprika, and water. Bring to a boil. Cover and cook over low heat until tender, about 45 minutes, adding a few tablespoons water if pan becomes dry during cooking. Add raisins; uncover pan if too much liquid remains. Cook 5 minutes, then add cayenne. Taste and adjust seasoning.

Makes 3 or 4 side-dish servings

VARIATION: **Turnips with Raisins**
   Substitute 2 pounds turnips for the rutabagas. Use only ½ cup water. Cook turnips only 15 minutes before adding raisins.

FINNISH RUTABAGA PUREE

Rutabaga is popular in Scandinavia. The Finns prepare a delicious orange-hued puree from the vegetable by combining it with potatoes, allspice, and a touch of butter. The puree makes a good accompaniment for roast lamb or chicken.

1 pound rutabaga
Salt and freshly ground pepper
½ pound potatoes
1 to 1¼ cups milk

1 tablespoon butter (optional)
½ teaspoon sugar
¼ teaspoon ground allspice

Peel rutabagas and cut each in 8 pieces. Put in a large saucepan, add water to generously cover, add a pinch of salt, and bring to a boil. Cover and cook over low heat for 10 minutes.
   Meanwhile, peel potato and cut in 8 pieces. Add to pan with rutabaga and cook about 25 minutes, or until vegetables are tender. Drain vegetables and transfer to a bowl. Mash them with potato masher or food mill. Return puree to pan and heat it. Gradually stir in milk over low heat. Add butter, sugar, and allspice. Season to taste with salt and pepper. Serve hot.

Makes 3 or 4 side-dish servings

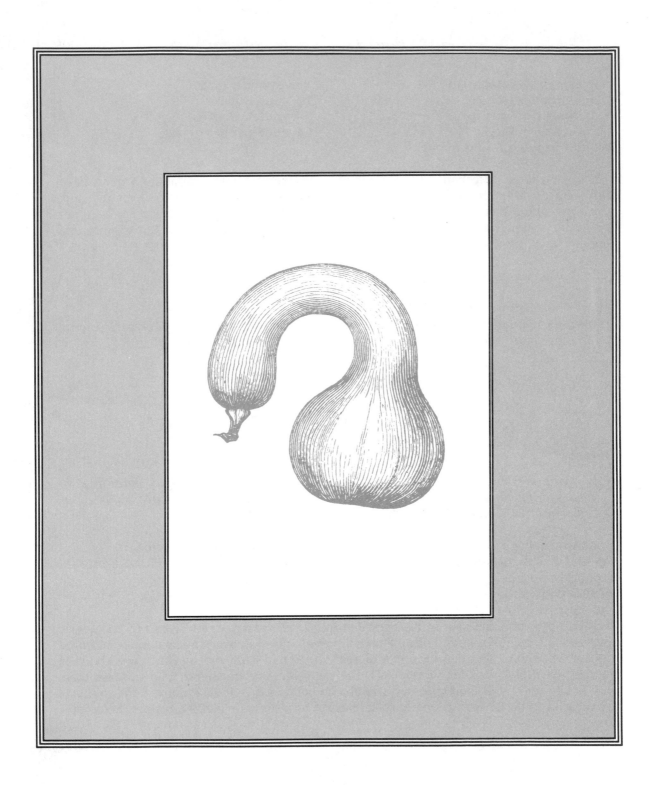

28

Winter Squash and Pumpkin

Piles of pumpkins everywhere remind us not only of the approach of Halloween but also of the culinary possibilities of the vitamin A–rich pumpkin and other members of the culinary winter squash family.

Pumpkins have been known to grow to huge sizes; last year's contest for the biggest pumpkin hit a new world record—over 800 pounds! These giants are best left for exhibits at county fairs or for carving jack-o'-lanterns, however. Relatively small ones, especially sugar or cheese pumpkins, are better suited to cooking.

Many traditional recipes call for baking pumpkin and firm-skinned winter squash for an hour or two. But there's a faster way. You cut off the peel, cut the flesh into cubes, and steam the vegetable in a steamer or in a little water in a saucepan. It's the tough skin of a winter squash that makes the heat take long to penetrate. The flesh itself is tender and cooks quickly. Another way to drastically cut the vegetable's cooking time is to use the microwave, if you're not cooking a large amount of squash.

For savory recipes, sugar pumpkin is interchangeable with winter squash such as hubbard, banana squash, acorn, or butternut. A tasty new variety in the market is sweet dumpling, a

335

ridged squash with a speckled white peel and bright orange flesh. Each does have its own flavor; experiment and find your favorite. Easiest to use are the newly available mini pumpkins, which don't even require peeling.

While pumpkin's sweet flavor and smooth texture motivated American cooks to use it in pies for dessert, cooks in other parts of the world utilize it differently. Moroccans make savory pumpkin salads with garlic, cilantro, and hot pepper sauce. Italians like to cook pumpkin in risotto; in the Abruzzo region on the central Adriatic coast, the flavor of the pumpkin-rice combination is enhanced with sautéed onions and pecorino cheese.

In Mediterranean, European, and Latin American countries, pumpkin is a favorite addition to vegetable and meat soups because its mild flavor harmonizes well with other ingredients. Brazilian cooks prepare a hearty soup of pumpkin simmered with beef, potatoes, carrots, and tomatoes. The Périgord region in central France is best known for its black truffles and

WINTER SQUASH AND PUMPKIN BASICS

✗ **Season:** Winter squash are available all year. In the peak season of fall and winter, more varieties are available.

✗ **Choosing:** Choose squash that feels heavy for its size. The rind of winter squash or pumpkin should be smooth and should not have soft spots. The meat of cut squash should have bright yellow or orange color and should not look stringy.

✗ **Storing:** Whole squash will keep for a month in a cool, dry place. Cut squash should be tightly wrapped; it will keep 1 week in the refrigerator.

✗ **Serving Size:** Allow 6 to 8 ounces squash or half a baked small squash per person.

✗ **Nutrients:** Winter squash is an excellent source of vitamin A and a good source of vitamin C. One cup of cooked squash has 80 to 110 calories.

foie gras, but in most kitchens you're more likely to find a modest vegetable soup of pumpkin or winter squash, white beans, carrots, leeks, and celery.

The French love pumpkin and other winter squashes also as the main ingredient of soups. For these delicate, velvety-textured soups, the pumpkin is simply cooked in water, pureed, and enriched with milk, cream, or butter. To emphasize the pumpkin's natural sweetness, sometimes a little sugar is added and so is nutmeg, as in pumpkin pie. The traditional garnish is sautéed croutons, but cooked rice, small pasta shapes, green vegetables, or toasted chopped nuts are other favorites for stirring into the soup or sprinkling on top.

Spaghetti squash is a different sort of winter squash. When cooked, its flesh separates into spaghettilike strands. Usually the squash is baked or steamed whole, or halved and microwaved. Because the vegetable is mild in flavor and resembles spaghetti, it is often served with pasta sauces.

Basic Preparation

Rinse squash. Cut it with a heavy knife, being careful not to let the knife slip. Remove the seeds and strings with a spoon. If cutting squash into cubes, it's easier to cut it first in pieces and then to cut off the peel from each piece. Sometimes the skin of butternut squash is tender enough so it can be peeled with a vegetable peeler.

I've had a problem cutting into some winter squashes because of their hard skin. The experts at Frieda's, the company that has introduced many exotic vegetables to U.S. markets, came to my aid. They suggested microwaving the squash briefly so the skin softens enough to cut it. It works perfectly! You can also bake or steam a whole squash until it's partially tender for the same purpose, but it will take longer.

To Microwave Squash

Halve the squash and remove the seeds and strings. Wrap each half in microwave-safe plastic wrap; or put squash cut side down in a microwave baking dish and cover with wax paper. Microwave on high until tender; 2 to 2½ pounds of squash will take about 15 minutes. Check by piercing the flesh in its thickest part with a fork.

WINTER SQUASHES

TYPE	DESCRIPTION	USES	AVAILABLE
acorn	acorn-shaped; green or gold skin with deep furrows, yellow flesh; slightly sweet, can be bland	halve, bake, stuff	year-round
banana	long, cylindrical shape; pale orange to creamy white skin, orange flesh; often sold in pieces; mild flavor	dice and steam, add to soups	year-round
buttercup	large, flat, round with turban on top; green skin with grayish flecks, orange flesh; sweet flavor	bake, steam, puree	summer, fall, winter
butternut	large or small, bell-shaped; tan-color skin, deep orange flesh; rich flavor	bake, stew, soups, casseroles	most of year
calabaza (West Indian pumpkin)	large, melon-shaped; hard, white and yellow spotted, greenish skin; yellow to orange flesh; sold in pieces; slightly sweet flavor, meaty texture	Caribbean and Latin American cooking; boil, stew, puree	most of year
golden nugget	small, round, looks like small pumpkin; hard-ridged orange shell, bright orange flesh; slightly sweet taste	bake, steam, or microwave halves	most of year

WINTER SQUASHES

TYPE	DESCRIPTION	USES	AVAILABLE
hubbard	large and round, tapered ends; golden, blue-gray, or green skin; orange flesh; rich flavor	bake, steam, or microwave; glaze or puree	June to January
kabocha (Japanese squash)	flattened ball shape; deep green shell, orange flesh; rich flavor	Japanese cooking; steam, stuff, glaze, puree, use in tempura	year-round
spaghetti	cylindrical, bright yellow shell; pale yellow, mild, crunchy, spaghettilike flesh when cooked	bake whole, steam or microwave halves; serve with pasta sauces or vinaigrette	year-round
sugar loaf	small, cylindrical, tan-and-green-striped shell; rich, sweet yellow flesh	bake, boil, steam, microwave; stuff; good for individual servings	June to November
sweet dumpling	small, ridged squash; hard, white-and-green-striped shell; sweet, yellow flesh	bake, steam, microwave; good for individual servings	June to February
turban	flattened orange base with white-and-green-striped knobs on top; orange flesh; rich flavor	bake, steam, boil	May to November

WINTER SQUASH WITH SWEET SPICES

Ginger, cinnamon, and black pepper make this Algerian squash dish quite spicy, but it has a hint of sweetness as well. I prefer butternut or sweet dumpling squash, followed by acorn squash. This makes a light and lovely accompaniment for roast chicken or the Thanksgiving turkey.

2 pounds winter squash, such as
    butternut, acorn, or sweet
    dumpling
2 medium garlic cloves, peeled
¼ teaspoon ground black pepper
½ teaspoon ground cinnamon

½ teaspoon ground ginger
1 tablespoon sugar
1 tablespoon vegetable oil
⅔ cup water
Salt to taste

Cut off squash peel, remove seeds and strings, and cut flesh into 1-inch pieces.

    Combine remaining ingredients in a large sauté pan and bring to a simmer. Add squash and stir until coated. Sprinkle with salt and heat until sizzling. Cover and cook over low heat, occasionally stirring gently, for 30 minutes or until squash is tender. Remove garlic, chop, and return to pan. If sauce is too thin, uncover and cook 2 to 3 minutes or until it thickens. Taste and adjust seasoning. (*Squash can be kept, covered, 3 days in refrigerator.*) Serve hot.

Makes 3 or 4 side-dish servings

WINTER SQUASH WITH RICE AND GREEN BEANS

In Italy I tasted pumpkin in risotto and other rice dishes. This is an easier, California-style adaptation using more readily available winter squash and seasoned with soy sauce and hot pepper sauce. If you cook the squash in the microwave, it makes a quick, easy supper dish.

I like to add green beans for a fresh, colorful accent, but you can use 1 to 1½ cups of any diced cooked vegetable or even a frozen vegetable.

1¼-pound butternut, acorn, or other
    winter squash
¼ pound green beans
Salt and freshly ground pepper
1 to 2 tablespoons vegetable oil
2 cups cooked white or brown rice

2 tablespoons water
2 teaspoons soy sauce, or to taste
½ teaspoon ground ginger, or to taste
Bottled hot pepper sauce to taste
2 to 3 tablespoons chopped green
    onion (optional)

Halve the squash and remove seeds. To bake squash, put halved squash in an oiled baking dish cut side down and bake at 400°F. for 45 minutes or until tender; check by piercing meat in thickest part with fork. To microwave squash, put halved squash in a glass baking dish cut side down. Cover with microwave plastic wrap and microwave on high for about 10 to 12 minutes or until tender; check by piercing meat in thickest part with fork. Remove flesh and cut into dice.

Remove ends from beans; cut beans into 3 pieces. Cook in boiling salted water about 7 minutes or until crisp-tender. Drain well.

Heat oil in a large, deep skillet over low heat. Add beans, salt, and pepper and sauté lightly to reheat. Add squash, rice, water, and soy sauce and sprinkle with pepper and ginger. Cover and heat gently until mixture is hot; stir occasionally and add more water if mixture is dry. Taste and adjust seasoning, adding hot pepper sauce to taste. Sprinkle with green onion and serve.

Makes 2 main-course servings

SQUASH WITH SAUTÉED ONION

An easy way to turn winter squash or pumpkin into a colorful accompaniment is to heat the steamed vegetable with sautéed onions, which complement the smooth, sweet flesh. I especially like to use sweet dumpling squash for this. The Italian-inspired dish is delicious with roasted or broiled chicken.

If you like, cook the squash in the microwave in its skin (see page 337) until nearly tender, and then sauté it with the onion for a super-quick side dish.

1½ to 2 pounds winter squash, preferably sweet dumpling, or pumpkin
1 cup water

1 tablespoon olive oil
1 medium onion, minced
Salt and freshly ground pepper

Cut squash or pumpkin in pieces and cut off peel with a heavy, sharp knife. Remove any seeds or stringy flesh. Cut flesh in 1-inch cubes. Put in heavy saucepan with water, cover, and cook over medium heat, stirring occasionally, about 20 minutes or until tender. If all the water evaporates before squash is tender, add a little more; if water is left when squash is tender, drain it.

Heat oil in a heavy, medium skillet or sauté pan. Add onion and sauté 7 minutes over medium heat. Add squash pieces, sprinkle with salt and pepper, and sauté, stirring lightly, about 2 minutes or until coated with onion. Serve hot.

Makes 3 or 4 side-dish servings

STUFFED ACORN SQUASH WITH APPLES AND PECANS

Baking squash with an American bread stuffing similar to the type used in turkeys has become a Thanksgiving tradition for many vegetarians. For nonvegetarians, it's delicious alongside roast turkey. This stuffing gains flavor from onions and toasted pecans and zip from fresh ginger.

3 acorn squashes, about 1½ pounds each, halved lengthwise and seeded
4 tablespoons vegetable oil or butter (½ stick)
1 medium onion, finely chopped
¼ cup chopped celery
Salt and freshly ground pepper
1 tablespoon minced peeled fresh ginger

2 cups peeled, finely chopped tart green apples (about 2 medium)
¼ teaspoon ground allspice
1 cup fresh bread crumbs (see Note)
⅓ cup pecans, lightly toasted (page 413), coarsely chopped
1 large egg, beaten

Preheat the oven to 400°F. Cut a thin slice from the bottom of each squash, if necessary, so it will stand straight when stuffed. Oil a large nonstick roasting pan, or line pan with foil and oil the foil. Place squash skin side up in prepared pan and bake about 45 minutes or until tender when thickest part of meat is pierced with a fork.

Meanwhile, heat 3 tablespoons oil in a large skillet over medium heat. Add onion, celery, and a pinch of salt and pepper. Sauté, stirring occasionally, until onion is soft but not brown, about 5 minutes. Add ginger and apples and sauté, stirring often, about 10 minutes. Stir in allspice. Transfer to a bowl; cool slightly. Add bread crumbs and nuts, and toss lightly until blended. Taste and adjust seasoning. Add egg, tossing lightly. (*Stuffing can be refrigerated up to 1 day in covered container.*)

Reduce oven temperature to 350°F. Fill squash halves generously with stuffing. Sprinkle remaining oil over stuffing; or melt remaining butter and sprinkle it. Cover and bake squash for 30 minutes or until stuffing is hot.

Makes 3 main-course or 6 side-dish servings

NOTE: To make bread crumbs, process 2 or 3 slices day-old or stale white bread in a food processor until you have fine crumbs.

SWEET-AND-SOUR WINTER SQUASH WITH RAISINS

The Kurdish people live in an area of northern Iraq, western Iran, and southeastern Turkey, and they have developed many hearty dishes for the cold winters. In this recipe, they stew the squash with tomatoes and onions, then finish the sauce with raisins and lemon juice. Use acorn, butternut, banana squash, or any other winter squash. When this dish is served as a main course, the traditional accompaniment is bulgur wheat, but it can also be served with rice or can accompany beef or chicken.

2 pounds winter squash
2 tablespoons vegetable oil
1 large onion, chopped
1 pound ripe tomatoes, peeled, seeded,
    and chopped; or 1 28-ounce can
    plum tomatoes, drained and
    chopped

⅔ cup water
Salt and freshly ground pepper
2 teaspoons sugar, or more to taste
⅓ cup dark raisins
2 to 3 tablespoons strained fresh
    lemon juice, or more to taste

Peel squash, remove seeds and strings, and cut flesh into 1-inch pieces.

Heat the oil in a large, heavy sauté pan, add onion, and sauté over medium heat about 7 minutes or until golden. Add tomatoes and cook uncovered for 5 minutes. Add squash, water, salt, pepper, and sugar. Stir and bring to a boil. Cover and cook over low heat, occasionally stirring gently, for 30 minutes. Add raisins and lemon juice, and cook 5 minutes or until squash and raisins are tender.

If sauce is too thin, uncover and cook 2 or 3 minutes until it thickens. Taste and add more salt, lemon juice, or sugar if desired. (*Squash can be kept, covered, 3 days in refrigerator.*) Serve hot.

Makes 4 side-dish or 2 or 3 main-course servings with bulgur wheat or rice

HOT PUMPKIN PUREE WITH GARLIC

Throughout North Africa this savory pumpkin puree is prepared and served as an appetizer. This spicy version with generous amounts of garlic and hot pepper sauce comes from Libya. For a Tunisian variation, add 1 teaspoon caraway seeds to the finished puree, use half as much harissa *and garlic, and garnish the puree with chopped cilantro. Whichever version you prefer, accompany it with fresh pita bread or toast.*

For a quicker dish, cook the pumpkin or squash in the microwave (see page 337); in this case there is no need to peel it before cooking.

3-pound sugar pumpkin
2 cups water
Salt to taste
2 or 3 large garlic cloves, finely minced
½ to 1 teaspoon Harissa (page 393) or
    bottled hot sauce
2 tablespoons lemon juice

2 tablespoons good-quality olive oil
1 teaspoon ground cumin (optional)
1 tablespoon chopped cilantro (fresh
    coriander) or fresh Italian parsley
Small sprigs of cilantro or Italian
    parsley, for garnish

Cut pumpkin in pieces and peel. Remove seeds and strings, then cut flesh into 1½-inch cubes. You should have 5 to 6 cups cubes.

In a medium saucepan, combine pumpkin cubes, water, and a pinch of salt and bring to a boil. Cover and simmer over low heat, stirring occasionally so that all pieces come in contact with the water, about 25 minutes or until very tender when pierced with a sharp knife. Drain thoroughly. Mash the pieces with a fork; leave a few small chunks if desired. Transfer pumpkin to a colander and leave to drain for 1 hour.

Transfer pumpkin to a bowl and add garlic, *harissa*, lemon juice, 1 tablespoon olive oil, and salt to taste. Add cumin if desired. Mix well, cover, and chill.

To serve, spread the puree on a flat plate. Sprinkle the center with chopped cilantro. Sprinkle the remaining olive oil over the surface of the puree and surround with cilantro sprigs.

Makes 4 to 6 appetizer servings

VARIATION: Substitute a 2-pound piece of winter squash, such as Hubbard or banana, for the pumpkin. (A smaller piece of squash is needed because there is less to peel and trim.)

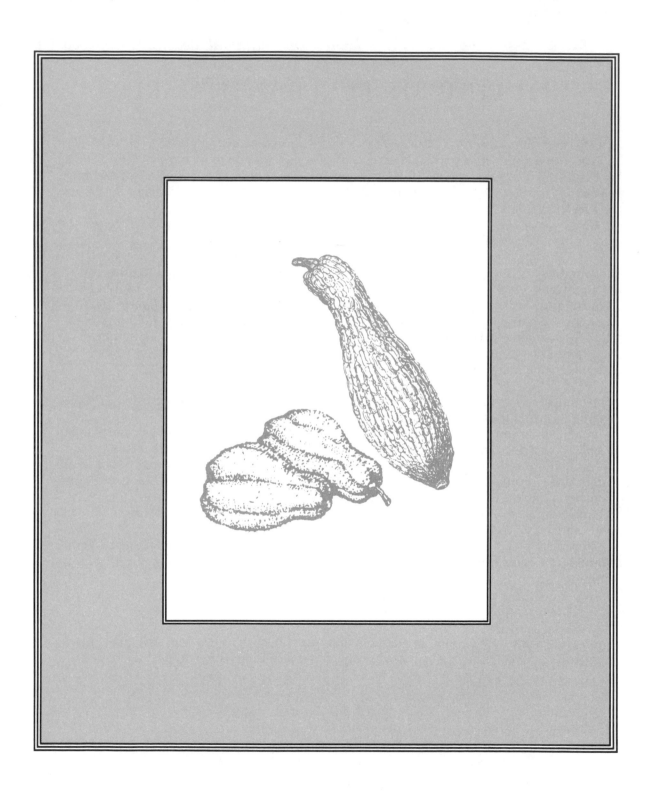

29

Zucchini, Summer Squash, and Chayote

Zucchini is also called Italian squash, and this is the cuisine in which there are the greatest number of recipes for the vegetable. In Italy zucchini might be braised with onions, tomatoes, and basil, as in Napoli Zucchini Casserole (page 355). It can be briefly boiled and served with oil and vinegar, or can be sautéed and tossed with pasta.

Throughout the Mediterranean area stuffed zucchini is a favorite, either halved, stuffed, and baked, or hollowed out and stuffed whole, simmered in tomato sauce. These stuffings are often based on lamb, rice, and cilantro, as for Lebanese Stuffed Tomatoes (page 317). Zucchini can also be used as a container for serving French-style vegetable purees, as in Zucchini Boats with Carrot Puree (page 356).

The vegetable can be cooked by a variety of techniques. Zucchini poached in broth is a frequent accompaniment for couscous in the Moroccan kitchen. Cooks in the Middle East like to simmer zucchini in tomato sauces, like the one used in Lebanese Green Beans with Tomatoes and Garlic (page 48) or in a delicate sweet-and-sour sauce with mint (page 352). In North Africa summer squash is made into salads, such as Tangy Tunisian Zucchini Salad (page 360) with its tart lemon-garlic dressing. Like eggplant, zucchini makes a good addition to Thai and Indian curries. In fact, zucchini and other summer squash can be substituted for eggplant in a great number of dishes.

Zucchini and other summer squash are also popular in northern and central Europe. Stewed with paprika and fresh dill (page 201), zucchini is a favorite accompaniment in the Hungarian kitchen. Baking it as a gratin is another well loved way to serve it, with a coating of cheese sauce or tomato sauce.

Zucchini is our most common summer squash, but there are others in the supermarket. All cook quickly but also overcook easily and can turn mushy. Yellow crookneck squash and straight yellow zucchini can be substituted for green zucchini in many recipes; when both green and yellow zucchini are available, they are best combined to make zucchini dishes more colorful. Other attractive summer squash are green and yellow pattypan, also interchangeable with zucchini in recipes that call for slicing or dicing the vegetable. Some markets feature baby summer squash; these are best cooked very simply—steamed, boiled briefly, or lightly sautéed.

Zucchini is very low in calories. If very fresh, it makes a good addition to raw vegetable snack trays served with a dip.

To quickly add vegetables to a menu, I often add green and yellow zucchini sticks to the cooking water of pasta about 2 minutes before it is done. Then I drain them together, so I have a cooked vegetable ready for tossing with the pasta. Other practically instant ways to serve boiled or steamed zucchini is to top them with Yogurt-Garlic Sauce (page 380) or toss them with a little Tarragon Vinaigrette (page 103). For an easy, festive dish, sauté thin strips of summer squash with carrots and snow peas (page 273).

Chayote, a pear-shaped green squash sometimes called a vegetable pear, mirliton, or christophine, is a Latin American vegetable that features in Mexican, Caribbean, and Creole cooking of the American South. Like other summer squash, it can be boiled, steamed, baked, stuffed, or stewed, as in Chayote Squash with Tomatoes and Caribbean Sofrito (page 359). Cooks in Puerto Rico also use them to make desserts.

SUMMER SQUASH AND CHAYOTE BASICS

✖ **S**eason: Summer squash are available year-round, although the peak of season is summer. Chayote squash is available in fall and winter.

✖ **C**hoosing: Zucchini are best when small or medium, not large. They should be firm and smooth without bruises or soft spots, and should feel heavy for their size. The stem ends should look green and fresh.

✖ **S**toring: Keep summer squash in plastic bags in the refrigerator. They can be kept about 5 days. Chayote squash will keep up to 2 weeks.

✖ **S**erving **S**ize: Allow 4 or 5 ounces summer squash per serving.

✖ **N**utrients: Summer squash are a fair source of vitamin C. One cup raw zucchini has about 18 calories; one cup cooked has about 28 calories. One cup cooked chayote squash has 38 calories.

✖ **B**asic **P**reparation: Rinse squash. Trim off ends. There is no need to peel summer squash. Chayote squash should be peeled; if the vegetable will be boiled, it is easier to peel after boiling. Most cooks also remove the seed.

ZUCCHINI WITH ROMANO CHEESE AND BASIL

This is a Sardinian formula for a very simple, aromatic way to embellish sautéed zucchini—simply add plenty of chopped fresh basil and a sprinkling of Romano cheese. In Italy the preferred cheese is pecorino Romano, made with ewes' milk, but you can use any type of Romano you like, or a mixture of Romano and Parmesan. Garlic toast is a good accompaniment.

1 pound zucchini
2 tablespoons olive oil
Salt and freshly ground pepper
3 tablespoons freshly grated Romano
     cheese, or mixed pecorino and
     Parmesan

⅓ cup chopped fresh basil

Cut off zucchini ends. Slice zucchini into ¼-inch rounds. Heat oil in a large skillet, add zucchini, and sprinkle lightly with salt and pepper. Sauté over medium-high heat, stirring and turning often, about 8 minutes or until tender and very lightly dotted with brown. Transfer to a shallow serving dish, add 2 tablespoons cheese and all but 1 tablespoon basil, and mix well. Serve sprinkled with remaining cheese and basil.

Makes 3 appetizer or side-dish servings

CROOKNECK SQUASH WITH DILL AND PAPRIKA

Summer squash is a popular vegetable in Hungary, often added to a sauce of flour, butter, and cream. In this lighter version, the squash is seasoned in the Hungarian style with sautéed onions, sweet and hot paprika, and fresh dill. It's delicious hot or cold. I like it as a supper dish with noodles or rice and a salad.

6 medium crookneck squash (1½ pounds)
2 tablespoons vegetable oil
1 medium onion, chopped
1¼ teaspoons sweet paprika
Pinch of hot paprika or cayenne pepper (optional)

Salt and freshly ground pepper
1 to 2 tablespoons water (optional)
1 tablespoon chopped fresh dill
1 tablespoon chopped fresh parsley

Cut off the thin neck of the squash. Quarter the rest lengthwise and cut each quarter into 2 pieces. Heat oil in a medium sauté pan over medium heat. Add onion and sauté 5 minutes or until golden brown. Add squash, sweet paprika, hot paprika, salt, and pepper and sauté 1 minute, stirring to coat. Cover and cook over low heat, stirring occasionally, for 10 minutes or until tender. Check and add 1 to 2 tablespoons water during cooking if needed. When squash is tender, if too much water remains in pan, uncover and boil to evaporate it. Add dill and parsley and toss. Taste and adjust seasoning.

Makes 4 main-dish servings with noodles or rice

VARIATION: Substitute green or yellow zucchini for crookneck squash. Quarter zucchini lengthwise and cut each quarter into 3 pieces.

SWEET-AND-SOUR YELLOW SQUASH WITH MINT

This dish is based on a recipe I received from a man I met on a long flight—Benny Mizrachi of Silver Spring, Maryland. It's a dish he learned as a boy from his Syrian-born mother, when she was in the hospital. He was the eldest of seven children, and realized his mother's food was missing at home while she was ill. So every day when he visited her, she told him how to make one dish, and he went home and made it for supper. This experience so marked him that he later became a chef and restaurateur, with a restaurant in the Washington, D.C., area.

This easy dish of stewed squash seasoned with lemon juice, dried mint, garlic, and sugar makes a good accompaniment for meat and rice.

2 tablespoons vegetable oil
1 medium onion, chopped
1 pound crookneck squash or zucchini,
   cut into ½-inch slices
Salt and freshly ground pepper
About ⅓ cup water

1 teaspoon dried mint, crumbled
1 large garlic clove, minced
2 teaspoons sugar
1 tablespoon plus 1 teaspoon strained
   fresh lemon juice

Heat oil in a medium sauté pan, add onion, and sauté over medium heat about 5 minutes or until golden. Add squash, salt, and pepper and sauté 2 minutes.

Add water, mint, garlic, sugar, and 1 tablespoon lemon juice. Cover and cook over medium heat, stirring occasionally, about 7 minutes or until squash is tender and absorbs most of liquid; add a little more water during cooking if pan becomes dry. Add remaining lemon juice. Taste and adjust seasoning. Serve hot or cold.

Makes 3 or 4 side-dish servings

QUICK ZUCCHINI AND EGGPLANT SAUTÉ WITH BASIL

Serve this easy Italian dish hot as an accompaniment or cold as an antipasto. Fresh basil makes it sing, but when it's not in season add some dried herbs; when combined with the garlic, olive oil, and tomatoes, they will still make a tasty sauce for the vegetables.

¾ pound zucchini
¾ pound Italian or Japanese eggplant
2 tablespoons plus 1 teaspoon olive oil
Salt and freshly ground pepper
2 large garlic cloves, chopped
½ pound ripe tomatoes, peeled,
    seeded, and diced; or 1 14-ounce
    can plum tomatoes, diced

1 teaspoon dried thyme, oregano, or
    basil (optional)
3 tablespoons chopped fresh basil or
    parsley

Quarter zucchini lengthwise, then cut in thirds crosswise. Cut eggplant in sticks of about the same size as zucchini pieces.

Heat 1 tablespoon oil in a skillet over medium heat, add zucchini, salt, and pepper and sauté 2 minutes. Remove with a slotted spatula to a plate.

Heat 1 tablespoon oil in skillet, add eggplant, salt, and pepper and sauté 3 minutes. Remove to a plate.

Add 1 teaspoon oil to pan and heat over medium heat. Add garlic and stir a few seconds. Add tomatoes, salt, and pepper. Sauté about 2 minutes or until thick. Add eggplant and dried herbs to sauce, cover, and cook over low heat 3 minutes. Add zucchini, cover, and cook 5 minutes or until vegetables are tender. Add basil. Taste and adjust seasoning. Serve hot, cold, or at room temperature.

Makes 3 or 4 side-dish servings

PARMESAN-COATED ZUCCHINI FANS

This festive zucchini recipe is a specialty of Parisian Chef Christian Simon of Le Delmonico restaurant. Before coating the lightly cooked zucchini fans in grated Parmesan cheese, he dips them in butter to help the cheese stick. I find brushing on olive oil works just as well and uses less fat.
Serve the zucchini fans with chicken, turkey, eggs, or brown rice.

4 zucchini, peeled (about 1 pound)
Salt and freshly ground pepper
About ½ cup grated imported
    Parmesan cheese

1½ to 2 tablespoons olive oil or melted
    butter

Cut each zucchini in thirds lengthwise. With a thin-bladed knife, make lengthwise cuts in each piece about ⅛ inch apart, leaving the slices attached at one end so that ½ inch of the zucchini piece is not cut.

Cook zucchini pieces in a pan of boiling salted water for 3 minutes. Rinse with cold water and drain well. Put on a cloth or paper towel and press slices gently so they fan out. Pat them dry.

Brush fans with oil on both sides and sprinkle them with pepper. Dip both sides in Parmesan, then arrange fans in one layer in a lightly oiled gratin dish or heavy shallow baking dish. (*Zucchini can be kept, covered, 1 day in refrigerator.*)

Preheat the oven to 400°F. Bake zucchini until just sizzling, about 10 minutes. Broil briefly, watching carefully, until lightly browned in spots. Serve hot.

Makes 4 side-dish servings

NAPOLI ZUCCHINI CASSEROLE

Fresh basil, Parmesan cheese, and tomatoes give this casserole a lovely, pizzalike aroma. Many versions of the recipe call for deep-frying the zucchini slices and layering them with a large amount of mozzarella cheese, but I prefer to sauté the vegetable and use just a sprinkling of Parmesan for a lighter dish.

3 tablespoons olive oil
1 pound small zucchini, cut lengthwise
    into ⅛-inch thick slices
½ large onion, chopped
1 pound ripe tomatoes, peeled, seeded,
    and chopped; or 1 28-ounce can
    plum tomatoes, drained and
    chopped

¼ to ⅓ cup coarsely chopped fresh
    basil
Salt and freshly ground pepper
4 large basil leaves, torn in pieces
3 tablespoons grated imported
    Parmesan cheese

Heat 2 tablespoons oil in a large, heavy skillet over medium-high heat. Add zucchini in batches enough to make 1 layer and sauté 1 minute per side. Remove to a plate.

Heat remaining oil in skillet, add onion, and sauté over low heat for 5 minutes. Add tomatoes and cook until thickened, 5 to 10 minutes. Add chopped basil. Taste and adjust seasoning.

Preheat the oven to 350°F. Lightly oil a 9-inch square baking dish. Add half the zucchini. Top with half the torn basil, half the tomato sauce, and 1 tablespoon Parmesan. Top with remaining zucchini and oil on plate. Repeat layering remaining ingredients. Bake casserole uncovered for 20 minutes. Let stand about 10 minutes before serving. Serve hot or at room temperature.

Makes 4 side-dish servings or 2 main-course servings with rice

ZUCCHINI BOATS WITH CARROT PUREE

Carrot puree is a favorite comfort food in France and much of Europe, and is lovely served in zucchini boats. These are delicious with light meats—braised or roasted turkey breasts, grilled veal chops, or sautéed scaloppini. For a vegetarian feast, serve it as one of several stuffed vegetable dishes.

You can also present carrot puree in flower-shaped pattypan squashes. And other good fillings for zucchini or squash are Duxelles (page 408), or tomato or red pepper purees.

1 pound carrots, peeled	3 tablespoons butter
Salt and freshly ground pepper	4 small zucchini (about 1¼ pounds),
½ teaspoon sugar	ends trimmed

Cut carrots into ½-inch slices. Put them in a medium saucepan with enough water to cover and a pinch of salt. Bring to a boil. Cover and simmer 25 to 30 minutes, or until carrots are very tender when pierced with a sharp knife.

Drain carrots. Put them in a food processor, blender, or food mill and puree until very smooth.

Return puree to saucepan and stir briefly over low heat to dry. Add sugar, salt, and 2 tablespoons butter and stir over low heat until blended in. Taste and adjust seasoning.

Preheat oven to 400°F. Add whole zucchini to a large saucepan of boiling salted water. Boil 2 minutes and drain. Rinse with cold water and drain thoroughly. Cut each zucchini in half lengthwise. With a small sharp knife, carefully scoop out seed-filled centers of each half, leaving a boat-shaped shell; be careful not to pierce the sides. Put zucchini in a generously buttered shallow baking dish. Dot them with remaining butter and sprinkle with salt and pepper. Bake for 5 minutes.

Spoon carrot puree into zucchini. Bake 10 more minutes or until ends of zucchini are tender when pierced with a sharp knife. Serve hot.

Makes 4 side-dish servings

PROVENÇAL ZUCCHINI OMELET WITH GARLIC

Sautéed zucchini are a great addition to omelets and scrambled eggs. In Provence omelets are often flat like Italian frittatas, instead of being rolled as in the rest of France. The pronounced garlic flavor of this omelet is because the garlic is not precooked. Sometimes grated Parmesan cheese is added to the eggs as well. Many other vegetables are also used in omelets in Provence; sautéed shredded spinach or chard leaves, sautéed sliced onions, or uncooked tomatoes.

½ pound zucchini
3 tablespoons olive oil
Salt and pepper

4 eggs
1 medium garlic clove, finely chopped

Scrub the zucchini, then cut into crosswise slices about ¼ inch thick. Heat 2 tablespoons oil in a heavy 9- or 10-inch frying pan, if possible with an ovenproof handle. Add the zucchini and sauté over medium-high heat, turning them over occasionally, about 5 minutes or until just tender. Season to taste with salt and pepper.

Thoroughly beat the eggs with the garlic, salt, and pepper. With a slotted spoon, transfer the zucchini to the eggs and mix gently. Dry the frying pan.

Add the remaining oil to the pan and heat over medium heat. Swirl the pan slightly so the oil coats the sides as well. Add the egg mixture to the hot oil. Cook without stirring, but occasionally lift the edge of the omelet and tip the pan so the uncooked part of the egg mixture runs to the edge of the pan. When the top of the omelet is nearly set, place the pan in the broiler. Broil until the top is set and lightly browned. Serve from the pan.

Makes 2 main-course servings

NOTE: If the frying pan doesn't have an ovenproof handle, finish cooking the omelet thus: When the top is nearly set, carefully slide a wide utensil such as a pancake turner under the omelet to free it from the pan. Cut the omelet in half and turn it over. Cook about ½ minute over low heat to brown the second side. Transfer to a platter or to plates and serve.

MOROCCAN GREEN AND YELLOW SQUASH SALAD WITH CUMIN

The summer squash cooks directly in its tangy garlic-cumin dressing in this easy, tasty recipe. Serve it as an appetizer or a refreshing partner for grilled chicken.

½ pound zucchini
½ pound crookneck squash or yellow
   zucchini
1 medium garlic clove, minced
1 teaspoon paprika
2 tablespoons vegetable or olive oil

¼ cup water
Salt and freshly ground pepper
½ teaspoon ground cumin
Cayenne pepper to taste
1 tablespoon strained fresh lemon juice

Quarter the zucchini lengthwise, then cut it into ¾-inch slices crosswise; it will form cubes. Cut crookneck squash in cubes of similar size.

   Put both squash in a medium sauté pan with garlic, paprika, oil, and water. Sprinkle with salt and pepper. Bring to a boil and cook uncovered over medium-high heat, stirring often, about 5 minutes or until squash pieces are crisp-tender and most of liquid evaporates. Add cumin and cayenne pepper, and stir over low heat for 30 seconds. Off the heat, add lemon juice. Taste and adjust seasoning. Serve cool.

Makes 3 or 4 side-dish servings

TANGY TUNISIAN ZUCCHINI SALAD

This very quick, easy salad of lightly cooked zucchini with a zesty garlic dressing makes a refreshing summer appetizer. I find that sun-dried tomatoes are a perfect garnish although they are associated with the cuisine of Italy. If you prefer to stay in the Maghreb tradition, garnish the salad with roasted red pepper strips.

6 medium zucchini (1½ pounds)
2 large garlic cloves, finely minced
2 tablespoons strained fresh lemon
   juice

2 tablespoons extra-virgin olive oil
Salt and freshly ground pepper
4 to 6 oil-packed sun-dried tomato
   halves

Halve zucchini lengthwise, put them cut side down, and halve again lengthwise. Cut each piece in thirds crosswise.

Add zucchini to a large saucepan of boiling salted water and boil uncovered over high heat about 2 minutes or until crisp-tender; do not overcook. Drain immediately in a colander, rinse with cold water, and drain very well.

In a small dish, mix garlic with lemon juice, oil, salt, and pepper.

Put zucchini in a shallow dish and sprinkle with salt and pepper. Pour garlic dressing over them and toss gently. Cover and refrigerate about 15 minutes. (*Can be kept, covered, 1 day in refrigerator.*) Garnish with tomatoes.

Makes 4 to 6 appetizer servings

CHAYOTE SQUASH WITH TOMATOES AND CARIBBEAN SOFRITO

This Puerto Rican dish is good on its own, served with white or brown rice. For a more substantial dish, stir in a little diced smoked chicken or turkey breast, or sliced heated turkey sausage; or you can add some beaten eggs and scramble them with the vegetable mixture. If chayote squash is not available, prepare this dish with 4 or 5 diced, briefly cooked zucchini.

2 chayote squash
Salt and freshly ground pepper
Caribbean Sofrito or Spicy Sofrito
  (page 396)

1 large ripe tomato, or 3 ripe or
  canned plum tomatoes, diced
1 tablespoon chopped cilantro (fresh
  coriander)

Halve chayote squashes lengthwise. Add to a saucepan of boiling salted water. Simmer uncovered over medium heat for 25 minutes or until just tender. Drain and rinse with cold water. Remove peel with a paring knife, then cut seed from center and spongy white meat around it and discard. Cut vegetable into ¾-inch dice.

Heat sofrito in a sauté pan over low heat. Add tomato, chayote, salt, and pepper and stir 2 to 3 minutes or until heated through. Taste and adjust seasoning. Serve hot, sprinkled with cilantro.

Makes 2 main-course servings with rice or 4 side-dish servings

MEXICAN BAKED CHAYOTE SQUASH SLICES

This dish is based on a recipe I learned from Mexican-born chef Jorge Villanueva and his wife, California chef Teri Appleton Villanueva. The original Mexican specialty is made of chayote squash slices sandwiched with Monterey Jack cheese, breaded and fried. I have simplified it by baking the breaded squash slices in one layer and topping them with cheese. For a lighter dish, omit the cheese. The Villanuevas recommend serving the baked squash slices with Chipotle Chili Salsa (page 389), which makes a colorful, delicious topping and turns the squash into a party dish.

When chayote squash is not available, you can make this dish with zucchini.

2 chayote squash (total about 1 pound)
1 egg
Salt and freshly ground pepper
¼ cup all-purpose flour

⅔ cup bread crumbs
2 to 3 teaspoons vegetable oil
About 12 slices Monterey Jack cheese,
about ⅛ inch thick

Preheat oven to 450°F. Lightly oil 2 baking sheets. Peel chayote squash and cut in lengthwise slices about ⅓ inch thick. Remove seed from each by cutting around it.

In a shallow bowl beat egg with salt and pepper. Spread flour and bread crumbs on 2 plates. Dip both sides of each squash slice in flour, egg, and bread crumbs. Transfer to baking sheets in a single layer. Sprinkle squash with oil.

Bake 15 minutes or until tender. Trim cheese slices so they are slightly smaller than chayote slices. Top each chayote slice with a cheese slice. Bake 3 minutes or until cheese melts. Serve hot.

Makes 4 appetizer servings

MARTINIQUE CHAYOTE SALAD

Chayote squash, also called vegetable pears, are becoming more common in our supermarkets. In this simple, light, and refreshing salad from the French Caribbean island of Martinique, the cooked squash is moistened with a garlic-scented dressing flavored with thyme and hot pepper sauce.

4 chayote squash, halved lengthwise
Salt and freshly ground pepper
2 to 3 tablespoons extra-virgin olive oil
1 tablespoon lemon or lime juice or
  white wine vinegar
1 medium garlic clove, finely minced

1 teaspoons chopped fresh thyme, or ½
  teaspoon dried thyme, crumbled
½ teaspoon Caribbean or other bottled
  hot pepper sauce
2 tablespoons chopped fresh parsley

Add squash to a large saucepan of boiling salted water. Simmer uncovered over medium heat 25 minutes or until just tender. Drain and rinse with cold water. Remove peel with aid of a paring knife. Cut seed from center and spongy white meat around it.

Keeping each squash half together, cut into ¼-inch slices. Transfer slices of each half-squash together to a platter; press slightly to flatten but leave slices overlapping.

Whisk together 2 tablespoons oil, lemon juice, garlic, thyme, salt and pepper, and hot pepper sauce. Taste and adjust seasoning; whisk in remaining oil if desired.

Pour dressing over squash. Serve sprinkled with parsley

Makes 6 appetizer or side-dish servings

30

Vegetable Medleys

The recipes in this chapter feature dishes in which no single vegetable is dominant. In every cuisine there are some dishes that include a variety of vegetables. Often these are braised dishes for which the vegetables slowly cook together. Ratatouille (page 372), the Provençal casserole of eggplant, zucchini, peppers, onions, and tomatoes, is the best known of this type of dish. A less familiar example is Givetch (page 370), the baked Balkan vegetable stew of eggplant, potatoes, peppers, onions, and green beans in an aromatic tomato sauce. These braised dishes are convenient to serve because they reheat well and thus can be made ahead.

Faster-cooking vegetable mélanages are the Chinese vegetable stir-fried dishes, such as Chinese Vegetables with Rice Noodles and Shrimp (page 366), which cook in no time. Also quick is Thai Vegetable Medley with Mint and Chilies (page 365), made of sautéed Japanese eggplants, zucchini, and bell peppers. Rapidly sautéed vegetables can be tossed with rice or noodles for a lively main course.

A wide assortment of vegetables makes for the most colorful salads. They are often mixed together, as in Mediterranean "chopped salads," or they might be served like the well-known French Crudités (page 374), for which each vegetable is dressed separately with vinaigrette and the resulting separate salads are served side by side as one dish.

In classic European cuisine there is the category of salads known as "composed salads," which contain mixed cooked vegetables but sometimes some raw ones as well. The most celebrated representative of these salads is the Niçoise Salad (page 371), which usually includes cooked potatoes and green beans as well as uncooked cucumber slices and tomato wedges.

THAI VEGETABLE MEDLEY WITH MINT AND CHILIES

Mint and chilies, a popular flavoring duo in Thai cooking, add zip to vegetables, as in this easy sauté of eggplant, zucchini, and bell pepper. We associate shallots with French cooking, but Thai cooks like them too. My Thai chef friend Somchit Singchalee told me that unlike the French, the Thais like to sauté their shallots until brown.

Fish sauce, a favorite seasoning sauce in Thai cooking, smells somewhat strong to Americans but adds a characteristically Thai taste. It can be found at Asian specialty shops, in some supermarkets, and through mail order (see page 437).

Serve the vegetable medley with rice, preferably Thai jasmine rice, and bottled Asian hot sauce. SEE PHOTOGRAPH.

½ pound Japanese eggplants or small Italian eggplants
½ pound zucchini
1 large red bell pepper
3 tablespoons vegetable oil
1 medium shallot, sliced
2 large garlic cloves, minced

1 or 2 hot peppers, preferably red—either jalapeño or serrano or Thai hot peppers, minced
2 teaspoons Thai fish sauce (*nam pla*)
2 teaspoons soy sauce
1 cup fresh mint leaves
Fresh mint sprigs, for garnish

Halve eggplants lengthwise; slice about ¼ inch thick. Cut zucchini the same way. Cut bell pepper into strips ½ inch wide; cut each strip in half crosswise.

Heat oil in a large skillet, add shallot, and sauté over medium heat until light brown, about 3 minutes. Add eggplant and bell pepper, and sauté 8 to 10 minutes, stirring often. Add garlic, hot peppers, and zucchini and sauté 1 minute. Add fish sauce and soy sauce, and heat over low heat for 1 minute or until vegetables are crisp-tender. Off the heat, add mint leaves and stir to wilt slightly. Serve garnished with mint sprigs.

Makes 3 or 4 side-dish servings or 2 main-course servings with rice

CHINESE VEGETABLES WITH RICE NOODLES AND SHRIMP

Ginger-scented stir-fried bok choy with baby corn and water chestnuts makes a light and colorful side dish. Here the vegetables become a tasty sauce for fresh rice noodles, which can be found in Asian markets. Shrimp provide good flavor and a pretty color, but you can omit them for a vegetarian dish. This dish is best if you use the tender baby bok choy.

2 baby bok choy (total ½ pound)
1 tablespoon plus 1 teaspoon soy sauce
1½ teaspoons cornstarch
1 cup Chicken or Vegetable Stock (pages 407, 406) or canned broth
2 tablespoons plus 2 teaspoons vegetable oil
¼ pound small or medium shrimp, shelled
1 pound fresh rice noodles

2 medium garlic cloves, minced
2 teaspoons minced peeled fresh ginger
12 canned baby corn, drained, rinsed, and halved crosswise
12 canned water chestnuts, drained, rinsed, and each cut in 2 rounds
Salt and freshly ground pepper
1 green onion, chopped

Divide bok choy by rib and rinse very thoroughly in cold water. Cut stalks and leaves into 1-inch squares; you will need about 1 quart of squares.

In a small bowl mix soy sauce and cornstarch until blended. Stir in stock and mix well.

In a large skillet or wok, heat 1 tablespoon vegetable oil, add shrimp, and sauté 1 minute. Remove from pan. Add 1 tablespoon oil to pan and heat it. Add bok choy squares and stir-fry for 2 minutes over high heat. Remove from pan.

Put rice noodles in a large bowl and pour boiling water over them. Let stand about 1 minute, lifting noodles often with tongs to separate them. Drain in strainer.

Heat 2 teaspoons oil in wok or large skillet over medium-high heat. Add garlic and ginger, and sauté 15 seconds. Add stock mixture and bring to boil, stirring. Add baby corn, water chestnuts, shrimp, and bok choy and bring just to boil. Add noodles, salt, and pepper and toss. Taste and adjust seasoning. Serve sprinkled with chopped green onion.

Makes 2 main-course servings

EAST MEDITERRANEAN VEGETABLE STEW WITH LAMB

This baked stew is common in Lebanon and Syria. It resembles the ratatouille of Provence at the opposite end of the Mediterranean, but this version contains small cubes of lamb for flavoring and its main seasonings are aromatic spices rather than the fresh herbs of Provence.

¾ pound small zucchini, cut into 1-inch slices
¾ pound red boiling potatoes, peeled and cut into ¾-inch dice
1¼-pound eggplant, cut into 1-inch dice
2 pounds ripe tomatoes, peeled and cut into ¾-inch dice; or 2 28-ounce cans plum tomatoes, drained and diced
1 large onion, thinly sliced
1¼ pounds boneless lamb shoulder meat, trimmed and cut into ¾-inch pieces

¾ to 1 teaspoon salt
½ to ¾ teaspoon ground black pepper
¼ teaspoon ground cinnamon
Pinch of ground cloves
Pinch of freshly grated nutmeg
¼ cup water
2 tablespoons (¼ stick) butter, cut in small cubes, or olive or vegetable oil

Preheat oven to 350°F. Mix all the vegetables with the lamb pieces in a large, heavy gratin dish or shallow baking dish. Mix salt, pepper, cinnamon, cloves, and nutmeg. Sprinkle spice mixture over vegetables and lamb, and toss with your hands to mix thoroughly. Add water and cover with foil.

Bake for 40 minutes. Dot with butter or sprinkle with oil. Uncover and bake, stirring often and pushing potatoes down into liquid, for 2 hours, or until all the ingredients are very tender and most of the liquid has evaporated. (*The stew may be prepared up to 2 days ahead and kept covered and chilled. Reheat it over low heat, covered.*) Serve the stew from the baking dish or from a heated serving dish.

Makes 4 main-course servings

VEGETABLE TEMPURA

For many people this is the most loved Japanese vegetable recipe. The vegetables are dipped in a light batter, deep-fried, and served with a simple dip.

When I was studying French cooking at La Varenne in Paris, a Japanese student demonstrated tempura-making for the other students and the teachers. The French chefs were impressed by her technique of taking small handfuls of haricots verts *and dipping them in the batter together to make bundles, rather than dipping them one at a time. Of course, very thin French-style green beans are perfect for this method. You can also dip small bundles of bean sprouts, using tongs; the batter connects in the oil and forms a lacy pattern.*

All sorts of vegetables that are served raw or that cook very quickly are suitable for making tempura. At a Japanese restaurant near my home, tempura is made from sweet potato slices, green beans, zucchini slices, mushrooms, wedges of kabocha squash, and little bunches of radish sprouts. You can also use asparagus pieces, cauliflower florets, or Japanese eggplant or cucumber slices. The chef of the restaurant gave me his recipe for making the dipping sauce, but instead of using dashi, *the standard Japanese seafood stock, I use vegetable stock.*

Tempura Dipping Sauce

1 cup vegetable stock or water
¼ cup *mirin* (Japanese sweet rice
    wine)

¼ cup soy sauce
½ teaspoon sugar

2 tablespoons grated fresh ginger
    (optional, for accompaniment)
½ cup grated daikon radish (optional,
    for accompaniment)
16 green beans, ends removed
8 slices zucchini, ¼ inch thick
16 medium broccoli florets
8 mushrooms, patted dry, halved

8 peeled sweet potato slices, ¼ inch
    thick
16 sugar-snap peas or snow peas, ends
    removed
1 cup bean sprouts, rinsed and patted
    dry
1 cup radish sprouts, rinsed and patted
    dry

Batter

¾ cup plus 2 tablespoons all-purpose
    flour
¼ teaspoon baking soda

1 egg yolk
1 cup ice water

Vegetable oil for deep-frying

Read the Hints on Deep-Frying (page 15) before frying the tempura. Prepare dipping sauce: Mix ingredients in bowl. Prepare ginger and radish and put on small serving plates.

Prepare all vegetables. Keep each type separate. Have ready a tray lined with paper towels.

To make batter, sift flour with baking soda. In a small bowl beat egg yolk. Gradually beat in ice water. Add flour mixture all at once. Mix gently so batter is combined but is slightly lumpy. Refrigerate while heating oil. Heat oil to 350°F. in a deep sauté pan, wok, or deep-fryer.

Dip one type of vegetable in batter to coat lightly; let extra batter drip into bowl. Put in oil; deep-fry, turning once or twice, about 2 minutes or until batter is light golden and crisp.

Drain on paper towels. Put in low oven (200°F.) to keep warm. Skim pieces of batter from oil. Continue frying remaining vegetables. To fry sprouts, use tongs to dip a small handful of sprouts in batter and to add to oil; fry about 30 seconds; remove with slotted spoon.

Serve as soon as possible. Serve dipping sauce in small bowls; each person adds grated ginger or daikon to his or her bowl, to taste.

Makes 4 to 8 appetizer servings

GIVETCH—BALKAN VEGETABLE CASSEROLE

This casserole is popular in Bulgaria, Romania, and other Balkan countries. I learned it from a Romanian friend when I lived in Israel. The slow-cooking vegetable casserole traditionally was cooked in the baker's oven in some communities. It is the Balkan version of the French ratatouille and contains many of the same ingredients—eggplant, peppers, tomatoes, and onions. But givetch *also contains green beans, carrots, celery, potatoes, and sometimes okra. Hot pepper flakes, garlic, and parsley are favorite flavorings, but thyme, rosemary, dill, or paprika might also be used.*

This is a summer version, but givetch *is also made in winter, and then it might contain cauliflower, mushrooms, celery root, or dried beans.* Givetch *can be vegetarian, as in this recipe, or can be cooked with cubes of beef or spicy sausages. Some people garnish their casserole at the last moment with green grapes.*

4 tablespoons olive or vegetable oil
2 medium onions, halved and sliced
    thin
1 red bell pepper, cut into strips about
    ⅓ inch wide
1 green bell pepper, cut in strips about
    ⅓ inch wide
1 large eggplant (1¼ pounds), cut in
    ¾-inch cubes
Salt and freshly ground pepper
1½ pounds ripe tomatoes, chopped; or
    1 28-ounce and 1 14-ounce can,
    drained and coarsely chopped
½ teaspoon paprika
4 medium boiling potatoes (1 pound),
    cut into ¾-inch cubes

4 ounces green or yellow beans, ends
    removed; or okra, stem trimmed;
    or half of each
2 medium carrots, sliced ⅛ inch thick
3 tablespoons tomato paste
¾ cup Chicken or Vegetable Stock
    (page 407, 406) or water
¼ teaspoon sugar
1 teaspoon dried thyme
1 large garlic clove, minced (optional)
½ teaspoon dried hot red pepper flakes
    (optional)
2 tablespoons chopped fresh parsley

Preheat the oven to 350°F. Heat 2 tablespoons oil in a large, heavy skillet, add onions and peppers, and sauté over medium heat about 7 minutes or until onion browns. Remove onions and peppers. Add remaining oil to skillet and heat it. Add eggplant, sprinkle with salt and pepper, and sauté, stirring, for 3 or 4 minutes. Remove. Add tomatoes and paprika to pan and cook about 10 minutes or until thick.

Oil two 2-quart shallow baking dishes and layer the vegetables in dishes, sprinkling each layer lightly with salt and pepper: Use half the onion mixture on bottom of each dish, top with potatoes, then beans or okra and carrots, then tomatoes, then eggplant, and finally add remaining onion mixture.

In a small bowl, mix tomato paste, ½ cup stock, salt and pepper, sugar, thyme, garlic, and pepper flakes. Pour sauce over vegetables. Pour remaining stock into bottom of baking dishes. Cover and bake 30 minutes; check and add a little stock to bottom of pan if it's becoming dry. Re-cover and bake 30 more minutes or until all vegetables are tender. (*Casserole can be kept, covered, 2 days in refrigerator.*) Serve hot or cold, sprinkled with parsley.

Makes 8 side-dish or 4 to 6 main-course servings

CAFÉ DE PARIS NIÇOISE SALAD

Niçoise salad is probably the most famous of French salads. Some ingredients change with the seasons and from place to place, but it always has tomatoes, black olives, and anchovies and usually cooked green beans. Other additions I've seen are cooked potatoes, cucumbers, capers, tuna, pickles, and hard-boiled eggs. It's good to know when to stop, so the salad keeps its original Mediterranean character. This is a version I frequently enjoyed at Café de Paris on the Champs-Elysées.

12 anchovy fillets
3 medium potatoes, unpeeled
Salt and freshly ground pepper
½ to ¾ cup Thick Mustard Vinaigrette
    (page 382), made with olive oil
¾ pound green beans

7 ounces tuna, preferably in olive oil
    (optional)
¼ cup oil-cured black olives, halved
    and pitted
3 ripe tomatoes, quartered
3 hard-boiled eggs, quartered

Soak anchovies in water while preparing the salad.

Cook potatoes in salted water about 25 minutes or until tender but not falling apart. Peel, slice, and put them in a shallow serving dish. Add about half the vinaigrette and mix gently.

Cook green beans in boiling salted water for about 6 minutes or until crisp-tender, rinse with cold water, and drain.

Flake the tuna but leave in fairly large chunks. Mix gently with beans and enough vinaigrette to moisten. Taste and adjust seasoning. Spoon mixture over potatoes.

Drain anchovies and pat dry. Decorate center of salad with anchovy fillets and olive halves, and garnish edges with tomato and egg quarters. Moisten them with vinaigrette. Serve salad at room temperature.

Makes 6 appetizer or 4 light main-course servings

RATATOUILLE

This aromatic stew of eggplant, peppers, zucchini, tomatoes, and onions with garlic and fresh herbs is one of the glories of Provençal cooking. It's wonderful hot or cold, as a main dish or as an accompaniment for grilled chicken, steak, or fish. Naturally it's at its best in summer, when tomatoes, peppers, eggplant, and zucchini are at the height of their season.

Ratatouille is great to have on hand for making quick supper dishes. Toss it with cooked rice or pasta, or roll it in a crepe. Some untraditional but delicious uses are as a filling for hot tortillas or as a topping for pizza.

1 small green bell pepper
1 small red bell pepper
½ pound zucchini (3 small)
¾ to 1 pound thin eggplant (1 small eggplant), peeled if desired
About 7 tablespoons olive oil
2 pounds ripe tomatoes, peeled, seeded, and chopped; or 2 28-ounce cans plum tomatoes, drained and chopped

Salt and freshly ground pepper
1 bay leaf
1 large onion, halved and thinly sliced
3 large garlic cloves, minced
1 teaspoon chopped fresh rosemary
2 teaspoons chopped fresh thyme
2 tablespoons chopped fresh basil
Basil leaves, for garnish (optional)

Cut peppers into strips about ½ inch wide. Cut zucchini and eggplant into ⅜-inch slices. Cut any large eggplant slices in half.

Heat 1 tablespoon oil in a heavy, medium saucepan or stew pan over medium-high heat. Add tomatoes, salt, pepper, and bay leaf and cook, stirring often, for 20 minutes. Remove bay leaf.

Heat 2 tablespoons oil in a large, wide casserole over low heat. Add onion and cook 5 minutes. Add peppers and cook over medium-low heat, stirring often, about 10 minutes. Add zucchini, reduce heat to low, and cook about 5 minutes or until barely tender.

Heat 2 tablespoons oil in a skillet over medium-high heat. Add half the eggplant slices and sauté 2 or 3 minutes per side or until just tender. Repeat with another 2 tablespoons oil and remaining eggplant slices.

Stir garlic, rosemary, and thyme into the tomato mixture and transfer to the zucchini mixture. Add eggplant slices. Mix gently. Bring to a boil. Cover, reduce heat to low, and simmer 5 minutes to blend flavors. Uncover, raise heat to medium-high, and cook about 5 minutes or until thickened to taste. All vegetables should be tender. Stir in chopped basil. Taste and adjust seasoning; season generously with pepper. Serve hot or cold.

Makes 4 or 5 side-dish or 2 or 3 main-course servings

RAW VEGETABLES WITH CHIPOTLE CHILE DIP

For a zesty dip for raw vegetables, combine potent chipotle salsa with mayonnaise; you can use reduced-fat mayonnaise and it will still taste good. Serve with any vegetables that you like raw, but be sure they are very fresh. Have ready a colorful selection of vegetables and arrange them on a platter around the dip.

6 tablespoons Chipotle Chili Salsa
   (page 389)

About 4 cups of a selection of the
   following:
   jicama, peeled and cut into sticks
   small radishes
   cucumber, cut into sticks
   carrot sticks

2 tablespoons mayonnaise, regular or
   reduced-fat

celery sticks
cauliflower florets
broccoli florets
zucchini, cut into sticks
mushrooms, cut into thick slices
cherry tomatoes

Mix salsa with mayonnaise. Spoon into a small serving bowl.

Arrange vegetables on a platter around dip, grouping each type together and alternating colors.

Makes 4 appetizer servings

CRUDITÉS

*W*hen I encounter "crudités" at parties, I am often disappointed at what they turn out to be—thick carrot and celery sticks and big raw cauliflower and broccoli florets served with dip. Some of the guests nibble halfheartedly on the vegetables because "they're good for you." I always wish the crudités *would be the kind I enjoyed in Paris.*

The French word crudités *comes from* cru, *meaning "raw." When prepared the classic way, this dish is a beautiful array of salads, each of a single raw vegetable, served side by side. The vegetables are grated or cut into fine pieces and seasoned carefully with a little vinaigrette.*

There are a few exceptions to this formula. The platter sometimes features a salad of a cooked vegetable—usually beets, which in France are sold at the market already cooked, or potatoes. Cucumbers might come with a creamy dressing instead of a vinaigrette, while celery root is moistened with mustardy mayonnaise. Baby radishes; small, flavorful black olives from Nice; or hard-boiled eggs might garnish the plate.

As familiar in France as cole slaw is in America, crudités *are the quintessential bistro appetizer. Some reviewers even judge restaurants by their* crudités, *although this dish is not the result of the chef's flight of imagination; rather, these simple, down-to-earth salads indicate the quality of the restaurant's produce and the chef's attention to detail.*

When the vegetables are fresh and well seasoned, this is the perfect first course. In fact, it can play a major part in the meal. Several times my husband and I ordered a platter of crudités *in Paris and had such a good time eating the salads with fresh baguette that we were satisfied before the main course arrived.*

Part of the attraction of this appetizer is its seasonal variations, as the choice of vegetables changes with what appears at the market. When the luscious produce of early summer arrives, the crudités *platters are at their best, featuring ripe tomatoes, crisp cucumbers, young carrots, and sweet peppers. You can also prepare the salads from other vegetables that taste good raw, like shredded zucchini or thin pieces of jicama.*

People in North Africa and the Middle East also love crudités. *In these areas, the salads are seasoned differently from those in France, and some might be spicy or tangy. You can make them by substituting Tangy Moroccan Dressing (page 381) for the vinaigrette.*

Crudités *are one of the most convenient appetizers for picnics. The salads can be prepared ahead and each kept in its own container. All you need do at serving time is spoon them onto a platter or plates.*

For a time-saving tip when preparing crudités, *don't forget your food processor. Perhaps you remember when these appliances first came out, and demonstrators impressed us by reducing cabbages or several pounds of carrots to shreds in no time? This is still one of the best uses of the processor, and it certainly makes preparing the vegetables a snap.*

For a colorful platter, it's good to have at least three kinds of vegetables. Of course, each vegetable also makes a good salad on its own. For accompaniment serve fresh French or Italian bread.

At least 3 of the following:
  4 large carrots
  ½ small head green cabbage
  1 pound ripe tomatoes
  3 red, green, or yellow bell peppers
  1 large cucumber
  2 pounds potatoes
  5 or 6 medium beets (about 1½-inch
    diameter)

Classic Vinaigrette (page 383)
3 to 5 tablespoons chopped fresh
    parsley (for tomatoes, potatoes,
    and beets)

2 to 3 tablespoons chopped green
    onion (for tomatoes and potatoes)
1 to 2 tablespoons thin strips fresh
    basil (for tomatoes)
2 to 3 teaspoons snipped fresh chives
    (for cucumber)
Baby radishes, hard-boiled eggs, oil-
    cured or Kalamata olives, for
    garnish

Prepare each vegetable as given below, adding just enough vinaigrette to moisten. Taste each salad for seasoning after mixing with vinaigrette. Spoon side by side on a platter and add the garnishes, if you like.

✗ *Carrots*: Coarsely grate. Mix with about ¼ cup vinaigrette.

✗ *Cabbage*: Shred in thin strips. Toss with about 6 to 7 tablespoons vinaigrette.

✗ *Tomatoes*: Prepare at the last minute. Cut them into slices, arrange on a dish, and sprinkle with 2 or 3 tablespoons vinaigrette and with 1 tablespoon chopped parsley, green onion, or thin strips of basil.

✗ *Bell peppers*: Cut into strips or dice. Mix with about 3 to 4 tablespoons olive-oil vinaigrette.

✗ *Cucumber*: Cut into thin slices and toss with about 2 tablespoons vinaigrette and 2 or 3 teaspoons snipped chives.

✗ *Potatoes*: Cook, peel, and dice. Mix gently with 6 to 8 tablespoons vinaigrette and 1 or 2 tablespoons each chopped parsley and green onion.

✗ *Beets*: Cook, peel, and slice or dice. Combine with about ¼ cup vinaigrette and 1 or 2 tablespoons chopped parsley.

Makes about 10 to 12 appetizer servings; each salad on its own makes 3 to 4 appetizer servings

MEDITERRANEAN DICED SALAD, CALIFORNIA STYLE

Jicama and bok choy are not Mediterranean vegetables, but they make a delicious new addition to the region's traditional vegetable salad. This colorful salad is pretty served in a fairly shallow glass bowl.

½ long European cucumber, 3 pickling cucumbers, or 1 medium cucumber, diced small
8 plum tomatoes or 4 medium tomatoes, cut into small dice
½ cup chopped red onion
1 small red, yellow, or green bell pepper, cut into small dice
⅔ cup finely diced peeled jicama
⅔ cup finely diced bok choy, white part only

3 to 4 tablespoons chopped fresh parsley or cilantro (fresh coriander)
1 to 2 tablespoons extra-virgin olive oil
1 to 2 teaspoons strained fresh lemon juice
Salt and freshly ground pepper
Hot pepper sauce to taste (optional)

Mix the diced cucumber, tomatoes, onion, pepper, jicama, bok choy, and parsley. Add oil, lemon juice, salt, pepper, and hot sauce to taste. Serve cold or at room temperature.

Makes 4 appetizer or side-dish servings

INDIAN CHICKPEA, TOMATO, AND CUCUMBER SALAD

"It's like Israeli salad with chickpeas added," commented a friend when we tasted this appetizer at an Indian restaurant in Santa Monica. The salad was lightly seasoned, in pleasing contrast to other spicy dishes on the menu. It may not be a traditional Indian dish, but it makes use of chickpeas and cilantro in a tasty, light, oil-free, and very quick dish.

1 15- or 16-ounce can chickpeas
   (garbanzo beans), drained and
   rinsed; or about 2 cups cooked
   chickpeas
4 plum tomatoes, diced
1 cup finely diced cucumber
⅔ cup finely chopped red onion
¼ cup chopped cilantro (fresh
   coriander) or parsley
4 teaspoons strained fresh lime or
   lemon juice
Salt to taste
Hot red pepper (cayenne) to taste

Mix ingredients, taste, and adjust seasoning. (*Salad can be kept, covered, 8 hours in refrigerator.*) Serve cold.

Makes 4 side-dish servings

CHICKPEA SALAD WITH FENNEL, PISTOU, AND TOMATOES

*F*avorite flavors of the French Riviera—olive oil, lemon juice, tomatoes, black olives, fennel, as well *as a* pistou *of basil and garlic—combine in this dish and turn humble chickpeas into an elegant salad.*

2 15- or 16-ounce cans chickpeas
   (garbanzo beans), or 3 to 3½ cups
   cooked chickpeas, drained
3 tablespoons Pistou (page 387),
   chopped fresh basil, or bottled
   pesto
1 tablespoon plus 1 teaspoon extra-
   virgin olive oil
1 tablespoon strained fresh lemon juice
⅔ cup thinly sliced fennel or celery
   stalks
Salt and freshly ground pepper
1½ cups diced ripe tomatoes
1 quart baby lettuces (sometimes called
   mixed European lettuces)
Black olives, for garnish

Mix chickpeas, Pistou, 2 teaspoons oil, and 2 teaspoons lemon juice. Add fennel, salt, and pepper. Marinate, if desired, for 1 or 2 hours. (*Salad can be kept, covered, 1 day in refrigerator.*) Add tomatoes to chickpea mixture. Taste and adjust seasoning.

Rinse lettuces and dry well. Mix with remaining oil and lemon juice, and season with salt and pepper. Divide lettuce among serving plates. Serve the chickpea salad on the green salad. Garnish with olives.

Makes 4 or 5 appetizer or 2 or 3 main-course servings

31

Sauces and Dressings

Use the sauces in this chapter to add pizzazz to vegetables. Whether you have cooked fresh or frozen vegetables, dressings and sauces will make them festive. Toss hot or cold cooked vegetables with a French Tarragon Vinaigrette (page 103) or Argentinean Chimichurri (page 388) for a flavorful salad. Add a little zesty Mexican Fresh Tomato Salsa (page 390) to vegetables, then roll them in a warmed tortilla. Heat vegetables with a Caribbean Sofrito (page 396) of sautéed peppers and onions spiced with cumin and cilantro, for a savory accompaniment. Or try mixing vegetables with Ten-Minute Tomato Sauce (page 394) and tossing them with pasta or spooning them over hot cooked rice.

In general, sauces for vegetables are quick preparations. Most require no cooking, just whisking together or whirling in a food processor. Unlike many sauces for meat that cook for hours, even the cooked sauces for vegetables need only a brief simmering time.

Many of the dressings are so quick to make that you can have them ready in the time it takes to cook a package of frozen vegetables. Serve, for example, Walnut Oil Vinaigrette (page 383) with cooked lima beans or potatoes, or a light, cumin-scented Tangy Moroccan Dressing (page 381) with green beans or carrots.

For raw vegetables, choose any of the lighter mixtures here as dips rather than using salt-laden packaged dips or those made from high-fat cheeses and cream. Turkish Yogurt-Garlic Sauce (below) is delicious with carrot, zucchini, or cucumber sticks. Chipotle Chili Salsa (page 389) makes a spicy dip for all sorts of raw vegetables, either on its own or mixed with a little mayonnaise as on page 373. And instead of using melted butter for dipping cooked artichoke leaves and hearts or asparagus spears, use a well-flavored vinaigrette as a light, tasty alternative.

TURKISH YOGURT-GARLIC SAUCE

This easy sauce is a traditional accompaniment in Turkey for sautéed carrots, sautéed zucchini, baked or fried eggplant, or roasted peppers. It's also great for dressing up baked winter squash, potatoes, and sweet potatoes.

1 cup plain nonfat or low-fat yogurt
2 small garlic cloves, minced very fine
½ teaspoon dried mint leaves,
    crumbled

Salt and cayenne pepper

Mix yogurt with garlic and mint. Season to taste with salt and cayenne pepper. Serve cold or at room temperature.

Makes 1 cup; about 4 or 6 servings

MOROCCAN GARLIC DRESSING

This dressing is delicious with tomatoes, zucchini, roasted peppers, and grilled eggplant, and for adding zip to green salads.

1 small garlic clove, finely minced
½ teaspoon paprika
½ teaspoon ground cumin
3 tablespoons extra-virgin olive oil

1 tablespoon lemon juice
Salt and freshly ground pepper
Cayenne pepper to taste

Whisk dressing ingredients together. Taste and adjust seasoning.

Makes ¼ cup; about 2 or 3 servings

TANGY MOROCCAN DRESSING

Serve this tangy dressing with sweet vegetables like cooked carrots, beets, and roasted peppers. It's also good with green beans.

1 teaspoon paprika
1 teaspoon ground cumin
2 tablespoons distilled white vinegar
    or lemon juice

2 tablespoons olive or vegetable oil
Salt
Pinch of cayenne pepper

Whisk ingredients together. Taste and adjust seasoning.

Makes scant ¼ cup; about 2 or 3 servings

CARIBBEAN LIME JUICE DRESSING

Use this zesty variation of vinaigrette on grilled peppers, cooked cauliflower, broccoli, carrots, zucchini, or chayote squash, or to moisten a simple tomato or green salad.

4 teaspoons strained fresh lime juice
Salt and freshly ground pepper
½ teaspoon ground cumin
4 tablespoons vegetable oil

½ teaspoon Caribbean hot sauce, Tabasco, or other bottled hot sauce, or to taste

Whisk lime juice with salt, pepper, and cumin. Whisk in oil and hot sauce to taste. Taste and adjust seasoning.

Makes about ¼ cup; about 3 or 4 servings

THICK MUSTARD VINAIGRETTE

Toss this dressing with strong-flavored greens like escarole or dandelion greens.

2 tablespoons wine vinegar
2 to 3 teaspoons Dijon mustard

Salt and freshly ground pepper
6 tablespoons vegetable oil

Whisk vinegar with mustard, salt, and pepper until blended. Gradually add the oil in a stream, whisking until the dressing thickens. Taste and adjust seasoning.

Makes ½ cup; about 4 to 6 servings

CLASSIC VINAIGRETTE

This is the salad dressing in France and Italy. It has become popular throughout Europe, Canada, and in the United States, where it's known in casual restaurants as "Italian dressing." The dressing is perfect for green salad because it lightly coats the greens, but is also good with almost any salad of raw or cooked vegetables.

There are so many different types of oil and vinegar on the market now that enable us to vary the dressing in numerous ways. Use extra-virgin olive oil, vegetable oil, or a mixture of oils; you can also try herb oils or a small amount of hot pepper oil. White wine vinegar or red wine vinegar can be used, or special vinegars such as balsamic vinegar, Champagne vinegar, sherry vinegar, or tarragon vinegar.

Always taste dressings for seasoning. Whenever possible, taste salads for seasoning after adding the dressing. Taste also for the balance of oil and vinegar; since vinegars vary in strength, you might want to add a little more of one element of the dressing or the other.

If you make the dressing without herbs or other fresh flavorings, it will keep for weeks in a jar in the refrigerator. Just shake it before using.

¼ cup wine vinegar or strained fresh
    lemon juice
Salt and pepper

¾ cup extra-virgin olive oil or
    vegetable oil

Whisk vinegar or lemon juice with salt and pepper until salt dissolves. Whisk in the oil and taste for seasoning. (*Dressing can be kept in a closed jar for 2 or 3 weeks in the refrigerator.*) Shake or whisk it again before using.

Makes 1 cup; about 8 servings

VARIATION: **Walnut Oil Vinaigrette**
    Instead of oil above, use ½ cup of walnut oil and ¼ cup of vegetable oil.

PROVENÇAL HERB DRESSING

This dressing is good on almost any vegetable, hot or cold, raw or cooked. Serve it with cooked green beans, sliced raw mushrooms, tomatoes, and raw or grilled bell peppers. It's also a delicious seasoning for salads of raw spinach or mixed greens.

3 tablespoons fresh strained lemon
    juice
Salt and freshly ground pepper
½ cup plus 1 tablespoon extra-virgin
    olive oil
2 to 3 teaspoons fresh thyme leaves, or
    1 teaspoon *herbes de Provence,*
    crumbled

2 teaspoons chopped fresh tarragon
    (optional)
1 tablespoon chopped fresh parsley,
    preferably Italian

Whisk lemon juice with salt and pepper. Whisk in oil, then thyme. Taste and adjust seasoning. (*Dressing can be kept, covered, 1 week in refrigerator.*)
    Whisk dressing before using and add chopped tarragon and parsley.

Makes ¾ cup; about 6 to 8 servings

CAPER-CHIVE VINAIGRETTE

Toss this zesty dressing with green salads or serve it with lightly cooked cauliflower, broccoli, or zucchini.

2 tablespoons white wine vinegar
Salt and freshly ground pepper
6 tablespoons extra-virgin olive oil or
    vegetable oil
1 tablespoon drained capers, rinsed
    and chopped

1 tablespoon chopped fresh chives
1 tablespoon chopped fresh parsley
    (optional)
1 hard-boiled egg, chopped (optional)

Whisk vinegar with salt and pepper. Whisk in oil. Stir in capers. (*Dressing can be kept, covered, 4 days in refrigerator.*) Whisk again to blend. Stir in chives, parsley, and chopped egg. Taste and adjust seasoning.

Makes about ½ cup; about 4 to 6 servings

ORANGE VINAIGRETTE

Serve this dressing to accompany asparagus, beets, winter squash, and baked sweet potatoes.

¼ cup vegetable oil
1 tablespoon strained fresh orange
    juice
1 tablespoon strained fresh lemon juice

1 teaspoon finely grated orange rind
Salt and freshly ground pepper
Cayenne pepper to taste

Combine oil, orange juice, lemon juice, orange rind, salt, pepper, and cayenne in a bowl. Whisk to combine. (*Dressing can be kept, covered, 2 days in refrigerator. Whisk again to blend.*) Taste and adjust seasoning.

Makes about ⅓ cup; about 3 servings

MALAYSIAN PEANUT DRESSING

Serve this zesty peanut dressing with salads like Malaysian Cabbage Salad with Spicy Peanut Dressing (page 124). It also perks up hot or cold cooked vegetables such as green beans, potatoes, cauliflower, or broccoli.

1 large garlic clove, peeled
¼-inch-thick slice peeled fresh ginger
1 fresh red Thai or other small hot
    chili pepper, seeded (optional)
1 tablespoon vegetable oil
½ cup peanut butter
1 cup hot water

¼ teaspoon turmeric
1 teaspoon brown sugar
½ to 1 teaspoon anchovy paste
2 teaspoons strained fresh lime juice
Oriental hot sauce or cayenne pepper
    to taste
Salt to taste

Grind garlic in a mini food processor with ginger and chili pepper; or finely mince with a knife. Heat oil in a medium saucepan over low heat. Add garlic mixture and sauté 2 minutes, stirring. Add peanut butter, water, turmeric, brown sugar, and anchovy paste and mix well. Cook over low heat, stirring often, for 2 minutes or until smooth. Remove from heat and stir in lime juice. Season to taste with hot sauce and salt. Transfer to a bowl and cool. Taste and adjust seasoning.

If cooled dressing is too thick to pour, gradually stir in 1 to 2 tablespoons water.

Makes about 1¼ cups; about 6 servings

SUN-DRIED TOMATO DIPPING SAUCE

This is a zesty garlic-scented sauce dotted with parsley and chopped sun-dried tomatoes. It's delicious as a dipping sauce for artichokes, and can also be spooned over hot or cold cooked broccoli or cauliflower.

2 tablespoons olive oil
4 teaspoons strained fresh lemon juice
1 teaspoon minced garlic
Salt and freshly ground pepper

4 teaspoons chopped oil-packed sun-dried tomatoes
1 teaspoon minced fresh parsley

Whisk olive oil with lemon juice, garlic, salt, and pepper. Stir in tomatoes and parsley. Taste and adjust seasoning. Serve at room temperature.

Makes about ¼ cup; about 2 or 3 servings

PISTOU

This simple French cousin of pesto does not contain nuts and not necessarily cheese, either. It is popular in southern France as an addition to vegetable soups and for tossing with pasta. It also makes a delicious flavoring for vegetables—fresh and dried beans, corn, potatoes, and even mixed frozen vegetables.

This version has less oil than usual and is actually a basil-garlic essence. I find a mini food processor convenient here, as it can blend the ingredients with the small amount of oil.

1½ cups medium-packed fresh basil
  leaves (about 1½ ounces)
4 medium garlic cloves, peeled
¼ cup extra-virgin olive oil

Salt and freshly ground pepper
2 to 3 tablespoons freshly grated
  Parmesan cheese (optional)

Rinse basil and pat dry. Chop garlic in a small food processor. Add basil in 2 batches and chop finely. Return all the basil to processor. Add olive oil in 4 batches and process after each. Scrape down sides and puree again so mixture is well blended.

To serve as a sauce, season to taste with salt and pepper, or stir in grated Parmesan cheese.

Makes about ⅓ cup; about 3 servings

CHIMICHURRI—"ARGENTINEAN PESTO"

The traditional role of this "Argentinean pesto" is to accompany grilled meat, and some versions of chimichurri *can be so strong in vinegar and chilies that you can only sprinkle a few drops on meat. But the version I've enjoyed at an Argentinean restaurant in Santa Monica reminds me of pesto made with parsley, with a distinct oregano flavor and a little zip from hot pepper and garlic. It's a great way to add zest to plainly cooked vegetables such as steamed potatoes, broiled eggplant slices, boiled zucchini, and cauliflower.*

1 medium garlic clove, peeled
½ cup parsley sprigs
3 tablespoons extra-virgin olive oil
1 tablespoon lemon juice

1 tablespoon wine vinegar
¾ teaspoon dried oregano, crumbled
½ teaspoon hot red pepper flakes
Salt and freshly ground pepper

Chop garlic in a food processor. Add parsley and finely chop together. Transfer to a bowl or jar and add remaining ingredients. Stir or shake to combine. Taste and adjust seasoning. Serve at room temperature.

Makes ⅓ cup; about 3 or 4 servings

CHILEAN HOT CILANTRO SALSA

Serve this chunky salsa with Chilean "Succotash" (page 66), or to add a lively touch to plain cooked beans, winter squash, zucchini, or potatoes. For the preparation I find it convenient to mince the hot peppers and garlic in a mini food processor.

2 jalapeño or other fresh hot chili
    peppers
½ cup chopped cilantro (fresh
    coriander)
½ cup minced onion

1 medium garlic clove, minced
3 tablespoons olive or vegetable oil
1 tablespoon wine vinegar
2 tablespoons water
Salt to taste

Wear gloves when handling hot peppers. Remove seeds and ribs from peppers if desired. Mince fine, then mix with remaining ingredients in a bowl. Taste and adjust seasoning. Serve cold or at room temperature. (*Can be kept 1 day in refrigerator.*)

Makes about ¾ cup; about 4 or 5 servings

☓ CHIPOTLE CHILI SALSA

This smooth, deep-red salsa is made of grilled vegetables—tomatoes, onions, and garlic. What gives it character is the chipotle chili peppers, which are smoked jalapeños. For this recipe you buy the peppers canned in adobo sauce, often labeled chiles chipotles adobados, *which can be found at Mexican specialty shops.*

I learned to make this salsa from two friends of mine, Mexican-born Jorge Villanueva and his wife Teri Appleton Villanueva, both chefs at Ocean Avenue Seafood in Santa Monica. In Mexican homes the vegetables are charred directly over a gas flame; they can also be grilled on a barbecue. I find a stovetop grill easiest to use. There is no need to seed or peel the tomatoes; the charred bits in the salsa are part of its charm.

Use the salsa to add zest to all sorts of cooked vegetables, such as baked or fried chayote squash, baked or boiled potatoes, broiled eggplant slices, cauliflower, or zucchini. It's also good with white or brown rice and makes a tasty spread for bread or warm tortillas.

1 large white onion, peeled and
    quartered
1 pound ripe plum tomatoes (about 10
    small tomatoes)

2 large garlic cloves, peeled
1 or 2 canned chipotle chili peppers in
    adobo sauce (see Note)
Salt and freshly ground pepper

Heat stovetop ridged grill on medium-high heat. Add onion quarters and grill them on all 3 sides, about 8 to 10 minutes per side or until charred. Remove from grill.

Add tomatoes and grill about 5 minutes per side or until charred and tender. Char garlic cloves about 2 or 3 minutes per side.

Remove 1 chili pepper from the adobo sauce. Cut cores off charred tomatoes. Puree tomatoes, onion, garlic, and pepper in food processor until smooth. Taste; if you would like a hotter salsa, remove another pepper from its sauce, dice it, add to food processor, and puree again until well blended. Add salt and pepper to taste; salsa should be salted fairly generously. (*Salsa can be kept, covered, 4 or 5 days in refrigerator.*)

Makes about 2½ cups; about 8 to 10 servings

NOTE: If chipotle chilies are not available, use 1 or 2 serrano or red jalapeño peppers; char them on the grill until blackened. Remove seeds and membranes if you would like the salsa to be less hot. Puree the peppers with remaining ingredients.

MEXICAN FRESH TOMATO SALSA

Fresh Mexican salsa is a wonderful way to flavor all sorts of cooked vegetables, from grilled eggplant to steamed potatoes to lima beans to cooked squashes of all types, without adding any fat. The best way to have good salsa is to make your own. Adjust the hotness of this Mexican salsa cruda *to your taste by leaving some or all of the seeds in the jalapeño peppers—the more you leave in, the hotter it is.*

2 fresh jalapēno peppers, seeds removed, minced; or 3 to 4 teaspoons canned diced roasted jalapēno peppers
¾ pound ripe tomatoes, chopped
½ cup chopped cilantro (fresh coriander)

2 large green onions, chopped; or ½ to ⅔ cup minced white onion
¼ teaspoon salt
Ground red pepper or freshly ground black pepper
3 to 4 tablespoons water (if using plum tomatoes)

If using canned jalapeño peppers, chop them into finer dice. Combine tomatoes, jalapeño peppers, cilantro, and onions in bowl. Season to taste with salt and pepper. Add a little water if mixture is dry; it should have a chunky, saucelike consistency. (*Can be kept 2 days in refrigerator.*) Serve at room temperature.

Makes about 2½ cups; about 4 to 6 servings

GARLIC-HERB OIL

Spoon this herb oil over grilled eggplant, zucchini, or peppers for a zesty marinade or sauce. If using the oil with salted eggplant, as in Grilled Eggplant Antipasto (page 188), do not add more salt to the flavored oil. This recipe makes good use of finest quality extra-virgin olive oil because the oil remains uncooked.

2 medium garlic cloves, finely minced
1 tablespoon coarsely chopped fresh basil
1 tablespoon minced fresh mint

6 tablespoons fine-quality olive oil
Salt (optional) and freshly ground pepper

In a small bowl, combine garlic, basil, and mint. Add oil. Season to taste with salt and pepper. Use at room temperature.

Makes about ⅓ cup; about 4 servings

MINT BUTTER

Serve this simple butter with steamed hot beets or with cooked carrots, peas, or zucchini. It's also good with baked sweet potatoes or winter squash.

1 tablespoon chopped fresh mint
3 tablespoons butter, softened

Salt and freshly ground pepper

Thoroughly mix mint leaves with butter and season to taste with salt and pepper. Serve at room temperature.

Makes almost ¼ cup; about 3 or 4 servings

HERB-LEMON BUTTER

A small pat of this flavored butter added to hot vegetables turns carrots, potatoes, cauliflower, or even frozen mixed vegetables into a treat.

4 tablespoons (½ stick) butter,
   softened
1 teaspoon strained fresh lemon juice
¼ teaspoon finely grated lemon zest

¼ teaspoon dried thyme, crumbled
Salt and freshly ground pepper
1 tablespoon chopped fresh Italian
   parsley

Beat butter in a medium bowl until very smooth. Gradually beat in lemon juice, lemon zest, and thyme. Season to taste with salt and pepper. Stir in parsley. (*Can be kept, covered, up to 3 days in refrigerator; or it can be frozen.*) Use at room temperature.

Makes ¼ cup; about 3 or 4 servings

GUACAMOLE

Serve this as an accompaniment for Mushroom Tostadas (page 243). In Mexico, guacamole is also served as a sauce for cooked cauliflower.

3 large ripe avocados (each 9 or 10 ounces), preferably Haas
½ cup minced green onions
3 tablespoon minced cilantro (fresh coriander)
3 fresh serrano chilies, seeded and minced; or hot pepper sauce to taste

2 tablespoons fresh lime or lemon juice, or to taste
1½ cups finely diced tomato (optional)
Salt

Halve and pit avocados, spoon pulp into a bowl, and mash pulp with a fork. Stir in green onions, cilantro, chilies or hot sauce, lime juice, tomato, and salt to taste. (*The guacamole may be made 2 hours in advance, covered with plastic wrap pressed directly on its surface, and chilled.*)

Makes about 3 cups; about 6 servings

GREEN ZEHUG

Like salsa on the Mexican table, this fiery pepper paste is a standard on the Yemenite table. Zehug is made in both green and red varieties, but the green is more aromatic because it contains cilantro in addition to the hot peppers and garlic. Make it hotter by using serrano instead of jalapeño peppers or by leaving in the seeds; or remove the seeds if you prefer it less hot.

You can mix zehug with cooked vegetables, even those that were frozen, to add a lively hot flavor—it will wake up anyone's tastebuds. My husband's aunt stirs a little of it into Mediterranean diced salad to give it a little bite. Zehug is also a great flavoring for mayonnaise or vinaigrette.

5 medium green jalapeño or 8 serrano peppers (about 2 ounces)
½ cup garlic cloves, peeled
2 to 3 tablespoons water, if needed
½ cup cilantro (fresh coriander)

½ teaspoon salt
Freshly ground black pepper to taste
1 tablespoon ground cumin, preferably freshly ground

Wear gloves when handling hot peppers. Remove stems from peppers; remove seeds and ribs, if desired. Put garlic and peppers in a food processor and puree until finely chopped and well blended. If necessary, add 2 or 3 tablespoons water, just enough to enable food processor to chop mixture. Add cilantro and process until blended. Add salt, pepper, and cumin. (*Can be kept in a jar in refrigerator for up to 1 week.*)

Makes ½ to ⅔ cup; about 4 to 6 servings

✕—HARISSA

*U*se this potent, brick red sauce, to accent Moroccan, Algerian, and Tunisian vegetable dishes or to season salad dressings. You can also mix a little with diced or sliced cooked vegetables to give them a spicy taste. For best results, use a mini food processor, which can easily blend the ingredients to a uniform paste.*

30 small dried red chilies, such as *chiles*
    arbol **or** *chiles japones* **(scant ½ cup)**
4 large garlic cloves

2 teaspoons ground caraway seeds
2 teaspoons ground coriander
Olive oil (optional)

Put chilies in a small bowl and cover with hot water. Soak 1 hour. Remove chilies, reserving soaking water. Put chilies and 3 tablespoons soaking water in a mini food processor or blender. Add garlic, caraway, and coriander. Process until blended to a paste. Some pepper pieces will remain. If processor blades won't blend mixture, add another tablespoon or two of the soaking water. (*Can be kept in a small container in the refrigerator, covered with a thin layer olive oil and a tight cover for up to 6 weeks.*)

Makes scant ½ cup; about 8 to 12 servings

TEN-MINUTE TOMATO SAUCE

In its simplest version, this sauce can be made of tomatoes sautéed in oil. All the flavorings are optional. Flavoring accents should highlight but not overpower the taste of the star ingredient. A little onion is a standard addition, but you can substitute shallots, which soften more quickly. Chopped garlic may be the most popular flavoring of all. Additional zip can come from a jalapeño pepper sautéed with the garlic, or dried hot pepper flakes added with the tomatoes. Green leafy herbs are best stirred in at the last minute so they keep their flavor. Thyme is a favorite in France, oregano and fresh basil in Italy, and cilantro (fresh coriander) in the Middle East and Latin America.

Depending on how finely the tomatoes are chopped, the sauce will be quite smooth or fairly chunky. If you like it completely smooth, puree it in a food processor or blender.

If you want a more intense color or a slightly thicker sauce, a spoonful or two of tomato paste does the trick. This quick tomato sauce is also a basic that enhances other sauces. For cold seafood appetizers, it is added to mayonnaise to color it pink and give it a tomato flavor more delicate than that of ketchup. When stirred into mushroom sauce, it beautifully complements the sauce's richness.

2 to 3 tablespoons olive oil, vegetable
  oil, or butter
½ medium onion or 1 large shallot,
  chopped (optional)
1 large garlic clove, minced (optional)
2 pounds ripe tomatoes, peeled,
  seeded, and chopped; or 2 28-
  ounce cans plum tomatoes, halved,
  drained, and chopped

½ teaspoon dried thyme
1 bay leaf
Salt and freshly ground pepper
2 teaspoons tomato paste (optional)
3 tablespoons chopped basil, tarragon,
  or parsley; or 2 tablespoons
  chopped cilantro (fresh coriander)
  (optional)

Heat oil or butter in a large skillet and add onion. Sauté over medium heat until softened but not brown, about 5 minutes. Stir in garlic, then add tomatoes, thyme, bay leaf, salt, and pepper. Cook uncovered over medium-high heat, stirring often, about 10 minutes or until tomatoes are soft and sauce is thick. Discard bay leaf. Add tomato paste and mix well. Taste and adjust seasoning. (*Sauce can be kept 2 days in refrigerator, or can be frozen.*) Stir in any fresh herbs after reheating.

Makes about 2 cups; 4 to 8 servings

COLOMBIAN TOMATO-ONION SAUCE

This thick, chunky sauce is a favorite in Colombia for seasoning beans, lentils, and potatoes. It is used as an accompaniment and as an element in cooking, as in Colombian Lentil Soup (page 77).

2 tablespoons olive oil
1 large onion, chopped
1 pound ripe tomatoes, peeled, seeded,
    and chopped; or 1 28-ounce can
    plum tomatoes, drained and
    chopped

Salt and freshly ground pepper
1 teaspoon strained fresh lemon juice,
    or to taste

Heat oil in large, deep skillet or sauté pan. Add onion and sauté over medium heat until lightly browned, about 7 minutes, stirring often. Add tomatoes, salt, and pepper. Stir and cook 5 to 10 minutes, or until tomatoes are tender and sauce is thick. Season to taste with lemon juice, salt, and pepper.

Makes 1½ to 2 cups; 4 to 8 servings

UNCOOKED TOMATO SAUCE

This uncooked sauce is rather like a light vinaigrette made with finely chopped tomato pulp. Starred restaurants in France love to serve it as an accompaniment to fish or vegetable terrines served cold, but it is also marvelous with simply cooked vegetables like hot or cold asparagus, green beans, or broiled eggplant. It is ideal for a hot weather dinner, and is the answer to the cook's summer dreams—a delicious sauce that doesn't heat up the kitchen.

1 large ripe tomato (½ pound), peeled,
    seeded, and finely chopped
1 tablespoon white wine vinegar
Salt and pepper

5 tablespoons good-quality olive oil
1 tablespoon chopped fresh herbs,
    such as basil, tarragon, oregano,
    thyme, or parsley

Put tomato in a bowl. Add vinegar, salt, and pepper and whisk to blend. Gradually whisk in olive oil, drop by drop. Sauce should be thick. Add the herbs and taste for seasoning. Serve immediately, at room temperature.

Makes about ¾ cup; 2–3 servings

CARIBBEAN SOFRITO

Sofrito is a mixture of sautéed peppers, onions, garlic, and cilantro loved as a flavoring in Puerto Rico, Cuba, and other Spanish Caribbean islands. Some Cuban sofritos are more spicy, as in the variation here. Many versions begin with diced salt pork, ham, or both, but I love it as a purely vegetable flavoring. People often make sofrito in large quantities and freeze it, then heat a few tablespoons to use as a flavoring.

Use Caribbean Sofrito to flavor cooked chayote squash, zucchini, corn, beans, cauliflower, or mixed cooked vegetables (even frozen ones). Another kind of sofrito is made in Spain (see next recipe). There, the tomato is much more dominant and the mixture does not contain cilantro.

2 tablespoons olive or vegetable oil
1 medium onion, finely chopped
1 small green or red bell pepper, finely
   diced

2 large garlic cloves, minced
3 tablespoons chopped cilantro (fresh
   coriander)
Salt and freshly ground pepper

Heat oil in a heavy, medium skillet or sauté pan over low heat. Add onion and bell pepper, and sauté about 15 minutes or until tender. Add garlic, cilantro, salt, and pepper and sauté 1 minute, stirring. (*Sofrito can be kept, covered, 3 days in refrigerator.*)

To use, stir mixture into 2 to 3 cups hot cooked vegetables and heat 1 to 2 minutes over low heat to blend flavors.

Makes about 1 cup; 2 to 4 servings

VARIATION: **Spicy Sofrito**
Add 1 teaspoon minced fresh or canned jalapeño or other hot pepper and ½ teaspoon ground cumin at the same time as the garlic.

SPANISH SOFRITO

This version of sofrito from Spain resembles a briefly cooked fresh tomato sauce. Mix it with vegetables like diced cooked potatoes or beans or serve it with pasta or rice.

2 to 3 tablespoons olive oil
2 medium onions, finely chopped
1 small green or red bell pepper, finely
    chopped (optional)
2 large garlic cloves, chopped
2 pounds ripe tomatoes, peeled,
    seeded, and chopped; or 2 28-
    ounce cans plum tomatoes,
    drained and chopped

Salt and freshly ground pepper
2 to 3 tablespoons chopped fresh
    parsley

Heat oil in a large skillet. Add onions and pepper, and cook, stirring often, for 10 minutes. Add garlic and sauté 3 minutes or until onions are soft but not brown. Add tomatoes, salt, and pepper and cook gently uncovered about 10 minutes or until mixture is thick. Stir in parsley.

Makes 2 to 2½ cups; about 6 to 8 servings

ROASTED RED PEPPER SAUCE

Serve this sauce as a colorful complement for Cauliflower Flan (page 100) or for simply boiled cauliflower, sautéed zucchini, or pasta with vegetables.

2 red bell peppers, roasted and peeled
    (page 281)
2 medium shallots, minced
1 to ½ teaspoons fresh thyme, or ½
    teaspoon dried

½ cup dry white wine
1 cup Chicken or Vegetable Stock
    (pages 407, 406) or canned broth

Halve peeled peppers and discard seeds and ribs. Drain well and pat dry. Puree in a food processor until smooth.

    Combine shallots, thyme, and wine in a medium saucepan and bring to a boil. Boil about 2 minutes. Add ½ cup stock and boil until liquid is reduced to about ½ cup. Stir in pepper puree and remaining ½ cup stock. (*Sauce can be prepared 1 day ahead and kept, covered, in refrigerator.*) Reheat before serving.

Makes about 1¼ cups; about 4 or 5 servings

DRIED MUSHROOM SAUCE

This luscious French sauce is a great accompaniment for asparagus or pasta. Morels give the sauce the most wonderful flavor. The Madeira Cream variation is a wonderful complement for Carrot Timbales (page 138).

⅔ to 1 ounce dried morels, cèpes, or
   porcini mushrooms
1 tablespoon butter
2 shallots, chopped
⅓ cup dry white wine

⅓ cup Chicken or Vegetable Stock
   (pages 407, 406) or canned broth
1 to 1¼ cups heavy cream
A few drops lemon juice
Salt and freshly ground pepper

Soak mushrooms in enough hot water to cover about 30 minutes or until tender; drain well. Remove mushrooms, rinse, and discard any tough parts. Halve or quarter any large pieces.

Melt butter in a sauté pan. Add shallots and cook over low heat about 2 minutes or until softened. Add the mushrooms and stir briefly over low heat. Pour in wine and bring to a boil, stirring.

Add broth and bring to a boil. Boil until the liquid is reduced by about half. Add cream and simmer, stirring occasionally, until sauce is thick enough to coat a spoon. Add lemon juice and taste for seasoning. (*Sauce can be kept, covered, 2 days in refrigerator.*) Serve hot.

Makes ¾ to 1 cup; about 4 to 6 servings

VARIATION: **Madeira Cream**
Omit mushrooms, stock, and lemon juice. To sautéed shallots add wine and boil until reduced to about 3 tablespoons. Add ¼ cup Madeira and bring to a boil. Stir in 1 cup cream, bring to a boil, and simmer until sauce is thick enough to coat a spoon. Season to taste with salt and pepper.

DUXELLES SAUCE

When you briefly simmer wine, stock, or cream with duxelles, *the mushroom taste permeates the liquid to quickly produce flavorful sauces for vegetables, fish, poultry, or light meats. This sauce is a light and easy adaptation of the classic* duxelles *sauce from Escoffier's culinary bible,* Le Guide Culinaire. *It is also good with roasted or poached chicken and with such vegetables as cauliflower, zucchini, and potatoes.*

Duxelles (page 408)
¼ cup dry white wine
4 teaspoons tomato paste
1½ cups Chicken or Vegetable Stock
    (pages 407, 406) or low-salt
    canned broth

1 teaspoon dried thyme, crumbled
1 tablespoon cornstarch dissolved in 2
    tablespoons water
2 tablespoons chopped fresh parsley
Salt and freshly ground pepper

In a medium saucepan mix *duxelles* with wine, tomato paste, stock, and thyme. Bring to a boil, then reduce heat to medium-low. Add dissolved cornstarch, stirring. Return to a boil and add parsley. Season to taste with salt and pepper.

Makes ¾ to 1 cup; about 4 servings

CHEESE SAUCE

Cheese and vegetables are a favorite partners on both sides of the North Atlantic. Gouda is often used in this sauce in Holland, cheddar in the United States, and gruyère in Switzerland and France. And Italian Parmesan is now loved in cheese sauce everywhere. Serve this sauce with cauliflower, Brussels sprouts, spinach, Swiss chard, zucchini, and mixed vegetables.

1¼ to 1⅓ cups Cream Sauce (page
    400) or Lighter Cream Sauce (page
    401)

¼ cup freshly grated Parmesan cheese,
    or ⅓ to ½ cup grated gouda,
    cheddar, or gruyère cheese

Heat sauce. Remove from heat and whisk in grated cheese. Taste and adjust seasoning.

Makes about 1⅓ cups; about 4 or 5 servings

VELOUTÉ SAUCE

Classic velouté sauce and its tomato variation are popular throughout Europe as a sauce to serve with vegetables. Often the sauce is made from the cooking liquid of the vegetable if it's flavorful, like that from root vegetables or mushrooms. Serve this sauce with cooked carrots, beets, celery root, parsnips, kohlrabi, or mushrooms. The tomato variation is good with cauliflower or zucchini.

1½ tablespoons butter or vegetable oil
1½ tablespoons all-purpose flour
1 cup Vegetable or Chicken Stock
   (pages 406, 407) or canned broth
Salt and white pepper

A few drops lemon juice (optional)
Cayenne pepper (optional)
1 tablespoon chopped fresh parsley,
   chives, tarragon, or dill (optional)

Melt butter in a small, heavy saucepan over low heat. Whisk in flour. Cook, whisking constantly, about 3 minutes or until mixture turns light beige. Remove from heat. Add stock, whisking. Bring to a boil over medium-high heat, then add a pinch of salt and white pepper. Simmer uncovered over medium-low heat, whisking often, for 5 minutes. Taste and adjust seasoning, adding lemon juice and cayenne pepper, if desired. (*If not using sauce at once, dab top with butter to prevent a skin from forming. Sauce can be kept, covered, up to 1 day in refrigerator; or it can be frozen.*) Reheat sauce and add chopped herb. Serve hot.

Makes 1 cup; about 4 servings

VARIATION: **Tomato Velouté Sauce**
   Add ¼ cup Ten-Minute Tomato Sauce (page 394) or packaged tomato sauce into Velouté Sauce. Makes about 1¼ cups sauce.

CREAM SAUCE

Cream sauce is a popular accompaniment in Europe and North America for almost every vegetable, from asparagus to zucchini. An alternative is Lighter Cream Sauce in the variation, made with low-fat or nonfat milk. Use it to accompany vegetables or to coat vegetables for baking as a gratin.

2 tablespoons (¼ stick) butter
2 tablespoons all-purpose flour
1½ cups milk
Salt and white pepper

Freshly grated nutmeg
¼ cup heavy cream (optional)
Pinch of ground red pepper, preferably
   cayenne

Melt butter in heavy, medium saucepan over low heat. Whisk in flour and cook, whisking constantly, until foaming but not browned, about 2 minutes. Remove from heat. Gradually whisk in milk. Bring to a boil over medium-high heat, whisking, then add a small pinch of salt, white pepper, and nutmeg. Reduce heat to low and cook, whisking often, for 5 minutes. Whisk in cream and bring to boil. Cook over low heat, whisking often, until sauce thickens and coats a spoon heavily, about 7 minutes. Remove from heat and add red pepper. Taste and adjust seasoning. (*Dab surface of sauce with butter if not using immediately. Sauce can be kept, covered, 2 days in refrigerator.*)

Makes about 1⅓ cups; about 4 or 5 servings

VARIATION: **Lighter Cream Sauce**
   Omit cream. Instead of butter, you can use margarine or vegetable oil. Increase flour to 2½ tablespoons. Use 1⅓ cups low-fat or nonfat milk.

TAHINI SAUCE

An Israeli friend claims that tahini sauce, or Middle Eastern sesame sauce, is good for everything that we normally think of using mayonnaise for. It's true that it has a multitude of uses in flavoring vegetables. In Israel it's sometimes added to the usual Israeli salad of tomatoes, cucumbers, and onions for a richer, more festive version. I've even had tahini sauce in an Ethiopian restaurant as a delicious dressing on a green salad.

Popular in Lebanon, Syria, Jordan, and Egypt, tahini sauce is a favorite flavoring for grilled eggplant, either for making Three-Way Eggplant Salad (page 186), or to accompany grilled eggplant slices. Tahini is served with cooked fava beans, cauliflower, potatoes, beets, and Swiss chard. Although not a traditional use, tahini makes a good dip for raw vegetable platters too.

Buy the thick tahini paste for making the sauce in Middle Eastern grocery stores; you can also find it in some supermarkets.

½ cup tahini (sesame paste)
½ cup plus 1 tablespoon water
½ teaspoon ground cumin
¼ teaspoon salt, or to taste

2 tablespoons strained fresh lemon juice
3 large garlic cloves, minced
Pinch of cayenne (optional)

In a medium bowl, stir tahini to blend in its oil. Stir in ½ cup water. Add cumin, salt, lemon juice, garlic, and cayenne. If sauce is too thick, gradually stir in more water. Taste, and add more salt or lemon juice if desired. (*Tahini thickens on standing, and may need a little water mixed in before serving.*)

Makes about 1 cup; about 6 to 8 servings

GARLIC MAYONNAISE

*S*pain and southern France each claim this zesty sauce, also known as áioli or alioli, as their own. It is delicious with a great variety of vegetables such as potatoes, roasted beets, artichokes, green beans, and cauliflower. You can also use it as a dip for raw vegetables. As with homemade mayonnaise, you can make this sauce with pasteurized eggs instead of raw eggs. The jalapeño pepper is not classic but it makes a tasty addition.*

4 to 6 medium garlic cloves, peeled
½ jalapeño pepper, seeds removed, cut
    into 4 pieces (optional)
2 egg yolks, at room temperature
About 2 tablespoons strained fresh
    lemon juice

1¼ cups extra-virgin olive oil, at room
    temperature
1 tablespoon lukewarm water
Salt and freshly ground pepper

Cut off any brown spots from garlic. Halve garlic cloves lengthwise and remove any green sprouts from center.

Drop garlic cloves and jalapeño pieces through the feed tube of a food processor, with motor running, and process until finely chopped. Add egg yolks, 1 tablespoon lemon juice, 1 tablespoon oil, and a pinch of salt and pepper, and process until thoroughly blended, scraping bottom and sides of processor container several times. With motor running, gradually pour in ¼ cup oil in a thin trickle. After adding ¼ cup oil, remaining oil can be poured in a little faster, in a thin stream. With motor still running, gradually pour in remaining tablespoon lemon juice, 1 teaspoon at a time. Add lukewarm water, 1 teaspoon at a time, to make sauce slightly thinner. Taste and adjust seasoning. (*Sauce can be kept, covered, 2 days in refrigerator.*)

Makes about 1¼ cups; about 8 servings

TARTAR SAUCE

This is a delicious dip for Cauliflower Fritters (page 98), cooked artichokes, or raw vegetables.

1 cup mayonnaise or reduced-fat
    mayonnaise
1 tablespoon Dijon mustard
2 tablespoons chopped fresh parsley
1 tablespoon chopped green onion
1 hard-boiled egg, chopped

1 tablespoon drained capers, rinsed
    and chopped
1 tablespoon chopped pickle
1 teaspoon wine vinegar or strained
    fresh lemon juice (optional)
Salt and freshly ground pepper

Mix mayonnaise and mustard in a bowl until blended. Stir in parsley, green onion, egg, capers, and pickle. Taste, and add vinegar, salt, and pepper if needed. (*Sauce can be kept, covered, 2 days in refrigerator.*)

Makes about 1¼ cups; about 8 servings

SPINACH WATERCRESS DIP

Use this sauce for dipping carrot, zucchini, cucumber, or jicama sticks; or toss it with cooked potatoes to make a rich and tasty potato salad. This herb-flavored sauce is usually made of mayonnaise alone, but I have lightened it by stirring in yogurt.

20 large spinach leaves, stems
    removed, rinsed
⅓ cup watercress leaves
¼ cup small parsley sprigs

1 cup mayonnaise or reduced-fat
    mayonnaise
½ cup plain nonfat or low-fat yogurt
Salt and freshly ground pepper

Put spinach and watercress in a medium saucepan of boiling water. Bring back to a boil and drain well. Rinse under cold running water and drain thoroughly. Squeeze to remove excess liquid.

    Puree spinach, watercress, and parsley in a food processor until smooth. If necessary, add 2 or 3 tablespoons of the mayonnaise to help make a smoother mixture. Add remaining mayonnaise and process until smooth. Transfer to a bowl and gradually stir in yogurt. Taste and adjust seasoning. (*Sauce can be kept, covered, 2 days in refrigerator.*)

Makes about 1½ cups; about 8 to 10 servings

32

Basic Recipes

Homemade stocks and doughs make the difference between a dish that tastes good and one that is very good. They are a fundamental part of traditional cooking around the world.

Stocks and doughs are easy to make. Stocks require simply putting the ingredients in a pot and leaving them to simmer. Making dough is a matter of whirling the ingredients in the food processor.

When time is at a premium, packaged substitutes are available for all these basic preparations. When you don't have time, energy, or desire to prepare your own stocks, crepes, and doughs, you can use canned or frozen stocks, packaged fresh crepes, or frozen pie or pizza dough.

VEGETABLE STOCK

Vegetable stock fulfills the same function as chicken and meat stocks—to add flavor to sauces, soups, vegetable braising liquids, rice, and other dishes—and can be substituted for either of these stocks. It is made essentially of the same aromatic vegetables used to make chicken or meat stock—mainly onions, leeks, carrots, celery, and mushrooms. You can include a small amount of parsnips, turnips, or celery root but cabbage family vegetables and strong-flavored greens should be avoided.

Flavor vegetable stock with garlic, thyme, bay leaves, and parsley stems, and if you like, a small amount of other herbs. The stock should be aromatic but fairly mild and neutral so that it will be good with a great variety of dishes. As with meat stocks, salt is not added in case the stock might be used in a dish that already contains salty ingredients. Instead, the dishes using the stock are seasoned to taste.

To make stock-making easy, you can freeze small pieces of the vegetables needed in bags or containers when you have extra vegetables or trimmings, and save them for stock. You can use the green tops of leeks, the stems of mushrooms, the ends of carrots, the leafy tops of celery, and even the skins of tomatoes to add flavor to the stock.

2 tablespoons vegetable oil, olive oil, or butter
2 large onions, coarsely chopped
1 medium carrot, scraped and diced
2 celery stalks, chopped
Dark green part of 1 leek, rinsed thoroughly and sliced (optional)
6 cups water
1 bay leaf
2 sprigs fresh thyme, or ½ teaspoon dried thyme

3 medium garlic cloves, peeled and crushed
5 parsley stems without leaves (optional)
½ teaspoon black peppercorns (optional)
1½ cups sliced mushroom stems or mushrooms (optional)

Heat oil in a large saucepan over low heat. Add onions, carrot, celery, and leek and cook, stirring often, about 10 minutes. Add water, bay leaf, thyme, garlic, parsley, peppercorns, and mushrooms and mix well. Bring to a boil. Simmer uncovered over low heat for 1 hour.

Strain stock, pressing on ingredients in strainer; discard ingredients in strainer. If not using immediately, cool to lukewarm. Refrigerate or freeze stock. (*Stock can be kept up to 3 days in refrigerator, or it can be frozen.*)

Makes about 1 quart

✗ CHICKEN STOCK

Chicken stock enhances the flavor of many vegetable sauces and soups, and adds great taste to braised vegetables. It is useful in creating lower-fat versions of traditional recipes that call for cooking vegetables with bacon or other fatty meats. You substitute chicken stock for the cooking liquid in these recipes to contribute a meaty flavor; if the stock is well-skimmed, it will add little fat.

The flavor of homemade stock is superior to commercial ones. Stock is easy to prepare and, although it cooks for 2 hours, this is practically unattended simmering time. Use whole chickens or cut-up chickens; if buying separate pieces, choose wings or dark-meat pieces for best flavor.

3- to 3½-pound chicken, or 3 pounds
    chicken pieces
2 medium onions, quartered
Green part of 1 leek, cleaned (optional)
2 medium carrots, quartered
2 bay leaves
5 stems parsley without leaves
    (optional)

About 4 quarts water
2 fresh thyme sprigs, or ½ teaspoon
    dried thyme, crumbled
½ teaspoon black peppercorns
    (optional)

Use all of the chicken, including neck and all giblets except liver, to make stock.

Combine chicken, onions, leek greens, carrots, bay leaves, and parsley in a stock pot or other large pot. Add enough water to cover ingredients. Bring to a boil, skimming foam from top. Add thyme and peppercorns.

Reduce heat to very low so that stock bubbles very gently. Partly cover and cook, skimming foam and fat occasionally, for 2 to 3 hours.

Strain stock into large bowls; discard mixture in strainer. If not using immediately, cool to lukewarm. Refrigerate or freeze stock. (*Stock can be kept 3 days in refrigerator; or it can be frozen several months.*) Before using, skim solidified fat off top.

Makes about 10 cups

NOTE: If you wish to substitute canned chicken broth for homemade stock, the low-salt varieties are best. You can also use frozen stock.

DUXELLES

*D*uxelles, *or a mushroom hash, is a time-honored French concoction of cooked chopped mushrooms flavored with shallots or onions. It is one of those magical mixtures that chefs in classic kitchens keep on hand to slip into their culinary creations.*

In fact, making duxelles *is the quickest way to cook mushrooms. They are done in just a few minutes, and their taste remains intense because they sauté briefly over high heat. Many classic formulas call for sautéing the mushrooms in plenty of butter, but I have found that vegetable oil works well too, and a tiny amount suffices.*

Cutting the mushrooms is a snap—you simply chop them in a food processor. When I studied at a Parisian cooking school, the chefs demonstrated that they could chop mushrooms for duxelles *with a knife as fast as we students could with a food processor. For home cooking, however, the convenience of chopping mushrooms in the processor is what makes* duxelles *suitable for quick meals.*

At the school we used duxelles *in many festive dishes. We enriched* duxelles *with cream and eggs and baked it in tart shells, or made it into a filling for puff pastry turnovers. But we learned that it is ideal for everyday cooking as well. We spread it on fish fillets as a stuffing or rolled it inside omelets. For stuffed mushrooms, we made* duxelles *from mushroom stems and used it to fill the caps. We discovered that the tasty mushroom mixture was perfect for stuffing other vegetables as well, like zucchini, tomatoes, and eggplant. (See Eggplant with Mushroom Stuffing, page 184.)*

Once you have this mushroom essence on hand, there's no end to what you can do with it. It's great mixed with rice or small pasta shapes like orzo because the little duxelles *particles give you a touch of mushroom flavor with every mouthful. Or spread* duxelles *on toast, sprinkle it with cheese, and brown it briefly in the broiler for an easy, tasty appetizer.* Duxelles *can be a good vegetable alternative to ground meat in many stuffings, spaghetti sauces, and other recipes. Stir* duxelles *into tomato sauce, for example, and you'll have a satisfying tomato-mushroom sauce for spaghetti or for your favorite pasta.*

Fortunately mushrooms are no longer an expensive extravagance for special occasions and can be used frequently. After all, most of us do not prepare duxelles *from pricey fresh cèpes or chanterelles, the way some top chefs do. A more reasonable recipe when you want an exotic flavor is to soak a few dried shiitake mushrooms in water, chop them, and add them to a* duxelles *made of common mushrooms. Another way to vary the taste of* duxelles *is to add chopped fresh tarragon or dried thyme or oregano to the cooked mushroom mixture.*

8 ounces fresh mushrooms, rinsed and
    patted dry
1½ teaspoons vegetable oil or butter

1 small shallot or green onion, minced
Salt and freshly ground pepper

Chop mushrooms in a food processor with pulsing motion so they are chopped in fine pieces but are not pureed. In a medium skillet, heat oil over low heat, add shallot, and sauté about ½ minute until soft but not brown. Add mushrooms and sprinkle with salt and pepper. Cook over high heat, stirring, for 3 to 5 minutes or until mixture is dry. (*Duxelles can be kept, covered, 2 days in refrigerator.*)

Makes about 1 cup

CREPES

*R*oll *cooked vegetables inside crepes made with white flour, or make them with buckwheat or whole flour as in the variations, to turn them into glamorous fare. These crepes are delicious and easy to cook, as they already contain melted butter; little or no additional butter is needed for greasing the crepe pan.*

Plain crepes have a pleasant buttery flavor, but for an extra touch, a pinch of nutmeg, white pepper, curry powder, cayenne pepper, or 1 to 2 tablespoons chopped fresh herbs can be added to the batter. If you like, you can use low-fat milk in the batter.

3 large eggs
1¼ cups milk, or a little more if
    needed

¾ cup all-purpose flour
¾ teaspoon salt
4 tablespoons (½ stick) unsalted butter

Combine eggs, ¼ cup of milk, flour, and salt in food processor and mix using several on/off turns; batter will be lumpy. Scrape down sides and bottom of processor container. With machine running, pour 1 cup milk through feed tube and process batter about 15 seconds. Scrape down sides and bottom again. Blend batter about 15 seconds.

Strain batter if it is lumpy. Cover and refrigerate about 1 hour. (*Batter can be refrigerated, covered, up to 1 day. Bring to room temperature before continuing.*)

Melt butter in small saucepan over low heat. Gradually whisk 2 tablespoons melted butter into crepe batter. Pour remaining butter into a small cup. Skim off foam to clarify. Batter should have consistency of heavy cream. If it is too thick, gradually whisk in more milk, about 1 teaspoon at a time.

Heat crepe pan or skillet with 6- to 6½-inch base over medium-high heat. Sprinkle with few drops of water. If water immediately sizzles, pan is hot enough. Brush pan lightly with some of clarified butter. (If using nonstick pan, no butter is needed.) Remove pan from heat and hold it near bowl of batter. Working quickly, fill a quarter-cup measure half-full of batter (to easily measure 2 tablespoons) and add batter to one edge of pan, tilting and swirling pan until its base is covered with thin layer of batter. Immediately pour any excess batter back into bowl.

Return pan to medium-high heat. Loosen edges of crepe with metal spatula, discarding any pieces of crepe clinging to sides of pan. Cook crepe until its bottom browns lightly. Turn crepe carefully over by sliding spatula under it. Cook until second side browns lightly in spots. Slide crepe out onto plate. Reheat pan a few seconds. Make crepes with remaining batter, stirring it occasionally with whisk. Adjust heat and add more clarified butter to pan if necessary. If batter thickens, gradually whisk in a little more milk, about 1 teaspoon at a time. Pile crepes on plate as they are done. (*Crepes can be kept, wrapped tightly, up to 3 days in refrigerator; or they can be frozen. Bring them to room temperature before using, to avoid tearing them.*)

Makes about 20 crepes

NOTE: To prepare batter in blender, combine eggs, 1¼ cups milk, flour, and salt in blender. Mix on high speed until batter is smooth, about 1 minute.

VARIATIONS: **Whole Wheat Crepes**
   Replace all-purpose flour with ½ cup whole wheat flour sifted with ¼ cup all-purpose flour.
   Buckwheat Crepes
   Replace all-purpose flour with ½ cup buckwheat flour sifted with ¼ cup all-purpose flour. Stir batter well before adding butter.

PIZZA DOUGH

Pizza dough is easy to make in the food processor or by hand. Use this dough for Pizza with Algerian Onion Compote (page 259). Use the thick crust in the variation for Mushroom Pizza (page 241) and Ligurian Tomato, Olive, and Caper Pizza (page 319).

1 envelope (¼ ounce) active dry yeast
   or 1 cake fresh yeast
1 cup plus 2 tablespoons warm water
   (105° to 115°F.)

3 cups all-purpose flour
1½ teaspoons salt
2 tablespoons vegetable oil

To make dough in food processor, sprinkle or crumble yeast over ⅓ cup lukewarm water in a cup or small bowl and let stand for 10 minutes. Stir until smooth. In food processor with dough blade or metal blade, process flour and salt briefly to mix them. Add remaining water and oil to yeast mixture. With blades of processor turning, gradually pour in yeast-liquid mixture. If dough is too dry to come together, add 1 tablespoon water and process again. Process about 1 minute to knead dough.

To make dough by hand, sift flour into a bowl and make a well in center. Sprinkle dry yeast or crumble fresh yeast into well. Pour ⅓ cup water over yeast and let stand for 10 minutes. Stir until smooth. Add remaining water, oil, and salt and mix with ingredients in middle of well. Stir in flour and mix well, to obtain a fairly soft dough. If dough is dry, add 1 tablespoon water. Knead dough vigorously, slapping it on work surface, until it is smooth and elastic. If it is very sticky, flour it occasionally while kneading.

Lightly oil a medium bowl. Add dough and turn to coat entire surface. Cover with plastic wrap or lightly dampened towel. Let dough rise in a warm draft-free area about 1 hour or until doubled in volume.

Makes enough for two 10-inch pizzas

VARIATION: **Thick Crust Pizza Dough**
Sprinkle yeast over ¼ cup water. Omit oil. Add 2 tablespoons more water and 1 extra-large egg to yeast mixture; use this as liquid for dough. Follow recipe above, using 1½ cups flour and ¾ teaspoon salt. Makes enough for one 10-inch pizza.

FRENCH PIE DOUGH

This dough makes a buttery, tender crust and lattice topping for Mushroom-Macadamia Tart (page 244). Follow the instructions below to shape it into tart shells for Leek Tart (page 263), and Swiss Onion Tart (page 262).

Instead of mixing this dough by hand, you can blend it in a food processor, following the pastry directions in the recipe for Tartlet Shells (page 416).

1½ cups all-purpose flour
⅜ teaspoon salt
½ cup (1 stick) cold unsalted butter,
    cut into bits

2 large egg yolks
About 2 tablespoons plus 2 teaspoons
    ice water

In a large bowl combine flour and salt, and blend in butter until mixture resembles coarse meal. Add egg yolks and 2 tablespoons ice water and toss mixture until liquid is incorporated, adding more ice water if necessary to form dough into a ball. Knead dough lightly with the heel of your hand against a smooth surface for a few seconds to distribute the fat evenly. Reform it into a ball. Refrigerate dough, wrapped in wax paper, for 1 hour. (*Dough can be kept, covered, 2 days in refrigerator.*)

Makes enough for an 8-inch tart with lattice topping, or for a 9-inch tart shell

VARIATION: Tart Shell

Butter a 9-inch fluted tart pan with removable rim. Roll dough on a lightly floured surface to a round about ⅛ inch thick and about 11 inches in diameter. Roll dough loosely around rolling pin and unroll it over tart pan. Gently ease dough into pan. Using your thumb, gently push dough down slightly at top edge of pan, making top edge of dough thicker than remaining dough. Roll rolling pin across pan to cut off excess dough. With your finger and thumb, press dough gently against pan so that it rises ¼ inch above the pan's rim. Prick bottom of shell lightly with a fork. Refrigerate for 30 minutes. (*Tart shell can be kept, covered tightly, 2 days in refrigerator; or it can be frozen.*)

TARTLET SHELLS

Fill these individual tart shells with Basque Pepper Stew (page 283) and goat cheese to make pepper and goat cheese tartlets. The dough for the tartlets is made in a food processor, but you can instead mix it by hand, following the method for French Pie Dough (recipe above).

2 large egg yolks
3 tablespoons plus ½ teaspoon ice
    water
2 cups all-purpose flour

⅜ teaspoon salt
¾ cup (1½ sticks) cold unsalted butter,
    cut into bits

To make pastry in processor, whisk egg yolks with 3 tablespoons ice water. Combine flour and salt in a food processor fitted with a metal blade. Process briefly to blend. Scatter butter pieces over mixture. Mix using on/off turns until mixture resembles coarse meal. Pour egg yolks evenly over mixture in processor. Process with on/off turns, scraping down occasionally, until dough forms sticky crumbs that can easily be pressed together but does not come together in a ball. If crumbs are dry, sprinkle ½ teaspoon water and process with on/off turns until dough forms sticky crumbs. Add more water in same way, ½ teaspoon at a time, if crumbs are still dry.

Using a rubber spatula, transfer dough to a sheet of plastic wrap, wrap it, and push it together. Shape dough in a flat disc. Refrigerate dough 1 or 2 hours. (*Dough can be kept up to 2 days in refrigerator.*)

Butter 12 fluted 3-inch round tartlet pans. Let dough soften 1 minute at room temperature. Set dough on a cold, lightly floured surface. Tap it firmly with a heavy rolling pin several times to flatten it. Roll it out, flouring often and working quickly, until it is slightly less than ¼ inch thick. Set 8 tartlet pans next to each other. Roll up dough loosely around rolling pin and unroll it over pans. With a small ball of dough (from edge of sheet of dough) dipped in flour, gently press dough into tartlet pans.

Using your thumb, gently push down dough a little bit at top edge of each pan, making top edge of dough thicker than remaining dough. Roll the rolling pin across pans to cut off dough at edges. With your finger and thumb, press up edge of dough around each pan so it extends slightly above rim. Prick dough all over with a fork. Cover lined pans and refrigerate at least 30 minutes. Refrigerate scraps. Roll out remaining dough and scraps, and line remaining tartlet pans. (*Tartlet shells can be kept, covered, 2 days in refrigerator; or they can be frozen for several weeks.*)

Makes twelve 3-inch tartlets

TOASTING NUTS AND SESAME SEEDS

A sprinkling of toasted nuts or sesame seeds adds a festive, tasty note to cooked vegetables.

Toasting nuts: Preheat oven or toaster oven to 350°F. Toast nuts on a small cookie sheet in oven until aromatic and lightly browned. Whole almonds and hazelnuts take about 10 minutes; walnuts and pecans take about 5 to 7 minutes; and slivered almonds, diced nuts, or pine nuts take about 3 to 5 minutes. Transfer nuts to a plate and let cool.

Toasting sesame seeds: Toast sesame seeds in small, dry skillet over medium heat, shaking pan often, about 3 or 4 minutes or until golden brown. Transfer immediately to a plate.

33

Menus

VEGETABLE MENUS

As with any menu, in planning menus that consist of all or mostly vegetable dishes, consider a good mix of colors, flavors, and textures. If you are including a rich dish, choose others that are light for balance.

Treat these menus as starting points for your own ideas. Prepare as many or as few dishes as you like; you can always complete the menu with rice, pasta, or fresh bread. The following menus can be served as vegetarian menus or you can add fish, poultry, meat, egg, or cheese dishes if you wish.

All the recipes here are in the book except for the dessert suggestions.

415

INDIAN VEGETARIAN DINNER

The appetizer is a zesty dish of spicy, sweet-and-sour eggplant from Sri Lanka, which is made ahead and served at room temperature. The aromatic chickpea casserole and the cauliflower with ginger and cumin can be prepared in advance and reheated. Fragrant Basmati rice is the perfect accompaniment. If you can get *naan* or *chapati*, you might like to serve them also. For a fresh cooling note, serve tomato and watercress salad with yogurt dressing. Seasonal fruit or sorbet make the best desserts after this hearty meal.

Sri Lankan Eggplant Relish (page 185)
Chickpeas with Spinach and Carrots (page 70)
Cauliflower with Fresh Ginger and Cumin (page 100)
Sri Lankan Tomato and Watercress Salad with Cucumber-Yogurt Dressing (page 322)
Sliced mango or mango sorbet

PIZZA AND STUFFED VEGETABLES PARTY

Pizza and stuffed vegetables are popular party foods and convenient to serve together. For this menu, the stuffed vegetables can be prepared ahead and heated at the last moment or served at room temperature. The pizza dough and toppings can also be made ahead, but it's fun to bake the pizza during the party so its enticing aroma during baking can be enjoyed by everybody, and so it will be served hot.

Pizza with Algerian Onion Compote (page 259)
Ligurian Tomatoes, Olive, and Caper Pizza (page 319)
Eggplant Stuffed with Scamorza Cheese (page 183)

Lebanese Stuffed Tomatoes (page 317)
Stuffed Peppers with Rice, Pine Nuts, and
Currants (page 284)
Mediterranean ''Chopped'' Salad (page 166)
Seasonal fruit with fresh strawberry sauce

LIGHT CALIFORNIA-STYLE LUNCH

The star of this light spring or summertime lunch is a salad of roasted asparagus tossed with roasted peppers and linguine. Serve it with a simple but elegant accompaniment like sautéed chanterelles or other wild mushrooms, or substitute jalapeño-accented Mexican sautéed mushrooms.

Salad of Baby Greens (page 215) or
Mediterranean Diced Salad, California Style
(page 376)
Roasted Asparagus, Red Pepper, and Pasta Salad
(page 40)
Sautéed Wild Mushrooms with Herbs (page 245)
or Mexican Mushrooms (page 238)
Fresh fruit salad with sorbet

LATIN AMERICAN VEGETABLE FIESTA

You can serve all these dishes buffet style. The hot dishes can be kept warm or served at room temperature. Be sure there are plenty of warm corn and flour tortillas. Chocolate cake or mousse is the perfect dessert—after all, chocolate originated in Mexico.

Raw Vegetables with Chipotle Chili Salsa (page 373)
Chilean "Succotash" (page 66)
Chilean Hot Cilantro Salsa (page 388)
Mexican Mushrooms (page 238)
Salvadoran Cole Slaw (page 126)
Potato Salad with Avocado and Cilantro (page 304)
Chocolate cake or mousse
Cherimoya, sapote, or other exotic fruit

ORIENTAL VEGETABLE LUNCHEON

For a light and colorful meal at any season, serve these three vegetable dishes. Only the broccoli dish needs to be finished at the last minute. The Japanese spinach appetizer is served at room temperature, and the Thai vegetable medley can be reheated. Serve the vegetables with plenty of hot cooked rice in attractive Chinese rice bowls, and for accompaniment serve Chinese or Japanese tea.

Japanese Sesame Spinach (page 200)
Thai Vegetable Medley with Mint and Chilies (page 365)
Broccoli with Chinese Mushrooms and Oyster Sauce (page 93)
Asian pears, tangerines, or kiwis

ELEGANT SPRINGTIME LUNCHEON

For this delicious menu for celebrating spring, serve crisp French or Italian bread as an accompaniment. A bottle of Chardonnay and a light strawberry tart or chocolate-dipped strawberries are just right for the festivities.

**Asparagus with Sun-Dried Tomato Vinaigrette
(page 36)
Carrot Timbales (page 138)
Green Peas with Mushrooms (page 270)
Steamed New Potatoes with Herb-Lemon Butter
(page 296)
Salad of Baby Greens (page 215)
Strawberries or a strawberry dessert**

MEDITERRANAN SUMMER FEAST

Everything on this colorful menu can be prepared ahead and served at room temperature, though you might want to reheat the filo pastries with their feta-accented filling just before serving them. Luscious summer fruit or a fruit tart makes the best dessert.

**Greek Spinach Pastries (page 204)
Armenian Pepper, Parsley, and Wheat Salad (page 285)
Caponata (page 179)
Spanish Green Bean and Red Pepper Stew
(page 49)
Lebanese Potato Salad with Tomatoes and Mint (page 302)
Mediterranean "Chopped" Salad (page 166)
Summer fruit or fruit tart**

FOURTH OF JULY LUNCH

An array of colorful salads and some vegetables on the grill make for a light and festive celebration of the Fourth of July. Fresh peaches and apricots with vanilla ice cream make a lovely seasonal sweet.

**Potato Salad with Avocado and Cilantro
(page 304)
Sugar-Snap Pea, Carrot, and Black Mushroom
Salad (page 275)
Black Bean, Pepper and Rice Salad (page 75)
Spinach Salad with Feta Cheese and Tomatoes
(page 205)
Grilled corn on the cob (see page 155)
Grilled red peppers (see page 281)
Peaches, apricots and ice cream**

SUMMER SALAD BUFFET

These tasty treats, most of which are from the North African culinary tradition, make wonderful light party fare. Fresh pita bread is the best accompaniment. You might also like to serve black and green Moroccan olives, and perhaps some feta cheese. For dessert make a salad of summer fruit or buy some fresh Greek or Middle Eastern filo pastries.

**Roasted Pepper Salad with Caper Dressing
(page 286)
Moroccan Tomato Salad with Red Onions and
Parsley (page 316)**

**Green Bean and Chickpea Salad with Tomatoes
and Olives (page 53)
Egyptian Eggplant Puree with Garlic and
Coriander (page 189)
Algerian Cucumber and Pepper Salad (page 165)
Salad of summer fruit**

AUTUMN DINNER À LA FRANÇAISE

This dinner is built around a festive leek tart accompanied by sautéed wild mushrooms. A beet and endive salad garnished with walnuts makes a light and tasty first course, or you might want to serve *crudités* instead, for a buffet-style appetizer. Most of the dishes in this menu are specialties of the region of Champagne, and so you might want to accompany it with the area's specialty for which France is best known—Champagne.

**Beet Salad with Walnuts and Greens (page 86),
or Crudités (page 374)
Leek Tart (page 263)
Sautéed Wild Mushrooms with Herbs (page 245)
Glazed Parsnips and Carrots (page 140)
Pears in red wine**

VEGETABLES FOR THANKSGIVING

Serve these vegetables as a basis for a festive holiday vegetarian dinner, or use some or all of them as wonderful accompaniments for the Thanksgiving turkey. Apple or pumpkin pie make good seasonal deserts with this menu.

Dinner Salad, American Style (page 216)
Stuffed Acorn Squash with Apples and Walnuts
(page 343)
Carrots with Wild Rice, Mushrooms, and
Tarragon (page 137)
Brussels Sprouts in Hungarian Mushroom Sauce
(page 113)
Apple or pumpkin pie

CELEBRATION OF THE WINTER HOLIDAYS

This colorful, tasty menu is great for a dinner or a party, as everything is easy to serve. Add a festive dessert like *bûche de Nöel* or chocolate truffles.

Leek and Butternut Squash Soup (page 262)
Mushroom-Macadamia Tart (page 244) or Sweet
Potato Latkes (page 310)
Red and Green Cabbage Salad with Citrus Fruit
(page 125)
Snow Peas with Baby Onions and Ginger
(page 272)
Chocolate Yule log or truffles

NEW YEAR'S PARTY ON A BUDGET

When I was a student in Paris, I went to a wonderful New Year's party where a simple soup—turnip cream soup—was served as the main dish. It was a surprising choice but was perfect for the cold winter night. Other rich, warming soups also make delicious party dishes. To complete the menu, serve two or three cheeses, such as brie, chèvre, and gruyère, and a selection of good fresh breads. Homemade brownies or chocolate truffles make perfect desserts.

Creamy Turnip Soup (page 331), Celery Root Soup (page 148), or Portuguese Green Soup (page 208)
Crudités (page 374)
Potatoes Dauphine (page 301)
Brownies or chocolate truffles

CASUAL WINTER SUPPER

This is an easy menu for enjoying at home with the family on a winter evening. If you prefer, make only one of the salads, or omit the rutabaga. The heart of this menu is the savory "unstuffed" cabbage, which can be served even without accompaniment.

Moroccan Radish Salad with Orange (page 231)
Carrot Salad with Garlic, Cumin, and Parsley (page 139)
"Unstuffed" Cabbage (page 121)
Rutabaga or Turnips with Raisins (page 332)
Ripe Comice pears

MAIN-COURSE VEGETABLE DISHES

The following recipes make especially good choices for satisfying main courses. If the dish doesn't already contain pasta, rice, or grains, serve it with one of these or with fresh bread. For more tips on menu planning, see Chapter 1, Why and How to Eat More Vegetables.

ARTICHOKES

Artichoke Hearts with Lima Beans and Dill
(page 23)
Breton Artichoke Omelet (page 25)
Artichokes and Mushrooms with Feta Stuffing
(page 26)

ASPARAGUS

Chinese Asparagus in Ginger-Scented Brown Sauce (page 35)
Asparagus with Shrimp and Dill Sauce
(page 38)
Roasted Asparagus, Red Pepper, and Pasta Salad
(page 40)
Baked Eggs with Asparagus (page 41)
Summertime Angel-Hair Pasta (page 42)

GREEN BEANS

Green Beans Basquaise (page 47)
Lebanese Green Beans with Tomatoes and Garlic
(page 48)
Ethiopian Spiced Green Beans and Carrots
(page 50)
Green Beans "Mimosa" with Feta Cheese and
Walnuts (page 51)
Indonesian Green Beans (page 52)
Green Bean and Chickpea Salad with Tomatoes
and Olives (page 53)
Green Bean, Shrimp, and Tomato Salad
(page 54)
Green (or Wax) Beans with Cèpes and Garlic
(page 55)
Chinese Long Beans with Black Mushroom Sauce
(page 56)

DRIED BEANS AND SHELL BEANS

Chilean "Succotash" (page 66)
Two-Bean Salad with Fennel (page 67)
Egyptian Beans with Greens (page 68)
Portuguese Lima Beans with Cilantro (page 69)
Chickpeas with Spinach and Carrots (page 70)
White Beans, Middle Eastern Style (page 72)
Tuscan Bean Soup (page 73)
Cuban Black Bean Soup with Cumin and Garlic
(page 74)
Cuban Black Beans with Peppers and Rice
(page 75)
Corsican Red Beans with Leeks (page 76)
Colombian Lentil Soup (page 77)
Middle Eastern Lentils with Rice (page 78)
Dutch Split Pea Soup (page 79)

BROCCOLI AND CAULIFLOWER

Broccoli with Chinese Mushrooms and Oyster
Sauce (page 93)
Couscous Pilaf with Broccoli and Garlic Butter
(page 95)
Algerian Cauliflower with Tomato, Garlic, and
Cilantro (page 96)
Czech Cauliflower with Onions and Eggs
(page 97)
Broccoflower and Rice Pilaf with Chipotle Salsa
(page 104)
Pasta Shells with Broccoli Rabe (page 107)

CABBAGE

"Unstuffed" Cabbage (page 121)
Romanian Braised Cabbage with Tomatoes and
Peppers (page 122)
Cabbage and Prosciutto Crepes (page 123)
Breton Cabbage Salad with Shrimp and Walnuts
(page 124)
Stir-Fried Bok Choy with Black Bean Sauce
(page 129)

CARROTS AND PARSNIPS

Ukrainian Carrot and Potato Stew with Dried
Mushrooms (page 136)
Carrots with Wild Rice, Mushrooms, and
Tarragon (page 137)

CELERY AND FENNEL

Fennel with Mushroom Stuffing (page 151)

CORN

Corn Maquechou (page 156)
Mexican Corn, Zucchini, and Pepper Stew
(page 156)
Light Corn Chowder (page 157)

EGGPLANT

Easy Eggplant with Ginger (page 176)
Chinese Eggplant and Peppers with Black Bean
Sauce (page 177)
Caponata (page 179)
East African Eggplant Curry with Chickpeas
(page 180)
Eggplant and Tofu Casserole with Tomatoes and
Garlic (page 181)
Eggplant Stuffed with Scamorza Cheese
(page 183)
Eggplant with Mushroom Stuffing (page 184)
Eggplant and Feta Crepes (page 191)

GREENS

Spinach Flans (page 203)
Spinach Salad with Feta Cheese and Tomatoes
(page 205)
Portuguese Green Soup (page 208)
Beet Greens with Rice (page 214)

JERUSALEM ARTICHOKES

**Jerusalem Artichoke Gratin with Walnuts
(page 226)**

MUSHROOMS

**Mushrooms with Red Peppers, Cumin, and
Thyme (page 239)
Thai Mushroom and Red Chili Curry (page 240)
Mushroom Pizza (page 241)
Sesame Mushroom Crepes (page 242)
Mushroom Tostadas (page 243)
Mushroom-Macadamia Tart (page 244)**

OKRA

**Okra, Egyptian Style (page 251)
Peppery Okra with Greens (page 251)**

ONIONS, LEEKS, AND SHALLOTS

Pizza with Algerian Onion Compote (page 259)
Swiss Onion Tart (page 262)
Leek and Butternut Squash Soup (page 262)
Leek Tart (page 263)

PEAS

Green Peas with Mushrooms (page 270)
Peas in Spicy Tomato Sauce (page 271)
Snow Peas with Baby Onions and Ginger
(page 272)
Stir-Fried Snow Peas, Carrots, and Yellow
Squash (page 273)
Sugar-Snap Peas with Sautéed Mushrooms
(page 274)
Sugar-Snap Pea, Carrot, and Black Mushroom
Salad (page 275)

PEPPERS

Hungarian Pepper Stew (page 282)
Noodles with Lecso and Chicken (page 282)
Basque Pepper Stew (page 283)
Stuffed Peppers with Rice, Pine Nuts, and
Currants (page 284)
Armenian Pepper, Parsley, and Wheat Salad
(page 285)
Pepper and Goat Cheese Tartlets (page 287)

POTATOES

Potatoes with Peanut Sauce and Cheese
(page 295)
Austrian Potato Soup with Chives (page 300)
Lebanese Potato Salad with Tomatoes and Mint
(page 302)
Potato Salad with Avocado and Cilantro
(page 304)
Russian Potato Salad (page 305)

SWEET POTATOES

Sweet Potato Latkes (page 310)
Tangy North African Sweet Potato Salad
(page 311)

TOMATOES

Lebanese Stuffed Tomatoes (page 317)
Easy Stuffed Tomatoes, Roman Style (page 318)
Ligurian Tomato, Olive, and Caper Pizza
(page 319)
Tomato and Corn Tortilla Soup (page 320)

TURNIPS AND RUTABAGAS

Algerian Turnips with Peas, Garlic, and Cilantro
(page 328)
Moroccan Winter Vegetable Stew (page 329)
Creamy Turnip Soup (page 331)
Rutabaga with Garlic and Greens (page 332)
Rutabaga with Raisins (page 332)

WINTER SQUASH AND PUMPKIN

Winter Squash with Sweet Spices (page 340)
Winter Squash with Rice and Green Beans
(page 341)
Stuffed Acorn Squash with Apples and Pecans
(page 343)

ZUCCHINI, SUMMER SQUASH, AND CHAYOTE

Quick Zucchini and Eggplant Sauté with Basil
(page 353)
Napoli Zucchini Casserole (page 355)
Provençal Zucchini Omelet with Garlic
(page 357)
Chayote Squash with Tomatoes and Caribbean
Sofrito (page 359)

VEGETABLE MEDLEYS

Thai Vegetable Medley with Mint and Chilies
(page 365)
Chinese Vegetables with Rice Noodles and
Shrimp (page 366)
Givetch (page 370)
Ratatouille (page 372)
East Mediterranean Vegetable Stew with Lamb
(page 369)
Café de Paris Niçoise Salad (page 371)
Chickpea Salad with Fennel, Pistou, and
Tomatoes (page 377)

MAIL ORDER SOURCES

I purchase the ingredients for these recipes in local supermarkets. However, if you can't find an ingredient, here are sources for ordering them by mail:

HOT PEPPER SAUCES, CURRY PASTES, DRIED CHILIES

Mo Hotta—Mo Betta
P.O. Box 4136
San Luis Obispo, CA 93403
800-462-3220

SPICES AND INGREDIENTS FOR CENTRAL EUROPEAN COOKING

Paprikas Weiss Importers
1572 Second Avenue
New York, NY 10028
212-288-6117

SPICES AND INGREDIENTS FOR INDIAN AND SOUTHEAST ASIAN COOKING

House of Spices
76-17 Broadway
Jackson Heights, NY 11373
718-476-1577

ORIENTAL INGREDIENTS

China Bowl Trading Company
169 Lackawanna Avenue
Parsippany, NJ 07054
800-526-5051; 201-335-1000

SPECIALTY GRAINS AND INGREDIENTS FROM EUROPE, ASIA, AFRICA, THE MIDDLE EAST, LATIN AMERICA, AND THE CARIBBEAN

G.B. Ratto & Co. International Grocers
821 Washington Street
Oakland, CA 94607
800-228-3515 (in CA, 800-325-3483);
415-836-2250

SPECIALTY OILS AND VINEGARS

Williams-Sonoma
Mail Order Department
P.O. Box 7456
San Francisco, CA 94120-7456
800-541-2233; 415-421-4242

WILD MUSHROOMS, DRIED BEANS, OILS, AND VINEGARS

Dean and DeLuca
560 Broadway
New York, NY 10012
800-221-7714; 212-431-1691

SPICES AND HERBS

Select Origins
Box N
Southampton, NY 19968
800-822-2092; 516-288-1382

Rafal Spice Co.
2521 Russel St.
Detroit, MI 48207
313-259-6373

The Spice House
1031 N. Old World Third Street
Milwaukee, WI 53203
414-272-0977

DRIED CHILIES, DRIED MUSHROOMS, FRESH SQUASH, SALAD GREENS, AND HERBS

Frieda's By Mail
P.O. Box 58488
Los Angeles, CA 90058
800-241-1771

CONVERSION CHART

LIQUID MEASURES

Fluid Ounces	U.S. Measures	Imperial Measures	Milliliters
	1 tsp.	1 tsp.	5
1/4	2 tsp.	1 dessert spoon	7
1/2	1 T.	1 T.	15
1	2 T.	2 T.	28
2	1/4 cup	4 T.	56
4	1/2 cup or 1/4 pint		110
5		1/4 pint or 1 gill	140
6	3/4 cup		170
8	1 cup or 1/2 pint		225
9			250 (1/4 liter)
10	1 1/4 cups	1/2 pint	280
12	1 1/2 cups or 3/4 pint		340
15		3/4 pint	420
16	2 cups or 1 pint		450
18	2 1/4 cups		500 (1/2 liter)
20	2 1/2 cups	1 pint	560
24	3 cups or 1 1/2 pints		675
25		1 1/4 pints	700
27	3 1/2 cups		750
30	3 3/4 cups	1 1/2 pints	840
32	4 cups or 2 pints or 1 quart		900
35		1 3/4 pints	980
36	4 1/2 cups		1000 (1 liter)

SOLID MEASURES

U.S. and Imperial Measures		Metric Measures	
Ounces	Pounds	Grams	Kilos
1		28	
2		56	
3 1/2		100	
4	1/4	112	
5		140	
6		168	
8	1/2	225	
9		250	1/4
12	3/4	340	
16	1	450	
18		500	1/2
20	1 1/4	560	
24	1 1/2	675	
27		750	3/4
28	1 3/4	780	
32	2	900	
36	2 1/4	1000	1
40		1100	
48	3	1350	
54		1500	1 1/2

OVEN TEMPERATURE EQUIVALENTS

Fahrenheit	Gas Mark	Celsius	Heat of Oven
225	1/4	107	Very Cool
250	1/2	121	Very Cool
275	1	135	Cool
300	2	148	Cool
325	3	163	Moderate
350	4	177	Moderate
375	5	190	Fairly Hot
400	6	204	Fairly Hot
425	7	218	Hot
450	8	232	Very Hot
475	9	246	Very Hot

INDEX

Acorn squash, 338
  stuffed with apples and pecans,.
    343
Afghan cuisine, cucumber salad with
    yogurt, walnuts, raisins, 164
African cuisine, 6
  mail-order sources, 438
  see also East African cuisine; North
    African cuisine; West African
    cuisine; specific countries
Áioli, 402
Algerian cuisine
  cauliflower with tomatoes, garlic,
    cilantro, 96
  cucumber and pepper salad, 165
  onion compote with tomatoes,
    259
  turnips with peas, garlic, cilantro,
    328
  vinegar-scented peppers, 286–87

winter squash with sweet spices,
    340
Anaheim chilies, 288
  grilling, 281
Argentinean cuisine, *chimichurri*,
    102, 176, 388
Armenian cuisine
  beet greens with rice, 214
  pepper, parsley, and wheat salad,
    285
Artichokes, 19–29
  basics, 21–22
  bottoms, 22
  eating whole, 22
  hearts, 20
  hearts with lima beans and dill,
    23
  marinated, Greek, 27–28
  and mushrooms with feta stuffing,
    26–27

omelet, Breton, 25–26
  and orange salad, Moroccan, 29
  salad with olives and capers,
    28–29
  stuffed, Moroccan, 24–25
  whole with dipping sauce, 24
  see also Jerusalem artichokes
Arugula (rocket), 197
  salad with bean sprouts and enoki
    mushrooms, 217
Asian cuisine. *See* Oriental cuisine;
    specific countries
Asparagus, 31–45
  and angel hair pasta, 42
  and baked eggs, 41
  basics, 33–34
  feuilletes with dried mushroom
    sauce, 43
  in ginger-scented brown sauce,
    Chinese, 35

441

Asparagus (*continued*)

with herb-lemon butter, 37
with mustard-shallot sauce, 37
peeling tip, 33–34
roasted, 39
roasted, in pasta and red pepper salad, 40
sautéed, 34–35
with shrimp and dill sauce, 38
with sun-dried tomato vinaigrette, 36
Austrian cuisine
cucumber salad, 166–67
potato soup with chives, 300
Avocado
guacamole, 392
potato and cilantro salad with, 304–5

Baby vegetables
bok choy, 128
Brussels sprouts, purple, 112
Chinese, with rice noodles, shrimp, 366
corn, 154, 159, 366
greens, 215, 330
onions, 261, 272
summer squash, 348
Baking, 16
Brussels sprouts, 115
eggplant, 173
squash, 343, 360
sweet potatoes, 309
Basil
in *pistou*, 387
roasted eggplant with garlic and, 182
zucchini and eggplant sauté with, 353
zucchini with Romano cheese and, 350
Basque cuisine
green beans, 47–48
pepper stew, 283, 287
Bean sprouts, 62
Beans. *See* Chinese long beans; Dried and shell beans; Green beans; *Haricots verts*
Beets, 81–87
basics, 82
as *crudités*, 375
greens, 197

greens with rice, 214
roasted with dill dressing, 84
salad with horseradish dressing, Swedish, 85
salad with walnuts and greens, 86
salad with yogurt and mint, Persian, 87
steamed with mint butter, 83
Belgian endive. *See* Endive, Belgian
Bell peppers. *See* under Peppers
Bibb lettuce. *See* Butter lettuce
Black beans (turtle), 64
with peppers and rice, Cuban, 75
sauce, eggplant and peppers with, Chinese, 177
sauce, stir-fried bok choy with, 129
soup with cumin and garlic, Cuban, 74
Black-eyed peas (cowpeas), 64
braised celery with, 146–47
Hoppin' John, 71
Blanching, 12, 118
Boiling, 11–12
artichokes, whole, 24
Brussels sprouts, 112
corn on the cob, 155
Bok choy
baby, with Chinese mushrooms, 128
in Chinese vegetables with rice noodles and shrimp, 366
stir-fried with black bean sauce, 129
Borani, 206
Boston lettuce. *See* Butter lettuce
Braising, 13
cabbage, 118, 122
celery, 146–47
endive, Belgian, 213
vegetable medleys, 370–71, 372
Broccoli, 89–107
basics, 91
broccoflower and rice pilaf with chipotle salsa, 104
broccoflower and tomato salad, 105
with Chinese mushrooms and oyster sauce, 93
in couscous pilaf with garlic butter, 95
garlic-scented, 92
gratin with pecans and cheddar, 94
rabe, pasta shells with, 107
rabe with garlic, 106

salad with Caribbean lime juice dressing, 102–3
salad with *chimichurri*, 102
Broiling, 16
eggplant, 176
peppers, 278
Brussels sprouts, 109–15
baked in cream sauce, 115
basics, 111
boiled, 112
in Hungarian mushroom sauce, 113
purple baby, 112
with shallots, 114–15
with water chestnuts and ginger, 114
Bulgarian cuisine, parsnips with yogurt-dill sauce, 141
Butter
garlic, 95
herb-lemon, 296, 391
mint, 83, 391
Butter lettuce (Bibb, Boston), 197
in beet salad with walnuts and greens, 86
Butternut squash, 338
and leek soup, 262–63

Cabbage, 117–29
basics, 119
braised with tomatoes and peppers, Romanian, 122
cole slaw, Salvadoran, 126
as *crudités*, 375
and prosciutto crepes, 123
red, with apples, Dutch, 127
salad, red and green, with citrus fruit, 125
salad with shrimp and walnuts, Breton, 124
salad with spicy peanut dressing, Malaysian, 124–25
sautéed, 120
"unstuffed", 121
see also Bok choy
Capers
artichoke salad with olives and, 28–29
dressing, roasted pepper salad with, 286
in tomato and olive pizza, Ligurian, 319
vinaigrette, chives and, 385

Caponata, 179
Caribbean cuisine, 9–10
  chayote salad, Martinique, 361
  lime juice dressing, 102–3, 382
  mail-order sources, 438
  okra salad, 253
  sofrito, 359, 396
Carrots, 131–32, 134–40
  and baby onions with raisins, 261
  basics, 132
  chickpeas with spinach and,
    70–71
  as *crudités*, 375
  with *gremolata*, 134
  parsnips and, glazed, 140
  puree, zucchini boats with, 356
  salad, apple and, Danish, 138–39
  salad, celery root, apples, walnuts
    and, Polish, 149
  salad, daikon radish and, 230–31
  salad with garlic, cumin, parsley,
    Moroccan, 139
  salad, sugar-snap pea, black
    mushroom, and, 275
  sautéed with yogurt, 134–35
  snow peas, yellow squash, and,
    273
  spiced green beans and, Ethiopian,
    50
  in stew with potatoes and dried
    mushrooms, Ukrainian, 136
  timbales, 138
  with wild rice, mushrooms, and
    tarragon, 137
  with zucchini, Korean, 135
Cauliflower, 89–107
  basics, 91
  beer batter fritters, 98–99
  flan with roasted red pepper
    sauce, 100–101
  with ginger and cumin, 98
  with onions and eggs, Czech, 97
  puree, spicy, 100
  with tarragon vinaigrette, 103
  with tomatoes, garlic, and
    cilantro, Algerian, 96
Ceci beans. *See* Chickpeas
Celeriac. *See* Celery root
Celery, 143–44, 146–48
  basics, 144
  braised with black-eyed peas,
    146–47
  stuffed with ground turkey,
    147–48
Celery root, 143–44, 145, 148–50
  basics, 145

and carrot salad with apples and
    walnuts, Polish, 149
  rémoulade, 150
  soup, 148
  in split pea soup, Dutch, 79
Cèpes (porcini mushrooms), 236
  wax beans with garlic and, 55–56
Chayote squash, 348, 359–61
  baked slices, Mexican, 360
  basics, 349
  salad, Martinique, 361
  with tomatoes and *sofrito*, 359
Cheese sauce, 399
Chickpeas, 64
  braised celery with, 146–47
  eggplant curry with, East African,
    180
  salad with fennel, *pistou*, tomatoes,
    377
  salad with green beans, tomatoes,
    olives, 53
  salad with tomatoes and
    cucumbers, Indian, 376–77
  with spinach and carrots, 70–71
Chilean cuisine
  hot cilantro salsa, 388
  "succotash", 66
Chilies
  basics, 280
  in green *Zehug*, 392–93
  grilling, 281, 289
  in guacamole, 392
  handling, 280
  in harissa, 28, 96, 393
  jalapeños, grilled, 289
  mail-order sources, 437, 438
  okra with garlic and, 252–53
  poblano strips with onions, 288
  salsa, chipotle chili, 104, 373, 389
  salsa, hot cilantro, Chilean, 388
  types, 277
  in vegetable medley with mint,
    Thai, 365
Chimichurri (garlic-herb dipping
    sauce), 176, 388
  broccoli salad with, 102
Chinese black mushrooms
  baby bok choy with, 128
  broccoli with oyster sauce and, 93
  salad with sugar-snap peas and
    carrots, 275
  sauce, 43, 56
  with sesame seeds, 246
Chinese cuisine, 7
  asparagus in ginger-scented brown
    sauce, 35

baby bok choy with Chinese
    mushrooms, 128
  baby corn and long bean salad,
    159
  bok choy, stir-fried, with black
    bean sauce, 129
  broccoli with Chinese mushrooms
    and oyster sauce, 93
  Chinese long beans with black
    mushroom sauce, 56–57
  cucumber salad, Sichuan, 169
  eggplant and peppers with black
    bean sauce, 177
  sugar-snap pea, carrot, and black
    mushroom salad, 275
  vegetables with rice noodles and
    shrimp, 366
Chinese long beans
  with black mushroom sauce,
    56–57
  salad, baby corn and, 159
Chipotle chili salsa, 104, 373, 389
Chives
  cucumber salad with smoked
    salmon and, 168
  potato soup with, Austrian, 300
  vinaigrette, caper and, 385
Christophine. *See* Chayote squash
Cilantro
  cauliflower with tomatoes, garlic,
    and, Algerian, 96
  in green *Zehug*, 392–93
  lima beans with, Portugese, 69
  potato salad with avocado and,
    304–5
  in salsa, Chilean, 388
  turnips with peas, garlic, and,
    Algerian, 328
Cole slaw, Salvadoran, 126
Colombian cuisine
  lentil soup, 77
  tomato-onion sauce, 77, 395
Compotes
  onion, French, 260
  onion with tomatoes, Algerian,
    259
Conversion chart, 439
Cooking techniques; 11–17; *see also*
    specific methods
Coriander, eggplant puree with
    garlic and, 189
Corn, 153–59
  baby, 154, 159, 366
  basics, 155
  chowder, 157
  hominy, 154

Corn (*continued*)

maquechou, 156
on the cob, 155
popcorn, 154
salad, baby corn and Chinese long
bean, 159
stew, zucchini, pepper, and,
Mexican, 156–57
succotash, American, 158
"succotash", Chilean, 66
Couscous pilaf, 95
Cowpeas. *See* Black-eyed peas
Cream sauce, 400–401
Crepes
batter, 409–10
cabbage and prosciutto, 123
eggplant and feta, 191
sesame mushroom, 242–43
Crookneck squash, 348
with dill and paprika, 351
Crudités, 374–75
Cuban cuisine
black bean soup with cumin and
garlic, 74
black beans with peppers and rice,
75
Cucumbers, 161–69
basics, 163
as *crudités*, 375
salad, Austrian, 166–67
salad, chickpea, tomato, and,
Indian, 376–77
salad, chopped, Mediterranean,
166
salad, eggplant with tomatoes and,
186
salad, pepper and, Algerian, 165
salad, Sichuan, 169
salad, smoked salmon, chives and,
168
salad, watercress and, 322
salad, yogurt, cumin seeds and,
167
salad, yogurt, walnuts, raisins and,
Afghan, 164
and yogurt dressing, 322
Cumin
in black bean soup, Cuban, 74
in carrot salad with garlic and
parsley, Moroccan, 139
in cauliflower with ginger, 98
in cucumber salad with yogurt,
167
in green and yellow squash salad,
Moroccan, 358

in mushrooms with red peppers
and thyme, 239
Curries
eggplant with chickpeas, East
African, 180
mushroom and red chili, Thai,
240
Czech cuisine, cauliflower with
onions and eggs, 97

Daikon radish and carrot salad,
230–31
Danish cuisine, carrot and apple
salad, 138–39
Deep-frying, 15
fritter batter, 99
onion rings, 260–61
potato puffs, 301
tempura batter, 368–69
Dill
artichoke hearts with lima beans
and, 23
crookneck squash with paprika
and, 351
dressing, roasted beets with, 84
oyster mushrooms with, 247
sauce, with asparagus and shrimp,
38
-yogurt sauce, Bulgarian, 141
Dips
spinach watercress, 403
tomato-pepper, Moroccan, 321
see also Salsas
Dough. *See* Pastries
Dressings, 379–403
caper, 286
cucumber-yogurt, 322
dill, 84
garlic, Moroccan, 381
Greek salad, 205
herb, Provençal, 384
horseradish, 85
lime juice, Caribbean, 102–3, 382
olive oil and mint, 165
orange, 309
peanut, Malaysian, 386
peanut, spicy, 124–25
tangy Moroccan, 381
tomato-yogurt, 322
see also Oils; Salsas; Sauces;
Vinaigrettes
Dried and shell beans, 59–79
basics, 63
chart, 64–65

with greens, Egyptian, 68
mail-order sources, 438
soup, Colombian, 77
soup, Cuban, 74
soup, Dutch, 79
soup, Tuscan, 73
"succotash", Chilean, 66
two-bean salad with fennel, 67
see also Lentils; specific kinds
Dried mushrooms. *See* Mushrooms,
dried
Dutch cuisine
red cabbage with apples, 127
split pea soup, 79
Duxelles, 234
in mushroom-macadamia tart,
244–45
recipe, 408–9
sauce, 399

East African cuisine, eggplant curry
with chickpeas, 180
Eastern European cuisine
latkes, 310
stewed kohlrabi, 228
see also specific countries
Eggplant, 171–91
antipasto, grilled, 188
basics, 174
bharta, 190
broiled slices, 176
caponata, 179
Chinese, with peppers in black
bean sauce, 177
curry with chickpeas, East African,
180
and feta crepes, 191
with ginger, 176–77
with mushroom stuffing, 184
puree with garlic and coriander,
189
ratatouille, 372
relish, Sri Lankan, 185
roasted with basil and garlic, 182
salad, roasted with pepper,
Catalan, 187
salad, three-way, 186–87
salad with garlic and yogurt,
Turkish, 187
salad with tomatoes and
cucumber, 186
salting, 172, 174–75
sautéed, 175

sautéed with fresh tomato
topping, 178
stuffed with scamorza cheese, 183
and tofu casserole with tomatoes
and garlic, 181
in vegetable medley with mint
and chilies, Thai, 365
and zucchini sauté with basil, 353
Egyptian cuisine
beans with greens, 68
eggplant puree with garlic and
coriander, 189
garlic sauce, 207
okra, 251
rutabaga with garlic and greens,
332
Endive, Belgian, 197
in beet salad with walnuts and
greens, 86
braised, 213
English cuisine, peas, 269
Enoki mushrooms, 236
arugula salad with bean sprouts
and, 217
Escarole, 198
bean soup, Tuscan, 73
Ethiopian cuisine, spiced green
beans and carrots, 50
European cuisine, 4
Brussels sprouts with cream sauce,
115
cabbage salad, red and green, with
citrus fruit, 125
celery root soup, 148
glazed parsnips and carrots, 140
mail-order sources, 437, 438
roasted beets with dill dressing, 84
see also Eastern European cuisine;
specific countries

Fava beans, 61
with artichoke hearts and dill, 23
with greens, Egyptian, 68
two-bean salad with fennel, 67
Fennel, 143, 144–46, 150–51
basics, 146
chickpea salad with *pistou*,
tomatoes, and, 377
with fontina, 150–51
with mushroom stuffing, 151
two-bean salad with, 67
Feuilletes, asparagus with dried
mushroom sauce, 43

Finnish cuisine, rutabaga puree, 333
Flans
cauliflower with roasted red
pepper sauce, 100–101
spinach, 203
French Canadian cuisine, carrots
with wild rice, mushrooms, and
tarragon, 137
French cuisine
áioli, 402
artichoke omelet, Breton, 25–26
baked eggs with asparagus, 41
beet salad with walnuts and
greens, 86
cabbage salad with shrimp and
walnuts, Breton, 124
Café de Paris Niçoise salad, 371
cauliflower flan with roasted red
pepper sauce, 100–101
celery root rémoulade, 150
chickpea salad with fennel, *pistou*,
and tomatoes, 377
couscous pilaf with broccoli and
garlic butter, 95
dried mushroom sauce, 43, 398
green bean, shrimp, and tomato
salad, 54
green beans "mimosa" with feta
cheese and walnuts, 51–52
green beans with sautéed onions,
51
haricots verts maître d'hôtel, 57
leek tart, 263–64
mashed potatoes, 299
mushroom-macadamia tart,
244–45
onion compote, 260
pie dough, 411–12
pistou, 387
potatoes Dauphine, 301
potato salad, Périgord, 303
Swiss chard gratin with cheese
sauce, 209
turnip soup, 331
French cuisine (Provençal)
eggplant with mushroom stuffing,
184
fennel with mushroom stuffing,
151
green bean and chickpea salad
with tomatoes and olives, 53
green beans Basquaise, 47–48
herb dressing, 384
Jerusalem artichoke stew, 227
pistou, 176
ratatouille, 372

roasted garlic cloves, 265
zucchini omelet with garlic, 357
see also Basque cuisine
Fritters, beer batter cauliflower,
98–99
Frying. *See* Deep-frying; Sautéing;
Stir-frying

Garbanzo beans. *See* Chickpeas
Garlic, 256, 265
basics, 257
black bean soup with cumin and,
Cuban, 74
broccoli rabe with, 106
broccoli with, 92
butter, 95
carrot salad with cumin, parsley,
and, Moroccan, 139
cauliflower with tomatoes,
cilantro, and, Algerian, 96
chimichurri, 102, 176, 388
dressing, Moroccan, 381
eggplant puree with coriander
and, 189
eggplant, roasted, with basil and,
182
eggplant salad with yogurt and,
Turkish, 187
eggplant, tofu, tomato casserole
with, 181
forty roasted cloves of, 265
green beans with tomatoes and,
Lebanese, 48–49
and herb oil, 390–91
mayonnaise (áioli), 402
okra with hot pepper and, 252–53
peeling, 258
in *pistou*, 387
pumpkin puree with, 345
rutabaga with greens and, 332
sauce, Egyptian, for kale, 207
sauce, yogurt and, Turkish, 380
turnips with peas, cilantro, and,
Algerian, 328
wax beans with cèpes and, 55–56
zucchini omelet with, Provençal,
357
German cuisine, green bean salad
with red onions, 55
Ginger
asparagus in brown sauce with,
Chinese, 35
Brussels sprouts with water
chestnuts and, 114

Ginger (*continued*)

cauliflower with cumin and, 98
eggplant with, 176–77
snow peas with baby onions and, 272
Givetch, 370–71
Glazing
parsnips and carrots, 140
radishes, 230
Great Northern beans, 64
Middle Eastern style, 72
Greek cuisine
country salad, 323
marinated artichokes, 27–28
spanakopitas, 204
spinach salad with feta cheese and tomatoes, 205
Green beans, 45–57
basics, 47
Basquaise, 47–48
with cèpes and garlic, 55–56
Indonesian, 52–53
"mimosa" with feta cheese and walnuts, 51–52
salad, chickpea, tomatoes, olives and, 53
salad, shrimp, tomato and, 54
salad with red onions, German, 55
with sautéed onions, Lyonnaise, 51
spiced, and carrots, Ethiopian, 50
stew, red pepper and, Spanish, 49
with tomatoes and garlic, Lebanese, 48–49
winter squash with rice and, 341
see also Chinese long beans; *Haricots verts*
Green onions, mashed potatoes with, Irish, 298
Green peas. *See* Peas
Greens, 193–217
arugula with bean sprouts and enoki mushrooms, 217
basics, 195
beans with, Egyptian, 68
beet, with rice, 214
beet salad with walnuts and, 86
chart, 197–99
mail-order sources, 438
okra with, 251–52
with onions and mushrooms, 211
with red pepper, 211
rutabaga with garlic and, 332
salad, American-style, 216

salad of baby, 215
soup, Portugese, 208
soup, with leeks and potatoes, 212
turnip timbales on a bed of, 330
see also specific types
Green squash. *See* Zucchini
Green *Zehug*, 392–93
Gremolata, 134
Grilling, 16
corn on the cob, 155
eggplant, 172, 188
peppers and chilies, 278, 281, 289
Guacamole, 392

Haricots verts, 45, 46, 51
maître d'hôtel, 57
Harissa (hot pepper sauce), 28, 96, 393
mail-order source, 437
Herbs
butter, lemon and, 37, 296, 391
-garlic dipping sauce, 102, 176, 388
and garlic oil, 390–91
mail-order sources, 438
see also specific kinds
Holiday cuisine, 137, 272
Hanukkah, 310
menus, 420, 422–23
New Year's Day, 71
Thanksgiving, 262–63, 343
Hominy, 154
Hoppin' John, 71
Horseradish dressing, 85
Hot peppers. *See* Chilies; Harissa
Hungarian cuisine
mushroom sauce, 113
pepper stew, 282

Indian cuisine, 6–7
chickpeas with spinach and carrots, 70–71
chickpea, tomato, and cucumber salad, 376–77
eggplant *bharta*, 190
mail-order sources, 438
okra with hot pepper and garlic, 252–53
Indonesian cuisine, 7
green beans, 52–53

Iranian cuisine
beet salad with yogurt and mint, 87
spinach borani, 206
Irish cuisine, mashed potatoes with green onions, 298
Italian cuisine
asparagus with lemon and anchovy, 37
bean soup, Tuscan, 73
broccoli, garlic-scented, 92
broccoli rabe, pasta shells with, 107
broccoli rabe with garlic, 106
caponata, Sicilian, 179
chickpeas with spinach and carrots, 70–71
easy stuffed tomatoes, Roman, 318
eggplant antipasto, grilled, 188
eggplant, roasted, with basil and garlic, Sardinian, 182
eggplant stuffed with scamorza cheese, 183
fennel with fontina, 150–51
gremolata, 134
mashed potatoes with peppers, Calabrian, 297
red Swiss chard with oil and lemon, 210
tomato, olive, and caper pizza, Ligurian, 319
zucchini and eggplant sauté with basil, 353
zucchini casserole, Napoli, 355
zucchini with Romano cheese and basil, Sardinian, 350
Italian squash. *See* Zucchini

Jalapeño peppers
in green *Zehug*, 392–93
grilled, 281, 289
in salsa, hot cilantro, Chilean, 388
in vegetable medley with mint and chilies, Thai, 365
Japanese cuisine, 7
daikon radish and carrot salad, 230
spinach, sesame, 200
vegetable tempura, 368–69
Jerusalem artichokes, 219–21, 225–27

basics, 221
gratin with walnuts, 226
sautéed with peppers, 225
stew à la Provençal, 227
Jicama, 223, 229
basics, 223
salad with orange and lime juice, 229

Kalamata olives, 28–29, 53
Kale, 198
with Egytian garlic sauce, 207
Kohlrabi, 222, 228
basics, 222
stewed, Eastern European, 228
Korean cuisine, carrots with zucchini, 135

Lamb's lettuce. *See Mâche*
Latin American cuisine, 9–10
mail-order sources, 438
see also specific countries
Latkes, sweet potato, 310
Lebanese cuisine
artichokes and mushrooms with feta stuffing, 26–27
green beans with tomatoes and garlic, 48–49
potato salad with tomatoes and mint, 302
stuffed tomatoes, 317
Leeks, 255, 256, 262–64
basics, 257
cleaning, 258
red beans with, Corsican, 76
soup, butternut squash and, 262–63
soup, watercress with potatoes and, 212
tart, 263–64
Leftover cooked vegetables, 97
Legumes. *See* specific beans and peas
Lentils, 60–61, 64
with rice, Middle Eastern, 78
Lesco, 282
Lettuce, 197, 198
see also Greens; specific kinds
Lima beans, 65
artichoke hearts with dill and, 23
with cilantro, Portugese, 69
with greens, Egyptian, 68
in succotash, American, 158

in "succotash", Chilean, 66
in two-bean salad with fennel, 67

Mâche (lamb's lettuce), 198
in beet salad with walnuts and greens, 86
Mail-order sources, 437–38
Malaysian cuisine, 7
cabbage salad, 124–25
peanut dressing, 386
Marinades, Greek, 27–28
Measures conversion chart, 439
Mediterranean cuisine, 5
"chopped" salad, 166
ground turkey stuffing, 147–48
red beans with leeks, Corsican, 76
vegetable stew with lamb, 367
see also French cuisine (Provençal); Middle Eastern cuisine; Italian cuisine; North African cuisine
Menus, 415–35
Mexican cuisine
chayote squash slices, baked, 360
corn, zucchini, and pepper stew, 156–57
guacamole, 392
jicama salad with orange and lime juice, 229
mushrooms, 238
tomato and corn tortilla soup, 320–21
tomato salsa, 390
Microwaving, 17
corn on the cob, 155
winter squash, 337
Middle Eastern cuisine, 5
beet salad with yogurt and mint, 87
eggplant sautéed with fresh tomato topping, 178
lentils with rice, 78
mail-order sources, 438
sweet-and-sour winter squash with raisins, 344
tahini sauce, 401–2
white beans, 72
see also Mediterranean cuisine; North African cuisine; specific countries
Mint
beet salad with yogurt and, Persian, 87
butter, 83, 391
dressing, olive oil and, 165

potato salad with tomatoes and, Lebanese, 302
sweet-and-sour yellow squash with, 352
vegetable medley with chilies and, Thai, 365
Mirliton. *See* Chayote squash
Moroccan cuisine
artichoke and orange salad, 29
artichokes, stuffed, 24–25
carrot salad with garlic, cumin, and parsley, 139
dressing, garlic, 381
dressing, tangy, 381
green and yellow squash salad with cumin, 358
radish salad with oranges, 231
tomato-pepper dip, 321
tomato salad with red onions and parsley, 316
winter vegetable stew, 329
Mushrooms, 233–47
and artichokes with feta stuffing, 26–27
basics, 235
carrots with wild rice, tarragon, and, 137
chart, 236–37
cleaning, 234
crepes, sesame and, 242–43
curry, red chili and, Thai, 240
duxelles, 408–9
and eggplant sauté, 175
green peas with, 270–71
greens with onions and, 211
mail-order sources, 438
Mexican, 238
pizza, 241
with red peppers, cumin, and thyme, 239
sauce, *duxelles,* 399
sauce, Hungarian, 113
slicing button mushrooms, 235
stuffing, 151, 184
sugar-snap peas with, 274
tart, macadamia and, 244–45
tostadas, 243
wild. *See* Wild mushrooms
see also specific types
Mushrooms, dried
mail-order sources, 438
sauce, 43, 398
soaking, 235
stew, carrot and potato with, Ukrainian, 136
see also Chinese black mushrooms

Niçoise olives, 53, 371
North African cuisine
  harissa, 28, 96, 393
  pumpkin puree with garlic, 345
  rutabaga with raisins, 332–33
  sautéed Jerusalem artichokes with
    peppers, 225
  tangy sweet potato salad, 311
  see also specific countries
North American cuisine, 8–9
  corn chowder, 157
  succotash, 158
  see also French Canadian cuisine;
    Mexican cuisine; Southern
    (U.S.) cuisine

Oils
  for deep-frying, 15
  garlic-herb, 390–91
  mail-order sources, 438
Okra, 249–53
  basics, 250
  Egyptian style, 251
  with hot pepper and garlic,
    252–53
  peppery with greens, 251–52
  salad, Caribbean, 253
Olives
  Kalamata, 28–29, 53
  Niçoise, 53, 371
  pizza, tomato, caper, and,
    Ligurian, 319
  salad, artichoke with capers and,
    28–29
  salad, eggplant with capers and,
    Sicilian, 179
  salad, green bean, chickpea,
    tomatoes, and, 53
Onions, 255–56, 259–62
  baby, carrots and raisins with, 261
  baby, snow peas and ginger with,
    272
  basics, 257
  and cauliflower with eggs, Czech,
    97
  compote, French, 260
  compote with tomatoes, Algerian,
    259
  greens with mushrooms and, 211
  peeling, 257, 258
  poblano chili strips with, 288
  in ratatouille, 372

rings, 260–61
  sauce, tomato and, Colombian,
    77, 395
  sautéed, green beans with, 51
  sautéed, squash with, 342
  slicing and chopping, 258
  tart, Swiss, 262
  see also Green onions; Red onions
Oriental black mushrooms. *See*
  Shitake mushrooms
Oriental cuisine, 7
  mail-order sources, 438
  see also specific countries
Oven temperature equivalents, 439
Oyster mushrooms, 236
  with fresh dill, 247

Pakistani cuisine, eggplant *bharta*,
  190
Parsley
  carrot salad with garlic, cumin
    and, Moroccan, 139
  tomato salad with red onions and,
    Moroccan, 316
  wheat salad with pepper and,
    Armenian, 285
  see also Cilantro
Parsnips, 133, 140–41
  with Bulgarian yogurt-dill sauce,
    141
  and carrots, glazed, 140
Pastries
  choux dough for potatoes
    Dauphine, 301
  feuilletes, asparagus, 43
  French pie dough, 244–45,
    411–12
  onion tart, Swiss, 262
  pizza dough, 410–11
  spinach, Greek, 204–5
  tart and tartlet shells, 412–13
Pattypan squash, 348
  and carrot puree, 356
Peanut sauce, 295
Pearl onions, peeling, 258
Peas, 267–75
  basics, 268
  English, 269
  with mushrooms, 270–71
  with peppers, 270
  in spicy tomato sauce, 271

and turnips with garlic and
    cilantro, Algerian, 328
  see also Black-eyed peas; Snow
    peas; Split peas; Sugar-snap
    peas
Peppers, 277–89
  basics, 280
  bell, 278, 281
  black beans with rice and, Cuban,
    75
  cabbage with tomatoes and,
    Romanian, 122
  as *crudités*, 375
  dip, tomato and, Moroccan, 321
  and eggplant with black bean
    sauce, Chinese, 177
  grilling, 278, 281
  Jerusalem artichokes with, 225
  mashed potatoes with, Calabrian,
    297
  peas with, 270
  in ratatouille, 372
  salad, cucumber and, Algerian,
    165
  salad, parsley, wheat, and,
    Armenian, 285
  salad, roasted eggplant and,
    Catalan, 187
  salad, roasted, with caper dressing,
    286
  sautéed tricolor peppers with
    herbs, 281
  in stew, Basque, 283, 287
  in stew, Hungarian, 282
  in stew with corn and zucchini,
    Mexican, 156–57
  stuffed with rice, pine nuts, and
    currants, 284
  tartlets, goat cheese and, 287
  in vegetable medley with mint
    and chilies, Thai, 365
  vinegar-scented, 286–87
  see also Chilies; Red peppers;
    specific types
Peruvian cuisine, potatoes with
  peanut sauce and cheese, 295
Pistou, 387
  chickpea salad with fennel,
    tomatoes, and, 377
Pizza
  with Algerian onion compote, 259
  dough, 410–11
  mushroom, 241
  tomato, olive, and caper, Ligurian,
    319
Poblano chilies. *See* Chilies

Polish cuisine
  asparagus with shrimp and dill sauce, 38
  celery root and carrot salad with apples and walnuts, 149
Popcorn, 154
Porcini mushrooms. *See* Cèpes
Portugese cuisine
  green soup, 208
  lima beans with cilantro, 69
Potatoes, 291–305
  basics, 294
  as *crudités*, 375
  Dauphine, 301
  mashed, 292–93, 299
  mashed with green onions, Irish, 298
  mashed with peppers, Calabrian, 297
  new, steamed with herb-lemon butter, 296
  with peanut sauce and cheese, 295
  salad, Périgord, 303
  salad, Russian, 304–5
  salad with avocado and cilantro, 304–5
  salad with tomatoes and mint, Lebanese, 302
  soup, watercress with leeks and, 212
  soup with chives, Austrian, 300
  stew, carrots, dried mushrooms and, Ukrainian, 136
  see also Sweet potatoes
Pots and pans, 12, 13, 14, 15
Puerto Rican cuisine, chayote squash with tomatoes and Caribbean *sofrito*, 359
Pumpkins, 335–37, 342, 345
  basics, 336
  puree with garlic, 345
Purees
  carrot, 356
  cauliflower, spicy, 100
  eggplant with garlic and coriander, 189
  pumpkin with garlic, 345
  rutabaga, Finnish, 333
  shallot, 264–65

Radishes, 224–25, 230–31
  basics, 224
  glazed, 230

salad, carrot and daikon, 230–31
salad with oranges, Moroccan, 231
Ratatouille, 372
Red beans, 65
  with leeks, Corsican, 76
Red cabbage. *See* Cabbage
Red onions
  green bean salad with, German, 55
  tomato salad with parsley and, Moroccan, 316
Red peppers
  black beans with rice and, Cuban, 75
  greens with, 211
  mushrooms with cumin, thyme, and, 239
  salad, roasted asparagus, pasta, and, 40
  sauce, roasted, 100–101, 397
  stew, green bean and, Spanish, 49
Relish, eggplant, Sri Lankan, 185
Roasting, 16
  asparagus, 39, 40
  beets, 84
  eggplant, 182, 187
  garlic, 265
  peppers, 278
  red pepper sauce, 100–101
Rocket. *See* Arugula
Romaine lettuce, 198
  in beet salad with walnuts, 86
Romanian cuisine
  braised cabbage with tomatoes and peppers, 122
  Givetch, 370–71
Russian cuisine
  oyster mushrooms with dill, 247
  potato salad, 304–5
Rutabagas, 325–26, 332–33
  basics, 327
  with garlic and greens, 332
  puree, Finnish, 333
  with raisins, 332–33

Salads
  artichoke and orange, Moroccan, 29
  artichoke with olives and capers, 28–29
  arugula with bean sprouts and enoki mushrooms, 217

asparagus, roasted, with red pepper and pasta, 40
baby corn and Chinese long bean, 159
baby greens, 215
beet with horseradish dressing, Swedish, 85
beet with walnuts and greens, 86
beet with yogurt and mint, Persian, 87
broccoflower and tomato, 105
broccoli with Caribbean lime juice dressing, 102–3
broccoli with *chimichurri*, 102
cabbage, red and green, with citrus fruit, 125
cabbage with shrimp and walnuts, Breton, 124
cabbage with spicy peanut dressing, Malaysian, 124–25
Café de Paris Niçoise, 371
carrot and apple, Danish, 138–39
carrot with garlic, cumin, and parsley, Moroccan, 139
celery root and carrot with apples and walnuts, Polish, 149
chayote, Martinique, 361
chickpea, tomato, and cucumber, Indian, 376–77
chickpea with fennel, *pistou*, and tomatoes, 377
"chopped", Mediterranean, 166
country, Greek, 323
cucumber, Austrian, 166–67
cucumber, Sichuan, 169
cucumber and pepper, Algerian, 165
cucumber with smoked salmon and chives, 168
cucumber with yogurt and cumin seeds, 167
cucumber with yogurt, walnuts, and raisins, Afghan, 164
daikon radish and carrot, 230–31
diced Mediterranean, California style, 376
dinner, American-style, 216
eggplant, roasted, and pepper, Catalan, 187
eggplant, three-way, 186–87
eggplant with capers and green olives, Sicilian, 179
eggplant with garlic and yogurt, Turkish, 187
eggplant with tomatoes and cucumbers, 186

Salads (*continued*)

green bean and chickpea with tomatoes and olives, 53
green bean, shrimp, and tomato, 54
jicama with orange and lime juice, 229
okra, Caribbean, 253
pepper, parsley, and wheat, Armenian, 285
pepper, roasted, with caper dressing, 286
potato, Périgord, 303
potato, Russian, 304–5
potato with avocado and cilantro, 304–5
potato with tomatoes and mint, Lebanese, 302
radish with oranges, Moroccan, 231
spinach with feta cheese and tomatoes, 205
squash, green and yellow, with cumin, Moroccan, 358
sugar-snap pea, carrot, and black mushroom, 275
sweet potato, North African, 311
tomato and watercress with cucumber-yogurt dressing, Sri Lankan, 322
tomato with red onions and parsley, Moroccan, 316
two-bean with fennel, 67
zucchini, Tunisian, 358–59
Salsas
chipotle chili, 104, 373, 389
hot cilantro, Chilean, 388
tomato, 42
tomato, Mexican, 390
Salting
cabbage, 118
eggplant, 172, 174–75
Salvadoran cuisine, cole slaw, 126
Sauces, 379–403
black bean, 129, 177
brown, ginger-scented, 35
cheese, 399
cream, 115, 400–401
duxelles, 399
garlic, Egyptian, 207
garlic-herb, 102, 176
garlic mayonnaise, 402
guacamole, 392
harissa, 28, 96, 393, 437

mail-order sources, 437
mushroom, black, 56–57
mushroom, dried, 43, 398
mushroom, Hungarian, 113
mustard-shallot, 37
peanut, 295
pistou, 377, 387
rémoulade, celery root, 150
roasted red pepper, 100–101, 397
shrimp and dill, 38
sun-dried tomato dipping, 387
tahini, 401–2
tartar, 403
tempura dipping, 368
tomato, 201
tomato, spicy, 271
tomato, ten-minute, 394
tomato, uncooked, 395
tomato-onion, Colombian, 77, 395
velouté, 400
yogurt-dill, Bulgarian, 141
yogurt-garlic, Turkish, 135, 380
see also Dressings; Oils; Salsas; Vinaigrettes
Sautéing, 14
asparagus, 34–35
cabbage, 118, 120
carrots, 134–35
cèpes, 55–56
eggplant, 175, 178
Jerusalem artichokes, 225
mushrooms, 238, 245, 274
onions, 51, 342
peppers, 281
Scandinavian cuisine. *See* specific countries
Serrano peppers
in green *Zehug*, 392–93
in guacamole, 329
in vegetable medley with mint and chilies, Thai, 365
Sesame
black mushrooms with, 246
and mushroom crepes, 242–43
sauce (tahini), 401–2
seeds, toasting method, 413
spinach, Japanese, 200
Shallots, 256, 264–65
Brussels sprouts with, 114–15
peeling, 257
puree, 264–65
sauce, mustard and, 37
slicing and chopping, 258
Shell beans. *See* Dried and shell beans

Shitake (Oriental black) mushrooms, 237
in sesame mushrooms crepes, 242–43
Sichuan cuisine. *See* Chinese cuisine
Sicilian cuisine. *See* Italian cuisine
Simmering, 11–12
Snow peas, 269
with baby onions and ginger, 272
stir-fried carrots, yellow squash, and, 273
Soaking
dried beans, 60
dried mushrooms, 235
Sofrito, 396–97
chayote squash with tomatoes and, 359
Soups
bean, Tuscan, 73
black bean with cumin and garlic, Cuban, 74
celery root, 148
corn chowder, 157
green, Portugese, 208
leek and butternut squash, 262–63
lentil, Colombian, 77
potato with chives, Austrian, 300
split pea, Dutch, 79
stocks, 406, 407
tomato and corn tortilla, 320–21
turnip, 331
watercress with leeks and potatoes, 212
South American cuisine. *See* Latin American cuisine; specific countries
Southeast Asian cuisine. *See* Oriental cuisine; specific countries
Southern (U.S.) cuisine, 8
corn maquechou, 156
hominy, 154
Hoppin' John, 71
Spaghetti squash, 337, 339
Spanakopitas, 204
Spanish cuisine
garlic mayonnaise (áioli), 402
green bean and red pepper stew, 49
green beans Basquaise, 47–48
roasted eggplant and pepper salad, Catalan, 187
sofrito, 359, 396–97
see also Basque cuisine
Spices. mail-order sources, 437, 438

Spinach, 199, 200–206
  basics, 196
  borani, Iranian, 206
  chickpeas with carrots and, 70–71
  dip, watercress and, 403
  flans, 203
  nutmeg-scented, 202–3
  pastries (*spanakopitas*), 204–5
  with pine nuts, 202
  salad with feta cheese and
    tomatoes, 205
  sesame, Japanese, 200
  substituting frozen for fresh, 196
  in tomato sauce, Zairian, 201
Split peas, 65
  soup, Dutch, 79
Squash. *See* Pumpkins; Summer
    squash; Winter squash;
    Zucchini; specific types
Sri Lankan cuisine
  eggplant relish, 185
  tomato and watercress salad with
    cucumber-yogurt dressing, 322
Steaming, 12–13
  beets, 83
  new potatoes, 296
Stewing
  eggplant, 172
  kohlrabi, 228
Stews
  carrot and potato with dried
    mushrooms, Ukrainian, 136
  corn, zucchini, and pepper,
    Mexican, 156–57
  green bean and red pepper,
    Spanish, 49
  Jerusalem artichoke à la
    Provençal, 227
  pepper, 278–79
  pepper, Basque, 283, 287
  pepper, Hungarian, 282
  vegetable with lamb, East
    Mediterranean, 367
  winter vegetable, Moroccan, 329
Stir-frying, 14
  bok choy, 129, 366
  snow peas, carrots, and yellow
    squash, 273
Stock
  chicken, 407
  vegetable, 406
String beans. *See* Green beans
Stuffed vegetables
  artichokes, 24–25
  celery, 147–48
  mushrooms, 24–25

peppers, 279, 284
squash with apples and pecans,
  343
tomatoes, 317, 318
zucchini, 356
Stuffings
  carrot puree, 356
  feta, 24–25
  ground turkey, 147–48
  mushroom, 151, 184
Succotash
  American, 158
  Chilean, 66
Sugar-snap peas, 269
  salad, carrot, black mushroom,
    and, 275
  with sautéed mushrooms, 274
Summer squash, 347–59
  basics, 349
  mail-order sources, 438
  see also specific types
Sun-dried tomatoes, 314
  dipping sauce, 387
  vinaigrette, asparagus with, 36
Swedish cuisine, beet salad with
    horseradish dressing, 85
Sweet potatoes, 307–11
  baked with orange dressing, 309
  basics, 308
  latkes, 310
  oven-fried, 309
  salad, North African, 311
Swiss chard, 199
  gratin with cheese sauce, 209
  red, with oil and lemon, 210
Swiss cuisine, onion tart, 262

Tahini sauce, 401–2
Tarragon
  carrots with wild rice,
    mushrooms, and, 137
  vinaigrette, cauliflower with, 103
Tartar sauce, 403
Tarts and tartlets
  dough, 412–13
  leek, 263–64
  mushroom-macadamia, 244–45
  onion, Swiss, 262
  pepper and goat cheese, 287
Tempura, vegetable, 368–69
Thai cuisine, 7
  mushroom and red chili curry,
    240

vegetable medley with mint and
  chilies, 365
Thyme, mushrooms with red
  peppers, cumin, and, 239
Timbales
  carrot, 138
  turnip, 330
Tomatillos, 315
Tomatoes, 313–23
  basics, 315
  cabbage with peppers and,
    Romanian, 122
  cauliflower with garlic, cilantro,
    and, Algerian, 96
  chayote squash with Caribbean
    sofrito and, 359
  as *crudités*, 375
  dip, pepper and, Moroccan, 321
  dressing, yogurt and, 322
  eggplant and tofu casserole with
    garlic and, 181
  green beans garlic and, Lebanese,
    48–49
  onion compote with, Algerian,
    259
  paste, 314
  peeling and seeding, 316
  pizza, olive, caper, and, Ligurian,
    319
  potato salad with mint and,
    Lebanese, 302
  in ratatouille, 372
  salad, broccoflower and, 105
  salad, chickpea, cucumber, and,
    Indian, 376–77
  salad, chickpea, with fennel,
    pistou, and, 377
  salad, country, Greek, 323
  salad, eggplant, with cucumbers
    and, 186
  salad, green bean and chickpea,
    with olives and, 53
  salad, green bean, shrimp, and, 54
  salad, spinach, with feta cheese
    and, 205
  salad, watercress and, with
    cucumber-yogurt dressing, Sri
    Lankan, 322
  salad with red onions and parsley,
    Moroccan, 316
  salsa, Mexican, 390
  sauce, 313–14
  sauce, for angel hair pasta, 42
  sauce, onion and, Colombian, 77,
    395
  sauce, spicy, peas in, 271

Tomatoes (*continued*)

sauce, spinach in, Zairian, 201
sauce, ten-minute, 394
sauce, uncooked, 395
soup, corn tortilla and, 320–21
in stew, Basque, 283, 287
stuffed, Lebanese, 317
stuffed, Roman style, 318
topping for sautéed eggplant, 178
see also Sun-dried tomatoes
Tunisian cuisine, zucchini salad, 358–59
Turban squash, 339
Turkish cuisine
eggplant salad with garlic and yogurt, 187
sautéed carrots with yogurt, 134–35
yogurt-garlic sauce, 380
Turnips, 325–31
basics, 327
greens, 199
with peas, garlic, and cilantro, Algerian, 328
soup, 331
timbales on a bed of greens, 330
in winter vegetable stew, Moroccan, 329
Turtle beans. *See* Black beans

Ukrainian cuisine, carrot and potato stew with dried mushrooms, 136

Vegetable medleys, 363–77
chipotle chili dip for, 373
crudités, 374–75
eggplant, tofu, tomatoes, and garlic, 181
Givetch, Balkan, 370–71

with mint and chilies, Thai, 365
ratatouille, 372
with rice noodles and shrimp, Chinese, 366
tempura, 368–69
see also Salads; Stews
Vegetable pear. *See* Chayote squash
Vegetable stock, 406
Velouté sauce, 400
Vietnamese cuisine, eggplant with ginger, 176–77
Vinaigrettes
caper-chive, 385
classic, 383
herb, 54
mustard, Dijon, 124
mustard, thick, 382
orange, 385
sun-dried tomato, 36
tarragon, 103
Vinegars, mail-order sources, 438

Watercress, 199
in beet salad with walnuts and greens, 86
dip, spinach and, 403
salad, with tomato and cucumber-yogurt dressing, Sri Lankan, 322
soup, with leeks and potatoes, 212
Wax beans, with cèpes and garlic, 55–56
West African cuisine, okra with greens, 251–52
White beans
Middle Eastern style, 72
soup, Tuscan, 73
Wild mushrooms, 233–34, 236–37
mail-order source, 438
sautéed, with herbs, 245
Winter squash, 335–44
basics, 336–37
chart, 338–39
mail-order sources, 438

microwaving, 337
with rice and green beans, 341
with sautéed onion, 342
stuffed with apples and pecans, 343
sweet-and-sour with raisins, 344
with sweet spices, 340

Yams. *See* Sweet potatoes
Yellow squash
salad, with green squash and cumin, Moroccan, 358
stir-fried snow peas, carrots, and, 273
sweet-and-sour with mint, 352
Yemenite cuisine, green *Zehug*, 392–93

Zairian cuisine, spinach in tomato sauce, 201
Zehug, green, 392–93
Zucchini, 347–59
basics, 349
boats with carrot puree, 356
with carrots, Korean, 135
casserole, Napoli, 355
and eggplant sauté with basil, 353
omelet with garlic, Provençal, 357
Parmesan-coated fans, 354
in ratatouille, 372
with Romano cheese and basil, 350
salad, Tunisian, 358–59
salad, with yellow squash and cumin, Moroccan, 358
stew, with corn and pepper, Mexican, 156–57
in vegetable medley with mint and chilies, Thai, 365

ABOUT THE AUTHOR

Award-winning author Faye Levy has explored the finest culinary preparations for vegetables around the world. She has cooked vegetable specialties in three continents—Europe, Asia, and North America—has written about her favorite vegetable dishes for national publications, and has taught cooking classes devoted to vegetables.

The first article that Faye wrote for the prestigious *Gourmet* magazine was on cabbage. Later she wrote articles for the magazine on Jerusalem artichokes and on eggplant. Through the years she published many vegetable recipes in her feature articles for *Bon Appétit* magazine and in her column, "The Basics." Professional chefs, too, have been inspired by Faye's articles on vegetables in her monthly column in *Western Chef* magazine. When *Cook's* magazine planned a feature story on classic spring vegetable recipes with a new twist, the editors turned to Faye to create the recipes.

Faye is a nationally syndicated cooking columnist for the Los Angeles Times Syndicate, with a biweekly column called "Quick and Classy." She has published articles on cooking vegetables in the *Boston Globe*, the *Washington Post*, the *Chicago Tribune*, the *New York Post*, the *Detroit News*, the *Portland Oregonian*, the *Los Angeles Herald Examiner*, the *Saint Louis Post-Dispatch*, the *San Diego Union*, the *Dallas Times Herald*, and other major newspapers across the country.

Faye holds the Grand Diplôme of the first graduating class of the famous Parisian cooking school La Varenne, where she spent nearly six years working closely with the school's chefs, and is the author of the highly regarded three-volume *Fresh from France* cookbook series.

Faye and her husband and associate Yakir Levy live in Santa Monica, California.

Charity Begins at Home

CHARITY BEGINS AT HOME

Generosity and Self-Interest Among the Philanthropic Elite

TERESA ODENDAHL

Basic Books, Inc., Publishers

NEW YORK

Library of Congress Cataloging-in-Publication Data

Odendahl, Teresa Jean.
    Charity begins at home: generosity and self-interest among the
philanthropic elite / Teresa Odendahl.
        p.   cm.
    Includes bibliographical references.
    ISBN 0-465-00962-X
    1. Charities—United States—Case studies. 2. Philanthropists—
United States—Attitudes—Case studies. 3. Upper classes—United
States—Case studies. I. Title.
HV91.O33 1990
361.7'4'0973—dc20   89-43095
                                                                    CIP

For Michael Bernstein

In many cases throughout this book, pseudonyms for individuals are used. I have also created composites based on the similar attributes of several people. (This technique is described on page 79.) When a pseudonym or composite is introduced, it is signified as such in the text or cited in the notes. If a pseudonym I have used happens to be the name of any person, the choice was inadvertent and that individual is unknown to the author.

In other cases, philanthropists are identified by their real names and discussed at some length. Information on Brooke Astor, as well as the Bass, Bingham, Mellon, Packard, and Pillsbury families, was drawn from published sources that are cited in the notes. Tracy DuVivier Gary, Swanee Hunt, and Jan Whiting are also named.

All unattributed quotations are from transcribed interviews with study participants.

CONTENTS

Preface   ix

Part 1
Commonalities

1   Culture, Generosity, and Power   3
2   Giving and Volunteering   19
3   The Political Economy of Philanthropy   43

Part 2
Distinctions

4   Dynasty and Philanthropy   71
5   Lady Bountiful   100
6   First-Generation Men and Their Families   118
7   Elite Jewish Giving   138

Contents

Part 3
Prospects

8   The Alternative Fund Movement   163
9   Wealthy "Feminist" Funders   187
10 Advisers and Professionals   209
11 The Restructuring of Elite Philanthropy   232

Methodological Appendix   247
Notes   251
Bibliography   281
Index   291

PREFACE

My initial insights about "the culture of philanthropy" came from experiences at Yale University. When I joined the research faculty in 1983, I was relatively unfamiliar with private educational institutions. Although I had grown up in an academic environment, I had been educated in southwestern public schools. Ivy-covered buildings and the traditions that went with them were new to me.

On my first day I was taken by a prestigious colleague to lunch at Mory's—a famous private club adjacent to the campus. It is a small structure of the federal period; the exterior looks like an affluent New England home.[1] Inside, most of the old wooden tables, scarred by carved initials and slogans, were full. All around on the walls were photographs of former Yale sports teams: boxers, crew members, and football players.

Like many private eating clubs, Mory's is exclusive. People may join if they can afford the fees; are alumni or students of Yale College, the undergraduate division of the university; or are faculty or other designates of the "Yale community." The food is expensive and famously mediocre. It is thought to be an impressive place to bring guests.

Although I did not know it then, for a young member of the culture of philanthropy there is nothing special about Mory's. By the time they get to college, children of the charitable elite are accustomed to bad meals in glorified settings and good food whenever they choose. Most of them take their privilege for granted; they have done so all their lives. As for Yale, many expected to go there or to some other Ivy League or elite institution. In many cases their parents attended Yale or a similar private university.

A few days after that lunch at Mory's I met my first "Yalie," a lower-division student. I asked her where she came from, meaning where was her home or where did her parents live. I was surprised when she said Andover, referring to the Phillips Academy, a boarding school in Massachusetts.[2] But this turned out to be a fairly common reply to a question like mine; it is a way for elite students to proclaim their educational pedigree.

In addition to high admission standards, I was to find, there are some less pedagogical traditions and rituals that are important at Yale and other elite universities. One of them is football. The Yale-Harvard game was played later that fall, and some acquaintances invited me to go. Along with hundreds of people, we had a tailgate party—a lunch adjacent to a truck— before the actual event. Not your average tailgate picnic; ours was grand. Yet it suffered in comparison with others we witnessed. And, I was told, in the fields just outside the stadium men in tuxedos and women in furs were hovering around tables decorated with candelabras. Champagne was served in crystal glasses, accompanied by exotic foods. This was an annual event, a day for Harvard and Yale graduates, their spouses and friends to revel with equals or aspirants in upper-class solidarity.

I also partook of the high culture at Yale. I attended concerts at the elegant Woolsey Hall. I visited the very fine modern art gallery on campus, a special project of the millionaire John Hay Whitney. I made an occasional foray to the Yale Center for British Art, Paul Mellon's pet charity.[3] I enjoyed plays at the Yale Repertory Theatre. And I had the good fortune to use the Sterling Memorial Library, one of the best in the world.[4]

Yale, Harvard, and many other private universities are elite institutions endowed by philanthropy. Phillips Academy and comparable prep schools are also nonprofit organizations. The students they educate are socialized to follow the mores of the culture of philanthropy. In addition, they attend and learn to value concerts, museums, and the theater.[5] They understand that the great libraries are theirs. After they graduate they are expected to contribute generously. Many of them already have because they came into their trust funds at age twenty-one, while still in college. Their first donation is only the beginning of a lifelong commitment to philanthropy.

The Harvard-Yale party referred to earlier, or the "P-Rade"—a Princeton end-of-the-school-year commencement and reunion spectacle[6]—might not immediately appear to be philanthropic events. But in addition to bringing old friends together, rituals of this sort are successful forums for raising money. At these and other reunion functions, former students are reminded of their college days, and urged to support the school that provided them with so much.

In 1988, for example, Yale had record contributions to its alumni fund. Some 46,000 donors made a total of over $35 million in gifts, averaging $761.00 per person. The total endowment is more than $2.1 billion.[7] Private higher educational institutions are the largest beneficiaries of elite charity, but they are by no means the only recipients, nor are the rich the only donors.

There is a strong tradition of individual giving and volunteering in the United States.[8] The wealthy have always funded their favorite benevolent activities. The poor and middle classes have also been generous, especially to religious causes, but as individuals they have of course had less to give. The largess of millionaire philanthropists has produced lasting institutions. Hospital wings, libraries, museums, opera houses, symphony halls, university buildings, and professorships across the country carry their names.

This book draws on material from several research projects as well as personal experience. I have been studying modern American philanthropy and especially, though not exclusively, the private grant-making foundation for the past ten years.[9] I worked at the Business and Professional Women's (BPW) Foundation for four years, and this was my entrée to the world I describe here. At regional and national meetings of grant-makers I met other foundation employees as well as wealthy trustees; both groups were helpful in arranging the confidential interviews my colleagues and I were to undertake.[10]

In the early 1980s, along with Elizabeth Boris and Arlene Kaplan Daniels, I investigated the career patterns and job duties of foundation staff members[11] on behalf of Women and Foundations/Corporate Philanthropy, with funding from the Russell Sage and John Hay Whitney foundations. A few years later I managed a multidisciplinary research project on foundations at the Yale University Program on Non-Profit Organizations. PONPO was the first university-based research center of its kind.[12] The project on which I worked was co-sponsored by a national trade association, the Council on Foundations. We received grants from the W. K. Kellogg, Charles Stuart Mott, and Andrew W. Mellon foundations.[13]

In the three years after the Yale project ended, I undertook additional interviews with wealthy donors, some of whom did not ask for anonymity. Though most of the personal interviews were confidential, material in the public record was also examined. For example, the Bass family of Fort Worth, Texas, serves as an initial case study in chapter 2 and the Mellon dynasty is highlighted in chapter 4.

The interpretation presented here is my own and does not necessarily represent the views of co-sponsors, funders, other researchers, or study participants in the various projects. Of course, I gratefully acknowledge their contributions to the data collection effort and to my thinking. This book (and the interviews I have conducted since the Yale study ended) was written without philanthropic support.

Many colleagues and friends have read and commented on various drafts of this manuscript. I am particularly grateful to Michael Bernstein, Elizabeth Boris, Elise Boulding, Steve Fraser, Gerald Freund, Eric Odendahl, and Sabrina Youmans for their painstaking reviews. Leah Brumer, Mary Ellen Capek, Arlene Kaplan Daniels, Susan Davis, Ernestine Friedl, Judith Gregory, Steven Hahn, Peter Dobkin Hall, Heidi Hartmann, Virginia Hodgkinson, Estelle James, David Johnston, Stanley Katz, Richard Magat, Richard Male, Leeda Marting, Arno Mayer, Winnifred Mitchell, Mary Odendahl, Phyllis Palmer, Patricia Read, Nan Rubin, Dan Schiller, James A. Smith, Peter Swords, Sylvia Tesh, Suzanne Wagner, Kay Warren, and David Weiman were helpful with portions of this work. All these individuals, as well as those who were interviewed for this study (a few of whom also read and approved sections where they were quoted), have my wholehearted thanks.

I have used anthropological methods in analyzing the interview data, but in this book I do not take the stance of the disinterested social scientist. I have tried to be honest about my biases. No scholarly account is totally comprehensive. This one is specifically limited by the confidentiality I promised to the study participants. I am not a member of the class I describe. My personal experiences and research have been at the edge and the receiving end, rather than at the heart, of the culture of philanthropy.

On the whole, given the objectives of my study, it is not the activities of specific individuals that are important, but rather the social structure in which they live—an economic and social system that often promotes inequality. In my view, if this inequality is a fact of life, basic human services must then be provided either by the State or by charity. In the 1980s, by default, and in the name of "less government," a disproportionate amount of charitable power has been conferred upon the wealthy. And, of course, this private system lessens public control. It is the burden of my argument that the rich do not find it in their interest to fund or provide social programs on a sufficient scale. My task in this work, however, is not to define "sufficient scale," but rather to demonstrate the possible consequences for the wealthy, as well as for the general social welfare, of a particular way of mobilizing income redistribution and human services in our nation.

Perhaps in spite of my best efforts I may be accused of overstatement, of submerging individual observations in general trends. The reader, of course, will have to decide. Whatever the verdict, it will be gratifying if my arguments are persuasive enough to encourage others to investigate farther, using similar and different methods; to dispute, modify, and expand these ideas; and to add to the data on which this study is based.

This book is divided into three parts. Part 1 presents the attributes, behavior, lifestyle, and values shared by the majority of the philanthropic elite I investigated. These commonalities not only set the stage for the general findings of this work but also establish a framework within which other aspects of the culture of philanthropy may be explored. My examination centers on the political economy of giving by the wealthy and contrasts the elite and the poor in this country and other industrialized nations.

In part 2, distinctions among various groups that are not necessarily mutually exclusive are analyzed. Philanthropists with "old money," men and women, self-made millionaires, and Jews are enculturated differently from each other. They also have particular approaches to giving and volunteering, as well as varying status in the hierarchy of elite philanthropic culture.

The last part of the book offers an assessment of the future of philanthropic behavior and activity in the United States. The emergence of public foundations as an alternative to elite control and its corollaries, traditional giving and grant-making, are highlighted. Social change and women's funds have attempted to build bridges between classes where mainstream philanthropy has created chasms. Advisers and professionals who do not simply serve the interests of the wealthy can also take on advocacy and mediating roles that challenge the status quo. Finally, I will argue that despite its inherently conservative tendencies, philanthropy can and does offer innovative solutions to social problems when government takes care of basic human needs.

PART 1

COMMONALITIES

Chapter 1

Culture, Generosity, and Power

Elite American philanthropy serves the interests of the rich to a greater extent than it does the interests of the poor, disadvantaged, or disabled. This book is concerned with the personal charity of millionaires as well as the consequences of their nonprofit activity. Voluntary organizations supported and directed by wealthy philanthropists divert decision making in the arts, culture, education, health, and welfare from public representatives to a private power elite.

Paradoxically, although people of all classes participate in nonprofit groups, most of these organizations are controlled by a few, and many charities benefit the rich more than they do the poor. The vast majority of nonprofit agencies and programs do not primarily serve the needy.[1] Many elite philanthropists are civic-minded and sincere, but the system they help to maintain may actually reduce the extent to which basic human services are provided on a democratic basis.

By studying rich people and their charitable endeavors,[2] I have identified a nationwide "culture of philanthropy." Those who inherited "old money"[3] and the richest Americans, usually with "new money," tend to be the most involved in voluntary activities. But they contribute disproportionately to private universities, the arts, and culture, rather than to community health clinics, legal aid programs, or other projects for the poor. There are thousands of good causes in which millionaires have little interest. Those are not the subject of this book, although they are certainly affected by the neglect of the wealthy.

Not all millionaires in the United States are serious philanthropists. My guess is that fewer than half of the wealthy are charitably minded. Those who regularly contribute large sums of money to nonprofit organizations, serve on several volunteer boards of directors, and spend much of their time raising additional resources for charity from colleagues, friends, and relatives belong to a select social group.

The 140 millionaire philanthropists who were interviewed for this study were active in local and national networks with others who give and volunteer. The vast majority of these men and women are white, Protestant, well-educated, and married with children. They tend to be older adults, although all ages are represented. These philanthropists are trustees of art museums, hospitals, libraries, social service agencies, symphony orchestras, think tanks, universities, and zoos. Most are also active in the work of private grant-making foundations that bear their surnames. Many are directors of more than one foundation. Individual giving, foundations, and other charitable devices provide them and their families with authority, power, and the self-approbation that generosity bestows.

In addition, and of great importance, is the fact that through their charitable activities wealthy philanthropists and their advisers sponsor what we think of as "high culture"—ballet, opera, symphony, theater, and the visual arts. Rich children learn to value these "serious" cultural forms that on the whole are produced by nonprofit organizations.[4] But there is more to philanthropic culture than breeding and taste.[5]

Through their donations and work for voluntary organizations, the charitable rich exert enormous influence in society. As philanthropists, they acquire status within and outside of their class. Although private wealth is the basis of the hegemony of this group, philanthropy is essential to the maintenance and perpetuation of the upper class in the United States. In this sense, nonprofit activities are the nexus of a modern power elite.[6]

The culture of philanthropy is manifest in the common behavior and manners, economic status, and sociocultural institutions, as well as in the shared attitudes, ideas, perceptions, tastes, and values of this group whose members frequently interact with one another. The "established" wealthy are socialized in the family and by exclusive preparatory schools and private colleges. Their interaction continues throughout adulthood as business associates, friends, leaders of local and national voluntary organizations, and relatives by birth and marriage. Elite culture is passed from generation to generation, and from those with old money to the newly rich.

Class and culture are related but not identical. Although the elite who participate in the culture of philanthropy are usually members of the upper class, not everyone in this class endorses a particular way of life. And some middle-class individuals—notably certain "professionals" who serve the wealthy as, for example, personal advisers and private foundation staff—often have perspectives and values similar to their employers and exist within the same charitable system.

My use of the term *culture* in connection with philanthropy is intentional: the word carries so many subtle applicable meanings. The rich are integral members of the wider society. In certain respects the charitable elite are so aware of prevalent middle-class cultural norms that they deny their affluence and privilege and do not present or even think of themselves as being upper-class. This book is primarily about wealthy people who belong to a distinctive culture that is, in the anthropological sense, a subculture.[7]

In general, the charitable wealthy live well below their means. They are conspicuous contributors rather than conspicuous consumers. Nonprofit work, more than anything else, engages them, giving them a sense of identity and meaning. This is particularly true for rich women, who view themselves as having fewer options than wealthy men owing to a relatively rigid division of labor by gender in the upper class. Historically, charity work has been a meaningful activity allowed but not limited to wealthy women.

One of the first interviews conducted for this study—with a middle-aged woman—was among the most memorable. We had met at a conference on philanthropy. When she learned about the project she kindly invited me to visit her. After an exchange of letters and phone calls, the arrangements were made. I drove through beautiful, wooded countryside into what I knew to be one of the wealthiest counties in the United States. At one juncture I passed through a stone gateway that I had been told would mean I was close to her house. I had not expected the mansion that awaited me.

The woman I was to speak with opened the door herself. She was dressed elegantly but informally. I was wearing my "interview outfit," a subdued brown business suit and a silk blouse, and carrying a leather attaché case. We exchanged pleasantries, and she asked if I would like a tour of the house. She explained that the downstairs was intended for formal entertaining and was not regularly used by the family. We walked through a large entry hall, adorned with a tropical flower arrangement, past a massive, thickly carpeted central staircase with carved wooden banisters. The furnishings were relatively sparse, as if the area was indeed intended for parties of people standing and milling about, and not for everyday living.

Two of the formal rooms stand out in my mind. The dining room was huge and long, probably at least twice as big as my middle-class parents' living room. An immense, highly polished dark wood table and matching chairs nearly filled the space. It was clear that a staff would be necessary to serve a meal in these surroundings. My hostess waved vaguely toward a doorway at the end of the room and said that was the "big" kitchen. She did not offer to show it to me but steered me toward the "music room," which was parallel to the dining room and about the same size. A grand piano graced one end of this area, with plenty of space for a small audience.

I have to admit that I started thinking about the board game "Clue." I just was not sure that everything around me was real, and I was nervous enough to wonder when the crime would be committed. Later in the research I became more accustomed to the trappings of wealth.

Upstairs the whole atmosphere changed. This, my hostess said, was where the family lived. We walked into a "normal-sized" living room, with well-worn overstuffed chairs and a comfortable floral-patterned blue couch. At her invitation I sat down and sank into the cushions. She did not show me around the "private" area of the house. She offered coffee, and got it herself.

While she was away I oriented myself, found a comfortable sitting position, and placed my tape recorder next to a small vase of spring flowers on the coffee table. It struck me that if I had not just come through the formal part of the mansion it would have seemed as if I were sitting in a well-appointed suburban house. The upstairs decor reminded me of many of my parents' friends' homes. It was tasteful, yet did not appear terribly expensive. The interview was conducted in this room.

The environment where any interview takes place has a bearing on the richness of the data collected. Some of the best, most informative meetings held during this research, those where sensitive or subtle ideas were expressed, were conducted in people's homes. The majority of home interviews were with women, but a few were held with young or elderly men.

I had been invited to stay for lunch. My hostess showed me through the "small" kitchen. It was about as big as my own, perhaps six by ten feet. There was food on the counter that had already been prepared. I asked if there was anything I could do to help. She said no, it would only take a moment. Would I like to wait on the balcony? She pointed the way.

Sitting in the sun, looking out at the sweeping, unobstructed view of a large body of water was the high point of my day. The white wicker table had already been attractively set. Sailboats glinted in the distance. The view distracted me as she served lunch and we chatted. We ate cold chicken, a salad, and toasted croissants. I did not see any servants, but I had the impression that they were around at least part of the time. Everything I observed was organized and spotless. My hostess was charming, gracious, and helpful—all aspects of philanthropic style.[8]

Although the downstairs was uncharacteristic, I chose to describe this particular house for three reasons. It was the setting of the first official interview for the study, my introduction to the private world of the philanthropic elite. The two ambiences within one home, the separate physical arrangements, were fascinating. But, most germane, this house is a vivid symbol of the conflict, psychologically "close to the surface," that many of the philanthropic rich feel about their wealth. Although they have an abundance of money, they do not actually want to live in opulence. Still, this particular family would not let themselves forget or hide their wealth. Every day they walked through the formal part of their mansion.

This is not a psychoanalytic study, but it is clear that many elite philanthropists have psychological "complexes": anxiety about their place in the world, denial that they are rich, and fear that people or the government are after their money, along with a lack of self-confidence or its counterpart—arrogance.[9] Like everyone else, the wealthy harbor prejudices and stereotypes about themselves and others. Their world is framed by a "we" and "they" perspective.

"They" are government officials who are not of the upper class, as well as the masses, who might take away private wealth through misappropriation, taxation, welfare, or revolution. In contrast, the "social change funders," a young minority group who are sometimes known as the "rich kids,"[10] think that the other "they" are conservative, mainstream, or traditional grant-makers. In many cases, then, "they" may be the parents of these younger philanthropists.

For the charitable wealthy of all ages, giving and volunteering is the "proper" thing to do. The improper, other rich are also "they," who spend too lavishly on themselves.[11] Feeling self-conscious about having so much wealth but wanting to retain it, the philanthropic rich assuage their guilt by living relatively modestly and contributing some of their income to "good causes."

Most of the houses of the people I visited are situated in upper-middle-class neighborhoods. They are pleasant, large, and appear to have been furnished by a decorator, but as structures they are not particularly remarkable. Fine art collections, especially modern paintings and sculpture, distinguish these homes from typical upper-middle-class dwellings. The artwork is displayed so that it seems lived among, unlike the works displayed in a formal museum.

Usually the grounds are a bit larger than normal. Depending on the part of the country where the house is located, there may be swimming pools or tennis courts. When small children are in the family, there may be elaborate swing sets and other play equipment outside. Most of the philanthropic elite do not live in mansions; doctors, lawyers, and other well-paid professionals might have similar houses.

Occasionally, interviews were arranged by the subjects or their advisers at their "clubs." I met men at the Princeton, Harvard, and Yale clubs in New York. These are the less exclusive, and hence less prestigious, clubs, but because of my gender I would not have been welcome in the more elite sanctuaries like the Century Club in New York or the Pacific Union in San Francisco. I went to country clubs for a few social functions. I was served cookies and tea in the late afternoon at a women's club in downtown San Francisco. The clubs I visited fit several stereotypes, with furnishings ranging from deep leather chairs and animal heads on the walls to antique Victorian furniture and lace curtains. They were normally quite formal. Uniformed or formally dressed personnel spoke in hushed voices while members conducted business.

The most typical scenario for an interview was an office, usually in a large downtown building. When this was the case, there was less to observe than in a person's home. Offices were frequently quite businesslike, although generally well-appointed, sometimes with original paintings hanging on the walls. Occasionally the informant referred to the artwork or boasted about his collection. In general, however, the study participants were modest in displaying their wealth. Almost all the men and advisers met me in their offices, where less about their private lives was revealed.

Wherever the interview took place, however, I consistently learned that the charitable wealthy and their institutions encourage personal social responsibility, or noblesse oblige. In addition, they consider themselves virtuous in comparison to other wealthy people who do not give. They have a vision of the world that they want to promote, not just to their families, but to others. They see themselves as upholders of an American democracy in which they are the natural leaders. They believe they set an example in their local communities and nationally. In this regard, much of their charity work is paternalistic.

Furthermore, the philanthropic elite think that they have greater knowledge than the average citizen. This is mirrored by a perception on the part of the middle and working classes that the wealthy are in fact the bearers of high culture and sophistication. Fundamentally, the ideology of the elite concerning their legitimate role in society depends on this perception of the middle and working classes—that the wealthy deserve their status. Conversely, the belief of the mass of citizens that a special minority must have special authority depends on the elite maintaining a posture of noblesse oblige. These complementary ideologies help explain the perennial fascination with wealth and the wealthy that is so notable a part of the attitude of the American people.

As I have argued, participants in the culture of philanthropy have more power than most Americans because they have more money and time to invest in the causes they endorse. They sit on the boards of important institutions ranging from Harvard University to the United Way. Yet the rhetoric of altruism and "doing good," as well as the tax deduction for charitable giving, allows them to promote their ideas and often to support upper-class institutions with little accountability to or scrutiny by the general public and elected officials.

When the Reagan administration drastically reduced funding for basic welfare services and called on the "private sector" to defray these former government costs, this policy placed the provision of many basic services more squarely in the domain of charity, dependent on the marketing skills of nonprofit organizations as well as the interest and whims of corporations, foundations, and private givers. The wealthy have disproportionate influence in the private sector because they own the assets, control the corporations and foundations, and often make large individual charitable contributions.

In 1987, the largest widely reported individual gift to a nonprofit organization other than a foundation was $25 million contributed by John W. Kluge to Columbia University. That year alone, which was thought to be a "down year" for charity,[12] at least eighty-nine personal philanthropic donations exceeded $1 million each. Some $210 million of this money went to nonprofit universities and over $143 million to public educational institutions. The Metropolitan Museum of Art in New York was the single cultural organization to receive philanthropic funds of this magnitude from individuals: Henry R. Kravis gave the Museum $10 million, and Iris and Gerald B. Kantor donated $7 million. Charles Allen, Jr., and his brother Herbert Allen contributed the largest gift in the health field: $15 million to the Presbyterian Hospital of New York. Paul W. Mellon gave $10 million to his prep school, Choate Rosemary Hall.[13]

The only publicized individual contributions for human services in excess of $1 million during 1987[14] went to establish and operate the Hole in the Wall Gang Camp, which opened that year and serves children with cancer and many blood-related diseases. The camp was conceived and funded largely by the actor Paul Newman through personal donations and Newman's Own, his food company.

In 1985, the largest philanthropic "transfers," totalling $2.4 billion, went from individuals or their trust funds to endowed foundations. Gifts to only thirty-one of these grant-making organizations, which each received at least $10 million, accounted for more than two-thirds of the total.[15] The majority of such foundations have been controlled by donors and their family members for as long as three generations.

Perhaps the most famous trust fund of the decade, now called the Marin Community Foundation, received assets worth $447 million on January 1, 1987. Originally known as the Buck Trust, it was established in 1973 by the will of Beryl Buck, an elderly widow with vast oil holdings and stocks, who stipulated that giving would be limited to Marin County, California, her former home and one of the wealthiest areas in the United States. During an extensive court battle the initial manager of the trust, the San Francisco Foundation, argued that the donor had not understood the extent of her fortune and asked that the foundation be allowed to make grants from the trust to projects throughout the Bay Area. The foundation failed, however, to break the binding stipulation,[16] and as part of the judgment a new organization, the twenty-third largest foundation in the country, was established.[17]

Whether it be high culture, "high education," such as that provided at Ivy League universities, the "high philanthropy" of foundations, or the "high medicine" of private nonprofit hospitals, the rich fund and make policy for these institutions, while on the whole the middle class produce the cultural and intellectual products and services.[18] There has always been a tension between wealthy philanthropists and professionals. Just who are the experts and who is or should be running the shows? Ultimately, and according to the law, the trustees are responsible, and even the chief staff officer serves at the pleasure of the board.[19]

A growing number of middle-class people work in the charitable system as administrators; artists and performers; attorneys; doctors and nurses; and ministers, scientists, social workers, and university professors. Their livelihood depends on the nonprofit grants economy, so this professional group, particularly the managers, may consider it in their interest to maintain the system. The wider middle class also earn enough to enjoy events of high culture, but they are less engaged in such endeavors than the philanthropic elite.

What about the neediest citizens, those who are generally thought to be the beneficiaries of charity? It could be argued that philanthropy as currently practiced creates an unequal reciprocity between the upper and lower classes that may stifle rebellion or reform.[20] A system of private charity is not in the interests of the disadvantaged. The material benefits and the extent of control over their own destinies that are provided them by philanthropy are considerably less than in the Social Democratic countries of Western Europe, the Communist East European states, and even some "developing" nations. For example, in 1980, the United States ranked thirty-first in comparison to other countries on the percentage of national income received by the poorest 40 percent of the population.[21]

The charity system as organized today warrants investigation not only because it benefits the rich to a greater extent than others but also because of the frequency with which philanthropy is invoked by its proponents as an argument against redistribution of wealth by the government. Public policy, enacted through tax codes, allows and encourages a relatively small group of rich people and their advisers to hold much more power over the shape of society than the vast majority in the middle and lower classes.

WEALTH DISTRIBUTION

In former president Ronald Reagan's final State of the Union Address, he claimed that his tenure had witnessed

> not just the longest peacetime expansion in history, but an economic and social revolution of hope, based on work, incentives, growth, and opportunity; a revolution of compassion that led to private sector initiatives and a 77 percent increase in charitable giving; a revolution that—at a critical moment in world history—reclaimed and restored the American dream. (25 Jan. 1988)[22]

Many Americans were lulled by these words because they wanted to believe them. Private contributions to nonprofit organizations had been increasing, at least in part as a response to government cutbacks.[23]

The ideology of small government, more "private sector initiatives," and charity go hand in hand. When President George Bush was running for office, he echoed this rhetoric. He spoke metaphorically of "a thousand points of light," referring to associations and voluntary organizations.

> This is America: the Knights of Columbus, the Grange, Hadassah, the Disabled American Veterans, the Order of Ahepa, the Business and Professional Women of America, the union hall, the Bible study group, LULAC, Holy Name—a brilliant diversity spread like stars, like a thousand points of light in a broad and peaceful sky. . . .
>
> I will keep America moving forward, always forward—for a better America, for an endless, enduring dream and a thousand points of light. (18 Aug. 1988)[24]

He fails to mention in his thousand points of light analogy the elite institutions he attended that receive most of the funding. And the private groups to which he does refer are not solving and will not solve the persistent problem of inequality in our country.

Despite the Reagan and Bush rhetoric, America has not realized her dream, and many people's living standards are not adequate. In 1986 over 19 percent of American households had annual incomes of less than $10,000; another 21.4 percent earned between $10,000 and $20,000. In both categories, when controlling for inflation with constant 1986 dollars, there has been little change in the percentage of the population with these annual household income levels since 1970. In the middle-income groups combined, 46.1 percent of households made between $20,000 and $50,000 in 1970, but that figure dropped 3.4 points to 42.7 percent by 1986. However, the most affluent households, those with over $50,000 in income, increased from 11.5 percent in 1970 to 16.8 percent in 1986.[25] More people are getting richer, but more people are staying poor as well. In the last fifteen years, the opportunity and upward mobility we Americans tout seems to have been available to very few.

As Americans we like to think that we live in a democratic country wherein merit is rewarded and everyone has equal opportunity. We speak of the vast middle class, and even of a lack of class. We have not paid much attention to those who question these assumptions.[26] We want to believe that we have eradicated poverty, although we are noticing more homeless people on our streets.[27] In a sense, we have been willing to ignore the poor as well as the rich.[28]

The extreme concentration of private capital is a striking fact of American society. The super-rich[29] make up about half of 1 percent of the U.S. population. In 1983 they owned 26.9 percent of all wealth, compared to 25 percent in 1963. The richest 10 percent of the population hold almost 68 percent of the national net worth, an increase of just over 4 percent in a twenty-year period.[30]

Congressman David R. Obey of Wisconsin, chairman of the Joint Economic Committee, which released the above-mentioned figures, commented in 1986:

> The 90 percent of American families who are not on the top end of the economic totem pole appear to have suffered a loss of almost 10 percent in their share of national net worth between 1963 and 1983. This trend runs counter to the belief of our citizens that wealth is being more equitably distributed.[31]

There are probably around 500,000 millionaires in this country.[32] This means that there are only two or three for every one hundred people living in poverty. Furthermore, even among the rich, wealth is distributed like an inverted pyramid. In 1983, 1 percent of wealth-holders owned 34.3 percent of all assets while the remaining 9 percent owned slightly less, 33.6 percent.[33]

This is hardly a full statistical analysis, nor is such an undertaking the intent of this book. However, my interpretation of the summary data is that in the United States the poor have become more numerous; the working class are barely maintaining their standard of living; some of the middle class are poorer and some are richer. Only the wealthy are doing unambiguously well. There is a declining middle class and an increasing bifurcation of income distribution.[34]

The trend in much of the world has been for the State to determine which institutions and services are necessary for its citizens to enjoy a certain quality of life. In Western Europe, for example, much wealth is redistributed through taxation, and decisions about funding are made by elected officials or their appointees. In the United States wealth is also distributed this way, but to a lesser degree. In the modern era, increased government funding for nonprofit organizations has been combined with tax deductions and incentives that permit individual discretion about charitable recipients. Viewed as an alternative kind of taxation, these policies have contributed to the growth of voluntary efforts.

Unequal distribution of resources is firmly established in the United States, aided by the charity system. Since the advent of the Reagan administration, more "initiative"—translated "power"—has been given to the "private sector"—that is, the wealthy and the corporations they control. Inequality is apt to become even more pronounced in the future if the federal government continues to move away from financing basic human services.

THE PHILANTHROPY SYSTEM

Studies of the power elite have tended to examine strict economic or government control and have mentioned only briefly or completely overlooked interconnections with charity. The culture of philanthropy extends far beyond the glittery charity balls and gala events that fill the society pages of local newspapers. Indeed, the heart of the philanthropic exchange system is a $300 billion industry that supports most of the 950,000 nonprofit agencies in the country. The number of organizations, total employment, wages and salaries, and share of national income of voluntary agencies has been growing in the United States for at least fifty years. Almost seven million paid employees and five million volunteers ran nonprofits in 1984. In comparison, businesses employed some eighty million people, and government had twenty million workers.[35]

The legal and tax status of any given private organization is determined under the Internal Revenue Code, which recognizes certain agencies as nonprofit and therefore in some manner as tax-exempt. Religious organizations operate tax-free. Most arts and cultural agencies; foundations; private schools and universities; professional and other associations; think tanks and scientific groups; and such civic and service-providing entities as child-care centers and drug-rehabilitation programs are designated as nonprofit. Many hospitals and health facilities are nonprofit as well, although hundreds have been organized on a profit-making basis. Certain advocacy organizations qualify as nonprofit, as do chambers of commerce.[36]

The irony here is that a government decision defines what many would like to think of as a private effort. The distinctions are somewhat vague, for although nonprofit organizations may generate a profit, individuals directly involved must not personally benefit monetarily. The profit "test" does not pertain to taxable salaries in all ranges (including some very high salaries at elite charities) or to the non-taxable expense accounts of employees and trustees. Once the IRS has made the determination, nonprofit organizations operate with very little regulation, although often with at least some government funds.

The demand for services and the higher expectations of Americans since the New Deal led to an increase in government funding to charities. The United States does not actually provide many of the services for which we think it is responsible but contracts them out by partially financing nonprofit organizations. The political scientist Lester M. Salamon and his staff at the Urban Institute undertook the most comprehensive investigation of nonprofits to date. They found that federal support to the nonprofit sector alone amounted to $40.4 billion in 1980, which represented about 36 percent of total federal spending in these fields (Salamon & Abramson 1982, 37–42). State and local government own-source revenues would likely add another $8 billion to $10 billion to this total.

Salamon points out that voluntary organizations also received in 1980 over $8.4 billion in indirect government support from revenue that would be collected by the U.S. Treasury if it did not go to nonprofits and provide tax deductions to the contributors.[37]

Earned income in the form of dues, fees for services, and other charges is the largest source of revenue for nonprofit organizations, providing them with 38 percent of their overall receipts. Personal donations or bequests, and foundation or corporate grants, provide 27 percent of the total support. Government payments from federal, state, and local sources combined account for an additional 27 percent.[38] The remaining 8 percent of nonprofit funding comes from endowment and investment income.[39]

The increasing dependence of nonprofits on fees for service has the greatest detrimental effect on the poor. In the early 1980s charitable organizations serving the neediest clients suffered the worst federal budget cuts. For example, nonprofit legal services lost 28.8 percent of the government funding they had previously received, and even with increases in private giving and fees raised by 19.2 percent, their total revenues still decreased by 15.5 percent. Support from the government for nonprofit employment and training programs went down by 12.7 percent, and State funding to social services decreased by 8.8 percent.[40]

By the end of the Reagan administration the nonprofit fields most severely affected were in employment and training, "where spending by FY [fiscal year] 1989 would end up 73 percent below its FY 1980 level . . . ; community development, where the reduction would be 66 percent; higher education (down 57 percent), health services (down 42 percent), social services (down 37 percent), and arts and culture (down 33 percent)."[41] Private contributions offset these reductions by only 7 percent. Most nonprofit organizations could barely maintain their former level of services, much less increase them to accommodate government cutbacks.[42]

Although nonprofit agencies are extremely diverse, they may be characterized by the concentration of financial resources among a small number of institutions. In 1982, 81 percent of total nonprofit assets were controlled by only 6 percent of all charitable organizations. Financial resources were also unevenly distributed across nonprofit institutions: 4 percent received 75 percent of the revenues. Furthermore, about 6 percent of all nonprofit organizations spent 74 percent of the available funds.[43]

The general tendency of the wealthy to contribute to upper-class-specific programs and institutions[44] aggravates the problems of inequality. A West Coast millionaire told me: "I only give to the things that I like. Oh, I give to the things that are good for the community. I give to the ballet, the opera, the symphony. I give to hospitals. I give to universities. . . . We give to everything." Yet everything he mentioned benefits the elite more than others. Few rich people give to county or public hospitals, donating instead to nonprofit hospitals, whose patients nearly all have insurance. A small percentage of large nonprofits such as Ivy League universities are financed by government grants and gifts from the wealthy. Thus philanthropists oversee the policies of many of the largest and most influential nonprofit institutions, where assets are concentrated.[45]

Philanthropists have increasingly begun to finance public institutions, especially prestigious state universities. In 1987, for example, Curtis L. Carlson gave the University of Minnesota $25 million, and Marion and John Anderson gave the University of California, Los Angeles, $15 million.[46] At one time such grants went primarily to private institutions. In addition to improving the programs at public universities, such gifts enhance their reputation. But donations of this type may also shift public perception of the need for state legislatures to fund higher education. Ultimately such donations could also mean that the viewpoint of the rich is more prevalent in any university—private or state.

The stake of the rich in philanthropy is rarely articulated. Few wealthy people actually talk with each other about the benefits of philanthropy to the upper class. The charitable rich feel that they are entitled to their special position, and on the whole they do not question their privilege. If anything, the philanthropic elite congratulate themselves for their civic leadership, viewing their voluntary work as promoting decency, morality, and the general quality of life. They believe that they fund worthwhile causes, and often they do.

Public relations discourse on philanthropy was originally framed by the wealthy people it would benefit. John D. Rockefeller III is credited with inventing or at least popularizing the phrase "the third sector." By this he meant

> not business or government but those nonprofit institutions, such as colleges, universities and research centers, museums and orchestras, churches and social welfare agencies which he held to be crucial to the nation's cultural and moral life.[47]

This word *sector* is in vogue among those who study, talk, and write about philanthropy. In all likelihood, one of four phrases—*independent sector, nonprofit sector, third sector,* or *voluntary sector*—will soon come into popular usage. I am resistant to this formulation, question its basic meaning, and consider it misleading.[48] If we look only at sectors of society, then it is easy to ignore the relations among different classes and their interests, as well as gender and race relations.

Indeed, the rhetoric surrounding voluntary agencies usually highlights what is taken to be the pluralistic nature of the services provided. Brian O'Connell is president of the Independent Sector, "a nonprofit coalition of over 600 corporate, foundation and voluntary organization members. The organization's mission is to create a national forum that encourages the giving, volunteering and not-for-profit initiative that help all of us better serve people, communities, and causes."[49] As early as 1976 he wrote:

> We Americans are organizing to influence every conceivable aspect of our human condition. . . . And in the process we raise money and votes for a staggering array of causes we believe in. . . . Today a far greater proportion of our population is involved in volunteer efforts than at any time in our history.[50]

O'Connell claims that elite control is no longer a feature of philanthropy, that "democracy has truly come alive with all the population joining in the traditions of service and reform. Today, anyone who cares and is prepared to do something about the caring can make a difference."[51]

The basic idea is that when a number of people with different interests make individual decisions about where to put their volunteer time and money, a variety of types of organizations end up getting funded and running smoothly. Yet a 1986 survey of national health agencies counted a decline of over one million people in the number of volunteers.[52] And the "worker bee" or "foot soldier" volunteer has much less influence than the board member.[53]

All people have leadership and social needs. The middle class also work in hundreds of thousands of voluntary efforts across the country. Their charities tend to be churches, neighborhood groups, and professional associations. These are the kinds of organizations said to promote pluralism. But the lack of funding, sheer numbers, and small size of most middle-class and lower-class nonprofit ventures, as well as minimal coordination, counteract their concerted potential for power.

Many nonprofit ventures, especially those that are not elitist, are essential for the generation of new ideas and programs. They may also serve as an avenue by which grassroots and other popular causes may ultimately influence government policy. A positive aspect of voluntary efforts has been the creation of vanguard charities, such as battered women's shelters, that the State would not initially fund. But once the necessity for such agencies has been demonstrated, should they remain dependent on the largess of private individuals? This is a question that is rarely if ever posed.

In the next chapter I describe the common personal histories, enculturation, and lifestyle of wealthy philanthropists. I pay specific attention to charitable recruitment. I am most interested in the process by which members of the culture of philanthropy acquire the habits, beliefs, and accumulated knowledge that epitomize their membership in this group.

Chapter 2

Giving and Volunteering

I went to [a well-known prep school] and to [an Ivy League university], and I worked for [a large multinational company] for over forty years. In the course of those experiences I guess I became interested in giving, both money and ideas. Subsequently, I have been involved in both the giving and the receiving end of philanthropy. Then, of course, my work with the ———— Foundation has brought me into the foundation field, which has been going on for thirty-five years now. I guess that much background shows my interest in and concern for philanthropic giving.

An archetypal philanthropic millionaire, this man is quite aware that the schools he attended, his role in a large corporation, and his association with a large foundation contributed to his charitable impulses and outlook.[1] Like him, a majority of philanthropists come from long-established families of wealth in which donating to charity is an accepted responsibility.[2] "I was brought up to give, and I always have given," explained one person with old money. Other members of the subculture are recent inheritors or self-made millionaires who acquired charitable habits as they and their families entered higher economic and social circles.[3]

Money alone is not enough for acceptance into high society.[4] Socialization in the culture of philanthropy is a childhood matter, as well as a lifelong and intergenerational process. The relatively new Bass dynasty (see figure 2.1), for example, is reported to be "the fastest-growing family fortune in America."[5] A substantial inheritance, an elite education, business acumen, and philanthropy are important aspects of the Bass ascent. Four young brothers from Fort Worth, Texas—Sid Richardson Bass, Edward Perry Bass, and Robert Muse Bass, who are in their forties, and Lee Marshall Bass, in his early thirties—are worth billions of dollars. *Forbes* listed three of them as individual billionaires in 1988, but estimated Edward's worth at only $755 million.[6] All are graduates of prep schools and Yale University. Sid, Robert, and Lee Bass, along with their wives, are prominent participants in several nonprofit endeavors, both in Fort Worth and nationally.

The Bass wealth-maker was their great-uncle Sid Williams Richardson, a Texas oil wildcatter and rancher, who "made and lost three fortunes, finally holding on to the fourth and largest."[7] When Richardson died in 1959, his estate was valued by the federal government at $105 million. The bulk of it went to the Sid W. Richardson Foundation.[8]

Richardson had created the foundation in 1947, and for over a decade it was apparently a pass-through vehicle for his company and his personal philanthropy.[9] The foundation's $78 million in assets in 1962[10] had almost tripled by 1986, when they reached $211 million. That year the foundation made over $6 million in grants to education, health, the arts, and social service programs in Texas, primarily in the Fort Worth area. The foundation is the sixtieth largest in the United States. Most of its trustees are Bass family members. Perry Richardson Bass (the brothers' father) is president; his wife, Nancy Lee Bass (their mother), and Sid and Lee Bass are vice presidents.[11] The Sid W. Richardson Foundation has "donated more than $5 million to the Fort Worth Country Day School, a private school Perry helped found so that his grandchildren, unlike three of his sons, would not have to go up North to prep school."[12]

During the Depression Perry Bass's mother had lent her brother, Sid Richardson, forty dollars to invest in oil. Later, Perry, a graduate of Yale, became his uncle's lawyer and partner. Richardson left "$14.5 million to family and friends. Each of the current Bass brothers inherited cash and property worth $2.8 million."[13] When his uncle died, Perry Bass had at

FIGURE 2.1
The Bass Family

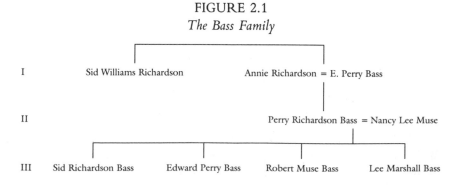

least $12 million in the business. "He disclaimed any share of Richardson's estate except for $450,000 worth of cattle, and in 1960 he set up Bass Brothers Enterprises, Inc., a convenient vehicle for turning over the business to his sons."[14]

"Perry has done everything in his power to prepare these kids for this type of life, just as a king might prepare his sons for their succession to the throne."[15] He is also an active philanthropist. He chairs Boy's Incorporated of America, in Dallas, Texas (Sid and Robert Bass are also directors); is vice president of another large Fort Worth grant-maker, the Anne Burnette and Charles D. Tandy Foundation, ranked seventy-first in size in the country;[16] and sits on the board of the Smithsonian Institution in Washington, D.C.

The eldest of the Bass brothers, Sid, is said to run the family business. Over the years the brothers have formed separate endeavors as well. Robert and Edward Bass have their own business and philanthropic interests, although the family foundation, as well as much of the oil and real estate, are still jointly held. Bass Brothers Enterprises has been liquidated and divided four ways.[17]

In 1988 Sid Bass was in the middle of a "divorce settlement, rumored near $500 million," although published confirmations of the final stock transfers were closer to $100 million.[18] He is currently married to Mercedes Kellogg, a New York socialite.[19]

The youngest brother, Lee, who holds an MBA from the Wharton Business School, has taken on increasing responsibilities in the family firm. He is married to Ramona Seeligsons Bass, from "one of San Antonio's richest families."[20] Sid and Lee's "share of family assets, [and] private partnerships, [are] worth an estimated $2 billion."[21]

Edward Bass funded an elite intellectual "cult" of futurists. He also built the avant-garde nightclub Caravan of Dreams in downtown Fort Worth. He is a "passive investor in some family deals: 'A lot of things I just have to read about in the paper.' "[22]

Robert, who like his older brother Sid is also an Andover, Yale, and Stanford Business School graduate, created the Robert M. Bass Group in 1983. His offices and staff are located one floor down in the "Bass-built Fort Worth office tower." Like his father, Perry, he is reported to be publicity-shy. "Rumored political ambitions may change that." He is the richest of the Bass brothers, with a "net worth estimated at at least $1.6 billion."[23] He recently clinched a "$2 billion deal with the Federal Home Loan Bank Board to take over the ailing American Savings and Loan Association of California."[24]

Robert and Anne Bass spend a fair amount of time in Washington, D.C., where they own a historic Georgetown house. In September 1988 they presided over a benefit dinner dance at the newly restored Union Station, held on behalf of the National Trust for Historic Preservation. Robert is chairman of the board of the National Trust; a member of the Collectors' Committee of the National Gallery of Art; and a major donor to the restoration of the presidential guest house, Blair House, as well as the diplomatic reception rooms at the Department of State. Anne Bass is a trustee of the World Wildlife Fund and the Conservation Foundation. The couple were also the principal donors to the Robert M. and Anne T. Bass Center, a Stanford University residential study center and intern program in the nation's capital.[25]

The president of the Conservation Foundation, William K. Reilly,[26] said that Robert and Anne Bass "are very much a team. They both are extraordinarily earnest, serious people and I am endlessly surprised to discover that people who operate at the level they do are interested in ideas. They don't talk in terms of wielding power and influence. They talk about making a contribution." A friend of Robert Bass is reported to have observed that Washington, D.C., interests them because "it has a sense of culture and history that they appreciate, and it is the center . . . of public policy issues and activities. . . . I think it is an interesting choice for Bob. It is a reflection of the man that they didn't go to New York."[27]

One of the reasons that Robert and Anne Bass did not choose to make New York a second home may be that this is precisely what Sid Bass did. "Ultra-private" Sid and his ex-wife Anne had entered New York City high society at her "urging."[28] She joined the Chairman's Council at the Metropolitan Museum of Art. They purchased an apartment, "stuffed it with Monets, and became increasingly familiar fixtures on the Manhattan and European social circuits. Anne became an active benefactor of the New York City Ballet and received widespread—and not so favorable—publicity when director Lincoln Kirstein and his supporters accused her of trying to take over the ballet company's school."[29] Anne had studied ballet as a girl.[30] Sid and Anne's two daughters have taken lessons at the school. A few years earlier, Anne had led "a $10-million fundraising campaign for the 50th anniversary of the School."[31]

In spite of the controversy, Kirstein seems to hold Sid Bass in high esteem. "He really looks at things in museums. Of all the rich men I know, Sid Bass is the only intellectual. He really cares about culture." Bass is also a trustee of the Museum of Modern Art in New York and of his alma mater, Yale.[32]

Again, most significant giving by people like the Basses goes to prestigious, traditional endeavors and institutions where they have a specific interest
or where family and friends are personally involved. An Eastern multimillionaire commented:

> I would say, in terms of dollar volume, that 90 percent of what I do each year
> . . . is given to the organizations with which I am directly associated. The other
> 10 percent are small gifts to local community things that need support, but do not
> need massive amounts from any individuals such as myself. . . . I tend to give to
> organizations that I know the most about, and I know the most about the ones
> that I personally serve.

He is on the board of a leading private university, a metropolitan hospital,
and several smaller nonprofit organizations.

Being interested primarily in elite institutions, most wealthy individuals
are never exposed to the many nonprofit agencies that must struggle for
funds. As one candid philanthropist explained:

> Groups limp along unless they have a wealthy patron. . . . It is pretty hard for an
> out-on-the-fringe organization to survive. . . . The [wealthy] people who care about
> XYZ organization have to work and help raise money. It is very interlocking. It
> is tremendous business.

An "out-on-the-fringe organization" is not mainstream, prestigious, or
traditional. Its trustees are not money or power brokers, nor are they on
the boards of several other nonprofit groups.

The philanthropic wealthy range in behavior from people who treat charitable donations as they would paying any other bills to those whose lives
are defined by their voluntary work. A millionaire at the least concerned end
of the scale stated: "Giving to charity is an expense. It is not an optional
thing. It is something you have got to do, like paying taxes." The wife of
one of the richest men in the world is representative of those on the other
side of the spectrum. She said of her philanthropy: "My life revolves around
it."

THE PHILANTHROPIC LIFESTYLE

> I have always had more money than I needed. My father was wealthy, and
> I was also lucky in business. It has always seemed to me that the opportunities
> of using money, for whatever the philanthropic organization, are just so
> much sounder, or appealing to me, so much more gratifying to me, than
> spending money on a yacht or airplane or whatever else.

In addition to a privileged background and a special process of socialization, members of the culture of philanthropy have a distinctive lifestyle that

ramifies into every aspect of their existence. Not only in their choice of charities but also in their decisions about personal consumption do the philanthropic elite establish and maintain a unique pattern of behavior.

Charitable rich people, for example, view expensive cars, yachts, and airplanes as ostentatious and incompatible with their social obligations. Ironically, collecting works of art is an acceptable expenditure because it falls in the realm of high culture.[33] In addition, whether women or men, with inherited fortunes or self-made millionaires, the philanthropic elite regard charitable giving as an alternative to consumption. An elderly Midwesterner with inherited wealth said:

> I think that one of the big differences between people is whether they want to spend their money living lavishly—throw their money away—or do they want to put their money where it will amount to something, and do the greatest good for the greatest number of people?

Many of the charitable rich own boats and planes, but few with whom I spoke mentioned having them.

Generally, these people are not like the New York real estate developer Donald Trump, who is the proud owner of "the biggest apartment . . . the biggest country houses . . . the biggest yacht . . . and the biggest plane."[34] Members of the culture of philanthropy do not flaunt their wealth. They are not of the jet set. If they allow their names and pictures to get into the newspapers, it is usually in connection with some "good cause" that they are supporting.

Virtually all of the philanthropic elite believe that they have a special obligation to society because they are rich. This sense of responsibility is integrally related to their relatively modest consumption patterns. In fact, many describe their lifestyles and material belongings with some embarrassment, while reinforcing their view that charity is an obligation. An Eastern woman with inherited money offered a typical comment:

> I was raised in a family where there was a great deal of feeling that you have a responsibility and obligation that wealth carries with it. It isn't just how many pieces of clothing can I have, [or] how many jewels. . . . I mean I drive a very nice car, but I don't need a Mercedes. That kind of thing has never been terribly important to me. . . . I don't want for anything. . . . We have a very nice lifestyle . . . domestic help . . . a vacation home.

These beliefs and behavior patterns stem from socialization and class guilt, as well as a fear of government intervention or social disorder that might erode privilege.

One self-made millionaire touched on several common themes that point to contradictions embedded in philanthropists' lifestyles and presentations of self.

> I do a lot of things that are certainly not frugal, but we have a nice simple house, and do not have a big yacht. Our vacation places are very simple. . . . The wife is even more frugal than I am. . . . I do not find gratification in having a big car, big boat, big house, servants, these kind of things, nor fancy things. We both feel very comfortable.

Notice this man's use of the plural "vacation places." Any one car, home, or boat should not be too big or fancy. Apparently, having several modest vacation places is acceptable so long as none looks opulent. Along with other philanthropic wealthy people this man manages to appear as if he is upper middle class. He does not want to seem too rich, because he feels guilty about his wealth. He actually thinks of himself as leading a simple, unpretentious life.

Privileged children studied by the psychologist Robert Coles also used the word *comfortable* as shorthand to describe and summarize how they live. "Comfortable, comfortable places," said a little girl growing up in a spacious apartment on Lake Shore Drive, Chicago; a ski lodge in Aspen, Colorado; and a cottage on Cape Cod.[35] As noted by the philanthropist quoted above, each home is comfortable, none is considered excessive. Coles also wrote about the importance of appearances.

> Old, worn Persian carpets are valued, among other reasons, precisely because they give just the slightest impression of shabby gentility to homes owned by people determined to indicate how casual and relaxed they have become about their considerable wealth.[36]

Philanthropy contributes to these feelings of comfort and relaxation by ameliorating guilt and adding meaning to rich people's lives.[37]

Along with other Americans, the rich are prone to believe "the myth of the middle class," an inaccurate idea that the vast majority of people in the United States make up an affluent, homogeneous group.[38] The philanthropic wealthy want to appear as if they too conform to the image of the contented and secure upper middle class, in spite of their considerable capital.

In fact, several verified multimillionaires expressed surprise that I would want to interview them, as they did not consider themselves wealthy. Some may have earnestly believed what they said.[39] Such denial is partly motivated by a personal desire for privacy, but there is also the issue of safety. An elderly study participant said that in the aftermath of the Lindbergh kidnapping case (1932), the children in his family had gone to school in the basement of their home with bodyguards constantly present. Even today, Sid Bass and his family travel with bodyguards.[40]

Inconspicuous lifestyles serve another purpose for members of the culture of philanthropy: to mask disparities between their own lives and those of the people ultimately receiving their charity. In maintaining lower public profiles and standards of living than their wealth would allow, the elite are protected from public exposure and criticism. Until recently, for example, the Bass family was relatively unknown;[41] along with other rich people they were shielded from unwanted solicitations for money.

Those who give anonymously are even more successful in maintaining their privacy. Unnamed philanthropists are the least accountable to the public or to government and the least besieged by fundraisers. But they are a minority compared to those who want to be known for their giving. In 1987 at least seventy-five donors made well-publicized contributions of over $1 million dollars each; in contrast, only fourteen gifts of this size were anonymous.[42]

The self-made millionaire with several vacation homes quoted earlier claimed that he did not set out in business to become rich, and he sees himself as different, perhaps better, than those who do aspire to wealth.

> I have never had any interest in accumulating wealth. . . . I happen to have started a company which became successful and went public. The value of the stock increased. I sat on an acorn and an oak tree grew. . . . Personally, I would rather be known for the amount of money I give away than the amount I accumulate.

The desire for recognition alluded to here is the key to most elite philanthropy.

An attorney recounted the words of a client hospitalized with terminal cancer who decided to rewrite his will so that a sizable portion of his estate would go to charity. "I want the sons-of-bitches to know who I was." None of my wealthy informants were quite so graphic, but fundraising professionals have long recognized the advantages of appealing to the desire for a memorial to one's life. In general, status motives underlying philanthropy to nonprofits are not readily expressed, except when the conversation turns to other people's incentives for giving.

Although there are rare exceptions, most philanthropists retain and safeguard capital, spending only income. A young man who inherited two modest trust funds (amounting to less than $250,000) explained: "Part of my background, and I think you probably find this in a lot of old monied people, is you do not spend capital. You just don't." And an elderly man from an old family concurred: "I gave some out of capital. . . . I guess I'm a conservative financially. . . . [My philanthropy] was mostly out of income."

There are various channels through which charitable donations can be made. The most popular and widely used besides the direct gift of cash is the donation of appreciated assets—stock, real estate, or other property[43]— to a nonprofit entity. This method offers the best tax advantages because the donor pays no taxes on the profit. A substantial contribution also leads to the greatest direct involvement and personal recognition.

Private foundations offer an alternative means for charitable giving, although they are subject to greater federal and state control. A foundation can be established as a pass-through vehicle that awards grants to nonprofit groups from the annual contributions of the donor, or the donor can endow the foundation and make grants from income earned on the foundation's investments.[44] In other cases, people who sit on the boards of foundations established by their family exercise control over grant-making whether or not they make additional contributions to the foundation's endowment holdings.[45]

Family foundations provide wide flexibility in the timing of charitable gifts and can confer a great degree of status and power on wealthy donors. A New Yorker who has established a private foundation noted: "If you are an individual making small contributions, you are magically transformed when you become a foundation making small grants. . . . I feel that I am taken very seriously. Embarrassingly so. I think some people listen to my counsel a little too carefully."

Community foundations offer yet another vehicle for giving that minimizes administrative and regulatory concerns associated with private foundations. Most large American cities have community foundations. The more than 300 community foundations in the United States[46] are often umbrella organizations for a number of modest and a few large philanthropic endowments. Individuals may establish donor-advised or donor-designated funds with a local community foundation that enable them to specify or suggest groups or causes they wish to support. Like those who endow them, community foundations are notorious for funding mainstream, non-controversial causes.[47]

Estate tax law provides a framework for philanthropy.[48] Types of charitable trusts vary, but all of them benefit the people who establish them, their heirs, and nonprofit organizations.[49] For example, in 1988, Edra E. Brophy set up a $17 million charitable trust with some of the proceeds of the sale of Farmers Insurance Group, which her father co-founded. In twenty years it will be distributed to the University of California at Irvine, the Orange County Performing Arts Center, and three other Orange County arts groups. In the meantime her family will have tax-free use of the interest on the capital.[50] In some trusts the opposite occurs. Income goes to charity for a specified number of years; the capital then reverts to heirs. Still other charitable trusts skip generations. Various types of funds at nonprofit institutions such as universities and hospitals are available or can be formed for similar purposes. It is even possible to create new nonprofit entities such as churches, schools, and support organizations.[51]

Whatever method they use, philanthropists have more visibility through giving than through consuming. A prominent middle-aged woman alluded to the value and meaning of money by contrasting the spending decisions of wealthy givers and non-philanthropists. Because the following quotation makes a number of important points, it is presented here, and then discussed by topic.

> You hear about these new millionaires. It is incredible. So and so has a home in Sardinia and a yacht he keeps parked off of blah-blah. Nobody knows him. . . .
>
> Money is such a sensitive subject. It is incredible. When people get older, particularly, money becomes so sentimental to people.
>
> You can have the most marvelous relationship with somebody and then you talk about money and suddenly their whole body language changes. . . . Nobody can tell anybody else what they should give. You can say, "Would you consider a gift of . . . ?"

"Nobody" who matters "knows" these new millionaires who spend so lavishly. They are clearly unworthy of being members of the culture of philanthropy. Here again, there is more to "class" than simply having a fortune. Wealth brings recognition and status only if used correctly.

Money is extremely important, private, even "sensitive" and "sentimental." Discussing it directly is taboo:[52] "Suddenly their whole body language changes." A younger informant from a multigeneration family of wealth said: "People talk less about money than they do about sex. . . . Any number of friends, I know everything about their sex lives. . . . But when it comes down to asking how much money do you have, they look at you like you gotta be out of your mind."

"Nobody can tell anybody else what they should give." Giving is a personal decision. Philanthropy allows the wealthy to be individuals, permitting them choices that others do not have. And money becomes more important as people get older. Philanthropists usually have more and give more as they age. They begin to care more about the personal stamp they will have made in their hometowns or the nation.

Wealthy philanthropists, who can afford almost anything, buy whatever they want. It struck me that these people wear clothing that on the whole cannot be distinguished from that of the middle class. A lack of distinction in clothes is another part of their denial of wealth and attraction to the simple life. Yet most employ at least one servant and a personal secretary. They travel extensively and frequently, for both business and pleasure.

Many philanthropists have at least one Mercedes in the garage, others drive beat-up clunkers of all varieties.[53] The choice of car probably has great personal significance, but the meaning attached and the patterns of ownership are inconsistent. A young Midwestern heiress told me: "I am not a Cadillac liberal. I call myself a Volvo liberal." To this person, Cadillacs represent showiness, and possibly bad taste, whereas Volvos are well-built, dependable transportation. Her remark also demonstrates how unaware, in a certain respect, she and many other rich people may be of cost, since, for them, the price difference between any two makes of car is negligible.[54]

In the privacy of their homes, the philanthropic elite feel less constrained about expressing themselves and their wealth. The exteriors of their residences, at least the side facing the street, do not stand out from those of their middle-class and upper-middle-class neighbors. However, the interiors and back yards tend to look significantly more personalized and costly. All of the homes I saw displayed some type of artwork that appeared to be original. A few had magnificent sculpture gardens. Many upper-class people like antiques; others prefer the high-tech, more modern look; but either way the decor has "character."

Most of the charitable wealthy have a primary residence, although several regularly commute between an ancestral location and a big city. Although the Basses still call Fort Worth home, Sid and Anne Bass had a Fifth Avenue apartment in New York City, and Robert and Anne Bass own a house in Washington, D.C. For other philanthropists, additional residences tend to be vacation places in resort or rustic settings. The homes that I visited ranged from large urban apartments to suburban houses; there were only a few mansions. They might be quite old or brand-new and represented every possible style.

Extended families of several generations often maintain a secluded country estate or ranch that is used for holidays and retreats. For example, the "Rockefeller estate in the Pocantico Hills of New York, overlooking the Hudson River, offers an idyllic and very private setting for the homecomings of the family's younger members."[55] The important fact here is seclusion. One mansion may house a large number of guests; cabins and cottages[56] are usually available for those who desire more privacy. Regular family reunions are often held on the estate, which may serve to promote or be a symbol of family dynasty, unity, and wealth. Such estates may have been the primary home of the founder of the family's fortune.

Many wealthy families have a history of political and social prominence, as well as philanthropy, in ancestral communities. They are rooted in a given area or city where they have been among the leading families for generations. When asked about the history of his charitable activity, an elderly man with old money unself-consciously described a kind of noblesse oblige that he had been taught throughout his life.

> One of my earliest recollections is taking a turkey down to a family in [a rural Midwestern area] with my father. We seemed to do that every year. . . . [At prep school] it was very much part of the values of the community. . . . And this was certainly reinforced at Yale. . . . The whole idea of leadership and responsibility for others was very much a part of the culture of that society.

He uses words like *leadership* and *responsibility* to describe activities that are inherently paternalistic.

Giving turkeys or food baskets to poor neighbors is symbolic of a type of charity that is widely approved of in the United States. Every holiday season children of all classes are asked to bring canned goods to school for distribution to the needy. The difference for the rich, as this example illustrates, is that they are involved more directly. The father mentioned above took his young child with him when he distributed charity, to teach his son the responsibility of wealth. It is also meaningful that such an event is among the first memories of a now-old man. Taking the turkey to a poor household helped this rich child to understand that he was different and superior.[57]

In vivid contrast to the people who received the turkey, this child, even during the country's biggest economic downswing, was sent to costly schools where he associated with others who were learning about their privileged place in the world. Education for wealthy children typically begins at the private "country day school," and many later attend nonprofit boarding schools.

Elite precollegiate schools such as Choate, Hotchkiss, and Miss Porter's in

Connecticut; the Culver Military Academy in Indiana; Deerfield, Groton, Phillips Exeter Academy (Exeter) and Phillips Academy (Andover) in Massachusetts; St. Paul's in New Hampshire; and Lawrenceville in New Jersey attract a rich student population from around the country. With the exception of Choate, each school listed here graduated several members of the *Forbes* list of the 400 wealthiest people in the country. Most of these prep-school–trained individuals had inherited their wealth. Self-made millionaires have not usually themselves attended such institutions but do send their children or grandchildren to them.[58]

Prep schools are at least as good a predictor of future prominence as the higher educational institution a person attends.[59] They prepare students for admission to the "best" private, nonprofit colleges and universities such as Harvard, Princeton, Stanford, and Yale.[60] They instill values of obligation, public service, and superiority. They also bring together young wealthy people and others who may be the future elite to form lifelong associations.[61] This is most important for male philanthropists. The lifestyles of men and women in the culture of philanthropy are significantly different.

THE BUSY MEN

Unlike their wives, most wealthy men have responsible jobs—in a business they formed; in a family firm, holding, or investment company; or in their chosen occupation. Nonprofit activities take up a substantial portion of their time, in part because usually they do not fully relinquish control of the funds they contribute to charity. An Eastern donor explained:

> I am a director of too many, eighteen or twenty, [nonprofit] institutions. And so I have something to do with the way the money is used and spent. That includes [an art museum], [a performing arts center], [a university], and so on down the line.
>
> When I give these institutions money, I get involved in the management of the institution, deeply involved. So much so that I spend currently over half my time in institutional work. I'll spend this afternoon, the entire afternoon, at the [art museum] board meeting. Friday, I have to go spend six hours at ——— University. . . . Yesterday I had lunch at the ———; I am a former chairman. It took me two hours. And so these things consume a great deal of time, but that is my interest.

Charitable rich men often choose to be volunteers because this work gives their lives meaning. Their wealth allows them to indulge in whatever they choose. He continued:

> There are so many things that a rich man can do for fun. He can buy . . . sports teams. He can go sailing. He can keep women. You don't have to be a rich man to do that. My wife wouldn't like it, so I don't do that. You can do all sorts of

different things. I am fully involved in all the pleasures. I play a lot of golf, and go skiing when I want to. But I cannot make a life out of those things.

He is cognizant of his privilege.

Most human beings have discretion of only a very small part of their lives. They work forty hours a week. . . . I don't have to work for a living. . . .

When I get up in the morning, there isn't a human being that can tell me what to do. . . . But I have assumed many obligations.

This man's manner was arrogant, but jocular. His ironic asides indicated that he was conscious of his class position. He also made it clear that voluntary activities were more important to him than business and leisure pursuits.

THE ACCOMMODATING WOMEN

Charity is an even more central part of the lives of female than of male philanthropists. Whereas many rich men are active in managing the growth of their fortunes, this is less usual for their wives. Husbands tend to be entrepreneurs or investors, while their wives tend to be full-time philanthropists. Married couples often make joint decisions about philanthropic gifts, but the women spend more time in volunteer work with local-level organizations. An Eastern woman donor and volunteer noted, "Women particularly spend a lot of time and give a lot of hours . . . on many, many philanthropic efforts, either boards of hospitals, churches, schools, what have you." In addition, women increasingly use their inheritances to establish foundations and charitable funds that they themselves manage.[62]

Women of wealth are usually homemakers, unlikely to have paid employment. Occasionally they have outside offices, especially if they run the family foundation. In addition, and of great importance, they are responsible for socializing the next generation. A Californian talked about her role in passing aspects of the culture of philanthropy on to her children. "I struggled with how to teach values to the kids when they have so much. . . . It is really important that they turn out strong, and think for themselves." In addition to dedication to their families, upper-class mothers feel they need creative, productive outlets for their energy and talents. For privileged women of all generations, philanthropy is a meaningful, prestigious occupation.[63]

This California heiress is on the board of the family foundation her parents established. Her elderly parents, husband, brother, sister, their spouses, and a family adviser are trustees. "It was well instilled in us when we were growing up—the importance of sharing with other people. My parents did give away a lot of money. We have been exposed to this all our lives, and we realize it is an important thing to do.''

Apart from the foundation, she and her husband are active in the elite charitable scene in their community. ''Most of our personal giving is very much geared to those things [to] which we have a commitment, whether it be through the schools—my husband and I are very committed to education and to the arts.'' She is much more involved than her husband as a member of several local nonprofit boards, many of them funded by the foundation. She spends time fundraising for these causes and planning special events. Women like her are also primarily responsible for another component of the maintenance and intergenerational replication of the culture of philanthropy: the process of charitable recruitment.

CHARITABLE RECRUITMENT

Philanthropists are drawn to volunteer work in a variety of ways. One woman claimed: ''I was weaned on social responsibility. . . . It was so much a part of our lives that I never questioned it.'' Others are recruited by being asked to contribute money or time. The nouveau riche seek acceptance by joining various nonprofit efforts.[64]

Wealthy women from across the country pioneered the strategy of gaining philanthropic and social prominence by contributing to New York causes that are nationally recognized. ''Ann Getty, of San Francisco, became a major benefactor of both the Metropolitan Museum and the Metropolitan Opera a few years ago and proceeded to vice-chair the opera's centennial gala.''[65] The Gettys are rich enough and have had money long enough to gain entrée wherever they wish. Anne Bass (the former wife of Sid) used a similar method to join the national culture of philanthropy.

A man with old money is representative of the general pattern of philanthropic leadership development. Being asked to serve on the boards of directors of nonprofit institutions was what began his career as a philanthropist; knowing the bounty that he could bestow, employees in an organization or other board members would recruit him to their cause.

Activity and involvement institutionally were what got me interested. . . . It was very much of an evolutionary process. I would tend to give larger gifts to the institutions where I was very close and had confidence in—especially if I were chairman or something. Then I would probably give a leadership gift to that enterprise.

This type of donation is generally the first made to a capital campaign. It is usually very large—at least $1 million to a nationally prominent institution like a university, perhaps $25,000 for a new community theatre company—and is viewed as an encouragement to others to contribute generously. It also establishes or maintains the giver's role as a power broker within the institution.

Board membership is often a reward for large contributions or successful fundraising; such activities are also expected of most trustees. One multimillionaire commented on the prestige or status he gains from charitable work, particularly from board service.

> There is a certain amount of ego satisfaction in this. . . . The fact that I am an officer of a lot of different things . . . there is no doubt that that contributes to my willingness to give a lot of time. . . . And why do you do your duty? It is not only because you are such a public spirit. It is partly because that is the price you pay if you want to be a big shot—if you want to be known as someone who is active, if you want a certain amount of credit in the community.

Local elite philanthropists are usually trustees of such nonprofits as large arts organizations, colleges, and hospitals, whose boards are "dominated by men holding multiple corporate directorships. . . . 'Less vital' nonprofits include social service agencies whose boards more often consist of women and men with few corporate ties."[66]

Nonprofit boards tend to be self-enclosed, self-referencing, and self-reaffirming. Most members of the culture of philanthropy sit on several boards where they have the opportunity to meet, influence, and be praised by fellow philanthropists whom they recruit to their special causes. Women tend to serve as trustees of local nonprofit enterprises, whereas men are also on for-profit and national voluntary organization boards. One man indicated: "I have served on something like sixty national and international boards." There is often strong crossover in the composition of boards and interlocking directorates at the local and national levels and between corporations and nonprofit organizations.[67]

A prominent Easterner who serves as trustee of several nonprofit organizations discussed his experience in moderating a conflict between a new president, the board, and the faculty of a private university. This man had graduated from the institution but said he was "viewed as having no particular axe to grind, other than an abiding love for the school."

A new president came in . . . and, being a most brilliant man, he was somewhat controversial. The board was divided over him, as was the administration. I was approached by different factions of the faculty, the administration, and the board.

The president was perceived to have political ambitions and to lack a commitment to academic values; his leadership style was questioned as well. There was both faculty and administration opposition to his appointment, and an unsuccessful petition was circulated against it.

The philanthropist wielded his influence in support of the new president. The board made it clear that they, rather than the faculty, had the power to set policy and select the chief executive officer. Later:

> I involved myself in a series of things, not merely fundraising, although I am very active on the development committee, but I am also on their planning committee and university policy, the community relations committee. . . . That takes up a fair amount of my time, and I enjoy it.

This particular man's fortune, his mediation at the beginning of a new university administration, and his national prominence reinforced his power base at that institution.

The same man serves on the board of an orchestra. "It is obviously a very well-established institution in this city. It probably gets the most prestigious board." He explained how the board's composition changed as leadership shifted from those with "old school ties" (referring to elite prep schools and colleges) to newer business leaders.

> It had gone along with a fairly narrow fundraising constituency [the philanthropic wealthy]—until the last few years when it was realized that expenses were catching up and exceeding our revenue-raising capabilities . . . and that we were going to have to raise the amount of contributions and therefore broaden the constituencies. And what happened was that it became a conflict between the old tie and the new tie. And the most dynamic individuals on the board, by and large, were not the old school ties but the newer people of the city who were very accomplished individuals in the corporate world.

Here is evidence of the exclusionary, but changing, nature of certain elite institutions. Only those people who can make or raise large contributions are allowed access to policy-making positions. But "new constituencies"— the newly wealthy and corporate executives—made their way onto this orchestra board because they or their businesses had money to give. Class snobbery may be tempered by the necessity of getting additional funds,[68] and this often means that the longtime elite must share control with newcomers.

Different philanthropists want different kinds of control, and there is usually considerable variation in how the same person may behave with a range of nonprofit organizations. A businessman with inherited wealth stated: "Entrepreneurs have a great need to control. If you give them a controlling reason to give philanthropic money, you have all of the sudden got a philanthropist that might not otherwise be there." A funder of social change mused:

> It would be a little disingenuous to say I have no interest in controlling or affecting where the money goes. There is a sense in which [my philanthropy] embodies a concept of the types of places I want my money to go and where I think other people's money ought to go. So a major motivation is influencing where wealth will be distributed.

A Midwesterner with inherited wealth gave an example of how control is exercised: "We put a couple of hundred thousand dollars in [a nonprofit organization] every year. . . . Last year I said, 'I don't see that they are using the money the way we asked them to. Let's give them half. . . .' "

Wealthy philanthropists have a "double standard" with regard to elite as compared to grassroots or broadly based organizations. For example, when a performing arts complex was destroyed by fire some years ago, the funds to rebuild it were almost immediately forthcoming. The center was located in the suburbs of a large metropolitan area and served an affluent population. According to Pablo Eisenberg of the national Center for Community Change in Washington, D.C.:

> Every major foundation, corporation, individual donor, as well as the federal government, gave large sums of money without assessing whether the theater corporation was well-run or accountable.
>
> At the same time, a number of grassroots organizations serving the poor and other disadvantaged families in the same metropolitan area could not raise a dime from many of the same donors, although their leadership, management and programs were of the highest quality.

He asked: "Why should a fourth-rate orchestra, ballet, or museum be funded when it's so difficult to support first-rate community groups or alternative service agencies?"[69] These struggling nonprofits generally have boards that are representative of the total community or their constituency. Precisely because they do not have elite boards and staff, they have difficulty raising funds.

"Give, get, or get off" is an old adage among fundraisers in referring to nonprofit board service. In order to get money, how much board members give and whom they know is of utmost importance. "Philanthropy has a lot to do with peer pressure, and fundraising involves a snowballing effect, circles of people who are in the fundraising tradition, who are also giving," a wealthy man explained. Although board service is essential for maintaining the interest of the elite in nonprofit matters, fundraising is the activity that really pulls them into leadership positions in the "third sector."

One prominent businessman said:

> The more people you get to know, the more people who know you. If you are successful in any of it, even including your own giving, then that sort of brushes off on other people. I go to them and talk about why they should give money. It just keeps on expanding. And the first thing you know, you believe everything you say.

Over time, the elite broaden relationships within their socioeconomic group as they ask for and give money. Influential philanthropists are those most tied into giving, getting, and brokering for prestigious charities. The successful fundraiser becomes a "star"[70] in the nonprofit world. Giving one's own money can be a private commitment, but once an elite person has asked others to contribute, he or she is generally more invested in that particular organization and the culture of philanthropy. He or she then publicly appears to be responsible for the success of the charity.

When soliciting a substantial gift from an individual or grant-making entity, a trustee or executive of the applicant group must usually know personally the donor, director, or an officer of the grant-making organization. A Southerner declared: "I have found out that no corporation, no foundation, or no individual ever gives to an organization. Individuals give to individuals."

The successful solicitor is usually a peer of the potential donor; one millionaire explained:

> The person who asks you [to give] can be significant. Certain people, in my view, have great influence. If one of those asks someone else of that caliber, it becomes important for the other person to respond—in part because next month I will have something cooking. If you scratch my back, I'll scratch your back type of thing.

In order to raise funds from their peers, philanthropists must themselves make sizable contributions. "The ones who are givers are raisers; those who don't give, don't raise," commented another man with whom I spoke.

I have an A list, and the A list are the CEOs of companies that have been after me for money about something. You run up these due bills back and forth. So, if I get $10,000 from this fellow's company for whatever it might be that I am interested in raising money for . . . If he gives $10,000 at my request, I want to hear from him in six months. And this time it is going to be whatever he is interested in.

This is an example of philanthropic exchange in the "old boy network."

The subculture of philanthropy is not wholly self-generating, and there is a need to attract new money and recruits who have the appropriate perspective. For example, William Gates III of Seattle, Washington, a man in his early thirties, is the chairman of Microsoft, one of the country's largest personal computer software firms, which he co-founded after dropping out of Harvard. Personally worth over a billion dollars, he is credited with being the youngest person ever to make that much money. In 1987 he joined the national board of United Way at the request of John Akers, the chairman of IBM. Gates says he is not yet ready to be a serious philanthropist. "I'm in a phase for the next ten years where my work is my primary contribution. The idea of funding other things is some time off."[71] But he is probably in training for the culture of philanthropy. If he were married, his wife could do some of the advance work while he concentrated on the business.

Because high culture is the domain of the wealthy, it is a good investment for those who wish to become well-known members of that class. A second-generation West Coast giver spoke about the charitable interests of her family. "We mostly donate to the arts. We give quite a bit to the opera, to the symphony, to the ballet, the theater, and the museums, all that sort of thing." Her remarks are characteristic of those with new money.

Many self-made millionaires and their offspring consciously set about joining the culture of philanthropy. They admire, envy, imitate, and compete with those who have old money. Frequently they attempt to "pass" into the upper class, or at least increase their influence and status among the charitable power elite, by making big donations to the high arts and by sending their children to elite schools.

One of the reasons that some people with new wealth are able to pass into the world of the charitable rich is that by the fourth and fifth generations of inherited wealth fortunes have often been broken up and spread among multiple great-grandchildren, not all of whom participate in the culture. Some old families maintain their philanthropic position through their leadership and work, rather than through monetary gifts. But nonprofit institutions are constantly foraging for new money.

CHARITABLE EXCHANGE AND PHILANTHROPIC NETWORKS

> An exchange seems to go on, particularly between individuals with a lot of
> resources, who are often localized in business communities. They just
> exchange favors with one another. If the head of IBM's wife is into crippled
> children, then the head of IBM will call the head of Chrysler, and the head
> of Chrysler will send in the contribution.

A nationally known professional development consultant described a typical exchange. One philanthropist telephones another: "I hope you will call ——— in the development office about ———. And, by the way, did you get my check?"

Why should anyone ask another to give $10,000 to one charity, knowing that within the next week or month or year he or she will be asked to respond in kind? Obviously, each could have donated the extra $10,000 to his or her own charity and the recipient organization would have been in the same financial position. My explanation is based on the principles of exchange and reciprocity, and the benefits of this behavior in maintaining an exclusive and cohesive social group or network.[72,73]

Rich people contribute to the favorite causes of their business associates, family, and friends, expecting them to reciprocate. One young woman of wealth said that she has developed her own system to keep track of charitable debts that are owed her. "There is a certain amount of 'if you help my cause, I will help your cause.' "[74] Some exchanges operate at this direct level, while others are more elaborate or indirect—but wealthy people generally get something in return for their generosity.

Exchange occurs within and across levels in the charitable hierarchy. The most real power belongs to the givers[75]—the corporations, the government, and the charitable individuals who pay for the services provided by nonprofit organizations. Givers may also get better public relations and visibility, and a host of different types of personal gratification. In addition, a charitable agency may be asked to return the favor.

For example, the executive director of a small nonprofit organization in the West was told by a program officer at one foundation that the foundation would make a contribution to his group if the agency would help support certain proposed regulations favorable to the parent company of the foundation. The requested exchange may be direct, or it may be veiled, as in: "Our expectation is that those organizations we support will be supportive of us."

In some cases the gift exchange may be relatively, even ludicrously, trivial, as in this case of an important contributor to Ohio State University, who said:

You will be amused at my motivation. . . . Ohio State has one of the greatest football teams in the world, and we are a football-crazy town. There are eighty-some thousand seats there and never one for sale to the public. The only way that you can get a seat at that stadium is to join the President's Club, or be an alumnus, faculty, or student.

The man made a donation to the President's Club.

Another scenario is the following. A prominent millionaire said, "When John D. Rockefeller was setting up Lincoln Center, I gave him $25,000 for a chair in each house. At that time he was active in the Rockefeller Foundation." Shortly thereafter, the man said, three of "his" organizations—a regional school for the arts, a chamber orchestra, and a dance theatre—received grants of between $125,000 and $200,000 from the Rockefeller Foundation. "So, I call those attention-getting grants," he laughed. "Not entirely happenstance."

The most common "payoff" for charitable giving is often described as simply a good feeling, a sense of personal achievement—satisfaction. A woman with inherited wealth living in the mid-Atlantic region said: "There is a part of me that really enjoys giving." An older man in San Francisco explained: "Sure, there is a lot of need, but it is fun giving. It is exciting to give." A woman in Texas exclaimed:

I picked up the newspaper and on the front page there was a story about two wonderful things that I had funded. I was filled with joy. My gosh—I am on the right track! That was such a good feeling!

It may be that part of the joy was the pride that a public authority—the newspaper—had lent additional justification to the donor's sense of being right. In addition, she received public recognition for her projects.

Although increased social status and peer recognition are widely viewed as motives for giving and volunteering, wealthy people do not usually acknowledge them as being among their own reasons for such activity. A young woman who works as her father's charitable adviser explained unabashedly why her family contributes large amounts to local arts organizations.

My father is trying to get the most benefit out of his money. . . . We want our name to be heard. . . . Besides our feeling for the arts . . . the social scene is a very strong reason. . . . We want good seats. We want to be invited to all the events, so that is the reason why we give.

As we have seen, once a newly rich family turns to philanthropy, its members have a better chance of being accepted into upper-class society. For one thing, they are demonstrating the proper values by giving rather than by displaying wealth. It is also likely that they will assume increasing monetary and political responsibilities over time and can thereby help to ensure the perpetuation of the institutions and values of the upper class.

Most wealthy people are not as open as the young woman quoted above in attributing their philanthropy to status concerns, preferring to cite more positive and socially acceptable motivations. The study, however, encountered some notable exceptions. One millionaire claimed that "very little of [my giving] is motivated by a genuine understanding and commitment to philanthropy. Most of it is motivated by either the harassment of a friend who is trying to solicit money, the status . . . or to benefit them in their business." And the elderly patriarch of a leading family in the Northeast replied that his prime motive for being involved with charity was "vanity, vanity, vanity."[76]

Having the opportunity to interact closely with others of like means and values is another of the rewards for philanthropic activity even for the established wealthy. Members of the culture of philanthropy spend a good deal of time associating with each other at charitable, political, and social functions. "I mostly do [my charitable work] . . . with the network of friends that I trust who share my interests, chatting with them," said one donor. There are obvious advantages in belonging to a social group with common values and having friends with whom to do things. People maintain their class position in a community by being benevolent funders and insuring that they have the proper social connections for themselves and their children. "I happen to have enough money and those around me do."

Charity balls, where everyone attending pays a large sum, typically $500 to $1,000, for the benefit of a particular nonprofit organization, are the most public example of philanthropic social interaction. These are the kinds of "rituals of class solidarity" to which sociologists Paul DiMaggio and Michael Useem refer.[77] There is often a theme at a charity ball, and an elegant dinner dance. According to a Palm Beach millionaire:

> Probably the Heart Association raises more money than anybody else. They not only have a ball. They have an auction night where they get people to give valuable gifts, including businesses and trips, which they auction off. I think they raised two, three hundred thousand dollars in one night.

The Heart Association is well known. Heart attacks are the second leading cause of death in the United States, which may be especially meaningful among the highly successful older population of Palm Beach.

Charity balls engage most of the people who attend them for only a single evening. They produce relatively less money than other fundraising methods—often only thirty cents on the dollar—and take immense amounts of time to plan. However, they bring the elite women who organize the balls together for extended periods and make work for them. At the charity ball, all the "right" people see each other, the local press covers the event, and such things are thought to increase status.[78]

In the asking, giving, and exclusive interacting, corporate heads and rich people establish greater solidarity among themselves, their spouses, and within their class. Although the nonprofit agency receives no additional monies, it has a wider base of support for its activities. Following on this, potential funders usually review an organization's list of donors before making a contribution. If certain corporations or wealthy individuals are on the list, this may be the persuasive factor that brings others on board. One of the direct effects of fundraising by the wealthy for their favorite organizations is that other causes failing to receive elite support will suffer.

This outcome is not, however, simply the result of individual choices made by wealthy people. It is one of the symptoms of a privately based political economic structure for redistribution of income in this country. This is the theme of the next chapter.

The Political Economy of Philanthropy

The capitalist system produces wealth so unevenly. . . . There has to be a
public system to balance things out, but it is also incumbent on individuals.
And of course, it is better when it is done by individuals. . . . The alternative
to capitalism—which is private ownership—is socialism—which is public
ownership. And then you get people trying to play God, deciding who is
going to work where and where the money is going to be. Whereas in the
capitalistic system no one is playing God. The marketplace is the determi-
nant. And, of course, the marketplace is extremely cruel. But it is nothing
more than economic democracy.

The wealthy man quoted above does not seem to think that he is playing
God when he makes charitable funding decisions but feels, rather, that public
officials in socialist systems practice their own kind of theocracy. Obviously,
the rich would have the most to lose in a less capitalistic system: their profits
might be more rigorously regulated, and they might pay a heavier tax bill.
The political economy in the United States operates in the interests of the
wealthy under an ideology concerning the merits of private charitable giving
that supports the status quo.

The philanthropic wealthy and others contend that private contributions
and nongovernmental organizations are integral to the American way of life.
They contrast individual philanthropy with the taxation policies of European
welfare states. Rich people want to make their own decisions about where
their surplus money goes; they think their funding is better than the State's

43

and believe that services are provided most effectively by voluntary agencies. This ideology is the basis of their involvement in and control over certain charitable organizations.

In this chapter I analyze elite philanthropic rhetoric and ideology, as well as the political economic consequences of the charitable practices of the rich. My interpretation is that philanthropy interacts with business and government, and cannot be fully understood outside of this context. A fiction has been promulgated that there are three sectors of society—business, government, and nonprofit enterprises—which operate independently.[1] Yet the freedom to amass and protect fortunes and to transmit them across generations is linked with tax policy and philanthropy. Recent income tax legislation has been increasingly less redistributive. The charitable deduction is available only to the affluent who itemize. Philanthropic provisions in estate law favor the accumulation of private wealth for use by nonprofit organizations.

The U.S. government contracts out most of its services. For example, many roads that are funded by tax dollars are built by private firms owned by the rich. Medicare payments go to both nonprofit and for-profit hospitals where philanthropists serve as board members. Social services provided by nonprofit organizations are financed almost equally by the government and private contributors. This means that the philanthropic elite often have authority over both public and private funds; the charitably wealthy are not making decisions about "their" money alone.

Finally, and of greatest concern, philanthropy has recently served as a justification for minimizing the welfare role of government. Yet the amount and the reality of where private grant money goes do not support this rationale. The erosion of the federal safety net has contributed to increasing poverty that charity will not eradicate. The rich do not necessarily get richer because of their philanthropy, but the poor are rarely made better off because of it either.

PHILANTHROPIC IDEOLOGY

> If there were not a nonprofit community out there, two things would have happened. I do not think we would still be a democratic country. This may be exaggerated, but the public demand for the government to do this, that, and the other would be to such a degree because of their needs. . . . We would probably be a huge big government doing all these things—Socialistic.

Members of the culture of philanthropy equate their freedom to make individual decisions about dispersing their wealth with capitalism and democracy. Most are opposed to the politics of the welfare state and distrustful of government. Like most Americans they are subject to a prevailing fear of socialism, which they assume is the opposite of democracy. Or rather, as in the case of the millionaire quoted above, their view of democracy is closer to that practiced in the democracies of the late eighteenth and early nineteenth centuries, wherein only the propertied class had the right to vote. They do not believe that the common people constitute the source of political authority. They hold that although the masses may have the vote, the elected government should be limited in its power. The "public" cannot "demand" too much, whatever its "needs" might be.

A middle-aged northeastern woman expressed her views: "We get closer and closer to an undemocratic society if we shift all the responsibility onto government. And that is what is going to happen if private philanthropy is discouraged." Once again, a peculiar idea about democracy is voiced wherein it is undemocratic for the State to have the lion's share of the responsibility—although this woman does not specify the type of responsibility to which she is referring. There is little recognition of the extent to which the U.S. government already funds nonprofit organizations,[2] but there is a notion that private charity can counteract or balance economic and State power.[3]

This very rich woman continued: "Somebody has got to take over or we are all going to be ciphers in some government-sponsored social agency. I think it would be disastrous." She has an unabashed view about where control should rest. "Somebody"—presumably an individual philanthropist and not the government—should wield power.

A millionaire with inherited wealth who lives in Los Angeles said:

> I put back into society something that I had taken out of it. . . . Nobody has to do that. When they don't, they simply take the social system for granted [or think] that somehow the little bit they pay in taxes makes it run. They are increasingly, by default, giving to one petty bureaucracy or another. . . . Then they get irritated that things are not going well, or the government seems unresponsive to the communities. Well, what do you expect if you don't participate in it yourself? People who are doing the bureaucracy functions are just sitting at their own desks. Why not? They don't give a damn. Why should they?

Presumably, "they" are members of the civil service. His antibureaucratic sentiments are typical of the charitable elite. He does not seem to consider the fact that he has the resources to "participate" more actively than other citizens.

A set of beliefs like those of philanthropists is plausible because of an even more widely held ideology that bolsters an artificial separation between the economy and politics, business and government, the private and public sectors. According to Robert B. Reich, "American political rhetoric often frames the decision in the dramatic terms of myth: Either we leave the market free, or the government controls it."[4]

Another flawed myth holds that pure capitalism operates as if under natural law, that any interference with laissez-faire processes will lead to an economy in shambles. Government intervention and welfare provision must therefore be severely limited. Frances Fox Piven and Richard A. Cloward traced the development of this idea in a more historical context, and argued cogently that popular ideology has reinforced that fallacious interpretation. "Poverty and riches were evidence, not of injustice, but of the fact that the market and its unerring laws had duly punished the slothful and untalented while rewarding the industrious and meritorious."[5]

This notion has been supported by the guarantees of property rights embedded in the U.S. Constitution.[6] Since the founding of the U.S. government, the propertied have been politically dominant. "The political ascendance of capital was made possible by a doctrine that was so successfully translated into popular ideology that people were led to treat economic life and economic conflict as if they were distinct from politics."[7] In reality, the State has always intervened, but more often on the side of the wealthy.

An implicit social Darwinism that harks back to the late nineteenth century is conveyed by many in the culture of philanthropy:[8] as if the elite are rich because they have greater ability than common people and are thus better qualified to make decisions for the masses. A self-made Texan put it succinctly: "If you have got enough sense to make the money, you ought to have enough sense to give some direction as to what you are going to do with it."

Leaving aside the questions of what means were used "to make the money" and whether a different type of knowledge and practice might be required for philanthropy, there is inconsistency between the social Darwinist view and the reality of inherited wealth. Second-generation to fifth-generation rich people have been taught that they are better than others, and feel that their superior culture and education have prepared them to be leaders. Thus, in this context as in others, social Darwinism becomes a self-fulfilling philosophy. The wealthy begin with money, and their advantages continually accrue because they can afford them and their philanthropy supports the kinds of institutions that they believe prepare them to be more fit.[9]

Robert Reich has argued that there are four enduring "core parables" of

"American political mythology" and culture that we modify and rearrange in order to comprehend our place in the world. Variations of these four parables are found in elite philanthropic ideology. For the wealthy, Reich's "mob at the gates" is the common people; "the triumphant individuals" are themselves, who fund "the benevolent community"; and the government represents a "rot at the top."[10]

Rich people of every political persuasion with whom we spoke talked of the importance of private nonprofit endeavors.[11] They referred proudly to the history of charitable giving in this country, as well as to their desire to fund projects that perpetuate traditional "American" values. Several different interpretations of what actually constitutes that tradition emerged, although an ethic of individualism and ethnocentrism pervaded most people's comments.[12]

When referring to his family and company giving, a conservative Western grant-maker stated:

> We are defenders of the American Way. We believe that it is in danger. So organizations that address themselves to the preservation of the traditional rights, the traditional freedoms, and particularly the traditional responsibility of the great American citizen, we favor.

He is interested "primarily in education. I support things like the boys' club . . . and universities that appeal to me."

A liberal Easterner said that she thinks people give

> because of a very strong Judeo-Christian, American principle. I think de Tocqueville observed it, and it is true. We do believe, as American people, that we can change life for other people and for ourselves, and make it better. We really do believe that. Other societies I don't think have that belief.

She funds "high-risk, interesting ventures." These include the ballet, education, and religious organizations. From her descriptions of these projects, only the private schools she supports represent any kind of risk. They seem to be on financially shaky ground—in part, she implies despite her professed liberalism, because they are ethnically and racially integrated and provide scholarships for poor students.

This liberal philanthropist might appear to be at odds with the conservative quoted before her, but their basic philosophies are close. They both think it is up to the individual philanthropist to determine what makes life better and to act on it; they do not want to leave this responsibility to others.

Another example sharply highlights inconsistencies among political views, perspectives on charity, and practice. A young funder who inherited his money and described himself as a "leftist" stated:

> I think the philanthropic tradition in the United States is very important. It is different from Europe. . . . Europe does not give tax deductions for charitable giving. . . . Individuals are not encouraged to give money there. So when they do, they give less. . . . The needy organizations fall under the government and the attendant bureaucracies. I think those societies move more slowly and individual initiative is not rewarded as fully. There is a rigid structure that has to do with this interweaving of politics, bureaucracy, and the existing order.

He has joined with other young rich people in an alternative foundation that has made grants to small local groups such as the La Raza Legal Center and the Medical Coalition for the Rights of Women. In spite of his avowed politics, his outlook is totally consistent with philanthropic ideology, including what amounts to a kind of bald nationalism.[13] He is at odds with many of the positions of the Reagan and Bush administrations, but he supports the American political-economic system, especially individualism in philanthropy.

Philanthropists, whether conservative, liberal, or radical, may not consciously understand the way in which their giving maintains the status quo and can even perpetuate inequities, but by starkly contrasting American politics and values with those of other countries, they congratulate themselves on their heritage and what they consider their own ingenuity.

The charitable wealthy do not all publicly endorse the ideology just described, although most accept parts of it. A distinct minority of young activists with inherited money, especially women, are giving grants for projects aimed at social change. They may not like the current economic or political system, but through their philanthropy they use it to promote their ideas. One feminist funder dissented radically from even her progressive peers in being the only person whom we found to say: "I am against the profit motive."

This woman views the world as an interconnected "global political economy," where decisions and developments in one country ultimately affect other nations. Unlike most philanthropists, in addition to donating money to causes at home, she funds international, especially Third World, projects. She gives away about $800,000 each year. On this she commented:

> I know it is a lot, but there are people with a whole heck of a lot more money than I have. . . . [Where I come from] we had a big house, but there were an awful lot of other people who did too. The money is there. It's an unusual situation

on the face of the earth, where there is such a widespread group of people with money, even though it is small compared to worldwide poverty.

Along with a minority of wealthy grant-makers, she questions both America's business system and its governmental system, but in the final analysis, she is in a position to exert her influence by choosing which projects to fund and which not to fund, and can exercise power over those she selects and supports.

BUSINESS AND CHARITY

Directly and indirectly, about half of all private philanthropy comes from the rich—from companies, from foundations, and from individuals. Although far fewer in number than the poor and middle classes, the wealthy, collectively, have far more money to give. As we have seen, whereas most people contribute a majority of their charitable donations to religious organizations,[14] the rich fund upper-class institutions. In 1986, wealthier itemizers increased their philanthropic donations; the lower classes contributed less than they had in previous years. Those who reported $100,000 or more in income contributed over $32.5 billion; other itemizers gave about $24 billion.[15]

In 1987, an estimated $94 billion was contributed from private sources to nonprofit organizations. Less than 5 percent of all donations came directly from corporations, compared to nearly 6 percent from bequests, 7 percent from foundations, and 82 percent from individuals of all classes. Business gave $4.5 billion.[16] Exactly what portion of the nearly $6 billion in bequests was made by the very rich in 1987 is unclear, but it is obvious that only the affluent have accumulated enough capital to make bequests.[17] Foundations gave away more than $6 billion to charity.[18] Individuals contributed almost $77 billion.[19]

By adding the conservative $32 billion reported on income tax returns by the affluent in 1986 to $4 billion in corporate giving,[20] $5 billion in bequests,[21] and $6 billion in foundation grants, I estimate that roughly $47 billion—half of the total $94 billion of gifts in 1987—came from the rich.

The corporate, charitable, and personal interests of wealthy people are interrelated. Business and investments provide the profits for philanthropy. Many companies, both small and large, are family-controlled.[22] Most of those who determine corporate giving (usually chief executive officers) are rich.[23]

The assets of family foundations are invested in the general economy. Large educational institutions and hospitals keep their funds in stocks and bonds. In this sense, organizations supported by philanthropy are not strictly nonprofit.

A Minneapolis businessman explained that philanthropy was vital in his community because "we have a relatively small number of very wonderful families on the one hand, and the leadership of the business community on the other hand." In the Twin Cities, the leading families own or have controlling interests in many of the big companies. The mix of corporate and individual wealth varies by location, but all rich people have business interests. Both today and in the past we find business leaders and the wealthy to be the philanthropic leaders,[24] and, as such, unlikely to fund projects that might jeopardize their profits. One Midwestern millionaire admitted, "We pretty much give to the same things, the safe things." He said, "It is a club. What is the phone company giving? What is the bank giving? What is the other bank giving? And everybody else falls into line, in proportion." He and his relatives own a bank and part of the regional phone company. "That is pretty much family. However, they do have boards. Well, the bank is family-owned, period. The phone company is only 20 percent family-owned. We have a board meeting and approve the budget every year."

Corporations not only fund safe projects; they systematically keep certain organizations from getting funds. The man continued:

> If one guy [head of a company] has a problem with a neighborhood group, more than likely other corporations will have problems with the same neighborhood group—like neighborhood groups that go after banks for not making loans. . . . Well, suddenly, everybody's bad-mouthing this neighborhood group. I would guess they have never taken the time to personally visit the people about their concerns.

The particular case he spoke of is related to the nationwide phenomenon of "red-lining" (drawing a line around) poor, frequently inner-city communities, and refusing them loans and other services.

The Salt Lake Citizens' Congress (SLCC), an example of the kind of neighborhood group to which the philanthropist quoted above referred, constantly faces a severe funding shortage. This grassroots organization was formed in 1983 because of the frustration of low-income residents about the lack of city services, high unemployment among the low-skilled and minority population, escalating utility rates, toxic sites in neighborhoods, a crumbling infrastructure, insufficient drainage systems, and excessive commercial development overpowering low-income residential areas.

The SLCC has been organizing against red-lining, mixed-use commercial zoning in certain poor neighborhoods, and utilities deregulation. According to its executive director, Barbara Toomer, "We went after the banks . . . the city council, and . . . the telephone company." There have been reprisals: an activist employed by SLCC lost his appointment to the Community Development Block Grant Program, and previously pledged grants from utilities were not forthcoming, or were much delayed, apparently as a warning to the group.

"There's nothing that we can put our fingers on," said Toomer. "I do know there are people in town who say they sleep better because we are around. . . . The banks are a little more [careful] as a whole not to be discriminatory . . . because of the [bad] publicity" they have gotten in the past. Most of SLCC's funding, however, has had to come from foundations and religious organizations outside of Salt Lake City.

Private and community foundations, especially the largest institutions, have a better record than corporations for funding welfare programs. According to a Foundation Center survey of 375 foundations conducted in 1986, almost 25 percent ($466,875,000) of their grants went to human service or public and society benefit activities. The health field received 22.5 percent ($423,007,000); education, 21.9 percent ($410,866,000); the sciences, 15.1 percent ($282,381,000); the arts and culture, 14.2 percent ($265,562,000); and religion, 1.4 percent ($26,596,000).[25]

This funding pattern is a response to government cutbacks and represents a distinct shift from earlier years, when foundation grants went primarily to education. Since 1982, when it received 42.5 percent, education's share of foundation awards has been steadily declining. But the shifts in foundation priorities cannot make up for the loss of federal funding to social services. Foundation support constitutes about 10 percent of that provided by government to nonprofit organizations.[26]

In 1987, the 21,200 noncorporate foundations in the country had assets over $122 billion,[27] which are administered by trustees, outside money managers, and banks. Although individual board members and officers are not permitted to benefit personally from their foundation activities, they can send business to friends and associates. Foundation investments contribute to the stability of the overall economy. By law foundation assets are required to be distributed at a rate of only 5 percent per year.[28]

To a greater extent than the giving programs of foundations, company giving programs directly reflect corporate interests and objectives and the personal opinions of the chief executive, officers, and owners. Corporations give nonprofit organizations cash, securities, and other property, as well as their executives' time and the use of company facilities, and sometimes lend them money at below-market rates. They also donate company inventory and products.[29] Apple, Hewlett-Packard, and IBM, for example, have all contributed computers to schools and colleges.[30] When a company funds research related to its product, this is also considered a charitable donation.[31] According to a study by Yankelovich, Skelly and White, Inc., "Corporate giving is an expression of enlightened self-interest."[32]

In many instances, corporate philanthropy is not part of a charitable contributions or company foundation budget, but is rather a part of the budget of the community and public relations departments. If the group that is receiving the gift has been designated as nonprofit by the Internal Revenue Service, then the company may choose whether to take a charitable tax deduction or to count the gift as a tax-deductible business expense (known as "expensing it out"). The bottom-line financial benefits are usually the same, to both donors and recipients.[33]

The predominant opinion across the country is that business comes before charity. In a temporal sense, this is obviously true, but once the money has been made, it can be used in any number of ways: reinvested to generate more income and profit, spent on consumer items, or contributed to charity. A California entrepreneur stated:

> The prevalent view is that a corporation's job is to make the shareholders' net worth grow. Then it is the shareholders' function to decide what they want to do with their money. In this company we take a very narrow view of what our philanthropic obligation is. If it does not relate fairly directly to the interests of the company or to our employees, we pass it by.

Corporate gifts may be clear-cut contributions to charity or may fall into the gray area of advertising, public relations, or marketing.[34] This is particularly true when a company sponsors a cultural event. And it should be noted that the putative distinction between corporate sponsorship of tax-deductible public television programs and those of commercial television is overstated. Both are actually advertising.[35]

Several examples of creative, high-visibility funding are illustrative of corporate giving. American Express was a principal contributor to the highly touted renovation of the Statue of Liberty. Donations from the company to the statue renovation were based on charges made by consumers on credit card accounts. American Express called this type of fundraising "cause-related marketing," and trademarked the phrase. Other credit card companies are now engaged in similar schemes. The Scott Paper Company has a coupon on certain of its products; if the consumer mails in this coupon, Scott will make a contribution to a designated charity. Coca-Cola and CitiCorp sponsored the "Hands Across America" mega-fundraising event to aid the homeless. "Hands Across America" was a great bargain for its corporate sponsors, who reached a big audience and got volunteers to do the work. These activities serve both as advertising and as a show of goodwill.

One Eastern businessman was unusually straightforward. "Philanthropy," he said, "is not a question of commitment, but one of economics." When asked about the process by which he makes his individual charitable decisions he claimed:

> It is what is good for the business. An example of that would be that somebody we are in business with is really strongly advocating their favorite charity. Or we do it because of the connection of the individual, or because the charity is so linked with some business activity we are doing. A good example of that would be the [a private] University, which is a large client of the firm. We do a lot of business with them, and therefore we give to the university.

More examples of business connections with philanthropy were offered by a man from Chicago.

> We support well-made, basic charities. A typical example would be United Way and things of that sort. And [we] engage in special projects of public benefit which bear a significant relationship to our business, with particular emphasis on projects designed to prevent or reduce socioeconomic losses. . . . We are primarily in the insurance business. We pay for losses that people suffer, so we are very heavy into such things as traffic safety, worker safety, things that get into efforts to control arson, crime.

Much funding that relates to business interests is described as being "for the good of the community"—and often that community is the corporate community.

A woman philanthropist whose husband is a commercial real estate developer spoke of the advantages and disadvantages of attending charitable functions for business reasons:

> There are some people that we do pay back. . . . The reason that we are going to the [charity] ball tomorrow is not because we want to. We went last year and we both looked at each other and thought, "What a crock. I am never going back. I'll buy a table." I could care less [about this particular event] and he could either. We are going because five or six people in his office wanted to go, so he is doing

it as an office morale thing. . . . People will come up to him all night tomorrow night to make a deal here and cut a deal there. People will come up to me and ask to be introduced and so on.

Though she says she does not enjoy these activities, this woman is clear about their other-than-strictly-philanthropic value. Even if the couple could have come up with an excuse for not attending the ball, their company still would have paid the $10,000 fee for a table out of indebtedness to one of the organizers of the event.

A well-known philanthropist claimed:

There is only one excuse for American business and it is to serve society. Profit is our reward. If we do not serve society, we will be punished and we will not be allowed to make as much of a profit. When business does not do its job, then we get punished with adverse legislation, stringent regulations, pressure groups of all kinds. . . . It is in business's and the nation's best interest to have as large a proportion of the demand for services, whether it be social, cultural, educational, medical, or whatever, filled in the private sector.

Here is one of the clearest explanations of the business component of philanthropic ideology. If the business community takes the lead and funds "for the public good," then its other, profit-making activities are less constrained. The government will not interfere. In this straightforward way philanthropy serves capitalism, but business does not necessarily serve the whole society.

Whereas capitalism has shown itself to be effective in amassing wealth, it has often had difficulty in sustaining egalitarian redistribution.[36] In most democratic countries, the reallocation of resources has been a vital role of government, accomplished through a political process.

PHILANTHROPY AND POLITICS

Despite their avowed suspicion of government, many of the charitable wealthy are engaged in politics, an activity that is a link between philanthropy and the political economy. One millionaire said, "I have always been on [philanthropic] boards, even in my political years." Many rich people have held or have run for public office. There is a well-recognized "turnstile" between posts in government, large nonprofit organizations, and business.

Most of the charitable elite are committed to promoting particular causes through their philanthropy. A fairly representative member of the culture of philanthropy told us, "I have always been politically active, if you define *politically* broadly, not just as electoral politics." In this sense, the giving practices of most philanthropists are related to their political beliefs and involvement. Except for tax purposes, no distinction is usually made between political and other activities.[37] When asked about charity, a funder from the Mid-Atlantic region said: "I give my money to conservative causes." Another said: "My original fundraising and giving away money was really encouraged in the political arena. I was head of [a committee] for George McGovern's presidential candidacy."

In some cases the commitment is recognized as being primarily political. One young man admitted that his motives for charitable giving were "almost purely political." A funder who lives in Washington, D.C., said that she had "decided that I wanted to have an impact politically and that one of the things people in politics listen to is money."

Federal campaign law sets limits on contributions that any company or individual may make to political candidates. This policy was specifically formulated to limit the influence of the wealthy and insure equal political participation by people of all economic means. To be eligible for federal matching funds, for example, a presidential aspirant may receive no more than $1,000 from any one person or group. One philanthropist described a fairly widespread practice. She and her husband give all the major candidates a full contribution, apparently "hedging their bets" so that they are in favor with whoever wins. Of course, rich candidates still have an additional advantage because they can personally finance part or all of their campaigns.

There are many ways around the $1,000 limitation, including buying tickets in friends' names for political dinners and other events, contributing to political action committees (PACs), and giving funds directly to political parties rather than candidates. In 1988, Nicolas Salgo, former ambassador to Hungary and a Reagan State Department appointee, gave the Republican party over $500,000—the largest of many such contributions given by rich people to help elect George Bush. Nathan Landau, a Washington, D.C., real estate developer, and some 125 other wealthy people, gave checks for $100,000 each to the Democratic party on behalf of Michael Dukakis. The Atlantic Richfield Company contributed $135,000 to the Republican party and $35,000 to the Democratic party. "This private cash has been dubbed 'soft money' because it is being raised and spent through a loophole in federal law. The law prohibits corporate contributions to presidential campaigns and sharply limits individual contributions, but individuals and corporations are free to give as much as they choose to political parties."[38]

Political activity encompasses more than individual or small group efforts, candidacies, and funds. Ideas, policy formulation, and the organization of political agendas are increasingly apt to come out of nonprofit higher educational institutions and so-called independent policy research institutes—"think tanks." These organizations usually take the stance of impartial experts outside of government. But many of the think tanks have political agendas.[39]

The Heritage Foundation is a recent example. This right-wing nonprofit think tank gained prominence in the early 1980s with the financial support of conservative philanthropists. Less than a week after Ronald Reagan was elected president, Heritage released a book[40] outlining its recommended policy programs and sent resumés of potential appointees to the White House transition team. The foundation had been formed seven years earlier with the express purpose of serving conservative Congressmen in need of intellectual support for their positions.

Expert marketing and public relations, as well as substantial contributions, help explain the success of the Heritage Foundation and similar organizations. The historian James A. Smith, who has studied public policy research institutions, has documented their advocacy techniques. But Heritage is only one case; there are more than 1,000 nonprofit policy research institutions in the United States and Canada. In Washington, D.C., alone at least one hundred think tanks were operating in the 1970s and 1980s.[41]

The election of Ronald Reagan marked what had been a gradual movement of middle, or moderate, politics to the right, and think tanks played a central role in this shift. The Heritage Foundation has at least three strong "rivals" and allies for influence on the right: the American Enterprise Institute (AEI), the Center for Strategic and International Studies (CSIS), and the Hoover Institution. Barry Goldwater's lead policy adviser during his unsuccessful 1964 presidential campaign was William Baroody, Sr., president of the AEI from 1960 to 1978. In the 1976 and 1980 presidential campaigns, Martin Anderson of the Hoover Institution was responsible for bringing together Ronald Reagan's domestic policy team; later, Anderson was given a prominent post as a White House adviser.

For some time, conservatives had been building their own institutions to challenge what they viewed as the "liberal policy Establishment." The Brookings Institution, on which many of the think tanks were modeled, was perceived as the leading liberal organization of its kind; however, Smith argues that this characterization was made primarily by the right wing. Conservative rhetoric has led institutions formerly considered centrist to be labeled left-wing;[42] a fate that was met by the Carnegie Endowment for

International Peace and also the Council on Foreign Relations—an elite discussion group with research capability.

Each of the think tanks has been accused of leaning in one direction or the other on the political spectrum. Although this diversity of policy approaches might promote pluralism, significant segments of the population who do not have the means to fund think tanks or other intellectual activity are not heard.

Instead, the conservative ascendancy and an ideological reliance on the merits of philanthropy has led to an outright war on public welfare.[43] Ironically, however, because of the manner in which social services are provided in the United States, this assault has not been focused on government programs alone.

We have in the United States a mixed political economy of giving—what political scientist Lester M. Salamon has termed a partnership between government and voluntary organizations.[44] In 1980, nonprofit organizations were providing more than half of the nation's social services, with funding from both the government and private sources. In the welfare field, slightly more federal tax revenue went to nonprofits than to government agencies.[45] Funds from philanthropy actually constitute less than half of the budgets of every kind of nonprofit organization except arts and cultural groups.[46]

According to a historian of welfare provision, Michael B. Katz,

Voluntarism never met most of the needs of dependent Americans. Some form of public assistance has always been crucial. . . . As inadequate as they were to meet the crises in the past, voluntary agencies have become even less capable in the present. Not only have they lost their role in income maintenance; more recently, escalation of government contracts for services with the private sector made them dependent, as never before, on money from public sources. Serious cutbacks in public funds, therefore, have left voluntary agencies with less money to spend on the increased numbers of needy people whose benefits have been terminated or reduced by the war on welfare.[47]

Thus the federal safety net of basic human services carefully woven together since the 1930s has been torn apart. To those in power, the idea that no American should go hungry or be without shelter has become passé. Martin Anderson, a former Hoover Institution fellow, spoke on behalf of the Reagan administration: "Providing a safety net for those who cannot or are not expected to work is not really a policy objective."[48]

According to the rhetoric of the philanthropic elite, private giving plays a special role that the State cannot, does not, or should not play. In fact, however, governmental, corporate, foundation, and personal spending has generally been complementary. A philanthropist provided an example of a social service program he supports:

> In the first year our company put up $400,000 and the state put up $400,000. And then I put in $400,000 which I had agreed to personally, so there would be some flexible funds there. In the second year the company had no obligation to continue, but did put in $250,000 and the state put in $3.8 million. Now in the third year the company put in $50,000 and the state is putting in $4 million to continue the programs.

I chose this case specifically because it is in the welfare area, and although exceptional in that regard, it graphically illustrates the policy role that wealthy people can and do play.

These types of "public-private initiatives," as they are called, have been around for a long time, but they are increasingly popular.[49] The broker may be a public or private entity or may be an individual. City and state officials with budget problems also try to sell their ideas to private investors. Joint projects may be undertaken in almost any type of venture, from the arts to welfare.[50]

The millionaire quoted above was personally involved in the nonprofit health and poverty project to which he refers. He acted as a broker, using his political influence and money to interest state officials in the program. His closely held business made a sizable initial grant, with matching funds from state government. He himself donated the same amount, bringing the total first-year budget to at least $1.2 million. These identical contributions gave the appearance of equivalency, but during the program's formative period the man in question had obviously invested more than the state when his company's money is also considered. He undoubtedly had a good deal to say about the project, how it would develop, and whom it would serve.

Later, presumably after the project had proved successful, the millionaire's company and personal contributions declined substantially, and the state was footing an increasing bill. Though the program was created by private initiative, its ongoing budget is now funded by the government. The state is not running the project, but it is providing the bulk of the money. The original broker and other trustees continue to make policy decisions about agency operations, although there is government oversight. Ongoing funding is not guaranteed but is linked now to political decisions. This particular health and poverty project will probably stay in good standing because of ties between its board and state officials.

Although this kind of interest in welfare services is relatively rare, the philanthropist spoken of here is typical in that he wants to exert control in the organizations he chooses to support. Here is a wealthy individual deeply concerned about social problems and willing to commit his own resources to finding solutions. But even if a majority of millionaires and their companies chose to donate money to welfare programs rather than to universities and the arts, we must ask whether we would want them, as a class, to decide which projects will exist and which will not. Furthermore, unless the rich begin giving their capital away—which is highly unlikely—even this amount could never equal what could be provided by government sources.

The way that social services are funded and produced is illustrative of problems endemic to the political economy of giving in the United States. In basic human welfare, the government must be the primary financier or many services cannot be delivered. Churches and other voluntary agencies may sponsor soup kitchens and shelters in particularly bad times, but they cannot meet all the needs of the poor or homeless. And they do not solve the problems of, for example, unemployment, underemployment, or the lack of adequate housing.[51]

One rationale for the tendency of the rich to donate money to elite organizations is that until recently they have expected the government to take care of primary human services. Most wealthy people, along with those of lesser means, assume that the federal government is responsible for a welfare safety net. A recent survey of charitable behavior indicated that a majority of Americans in all income groups agreed that "the government has a basic responsibility to take care of people who can't take care of themselves."[52]

The belief that the government is responsible for its neediest citizens is voiced by wealthy people whether or not they condone federal safety net policies. In describing why they established a college scholarship program that assists middle-income students, a Texas couple commented:

> The government subsidizes the minorities and the ones who really cannot afford it at all. And we felt, from our own personal observation, that a lot of it was wasted. We wanted to help the brighter students who really were eager for education but just did not have quite enough to make it. . . . We empathized with these students that want to do well and have the capacity. With just a little help, they could get over the hump.

This couple have not always been rich. They struggled to make it through college and eventually to establish a business empire. They decided to give funding to young people whom they considered more "like us."

It seems reasonable that the U.S. government, which represents the interests of all citizens, would have priorities different from those of wealthy donors. For fifty years welfare provision has been considered a State responsibility. The Social Security system, introduced after the Great Depression, and the War on Poverty programs of the 1960s and 1970s, led Americans to expect that the government would fund certain primary services. This expectation continues, but as we know, drastic policy changes occurred with the Reagan administration, and social services were hardest hit in the budget cuts.[53]

According to Alan J. Abramson and Lester M. Salamon of the Urban Institute's nonprofit sector project:

> One of the avowed objectives of the Reagan administration's budget policies . . . has been to shift more of the responsibility for addressing community needs from public to private institutions, among them private, nonprofit groups. Reflecting long-standing conservative beliefs, the administration has taken the view that a conflict exists between government and voluntary institutions and that the best way to aid the nonprofit sector is therefore to get government out of its way.[54]

From 1980 to 1986, social welfare programs lost federal outlays amounting to $58.9 billion, a 42 percent decrease; education and research funding declined $19.6 billion, or 18 percent; and the arts and culture were cut by $6 million, or 15 percent.[55] In social welfare, the largest budget cuts were made in employment and training programs. Education was affected because social security benefits in higher education for adult students were eliminated, as well as other forms of financial assistance.

Recent changes in the shares contributed to these programs by private sources and by the State are clearest when viewed from the perspective of nonprofit budgets.[56] In 1977, the federal government was picking up more than half of the tab for private social service programs (53.5 percent). In 1984, however, conservative priorities had become well-established, and the State was contributing only 43.9 percent to these programs.[57] Between 1982 and 1984, the years for which published data are available, private giving made up for only 7 percent of the government spending reductions.[58]

Others have more than adequately documented and critiqued the political attack on welfare. My intention here has been to reiterate how philanthropy, think tanks, and voluntarism were and are effectively used in unsubstantiated political rhetoric that has allowed the federal safety net to be eroded.[59]

If education, health care, and social welfare services were adequately supported by the State, these services might be more equal for all citizens in both quality and availability. In all societies a host of needs, and differences of opinion as to what makes for a better quality of life, create tensions about funding priorities. The issues, however, are political ones, and they are best worked out in a political arena. But the concerns of the poor or even the middle class have not been paramount in tax legislation.

TAX POLICY

I try to maximize my philanthropy and minimize my taxes. You reduce the cost of giving because of tax considerations.

Charitable tax policy in the United States is not equitable; the charitable deduction is available neither to the poor nor to some of the middle class who do not itemize their deductions. Thus tax policy encourages affluent citizens to give to the nonprofit causes they choose without providing this opportunity to others.

In 1984, according to the Internal Revenue Service, the 16,295 individuals or couples with an annual adjusted gross income of $1 million or more claimed an average charitable contribution of $139,291 on their income tax returns. The average deduction taken by all 57.5 million itemizers was based on $1,223 in gifts, slightly above the average $1,133 donated by taxpayers in the $30,000 to $50,000 bracket and well over the $672 average of people who had made between $5,000 and $10,000 that year. In addition, nearly 23 million non-itemizers showed an average $51 donation. This was before 1986, when the charitable deduction for non-itemizers was revoked.[60]

Some hypothetical examples may clarify these figures. The "average" millionaire who gave $140,000 to charity might have made ten gifts of $10,000 each to a favorite nonprofit organization—or two gifts of $50,000 each—and divided the remaining $40,000 among several groups. A middle-class person probably wrote checks of a hundred dollars or less to ten or twelve causes. The $10,000 contribution, and almost certainly the $50,000 donation, would put the wealthy person in a position of influence with from two to ten charities. The hundred-dollar contribution, which for many Americans is sizable, would have gone into a pot of money over which the person donating it would have little control.

The real story is slightly more complicated. Only a portion of those 16,000-odd millionaire families are part of the culture of philanthropy: There is evidence that the leading philanthropists are the very wealthiest people in the country, the "super-rich."[61] An economic study on the charitable contributions of the wealthy, based on a stratified random sample of income tax returns filed between 1971 and 1975, found great variability in levels of giving, especially for those with the highest incomes. Researchers Gerald Auten and Gabriel Rudney suggest that "the reputation of the wealthy for generosity is largely the result of exceptional generosity on the part of a minority of high income givers rather than widespread generosity among the wealthy."[62] Auten and Rudney also indicate that "the proportion of generous givers rises with income."[63] Their study supports the notion that a small group of multimillionaires are actually those giving the most money to charity.

In the 1970s, according to Auten and Rudney, wealthier donors who gave more to charity made annual median contributions of about $435,000.[64] Let us assume, along with the economists, but discounting inflation, that this figure is more accurate for prominent members of the culture of philanthropy than the average $140,000 that includes those who are not particularly charitable.

The hypothetical multimillionaire philanthropist has contributed $400,000 to selected causes. He can exercise great influence in one organization, or he can have substantial leverage by donating $100,000 to four different organizations. He may give $40,000 to ten different groups—and still have authority. Actually, he probably gave two or three large grants and several smaller ones in the range of $10,000, which would offer him a significant voice in several organizations.

"I am sure I give away more because it is deductible than if it was not," said one millionaire, "because I am sharing it with Uncle Sam. Instead of a congressman telling me where my dollars are going to go, I am telling them where their dollars can go."

Millionaires generally contribute up to the maximum for which they receive a deduction. Few in this study claimed that taxes had no influence on their giving levels, but only a small number said that taxes were the prime reason for their philanthropy. A typical statement was: "We give as much as is allowed." (Their charitable contributions were determined by the deductibility limits established by the federal tax code.)

One of the most influential philanthropists in the United States told us:

> I have been a donor since I was giving to the church as a small boy. . . . Then, when I came into some money of my own, upon reaching twenty-one, I began to think about giving in a more organized way. I was made aware of the tax advantages

of giving up to a certain percentage of income. So, each year I would tend to budget myself approximately the amount that I could give away with some tax advantage.

Another told us:

> The government makes it pretty attractive to you [to make charitable donations] in two ways: giving you a deduction for what you put into philanthropic purposes, and also taxing you at a very high rate if you do not [1985].[65]

Thus charitable tax incentives are of special benefit to the wealthy because they can substantially reduce the taxable portion of their income through their philanthropic contributions; the larger the gifts, the more they save in taxes, and the greater the influence they can wield.

In the last thirty years, for those in the highest tax bracket, individual income tax rates have declined from 92 percent to 28 percent; the 1986 Tax Reform Act (TRA) dramatically reduced the top rate from 50 percent to 28 percent. But although there will be a greater direct economic cost to giving by individuals than in the past, rich philanthropists will still receive a deduction. The price of giving for high-income individuals is 72 cents for every dollar donated to charity. In other words, when a donor makes a $10,000 gift, the cost to that donor, because of savings in taxes, is only $7,200. This means lost revenue to the government but probably increased funds to nonprofits.

The professed goal of the 1986 TRA is to encourage investment and productivity by taxing them less. In real terms, however, the effect of the TRA is to make the tax code less redistributive. The full impact of this new law will not be felt for several years. Although the 1986 tax code reduces rates, and thus deductibility for charitable giving, more money will be available to the wealthy who will pay less in taxes.

Several people voiced the view that tax policy was more important to charitable giving in the past than it is today. One millionaire from New York said:

> [Taxes] were extremely important because I could give away securities and end up with the same amount of money, after tax, as if I sold them. And, if I gave them away, they went where I wanted. If I sold them, they went to the U.S. government. . . . The laws have changed so it is not so advantageous to give away securities rather than selling them. Just the change in the tax brackets from 70% to 50% [1986].

This quotation introduces another complication into our consideration of the relationship of taxes to philanthropy. Contributing certain types of assets—

for example, stocks or real estate—to different kinds of nonprofit organizations offers different kinds of advantages, disadvantages, and deductibility levels.[66]

Many members of the culture of philanthropy are not happy with what they consider a lack of charitable incentives in the 1986 law. A Midwesterner complained:

> The thing that just frosts the hell out of me is the fact that we now have an administration that is saying the private sector ought to do it, on the one hand. And, on the other hand, they are doing everything under the sun to prevent the private sector from doing it. The most important thing is the most ungodly example which our president sets, of not giving anything himself. *And he is telling the private sector to do it* [1986].

Even conservative philanthropists who supported the Reagan philosophy had questions about the 1986 legislation. An oilman said:

> I think anyone who is concerned about charitable contributions . . . for the good of society, should be concerned about what will happen to the future tax laws. If the federal government is going to get out of the contributing side, which I think it should, and it gets back to private individuals to do it, then it is necessary that we have laws that encourage that [1986].

A possible but unlikely effect of diminished charitable tax incentives is that the wealthy will simply pocket the extra funds. The culture of philanthropy, however, is well-established, pervasive among the super-rich, and strong enough to adjust to lowered direct economic incentives.

Taxes, although they are important, are not the prime motivation for charitable giving among the wealthy. The other benefits of philanthropy— business connections, control, influence and status, as well as personal pleasure—will prevent any great loss of contributions to nonprofit organizations.

Taxes are, however, essential for the redistribution of wealth. In Western Europe, where there is a variety of political and tax systems, philanthropy is generally much less important than it is in the United States. In fact, the scope of charitable giving is broader here than in most other countries because less private money abroad finances nonprofit endeavors. Worldwide, philanthropy is insignificant and governments are the primary source of funds for nonprofit organizations.[67]

Detailed information on nonprofit activities in foreign countries is much more limited than statistics for the United States. Economist Estelle James compiled 1982 data on the Netherlands and Sweden, two European countries with widely differing methods of service delivery. In the Netherlands, voluntary agencies are the primary source of education, health, and welfare programs, whereas in Sweden the government takes direct responsibility for these activities. In both cases the government or compulsory insurance funds a majority of basic services, as well as cultural and recreational activities.[68] The Swedish have practically no nonprofit groups outside of religious and advocacy organizations.[69] According to James, what matters in countries other than the United States is not that certain services are privately provisioned, but the extent to which they are publicly funded.[70]

Throughout Western Europe there is substantial diversity in the methods of providing basic human services. Nonprofit activity is sizable in some countries and in a few instances even proportionally larger than in the United States. In all cases, however, the funding comes from government. The system in West Germany is similar to that of the Netherlands. About half of social services are subsidized by the State but are provided by nonprofit agencies. The United Kingdom is more like Sweden, "because of the dominance of its statutory agencies." France is in between, but closer to the United Kingdom than to the Netherlands.[71]

The key variable for determining the quality of life and the welfare of the general population does not seem to be whether or not nonprofit organizations deliver services, but whether or not the government funds them. On a variety of measures, many of the Western European countries consistently rank higher than the United States in public expenditures on social welfare, percentage of national income received by the poorest 40 percent of the population, and the physical quality of life.[72] In nonprofit provision, Canada falls somewhere between Great Britain and the United States.[73]

West Germany spends 49.58 percent of its budget on social welfare; Sweden, 45.17 percent; France, 43.92 percent; the Netherlands, 37.06 percent; the United States, 34.10 percent; Canada, 32.77 percent; and the United Kingdom, 26.15 percent.[74] In the percentage of national income received by the poorest 40 percent of the population, Sweden ranks highest with 19.7 percent. In the United Kingdom, this figure is 18.9 percent; in West Germany and Canada, 16.8 percent each; the United States, 15.2 percent; and France, 14.1 percent. The Netherlands and Sweden, along with Iceland and Japan, rate highest on a physical quality of life index that is calculated by averaging life expectancy, infant mortality, and literacy. They are followed a few points behind by Canada, France, and the United States. The United Kingdom and West Germany trail by a few more points.[75]

Although rhetoric on the subject abounds in all Western countries, there is little evidence that services provided outside of government are any more efficient or effective than those provided by government. Non-governmental programs may be less costly, however, because they depend on the unpaid work of volunteers.[76]

Efficiency, effectiveness, and quality are difficult to measure, but cost cannot be the only criterion. The Personal Social Services Research Unit at the University of Kent at Canterbury is doing some pioneering work in trying to evaluate efficiency in public and private day care delivery, both for children and the elderly. Martin Knapp and his colleagues have found that the size of an operation, rather than its public, private, or voluntary status, has a bearing on cost. Generally, the smaller the organization, the less expensive its services.[77]

In his comparative study of voluntary and government programs for the disabled in four countries—the Netherlands, England, the United States, and Israel—Ralph M. Kramer drew some surprising conclusions. The largest and most bureaucratic or professional agencies he investigated, rather than the smallest groups, were the leading initiators of new programs. Sometimes these large agencies were government agencies. When the State is responsible for basic services, nonprofit groups that specialize are the most effective, but they can also suffer from fragmentation. Voluntary groups are vulnerable to institutionalization, goal deflection, minority rule, and ineffectuality. Whatever their size, they are extremely dependent on the quality of their executive leadership. One of the greatest strengths of voluntary organizations is advocacy—the monitoring and pressuring of government to safeguard and raise the quality of public services.[78] Because of the financial squeeze and lack of support from a conservative government, advocacy has been a diminishing function of nonprofit groups in the United States.

THE CONSEQUENCES OF ELITE CONTROL

> We like to have somebody on every school board, every hospital board, and we have got it pretty blanketed now. Every year we get into more and more things. This is good for us.
>
> We want control of where our money is going. I know we can have that type of control, but I think it is still not quite as much as we want.

The business and political advantages of charitable giving, as well as an individualistic and acquisitive ideology, support the culture of philanthropy.

The Political Economy of Philanthropy

A self-made millionaire voiced the prevailing view that rich people in the United States should be entitled to make many kinds of decisions that in other countries are handled by the State.

> I think we are much better prepared to make the money go to places where it really should be utilized and utilized without wastage than occurs when it goes through the government's hands.

The rationale for elite control is that the system will work more efficiently, but the available evidence indicates that the bulk of private funds goes to services that are unavailable to many of the very neediest.

The advantages that philanthropy confers on the upper class are both direct and indirect. At the individual level, the families of those who participate in philanthropy receive an excellent private education and high-quality health care, and have greater opportunities to partake of high-culture leisure activities. Even when the person directly funding a particular institution—for example, through alumni donations—does not personally receive services, upper-class institutions are still maintained and perpetuated through such philanthropy.

Of course, not all elite philanthropy is aimed at privileged people. Some wealthy people and foundations do fund programs in the social services or in public education. Scholarships are normally provided for selected students who cannot afford private school and university fees. Certain nonprofit civic improvement projects benefit a broad spectrum of users.

But most philanthropists want to promote opportunities for those with whom they identify or who may be at least upwardly mobile. The newly rich often remember their own early difficulties, and their charitable donations may reflect their associations with the past. For example, an orphan may eventually help fund an orphanage. The Horatio Alger role model, or the philosophy of "pulling oneself up by one's bootstraps," lies behind the giving of many wealthy philanthropists.

If the government were insuring basic human services, especially for its neediest citizens, then philanthropy by the wealthy to the middle class might be considered progressive. Or, if tax dollars were redistributed equitably to provide for the general welfare, a system based on elite funding for the arts and culture might be acceptable. At one time this was the understood sphere of philanthropic donations by the wealthy. But, as we have seen, since the Reagan administration, the provision of many basic human services, as well as the arts, private education, and small-scale health care, has been left to the discretion of private individuals and nonprofit organizations.

Another problem with the operation of the philanthropic system is that most givers require some kind of immediate personal gratification for their contributions. For example, a funder in the South explained: "[A university] had a new building to build, so we raised the money. . . . Now, if you need money for expansion and that sort of thing, you raise money, and you see the results right then and there." Long-term and root problems are rarely approached, and there is little coordination or planning among philanthropists.

Private grant-makers often cut funding to organizations after a few years, explaining that they have been giving to that group for too long. Many philanthropists think that they should choose and fund projects they deem worthy and that if these endeavors prove successful then the government should take over. This role for private philanthropy will not be effective if the federal government continues to withdraw from providing basic services. The upshot of the Reagan administration's budget policies is that rich people now have more money in their pockets, poor people have less, and there are fewer incentives for redistribution. One wealthy person expressed other incentives for giving well: "There is a feeling of power that goes along with all this, and a feeling of being able to hand it out." This attitude is what many elite philanthropists have in common.

In the next four chapters I shall explore the fundamental distinctions among wealthy donors in greater detail. Those who inherited their money are raised in the culture of philanthropy, whereas self-made individuals and their spouses come to it later in life. In a larger society where gender frames experience, wealthy women resemble each other more than they resemble rich men. And, in a parallel manner, elite Jewish philanthropists tend to feel themselves outside the dominant Christian giving establishment.

PART 2

DISTINCTIONS

Chapter 4

Dynasty and Philanthropy

This was a philosophy that I learned, as many of us do, from our families. My father particularly was involved in the community, both from a tradition of donation and of service. I continue that. I think in a larger measure all of us have had that history. . . . We have followed our parents and grandparents.

Wealth and philanthropy often inhere within a family dynasty—a group of relatives who maintain their prominent position within a community or in the nation for a considerable period of time. In the modern American context, the accumulation, preservation, and transmission of capital through several generations is the key to dynasty. Estate plans that include gifts to heirs as well as to nonprofit institutions provide the wealthy with the legal means of perpetuating dynastic succession. Family members, depending upon their interests as well as their business, philanthropic, and political activities, assume varying amounts of authority and power.

People with old money, almost by definition, come from dynastic families. But some dynasties are richer, more powerful, or longer lasting than others. Where there is great wealth, several dynasties may be formed through branches of a family. But by the fourth or fifth generation, except in rare cases, family authority, pooled capital, and unity wane. In some instances, wealth is nearly lost, but remade by heirs. In any event, new names are constantly added to bronze plaques at museums or symphony halls and mentioned in association with this or that nonprofit organization. Philanthropists with new wealth create dynasties. Over time, new money becomes old money.[1]

Building a dynasty requires complex and creative combining of the assets of the founder's progeny—either with the consent of relatives or by the establishment of such irrevocable legal instruments as charitable and non-charitable trusts and foundations. Decisions and actions that lead to dynasty are normally formulated within the first few generations of wealth. Obvious obstacles may arise for inheritors who share smaller family fortunes with many siblings and other relatives. They must keep expanding and protecting the capital in order to live comfortably, provide for their spouses and children, and give funds away. Over generations and time, fortunes are often broken up and used up. In the case of the Mellon family, discussed below, the wealth, although dispersed for five generations, continues to grow.

THE MELLONS

The Mellon family dynasty[2] and philanthropy are prototypical of modern-era old money. The Mellons and their relatives are by far the wealthiest old money family in the United States.[3] In the late 1800s, Andrew W. and Richard B. Mellon began running their father Thomas's bank, from which they made loans to other companies, in which they also invested. Two of the enterprises were to become the Aluminum Company of America and the Gulf Oil Company.[4] Andrew Mellon's branch of the family became philanthropists of national repute and influence; Richard Mellon's offspring remained more active in family business and in local philanthropy.

Andrew Mellon was the U.S. Treasury Secretary from 1921 to 1932, as well as founder of the National Gallery of Art.[5] Although at this time he was less active in the family's business, it is safe to assume that as the nation's chief fiscal officer he was in a unique position to pursue his private interests while executing public responsibility. His tenure as Treasury Secretary has been noted by historians for its sustained effort in cutting taxes while reducing the national debt. Perhaps it is not simply hyperbole that he has been labeled "the man under whom three presidents served."[6]

The Mellon brothers' children—Richard King Mellon, Sarah Mellon Scaife, Paul Mellon, and Ailsa Mellon Bruce—each inherited fortunes that included stock in "three companies: Gulf Oil, Aluminum Company of America, and Koppers. . . . These two branches of the Mellon family also held large blocks of stock in several other enterprises such as Mellon National Bank, Carborundum, and Pullman."[7]

FIGURE 4.1
The Mellon Family

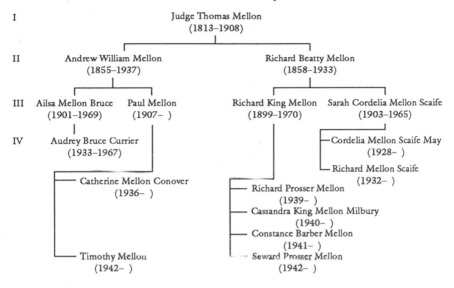

The eldest of these cousins, Richard King Mellon, was the "dominant businessman" in his generation; he administered the "family empire" from the 1930s until his death in 1970.[8] As a philanthropist, he was also "actively involved in the redevelopment of downtown Pittsburgh."[9]

Sarah Mellon, Richard's sister, married Alan Scaife, "the scion of an established Pittsburgh family."[10] According to biographer David E. Koskoff, "Alan easily took up his new role as a Mellon." Scaife followed his father-in-law as chairman of the board of Pittsburgh Coal, and he became vice president of Gulf Oil and chairman of the Mellon National Bank. His nonprofit board memberships included the Mellon Institute (a local hospital that his own family favored) and the Yale Corporation (the governing body of his alma mater). Through most of the 1950s Scaife was chairman of the University of Pittsburgh, "generally regarded at the time as a Mellon family trust."[11]

Sarah Mellon Scaife led the life of an upper-class woman, collecting art, entertaining, mothering, traveling, and practicing philanthropy.[12] Before her marriage, she had been the third president of the Junior League of Pittsburgh. Later, she gave a zoo to the city and donated "significant gifts of art to the Carnegie Museum."[13]

A foundation named after Sarah Scaife was initially established as a trust in 1941.[14] While she lived, the foundation awarded at least $26 million to various Pittsburgh universities, hospitals, and museums. "Her most notable outside gift was $750,000 in 1964 for a building at Stanford's Hoover Institute to house papers related to President Herbert Hoover, one of her son's heroes." However, she never headed the foundation, which was chaired first by her husband and then by her son.[15] After her death, $66 million of the Sarah Scaife estate went to the foundation.[16]

In the 1970s, the Sarah Scaife Gallery, a wing of the Carnegie Institute, was established with more than $12 million in funding from various Mellon, Scaife, and allied family foundations and relatives. The core of the gallery holdings is Sarah Scaife's art collection, as well as "paintings donated by a wide variety of Mellons and allied families."[17]

By 1986 the Sarah Scaife Foundation had more than $173 million in assets and that year alone made grants of $8.5 million to fewer than seventy organizations. The foundation funds local Pittsburgh philanthropies and national public policy groups. Sarah's middle-aged son, fourth-generation Richard M. Scaife, is chair of the board of trustees.[18]

Richard M. Scaife publishes several newspapers, "which must promulgate his conservative ideology." According to *Forbes,* he is "the most prominent Mellon of his generation." He makes large contributions to right-wing politicians and think tanks. He is worth over $550 million, which he "vigorously denies."[19]

Richard Scaife is known to have given large sums to the campaigns of Barry Goldwater, Richard Nixon, Max Rafferty, and Ronald Reagan. In 1974, for example, he "contributed an even one million dollars to President Nixon's re-election drive." The donations were made with 332 $3,000 checks and two $2,000 checks, written out to different Republican campaign committees. At that time, political contributions exceeding $3,000 were taxable, but Scaife avoided paying any taxes on those gifts.[20]

Relatively little has been published about Cordelia Scaife May, Sarah Scaife's daughter. It has been reported, however, that she "lives modestly, supports population control, [as well as] other liberal causes." Most of her capital assets are in trusts. Her estimated worth is over $400 million.

The fourth-generation cousins of the Scaifes, the adopted children of their Uncle Richard King Mellon, are referred to as the "Pittsburgh Mellons." Except for the non-biological relationship, they follow a typical family pattern of capital preservation. Seward Prosser Mellon, who followed in his father's and grandfather's footsteps, is a director of the Mellon Bank, where he "trained" in the trust department, and is "president [of the] family investment firm Richard K. Mellon and Sons. [Seward's] brother Richard [Prosser Mellon] tried banking, switched to conservation and oceanography; [and is]

chairman of [the] Richard King Mellon Foundation, [the] family philanthropic organ."[21]

A 1947 trust formed the Richard King Mellon Foundation. In 1985, the
foundation had assets in excess of $564 million and made grants and loans
of more than $21 million, primarily to about one hundred organizations in
Pittsburgh and Western Pennsylvania. The exceptions are nationwide conservation programs, the special interest of Richard Prosser Mellon. A smaller
grant-making organization with $19 million, the R. K. Mellon Family
Foundation, was formed by Richard King Mellon's heirs, Richard, Constance, Seward, and Cassandra,[22] who is "active in philanthropy, [as well as]
public affairs."[23] Together these siblings "preside over trusts said to be
worth at least $500 million."[24]

Their uncle Paul Mellon, Andrew W. Mellon's son, is the wealthiest
living member of the Mellon family. In 1988, *Forbes* estimated his net worth
at over $850 million. During the years when his father was in government
service, Paul Mellon attended boarding school at Choate Rosemary Hall and
then went to Yale University.[25]

In 1926, Paul's sister, Ailsa, married David K. E. Bruce, who was later
to become ambassador to four countries.[26] She had "finished" at Miss
Porter's School and served as a hostess for her father in Washington, D.C.
Bruce was also "born to wealth and power;" his father was a U.S. senator.
The couple were eventually divorced in 1945. "Working out the separation
. . . was staggeringly complex because of the extent to which their tremendous interests had in fact become merged."[27] Ailsa took pride in her
"philanthropies and her art collection, much of which she donated to the
National Gallery of Art."[28]

After college, Paul "floated into and out of family businesses." Today he
"collects art on a giant scale."[29] In spite of his generous philanthropic gifts,
his wealth has more than tripled during his long lifetime. From 1979 to
1985, he was chair of the National Gallery of Art, to which he contributed
at least a third of the $94.4 million it cost to build the new East Wing.
"He also donated 93 objects of art worth up to $1 million dollars each to
the gallery." He gave over $18 million in cash and art to Yale University's
Center for British Art, in addition to establishing the Paul Mellon Arts
Center at his prep school, Choate.[30]

After their father's death in 1937, Paul Mellon and his sister each created
foundations. When Ailsa died, "she left the bulk of her estate, valued at
$570 million, to the Avalon Foundation,"[31] which later "merged with the
Old Dominion Foundation, and [was] renamed The Andrew W. Mellon

Foundation in 1969.'' Paul's son Timothy sits on the board of trustees of this national independent foundation in New York City. It is valued at almost $1.5 billion.[32]

Fourth-generation Catherine Mellon Conover and her younger brother Timothy each inherited $100 million trusts from their grandfather. ''Conservatively invested, each should be worth $225 million.'' Catherine lives in Washington, D.C. She contributes to environmental issues in the Rocky Mountain region,[33] and has been described as an ''anti-war activist.''[34]

After graduating from Yale, Timothy Mellon, who resides in New Hampshire, established a computer programming company. Several years later he co-founded a firm to pressure-treat railroad ties, and ''acquired Guilford Transportation for $50 million.''[35] He is the donor and president of the Sachem Fund in Washington, D.C., and ''reportedly has long been involved with energy conservation, ecology, and human rights.''[36]

I have dealt at length on the history of the Mellon family because it illustrates various forms of family and philanthropic dynasty formation at both the national and local levels. Members of upper-class families may either cooperate or clash. For example, the Scaife side of the Mellon family is at odds. Siblings Richard and Cordelia are reportedly not on speaking terms. The children of Sarah Mellon Scaife fund different, often opposite types of causes ranging from conservative to liberal. But each of them is rich enough to have substantial personal power.

Those who disassociate themselves from direct involvement in family financial affairs in order to increase their civic and philanthropic activities still benefit, of course, from the income produced by the family's wealth. In the Mellon family, by late in the life of the second generation there was enough surplus for one branch of the family to move into politics and national affairs while other members ran the family banking and corporate interests in Pittsburgh.

Two generations of Mellons, starting with Andrew Mellon, built the National Gallery of Art; their personal collections formed the initial core of this outstanding public museum. Paul Mellon's children are philanthropists and business people. As is typical of male heirs, Timothy Mellon shows a renewed interest in entrepreneurship. It is quite possible for fortunes to be increased, or remade, thus starting a new cycle of dynasty.

The other side of the family has mostly remained in the Pittsburgh region, maintaining its dynastic control by consolidating business matters in the investment firm at Richard K. Mellon and Sons (which is now run by Seward Prosser Mellon) and concentrating its philanthropy in the Richard K.

Mellon Foundation, which is overseen by both Richard Prosser Mellon and his brother, Seward.

In strong dynastic families, the course of development generally runs toward a corporate structure like that of the Pittsburgh Mellons. A "family office" is frequently the center of family decision making, especially when there is more than one heir. Pooled resources are invested in diversified concerns, both financial and charitable. A few male heirs may be closely engaged with family business matters, especially if the family company is still intact. But most inheritors choose careers in philanthropic and public life.

Literally and figuratively, the family offices can rarely hold more than a few relatives, each of whom may want individual control. Many members of the family who are not entrepreneurs are members of the culture of philanthropy and depend on those in the family office to build, organize, and protect the family's wealth.[37] Financial activities are not usually directed by heirs, unless one of them, like Seward Mellon, is especially suited to business. The decision to keep family assets together may break down in future generations depending on the interests, skills, and situation of the heirs.

Institutionalized philanthropy is an important aspect of the perpetuation of dynasty. Endowed foundations may last into perpetuity, carrying on the family name if not the family interests. Relatives of the founder usually sit on the board for several generations. More than a handful of foundations were created by the turn-of-the-century Mellon fortune. Three of them, as shown in the chart of selected Mellon philanthropies (figure 4.2), are among the one hundred largest in the country.[38] Foundations remove capital from certain types of taxation but often leave it under the control of heirs active in the culture of philanthropy.

Only one Mellon grant-making organization—the Andrew W. Mellon Foundation, which is ranked ninth in size among all foundations in the country—is national in scope. Fourth-generation heir Timothy serves on the board of this foundation and has his own, much smaller foundation as well. Both the eighteenth-ranked Richard King Mellon and eighty-second-ranked Sarah Scaife foundations are still largely family-controlled and local in distribution, with third- and fourth-generation Mellon descendants serving as chairs.[39]

The private foundation may be viewed as a symbol of family dynasty,[40] implying that the family has reached a stage where it can easily give money away. In some cases the personal wealth has not grown, but a foundation continues a family ethos and gives relatives meaningful work. Legally no one

FIGURE 4.2
Selected Mellon Family Philanthropies

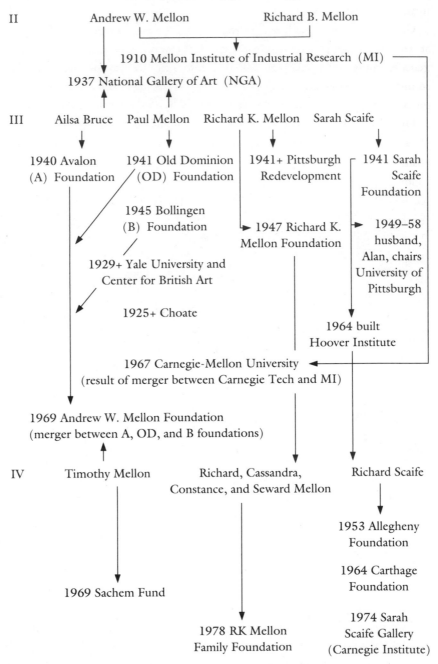

in the founding family or on the board of trustees may benefit financially from the activities of a foundation, but the accumulation of wealth in this form is in itself valued.

Generally, by the third generation, a private foundation has paid staff and at least a few individuals outside the family serving on the board. Over generations, control tends gradually to shift from the family to professional administrators.[41] However, even when wealth has declined, foundations often go on funding family interests.

Dynasties are cyclic. They are typically most stable in the third generation of wealth. Individuals of that generation are more confident about their position in the world than their parents were or their children and grandchildren will be. In the second, fourth, and fifth generations in particular, the wealthy tend to harbor a great deal of ambivalence about their standing. Second-generation inheritors are caught in the transition between new and old money, although there is probably more money at this stage. They compare themselves to the father who made the fortune and fear that they may not measure up. But they also look at those with old money and worry that their money is not old enough.[42]

In this and the next three chapters, I present composites of the people interviewed for this study. This method of presentation does not reveal the identities of study participants but allows a closer look at patterns and nuances of beliefs and behavior. The personal features and life experiences are factual and realistic. They have been combined from the accounts of several people who are similar in age and gender and, except where indicated, the same generation removed from the family's original wealth. At least one and usually several individuals have each of the attributes reported in a composite vignette. They were selected for presentation because of common activities, outlook, and philosophy. I use actual quotations from these people, but in any one composite several different study participants are quoted with remarks representative of a number of the individuals in the group. Pseudonyms were invented for each of the composite characters.

The following four composites are characteristic of philanthropists with old money. Though their age, generation, gender, and personal experience vary, their background and behavior are remarkably similar. All of them refer to a family tradition of giving. All attribute at least part of their philanthropic values to religious training, three in Protestant denominations and one as a Jew. They followed the "class curriculum"[43] by attending private nonprofit schools and cultural functions. Family foundations played a role in their socialization as philanthropists and, except in the last generation, continue to be a major vehicle for their giving.

SECOND-GENERATION MIDDLE-AGED MAN

I had a father who worked very hard, [was] very successful, and simply passed on the need to do as much public service work as I [could]. So, that's what's going on. I may have been very different if I had had to earn all of this myself. My personal interests are in education, primarily at the university level. I am also involved in activities related to the performing arts, and health.

Unlike his two older brothers, who went into the family business, David Stein graduated from Harvard University in the late 1950s and spent the next fifteen years running the foundation established by his father.[44] After a brief stint in Congress, he went back to a philanthropic career. Although he is in charge of the foundation, he considers it a family endeavor.

This composite shows how many second-generation heirs can promote dynasty without direct involvement in the family company or other strictly economic pursuits.[45] In Stein's case, he chose a personal occupational niche that combines politics and philanthropy. Because of his wealth, he does not need a salaried position, yet he wants to work. By redirecting family giving from a local to a national scale and having served in Congress, he has gained national prominence for his family.

Like many inheritors of his generation, Stein is "giving" his way into higher society. He is typical in his hearty endorsement of an interrelated capitalist and philanthropic ideology; he sees himself as an expert on charitable donations and supports individual decision making in this area. He comments on the mixed motives of philanthropists in general but stops short of admitting that his own motives are not altogether altruistic.

I interviewed him in the conference room on the top floor of his family's company, whose executive offices were similar in atmosphere to those of other corporations I had visited. The carpeting was plush, the furniture elegant but utilitarian, and the view spectacular. Stein was wearing a well-tailored gray suit and a paisley tie. After our meeting, he took me to see his collection of black-and-white photographs by a famous artist.

Stein inherited substantial capital, and he has become more deeply involved in his own philanthropy as his income has increased. "I decided to spend my time on the appropriate use of my inherited wealth, and less time in the management of it.'' His family's net worth is estimated at $200 million, although he did not comment on his share. As the full-time administrator of the family foundation, Stein changed the grant-making focus from local programs in New York City to national and international issues. This reflected his personal interests and politics.

When he was in his late thirties, Stein made a successful bid for a seat in Congress, which he held for two terms. Today about 20 percent of his income goes to political causes. He spends half his time on politics and half on philanthropy, giving and raising money for organizations he endorses: ''I've sat on every nonprofit board in town. . . . Recently, the pace seems to have quickened.''

As a professional giver Stein told us that he divides his philanthropy into four categories:

> One, those things that are pure philanthropy, meaning taking care of the sick, aged, helping of one sort or another. That would be giving money to a hospital or to a community center or something of that sort.
>
> Another would be . . . institutional philanthropy—giving money to Harvard, the Council on Foreign Relations, or whatever.
>
> The third category is religious. Being Jewish, it would be to a Hebrew home for the aged . . . to Israel in the gray area of what may or may not be religious.
>
> Then there is another area of civic work I still try to encourage. Let's say the restoration of the Statue of Liberty, giving money to a museum.

He and his family give out of a sense of obligation, what he calls ''self-tithing.'' His brothers have a similar perspective, but they spend less time than he does on nonprofit causes.

Stein elaborated on the family tradition.

> This goes back as far as our memory of the family, through my great-grandfather and beyond, when we were not wealthy people, as we are now. There was always a tradition of involvement in community affairs. The earliest record we have of the family is in the 1850s. As a matter of fact, the family arrived in America in 1870, already having been involved in voluntary charity groups. And it was continuous.

When his father set up his business, the principles of the company included ''a basic obligation to humankind to share the benefits of the system in which we live.'' The Steins follow both a family and a Jewish tradition, and their sense of social responsibility applies to business endeavors as well.

Stein discussed his father's views on philanthropy. ''It was important to him to leave the foundation behind.'' The foundation is worth almost $30 million, owing partly to money from his father's estate and partly to gains in securities. His father, Stein said, wanted the foundation to perpetuate his name and lifestyle and also to "serve as the focus of the family, some nucleus that we can get around and all have in common." These motives for forming a foundation are extremely typical. The picture Stein presents of his father is that of an active businessman, a mover and shaker in town. "He never considered himself a politician, but he felt that he had a civic obligation."

Although he does not characterize his father as a philanthropist or politician, the younger Stein believes he is following a path that his father charted.

> It's a responsibility to deal out the money in an intelligent way. And it's also a responsibility to deal with the family situation in an intelligent way. Somebody's got to do it. And one of the kicks I get out of it is that it helps me become more central to my family, which is important to me. It makes me a better uncle and so forth.

Stein is clear about his desire for authority. He referred to the sense of "power that goes along with all this" and continued: "I guess there is a feeling of being courted, you know." In the interview, he did not explicitly make a connection between his philanthropic and political ambitions.

Although he does not control the family business, Stein does want the family philanthropy to continue beyond his lifetime. "I don't have long-term plans, but I have it in my head that this foundation should pass onto the next generation." His nieces and nephews have been brought onto the foundation board. "They are really interested, and they are looking forward to inheriting."

Stein was not old enough to serve in World War II, but he remembers it well. He was in college during the Cold War, and is similar to others of his age, generation, and nationality in lauding the American business system and endorsing the ideology of the nonprofit sector. He said: "We are beneficiaries of the system of free enterprise and capitalism, which enables us to have these principles . . . [and] to live well. . . . Beyond that, we have an obligation to help." He views himself as a "beneficiary" rather than an active capitalist.

Philanthropy has been his life avocation, and he was well-informed and thoughtful in talking about these matters. He was critical of the emphasis on foundations in my research.

> I think the rather broader and more important subject is volunteerism in this country. . . . From my point of view, this is much more valuable than giving money. Volunteerism has been deeply an American enterprise. . . . All over the

world, countries [and people] have marveled at the ability of Americans to get themselves together with little direction from above and organize themselves to meet some particular community need.

In fact, volunteerism is currently Stein's full-time pursuit. Giving his time motivates him more than donating money. But his vision is a delusion. Because Stein is wealthy he has the luxury of being a full-time volunteer.

Stein fears that volunteerism is becoming a thing of the past. He said, "There is very much less of that in this day and age. There is a lot more spending with money, especially through foundations, who I don't think for the most part spend very wisely." Yet this is exactly what he does.

Stein believes that generosity depends on the individual. But he does not have a clear idea about why people give and points to their mixed motives. Nor does he have a comprehensive theory about philanthropy, but he generally believes that "good" prevails whatever an individual's motives might be. For example, he said:

> I know some people who inherited a lot of money. They're very rich, and they're just as tough to get money out of as somebody who's made it quick. On the other hand, I can think of different situations, too, precisely the reverse, where there are some terribly generous people who are both self-made and have inherited money. So much of it is an attitude.

What he calls an "attitude" I see as variations of response or behavior within a culture. Stein took the old-money curriculum, and is helping to transform his family from new- to old-money status. He especially admires the leading families of the culture of philanthropy.

> You read about the Rockefellers. I don't know firsthand, but they act as though somebody must have told them because they've done it as a family . . . pretty doggone well. . . . They have had this tremendous urge to support the public sector, and do some things that count.

He thinks that "people give to charity because they want to help." But he does not stress altruistic motives as much as self-serving ones for other philanthropists.

> I'm sure they want to be well thought of in the communities where they live. I think the economic incentives are often overplayed because there is some notion that somehow you get wealthy and make money by giving people charity. You don't. . . .

There are obviously the secondary gains: respect and social status. But, I think it really is, for most of us, secondary. Obviously, there are those who like to buy their way to social acceptability by making charitable contributions. I can also add that I don't really think it matters why somebody gives.

This last statement reveals Stein's uneasiness. Often, when people talk about others they are actually referring to themselves. Stein wants to be "well thought of," but he also understands the "economic incentives" of philanthropy. He magnifies his first statement by adding that "respect and social status" are outcomes of giving. He includes "buying your way into social acceptability." And he concludes the thought with a rationalization. It does not matter why a person gives.

Stein elaborated with a curious drowning fable that vividly embodies images of power.

> Think of the man who saves another man from drowning. [He] doesn't save the other from drowning because he knew there was going to be a reward. . . . A life got saved. . . . What was he going to do? Let the man drown because the reason for saving him might have been one that was not socially good?

He places himself or any philanthropist in a very powerful position when he imagines saving someone's life.

He continued his musing with references to well-known philanthropists of historic and current time.

> I think the record is pretty clear that the really great benefactions in the history of the world were made by those whose motives, at least in making the money, were not the motives that you and I might choose. The Medicis were hardly what you would call pillars of the community, except they literally wrote the rules of the community and wrote themselves at the top of it. And so most of the big fortunes that have been the backbone of philanthropy in this half of the century— the Rockefellers and the Mellons and so forth. For whatever reasons they recognize the importance for selfish reasons of having a better community around them. One way to do this is to choose to give at least part of their money for charitable purposes.

Stein's own mixed motives are apparent in these quotations, although he was not able to come right out and say that his own involvement in philanthropy is complex. This interpretation is reinforced when he repeats himself later in the interview by saying, "Philanthropy is a way of buying into acceptable society."

THIRD-GENERATION MIDDLE-AGED WOMAN

> They look to our family to do most of the stuff around here in the most
> charitable manner. . . . We look to it as the company family will look to
> take care of their people. . . . Our family has traditionally felt their obliga-
> tions. That's the way the foundation is set up, to perpetuate responsibility
> of the family to the area.

All of her life Caroline Stockton has played traditional roles and met her
family's expectations. She has been a good daughter, mother, philanthropist,
volunteer, and wife.[46] Stockton and her husband live in the South. Both of
them come from "leading" families in their area. Wealthy families are often
rooted in a particular town and have a history of responding to charitable,
civic, and cultural affairs of that community.

Caroline Stockton is an avid proponent of the nonprofit sector. Like David
Stein, she thinks that a well-informed person of wealth is in the best position
to make good decisions about which organizations deserve funding. But she
has the weight of an extra generation of wealth behind her that Stein does
not. She is confident about her cultural responsibilities, and does not question
them as much. She inherited a large foundation that gives regionally. The
foundation takes up most of her time. She enjoys the authority that this
work confers upon her. She is especially cognizant of the need to pass
philanthropy down to her children.

Stockton chose to be interviewed at her home. It is located in an affluent
part of town, but the lot and house are neither huge nor imposing. A black
servant, in uniform, was working quietly in the the kitchen while we talked.
I glimpsed this woman when I arrived, but she was not spoken to, or of,
during my stay. The living room was decorated with formal, highly polished
furniture. The walls were adorned with oil and watercolor landscapes.

The Stocktons administer several family foundations. She is primarily
responsible for the larger staffed foundation that her mother established. She
explained that the foundation was initially set up to help build the community.

> So many people, it seems to me, have had their sights set on things that were
> happening up North and wanted to emulate educational organizations, libraries,
> museums, musical activity, which were going on there.

She endorses the idea of promoting "culture" in her region and plans to
follow her mother's example by leaving her money to the foundation. She
is, by others' accounts, a lady bountiful of the community. She explained

that she is on the board of a local hospital, but "that's something the foundation funds." In addition, she is a trustee of the private college she attended.

Conscious of the importance of heritage, Stockton traces her philanthropic impulse back to her childhood. Early memories of church stand out in her mind.

> When I was a little girl growing up . . . I had wonderful times with all my friends at various clubs and church activities that had wonderful things for young people. I remember, particularly, that for a couple of years I was in the choir. . . .
>
> I remember being so struck by the minister and his wife and their five children. They were wonderful people. One time I came in and there was a blackboard up and it listed the budget of the church for the year. This was in 1943, '42, '41, I don't know, but somewhere in that time. His salary for the year was something like $2,500—with all those children! Of course, they [the church] gave him a house, but I remember thinking what wonderful people they are to give so much of themselves. Mrs. Minister was as much involved in the church as the minister was. I cannot remember their names, but I remember being so struck by the goodness and the giving of these people, and how little they had at the time. Maybe it was $2,000. It was such a small amount of money for children in high school and college, even in those days. . . . There were wonderful people like that that made me very aware of what it is like to sacrifice and give.

Her memory has provided her with a powerful fantasy of comparison to the poor, struggling, and selfless. Here, without saying it, she was surely comparing her circumstances to that of the minister's family. She lived in a big house, and though money was not discussed she somehow knew that the pastor's salary was low.

Most of us have fantasies about our childhoods. This particular memory might have served as a lesson in reality for Stockton, that other people had far less than she and her family. It might have made her more sensitive to the plight of the poor.

> I don't think I thought too much more about it until we got married and started a family . . . and started our own giving. But, it became very important to me to be able to share the advantages that I had in some way.
>
> And now I am so fortunate. I have just had the most wonderful things happen to me, and the most marvelous experiences with the people in the foundation, the people who come to our foundation for grants, the people I have met doing wonderful things in the world. It is so thrilling to me, to be able to help.

Again, as in the Stein case, Stockton purports to believe that wealth just happened to her. She is clearly conscious of her class position, but she never refers to it directly.

Stockton has found meaning in her life through her foundation activities, and this is especially true now that her children are grown. She spoke about them a great deal throughout the interview. They have graduated from college. One of them still lives in the South. The two others have left the area, but they are both philanthropists in their own right. Her older daughter is active in a ''progressive'' foundation in the West, formed by a group of wealthy young people.

> We were very anxious to imbue our children with this kind of feeling [about philanthropy and foundations]. So now our daughter is on the ——— Foundation [the larger long-standing family foundation]. Our son is on the foundation named for me, which my husband set up. . . . You don't like to push [the children] too much, else they feel that they are supposed to be just like us. I don't think that is a very good idea. But, I noticed that on her own she [daughter] contributed to Ethiopian relief.

Stockton indicated that the smaller foundation was established specifically to encourage her children to learn to give, to socialize them to their class ''responsibilities.''

> It was an effort to get our children involved in my gift giving. . . . We wanted a vehicle which the children could make decisions about. . . . We wanted the children from the time they were quite young to become interested and accustomed to being responsible in giving money away. Now, this was when they were still in high school and college.

Foundations, especially the smaller ones of the type she describes, may emerge as playthings, boredom breakers, or even genteel instruments of revolution. A few million dollars is put aside for the children, with tax breaks for the parents. Although never presented in this light by the wealthy themselves, such foundations also teach young upper-class adults, in a tangible way, how to become powerful through philanthropy.

Stockton rather proudly recounted an episode about her elder daughter.

> In the '60s, during high school years, my daughter was going to boarding school. She and some of her friends came home. They, of course, were at the tail end of the '60s, [and believed] you know, 'This world's a terrible place' and so on. . . . It was interesting because they were complaining about all these things—don't we all? But, it began to sound a little serious, so I said, ''The thing for you all to do is talk to trustees.''

> So one day I had my foundation material. . . . I had this little notebook with about 100 summaries of organizations for a particular project. . . . I brought out this notebook and I said, "Girls, there are people trying to do something about all these problems in the world. And they are all in the nonprofit community." So, they pored over this book of proposal summaries. And I think that's how they got interested . . . because they discovered, as I said, "They're asking us for grants?"

Wealth gives people the sense that they can marshal change in the direction they desire. It also allows them to define what are and what are not problems.

Orienting her children toward philanthropy was particularly important to Caroline Stockton because of her wish that she herself had had such training when she was young. "We didn't talk a whole lot about philanthropy, because it was considered sort of appropriate not to." Her family did not discuss their charitable activities, but she knew she was expected to become a volunteer leader in the community.

She explained: "We [her siblings and she] were all put on [the foundation board] as lifetime members as soon as we became twenty-one. So we were introduced to philanthropy at a very young age." She worried, however, that it may not have been soon enough.

> Everyone that comes on the foundation, I can tell you, knows nothing about sophisticated philanthropy. And you don't learn overnight. You can't read a book. There's no how-to. It takes a long time.

I asked her to tell me what she meant by "sophisticated philanthropy." And she replied:

> My definition of that would be running a professional organization. Obviously you need a staff, but the board members should participate to a large extent. The board members should spend plenty of time on the outside learning more about all there is out there to which the grants may go at some time. Not leaving it all up to staff. Plenty of foundations are run that way, but then the board is just rubber-stamping the staff. . . . I don't call that sophisticated.

Like Stein, Stockton stresses personal contact and involvement. The activities she prescribes for board members, like proposal review and site visits in addition to meetings, are such that they consume large amounts of time and are therefore easier for those without such commitments as a paid job.

These are the kinds of roles that wealthy philanthropists, both women and men, have created for themselves. They are also part of a more general tendency in the foundation field, as in the professions, to routinize duties of staff and trustees.[47] A professional cadre masks the control that the elite in most foundations continue to exercise over the grant-making process.

Later in the interview Stockton commented: "I think all of us—and I can speak for all of us, my husband and my children—we all want to be able to make the decisions ourselves."

Stockton values her staff, but she is critical of certain philanthropic operations.

> I think advisers can be influential to a fault in some small foundations—where people have left foundations [to] some trust department of their bank—where some attorney just sort of gives to a bunch of scholarships every year in order not to be bothered.

She does admit that professionals "can keep you on the straight path, keep you out of trouble." She praised a longtime foundation employee in this regard.

> It was the businessman, the thoughtful, personal businessman [in the family office], who kept the foundation from being a routine kind of thing. And mother thought so much of him, and knew he was a very dedicated, very religious man. And she knew that anything he said was well thought out.

It sounds as though her mother had been socialized into a semi-dependent relationship with the family adviser.

Third-generation Stockton is not so sanguine about the advice of retainers: "I think that attorneys can be coldly involved, and they can cut down on the compassion of the foundation." In a similar way, professionals may also threaten the domain of charity, which in upper-class families is often controlled by women.

THIRD-GENERATION ELDERLY MAN

> Going back many years, I guess our family, which is made up of three families, started from my grandparents. . . . We were the principal foundation in the county.

"As long as I can remember, the family has been doing good works," said Jonathon Clifford, a man in his eighties, the eldest grandson of Western pioneers and the current patriarch of his family's fortune.[48] This composite illustrates the basic principles of noblesse oblige.

Clifford speaks of his elite but modest and trustful family working together on behalf of their community and employees. But in his account inconsistencies emerge. He claims that his family established a foundation to "give back" to the community, but the Cliffords decide what to give and where. They determine what constitutes "good works." As in most instances of noblesse oblige, the employees or townspeople have little voice in decision making.

The interview was conducted at the Clifford family office, a modern, one-story structure nestled in a grove of trees. I announced myself to a receptionist. The casually dressed Clifford came out to greet me, offered a warm handshake, and we walked a short distance to his spacious private library and office. The high-backed wing chairs were upholstered in deep brown leather. The bookcases along all walls were interrupted only by windows. There were books of every size, many of them leather bound, displayed in the cases along with small cast sculptures. Through some architectural and landscaping feat, it seemed as if we were protected, safe, in the center of the grove. Sunlight filtered through the swaying branches all around, and through skylights in the ceiling.

> It's just bred in us that you put something back. God or whatever has been pretty good to us, and the people of the area have been good to us, and we have got to pay our dues. . . . That's the attitude of our family and always has been.

He continued: "We confine our contributions to this area that's made us wealthy as a family, to say thank you and to do something for the people who really don't have many places to go when they need help."

In both the Stockton and Clifford cases, the family business has been one of the largest in the area, and the family are the local elite. Many inheritors feel obligated to practice philanthropy in the region where their wealth was created, speaking of a desire to solve serious social problems and to "give back" to the community. Such expressions of social responsibility indicate that some rich people do recognize they have their wealth at the expense of others. Clifford himself is clearly aware of the economic inequality in his region. But most wealthy people in the United States, especially elite philanthropists, do not want to own up to their class power.

For the Cliffords and others, the perspective and expectation of gift giving and return have a religious basis. "Give, and it will be given to you; good measure, pressed down, shaken together, running over, will be put into your lap. For the measure you give will be the measure you get back."[49] The value of charitable donations is practiced and taught in churches and temples around the country, which rely on and encourage contributions.

Dynasty and Philanthropy

Clifford has retired as chair and chief executive officer of the family businesses. Before doing so he sold a large part of the business to a *Fortune 500* corporation. He sits on the board of that now-parent company, an arrangement which was negotiated as part of the takeover deal, although he is thinking of getting off soon.

In addition to personal and company giving, the Clifford family has several charitable trusts, but the center of their philanthropy is a $15 million foundation.

> The foundation was started by my father at the time of my grandfather's death . . . primarily to help ex-employees and their families, because in those days we did not have a pension, nothing like that, no organized effort. . . . We had all of these employees, so we made small checks monthly to them and that was allowed in those days. It wasn't adequate in a sense, but it was a good step. It was a great thing in those days.

It was also classic paternalism. The original foundation board consisted of "my father, two uncles and later an aunt and myself. . . . You know, we have never been much on titles because anybody's ideas would be accepted and listened to." However, anybody who was listened to had to be in the family.

> The whole ethos has been the family matter. I guess now the fifth generation is there [on the foundation board]. Remember, this was a device to maintain our charitable obligations. And the charitable obligations would be undertaken by family members, as always.

The corpus of the Clifford Foundation has been supplemented over the years by contributions of individual family members and the estate of Clifford's aunt. Here again, he emphasized the religion and humble lifestyle of the donor. Many rich families have these kinds of stories, because it makes them seem, or helps them to believe that their backgrounds are just like those of everybody else.

> My Aunt Edith was a wonderful Christian woman. She was a widow, and had been for many years. I don't believe Aunt Edith spent three hundred dollars a month. She had a comfortable house. My father made her get a decent car. She thought, as did all of the family at that time, that it was sinful to spend money on yourself. She wasn't a freak or anything. She just thought it was wasteful. . . .
>
> One day, when Aunt Edith was getting on—I guess she was about seventy— she was riding back from town with me and I asked her, I said, "Aunt Edith, have you thought about what you are going to do with your wealth when you inevitably pass away?"

And she said, "Ohhh, I don't like to talk about money."

And I said, "Whether you like to talk about it or not, you are a very wealthy person and you really ought to give some thought to it."

She said, "Well, all of it came from the company [that her father started] and I just want to give it back to the company."

Aunt Edith did not consider the money her own; it belonged to the company. The younger Clifford urged her to think of it as "the people's money."

I said, "Aunt Edith, you don't do that. Don't you mean you would really like to put it in a trust or something that would help the people who worked for the company, the neighbors who lived on our land. . . . Aren't you really thinking you would like to do something like that?"

She said, "That's what I would like to do."

So we merged it into the Clifford Family Foundation. Now she made several significant contributions to it during her lifetime. Other members of the family including myself have made contributions to it.

We adopted the principle (it is not in writing except as a guideline) that we would confine our activities to this area where we are dominant landowners, where we have an effect on almost everything that happens. We use it for all sorts of good work.

But they do not give it to the people directly, or even give the larger community any control over its distribution.

When the foundation got larger, a few individuals outside the family were put on the board. Clifford explained:

Well, we have always had more or less somebody outside of the family in the sense that they were not family members but they were usually very close associates and friends of ours. They usually worked with us.

These other trustees are presumably like-minded types and professionals, not the workers in the family company.

Today, the foundation makes contributions to museums and libraries, a leading hospital, and several community organizations in the county. "Our principal interest at the moment is to provide for the needy through organized [or legitimate by their standards] activity that exists already. There has been a great need in the last couple of years. . . ."

The foundation provides "matching grants" to many of these groups, "on the theory that if local people are willing to sacrifice for it, it is pretty good evidence that it's worthwhile." They have also teamed up with another major funder to work on economic development. "We did that with the caveat that it would be spent on a project in this state."

"I think in the future we are going to do more research which may benefit the general good." When asked what had led to this decision, Clifford said, "The fact that we have got so damn much money now. You know, with returns on investments as high as they are now, we probably have more money than we can give away in a [systematic] manner."

At one point Clifford paused and waxed philosophical.

> I don't know, if you want to look back on it, I'm not sure. Maybe it was an ego trip too. Having a foundation in your name is appealing. I never even thought of that, but I can maybe be honest about it now.

Later he used the word *vanity* in connection with his philanthropy. (Many of those interviewed began by giving only pat answers to our questions but as the interview progressed became more thoughtful and frank.)

Clifford serves on several nonprofit boards, both within and outside of his region. He has long been associated with a private boarding school in the East, "where I went to school. I'm retiring. I've been on too many years. I'm too old." He is a director of the art museum in the closest big city, "where I've got an interest."

> But in the last seven or eight years we have given in that area [the arts]. . . . So many of our employees benefit from being near [the city], which is a cultural center. And some of the bigger corporations were supporting it. We felt left out. You see, they wouldn't help us over here. They were very short sighted.

Here Clifford seeks a justification for giving funds outside the region. Apparently, although he does not consider his own strong personal interest in the arts a legitimate enough reason for giving company funds, promoting "culture" for employees is a different matter.

Clifford recalled that he supports several other nonprofit organizations outside his area. In certain years his personal donation to his alma mater, Princeton, "is top on their list." He has established several charitable trusts that benefit Princeton until his grandchildren are older, when the corpus will come to them. "Meanwhile, Princeton can use it." He said he chose the trust vehicle primarily because he did not want to spoil his grandchildren at an early age with all that money. With the types of trusts he mentioned, it is likely that the fortune will pass on to his grandchildren tax free.

Clifford wants to be sure that his estate is in order before he dies and that his heirs will pay as little in taxes as possible. He was obviously nervous and somewhat preoccupied about these matters. This was probably on account of his advanced age, which he mentioned several times, as well as an upcoming appointment with the estate attorney. (Such family retainers are often responsible for devising and implementing these objectives, and sometimes for protecting "the founder's legacy from divisive family quarrels.")[50]

Clifford then returned to the discussion of his philanthropic donations. "I give quite a few contributions to colleges." But, he claimed: "It doesn't thrill me to give money to Yale, or even Harvard." (Here, as a Princeton man, he was teasing me because he knew I was doing research at Yale.) He is a trustee of another elite but non–Ivy League university, and he takes great pride in that appointment. "I've given them a little money, but I went on the board with the understanding that I wasn't going to give anything." However, his name on the board list lent credibility for the institution's fundraisers, and Clifford brokers gifts from other wealthy people.

Clifford contributes to his political interests both inside and outside the state, but he refused to be specific about the beneficiaries. In response to a direct question, he indicated that he had made a grant to the Heritage Foundation in Washington, D.C., a policy think tank influential with the Reagan and Bush administrations. "I do give money to conservative causes. Not always conservative—something I believe in."

Clifford seemed to me to be quite a savvy individual, much more than the "old country boy" image he projected. He is, after all, a very influential power broker. He is on the board of at least one *Fortune* 500 corporation, an elite university, and a prestigious arts organization. He funds successful conservative causes. And these are only the things he told me about. He may have thought that I wanted to hear how the family was serving the poor in the county, acting out a scenario of noblesse oblige.

FOURTH-GENERATION YOUNG WOMAN

> I personally learned from my family the value of giving, because they were regular philanthropic supporters of the community. . . . My family has traditionally given away substantial amounts of money. I assumed the values of supporting the local church, hospital, and so on—the cultural and civic responsibilities. I was raised with basic values that one gives away, is both responsive to one's community and supports it with one's wealth. . . . I inherited that from my family.

Jane Bennett is a thirty-four-year-old woman of wealth.[51] She is characteristic of the philanthropic "rich kids," who grew up in the 1960s and

1970s, feel uneasy about their wealth, and are politically progressive. They begin by giving to such traditional nonprofit institutions as their prep schools and colleges but eventually look for other kinds of causes to support. They are keenly aware of inequality and seek out projects that attempt to empower the oppressed. Through their commitment and gift giving they are also searching for a sense of their own identity.

Bennett inherited a substantial fortune when she turned twenty-one. While growing up, she had known that she and her siblings had trust funds that had been established by their grandfather. She understood little about them, however, and was not fully prepared to deal with either the psychological or fiscal realities of her wealth. "I did not know what I was doing, to be honest. I think there must be an awful lot of wealthy people who turn of age and don't have a clue as to what they are doing." She continued:

> It just horrified me, the amount of money. I don't remember how much money it was, for one thing. The other [issue was] how much I was supposed to give away. I just kept forgetting the totals, the subtotals, and everything. I was in shock. But the people in the family office just kept nudging me on.

Her family is a large shareholder in several business enterprises as well as having a prominent family-owned company. The family's financial interests, other investments, and philanthropy are managed by the family office, which is staffed by several accountants and lawyers and a full-time philanthropic adviser.

Bennett explained:

> Well, there is the legal person, and there's somebody who does my financial investment, and there are a number of people. . . . There is a person in the family business, which is the same office as the charitable funds, who is an accountant and a lawyer. He has grown enormously in the job, and has double the experience or training [that I do]. So, I consult him on philanthropic matters. This adviser, Arthur, has been working for the family for several years.

Before she inherited her money, Bennett had never needed to deal directly with the family office. In her youth she had simply approached her parents if she wanted funds. She felt timid about the professional retainers, although she had been acquainted with Arthur for some time. She viewed him as her father's friend.

> I wasn't willing to ask questions, or I didn't know the questions to ask. I was nervous to ask the more personal questions about the family situation. I knew that the money came from my family, so I felt a sense of obligation that it wasn't my money, personally. . . . And the money is tied up in certain ways.

Thus it took her several years to begin thinking of the money as hers and to assume control of decision making.

When her trust matured, Bennett was attending a Seven Sisters college, where her mother had also gone. "When I first started giving it was to scholarship kinds of things, because I was still in school." The family's philanthropic adviser suggested that she might begin by donating to her prep school. "We give to all our schools because we feel that they need our support and they helped us to get to where we are today."

After her graduation Bennett volunteered to raise funds for her college, and was disappointed by a lack of response on the part of her peers. Only half of the thirty alumnae to whom she wrote gave money, and none made contributions larger than fifty dollars each. In contrast, she was in a position to donate a sizable gift, and was encouraged to do so by the family advisers because of her tax situation. "We gave a large amount to ———, because my Mom and I went there, in both our names, but they decided how much to give."

Bennett was gradually beginning to understand that her wealth was far greater than that of most of her affluent classmates and peers. At first, she did not want to admit to the disparity and attributed it to a difference in values. She was critical of her local friends, who she thought were "such conspicuous spenders. They seemed to spend and spend. And everyone went out. They belonged to clubs, whether it was a health club or a country club. They all drove nice cars, but they did not think to give to community organizations." To her, they were the "other rich." She had been taught to display less and be less visible. She felt conflicted about her privilege, and began searching for some meaning in her life.

Not only was Bennett's wealth growing, but she also knew she would inherit a large portion of her parents' estate when they died. Her charitable funding in the mid-1970s was not public because she was embarrassed by her money.

> I was totally anonymous as a donor, and I didn't want anybody to know that I had anything to do with it. So I didn't want to go out and investigate all these different projects, because then people would wonder why that was happening. But I was getting increasingly uncomfortable giving large sums of money to projects that hadn't really been investigated by anybody. So, I was getting kind of stymied. At just about that time I started talking to [another wealthy young person].

Bennett was trying to find her place in the world, but her wealth still confused her. There seemed to be no one to talk with about her situation, and she was richer than everyone she knew, until she met another wealthy, young, politically conscious person. Although they came from different parts of the country, their personal circumstances were similar.

He had participated in "alternative" funding projects with other wealthy heirs in another city, and was organizing a similar group in the town where they lived. Bennett recounted her experience in the group that he formed.

> People who had inherited wealth became aware of themselves and each other, and the phenomena, and the embarrassment of inheriting wealth in a society in which money was the thing. If you had money you had power.
> I was born with what everybody else wants.
> I went through an interesting psychological self-awareness in recognizing that money isn't what makes one happy. . . . Often the very things that give financial security cut off a feeling of warmth and love and the emotional side of being close to people—outside of the family.

It was a new experience for her to talk openly with other young people of means about issues that bothered them. She had never felt she could be totally candid before, because she did not want to disclose her wealth. Along with her new peers, Bennett was able to recognize and identify her money as one of her difficulties.

> Within circles of people who have inherited wealth . . . we see it as a source of problems. . . . As these people who had inherited these problems began getting together, we began realizing that there is something very ambivalent and paradoxical about having power. . . . In other words, there is something very ambiguous about the issue of having money. . . .
> People came together to talk about the problems associated with money, the personal problems, the self-worth problems, being able to work without being asked to work, doing volunteer work. How do people get their sense of self-worth, self-identity, if they are not in a society that rewards them for doing a job and getting paid for doing a job?

She made friends with some of the group members and started to feel comfortable about her role as a funder.

Thus, unlike her parents and grandparents, Bennett questioned her privilege. Before she had formed strong opinions, the country was being challenged by strong social and political movements for equality—the civil rights movement, the women's movement—that shaped her thinking. She was maturing when consciousness-raising, encounter, and T-groups were the rage. Like many women her age, she was unmarried by the time she reached thirty. She and others of her age and class embraced what they thought of as a new movement, which engaged the wealthy in progressive social change through philanthropy.

By the early 1980s Bennett had become a leader in the alternative funding movement.

> We have gone from working through the problems of guilt and money and social change and empowering—thinking of ourselves as agents of social change. It is a whole evolutionary thing. . . .
>
> The basic substratum [of new recruits?] is dealing with the problems of money. But historically . . . we have gone from concern for human rights and poverty and social change, and now more and more people are concerned with the survival of the planet.

In the last few years, she and her friends have been working through a group of funders that support "whole war and peace," their phrase for antinuclear and arms control programs. "For a while, I was involved with a woman's group," but that lapsed as she became more and more specifically committed to peace issues.

It seems that as these wealthy young people grew accustomed to their new sense of power, they broadened the possibilities available to them.

> We begin to perceive it not as a social phenomenon but as a spiritual phenomenon, in which we are a generation of people that have become aware of the potential destruction, not just of a class of people, but of the whole earth itself. And that generates a sense of responsibility not for my local community . . . but a sense of responsibility for the planet as a whole. And now more and more people are involved in using their wealth, their philanthropic resources to form networks around the planet to begin solving local problems.

Once again, the rich kids with old money express a special responsibility because of their money and insight. They attempt to be different from their parents in turning their inheritances into good deeds, and they consciously endorse social change. Their work, however, is functionally similar to that of preceding generations.

AMBIVALENCE, RESOLUTION, AND DECEPTION

Elite philanthropy is a symbolic reconciliation between the ideal of a democratic society and the reality of inequality. For most Americans, the inherent contradictions between amassing wealth and espousing equal opportunity are abstractions. But for people with old money, the paradox is ever-present and frequently poignant. They can never be sure that their accomplishments are recognized as their own. They did not earn but were born to obvious cultural and financial advantages. Among many of them, this situation causes great self-doubt and often self-deception.

For example, Jonathan Clifford does not allow himself to see that increasing local needs might be related to the fact that "we have got so damn much money now," that wealth has shifted upwards. He views poverty as an accident that happens to other people, just as Stockton sees philanthropy as a "wonderful thing" that just happens to the wealthy. In this regard, both of them, other philanthropists, and the general public are deluded.

In their lifestyle and rhetoric, rich philanthropists are constantly trying to make themselves smaller, more folksy than they could ever actually be. Stein's family were all "little people from the old country." Clifford's wealthy Aunt Edith lived on three hundred dollars a month. In so doing, they deny what wealth really means and conceal it from themselves as well as the rest of the world.

But the fantasies and recollections of philanthropists have common themes of power. Stein imagines himself saving someone else's life, or even "writing the rules of the community." Stockton does her best as the poor, honest pastor of a foundation rather than a church. She thinks of herself as the leader of a congregation of grant seekers. The "rich kids" like Bennett actually take up an old mythology of Robin Hood and his Merry Men, wealthy aristocrats and clerics in coalition with the downtrodden, seeking to overthrow an evil government. Yet they do not wish to give up their riches or truly confer power to the people. These composite philanthropists are all "giving back" to those who have "given," in a very personal manner that gives them control, ego gratification, and power.

"Doing good" helps assuage the personal internal conflict of the rich, and provides an ideological rationale for wealth holding. This ideology, in particular, corresponds with traditional expectations about women's aspirations and interests—a theme to which I now turn.

Chapter 5

Lady Bountiful

Most rich women are invisible; we are the faces that appear behind well-known men, floating up to the surface infrequently, palely; the big contributors, often anonymous, to approved charities, or the organizers of fundraising events. Rich women have been so well rewarded by an unjust system that we have lost our voices; we are captives, as women are captives, of a system that deprives us of our identities.
—SALLIE BINGHAM, "The Truth About Growing Up Rich," *Ms.*, June 1986

American women of wealth are both privileged and subordinate. They have less power than the men of their class, yet they have more authority and status than most people because of their connections to powerful men, their philanthropy, and their money. The social construction of gender in the wider culture dictates that women are inferior to men and assigns different duties to each sex. The class system sorts people further, complicating gender distinctions. Rich women are in a position to exploit other women, as well as working- and middle-class men, but their status is lower than that of their fathers, husbands, and brothers.

Gender and class are interactive. Feminist theorists have been calling for more work on "the combination of patriarchy and capitalism."[1] Studying upper-class women contributes to the development and refinement of feminist theory,[2] as well as our understanding of the culture of philanthropy. As members of social categories, wealthy women are differentiated from men on the basis of gender,[3] and from people in lower classes on the basis of economics and culture.

Sexism is as prevalent among the rich as elsewhere in society. The wealthy, however, are better able and more likely than others to follow a strict division of labor by gender. Upper-class women do not need to work for pay and indeed face sanctions against taking jobs unless with the family philanthropy. Poor women have always joined the labor force out of economic necessity but have had to settle for low-wage jobs and have often felt guilty that they were not at home with their children.

Historically, the fact that rich women have appeared to dedicate themselves to motherhood may have set unrealistic standards for other mothers. Yet, paradoxically, women of means have long recognized the constraints imposed by full-time childrearing and housekeeping and have hired other lower-class women to do much of this work. Many wealthy women have themselves put their energy into entertaining, giving, volunteering, and the promotion of high culture.

This chapter focuses on rich women philanthropists.[4] Through the socialization of their children, the support of their husbands, and their nonprofit activities, these elite women maintain the class system and do not seriously contest the gender inequality that exists in America.[5] Using examples from the public record and composite biographies, I describe the common multigenerational life cycles of women philanthropists with varying backgrounds and personalities.

The typical "lady bountiful" is trained to assume her cultural duties early in adulthood and will remain an active volunteer throughout her life. She usually both inherits wealth and marries a professional or a rich man, although she may simply "marry into money."[6] There are fewer rich women than wealthy men in the United States, although the average net worth of an upper-class female is greater than that of a comparable male.[7]

In most elite philanthropic families, the wife is responsible for child rearing, household management, social life, and charitable as well as cultural activities.[8] She may choose any combination of these duties, but she is neither encouraged nor supported if she deviates from prescribed gender roles.[9] A wealthy husband has many options, including philanthropy, although he usually works more actively in business or perhaps politics. The newly rich are clearly concerned with money-making endeavors, but even men with inherited wealth tend to invest their own money in entrepreneurial projects. The assets of women in the same position are usually managed by their husbands, brothers, or male financial advisers.

Whether they are the daughters, granddaughters, or sisters of millionaires, whether they have married "up" or "down," elite women's lives follow similar patterns because they are structured by gender, class, and culture.

Their status is derived from that of the husbands, fathers, or brothers who made or manage the family fortune.[10] Their class standing is contingent on having surplus money that they did not earn, much of which is tied up in trusts.[11] Their cultural prestige is based on giving away interest income to the right causes and working as volunteers with nonprofit organizations. Most wealthy women have little economic independence.

Caroline Stockton, whose composite biography was presented in chapter 4, is characteristic of elite women. She explained how the tradition of philanthropy was passed down through the women in her family.

> You remember bits and pieces from your childhood. . . . My mother was always interested. . . . Then my grandmother sort of nabbed me, got hold of me, when I was in high school. . . . She said, "Now, I want you to get interested in [a particular family charity]". . . . I went to all kinds of dedications and unveilings, and what have you.

As a young adult at a private college, Stockton had a mentor who both reinforced her childhood training and expanded her horizons.

> I had a very strong dean when I was in college, and I got very close to her. . . . She pushed us very, very hard into just about everything that you can imagine. She urged us to go into public life. She urged us to go into philanthropy . . . to make something of ourselves.

Stockton had educational advantages that in her youth were primarily available only to men and upper-class women. Yet then and now, "making something of herself" did not mean pursuing a career but rather assuming the proper roles of a daughter of wealth. She married a rich man in her community, and administered the family philanthropies. She taught her children, especially her daughters, similar values of giving.

UNMARRIED DAUGHTERS AND SISTERS

> When I was fourteen, I was told that I would have enough money to never have to work in my life. . . . I was told that the money would be enough to live on forever, and that I could afford to do good for other people.

Wealthy daughters are the youngest initiates into the culture of philanthropy and later the most dedicated proponents of that way of life. From their earliest years, girls born with old money are socialized by women—their mothers and their nannies. They understand that they are like their mothers, and they generally want to follow in their mothers' footsteps. At the same time, they realize that the family money was made by men.

Jane Bennett, the thirty-four-year-old composite fourth-generation heiress introduced in chapter 4, learned from observing her parents' activities.

> My earliest memories revolve around their social events. They [still] attend between three and four charity [meetings] a week, and are very involved in philanthropy. [My mother] put on the [a large health organization] Ball, which made a million dollars a year for years and years. It would be a six-month organizing project. She would usually do two or three of them a year. . . . [In addition], she worked for twenty-five years raising hundreds of thousands of dollars for [a boys' youth group].

Bennett's training was also practical.

> My mother's friends would come over and they would be doing fundraising letters. The kids would lick stamps, seal, and stuff envelopes . . . when we were eight or nine years old.

She vividly recalled that when she was given her first quarter she received a lesson in noblesse oblige. Her mother said, "There are many ways to spend it, but here is what I recommend. You [should] really think about how you can contribute to the society around you." She was advised to use only five cents for herself, put some into savings, and give the rest to a worthy cause. This lesson reflects the value that the philanthropic wealthy place on accumulating assets and living relatively modestly.

When Bennett became a teenager, her father began to take a more active interest in her philanthropic upbringing. "I used to go to board meetings with my father. . . . Once, when I was probably about fifteen years old, I went to a corporate contributions meeting with him, and was fascinated."

Her brother's training was different.

> My brother was directed more toward money-making activities, and I was directed, as a young woman, toward philanthropy. . . . He was sent off to work in stock brokerage firms, and I was sent to the public library to do work with children. There was definitely a gender bias.

Later, Bennett was given specific volunteer responsibilities.

> My family sat on a number of boards [of nonprofit organizations], and I think it was early on, when I was eighteen or nineteen [that I began to serve on these boards]. I have constantly gone to trustee meetings and staff meetings, and been the loudest voice and the youngest one for many years.

In spite of her gender and youth, Bennett found that she had authority and influence as a volunteer. Other people listened to her. "I understood very early on what the satisfaction was. . . . I loved the excitement of it. I loved the culture. It was a very social activity."

Bennett realizes that, in essence, her mother's situation is also hers. "My mother is very oriented, driven by a sense of duty, a sense of obligation. . . . It is very compulsive. I caught it." She has had trouble in establishing psychological boundaries between her own and her mother's life. She believes that she has internalized a sense of inferiority.

> In my mother's case . . . in both our cases, we have a lot of shame, low ego development, low self-esteem. And so I learned from her that by doing for other people, or by extending, or being with people that were of either an image that we wanted, who were living a life that was either more humble than ours, or living a life that was more exciting than ours—you don't have your own ego. You feel connected in a certain way. You aspire to be like those people.

Bennett and the heiresses of whom she is a composite have great difficulty in knowing who they are; they have no firm identity. From an early age their gender leads them to look to their mothers, but they are not rewarded with a sense of personal power. When they begin to understand that they are wealthy, their class becomes a dominant factor in their lives. Yet they see the attributes of class standing as being largely connected with men. Of course, they know that they are more fortunate than other young women. But their sense of self bears little relation to their own personal qualities. Their self-identity becomes attached to their philanthropy rather than to their individual personalities or talents.[12]

The socialization of Jane Bennett and Caroline Stockton is quite typical of the majority of women in the culture of philanthropy who have inherited money. Daughters of the newly rich usually have a different kind of initiation into the world of giving and volunteering; they begin their enculturation later in life.

Susan Jones[13] is in her mid-twenties, a graduate of a public university in her home state. She works at her father's firm in a Midwestern city about two or three days a week. She has no official title but is responsible for organizing, reviewing, and recommending charitable contributions in the family name. When interviewed she had held her position for less than six months, but the workload had been increasing along with the giving program. She was not concerned with company contributions, but there had been some talk about moving in that direction as she learned more of philanthropy.

Jones is a shy, rather retiring individual, in contrast to her father, a large man with a booming voice and authoritative air. In the middle of our discussion he burst into her office to tell her that he wanted to see her when we were done. Perhaps he intended this as a warning, for she became more reticent and ended our conversation shortly thereafter. Or perhaps she is simply accustomed to responding promptly when her father calls.

She is delighted that her father offered her the position, for she finds the work quite rewarding. "The reason I am so excited about my job is because I feel very lucky for everything that we have. So, it is a great opportunity to do something with it. It makes everything worthwhile." Here her developing ideology about wealth and philanthropy is quite similar to that of Caroline Stockton: Wealth "happened" to her and philanthropy makes it worthwhile.

She described the family's grants program. "Mostly we do hometown types of activities. . . . We do a lot with the arts . . . the museum, and the symphony. One of the major things we contribute to is a program for 'youths at risk,' . . . a ten-day survival, look-at-your-life type of course for problem kids. And apparently it's really turning their lives around."

Jones made clear that she does not have full authority over funding decisions but defers to her father and the rest of the family. Sometimes they contribute to projects that she recommends because she thinks they are good. In other instances they make grants in a more opportunistic manner. "Well, my father is trying to get the most benefit out of his money. We want our name to be heard . . . just because a lot of opportunities can come out of that." She has not yet learned the cultural norm that makes it inappropriate to make blunt, albeit honest, statements like this.

Recently the Joneses started having family meetings to make the most important charitable decisions.

> Everyone has an equal vote, but of course, if Dad recommends something strongly, it's like everyone realizes where the money is really coming from and goes along with that. [She laughed.] But he also listens and is really open-minded to what we are all saying.

She indicated that any one member of the family may make a funding recommendation. "And I can come across something and make a recommendation. But it isn't because of my position as an administrator." She thinks that her role as a family member is what counts here.

Sisters may also decide or be asked by their brothers to take on a philanthropic role. Pamela Richards[14] was a high-ranking professional when her self-made millionaire brother invited her to manage his foundation. Today, she works full-time at that job.

> My brother has a great desire to do things in a creative way. He wanted to build a company. . . . It so happens that he was at the right place at the right time, and he made a great deal of money. Once he had this money, he and his wife had no desire to live the jet-set life.
>
> [He] phoned me to join him when his foundation was established. He felt [giving] would be a very personal thing with him and his wife; that I understood them; that I could be pretty tough; and that with the things he would want to do, it would take those attributes. So, I did agree to resign the job that I had prepared myself for, and that I loved, to join him. I have never regretted it. It has been a fantastic experience.

It took her some time to decide to accept the position, but she said she now "adores" philanthropy.

Her brother is president of the foundation board; she is the vice president and manager. "I'm the one that does the day-to-day stuff," she said. Family members and a few other close friends and associates are also trustees.

> Working with my brother is tremendous, because he is so creative. He tells you what he wants you to do; then he walks away. He does not tell you how to do it. You know you have the authority to do your job. If you do not do it right, you are in a lot of trouble. The best thing about it is that I feel what I do is important. The second-best thing is that working with him is really a challenge, and it is gratifying.

Richards talks about having authority, but from her description she seems to walk a very fine line that always requires pleasing her brother. Luckily they share the same general philosophy and politics.

Most of the Richards' philanthropy, in contrast with the Joneses', is anonymous. Richards explained:

> We don't do this for publicity. We don't do it to get any pats on the back. We do it because we think it's the right thing to do. It's not something that we like to just go around and talk about. I think that's self-serving, and we have no desire to do that.

They would prefer that all their gifts be anonymous, but have been "unable to" make donations in this way because of the brother's image in the business world. Richards claimed that they tried to keep their philanthropy secret, but "anything that he does is going to be known. If we don't go ahead and admit that we gave this, then it almost looks like we're doing something devious. . . . Of course many things that we do are not known, and that's the best kind.''

Pamela Richards came to philanthropy later in life than Caroline Stockton, Jane Bennett, or Susan Jones. Over the years, she has been fully enculturated through her work, and it seems likely that Jones will have a similar experience. The power they hold, however, is somewhat illusory. Women accept the implication that their work is not as significant as that of their fathers, husbands, brothers, or male public figures.[15]

Neither Richards nor Jones explicitly indicated that they understood their roles in assisting fathers, brothers, and other family members to be accepted into the culture of philanthropy. But wealthy wives are well aware of this responsibility, especially vis à vis their children.

WIVES AND MOTHERS

> I have spent my child-bearing years working as a volunteer, as a board member. . . There is a flexibility that I very much like. On the other hand, there is nobody who can fire you, or really dare criticize you, because not only are you there working for free, but you are also contributing money and raising money.

Elite women do not work for pay, both because of conventional gender arrangements and because such behavior would subtly jeopardize their class standing. Even within the household they are primarily managers rather than laborers. Upper-class women usually hire domestic and child-care workers. They direct and organize their children's activities, but their relations with their children may be somewhat remote. "From childhood on, my mother was not around a lot," explained Bennett. Furthermore, most wealthy children leave home at an early age to attend boarding school.

As a consequence both of having money and of limited involvement with their children, rich women have the resources and time to devote to other causes. In this respect, they are more similar to men, both of their own class and outside of it, than they are to many other women. Their lives do not so clearly revolve around the more tedious aspects of home and family. They do not work the "double day" of most women.[16] Still, much of what they do is expected to benefit or at least reflect well upon their families.

A few of the younger, single women we interviewed did hold jobs, but once a baby is born, a wealthy woman is expected to concentrate on domestic management, socializing the children, and volunteering. One young second-generation woman who was employed until she had children explained:

> I don't see that there is any time for volunteer activity if you are working at a full-time job and have a child. I just don't see it. I mean, you drop your baby off, or the household help arrives, and you go to work. You work your hours. You get home in time for the day care to go home, or pick up the baby. Once you get home, you are there alone with the baby, and that is it. I think women are still in large part responsible for the household chores. I know that was true in my family, and it is true in my family.
>
> Women find that if they have a job and child they have little time for volunteering. Women have always been the backbone of volunteer communities. I mean the only way I can volunteer is because I am not working and I have day care.

Not only does she have day care, but she also has domestic "help." She could have a paying job if she wanted to. Volunteering allows her the ultimate in flexibility.

Volunteering is viewed by upper-class women as an activity of higher status than working for pay. As a result, a form of the we/they distinction has developed in certain elite women's associations. For example, in at least one Eastern city there are now business and professional divisions of the Junior League—a prominent, exclusive national women's organization with local chapters.

Alice Todd[17] referred to this phenomenon.

> They hold meetings at six o'clock at night once every two months or so. That is great for a working woman. She has got the child care situation taken care of. She just stops at this meeting on her way home from work. You could never do that with me. I would not come to a six o'clock meeting. I would tell you, "You are out of your mind. That is the time I am cooking dinner. I am waiting for my husband to come home, and yelling at my children in the kitchen."

She presents herself as a kind of harried housewife and obviously thinks of herself this way. Yet most of the day she is away from home volunteering. Her children go to a local country day school. She employs a younger woman to supervise their activities from mid-afternoon till early evening. A maid works for her several days a week. She enjoys cooking and so generally does it herself. She considers the evenings family time, although she and her husband go out several nights a week to charitable, cultural, and social events.

She continued on the subject of the Junior League and professional women.

So they are making a very conscious effort to deal with this group [of working women] as an individual group. It has its own identity, its own problems. They have special programs. They are geared just to the problems those women are experiencing. I think that hopefully, as we are talking, more and more successful couples with the double income will be able to perhaps give more money if they cannot give more time. By having to attend these kinds of meetings, they will have the interest kept up. . . . They are educated, and very well informed. . . . It is very important to keep trying to get them there. . . . [The women] at home, they kind of resent anything that slips in the middle.

She betrays her sentiments, especially in her final comments. She is one of the women "at home." Wealthy women who choose paid employment have obviously "slipped in the middle." They are not members of the culture of philanthropy: Although they may contribute, they do not volunteer.

Todd feels conflicted about and possibly threatened by the women of her class who have taken on non-volunteer jobs. She tries to validate her own position by pointing out that she has responsibilities at home, and she insinuates that a woman working for pay, who can attend a meeting only every few months, is contributing less to society, at least through traditional charitable organizations.

It is also significant that Todd underrates the continuing family responsibilities that even employed women of wealth are likely to have. She implies that child care is easy to arrange. She suggests that perhaps they (notice here how the professional woman is still connected to her husband) will contribute money instead of time to charity.

The unspoken criticism is that women who take paid jobs are shifting classes and cultures. Todd does not consider the disadvantages of her position: that lack of her own income, whether it be from investments or employment, translates into little personal independence. Nor does she recognize that the tasks an elite woman who volunteers undertakes, such as fundraising, are also part of the responsibilities of paid professionals, especially development officers and executive directors of nonprofit groups.

The fear of changes introduced by women's increased participation in the labor force is not limited to young women with children. At a country club in Texas an older woman bemoaned at length the fact that young women are now working outside the home rather than volunteering. As might be expected, older women tended to be more traditional than their younger counterparts.[18]

The activities of elite wives, whatever their personal background, are remarkably similar. Evelyn Marsh[19] spoke of her own modest upbringing and her friendship with a wealthy prep school roommate. When they first met, their families' financial circumstances were entirely different. But since each of them has married an upper-class man, they are "taking very parallel tracks. . . . I really feel that linkage with her."

Marsh's socialization in the culture of philanthropy began at the boarding school she attended, where her classmates were the daughters of either the wealthy or of parents with upwardly mobile aspirations. After marriage, Marsh learned more specifically about the culture of philanthropy and the role she was to play from her husband and his family, especially his female cousins.

She is very clear that as the wife of a wealthy man she has specific responsibilities. "I was given money as soon as we got married. I was given stocks so that I could contribute." She never seriously considered spending the dividends on herself or anything else. They were for philanthropy. Although not originally of her husband's or her former roommate's class, Marsh learned the acceptable behavior and absorbed the values.

The Marshes live in the city where his family had made their fortune. "My husband started doing some of the work of helping my father-in-law. We had the family office, and everything was run out of there, all the financial affairs."

> The foundation was one small part of it. It was always, "Well, now, we have got to do something with the foundation at the end of the year." My husband was bringing home proposals to me. I would review them.

Marsh eventually became the most active member of the family in foundation matters.

She did not question her assigned roles, but she wanted greater knowledge in order to undertake them as well as recognition for what she was doing. She began attending professional meetings in the region, and the national Council on Foundations annual conference. She brought some of the information she gathered back to her family. "Since the foundation should be a public foundation, I keep pushing on that with the family members. It is hard to bring the family along, but they are becoming educated." Thus, women who marry into wealth may play an important role in helping their conjugal families adjust to a changing world. They may even serve to introduce points of view from outside the culture of philanthropy.

"I cannot stand inefficiency. I like things to work. . . . I like doing long-range planning. I saw that we were going to have problems. And I also did not want anything to happen to our family that families break up over." More than those who were born into it, Marsh recognizes that hers is a dynastic family.

Giving money is very powerful. In families. And what do they have? Feuds. It is the money. And so I wanted to work out a system so everybody is comfortable as we go on. Now I have my own agenda for the future, because I can see the foundation changing. As the younger children are older, they are saying, "Oh, we've got a foundation?"

She thinks that she can interest and influence the next generation in philanthropy and that they will carry on the family tradition with a minimum of conflict.

At the same time she has built a more meaningful and prestigious life for herself in the context of wealthy women's traditional roles.

I came out of the kitchen, although I do not think many people ever associated me with the kitchen. I ran the foundation almost anonymously from my home for fourteen years while I was living the rest of my life and doing a lot of other interesting things: raising children, studying very seriously. . . . I was encouraged by a few different people to take my role in the foundation world more seriously and to demonstrate that seriousness by becoming more visible—taking an office, having a calling card. . . . Rather than taking a paying job, which I do not need, I was encouraged to be effective . . . and at a critical time in my life.

The content of Marsh's work has not changed although the form has. She is now more open about her family's financial contributions, but she still chooses to work as a volunteer. The difference may be that she now views philanthropy as a legitimate career.

BACKDOOR AUTHORITY AND CONTROL

Men who marry money suddenly wind up with power over that money, whereas women do not.

Women have less control over their wealth than men do.[20] Although attorneys, accountants, and bank trust officers serve upper-class clients of both sexes, male advisers are frequently blamed for keeping women's funds tied up. Bennett complained:

I think that while women are seen as having a lot of resources in this country, in fact it is not necessarily true, because even the money that women inherit is controlled by a bunch of men lawyers . . . a bunch of men accountants, who all give them advice as absolutes. "You cannot do this. You cannot do that." And, also, so much of your money is put into trusts that [you] cannot touch. Women do not control the assets. All they get is the income.

Middle-aged Stockton elaborated:

> The people in my generation have depended on their male financial advisers and lawyers. I do not think [the younger] generation is going to operate that way. The women in your generation are well educated and career professionals themselves.
>
> I have friends [my age] whose situations are controlled by lawyers and financial advisers. I am talking about friends who have a considerable amount of money.

Male attorneys and accountants are viewed as culprits, keeping money out of the hands of women. Ironically, though, it is usually the males of the family who established the original trusts that limit a female beneficiary's control over her assets.[21]

Thus, especially in rich families, wealth is not a guarantee of authority. Although volunteering in arts, cultural, and charitable organizations is viewed as suitable for upper-class wives, there are many cases in which making decisions about where money will go—even funds that the woman inherited, or those earmarked for charity—is not. I was told about one woman who had inherited considerable wealth that her husband subsequently managed. "She did not feel she had a right to do anything with the money. She would always go to him and say, 'Oh, please, give something to [a cause she endorsed].' He was giving her money to all these things she did not like!"

In general female philanthropists are not liberated. Wealthy women risk losing more economic security and status than other women in contesting a system that privileges them. On the surface, they have all they could want. But their options are limited—ideologically, psychologically, and materially.

A somewhat atypical wealthy woman fundraiser and giver, who was interviewed along with her husband, said:

> Most of the wives are not free to make the final decision. . . . I call and they say, "I'll ask my husband what I can give this year." . . . I have not had one woman say to me, "Yes, I will give you x number of dollars for my gift this year." I am always tempted to say to them, "Do you call up and ask your husband if you can buy a pair of shoes?" I mean, I just have to bite my tongue.

She continued:

> Most women do not have money, unless they are widows and have been left an estate. . . . It is the husband's money. . . . There is not much independent giving. . . . [I] find that disappointing.

Younger women like Todd did suggest that they should be more independent in determining their charitable contributions. "I used to think that you should deal with philanthropy as a couple, but I think that as more and more women gain financial independence the [decisions] should be dealt with separately."

Bennett wanted greater control of her inheritance but initially had to seek the assistance of professional male advisers. She went for advice to both a financial manager and a lawyer, but in her opinion neither was very helpful. "I guess I have talked to a few different lawyers, but have not been excited by any of them."

Sometimes, resistance to younger women like Bennett taking greater control comes from older women. Bennett's mother is dubious about her daughter's philanthropy, probably because it is now more public and less traditional. Bennett said:

[My mother] has had a lot of questions about my grant-making; she does not necessarily think it is the greatest thing. She has been a little worried about the whole thing, afraid that I am going to do something to get into deep water.

Wealthy women are generally expected to support conventional causes, and often to do their work behind the scenes.

Stockton described her strategy: "I always went, kind of, the backdoor way to what the needs were." But, she went on to say, "I did not mind speaking up. . . . I will give you an example."

I kept pushing the fact that there was no woman trustee. . . . Well, eventually that came about. One of the presidents retired and they appointed his sister. We all [wealthy women] participated in this pressuring, [but we had to be sure not to] bug people too much. I felt we were making points.

Some upper-class women are seeking more power, but many feel that they cannot be too obvious about it, and they use strategies traditionally acceptable for women.

Although Stockton thinks that women should have more philanthropic power, she also seems to endorse the dictum that those who do should be from the elite. She does not indicate that she sees anything wrong with the fact that the sister of a prominent man was the woman named as a trustee. The sister came from the "right" kind of family. It was not her personal characteristics that qualified her for the position, but rather those of her brother.

Bennett, who is actively encouraging women to take greater control of their money, said:

> I think it has been real difficult for us to convince ourselves as women that we can and should give large sums of money to different things . . . the financial piece is the last thing that we, through the women's movement, have come to realize that we need to grapple with. . . . We just have not recognized ourselves as having financial power with a financial responsibility.

She has been giving directly to charities and political organizations for a number of years, and is planning to set up a foundation. In this respect she is very similar to men who have established foundations so that they can have maximum control over the disposition of their charitable funds. She continued:

> Well, I certainly want the authority. There is no doubt about that. There is no other board [for my philanthropy] than me. When we legally form the foundation, there will be a three-person board, and it will be my best friend and my financial guy. It is very clear that the funding decisions are going to be mine.

Stockton agrees. "I want to be sure my interests are carried through."

There are only a few ways for a woman to escape the tyranny of upper-class expectations. One is to choose not to marry or to negotiate a different role with her husband and, in either case, face possible social ostracism. Another is to decide to work for pay. A third, less felicitous but more accepted route to independence is to have one's husband die. Even then, many widows perpetuate the giving patterns of their husbands.

Brooke Astor is New York City's best-known wealthy philanthropic widow and has been so for nearly thirty years. In 1988 she was lauded by *New York* magazine as one of "the big twenty," specifically "because she is New York's own lady bountiful in the midst of the greed decade." In that write-up Louis Auchincloss—peer, former corporate attorney, and leading author of fiction on the culture of philanthropy—described her as a "society leader."

> She has been not only a friend of all the arts; she has herself been a master of the art of living. Brooke believes that the good life is more than doing the best you can for your fellow man, vital as that may be; it involves doing the best you can, in a civilized sense, for yourself. There should be order and grace.[22]

When Brooke Astor's husband, Vincent, died, he left his wife a huge fortune, "half bequeathed to her outright and half to a foundation of which she has ever since been the very active president.''[23] According to Astor, her husband intended that she run the foundation, then one of the largest in the country. He told her to ''have a lot of 'fun' with it.''[24]

> To sit in an office and read ''meaningful in-depth studies'' of something I had never heard of before or would probably never see was certainly not a very stimulating or productive thing to do. Without a husband to look after, and with no one who needed me, I could direct all my energy to the Foundation. I wanted the best possible advice I could get.

She contacted John D. Rockefeller III. ''He gave me the advice that has been my principal guideline for the last twenty years—'The person who has control of the money should also be personally involved in the giving. It is a lot of work, but it is worth it,' John told me.''[25] She investigates every grant finalist, and says, ''It is my proud boast that the foundation never gives to anything that I do not see.''[26]

After she was widowed, Astor almost immediately began to enlist the cooperation of public authorities like Mayor Robert Wagner and the New York City housing authority in her philanthropic schemes;[27] later she involved Robert Kennedy, then a U.S. senator.[28] In her autobiography, she provides a particular example of her political pull with Lady Bird Johnson.

> As the years have gone by, she has become a good friend whom I have never ceased to admire. I was a member of her Beautification Committee when she was in the White House, and it was because of her that in 1966 we gave our only Foundation gift outside of New York: in Washington, D.C. [a park at a public school].

Later, as a board member at the Metropolitan Museum of Art, Astor asked Mrs. Johnson to intervene with her husband on behalf of the museum, which hoped to house the Temple of Dendur, a gift from the Egyptian government to the American people. The Smithsonian was vying for the same honor. ''I called Lady Bird, who said that . . . she would speak to the president but that naturally she could promise nothing, since he did not discuss decisions of that sort with her. I understood perfectly.'' The First Lady called Astor within a few days, ''and said that we had it.''[29]

Over a twenty-five-year period, the foundation has spent $136 million in grants, ''covering almost every area of urban life; education and museums received the most.'' Auchincloss ends his testimonial by writing:

> Brooke has gained much expertise on the cultural problems of the city by serving as an active trustee on the boards of her three favorite institutions, which she likes to describe as the ''crown jewels'' of New York: the Metropolitan Museum of

Art, the New York Public Library, and the Bronx Zoo. . . . She indeed merits the title some give her of Mrs. New York.[30]

Had her husband been alive, it is likely that he would have been praised as "Mr. New York," and Brooke Astor would have simply been his wife.

Rich women of every age and marital status have been taking increasing control of their financial assets, but most are doing so by setting up charitable funds and foundations that they then administer themselves. They are maintaining a tradition of philanthropy, just as their mothers-in-law, mothers, and grandmothers did before them. In doing so, they are increasing their personal authority and making meaningful work for themselves.

PHILANTHROPIC CULTURE AND GENDER

Women philanthropists are symbolic priestesses who organize the rituals and social functions of their culture, personally visit the worthy needy in classes below theirs, and remain pure by avoiding direct involvement in business and politics. Unlike women in the lower classes, rich wives are cloistered, almost guarded within their homes and temples away from home—the art galleries, museums, symphony halls, and traditional charities for which they volunteer.

Wealthy women belong to a "cult of domesticity" that bears a strong resemblance to that described by historian Nancy F. Cott as having existed in the United States two centuries earlier. Given the old-money reverence for history, the persistence of this arrangement in the upper class is not surprising. The ideology of women's domesticity is centered upon "its constant orientation toward the needs of others, especially men."[31] There is an aversion to "exploitation and pecuniary values"—ironically the very values that accommodate capitalism, the men who pursue wealth, and the philanthropy in which the women are involved.[32] This ideology also limits the prerogatives of philanthropic women and denies them a fully individual identity.

In addition, the popular image of the elite philanthropist, and therefore in a certain sense of the culture in which she participates, is "gendered" feminine and frozen in a previous time period. The "lady bountiful" portrayal need not be derogatory, but it is stereotypical. The lady is sometimes seen as interfering in the lives of others, especially in a maternalistic way. She is a naive but well-intended "do-gooder," sympathetic to the plight of the lower classes but not truly understanding. She has nothing better to do. The lady bountiful is utterly removed from the hardships of the world around her.

Normally, activities or things become "gendered" because of their close or predominant association with one of the sexes. For example, we can easily accept the idea that business endeavors are masculine in nature, because we see more men than women at the managerial level of companies. Two further instances of "gendering" are cooking and parenting. In general, women spend more time in cooking and in the everyday organization and work of parenting than men do. Yet those considered "great chefs" are men, and fathers often have a great deal of parental authority in their families. In the culture of philanthropy, young boys "prep" to become the head chefs of investment, wealth accumulation, and philanthropy; young girls, more often than not, are socialized to become the "help."

Nevertheless, it should be noted that the philanthropic work of wives, sisters, and daughters can serve as a particularly important means of entrée for self-made husbands into cultured society. Women have an easier time crossing class lines than men do, because women enter higher circles at a lower level. The most prestigious posts in nonprofit organizations are less available to women, even those with old money. Like capital, however, workers are always needed. The lady bountiful poses little threat to the powers that be, who want to hold on to their position and status. It takes years and very old money, or a lot of it, for a woman to make it to the top of the philanthropic hierarchy.

First-generation women of wealth faithfully do their duty so that their sons and daughters will be fully accepted into the old-money culture. As a result, they lead very busy social lives. In the meantime, their offspring are generally being socialized according to the philanthropic curriculum at prep schools and elite private colleges. Thus the transition is smoothed for those in the second generation of wealth, who will have learned the rules of inconspicuous behavior at an early age, and internalized them. The first generation of great wealth is not always the first in the culture of philanthropy. But "good works" and inconspicuous living can help new money become old money. This is the topic of the next chapter.

Chapter 6

First-Generation Men and Their Families

In the late spring of 1988, seventy-five-year-old David Packard, the co-founder of Hewlett-Packard, a leading computer and electronics firm, announced that he would donate $2 billion of his fortune to the David and Lucile Packard Foundation. Virtually all of his stock in the company will be transferred to the foundation, making it one of the ten wealthiest in the country. His decision is reported to have reflected a family commitment to charity.[1]

David Packard indicated that he and his wife, Lucile, who had died the previous year, had "decided early on this was what we wanted and worked twenty-five years to get to the point where we [could] do it. Assuming the market stays strong, the stock will be worth even more and the foundation will have $100 million to spend yearly."[2]

The charitable history of the Packards is characteristic of elite first-generation givers. Published accounts indicate that as their wealth began to grow, Lucile Packard increasingly dedicated herself to volunteering. As she became more involved in nonprofit activities during her child-rearing years and then throughout her life, her husband followed a distinctly masculine career pattern that combined business, politics, and philanthropy.[3]

In addition to managing his company, David Packard served as a deputy secretary of defense under Richard Nixon and was chair of President Reagan's Blue-Ribbon Commission on Defense Management. He has been a major donor to his and his wife's alma mater, Stanford University, to which he contributed $70 million in 1986.[4] He has also directed much of his volunteer time toward conservative public policy philanthropy. For example, Packard has been a board member of the American Enterprise Institute for Public Policy Research and the Herbert Hoover Foundation.[5] He supports political candidates as well.[6]

Self-made philanthropic millionaires are generally white men over sixty years old.[7] Most of the newly rich made their money in the computer and high technology industries; manufacturing; real estate; oil; or retail trade.[8] Their businesses are well-established and mature. They have reached a stage where they feel less pressure to put profits back into their companies. These aging men are more comfortable than they were in their younger years about giving to charity. With their wives, they may have been accepted into the culture of philanthropy, or may simply have recognized their mortality. Some of their younger counterparts—middle-aged men and women of new wealth—will probably go through similar stages as they get older.

David Packard and Lucile Salter were not born rich, but they did have the advantages of elite Stanford University schooling. They met "in the kitchen of her sorority house, where he was working to help finance his own education." After college, he took a job at General Electric in Schenectady, New York. In 1938, Lucile Salter joined him there, and they were married. A short time later, the couple decided to return to California and join William Hewlett in forming what was to become the Hewlett-Packard Company.

> The young company grew, and . . . [Lucile took] on tasks ranging from interviewing potential employees to baking metal panels for the company's electronic products in her oven. As more employees joined the company, she helped establish the tradition of care for them and their families for which the company is still known.[9]

In this quotation there is a clue to Lucile Packard's role in helping to build the business, as well as her advocacy of humanistic benefits for employees. She was the "do-gooder." David Packard "supplied the business acumen, Bill [William Hewlett] the engineering knowledge." Hewlett-Packard was the "first major U.S. company to adopt 'flextime' work hours."[10]

At some juncture, Lucile Packard became actively interested in philanthropy. Her interests were typical of newly wealthy women: she was to serve on the boards of the San Francisco Symphony, the Wolf Trap Foundation for the Performing Arts, the Castilleja School, and the Council on Foundations. "She also had a major role in the creation of the Monterey Bay

Aquarium, another family project. Her personal attention to detail was a major contribution to the beauty and success of the completed Aquarium."[11]

Aquariums are akin to zoos, popular with lady bountiful recruits. But the Packards had added incentives in supporting this enterprise. Two of their daughters, "Nancy Packard Burnett and Julie E. Packard, have graduate degrees in marine biology. Julie heads the Monterey Bay Aquarium . . . built by the Packards from their personal wealth."[12]

Lucile Packard had her own special charitable projects.

> Most important to Lucile was her deep concern for children. She dedicated herself to the early development of the Children's Health Council, eventually serving as its chairman. Her commitment to the Children's Hospital at Stanford was lifelong, from her student days as a volunteer to her recent service as board chairman. In her last years she worked tirelessly to bring about the creation of the New Children's Hospital at Stanford.[13]

In 1964 the Packards established a family foundation[14] "to support education, members of minority groups, health, and the arts. Last year [1987], the fund had assets of about $145 million and awarded $10 million in grants."[15] According to the annual report,

> Lucile Packard was the heart and soul of the David and Lucile Packard Foundation. For the first twelve years she was both staff and trustee; and even after it grew in assets and acquired a paid staff, she continued to not only point the direction, but to review the proposals carefully. Lucile said that her, and her family's active participation in what was going on around them was the motivation for creating a foundation, and the foundation, in turn facilitated greater understanding and involvement in the community. She said to be interested in others makes the donor come alive.[16]

During a period when Lucile Packard's health was failing and David Packard was recuperating from surgery, he said, "We spent a lot of time together formulating plans we hope will characterize what the foundation will do."[17] These included his particular interest "in improving scientific research and teaching. The foundation has already begun a fellowship program that will eventually award $10 million annually to encourage young science professors to remain in academe. The fellows will receive $100,000 annually for five years."[18] In addition, the foundation will probably make child health grants, "following the interests of Mrs. Packard," as well as population studies, programs on teenage pregnancy, and pre-collegiate education.[19]

Philanthropy has allowed each member of the Packard family, including the four children, to pursue his or her personal interest and thus to gain individual stature in the community. "Like the Rockefeller family, the Packard children were introduced early to philanthropy and took their places on the foundation board as young adults." The Packard's son, David, is "a classics scholar with an engineering degree." His favorite foundation projects fund ancient studies and work in archeology. One daughter, Susan Packard Orr, who holds a computer sciences degree, "has been developing software packages that will help non-profit organizations track their fundraising and grant-making activities and thereby improve efficiency."[20] The upcoming gift of company stock to the foundation will undoubtedly propel them all to old-money status, if they have not already acquired it.

Most of the newly rich intend to will at least half of their financial and charitable assets to their children. Others, however, are opposed to individual inheritance and plan to dispose of their money through lifetime giving and charitable bequests. Their reasoning is based in part on the extent of their confidence in their children and in some cases on concern about the perceived corruptive aspects of unearned wealth.

The following three composites explore the attitudes and types of personal history that contribute to the views of self-made philanthropic millionaires. This is not a representative sample of the nouveau riche but is intended to be illustrative of those who have been or are being recruited to the culture of philanthropy. In each case, although the family's wealth has been acquired by men it is women who have played the central role in bringing their families into upper-class society. In the end, the old-money culture renews itself and persists.

STARTING A DYNASTY

> I took a chance and I turned everything I had over to my children, so that I have nothing today. Everything that I had fifty years ago belongs to the trust. Everything since that time belongs to the trust.

"I was lucky enough to invent four or five extremely successful products," said George Klepper.[21] Although well beyond the typical retirement age, he is the chief executive officer of a manufacturing company owned by trusts that he established for his children; he is also a director of the bank that administers these trusts. Klepper is an avid opponent of taxation and a strong proponent of family cooperation in business and philanthropy. Although he has been generous during his lifetime, he is leaving no money to charity when he dies.

Klepper serves on the board of a regional community foundation, is a member of the local power elite, and is grooming others to take his place. "I have had four men who've worked for me ten to twenty years. . . . They've turned out to be very successful. . . . They've done very well and have assumed a proper place in the community. It is interesting how closely associated we are in many of these things."

When he moved to Texas over half a century ago, George Klepper claims to have had only fifty dollars in his pocket. Even today, he does not consider himself truly rich, but *Forbes* has labeled him one of the 400 wealthiest people in the country. Technically he is still only a company employee, but he continues to control the fortune he created.

Although the Klepper family is philanthropic, they very much enjoy their money. Klepper's wife, Helen, is particularly interested in the arts; according to her husband, "She's nuts about art. She's bought about $6 million of it." Helen Klepper is also active in local and national arts organizations. Their eldest son, who is beginning to assume management of the family company, is less involved with charity than his father, who admires his son's business acumen. The Kleppers' daughter oversees the family philanthropy.

I interviewed Klepper and his wife, who said very little, at a regional meeting of grant-makers. Both were dressed in professional-looking conference attire. As we sat around a table in a hotel restaurant, he told me that the business and philanthropic enterprises of the company, the family, and their trusts are managed by a host of professionals and tax experts.

> We have about eighty guys working on our income taxes. We have five members of the United States government who do nothing but check us . . . through the whole year. They sit and work on us. We had to rent another place for them.

Despite this cozy arrangement, Klepper considers taxation unfair and has set up trusts for his children specifically to avoid the income tax. By doing so he has also eliminated inheritance taxes. He explained:

> When I die I leave nothing. I already gave it. . . . There are very few fathers that are willing to gamble that their children will do the right thing, but I've been lucky that way.

He says his family deserves all the money that he has earned, and he praises them highly.

Like other self-made wealthy people, Klepper views philanthropy as part of his business interests. He and his family give over $4 million a year to nonprofit organizations. He indicated that they contribute to charity because

> the community has been very generous to my family and me. We have been active participants in the community's growth, and the more it grows, the more business we get. You help build your community and it helps build you. Without having a selfish motive, I want to pay my rent.

This attitude is similar to those with old money. It is a component of building a family tradition of giving, as well as part of the ideology of the culture of philanthropy.

Klepper wants to be sure that the family's charitable donations are coordinated. He explained:

> We started giving [on a large scale] about twenty-five years ago. We decided we couldn't let each [family member] give. That's silly. So instead of that we'd better all give to [each of] our charities.

He continued: "I made a decision that I didn't want a life of making money without balancing it with giving it away."

He learned about community foundations in the mid-1960s.

> I was at a directors' meeting of the bank and was sitting next to a Mr. ———. And for some reason or another, he told me about community foundations and their advantages. So after the meeting, I went to his office with him [to get the details]. I went back and started one [in our community].

The Klepper family established a special advised fund in the community foundation, wherein they could make decisions about the disposition of interest income. They leave the management of the money to foundation professionals but themselves select grant recipients according to criteria established by the foundation's board of trustees. Since Klepper, Sr., is the "grandfather" of the foundation, he has always had a good deal of influence over policy. The Klepper Family Fund is used primarily for local arts and civic projects. "What we have are several packages for contributions. We have to relate our giving as a group in the family and coordinate it with the community foundation's giving."

Joint family giving, according to Klepper, works very smoothly. "I've never had an argument, nothing. When I wanted to give $15 million to the university, I gave it and they [the family] paid for it." This is probably because the family still thinks of the fortune as his, just as *Forbes* does.

Of the family philanthropy Klepper said: "It's a way to see that our acquired wealth goes to a very useful purpose and it doesn't end up in Washington being spent by a bunch of politicians." His antitaxation sentiments are apparent in the charitable arena as well; he ruefully observed, "I'm paying taxes on what I give away."

As much as the Klepper patriarch is opposed to the income tax, the system seems to structure the family's charitable giving. "You're limited," he said, "in how much of your earnings you can give to charity. You know that?" In fact, Klepper could arrange with his family to give all the trusts' assets to nonprofit organizations, but he would not get a tax break for doing so. He takes pride in thinking that, with the help of his lawyers, he has kept up with income tax and estate law. His charitable activities have aided him in avoiding taxes.

Klepper has thought a good deal about a unified and informed family. He did not use the word *dynasty*, but he appears to have taken all the steps necessary to create one. As mentioned earlier, he started years ago to hold a monthly business meeting for all members of the family. From the beginning, he wanted his wife to learn about his business affairs, in case he died early. "So often, widows don't know a damned thing about what's going on and also lawyers get a hold of them and point out all your mistakes and show how stupid you've been," he explained.

Today, the monthly meeting includes members of the family, four bank officers, the head of a law firm, the head of the accounting firm, and an investment counselor, and they go into all aspects of the business operation. In addition, the family has frequent luncheon meetings at the bank in order to consider their investments. Klepper said, "The best thing about it is that you rarely or never do anything [where] you know [exactly] what you're doing. There are always some pros and cons to whatever you do. . . . But that's worked out fine. Whenever we do anything, we all know what's going on."

He also indicated that the content of the meetings has changed over time.

> It's a developing thing. In our monthly meetings, if anything has changed materially in the taxes or family relationships, those things can all be handled right then and there. It's not a locked-in pattern. It's something which reflects how things change. And that's one of the difficulties that's been encountered. [My wife's] father died, and he hadn't looked at his will, I don't believe, in twenty years. He was just as offbeat as a dodo. And it caused an awful lot of trouble for the family. That's something that has to be kept up to date.

Here is the only hint that there might have been a chink in the family unity, but the out-of-step father-in-law, having died, no longer poses a threat.

Although the elder Klepper is active in the nonprofit sector, he has complaints. He is not really concerned about causes to which he is not already contributing. "I get thirty letters a day asking for money. I'm so sick and tired of it. . . . I throw away more requests to charity. I don't know whether I should give to them, the old ones, the new ones. How do I know?"

He is particularly concerned about the expenses and overhead of nonprofit organizations. "If most of the money is going for the help, why should I give to them?" He therefore tries to be personally active with the organizations that he funds.

> If I show you my schedule, almost all of these are charities . . . almost every one that I go to. Each day somebody has a meeting. Each day. And I'm tired of it. My son refuses to go at all. He is probably one of the most successful young men in the world, and he says, "I'm too busy." But he goes occasionally.

"We are very active in the community. And we, along with others that are on our board, and people with whom we associate, keep in pretty good touch with everything that's going on in town. . . . [Young Klepper] is running so far ahead of me I can't keep up with him. He thinks I ought to retire, which is crazy. I'll retire when they put me away."

He continued,

> I know it sounds funny. Here I am an old man. The only thing I own is my home. Everything else is for the family. I'm the only one who is not a beneficiary [of the trust]. . . . It has worked out beautifully for me. We have that kind of a family— we're all one.

Klepper has the utmost confidence in himself, his family, and his son, the heir apparent. All of his close relatives have already been provided with an ample fortune, which they can choose to use as they like. His wife is collecting works of art; his son is making more money; his daughter is giving it away. This is a pattern typical of those with new wealth in the culture of philanthropy.

ENDOWING NONPROFITS, NOT THE NEXT GENERATION

> The kids are well taken care of, and too much money will kill you, just like liquor. . . . As a practical, down-to-earth matter, you do kids more harm than good if you give them too much money.
>
> If a person is successful and has had good fortune in making and saving funds, what else can you do with them? You can't take money away [with you when you die]. You could squander it if you wanted to, but I don't think anyone gets much satisfaction out of that.

Brian Dolan[22] owns a large construction and land development firm in Chicago. The windows in his spacious office, where we met, offer a magnificent view of the city. The walls are adorned with works of modern art. Dolan was wearing a three-piece business suit, but he reclined comfortably in his large office chair.

Dolan told me that he had concentrated almost wholly on his business enterprises until he was well into middle age. About that time, when his company and reputation were well-established, people began approaching him, often through his wife, to fund various nonprofit causes. His wife had come from old money, but Dolan presents himself as a self-made man. Today, he and his wife plan to put most of their wealth into a foundation or give it away to charity, rather than leave it to their children.

Dolan met his wife, Ginger, when he was in college at Harvard. He was the first member of his Irish immigrant family to receive an advanced education. Ginger Dolan has always been charitably minded and a volunteer. Dolan traces his wife's involvement to the Presbyterian church. She has consistently pledged a certain percentage of money, which increased as they became more successful. He explained:

> The church activities lead one into charitable activities of all sorts. Universities and schools that you attended seek funds. You're ordinarily pleased to give a certain amount of money to them. As time goes on, you get more sincerely interested in what you can leave to places that have helped you as you've come along. And sometimes through other schools also. It all depends on what the cause is and the availability of funds.

Ginger Dolan has contributed to many projects that interest her. She does most of her volunteer work at a day-care center for the elderly. She "relates" to these older women, while considering herself fortunate in comparison.

> She's very interested in the treatment of older persons. There have been sad cases where people don't have anyone left and no one to look after them. . . . She spends a lot of time when she's in town helping that particular group. . . . Some of them are such cute older ladies, she says, some up in their nineties that are just as cute

as can be. They're like little girls, interested in perfume and gold earrings and other things. She says they're fun to work with.

Now in his seventies, Dolan recalled his early ventures into land development and his single-minded approach to success. He said:

> If you're . . . trying to make your way in business in a narrow area, you're not looking outside to what makes other people run. You don't get exposed to it. First thing that happens, somebody comes to you for a contribution to the ———. Why the hell should I give to the ———? Well, there's the other one, the ———.

The solicitors eventually convinced him to give to causes that were also supported by people who could benefit him in his business.

> All of us have to learn how to give, why to give, and what to give to, and to learn that what you get back out of it is the sense of satisfaction of seeing something grow, something improve, all of which deals with people. So, it's sort of giving back to the general public what you have gotten from them in the position that you happen to be in, whatever that might be.

Dolan had made only small contributions before his company began to show a consistent profit and he saw that the corporate leaders in the community were involved with philanthropy.

"Probably a dollar or two when I was in college at different stages, and that's all it would have been, because money was awfully scarce in those days. . . . I guess the local institutions in Boston would seek funds, but it was very rare that a student working his way through college could contribute to anything like that." He continued: "However, we would buy season tickets to the symphony and other activities where they were trying to sell a certain number of tickets. Perhaps that was the start." The Dolans, possibly because of his wife's background and his ambition, were already interested in high culture. Many college students could not have afforded tickets to the symphony.

Like others who lived through the Depression, Dolan remembers the hardship of the thirties. He waxed philosophical about progress, especially in medicine and education.

> When I was working my way through college—and money was very scarce in the Depression days—I came to appreciate what a dollar is really worth. Unfortunately, they're not worth anywhere near as much as in those days. It's getting to be like pennies almost.
>
> It's just great to work with the medical institutions and hospitals and see them

advance in their fight against different diseases, and see people living tens of years longer than they did in the past. I wouldn't be surprised to see us live 150 or more years, five more generations down the line.

And then the educational side is so important. One reason we have as much poverty as we do in some parts of the country—to me, it's lack of education.

He attributes his success partly to a good education and is convinced that most personal problems can be solved through schooling.

As the son of an immigrant, he feels that he "made it" in his own right and has little sympathy for those who have not. Dolan did get into Harvard on his merit. He continued:

Just like our black contingent, which seems to have the toughest time in the country, everybody that deals with it in that circle, just to be sure that your children stay in school and get as much education as they can, because if they do, then they'll be able to get a fine job and be in the middle class and they can be successful or fail. I think the U.S. still has a long way to go in being certain that our youngsters stay in schools. . . . Well, if you can't control them by some means, they can curse the teacher and not come to class or do anything else. You don't have any means of educating them. And I think it's terribly stupid.

Dolan does not acknowledge the role that his wife's family money might have played in his success. He is obviously a skilled businessman, but his elite education, his wife's wealth, and his college and her family connections undoubtedly gave him a head start.

His attitude toward philanthropy changed, he said, "when I first started making a buck."

You start a business because you know something about it. And you think you can make a dollar, but you're risking a dollar, too—you might lose everything. Anybody who starts a new business in the United States faces those same things. A very high percentage of corporations or businesses go bankrupt within the first five years. So, it's a real challenge, in today's world, to build a good company.

It takes you twenty-five years to build a solid company. . . . Sometimes it doesn't even work. Sometimes you fall apart after twenty-five years. . . . Things happen step by step. You don't plan in advance to start a foundation, until you have enough money that it makes sense to start one. You only start thinking about it when you get there.

Today the Dolans' favorite causes are the arts, education, and medical research.

I guess we have made gifts to all the cultural groups here in town—the ballet and the symphony and the opera groups, and some of the theaters. I have been a trustee and director of the art museum.

The Dolans sent their children to preparatory schools, to which they now give generously. "We've made contributions to educational groups, schools, prep schools. . . . We have endowed a chair and scholarships and left money to Harvard. Contributions have gone to Stanford, where both children went as undergraduates."

Dolan's devotion to education is somewhat suspect, perhaps an easy way of avoiding the more disturbing reasons for poverty, including exploitation. His hypocrisy is rather striking. He does not give to public institutions, where most of the "black contingent" must go, but to exclusive prep schools and universities. Yet he speaks as if he is unaware of these inconsistencies.

The Dolans expect their children to use the good education they provided to "make it on their own." According to Dolan:

> You don't want to support your offspring so much that they have no motivation to succeed. Unfortunately, I've seen that happen in a number of cases in the past, where the offspring of a very fine family have really done nothing, sometimes squandered and lost the funds that were left to them, instead of building with them and contributing to society in general. But I guess we've structured ours to where, a number of years back, a good portion of this company went into their hands. So they're secure.

The Dolans believe that they are not coddling their children. Still, their offspring had more advantages than the vast majority of the population. And even if the estate of the older Dolans is left entirely to charity, Dolan has admitted that his children already own part of his company. Perhaps they will "make it on their own" the same way he did—with a little help from the family.

Ideas about the advisability of inheritance are clearly relative. As the composite Dolan case demonstrates, some newly wealthy families are conflicted about passing the money on. At a minimum, they want it to appear that the children are successful in their own right. Dolan and his wife have thought about this a good deal. He said:

> I was president of a hospital a long time ago. I've been on a lot of boards and I find that people with inherited wealth, particularly women with inherited wealth and men, too, are kind of cowardly. I suppose if they have enough money that may not be true. But for the most part they don't really have that much confidence in themselves. They don't trust themselves. . . . They tend to be less autonomous and more subject to doing things that everybody thinks are appropriate, rather than something they think ought to be done. . . . I think that if you have made the

money yourself, you have a lot less reluctance about either giving it away or worrying about what would happen if you needed it.

The compromise, for the older Dolans, between their concern about the effects on their children of too much money and their desire to give them some inheritance, has been to establish a foundation which the children will control; the Dolans' son John made this suggestion. The elder Dolan explained:

> One of my sons said, "You know, if instead of leaving your estate to us, if you set up a foundation with part of it, and assuming that we're going to be giving to charity, we can give more that way. That's an expense that we accept as a necessary expense in life. We can do better if you set up a charitable foundation because then the money will not be taxed. And when we give to charity we can give more that way." . . . So, to make a long story short, it paid. My will sets up a foundation. My children have the right to give money from it. And I have directed them—not specifically, but generally—that I would like it to go to the kinds of things that I was active in, involved in in my lifetime.

Like other wealthy people, the Dolans have a laissez-faire, anti-government, perspective. "I think," Dolan said, "that underlying all this is a kind of key factor. The donor feels that he can probably make better use of the money than the government can."

> When you're classified as an elder citizen, I think you need to start making contributions, because if you don't, they may count them for Uncle Sam and estate taxes will take most of it. Unfortunately, I feel that the government takes so much money. It is just a crime to let it go that way. They've squandered—I've seen billions of dollars go through the cracks just because the bureaucracy is so big and so uncoordinated and, in some cases, so selfish as far as individual purposes are concerned. They're not concerned about what's good for the country. It's what's good for them.

Dolan, failing to recognize his own paternalism, lambasts government officials for the same kind of behavior.

He believes that there is an amount of money that lends itself to establishing a foundation—enough money that individuals cannot intelligently give it away during a lifetime.[23]

> I guess we've set up a foundation in our will and set up a trust several years ago—a charitable lead trust. . . . Whenever we want to activate it, we can go ahead and start putting money into that foundation and as it stands now, we have not done that yet. We've been doing it more directly.

He explained: "We could set up something that would exist after we're dead and gone and would continue to do good things for society in general that otherwise wouldn't be done."

> Ordinarily my wife and I would make a direct gift to the college or cultural institution, hospitals, or the company would do the same. It's rare that we would run it through other foundations.

The prime advantage of a foundation is that it allows the Dolans to set their children up as philanthropists.

A POTENTIAL RECRUIT?

> It's never been a question of having more money than I knew what to do with. My wealth is almost all tied up in its own stock, which I let sit there. It doesn't rot or anything. It goes up and down, but it's not something I feel a burning desire to get rid of.

James Mitchell[24] has a good reputation in the computer industry of Northern California, but he still thinks of himself as a struggling entrepreneur. Although he is the chief executive officer of a competitive company as well as a millionaire, he does not consider himself rich nor present himself as such. He hopes to be wealthy, but business is volatile and Mitchell is a realist. Now in his early fifties, he has grown children, but his company is not yet mature. When he was a younger man, he became a millionaire and mistakenly thought he had "made it," only to lose control of a firm that he had started. Having begun again, he is counting on his experience and patience this time around. And whenever possible he is diversifying his business interests.

Several years ago, Mitchell's personal charitable contributions were minor and he handled them haphazardly. "I'd throw everything [solications] in a file, and once a year dig it out, sometime between Christmas and New Year's," he said. But his giving gradually increased as particular projects began to interest him.

Today his daughter, Christina, in her late twenties, manages the family contributions. She is college-educated, and married, and this is her part-time job. Mitchell does not have the time, and his daughter has the interest—a classic case of women bringing their families into the culture of philanthropy.

My daughter keeps my records and tries to get financial reports on all charities that we give to. We receive requests and try to ask them for their reports. She does an evaluation as to whether or not she feels their fundraising costs are in line. If so, we may consider them for a gift.

We're just trying to set up a program of giving. We usually, if everything works out all right, will probably give [a particular organization] the same thing next year, or slightly increase it, or if something happens that lowers our opinion of that particular charity, we'll decrease it. It's really very, very subjective. At this point, I don't know how to make it anything else.

But his daughter is learning. And it is significant that later in the interview he indicated that he watches attentively the charitable contributions of his business competitors the Hewletts and the Packards.

A native of California, Mitchell was educated in the state university system, from which he received an advanced degree in engineering. Neither big money nor old money was a part of his background. "I don't think I know anybody who inherited wealth. Out here that's not nearly so likely as in the rest of the country, I guess. I know an awful lot of millionaires, but I don't know any that inherited it."

He contended that the computer industry is not yet at a place where its people are thinking about contributing to charity.

It's a high risk industry. You have a lot of problems day-to-day. I'm not sure that the dynamics of the business leave much time to think about wealth and what you do if you're going to give it away. Usually you have to accumulate it. Then you start thinking about it. Wealth is a funny thing. While you're struggling to get it, it's always elusive. Then, after you get it, you've got to keep it. The sudden shift from how do you get it to where are you going to give it away is not something that just happens.

Unlike inheritors, self-made millionaires are quite aware that wealth does not just happen. Mitchell makes the clear connection between the need for massive accumulation of wealth and large-scale philanthropy.

Mitchell characterized the philanthropic activity in his region as relatively low.

This is an area that doesn't have a long-established history of that sort of thing. It's young. Most of the money here has been made relatively recently. I know even looking at the United Way, the per capita giving in this area is well below what it is in the more established industrial areas in the East. It is coming up, but that's as a result of a lot of work over the last several years. We are one of the fastest growing areas in the country. But it is clearly something that is not natural for the young companies.

Mitchell has been associated with the United Way for several years. He claimed that the older companies were always ahead in per capita giving and that many of the younger companies would not run a campaign; then he qualified this statement.

> There is a part of the community that is somewhat better established, where my generalization probably isn't true. For example, the Hewletts and the Packards have a tremendous history of charitable giving. In fact, I never see anything around here that either Packard or his foundation is not involved in, it seems like.

Mitchell also described the "enlightened-self-interest" kind of philanthropy practiced by computer companies in the "Silicon Valley."

> The tax law changes since 1979 [have] let companies give equipment to schools almost free—to universities in particular. And that has increased our giving of equipment rather dramatically.

He continued:

> Most of what my company does [philanthropically] relates to education. We depend on a continuing flow of well-trained people, so we consider supporting education to be in our enlightened self-interest.

This was particularly true, he said, with engineering departments, university programs that had a direct bearing on the business.

The industry association to which his company belongs has become concerned about housing and transportation problems in the area. "I think our orientation is more toward preventing disasters, if it's not too late, rather than really enhancing the area in which we live," said Mitchell. "I think we all appreciate the need to try to preserve whatever is left of nice living conditions in the area—and it sure has changed dramatically in the last thirty or forty years."

Ten years ago the area was composed of vast fruit orchards; they have since been replaced by no-frills industrial buildings like the one where our interview was conducted. Mitchell lamented: "This was really one of the most fertile agricultural valleys in the world. They cut down all the agricultural stuff, paved over the good land with parking lots—ridiculous." He mused: "People have a very real sense in this part of the country that they are individuals, that they have a capacity to impact on their destiny. [But] that feeling sometimes precludes coming together."

Mitchell believes that only a few business leaders really care about this situation.

I'll pick on the local industrialists, Hewlett and Packard [again]. . . . They've accumulated immense wealth. . . . They clearly are in a position to do something significant for the community, and I suspect that becomes a motivation for people who get way beyond what they imagined. . . . There's only so much you want to leave to your kids. You might as well spend whatever is left over, rather than let somebody else. I think that philosophy is not hard to come to. It is just that you don't want it to be a hassle. On the contrary. . . . Assuming I still have something left by the time I retire, figuring out what to do with it in a relatively hassle-free manner will be an interesting challenge.

He referred to the Hewletts and Packards several times throughout the interview. He obviously admires them for both their business leadership and their philanthropic leadership, and hopes to be like them someday. He is a potential recruit to the culture of philanthropy.

But Mitchell does not have complete confidence in the security of his wealth.

It is ridiculous how one can rationalize how much more he really needs to be secure. But most of the people around here who have significant paper worth—it might be in the order of several million dollars—have it in the stock of a company that doesn't pay any dividends. . . . I have an awful lot of stock, but actually it doesn't affect my standard of living—I haven't sold any in several years. I've given a little bit of it away, occasionally. But I don't feel a lot of cash flow that I've got to get rid of.

I live in the same house I lived in twenty-five years ago. I've got more automobiles than I might have, but not beyond what I can afford on my salary.

Mitchell has thought about forming a foundation but has always discarded the idea.

I've semi-seriously considered it. Frankly, the thing that keeps me from doing that as much as anything is what I would view as some kind of increased administrative hassles to set it up. The thing most precious to me is trying to save my time.

He said that he is too busy just keeping his business running to start a foundation and added:

[Time] gets taken away from me gradually anyhow by a variety of outside activities. Setting up a foundation requires some kind of administrative structure to run it. You have to make finances available on a regular basis—just exactly the kind of additional problem that at this stage I am not interested in undertaking. You have to figure out what you want your foundation to do. It's a bunch of problems that I'm not yet ready to spend any time on. I guess that I think that someday I'm going to work less than full-time, at which point it may be appropriate to set up a foundation.

Over the course of the interview it became clear that Mitchell does think about the future. And, although he touts the millionaire engineer mentality of many of his colleagues, Mitchell is already more of a philanthropist than they. "Eventually, I would like to control what happens to the bulk of my net worth. Assuming it remains roughly where it is now, it probably means that half to three quarters of it I would like to give away, or have it reasonably well-channeled before I die."

He has not firmed up his plans in this regard, although he has set up a charitable testamentary trust that would include the bulk of his estate should he die before making other arrangements. Mitchell has changed the charitable components of his will several times, and some of his decisions reflect the conflict he feels about great wealth-holding, his own sense that he is not really rich, and the fear that having money might adversely affect his children.

> Over a 20-year period you rewrite your will. I started out when my children were small. When I redid it last time, they were adults. It changed at that point. Well, and the other thing is my net worth grew like twenty-fold. That makes a bit of difference, too.

So, although he hates to admit it, it appears that Mitchell does hold sizable wealth. He continued more candidly:

> The will became a serious factor after I had established a fairly good confidence level in the ability of my children to deal with wealth. That, I guess, had coincided with the kind of major wealth that began to be available.

He trusts his children but is still undecided about how they will ultimately figure into his plans for his estate. "Personally, I would like my kids to be in a position where they could feel that what they earn is significant in their life," he said. "My older son lives on what he makes. He has a little money, enough to make a down payment on a house. That's about it. And I'm sure he will feel a lot better about himself for having done that rather than spending money, but, you know, various people have various feelings about that. It depends a lot, I think, on the personalities of the kids."

> It's a matter of both philosophy and economics. I think that what you earn—you get—the better you are for it. As far as the family is concerned, my obligation as a parent is to bring up my children and encourage them to be the best at whatever

it is they want to be; that they have the values that I think are desirable to have; and to do whatever it is they intend to do; and to assume responsibility for their own futures. And really, to get the same kind of satisfaction that I had in being able to do the things that I earned a right to do and [had] the ability to do. There's no substitute for that kind of feeling.

Mitchell qualified his ideas midway through.

I suppose that it would be a lot nicer if I could have gotten something from my parents, but I guess what I got from them are the values that I'm talking about right now. And I think I really discharged my obligation to my children since I equipped them with the best education available. And, they have the values to be responsible in society, maintaining the integrity and loyalty of the family. I don't think I have any obligations beyond that.

He modified these points further.

I have given them some capital . . . just a nest egg. . . . It's not what they would have reason to expect in [others' distributions of] fortunes to the family. So, that's all understood. It's all known. I think you have an obligation to do things for yourself. And inheritance really is a distortion of the processes of a free enterprise society. I believe in equality of opportunity as far as possible. I believe that inherited wealth tends to debilitate the character of people.

All this Mitchell said with great authority. But he is not quite sure. After all, he admitted that he never knew anyone with inherited wealth, and perhaps this contributes to his uncertainty.

He did not allude to the irony of providing his daughter with a job but not with an inheritance. Perhaps he, like some of his older counterparts with new wealth, will decide to bequeath a charitable legacy to his children, rather than hard cash.

Mitchell claimed he has recently been giving more because of a sense of responsibility for what's going on in the world. "To try and give back to those who are more needy. Or maybe I might have some excess," he pauses and begins again. "I won't say it's excess—I never have enough money. I think that when you make a lot of money, which I have, you can't spend it all, really. There is the fun and challenge of making money, and there is the challenge of giving it away." However, he said, "I have always felt it was terribly important for me to be primarily perceived in this community as a businessman, a person who's involved in the private sector." Here again is evidence of grappling with a personal sense of identity. Is James Mitchell's business secure in the long run? Will he be a prominent philanthropist? Will his children? That is yet to be seen.

HOW DOES NEW MONEY BECOME OLD MONEY?

Selected families with new money who behave appropriately are welcomed into high society because their donations are needed. It is in the interest of old money to find like-minded people with new money so that the culture of philanthropy is sustained.

Investing heavily in the visual and performing arts, as well as arts organizations, is a good strategy for the first-generation wealthy. Such donations are a rather straightforward way of announcing one's intention of participating in high society. Ownership of fine works of art, and dominion over their presentation and preservation in institutions, lie at the very heart of the old-money culture, distinguishing the upper class from others.

Newly rich men are busy ensuring the growth and perpetuation of their hard-earned assets. One difference between them and those with inherited wealth is that they feel confident that they gained their fortune in their own right. Guilt is not quite so evident among them; they see less need for philanthropy as a reconciliation between inequality and wealth concentration. They feel proud of their accomplishments. They feel that they worked as hard for their money as the people they employ.

In the American society of the 1980s, the prevailing ideology is at odds with reality: Equal opportunity is not available to all. Many first-generation philanthropists understand this but resist admitting it. So they say that they will provide their offspring with nothing more than good educations, but at the same time quietly pass their fortunes on to them, or bequeath them the power of seats on a foundation board. Self-made millionaires publicly adhere to the Horatio Alger myth that their own life stories help reinforce. But what are they going to do with all their money? Most despise the government, or at least taxation, so the alternatives are few: The wealth must go ultimately to the children or to philanthropy.

Elite Jewish giving, to be examined shortly, represents another variation on the theme of seeking acceptance into the culture of philanthropy. Because Jews have faced persecution and ostracism for centuries, they are keenly motivated both to provide for their own and to enter established society. Jewish philanthropy fills the first bill, giving to non-Jewish causes the second. But the balance between the two is delicate. Too much philanthropy to "WASP" (White Anglo-Saxon Protestant) causes is a threat to Jewish identity; too little condemns Jews to the role of perpetual social outcasts. To these matters I now turn.

Chapter 7

Elite Jewish Giving

All our ancestors came from the old country. You grew up in the atmosphere of refugees. You hear the stories. And you are constantly taught by them to give, and to give, and to give.

The history of Jewish charity in the United States parallels that of Protestant giving. For example, Jacob Henry Schiff was the leading Jewish philanthropist in America from the mid-1880s until his death in 1920.[1] Born to a wealthy German-Jewish family, he took pride in tracing his ancestry back to King Solomon. In the elite New York German-Jewish community of his time, family history was considered almost as important as wealth. There had been Schiffs in Frankfurt since the 1300s.[2] As a young immigrant, Schiff was readily accepted into the Jewish upper class of his adopted country.

Schiff's circumstances and prospects were quite different from those of the majority of Jews who would flee Eastern Europe to escape persecution during his era. He arrived in the United States with five hundred dollars in savings and partners ready and waiting to make Wall Street introductions. In 1867, at age twenty, he established a brokerage firm with two young friends. He had apprenticed with his father in this line of business in Germany. Schiff's pedigree, European contacts, previous experience, and presumed talent made him eligible to marry into the top of Jewish society that members fondly called "our crowd."[3]

When Therese Loeb became his wife in 1875, Schiff was made a partner in her family's banking house, Kuhn, Loeb & Company. He was an immediate success in his new position. Less than two years later he had earned a single $500,000 fee for selling Chicago & Northwestern Railroad stock abroad. Railroads were to "dominate the American financial scene" for the next three decades, and Schiff was a pioneer, innovator, and ultimately a kingpin in railroad financing and international banking. Within ten years, he was in control of policy at Kuhn, Loeb & Company. Schiff made deals with J. P. Morgan, E. H. "Ned" Harriman, and James J. Hill, "which would lead to the amassing of the greatest single railroad fortune in the world."[4]

Schiff was famous for personally investigating any railroad he considered backing, a pattern he would duplicate later in his support of philanthropies. His major charitable giving commenced in the late 1870s with aid "for the relief of Jews in the Ottoman Empire. He was almost immediately available for synagogue construction gifts to smaller communities."[5]

The sympathy and kinship with Jews around the world, as well as a willingness to support them generously in times of hardship, distinguishes elite Jewish philanthropy from its Protestant counterpart. Schiff became a foremost example of the "American *shtadlanim,* representatives with substance and propriety, 'court' Jews."

> Second only to riches in Schiff's shtadlanimdom was his stature as a patriarchal figure in the Jewish community. "Nothing Jewish [is] alien to his heart," Yahudim [Central European Jews] proudly told each other as they read news of his benefactions, and none dared commence major communal activities without first consulting him. Schiff would not travel on the Sabbath, said his prayers every morning, and kissed portraits of his father and mother. Yet he did not practice the Orthodox Judaism of his fathers. "He was attracted to [Reform Judaism] . . . by a number of circumstances," wrote his biographer, Cyrus Adler. "But the one he mentioned most frequently was that it satisfied the religious cravings of those who could no longer adhere to the ancient rabbinical religion and thus averted 'conversion' to Christianity."[6]

In the late nineteenth century, Americanization was acceptable and encouraged, especially for the less favored Eastern European Jews, but total assimilation was considered a threat to Jewish ethnic and religious identity.

Schiff believed in the Jewish principle of "tithing" 10 percent of one's income to charity. Philanthropy, he thought, consisted of anything above the tithe. He preferred that his gifts to institutions remain anonymous, or at least that the amount be undisclosed.[7] His perspective on giving was "individualistic" and his philanthropic interests wide-ranging. He is reported to have thought "that a man's giving should be done in his lifetime and, most important, under his personal supervision. In his spare time, he visited the Lower East Side looking for worthy 'cases' among immigrants."[8]

The dynamic Schiff was just as creative in the realm of charity as he was in that of finance, but like others of his day he was also decidedly sexist. He is credited with inventing the "matching gift" fundraising technique. Some of the projects he supported were given outright donations, others had to match or surpass his contribution in order to receive a donation. For example, one of his favorite nonprofit institutions was the Young Men's Hebrew Association (YMHA), to which he gave a building on Lexington Avenue that included a "gymnasium, library, clubrooms and classrooms." His interest in this organization is said to have led him to its "feminine counterpart," the Young Women's Hebrew Association. To that group he pledged a mere $25,000, and only if $200,000 could be raised from others during the year.

He put his daughter Frieda, then a young unmarried woman, in charge of the project.[9] After approaching everyone with whom she was acquainted, the younger Schiff still needed $18,000. Her father made up the difference in the name of her mother and uncle.[10]

Jacob Schiff's favorite and most durable philanthropy was the Montefiore Hospital. He was involved when it was founded, and became the second president of the board. "Montefiore was the only cause for which he would ordinarily solicit contributions; he personally acknowledged gifts from his desk at Kuhn, Loeb. Initial financing to begin the hospital came largely from two sources: a bazaar [that raised $160,000] . . . and his own checkbook."[11] He got to know patients by name, toured the wards on Sundays, planned special events, and supervised the staff.[12] His attitude was typically paternalistic, especially toward Eastern European Jews.

From the beginning of the mass migration of turn-of-the-century Eastern European Jews, the more affluent German-American Jews were to feel conflicted about the arrival of some two million additional co-religionists from the Pale of Jewish Settlement in Poland and western Russia. The language and culture of the Yidn (Eastern European Jews) were different from the Yahudim, but the major problem was class. The Yidn were poor. Their lot did not reflect well on German Jews, who were mostly Americanized. The Yahudim feared a loss of status in the larger society. They begrudgingly recognized a responsibility to their brethren, which took the form of patronizing charity. In return, the "Yidn differentiated between Our Crowd (them) and Our Kind (us) and decided the less help from uptowners, the better."[13] As a result, Eastern European Jews began setting up their own self-help organizations.

The tradition of giving is an important aspect of the community life, ethnicity and religion for Jews of all classes. While there is regional variation, a man from Minneapolis is fairly representative of his ethnic group.

> We have given in large measure across the strata. My principal gifts have been to the Jewish community. This is a philosophy I learned early. Jewish giving has got a special quality to it. It has a different kind of motivation than total community giving. Giving to the Jewish community is a much more intense response, has a much smaller base, and involves a frankly different set of motives.
>
> I think you're well aware that each ethnic group has a far greater sympathy for its own. That's expected and understood. That's simply what we have witnessed here in this community and throughout the United States.
>
> We have 21,000 Jews in the city of Minneapolis. Each year we give. This year our goal is $10 million. . . . Per capita, that's the highest in the country. Cleveland used to be ahead of Minneapolis, but no longer. Maybe that's because Cleveland has undergone some very difficult economic times.

Today wealthy Jewish people contribute generously to and are leaders in nonprofit enterprises across the country.[14] For example, although only 4 percent of the American population is Jewish, Jews have formed 19 percent of all the private grant-making foundations in this country.[15] Almost without fail, and with greater frequency than for those with other religious backgrounds, Jews referred to their Judaism as the primary reason for their charitable activity.[16]

Proportionally more of the Jews than other philanthropists whom we interviewed tended to be politically liberal. Several contribute to alternative foundations and other progressive causes. A young Jewish leader in the alternative funding movement explained:

> My mother in particular is a strong liberal. My dad is conservative by temperment, but a political liberal. . . . They were always supportive of [an alternative fund] and my work there. Once we started to expand a little bit past our own little circle, a lot of our fundraising was from their address book, essentially. There was a point when the older Jewish liberals, and others, but primarily Jewish at that point, did give to us—when progressive politics were more "in" than they have been in the last few years.

He continued: "I think it is true that, for whatever reason, a lot of Jews are progressive, or on the liberal side of center, and have some sort of social conscience."

Several Jews mentioned that they find it easier to raise money from Jewish people for charitable causes than from others. As one young man of wealth commented:

I would say, without being chauvinistic or anything, that probably Jews give more money away than other people. I think that's pretty obvious. . . . For someone from a Jewish background who's wealthy to give away $10,000—they have an experience with it. It's no big deal.

Yet an older Jewish woman questioned assumptions such as his. She said:

I am told that Jews are more philanthropic than non-Jews. Non-Jews flip out when they hear what United Jewish Appeal raises in the United States. They just can't believe that it raises so much more. And yet the largest, the greatest foundations are not Jewish foundations. The greatest philanthropists in the history of the country are not Jewish philanthropists. They are Christian philanthropists. Universities in this country were all started by Christians, with the exception of Brandeis.

I think that on a day-to-day basis if I were going around fundraising I would prefer to fundraise a Jewish person. But I'm not sure Jews are more philanthropic than Christians. And, of course, blacks and Puerto Ricans have never had enough money, by and large, to join the community of givers. I think that the thing they'd love most in the world would be to be in a position to give.

The speaker, Myrna Slote,[17] has had years of experience as both a fundraiser and a philanthropist. She is a leader in the Jewish community of New York and a sophisticated politician.

Slote casts doubt here on the folklore that Jews are more generous than Christians. (She may feel that comparisons of this type could be harmful, reinforcing anti-Semitism.) She is quick to mention the generosity of Christian philanthropists and their prominence in having established the foremost charitable institutions in this country. She also accurately alludes to the limited opportunities available to other minority groups, such as blacks and Hispanics. Yet she was the only Jewish person whom we found to express these views. And she admits that she would rather raise money from Jews than non-Jews.

An explanation for the strength of Jewish philanthropy is the historical oppression of Jews. "I think you can attribute it to persecution in prior generations . . . passed down," was a typical statement from a Jewish philanthropist. Conflict and opposition from outside an identifiable group can lead to greater solidarity and unity within that group.[18]

The Jewish community is a caste-like ethnic and religious group, incorporating the range of economic classes but still distinguished from a dominant WASP social world. Although many people of Jewish descent have assimilated through exogamy and other means, endogamy remains the norm. A leading authority on Jewish giving, Milton Goldin, has written that "philanthropy became the core around which Jewish life was organized."[19]

Jewish Federations in over 200 communities have been serving Jews since the early part of the century.[20]

The Holocaust reinforced Jewish identity. After the Second World War, American Jews felt fortunate to have escaped the "Final Solution," and were deeply affected by the tragedy. Their financial and political support of a Jewish homeland, now Israel, is an obvious outgrowth of what has become, for this ethnic group, a painful and unifying memory.

In 1946, the United Jewish Appeal raised over $100 million from American Jews, "in a campaign since legendary for its intimations of Jewish wealth."[21] Only two years later this amount was doubled. At the time there were only five million Jews in the United States out of a total population of nearly 151 million people. The continued success of Jewish fundraising has been attributed to a growing middle and upper class, as well as "superior techniques and aggressiveness."[22]

Myrna Slote explained the tradition of giving in her faith. She was well-informed about Judaic custom, philanthropy, and the minority group status of her people.

> You have to go into Jewish history and law to understand how deeply felt it is, and how very basic. The Talmud, which is the written law, makes one feel very strongly about *tzedakah*. The literal translation of it is righteousness, but in common usage, it's come to mean charity. . . .
>
> The fact that this is a guiding principle of our religion means that every Jewish child understands. They start out in their first Jewish educational experiences giving for some Jewish purpose. The reason that it's for Jewish purposes and why the Jewish community is so highly organized is because throughout our history, we have always lived a little bit outside of the general society. Often it has been the general society's wish that that be so. . . . It has been the feeling of both Jews and the general community that Jews must take care of their own needs.

She informed me about Jewish history, referring to the Sephardim, Jews from North Africa and Spain who settled in New Amsterdam in 1654.[23]

> Indeed, when the first Jewish colonists came to this country, they came with the understanding that they would be taking care of their own needs. [Much later], Jewish hospitals were organized to take care of Jewish needs, and often to take care of Jewish doctors, who couldn't practice in other hospitals. . . .

Like most wealthy philanthropists, she referred to a family tradition of giving.

I think that many Jews remember in their grandparents' homes—something that in a way has disappeared—called a *"tzedakah box."* It was a little can like you see standing out for muscular dystrophy or the March of Dimes. Every home had one in the kitchen, and coins that were left over from the day [were put in the box]. Even the poorest families would have a box. At the end of the week you would empty it and take it to the central place. There are some lovely antique ones around that have come literally from the Middle Ages. At the Jewish Museum you see them. . . . The concept of philanthropy, the concept of *tzedakah*, is very deeply ingrained in the Jewish psyche.

Jews have developed unique fundraising techniques. The matching gift, invented by Jacob Schiff, has been adopted by elite philanthropists of all religions. The practice of "calling cards," however, is widely used only in the Jewish community. "After rubber chicken or plastic roast beef, speeches praising the guest of honor, stale jokes, monotonous lists of needs, a recital of Jewish woes, and a recital of Jewish victories, the function gets down to business."[24] Sometimes exit doors are locked. A professional fundraiser gives the chair of the event a set of cards, one for each person present, which detail former donations. The chair (usually a man) begins by announcing his pledge for the past year and his increased pledge for the current year. He then announces, one at a time, generally from largest to smallest, the previous year's contribution of every other person in the room. All then increase their pledges, in the same general proportion as the chair. "None dare give less than the previous year; few dare give the same amount. Either alternative might be taken by competitors and friends alike as an indication that business is bad, a potentially disastrous intimation in this context."[25]

A San Francisco man claimed, "I do things in different ways because I'm Jewish. And because I'm Jewish, I give differently." Even those Jewish people who did not consider themselves religious traced their philanthropy back to Judaism. A woman from Baltimore explained, "It's hard to characterize. It's really a sense of cultural responsibility. We have strong religious identity. None of us practice the religion. We practice it in the way we live."

Non-Jews also commented on the extent and strength of Jewish philanthropy. And, though most wealthy Jews contribute to Jewish causes, they fund strictly secular activities of all types as well. An elderly California millionaire with a Protestant background commented, "The Jewish population has played a very important part in art, museums, music, and so on. They are very, very generous."

The following three composites illustrate patterns of Jewish giving by different generations, gender, and degrees of wealth in different cities. Except in New York where more Jews live and greater anonymity is possible, regional variations were not particularly pronounced.

FIRST-GENERATION ELDERLY JEWISH MAN

For me, there's two divisions in the philanthropic activity in the community. One is the Jewish community, with which I'm very involved and very active, where the greater portion of my time and money goes. The other is the non-Jewish community, which is represented primarily by the Community Fund here or United Way.

Joseph Mayer[26] was born in Chicago, where he raised a family. He got a law degree from the University of Illinois, then turned to banking and finance. Now a wealthy man, he cannot remember when he did not practice philanthropy in one way of another. He has been president of half a dozen leading nonprofit organizations. He proudly explained:

The Jewish community raised $35 million here for its philanthropic activities, both here, nationally, and overseas, which is a lot of money for 270,000 Jews. That's been going up a few million dollars every year. I remember when it was $10 million. So that's been successful in spite of difficult times now and then, even through so-called minor depressions we've had, spurred on every now and then by a crisis in Israel—there'd be a war or something like that. But, there's no war right now and this year we've raised more money than ever before. . . . If people don't give, they're not among the well-respected members of the community. . . . There are people who get away without giving, but by and large people are expected to give in proportion to their means

Mayer and his wife contribute at least a million dollars every year to causes they endorse. He continued, "A man who's making a good living here gives $10,000 or $25,000; a man who has an ordinary job may give $1,000 a year. But it is sizable money. In the non-Jewish community the figures are not that high, but on the other hand, there's a much higher base." Mayer described the motives of Jewish philanthropists. He said, "We give partly because of Jewish heritage and partly because of social pressure. No question about it."

He reminisced about his family's philanthropy and his own earliest philanthropic experiences. "My father was very active in charity work. He served on the boards of a number of things. . . . I got into it because of my father." The elder Mayer had a lower-middle-class income. "We lived a modest life," said his son. "But there was a Jewish National Fund, and the *tzedakah* box was at our house. When we went to services the [charity] plates were laid out on Yom Kippur. He would give modestly. If there was a health association created, he was a member of it. And we'd always have discussions about it."

> When I was young my father was at meetings a great deal. I said, "Not me. When I grow up I'm not going to spend all of my time going to charity meetings," and that's about all I do now. I'm on charity boards in New York and in Israel and everywhere else.

Mayer recalled:

> The whole cause of those days was Palestine. . . . When people make a few hundred dollars a month and give a hundred dollars a year, that's bread money. And yet, that's the tradition you found in Chicago, especially in the community that emigrated. The emigrés were much more generous, proportionately, than the old established community.
>
> When we organized the Junior B'nai B'rith back in 1924, one of our objectives was community service. We'd get some of the kids out of an orphans' home, and we'd take them out on a picnic, and we'd raise money among ourselves for that. What else can I tell you? From that point on, you get a little more money, you give a little more.

He also had some lessons to master. He recounted the following story. "I remember learning the tough side of charity, or giving. Romantically, we called it 'charity' in those days. I remember in 1929, when I was still in law school, there were some Arab riots." One of the leading Jewish men called together a big meeting.

> I was working nights to pay my way through [law school]. We had to raise money for the sufferers of the Arab riots in Palestine. In those days there was no hesitancy. You didn't call cards—"How much will you give, how much will you give?," and so forth. So one of the top professional men was asked how much would he give. And he said, twenty-five dollars. He was not greedy, but kind of a skinflint. It came my turn and I said fifty dollars. Then we went all the way around, and we raised a considerable sum of money. Then when we were through, that fellow that gave twenty-five dollars rose and made one of the burning speeches of my lifetime. Then he said, "I think everybody should now double what they gave." He'd given [only] twenty-five dollars.

Mayer obviously felt duped, and indicated that he had believed that experience was unique, until he said:

I became chairman of [a national Jewish philanthropy]. I went out to one of the five towns in New York, to a dinner in honor of a rabbinical friend of mine. After I got through with my speech, they called the cards. Whenever I went to those dinners I'd sit next to the chairman and I'd look at the cards. I was curious. They came to a fellow who didn't mention an amount. He said, "I'll double what I gave last year." I looked at the card, and he hadn't given anything last year. These are the kind of oddities you run into. For some people it's a game, for some people it's a way of life.

In my family there was no great wealth, but it was a way of life. You were expected to do these things. I don't want to be exclusive in it, but it is a part of the Jewish tradition. In any home that went to the synagogue, there was no escape. It was as natural as having something to eat. Maybe you didn't give as much as someone else gave, or someone else gave less than you did. There were many arguments about that. The only thing two Jews can agree on is what the third one should give to charity.

Mayer laughed at his own joke.

He indicated that there is more discussion about philanthropy and giving in the Jewish community than in other communities, and he tried to explain why:

If we are unique we are in the fact that we've got special problems, with a commitment to try to solve them. There isn't a comparison, in my judgment, between the outpouring of resources to causes in the Jewish community. . . . On top of which, we've lived through a period of time in which there's been such enormous change, the full impact of which will only be evaluated fifty to one hundred years from now—the creation of the State of Israel. People who would normally have given nothing, or five hundred dollars, have been known to give fifty thousand dollars in an emergency. The Holocaust. All of these things have had a special impact. We've just had more demands on us, and we've responded generously.

Mayer told another story about mostly non-Jewish businessmen to illustrate his points.

I was at a meeting this morning. We needed to raise a certain amount of money. Some of the top executives of Chicago were there. You take that same group—if they were Jewish, they'd be talking five to ten times as much money, and it would come easier. It's habitual. And it arises out of the special period in history. This was true in earlier periods, but only with respect to the very wealthy, who used to be the people who conducted all the charitable affairs in the community. Today, the amount of money given by modestly situated people is unbelievable.

After Mayer married and started a family, he began following in his father's philanthropic footsteps. He joined the Young Men's Jewish Council. The Council operated some boys' clubs in town.

I was doing nothing [philanthropically]. That was when I was determined I wasn't going to be sucked into doing that kind of thing. But the fellow who ran it called me up. I said, "I don't want to go out and ask people to give money." And he said, "Well, you'll learn about that. But in the meantime, why don't you come out to the the boys' clubs?" And I did, and it was kind of nice. I started a chess club. One night a week I went out and played chess with the kids. To make a long story short, I ended up going to all their weddings. I still see some of them. That's forty years ago. I became president of the organization eventually. One thing leads to another.

His tales of resistance to tradition, eventual acceptance, and systematic attempts by older Jews to socialize the younger generation toward philanthropy are representative.

Since that time, Mayer has figured prominently in the Council of Jewish Federations. He is on the board of governors of the Jewish Agency for Israel. He is on the board of the United Israel Appeal. He and his generation tend to concentrate more on Jewish charities than succeeding generations. However, Mayer has always funded non-Jewish nonprofit organizations as well, although he believes he has been excluded from participating in many of them.

His wife and children are also big contributors to charity.

They all give. I would say two of them are extremely generous, more generous than I would be. One is especially generous, and she is my oldest. She is more interested in the general community, although she gives her share. Our gift to the Jewish community is a family gift. We decide on it every year, and it's in six figures. The children contribute a modest share of the total. Mother and I are still giving most of it. But if there's an increase, they take the increase.

Everyone in the family, including Mayer's grandchildren, has been to Israel. "And a few of them are deeply interested in that. . . . How could they have escaped it? My wife and I have always, when the children were growing up, when we went to Europe or Israel, we'd take them with us. And they're doing the same with their children. We're creatures of habit."

In the 1950s the Mayers formed a foundation. Mayer explained, "It was named after and in honor of my father. It was formed by my children, and myself, and my sister and brother-in-law." The Mayer Foundation is a pass-through rather than endowed foundation. He said: "In those days we would put some money into the foundation, and when it was time to pay a charity bill or to give money to charity, we took it out of the fund. It was just a convenient holding spot."

The family still uses the foundation in this way. For example, he said:

My wife sold some stock the other day on which there was a large capital gain. Rather than take the money, she said to me, "We have some charity obligations, right?" I said yes. She said, "We might as well give the stock to the charity." The charity now sold the stock. There was no tax paid out of it. That money is sitting in the foundation, and a few months from now I'll write a check for about $50,000 and it will go out of the fund.

The Mayers plan to do their giving only during their lifetime; they will bequeath their estate to their children.

SECOND-GENERATION MIDDLE-AGED JEWISH COUPLE

> WIFE: My father was involved in charity, so I grew up with that as a background. It became very natural to just continue.
> HUSBAND: My first recollection of doing something significant was when I was in college. They passed a cigar box around for the Red Cross, and everybody put in a dime or a quarter. I put in a dollar.

Myrna and Benjamin Slote[27] are leading philanthropists in New York City. According to Myrna, "There isn't anything in New York that we don't support, unless they haven't sent us information. I don't turn anything down. There isn't a museum that we're not supporting. There isn't a dance group that we're not supporting that I can think of. . . . Whatever we can do for the culture of the city is very important to us." The Slotes give to Carnegie Hall, the Central Park Conservancy, the opera, and the New York Philharmonic.

"We are more heavily weighted to Jewish things but are trying to diversify . . . especially [in the] cultural things," her husband said. "The [Jewish] Federation takes care of local needs—136 agencies, but from the cultural viewpoint, we support a whole host of things."

The Slotes's money came from both sides of the family. She is more clearly in the second generation of wealth than her husband, whose father owned a store.

> That made me, in a sense, a wealthy person—even though it wasn't a big store and we didn't make any money. We survived out of the store. But I always felt I was rich.
> I worked for whatever I had, but I felt I had more than most. . . . Whenever I'd see somebody on the street, I'd give them some money, some poor person or something. And I remember my father made a pledge at synagogue, and he

really didn't have the money. I don't know however the hell he got to pay it. It might have taken him two, three years. . . . I saw that, and I had an attitude that I just had more than anybody else.

Ben Slote has made a fortune in real estate, and he believes that "in the real estate field it's just smart business for us to try and improve the quality of life in the city where we have our major holdings."

He remembers vividly one giving incident at about the time when Israel became a state. He was in college, living off veterans' assistance and working in his father's store, making about thirty dollars a week. Two women knocked on the door of his apartment. He said, "I didn't come from a Zionist background. . . . They asked me to make a contribution. They said something about Israel. . . . I wasn't that much oriented toward it. . . . I gave them twenty-five dollars cash. I'll never forget that." He claimed that this was the beginning of his philanthropy.

His wife teased, "That's the biggest contribution you ever gave!"

When they married, the Slotes moved into New York City, where her father was active with charity. The young couple both consider her father a role model for their philanthropy. Although they are not always in agreement, they still confer with him about some of their decisions.

Today the Slotes have both joint and separate charitable interests. But as Myrna explained: "Our giving is together. I don't have mine and he has his."

Ben is chairman of the board of a university and a leading secular cultural organization. He said, "It's getting a lot of time and attention from me, plus money."

Myrna attended a "Seven Sisters" college and serves on its board. She is a key fundraiser for the United Jewish Appeal, which, she stressed, gives locally and overseas to Jewish-sponsored charities, not only to charities that serve Jewish people. She also works with Planned Parenthood. Together, the Slotes give substantially to the UJA/Federation and to many projects in Israel. Myrna said, "We don't only do Jewish things—we do other things too. . . . I have to tell you that we give to many, many things, but we also wind up working for a lot of them!"

Myrna referred to differences in fundraising between the two institutions with which she works the most.

I would say the [Seven Sister] College fundraising is much more delicate, diplomatic, long-range. I mean you do a lot in the area of cultivation. You have to sort of get to be friends with somebody. Or even when you go out to a foundation, you have to supply them with a lot of information on why it is unique. It's a much slower process and a much softer sell. . . .

The UJA/Federation sell is much more survival, because we have ongoing agencies which cannot survive unless we raise x number of dollars. So, I would say it's more forthright, and one would call it a harder sell.

I mean, you never call a card at a [Seven Sister] College function. They would drop dead if you called their card, or asked them in public what they were going to give! So, you have to tailor your approach.

In the Jewish philanthropic community, people that I deal with, by and large, have a strong sense of conscience, a sense of responsibility that they must support the agencies that serve Jews all over the world. Whereas, in many cases in the [Seven Sister] world . . . it's much more "out-of-sight, out-of-mind." And a great percentage of them are even surprised that you even asked them for money.

As is common for wives, Myrna takes care of the family philanthropy; she has an outside office for handling these matters. There she meets with people, discusses projects, raises funds, and reviews various proposals to which her family might make grants. Her husband said, ''She's now in charge of that. It's so voluminous.''

Myrna spoke about Jewish charitable giving in general.

New York Jews give a lower per capita gift than in any other city. They give to Jewish charities much better in Cleveland, in Detroit, and in Philadelphia, because in New York you can be totally anonymous, whereas in other cities you don't get into the country club if you don't give. The temple, the synagogue will keep after you if you don't give. There's no escaping in the other cities because everybody knows everybody. But in New York you can be just as anonymous as you want to be. You can give to the Lincoln Center and the New York Public Library, but never really give to Catholic charities if you're Catholic, to Protestant welfare funds if you're Protestant, or to the Federation of Jewish Philanthropies/United Jewish Appeal. I think fundraising in New York has always been the toughest.

She gave an example:

I was just at the theater. . . . And there was this fellow, who I know is very wealthy, and there was his wife with him. And I went, ''Oh! I know I should be after her for [the Seven Sister campaign]!'' I mean, she just absolutely escaped. Whereas in Washington, D.C., the [Seven Sister] College Club is pivotal and they get them all in. What are you dealing with, 120 or 150 graduates? Whereas in New York, there are thousands. So New York is sui generis when it comes to charity. You've got the biggest givers and the smallest givers.

The Slotes offered their perspectives on reasons for charitable giving, each having different insights. They went back and forth, finally talking about political motives.

Myrna said, "In this city there's a tremendous amount of peer pressure: You give to mine and I'll give to yours."

Her husband said, "Also, you have a certain status if you're a philanthropic person. People ask you, and how do you say no?"

She said, "We have become involved in the political scene, taking a stand on certain issues and supporting the people who—"

He finished for her, "represent our views. But that's not philanthropic."

"No," she said. "But, it's also an area of giving that takes a lot of my time."

He claimed, "You become more responsible."

She agreed.

Ben continued, "You cannot say, 'It's not our issue. Let's not get involved.' You can't put your head in the sand. You have to take a stand and you have to support people."

The Slotes make their charitable and political contributions out of various funds they have established over the years. They do not have a foundation for their own giving, although at one time they considered starting one. They understand that foundations are more heavily regulated than other charitable vehicles, and they do not want to be questioned about their activities. "We don't want to start looking over our shoulders," said Myrna.

She added, "I think another reason we have avoided a foundation is that we are very emotional givers. That doesn't leave room for sitting down and taking a vote." They contribute to one project for intellectual or political reasons, and to others because the project touches their hearts.

The Slotes did, however, establish a small foundation for their children. Ben explained:

> We wanted our children to have the experience of working together to give out . . . a modest sum to begin with, and as it developed, a larger sum. They had to start working together, and decide how to give it. Did they want to divide it up, and each give twenty-five thousand? . . . Or would there be some idea of doing it together? It was for them to work out the method. We created the instrument, let them go work it out.

His wife elaborated:

> We did that because we thought that would be a training ground for what was to come, because we wanted to perpetuate in the next generation this feeling of giving and doing. We didn't want it to die with us. We didn't want them to put it in their pocket. They don't need it.

"If you don't expose them to the problems and the responsibilities, how else?" asked Ben. "So we thought that they should start to give some money away on their own," said Myrna, "without us knowing who, . . . what, where it was going. And they chose to have a public [rather than private] foundation." The older Slotes question this decision. He said, "To be public, you have to have a minority interest; a majority of the directors have to be nonrelated."

They have been looking into working with the New York Community Trust. "We have just started a conversation with them," said Myrna.

Our thinking is going in that direction for one reason. We've made a decision to do some funding in [a poor neighborhood of New York]. In order to do that, you have to really know the community. And these trust funds do, they work in them already. We wanted to be sure that what we plan is valid, and that we have some accountability.

They will set up a donor-advised fund in the community foundation earmarked for this project.

The Slotes, obviously thoughtful about their philanthropy, realize that they are unable to do much investigation or evaluation, and they are beginning to consider the need for follow-up. "We ask for financial statements now," said Ben. "We ask them to put things in writing." Myrna added, "We are asking for an end-of-the-year account before we will renew. . . . We're getting really organized, and starting to run it like a business."

Ben commented, "We just decided this year to deal with our children's giving [to Jewish causes] a little differently. We should not give their money away. Therefore, we have begun to deduct it from the overall gift. We'll say to the children, 'You should give.' That puts the responsibility on their back."

Myrna countered, "It also puts the responsibility on the UJA to go and solicit them and get it if they want it."

The Slotes realize that their children will make decisions different from theirs. "Both my son and daughter have feelings that they don't like the establishment," said Ben.

"That's right," mused Myrna. "My son is concerned with alternatives to established types of giving. . . . He might well take that amount of money and give it elsewhere—in Israel. I don't think he'll take it from Israel." They mentioned new Jewish organizations such as the New Israel Fund, the Radius Institute, Havarah, and the National Jewish Resource Center.

Ben contended, "It's like the youth are anti-establishment in the beginning. But eventually they're not so radical. They come around. They become establishment-oriented."

Myrna agreed: "They'll call themselves a counter-culture till they get older."

The Slotes are in the midst of changing their will. "It's lying on our desk. We haven't finished the latest changes. It's constantly going on." "The way we're doing it, I'm leaving everything to my wife. What she wants to do with it is up to her. . . . The children have already been provided for, by way of the business, so we don't have to leave them anything."

THIRD-GENERATION YOUNG JEWISH WOMAN

> My activities in the foundation and philanthropic world began in the past three or four years. So you have to take that into account in judging my remarks. They come from somebody who has not had vast experience, although I've had lifelong exposure to what goes on.

Wendy Levinson[28] is a political activist. Now thirty-two years old and married, she was an undergraduate at Princeton University and received an MBA from Stanford. She became a serious philanthropist when she was in her late twenties. The bulk of her charitable contributions go to feminist causes. She and her husband are among the founders of an alternative fund in the area where they live. Both inherited fortunes, but she is the more active philanthropist. Though raised in a Jewish family, she claims that she has only recently begun to identify as a Jew. Her first giving, however, was to Jewish causes.

Levinson's grandfather established a private grant-making foundation thirty-five years ago. Although she does not specifically acknowledge his influence, she seems to have modeled her giving after his. "My grandfather was always philanthropically inclined. Because he was a self-made man, he felt very privileged to have had the good fortune and luck and possibilities that he did."

For its first fifteen years of operation her grandfather's foundation was not well-known. Levinson said, "He gave, but he did not expect or require any publicity about his gifts. If anything, he requested anonymity. . . . But he was also the person—and this is true to this day—where if he perceived a need as genuinely important, he would be the first one in there giving substantial amounts of money to help the project get off the ground."

As the foundation began to fund more activities, it became better known, and the elder Levinson accepted public acclaim. His granddaughter continued:

> It's important to say that because he's from a Jewish background, I think that's an integral part of our religion and our cultural belief. And I think that whether it's at a conscious or unconscious level on his part, at an early age that's where he acquired [his philanthropic] behavior pattern.

Curiously, Wendy Levinson did not specifically refer to Judaism as an impetus for her own giving, although perhaps her statement about a "conscious and unconscious level" may be significant. Levinson commented, "I'm an atheist. I'm not even comfortable going into a synagogue."

She has been assessing the extent to which Jewish giving is different from that of others. She said: "As I work on a number of things outside of the Jewish world, and [continue to] associate with Jewish charities, I find it very disheartening. It's hard to raise money from people who are not Jewish." She went on:

> It's not a very nice thing to have to say, or to realize. . . . I don't see non-Jews committed to [philanthropy] to the same degree that Jews seem to give across the board. And I think that if you check what really happens, there are certainly many generous non-Jewish givers, but proportionately, it's outrageous. Just when you look at the number of white Anglo-Saxon Protestants who live very comfortably, and who think that a thousand-dollar gift to an organization is a major contribution. And there is no way to educate these people, at least not for me to go and educate them, and not at this point in my own development. I'm too young. I can speak to some of my peers, and I have.

About five years ago, the executive director of the Associated Jewish Charities (AJC) met with her parents and suggested that they consider establishing a philanthropic fund through the AJC to be administered by their children; he claimed that this would provide good experience and training in grant-making. The older Levinsons thought it an excellent idea. It happened to coincide with the divestiture of their company. According to Wendy Levinson:

> I am sure that [selling the company] went into the thinking and planning, but very clearly this was developed as a tool for us, the children, [as] our first exposure to direct responsibility for distributing and deciding how funds are going to be spent. The fund has continued to grow. The fund is not owned by us. It is not owned by our parents. The Federation/Association owns the assets. . . .

In very general terms, we are a committee who make suggestions to an executive committee. There would be no suggestions that would ever be turned down unless they were deemed detrimental to the Jewish community. For instance, we could not suggest a grant to the PLO, or underwrite the Arab League, or do a pro-Arab program in colleges.

They bring proposals to us. When we first started and were very inexperienced with all of this, that was where all of our proposals came from. As we began to [go further] we developed a more sophisticated understanding of what we want to be doing, and where we want to be going. We are now starting to develop proposals ourselves.

Levinson recalled an early mistake. Once, when she was serving on a panel at a conference concerned with charity, she put her personal address and phone number on the registration form, and the organization listed it in its roster. "Needless to say, I received tons of proposals at the house. I really didn't want to have twenty proposals coming in here a week to review."

She explained that a few years before she married

I had reached a point where I wanted to meet other young people who had inherited wealth. . . . An article appeared in the paper about [an alternative foundation created by rich young people], and I wrote ———— a letter and said that I wanted to meet for lunch. At that time I was particularly interested in meeting other young women who had inherited wealth. I think it's a lot easier for men in our society to have earned or inherited wealth. I think for women it's very different.

She continued:

I spent a lot of time educating myself, trying to figure out a lot of things [for which] most people, hopefully, have a bit of a longer learning period. You know, when you start working, you start earning a certain amount of money, and you hope that by the time you're fifty you'll be in a position to decide whether you want to put your money in stocks or savings. I didn't have that luxury. . . .

I wanted to meet other young people and talk. . . . There's a lot of emotional things that come with having inherited wealth, feelings about that. Having to write a will at a very young age, for example—the average person doesn't have to think about doing that. Or about getting married, and thinking through how do you structure, what part does money play in that, if the person has more or less than you. So, I was particularly drawn to [this alternative foundation group] because I hoped it would be a vehicle for meeting other young men and women who had inherited wealth.

Thus she got acquainted with others like herself, and through this group she met her husband.

Levinson thinks that she and her husband are becoming more systematic about their personal philanthropy.

> Up until about the past year or two, I had done most everything out of a checking account that I had from some stock that my father had given me five years ago. When we moved into this house, a lot of that money went into it, so that we are now making joint decisions that we never made before. We are beginning to develop that component of our relationship. I never had to ask my husband, "What do you think of x organization or y organization?" And now I do. It rankles me a bit, because there's an element of independence that's been lost, but at the same time I think it's helping us be more careful about the way in which we give money away.

She understands that some organizations are interested more in her name than in her skills. But she averred, "I am a good fundraiser. And I'm a good organizer. I can get people to do things."

After a few years in a new town to which they moved, Levinson and her husband created an alternative fund with other wealthy young people in the area.

> We sat around and had some meetings for a year to determine some policy and some guidelines. It was formed by [several] people who had inherited money. That's how it came to be.

Her husband is the family representative to the fund. She herself has become more active politically.

> Since then, I have wound up spending a significant part of my time working as a born-again feminist.
>
> Now I'm in a women's potluck that meets every two months. And there's about eight women at a time that meet, and we've become quite good friends. We're a good support system for each other. We share technical information. We talk about different issues in our lives, and try and discuss whether we are dealing with the issue in a certain way because we have inherited wealth or if we're dealing with it because it's a common issue for women our age.

Levinson is chair of a political committee that seeks to keep abortion safe and legal. In the last few years she has brought her philanthropy much more out into the open. "I had always sort of stayed in the background. . . . I have been much more open about putting our names on invitations . . . to the surprise of some of our friends."

Although they support each other's work, Levinson and her husband have different primary interests.

He and I have separated out our lives into three main areas of giving: economic development issues, women's issues, and Central America. . . . The only other [entities] that we fund are individuals. We will give money based on who's doing the project. That's one of the things we came to from gut instinct.

She does most of the political giving and has been urging her husband to become more active in that arena.

There are intergeneration conflicts in the Levinson family. She suspects, however, that along with her siblings she will soon be asked to serve on the board of the family foundation. She has some reservations about this. Her parents now use the "grandfather's foundation" as their primary charitable vehicle, and Levinson is critical of their methods.

I would guess that [the foundation] is the parents' generation's way of avoiding dealing directly with a lot of those decisions. Whereas I feel like our generation is a lot more willing to be out there on the front lines and more comfortable with saying directly [whether] this is a choice or not.

Her family has questions about the alternative fund that the younger Levinsons started.

My grandfather and father are both supportive of [the alternative fund]. But they think it's a lot of hot wind. They have no patience for it. "Why do you all need to get together and talk about giving money away? It's not such a goddamn difficult thing. Just give the money away!" And that is truly how they feel. In some respects they're absolutely right and in others they're wrong. They are wrong because of the way funding is going to be changing. Because the federal government [has] moved out of this area of basic support for human services, and if the private sector is not better developed and better organized, there are going to be some horrible human problems that we have got to meet. If we don't have these kinds of organizations that provide for the needy—a network—we'll be scrambling around trying to do it, or we'll be saying no to everybody.

She considers herself extremely political and sees philanthropy as a means of solving pressing problems. Thus, like most other elite givers, she endorses a philanthropic ideology.

She brought up the question of the next generation and what might motivate them to continue the practice of philanthropy.

In terms of the college-age generation, I don't know. I have no idea. I wish I did know. I think that reproductive rights on one level will be important. . . . I mean abortion has been legal. They don't feel any threat to that. And they think that we are paranoid. . . . That's why, cynically, I say the draft. I think if they're threatened with going to Central America they may become politically active. Other than that, I really don't know. There is a lot more campus activism on the divestment issue. . . . I feel like I am out of touch with it. I met a sixteen-year-old recently who was not suffering from testosterone poisoning, and I thought, here's hope. . . . So, there's one young boy who I know will have a social conscience, and other than that, I have no answers.

She says she has no answers, but she funds as if she did by the causes she selects. She thinks that having a social conscience and acting upon it is sufficient.

CONFLICTS AND TENSIONS

Wealthy Jews of all generations in the United States have been faced with a dilemma. They have wanted to maintain their distinctive Jewish identity but at the same time to be accepted into the dominant, elite Protestant culture of philanthropy. This conundrum has affected Jews with old as well as new money. In spite of anti-Semitism, many Jewish people have become members and even leaders of the culture because of its constant need for money.

Jews have proven themselves especially able in raising funds and have developed innovative techniques for doing so. The discreet suggestion that a large contribution will be made if a nonprofit agency finds others to match the gift has met with widespread approval. But practices such as the use of calling cards are still generally taboo in the culture of philanthropy.

There are similarities in the structural position of wealthy Jews and of women with new money in the culture of philanthropy. Both may be accepted into the culture if they follow the rules. They must enter at the bottom and do the hard background work first. They must follow the cultural mores of modest living, conspicuous giving, and high cultural patronage. And their children must go to the proper private schools.

Those Jews who wish to be accepted in both their own community and in the predominantly WASP culture of philanthropy have learned to adapt. As Myrna Slote explained, they use a ''hard sell'' method in fundraising for Jewish causes and a ''soft sell'' approach in soliciting for high cultural and educational organizations. This way, there is the potential to be at the top of both worlds, but a balancing act of this sort must be extremely difficult. It also takes a lot of money and time.

There are generational differences among elite Jews. Elderly, self-made millionaires like Joseph Mayer came up the hard way. They know they are Jewish and they are proud of it. Mayer has given to a few non-Jewish groups, primarily as part of his business interests, to consolidate his position in the corporate community. But he prefers to fund Jewish organizations. Such endeavors have repaid him grandly with recognition and honors.

The second-generation Slotes are caught somewhere in-between. They strongly identify as Jews but they are not Zionists. They are large donors to the Jewish Federation, but they also give to virtually every cultural cause in New York. Myrna Slote was educated at a prestigious college; she is a loyal alumna and works hard to raise funds for her institution. Like other "ladies bountiful," she runs the family charities and is opposed to hiring professionals to do this work. The third-generation Slotes, however, are, like Wendy Levinson, anti-establishment. The Slotes believe their children will eventually become less recalcitrant.

Wendy Levinson is not so sure about what her Jewishness means, except that she comes from a liberal or progressive tradition. She was educated with WASPs and learned their values. She has ties to Jewish organizations because her parents established a donor-advised fund within the Associated Jewish Charities. But she considers herself an atheist and along with her husband gives to nonreligious, highly political causes. They are committed to alternative, feminist, and social change funding.

There are tensions to be resolved between these two generations, as well as between the Jewish and non-Jewish philanthropic communities. Middle-aged, second-generation Jews straddle two worlds. Their third-generation offspring know that they are Jewish and rich but feel uncomfortable with both. Along with many other young people, they seek to change the world with feminist and progressive philanthropic commitments. The tensions and contradictions thrown up by these intentions are among the concerns of the next section of this book.

PART 3

PROSPECTS

Chapter 8

The Alternative Fund Movement

We're people who aren't satisfied to wait for our wills, just contribute to
our alma maters, or give in order to get on local cultural boards. Our motto
is change, not charity.
—GEORGE PILLSBURY, quoted in Michele Willens, " 'Rich Kids' Have a
New Way to Give," *USA Today*, 21 September 1984

The Haymarket People's Fund, created in Boston in 1974 to finance activist
and grassroots causes in the New England area, is part of a growing philanthropic movement among young people with inherited wealth. Haymarket
is different from its fellow alternative foundations, because although they all
award grants to a range of politically left or "progressive" organizations,
"Haymarket's funding decisions have been made by a board of community
activists, not by the rich people who donate the money."[1] Haymarket was
not the first alternative public foundation in the country, but early on its
founders pioneered a grant-making process representative of the communities
that were targeted for its funds.

This chapter is based on interviews with twelve individuals who have contributed to multi-issue alternative foundations. They may have also established a personal grant-making program that concentrates
on some combination of leftist activist, economic development, environmentalist, grassroots empowerment, peace, social change, "new age" spiritualist, or women's organizations. Additional material was
gleaned from public sources and interviews with non-donor staff members at three alternative foundations
and the Funding Exchange, a national network or umbrella organization of such funds.

There are now around twenty alternative funds or giving programs in the United States. To varying degrees, the wealthy young people who have formed this counter philanthropy movement have struggled to determine the extent of influence and control they should have in the foundations they finance and, by extension, over the groups that receive the money. Unlike the Haymarket People's Fund, most alternative foundations have developed a mix of some form of representative community participation as well as donor involvement in grant-making and policy matters. There has been no single organizational model or allocation practice. Several models have been tried in each of the alternative foundations. Each fund has evolved over time, depending on the perspectives of the founders, joiners, and recipients as well as the charitable or political climate of the area where it is located. A majority of these institutions, however, have moved in the direction of an increasingly representative governance and grant-making structure. Though there were contrast and contradiction among the original alternative fund models, over time they have tended to become similar to one another.[2]

THE PILLSBURY NETWORK

George Pillsbury, a founder of the Haymarket People's Fund[3] and heir to the baking goods and food company fortune, is a leading proponent of community, rather than donor, representation on the funding committees of alternative foundations. He was in his mid-twenties when his mother, Sally Pillsbury, told him about the Vanguard Public Foundation in San Francisco.[4]

The Vanguard Foundation had been established in the early 1970s "as a cooperative venture by several young wealthy people to support social change projects too controversial or too risky to find money at more conventional foundations."[5] After reading Vanguard's first annual report, George Pillsbury began fundraising and organizing the Haymarket People's Fund. He worked at this endeavor full time until 1977,[6] and continues actively to support both Haymarket and the alternative foundation concept.

Pillsbury personally recruited many others—including relatives—to the cause. He has claimed that "the movement started at Philadelphia in 1971 with the Bread and Roses Community Fund. The organizing grew directly out of opposition to the Vietnam War and concern about civil rights. There was a wish to fund social activism."[7] Within five years, Bread and Roses and the Vanguard Foundation, having formed independently, had been joined by Haymarket and then by the Los Angeles–based Liberty Hill Foundation. Liberty Hill was initiated by Sarah Pillsbury, George Pillsbury's sister, and other co-founders.[8] One of the early donors to Vanguard was Tracy DuVivier Gary, who had been urged by her cousin George to make contact with the fund. After several years' working with Vanguard, she helped to form the Women's Foundation in San Francisco, the first locally based fund that concentrated solely on women's issues and needs.[9]

Thus a movement as well as a social network was created by George Pillsbury, his relatives, and many other "organizers" of means. They use the term *organizer* because it symbolically connects them with the groups they fund—community, grassroots, and union-organizing efforts. Although the politics of these "rich kids" tend to be more left-leaning than the politics of their parents, the young progressive funders recruit money and people in the same way that their parents do.

The leaders of the alternative funds started by contacting college and prep school acquaintances, friends, relatives, friends of friends, and friends of relatives with wealth. They organized within their own class, in the regions where they lived, moved, or traveled. As a consequence of the efforts and tactics of all these organizers with inherited wealth, most are now known to each other and have multiple interrelationships. Several give to more than one alternative foundation, although they usually focus on their local institution.

Many wealthy young people in the alternative foundation movement have met, dated, and formed businesses or nonprofit enterprises, as well as joined potluck and support groups. Some have even married while setting up and working in social-change funds. Other young donors have sought out emotional and personal support from the elite network members, but self-consciously attempt to modify class boundaries by having friends, lovers, and spouses outside their class of birth.

Since the early days, Haymarket has expanded its base of contributors beyond the upper class. The fund is run by a staff of at least six in concert with nine regional grant-making boards of activists in New England. Haymarket has given to AIDS projects, environmental issues, groups organizing around a host of causes on the "activist left," such as civil rights and prison reform, as well as peace and women's organizations, and "solidarity work with the people of Central America and South Africa." Since its formation, Haymarket has distributed approximately $3 million.[10]

Only a handful of the donors to the Haymarket People's Fund are known to the public. The majority prefer anonymity, not wishing to reveal their economic status, their politics, or the nature of their philanthropy. Some are embarrassed by their privilege. Many value their privacy, in addition to the idea of giving without credit. Most do not want to be personally inundated with requests for funds. According to Judy Sutphen, a former member of the Haymarket staff collective, "Many donors appreciate the structure of Haymarket, which requires only a limited amount of input from them."[11] Like other more traditional foundations, such institutions shield the rich who do not desire publicity from grant seekers.

The unique aspect of the Haymarket approach is that its contributors, whatever their economic status, give up control of the money they put into the organization. Staff member Sutphen provided a blunt rationale for excluding major donors from decision making. "It's hard for ruling-class, white, rich, usually male people to judge what makes sense to fund in the left. It takes time to get inside it, and very few rich people have or take that option. It takes time to develop expertise."[12] However, the approach of strictly limiting donor involvement has not proven likely to attract many wealthy contributors unless they are provided with added incentives.[13]

The Haymarket People's Fund and many of the other alternative foundations have multiple purposes. They raise money from the privileged that will be distributed by activists to what they consider needy and worthy causes; provide a support structure for socially conscious people with wealth; and encourage and educate funders about progressive giving.[14] Most of the alternative funds teach untraditional philanthropy and provide a meeting place and supportive environment to young people of means.

After having contributed to an alternative foundation, a number of young wealthy givers have decided that they want more direct involvement with the groups whose work they endorse. One Northeastern woman's funding history and philosophy is illustrative.

> [My philanthropy] started with the Haymarket Fund, where I could just give a lump sum of money and they would deal directly with organizations. . . . It meant a lot less [work] than having to decide on my own, and it was a way to kind of help me get started giving money away. . . . As the amount of money I give has increased, I do more funding on my own, as well as supporting foundations like Haymarket.

Prior to her connection with Haymarket, this donor tried to separate the implications of having inherited wealth from her progressive politics, because they seemed contradictory.

I tried to live my life partly as if the money weren't there. . . . People often didn't realize that I had money, or was doing funding. Now I know much more [and] have integrated [having wealth with my politics]. I feel very good about the way I have been working with my money so the two can blend more together.

She explained what had attracted her to the Haymarket approach.

Haymarket was partially set up so that [rich] people would work with community activists. Community activists now decide where the money goes. But when donors are considering joining . . . it's so that they have someone to talk over proposals with. I think among my friends—I mean, a majority of my friends don't have money and aren't deciding where to give it away—those are things that it's not that easy to talk over with them. So that when we [wealthy donors] do get together to talk about giving money away, it helps break down some of that working in isolation.

The key concept in this quotation is "joining." This donor is committed to the idea of collaborating for change with grassroots activists and community people, but she stressed the emotional support and understanding she receives from other wealthy heirs. She has found a community of people like herself, a social group whose members have similar economic status and similar political and philanthropic values.

She elaborated:

Part of the business of the Haymarket Fund is to redistribute not only the wealth but also the power to make decisions over wealth. In giving to a foundation like Haymarket, it is sharing the control. It's basically redistributing the control over the money.

But, she indicated, she and others usually reserve some of their surplus income for funding activities outside of Haymarket.

I think it is kind of a trade-off. That's why people don't give all their money over to Haymarket. They still have their own goals, maybe different than the goals of the foundation; they want to fund other projects in other areas.

She admits that the community activists are "much more in touch with what is actually happening in the community, what projects are really successful." But as she has learned more about the funding process she has increasingly wanted to see the results of her own hunches and ideas, so that now

about half of my money goes to foundations like Haymarket . . . or the Film Fund, which gives to progressive films, or foundations which are set up to fund women's organizations. Half of my giving goes directly to organizations.

The social-change funders contribute to nontraditional organizations, and many give up power by sharing decision making about grants with community activists. But only a few of these funders have been willing to donate all their interest income, or even substantial sums out of capital, to either alternative foundations or recipient groups.[15] They want to remain personally involved; it gives their lives meaning. But in their hearts many are not confident that the system will change or that they, as members of the upper class, can be true catalysts for any transformation of society.

George Pillsbury has a sophisticated perspective.

It is encouraging when a black person is elected to Congress or a woman is chosen for the board of Standard Oil. But what are the overall benefits to all blacks, all women? As long as the system remains intact, no real change will take place.

All structural change in history has been the result of mass movements—though often in combination with chance events or outstanding individual leaders. Those in power have never given it away. The people took it away.[16]

In 1984 he explained: "We're not trying to divide the pie, but change the recipe of the pie. I want to spend my money to change the system that created this fortune."[17]

THE SAN FRANCISCO VANGUARD FOUNDATION

When I was in college I inherited some money so that I had a regular income. I felt that I should give some of it away, but there was no mechanism by which this could be done. . . .

I ended up in San Francisco by coincidence and ran into some other people that had inherited money. And we realized that together we could start a foundation. We could pool our resources.

The idea for an alternative foundation in San Francisco is attributed to a conversation between Philip Gerbode, a young inheritor who was active in antiwar and farm-worker organizing, and David Fuller, a consultant with a group called Pacific Change. Both were familiar with foundations and progressive funding. As part of his work, Fuller helped to match West Coast organizing projects with individual givers and foundations. Gerbode mailed a letter to thirteen other young people of wealth who he hoped would be interested in "innovative joint funding."[18] Gerbode was to move away from

California before his vision was realized, but he had inspired enough of his peers to take the project forward.

The six original donors to the Vanguard Public Foundation were all women and men of means between the ages of twenty-two and twenty-six.[19] Their number soon grew to a dozen, largely through the dedication and persuasive efforts of one of the organizers as well as referrals from "more established foundations." Altogether, these twelve individuals constituted the foundation's first official board of directors. This initial group of contributors is described as having "a variety of political perspectives, ranging from McGovern-type left to completely apolitical."[20]

Today the Vanguard Public Foundation has more than three hundred donors from all classes, who make contributions ranging from a few dollars to more than $20,000 a year. The allocation process at Vanguard was initially performed only by wealthy donors. Then they created a separate board of community activists who also distributed funds. Now the donor and community boards have been merged. Unless someone is a community representative, the minimum donation required to participate on the board of directors or allocations committee is $2,500. An early donor recalled that "in the beginning it was $200." He indicated that they are still

> constantly fundraising, beating the bushes for people who might have money and who might be interested in contributing to the foundation and getting involved. We are not finding as many people who are just coming out of college, but maybe that is starting to change as well. We have a new donor, just coming on, who is young. And there is a greater age range. We never had people older than our baby-boom generation until quite recently, but now we do. . . . We were recently considering one guy who is in his eighties, who had to drop out because of other time commitments.

The organization has a small endowment, but most of the funds raised in any given year are distributed to nonprofit groups.

More women than men have given to Vanguard. With some notable exceptions, these women donors have tended to be less public or visible than the men. Many wealthy women heirs have had to overcome a socialization that demanded their assumption of the role of a "lady bountiful."

Major contributors to the Vanguard Public Foundation have come and gone as their interests and lives have changed, but a few have remained active since the beginning.

> A lot of people have left just because they have moved away from here. I would say that is the prime reason. Some people's politics have changed. Some people have been there a long time. A lot of people have found, also, that they have learned

through the process what they would like to concentrate on. They don't want to fund this vast array of different issues and projects and communities but would like to concentrate more, and they do that on their own.

Several individuals created private foundations after their experience with Vanguard; some participants have helped establish new alternative groups in other areas of the country. At the national level these efforts have led to the Funding Exchange, a network of alternative foundations. At the local level, the Women's Foundation in San Francisco was partially inspired by Vanguard, and became a model for women's funds around the country.

A LONGTIME DONOR

One of the early and ongoing donors to Vanguard is a soft-spoken man who is now in his late thirties. I interviewed him in the sun-filled bedroom of his Victorian flat in San Francisco. We were meeting there out of consideration for the rest of his family, whom we occasionally heard through the door. He sat in a bay window seat overlooking the street and gave affectionate pats to two dogs as he remembered, "It seems incredible to look back on, now that we have quarterly meetings, but at first we actually met every two weeks to make granting decisions. And we would meet in between times every other week for just socializing."

He indicated that friendships and personal conversations were essential. "I think [they are] an important part of any political organization or effort. It is not always recognized as such, or given much credit. [But] that's a motivation for people to join. It was certainly true with us." There was a kind of safety, a feeling that they could discuss a host of personal and political issues with others in the same situation.

Although his own parents were liberal funders, this donor continued:

A lot of us were trying to grapple with some of the contradictions of having progressive political outlooks and having money, fairly opposing sorts of notions that were really felt as contradictions and conflicts. . . . Being able to talk about those kinds of issues with each other . . . helped us to grapple with them a little more concretely.

We have dealt with some people who have been very private and anonymous about it [giving to Vanguard]. I have always been pretty out front about what my position was, my class background and having money. To me, that's a good course. People can accept that. I have not found it to be a problem. . . . People who are not of the same economic status can accept and I hope even respect my choices.

A FOUNDING MEMBER

A member of the Vanguard founding group, who was interviewed in a New York restaurant and is no longer directly connected with the San

170

Francisco fund, also remembered his internal conflicts about having money. His family had not been philanthropic.

> I felt guilty that I had these extra resources. But that was a minor element of it. I felt it was simply a moral duty, if you have more, to share it somehow, and help other people out if you have the capability to do that. We decided we wanted to enlist other people with inherited money to give away what would be relatively small amounts—one thousand dollars a year to forty or fifty thousand. We were aware that to pool together . . . into a common attitude, that the influence would be magnified, both in terms of our own dollars and the way we could influence other foundations.

Many of the "rich kids" put their money and their time behind their ideas.

> At the beginning of Vanguard we felt that it was cheap to be able to write a check, put it in an envelope, lick it and put it in a mailbox. It takes a few moments of your time and it really doesn't hurt if you're rich. Not that anything has to hurt. But if we were committed to what we were supporting, then we should be able to commit our time as well. Which means, in a way, that anyone who works as a volunteer is a philanthropist.

Today this Vanguard founder is not contributing nearly as much money to nonprofit causes as he did earlier,

> partly because I gave a huge amount away of my liquid assets. And I consider the projects I am working on to be important as well. . . . At the same time, I am constantly advising people about how and where they can get money, from different sources. I find that is much more effective, and always has been, frankly, than my personal philanthropy.

THE EARLY YEARS

In 1972, the Vanguard board, composed only of donors, awarded $23,000 to a variety of alternative media, prison reform, and women's rights projects. An additional $14,450 went to causes specified by individual contributors. That is, this specified money was given to groups that might have been outside the established criteria but were still within the general progressive purview of the foundation. Such a flexible arrangement allowed donors the option of choosing exactly where their charitable funds went.

By then, two of the men on the board were volunteering full time at Vanguard. In the formative years, there was no paid staff, but the work of the foundation was continually increasing. Additional contributors were joining and more community groups seeking funds had learned about Vanguard. Grants rose to $210,000 in 1976, but only one out of ten applicants ultimately received financial support.

> Initially the grants were quite small: two thousand dollars generally. . . . Vanguard's fortunes—our fundraising—has increased through the years, but so have the number of groups we have funded. . . . At one point we were making grants of, say, four thousand to ten thousand, as high as ten, [but] that was very rare, [our] highest grant.

In the early years, said a founder, "we could fund community organizations, grassroots organizations, consistently to a level . . . which was awesome to them and see them move to getting support from larger foundations, more established foundations." The group's orientation and hence its funding were to become increasingly political.

THE AMALGAMATED RICH FOLKS AND A NEW WOMAN DONOR

> At that point [1974] they were forming something that was called ARF, which stood for Amalgamated Rich Folks. It was a national organization of people who had come from wealthy families that would meet once a year. These came to be the donors and supporters of the Funding Exchange [a national umbrella group of the alternative funds]. ARF has since changed its name. It is called the CNP, which stands for the Council on National Priorities.

> It was a chance for us to exchange [information], and look at political candidates, and talk about the labor movement, and other kinds of issues that we might not be hearing about in our own local communities. Then there were 30 of us; now there are well over one hundred.

A new donor to Vanguard, Tracy Gary recounted her history with the organization. "I first went to the ARF Conference, and from that met a bunch of Vanguard and other people. . . . I was very excited . . . I thought, 'This is a community of people who really care about change.' I was very moved by it, and wanted immediately to get involved with Vanguard." Like her peers, Tracy Gary was looking for her place in the world, an identity, some meaning in her life. She did not really know anyone in San Francisco, but was socially well-connected in the East.

> My cousin George Pillsbury had come out to visit [the people] who had just started Vanguard. He said, "You should get involved." And very soon after, I did.
> I moved out here in seventy-three. . . . I had "come out" in 1969 as a debutante. . . . This was not for me. I loved the parties, but I thought, "This is a ridiculous amount of money . . ."

> When I came out here it was really in reaction to not wanting to do the New York lifestyle. . . . I first went to a meeting in 1974. It did not seem like an East Coast group of people. . . . It was really clear that they had some of the values I did—from the sixties.

Her family was philanthropic in a traditional manner. She had had some experience from her boarding school and college days (she attended Sarah Lawrence) with contributing to nonprofit organizations, and she had volunteered over summers in a few inner-city projects with children.

> I worked from five to ten hours a week with Vanguard between 1975 and 1978. . . . I learned a great deal about going out on interviews [with potential grantees], but also got very impatient with what I saw to be a lack of sufficient organizational structure and planning.
>
> I was volunteering in other community groups during that time. Vanguard would be giving them two thousand dollars or something, but the technical assistance needs were so great. Oftentimes what would happen is I would stay and work with them on the organizational things. I would try to help them get other money, or think about a fundraising strategy.
>
> At about the same time I got involved with the first battered women's shelter here [Vanguard was the first organizational funder]—and was picked up quickly by the [women's] community as somebody who could—was willing to—write checks and help when I could.

Gary went on the board of La Casa de las Madres and within a few years was helping them to organize a conference on violence against women. "We could not find a physical space to put it in. It was at that point that a group of us decided to try to find a physical location where women's groups could be housed" (what was to become the Women's Building). Gary became more and more involved with funding women's issues and less active with the Vanguard group. Along with other women, she formed the Women's Foundation, and later the National Network of Women's Funds.[21]

THE DECADE-LONG TRANSITION

> It [Vanguard] was definitely a donor-controlled organization in the beginning. . . . We had a lot of very general ideas about what we wanted to do. . . . [We] experimented with this and that, different kinds of alternatives.

The mid-seventies was a period of tremendous administrative change and some upheaval for the Vanguard Foundation. The burnout of wealthy volunteer personnel, class conflict, an expanding network of alternative funds around the country with different structural models, and increasingly left-wing political values were all swirling at the center of the controversy, as well as contributing to an organizational evolution. The political component of Vanguard's funding was to develop and become clearer with time: "More and more community self-determination, community empowerment, community organizing." These principles were perceived by some to be at odds with the existing governance structure, which put the decision-making and funding power in the hands of economically privileged progressives.

The Vanguard founders and early donors were well-intentioned, but they were learning as they went along. "[Initially], we [had] wanted to operate it [Vanguard] ourselves, on principle," explained a member of the founding group, referring to the absence of employees. "We didn't want to hire someone to do the work for us. We thought that would distance us from the information that would allow us to make good decisions. In a way it was kind of copping out on our responsibility." He had thought the owner of the money should ensure that it was given professionally and used effectively. "I was very concerned that the money would be wasted. . . . The grantee organization had to be a good organization."

For the longtime donor

> the appeal of Vanguard was that it was a group of peers trying to do something . . . really moving philanthropy in a different direction, providing resources to the kinds of ideas, beliefs, values that we all shared. And it was a cooperative enterprise, at that point, even though we were donor controlled. It was a group of donors that wasn't related by family, which was sort of a new thing.

Over time, however, the initial participants in Vanguard were both psychologically "burning out" and developing new views about the need to enlist others in the granting decisions to a greater extent.

After several years, one of the original full-time volunteers left the office staff. In 1988 he recalled that decision in a faint voice.

> Part of it was just—there are those rare people who like to raise money. I do it because I feel it is where I can be useful. Not only this kind of thing, but I have gotten involved in local electoral political issues. . . . Fundraising, more than anything else, is what I can bring to an effort.

Then, in a firmer tone, he continued:

> I don't like it [fundraising]. I kind of hate it. And, doing it full time, not only, actually, for money, but also being the person who is screening the community organizations, and telling nine out of ten of them no, got to be quite debilitating, in a certain emotional sense, after a while. . . .

There was a real pressure, especially at that time, when politics were a little more confrontational. We were the screen for a certain amount of anger. . . . But more than that, it was just being in the position of always saying no.

It was certainly a good lesson to learn. I value the ability to say no, but on the other hand there is just a certain pressure of being in the middle between the wealthy community and the community community.

He laughed: "[I was] just feeling stretched both ways."

At first this wealthy heir believed that he could be "useful" or make a primary contribution raising money. Yet he found himself doing something he did not particularly enjoy. His usefulness was the result of his status as a member of the upper class and his connections, rather than personal skills or interests that he valued. As he talked it out, he realized again that he actually dislikes, even hates fundraising.

Then he changed the subject, turning to another important aspect of his former work, "screening the community organizations," and declining to give money to the vast majority of them. Although he understood that anger from the groups and people who did not receive funding reflected a more general frustration about a lack of resources, it was difficult for him not to take the hostility personally.

Finally, he touched upon his core conflict: He was between two worlds. He had rebelled against the elite advantages of his birth, but he could never belong to or be a part of the "community community," a connection for which he yearned. His work at Vanguard had helped him begin to establish his own identity. Ultimately he wrote a novel, a project clearly requiring his own special talents.

A new volunteer with inherited wealth took this young man's place after he resigned from the staff of Vanguard, although the longtime donor continues to do unpaid work for the organization. Many more groups needed to be investigated than in the early days. Eventually the board became convinced that despite the expense it would be necessary to hire paid staff. At the same time Vanguard changed its legal status from that of a private foundation to that of a public charity. And, "in perhaps the single most significant step in its evolution, [Vanguard] established a community board to share decision-making authority with the existing donor board."[22]

Part of the impetus to form a community board was the example of the more representative Haymarket fund. To some, Haymarket's very existence emphasized the hypocrisy of Vanguard's donors holding on to the power to distribute the money. As a staff member put it a decade later, in 1986:

Even though they were giving in a progressive direction, [they were] still imitating a pattern of philanthropy that they were very critical of. . . . They decided not to divest themselves of that activity, which was real important to them, but to create another board and to split the money that we raised down the middle.

By June 1977, seven local activists had been appointed to the new community board. "It was a majority people of color, a majority women, and covered not only a spectrum of ethnic communities but also the kind of issue areas we had been dealing with," explained the longtime donor. Each board was

autonomous and equal—equal amounts of money, equal amounts of say-so over money, that would make decisions autonomously . . . [but] generally funding the same projects. But there was some divergence. . . .

The donor board would fund certain kinds of issues that perhaps were mainly organizations of white people—maybe more middle-class white people—doing certain, what we would consider essential work. The community board would sometimes fund the project of a community that might not be the most incisive, but nonetheless the community had been underrepresented in our funding.

The disparity revolved around class and race differences.

There had been a certain level of comfort in working most closely with people from the same economic and social backgrounds, but that was to change over time when paid staff and community activists of different classes became part of the Vanguard decision-making group. Initially, some of the donors were not satisfied with the relationship that developed between the staff who were paid and the rich members of the board.

I felt from staff, who were not monied—it was a fairly troubled group of people [uneasy laughter]. I can't say troubled. I'll say it differently. PR and marketing was not their specialty in terms of personalities. . . . There was a whole wall that sort of happened with many of the donors, mistrust on the part of the staff, awkwardness about "How do we handle this group of wealthy people? What line do you cross over?" There was a lot of paranoia that was going on both ways, and it was not talked about enough.

Gary indicated that she had reservations about the dual board structure:

There was a desire to give power to the grassroots community members. Many of us on the donor board were trying to find our way with our power, were really trying to understand it. But the separation [two boards] in some way only exacerbated it, because what we got from the staff was a sort of attitude that we were all crazy—and did not know anything. And it was the community board who knew everything.

The group persevered, however, with the new staff, structure, and volunteers. The donors successfully worked out potentially difficult relationships with community board members and employees. Vanguard board members came and went. A few stayed active throughout the decade.

UNRESOLVED CLASS CONFLICTS

There was a huge little split[23] going on [at Vanguard] between the grant-making group that was from the grassroots community and the donor board—a lot of race and class stuff—that was unspoken. At that point, I did not have the equipment to know what was wrong. I felt like an outsider. I felt it was ridiculous having this wealth of information on the grassroots board and the donor board not working together [with them]. It symbolized the very thing I was trying to overcome. I was very interested in bridging those communities, in having the decisions made together.

For nearly ten years the Vanguard Public Foundation operated with two allocations boards. Working independently, each board tended to fund the same or similar projects and groups. The exceptions could typically be categorized on the basis of race, class, or both. The community board might fund a fledgling project in an ethnic or racially concentrated neighborhood if the organizers came from that community. The donor board was more likely to fund groups run by white, middle-class, but "seasoned" organizers, who encouraged empowerment. The community board members felt obligated to see that the constituencies they represented were funded. The donor board members were motivated by their politics and their sense of which groups were effective.

By this time Vanguard had diversified its sources of funds. A base of donations was assured each year—roughly fifteen times $3,500, or the number of members on the donor board times their contribution. Many board members paid more than the minimum amount. "$115,000 of our budget," said a staff member in 1986, "comes from donor board members. That is a fifth or a sixth of the budget. And we fundraise from individuals for the rest, which is now about $570,000 a year."

Within a year of that interview, the two boards were merged into one. "When we switched," said the longtime donor,

it became a unified board of directors that included both community reps and donors, as well as a unified allocation committee that also included community reps and donors. There is a lot of overlap. Community people have the slight majority of the allocations committee. The numbers are approximately equal, by design, on the board of directors.

Vanguard has also changed its process for appointing community people to the board. In the past they would widely distribute an announcement or call for resumés. Although they always received many, they generally chose only one person from any particular category such as Afro-Americans, Chinese, gays, or neighborhood groups. The longtime donor commented:

> That creates quite a bit of ill will from the many other people that we would have to say no to. It's a little late, but we finally decided that this was not the best way of approaching it.
>
> So from now on we are going to essentially try to build a pool of people who have been working with the foundation in other sorts of capacities, as volunteers, on one of the other committees, and try to go there first, or just reach out more quietly for a particular individual—somebody who could fit the bill of whatever slot we are looking for, [such as] someone who is black and works for a labor union.

In addition to eliminating the disappointment of declined applicants, this approach minimizes conflict by adding to the board people who are already well known to the organization. But it means that the recruitment process is less open.

The longtime wealthy donor was candid about his and others' fears and ongoing concerns.

> There was some trepidation at each step, before bringing on the community board in the first place and then merging the two boards. I like what has happened fine, but before we made this most recent move, I was not one who was speaking for merging the boards. It was other people. . . . Since this happened, I think it has worked very well.

However, according to this board member and major contributor, making decisions together has highlighted the contradictions between what had formerly been two groups.

> Bringing all that into one body has at times sharpened the debate around priorities, and particularly around race, whether we do fund [all-]white groups and how much we push them to become multiracial, and at what point we cut off their funding—that kind of thing.

The new funding board has had conflicts, "but not acrimonious ones on the whole," he stressed.

"I felt a good bit of concern that donors continue to be represented strongly, and if not fifty-fifty, at least close, that was important too," he continued. "It might sound odd or paradoxical, but to empower donors in the process, and not to play into guilt tendencies, to make sure donors have a voice."

"The problem is," he said with a show of irony, "that we have gotten more democratic. And that means that our grant money is spread pretty thin. We have taken some pains to have a very representative process, where all sorts of communities [have a voice] in the grant-making decision. And as a result," he laughed, "we have a whole spectrum of concerns that we cover, and nobody wants to have their area cut out."[24]

The Vanguard Public Foundation has distributed approximately $5 million since its inception.

AROUND THE COUNTRY

From the mid- to late seventies at least three new alternative foundations were created.[25] Either through individuals or organizationally, many of the old and new alternative foundations had informal ties with each other. In 1986, a Vanguard staff member recalled that

> in 1978 we formed ad hoc relationships with four other funds around the country that were similar to us: Haymarket, North Star in New York City, Liberty Hill in Los Angeles. Our main reason was to support each other, but also to try and encourage other foundations to set up around the country that would be like us.

By 1979, several alternative funds formally consolidated into what was to become the Funding Exchange, a national umbrella organization for such groups.[26]

The Vanguard staff member continued:

> Then we set up a national, donor-advised giving arm of the Funding Exchange, called the National Community Funds in New York City. That has grown way beyond our expectations. It gives away several million dollars a year. . . . This collection of funds doesn't take advice in any formal fashion. The staff . . . goes around and visits projects, receives proposals and sends them out to donors. The donors call up and say, "I want to fund this or that project." It is very much at the will of a donor. . . . And they get all the tax advantages of donating to a public charity.

On the average a new alternative fund has been created every year since the early 1970s. Altogether, over the course of fifteen years, these funds have distributed more than $30 million, $5 million of it in 1987. The Funding Exchange is launching a $15 million endowment campaign to pay for the operating expenses of the local funds. By 1988, the fund had raised nearly $5 million toward this endowment.

ONE OF THE NEWEST ALTERNATIVE FUNDS

In 1975 [his junior year of college] I heard what Vanguard was doing. . . . I was [visiting] in San Francisco. . . . So I went down, spent about half an hour with [a donor staff member], said, "This is great," and wrote him a check for three thousand dollars.

Considering that my total income was only about fourteen thousand a year from the trust—I had a lot of cash, but I was a student, and was paying for all my books and bills with that—it was probably a little more than I felt comfortable giving. I was so taken with the idea, so enraptured by it, that I wrote him a check.

I interviewed this busy thirty-six-year-old man at the kitchen counter of his home in Denver, Colorado. There were piles of papers stacked in various spots around us: architectural plans, fundraising materials, notes, and prospectuses for a business he was starting. Our conversation was interrupted by phone calls and by a brief visit from a colleague with whom he was working on one of his projects.

While he was taking his master's degree at a private Eastern university, the donor quoted above was also peripherally involved in the formation of the North Star Fund in New York City. He was friendly with the young man who was to become North Star's founder. "I got to know him, and [we'd] hang out. That's how I ended up talking to him about Vanguard. . . . He went out [to San Francisco] and ended up spending six months there as an intern. I still regularly take full credit for starting North Star myself," he said teasingly.

"If the . . . truth be known," he continued, "when he was starting North Star, I was in the middle of writing my thesis, and I did almost nothing." There had been a series of meetings.

I was on their mailing list. . . . They went so much more slowly and carefully than Chinook[27] [the alternative fund this donor was helping to start] did.

They really tried to incorporate a lot of people into this process, and had long meetings for nine months or a year—more than that, a year and a half to two years, I think—pulling it together. The whole process was so inclusive, so fair. Everything was documented. And they mailed out to everyone on the whole mailing list. Chinook just kind of came together. [He clapped his hands sharply.]

Two Colorado women independently had the idea of creating an alternative fund in their home state. Each had been giving to social-change causes or funds. One is the heir to a real estate fortune who had been in the Peace Corps in Africa and had worked for relief agencies there. Another is a socially conscious financial planner. Both contacted the Vanguard Foundation, which put them in touch with each other. "They didn't know each other at all. So [in the spring of 1986] they met and talked."

In July of 1986, my oil company was bought out. I bought an old convertible and drove to California. . . . I basically had a bunch of time on my hands, and had a bunch of money in my pocket. . . . I forget, my income was disgusting. You would resent it if I told you. I mean it was a lot of money.

He cleared his throat. "Anyway, right before I left on this trip, [one of the women] had gotten my name from North Star . . . because I had sent them money and they knew I was out here. . . . So she called me up and invited me to a planning meeting in September or October."

He attended the third meeting at one of the women's houses. It included a number of activists, mostly from the university town of Boulder. He already liked the idea. He liked the people.

Suddenly I had this time. And I had always had this sort of guilt. . . . I was giving all this money away, but I wasn't doing anything. It is so easy to write a check. To me, that is not the same level of giving as to really sit down and do something and invest time. That is giving. . . . Somehow it caught me at that time. I had time. There was no financial pressure on me.

I made the commitment in November, said I would do it. I was one of the few people, myself and [a founder], who had the time. A lot of other people were involved in a lot of other organizations and didn't really have a clear vision of what this could be, or what it was.

By January the meetings were more frequent, usually once a month. There were eighteen people on the planning committee of the Chinook Fund.

The majority of the work of putting Chinook together was done in 1987. The young man said:

Two or three people did 80 percent of the work. I called every one of the other Funding Exchange alternative funds . . . and talked to them about exactly how they were structured; how their board functioned; whether they thought that was successful; how or what they wished they would do if they had it to do over again. I made up a chart of each one: how much money they gave away; how many people were on the board; how many activists; whether they had two boards—a separate community board—and what their feelings were about that . . . just trying to bring together in one place all the information about all the different ones so we could decide what we wanted to do.

Chinook and the other new funds benefited from the experience of their predecessors. This donor explained that he originally had a preference for the old two-board system at Vanguard

because I knew them. But when I called them up and talked to them they were in the process of changing to a one-board structure. . . . They were not crazy about the two-board structure. . . . They thought it was unwieldy, and that it was a little weird having two groups giving away money. . . .

Talking to all the newer alternative funds, they all had one board, every single one.[28] There was more conflict within the one board, maybe, but it was much easier to resolve. You ended up with a stronger organization, a more centralized, cohesive organization in the end. On small points there would be some discussion, but there really weren't any conflicts or anything in terms of the structure of the organization, how it was going to work.

I sat down with a lawyer and worked out the bylaws, how it was all going to be. Then I took it back and gave it to the founders and one or two other people.

It was not just all the rich people putting together their organization. The activists had [a voice]. . . . To a true extent, it was the people who were willing to do the work. . . . Looking back on it, I can't see that there was all that much work that we did. You do the research and decide what the structure should be. But, it was a lot: hours and hours and hours.

The Chinook organizers also had to make their own hard decisions, had disagreements, and went through growing pains. They were concerned about how to determine who was a community activist, as well as how many and whom to appoint to their board. "That's a tough call," the same man mused. Some of the people on the planning committee wanted to serve on the board as activists. One was a forty-five-year-old college professor. "He dresses very nicely. He makes thirty-five grand a year. . . . We did not consider him a grassroots activist. We defined *grassroots activist* as someone who was from a particular ethnic community or was working in an organization on a grassroots level at promoting social change."

At this time, a donor who wished to be on the board was required to make a minimum $1,000 contribution to the fund.

> He [the self-identified activist] could probably have afforded that. Or before we had the minimum, he could have given five hundred dollars.
>
> It was a very tense situation on the planning committee, actually deciding who was going to be on the board. . . . Basically, there were some people who [the founder] and I had strong reservations about. She and I had been doing the work.

Others, especially some activists, had made promises but had not come through.

Class conflict was apparent in several meetings. The founder was verbally attacked or undermined by some of the activists after she expressed her ideas. The man I interviewed continued:

> The implication was that because she had money she thought she should be the one deciding. And that wasn't the case at all. She wasn't that way. She is probably the most democratic person that I can imagine.
>
> When all is said and done, she is the person who started Chinook. She is the person who continually pushed it, continually provided the oomph. . . .
>
> She's not a pusher and shover like I am. In a meeting like that, people are more reluctant to take me on. I can be very assertive.

In 1988 the Chinook Fund completed its first two funding cycles and distributed $50,000 to projects throughout Colorado. The central question for the grant-making committee was the definition of change-oriented work. Three of the fund's grantees are the Colorado Atomic–Agent Orange Veterans Coalition, which does advocacy for its members and has become a peace group; a farm-worker organizing project, Proyecto de Poder Trabajador Agricola; and Pueblans for Justice and Peace in Central America, a group that is 50 percent Latino and works among students at the high school and college level.

In Colorado, during the summer of 1988, the Council on National Priorities, a group of wealthy donors to Funding Exchange foundations from around the country, met for their annual retreat. Friction surfaced between certain Chinook community representatives and donors during a discussion about planning for that meeting. For example, an Afro-American community activist was upset that the conference would be open only to major contributors, and said something like: "I don't like these rich people making decisions for me." This provoked a discussion of the distance that the activists felt from the donors on the board. Unable to resolve her difference of perspective with other board members, this Afro-American activist eventually resigned.

Confrontation has been a part of the history of the Funding Exchange foundations, and the process of evolution has been at times extremely emotional and time-consuming. Conflicts because of differences in background are often resolved as wealthy contributors and community activists earn each other's respect.

IS ALTERNATIVE PHILANTHROPY A VIABLE ALTERNATIVE?

The critique of philanthropy offered by those in the alternative funding movement is quite similar to my own.[29] The wealthy young donors who organized the first alternative foundations and the activists who duplicated the model in other parts of the country understand that traditional giving by the upper class primarily supports elite institutions and the status quo.

The public foundation structure, especially the one created at the Haymarket People's Fund, offers a democratically representative alternative that is close to the kind of philanthropy that might truly be for the public good.[30] The donors are offered encouragement and moral support for contributing their money to projects for social change. But they give up control once the funds have been donated.

Structurally, foundations like Vanguard and Chinook are examples of a pragmatic compromise between traditional and progressive philanthropy, although they fund projects that are obviously less oriented toward the status quo. The decision-making process is shared by the donors with community activists and grassroots representatives. The process is democratic, although the rich donors still have proportionately more authority than those from the communities who are the ultimate recipients of the philanthropy. If these organizations really wished to be truly representative, there might be only one or two wealthy trustees.

It is perfectly understandable that donors want involvement with the groups they fund. The rich young people who tend to support the alternative foundations are especially committed to such endeavors, seeing themselves as stewards of their money and wanting to exercise this stewardship differently from their parents. As progressive as they may be as individuals, however, their interest in empowering themselves is nearly as great as their commitment to social change.

In certain regards the social consequences of alternative philanthropy differ little from those of traditional giving. Strengthening their egos and building community among themselves, as well as the continuing search for identity, are central parts of the alternative funding movement for the young people it attracts. Alternative funds assist them in their creation of community in the same way that the culture of philanthropy does for their parents, older relatives, or more conservative siblings. The funds provide a sense of identity, meaningful activity, and personal authority. By joining an alternative foundation, some of these young heirs begin to feel that they belong to something. The difference, of course—and this is a positive development—is that the alternative funds are less exclusive than elite philanthropy; part of their very raison d'être is to create bridges between classes and to redistribute wealth.

Internal tension is always seen in these funds: they would not, of course, be organized in the way they are if resources were distributed equitably in this society. Thus, there are still status differences on the boards of these funds. The community activists represent the needy; the donors represent private money. These two groups never actually become equal. And they remain separate from each other.

These rich young people do not give their wealth away; it is not redistributed. They give away their income and keep their capital. And, as embarrassed as it might make them feel, they symbolically carry this capital—and privilege—with them in all their endeavors. As donors they do not fully relinquish their power, although they try to share it. Sometimes they resent the fact that they are not more appreciated, that their opinions are sometimes discounted. It is difficult for them to escape the attitude of noblesse oblige with which they have grown up.

Another shortcoming of the alternative foundations is that in comparison to traditional philanthropy or the government, they actually have so little money to give. Altogether, the local funds and national grant-making programs of the Funding Exchange network distribute only about $5 million a year. There may be some merit to small-scale charity, especially because the recipient groups have modest budgetary needs. Alternative philanthropy of this type, however, represents less than .01 percent of the total giving of the wealthy.[31] Once again, if the government were providing for basic human services, then the alternative funds could play a significant role in supporting advocacy, innovative new projects, organizing among disenfranchised groups, and watchdog programs.

The alternative or public foundation model has much to recommend it, particularly if it becomes more widespread and better financed. The structure has already served as a prototype for the development of funds with other priorities—especially women's foundations, which are the subject of the next chapter.

Chapter 9

Wealthy "Feminist" Funders

In my first days of activism, I thought I would do this ("this" being feminism) for a few years and then return to my real life. . . . But like so many others now and in moments past, I've learned that this is not just something we care about for a year or two or three. We are in it for life and for our lives.
—GLORIA STEINEM, president, board of directors, Ms. Foundation for Women, *Campaign for a Second Decade* (promotional material), 1988

If one woman wins, all women win, and that ultimately will change things. We who have often been called upon to hold things together—families, marriages, businesses—must sometimes allow things to fall apart. Our compliance can only allow inequality to continue.
—SALLIE BINGHAM, founder and director, the Kentucky Women's Foundation, in the *Radcliffe Quarterly*, June 1986

Although the second wave of feminism[1] has helped change many of the ways in which women view themselves in the world, it has had less impact in the upper class, where gender roles remain more rigid than in wider society. Most of the wealthy women in this study did not mention the women's movement or, if they did, referred to it in a negative manner. They did not approve of women of their class taking paying jobs, and bemoaned the tendency of young women—who might formerly have volunteered—to join the labor force. In spite of this prevailing sentiment, eleven out of the fifty-six wealthy women in this study, from all parts of the country, said they favored changes in the status of women, and they devote much of their philanthropy to this goal.[2]

The women who are featured in this chapter and the women's foundations they help support are participants in a feminist funding movement that is burgeoning at the local and regional levels. They seek to redress the fact that in the last two decades only between 2 and 4 percent of institutional philanthropic money has gone specifically to programs for women and girls.[3] There are more than forty women's foundations in the United States, operating under varied models and philosophies. These foundations were inspired by the need of women's groups for money, the second wave of feminism, and the example of both the national Ms. Foundation for Women[4] and the alternative funds. As the number of local-level women's foundations increased, so did the personal grant-making programs of rich feminist women.

Beyond the fact that they are female and white, there is not a common demographic profile of the wealthy women interviewed who fund feminist issues.[5] In fact, the diversity of this small group is notable.[6] However, they tend to be younger than mainstream women philanthropists and proportionally more are single.[7]

Most of these women inherited their wealth and are at least three or four generations removed from the source of the family fortune. As is typical of those with old money, they spoke of a family tradition of philanthropy. One explained: "My family did charitable things for others. They mostly got into donating to things near home, to conventional charities such as hospitals." These elite "feminist" funders maintain the family tradition of giving, but they give primarily to battered women's shelters, programs for displaced homemakers, employment and training projects, rape crisis hotlines and prevention programs, and reproductive rights advocacy, as well as welfare reform and poverty projects. The foundations that they have established or support also fund these kinds of causes near to home.

A paradoxical uneasiness about acknowledging their feminist perspective or describing themselves as feminists was evident among most of these women. Only three actually used the word *feminism* during our interviews with them, but an additional seven chose to speak about the concerns of women and girls at some length. One woman managed to discuss women's issues without once referring to either feminism or women. But she told us that she gives money to NOW (National Organization for Women—she used only the acronym), is "pro-choice," and believes in sex education and teen pregnancy prevention.

This reluctance to identify themselves as feminists constitutes additional evidence for the strict division of labor by gender and subordination of women in the upper class. It is difficult for wealthy women to be feminists, for they are contesting a system that privileges them in other regards.[8] Curiously, the younger single women were more apt to avoid the term *feminist* than middle-aged or married women, despite the fact that these younger women are all activists, control their wealth, and give large amounts of money to feminist causes.

A middle-aged philanthropist with inherited wealth explained how her giving patterns had changed:

> After having become a feminist, which I did some seven years ago when I was getting my divorce, I went into a consciousness-raising group and became a feminist. . . . Here I was taking care of kids. All of my labor was free, as all women's labor has been free for centuries.

This woman developed a personal philosophy that equates giving with women's values. "I participated in this gift-giving economy rather than the exchange economy of the work world. . . . Women's work is gift-giving as opposed to exchange. I figure that is really the social basis of women's values. Another name for it is *nurturing*. . . ." She has established her own charitable and political contributions program.

> I really hope to inspire other women to do the same and feel the same kind of thing. The whole movement of empowering women is so important, when we do not slide outside our own values and take on men's values just in order to empower ourselves, which is the sad thing.

Several of the feminist grant-makers came out of the alternative funding movement, and have a similar philosophy. A number used the word *empowerment* and expressed solidarity with women of other classes, races, and nationalities.

These women and others across the country belong to organizations in common, interact frequently, and lend support to each other. One young woman with children said, "I think there is a real emerging network, a sort of changing network of women who talk to each other about this kind of thing." This woman married into wealth. She described how one of her husband's cousins had complained to him that she "did not approve of me because I could be doing something good for other people and I wasn't." Although our informant was angry at the time, "since then I have wound up spending a significant part of my time working as a born-again feminist." It is striking that the few women who did refer to feminism had experienced an almost religious conversion to the cause.

Most of the wealthy feminist funders with whom we spoke work hard at their charitable endeavors. They have differing explanations to validate their status. One young woman said:

> Instead of deciding to go to law school or business school, I sat on different boards of directors of different organizations. . . . I learned as a young person the same things I would have in law school and business school. . . . I made sure that I sat on the finance committees. And I listened for five to six years, absolutely learning from people who were pros.

Her wealth exempted her from the normal process of acquiring credentials and allowed her to learn as an apprentice philanthropist.

Another women with a large inheritance had taken a different path.

> I got my M.B.A. and in the process of getting it started learning more about how to manage [business and philanthropic affairs] and how to work with these guys, the old family retainer types that had been taking care of me. I became much more involved and aggressive in managing the money.

She was influenced by the women's movement to see herself as needing specific skills and training in order to conduct her affairs. She continued: "I say I have these three jobs. . . . I am an investor. I invest in real estate, the stock market, and small public interest organizations." She works out of the office of a charitable fund that she established. "It gives new meaning to the term, 'I gave at the office.'" The "offices" of the feminist funders are as varied as the governance structures and grant-making programs of the women's foundations. Some of the women work out of their homes. Others volunteer nearly full-time at a women's fund.

Not all of the women's funds are financed by wealthy women, although those with the largest endowments are; some feminist foundations have a broad range of support from women of all means. This is an examination of the role of rich women in three different foundations.

THE FIRST OF THE LOCAL WOMEN'S FOUNDATIONS

> Our commitment to diversity is one thing that distinguishes us. We feel that it is critically important to create an organization that is not just being run by a group of upper-class white women. So our board is 60 percent women of color, disabled women, older women.
> —TRACY DuVIVIER GARY, co-founder, The Women's Foundation, 1985

The Women's Foundation in San Francisco was the first local institution of its type. It was formed in the early 1980s as a public foundation to raise and distribute money to projects for women and girls. The foundation has been committed to participation in governance and grant-making by representatives of all sectors of the women's community. Money comes from women of all classes, and the board is diverse with respect to age, class, ethnic background, race, physical capability, and sexual preference. In the 1986 annual report, the foundation's president, Valerie Roxanne Edwards, wrote:

> At The Women's Foundation we believe that feminist philanthropy extends beyond raising and allocating dollars: it means a commitment to social change. Therefore, we not only fund programs that improve the economic, social, cultural, or political status of women and girls, but we also initiate new projects.

This language is similar to that found in the materials of most of the women's funds, but the Women's Foundation in San Francisco has a reputation for being more progressive than many of its sister organizations.

In 1980, Dr. Ruth M. McGuire, a psychotherapist in private practice, and one other San Francisco woman of means decided that they wanted to bequeath their estates to local women's causes. Tracy DuVivier Gary,[9] a wealthy woman donor to the Vanguard People's Foundation, engaged in discussions with them. "I tried to convince them to start a special fund at the Ms. Foundation or Vanguard. I was against starting a new institution. I said, 'You have to do a needs assessment to prove to the community of funders that this really is viable.' "

By 1981, after a good deal of study, as well as approaches to the San Francisco and Vanguard Foundations, Gary and the others were persuaded, if not even more convinced, that establishing a new women's foundation was the right thing to do. They were personally committed to women's issues. They believed that more women would contribute to an organization dedicated to funding women's projects than to the alternative foundations, which made grants to a range of causes. "There had been a very careful planning process," said Gary. "I left Vanguard realizing that there would be too much of a conflict of interest."

When Gary and her activist colleagues Marya Grambs and Roma Guy formed the Women's Foundation (with initial monetary pledges from Dr. McGuire and others), they had the Vanguard Public Foundation model, as well as their experience of working together at La Casa de las Madres, and with over fifty different types of nonprofit organizations to guide them. According to Gary:

All of us are from different class backgrounds—all white, but nonetheless different class backgrounds. We had at that point a six- or seven-year history of working together. We knew what each of our skills were and that we could take problems to each of our individual communities and catalyze people.

She did not make clear in which communities each was organizing, although she herself was presumably responsible for women of wealth.

Clinical psychologist Marya Grambs had established La Casa, one of the first shelters in the country for battered women. She is quoted as saying, "I grew up in a home where my mother was a battered woman for twenty years and that drew me into the work I do." But she stressed the difficulty of raising money for women's issues: "No matter how well-dressed you are or how well-written your request is for a grant, you will have doors slammed in your face because you are a woman."[10]

Roma Guy had been an organizer and project developer in the San Francisco Bay area for numerous women's causes such as La Casa, the Women's Building, Options for Women Over Forty, the Lesbian Agenda for Action, and the Action Committee for Abortion Rights.

According to Gary, "A lot of my energy in the early years [of the Women's Foundation] went into making sure that the systems were in place, that the institution would be long-living and not dependent on one or two people's ideas."

The founders produced a work plan, a committee structure, and a process for making decisions. Said Gary:

> We really wanted to create an organization that could be a catalyst for involvement for a whole new generation of people, women specifically, who would be interested in philanthropy.
>
> We were very careful in the formation. We took two years to research, plan, look, and interview—to create a model that we hope will be solid, have a strong foundation, reflect our politics and our belief that diversity creates a healthier organization.

Unlike the Vanguard Foundation in the early years, the Women's Foundation sought a base of funds from people of all classes and planned to establish an endowment.

> It was a massive organizing effort. . . . We raised three hundred thousand dollars in our first year. . . . We then began our allocations process, giving money away in 1983. We had decided to give away one hundred thousand, put one hundred thousand in endowment, and spend one hundred thousand on our first year of operation. The operation expenses were very high. . . . We were criticized.

But they were confident that they were launching a unique and creative model that, if fueled by adequate staff, would attract an essential core of volunteers who would assure the long-term goal of creating an innovative organization and greater possibilities for democratic management and new leadership. Since the formation of the Women's Foundation, this San Francisco model has been replicated, although not followed in every detail, at a rate of nearly five new women's foundations a year.

Within a three-year period the foundation had collected over a million dollars, "five," said Gary "in pretty small change ($5 to $500), except for some of the local foundations and corporations that have been very generous, in order to build our organizational base." By 1985, the Women's Foundation had over 2,000 donors. "The average contribution is two hundred dollars. We have a small handful who give one thousand and above—about forty or fifty people. But, for the most part, an awful lot of the lower end, like twenty-five dollars."

Initially Grambs and Guy were paid co-directors and also voting board members. One of them was responsible for fundraising and administration, the other for programming. Some 150 volunteers put in time on the board, on committees, or in doing office work. One of them was Gary, who explained in 1985, "I obviously don't need a source of income." But because she worked full time, she was considered a member of the staff.

Since it was created,[11] the Women's Foundation has dispersed $900,000 to 195 projects.

> We have had very little criticism of our allocation process. . . . We have a very strong conflict-of-interest policy. . . . We are very careful about everything we do. Because we have the volunteer support that we do, and are democratically managed, we give our volunteers opportunity every moment to give us input, and to evaluate, and to criticize the process. So it has constantly been improving.

The foundation has given away an average of $150,000 a year. In 1986, it allocated nearly $200,000 to some thirty-six organizations throughout the Bay Area. In addition, $1.5 million is pledged to the endowment.

The foundation also initiated financial education programs for low-, middle-, and upper-income women. Its Managing Inherited Wealth program, established in 1983, has had the highest profile. Gary commented: "I thought there would be twenty-five to forty women [interested]. In a year and nine months it had grown to four hundred women."

> We talk about philanthropy. We talk about managing money. We talk about socially responsible investments. We talk about the difficulties a woman who may have inherited twenty-five thousand dollars, who is from a very low-income situa-

tion, may have with her spouse when she inherits this money. It is a wide range. It's not just upper-class women in the group. (1985)

In six years, more than 1,200 women with inherited wealth have participated in some aspect of the program, which now holds four meetings a month in six locations throughout the Bay Area. In addition, a sister project, Women Managing Wealth, has been initiated in New York City.

Although the Women's Foundation offers these special programs for women with wealth, its leaders have not been willing to "privilege" rich donors. Gary has supported this policy, but told me that it has been an ongoing personal struggle for her and other contributors of means.

> If there is a way for me to step back from one of [my] privileges, have somebody else come forward, there is a tremendous benefit to society. . . . But it takes holding back what I have been trained to do, which is to assert myself, to be in control, to be in power. It means sitting on my hands a lot, deferring to other people, or saying there is somebody else over here who could really be a better speaker, or who has much more involvement with the community from which you need to hear.

Gary is convinced, however, that after seven years in the Women's Foundation "the class work" has not been done sufficiently.

> It is a complicated kind of thing. You do not want to be rolling out the red carpet [for wealthy donors]. You do not want to give [certain] people extra privilege. But if you really want to get people to give—I have been working on the endowment. I said that I would help them to get the additional million dollars in the endowment. I went to about twenty or thirty people and asked them to give. Well, there is no [additional] privilege in giving [large sums] to the Women's Foundation, at all.

She was clearly uneasy about this situation but continued: "I support it because the person who gives their ten dollars when they can only afford to give five deserves as much privilege. But it makes it a lot harder to find incentives [for wealthy donors]," and hence to raise funds.

In 1987, during a painful meeting with her co-workers, Gary resigned as a volunteer staff member at the Women's Foundation. Her action appears to have been highly symbolic and to have had multiple causes. She wanted what she considered her share of the recognition and status, although she claimed that she did not want any more status than her colleagues. She cited her anger at the way her colleagues had treated her, which she attributed to their discounting of her work because of her higher class standing. She admitted that she was also burned out. And she had been giving away her fortune to an extent that was beginning to affect her standard of living.

In 1988 Gary gave me her perspective on her resignation.

> When we formed the Women's Foundation board, I felt very strongly that since I had been on the board of another foundation, I did not need that experience. [I thought] that it was important, in fact, for me not to be on the board. But what I did not know was that if I was a staff person, and not being paid, and they were the co-directors, that the hierarchy would bother me so much. And suddenly, from what had been an equal partnership [a hierarchy developed]. They had pay, position, and were on the board. And I missed our equal-peer collaboration.

According to Gary, many of the status and structural problems were related to the rapid growth and even to the success of the organization.

For the first two or three years of the Women's Foundation there were four staff people, the original team of three and an administrative assistant. By the time Gary resigned there were ten staff people, who were supervised by the co-directors. "Their power increased, and influence. I started feeling less of an equal. That was the natural course of events, but it also affected my self-esteem."

Gary was expressive about her disappointment, as well as self-conscious about her own contributions to a difficult situation.

> While I think competition is a healthy thing between women, what I did not realize is the [personal] cost. It is one thing to have a philosophy about redistributing wealth and power, and another thing to be doing it, to be giving away your money and position.
>
> What happened was that I began to see myself acting out in the meetings. I would dominate, verbally, the discussions. Or, I was not being an effective communicator. I was chair of the planning committee for years. I became ineffective. The ideas that I had were not the ones that they [the board] followed. There was a certain way in which I did not have credibility, or the same amount of credibility as Roma and Marya.

She was also exhausted, mentally and physically. "I was getting very worn down, managing the inherited wealth program, doing major gift fundraising [working with emerging women's funds across the country]. I was essentially doing two or three different jobs and working fifty, sixty hours a week all the time, for three, four, five years, and getting very internally frustrated. I was not getting the recognition and support that the paid staff were."

Prior to what appeared to be a sudden decision to quit, Gary had spent six months conferring with a personnel consultant once a month, talking about her politics and self-worth issues, and planning out what she needed to do to improve her position at the Women's Foundation.

> And I had an economic reality, which is at that point I had given away about a million and a half of the money that I had [inherited] and had about a million dollars left, plus my home. At that rate, the habit that I have of giving away one hundred and twenty thousand dollars a year, I [knew I] was going to have to come to terms with the fact that I now have thirty or forty thousand to give away a year. I began thinking, "Wait a minute. I am thirty-five years of age, and I am going to run out of money. . . . The gig is up here."

She realized that she would have to start earning income.

> I began to feel, even though I believe in the redistribution of wealth and power, that it [what she had been doing at the Women's Foundation] was a job. And I deserved to be paid for the job that I was doing. I was willing to take ten thousand and not thirty thousand. But I was seeing my self-worth erode, and my credibility within the organization erode. I believed that I should have a place and be recognized for my work equally.

Gary went to the staff to explain why she thought she should be paid for her work.

> What happened, essentially, is that they said no. The process was horrendous in terms of the class stuff. It was such a discounting of the work that I had done that I resigned. It was a very, very painful two- or three-hour process. I had built up to [the meeting] for six months, making a very strong case.

Although she had been thinking about changing her role for half a year, Gary's request came as a surprise to her co-workers. The atmosphere was highly charged. Some of the other staff members reacted negatively. A mother with three children who makes under $20,000 a year—and will probably never make more—could not in a matter of hours understand Gary's dilemma.

After a period of months, with the consensus of the board, the co-directors did offer Gary a paid job. But she felt that a preponderance of people in the foundation thought that her usefulness was essentially at an end. For six more months she was depressed, and spent most of her time working at home.

> When I came out of my ego self, I really saw it as a happy thing. The organization I cared most about was up and running. I had played a key role, giving as much as I could. I felt at my core, pleased. I had to see and accept, however, that the

development of new and diverse leadership meant it was more appropriate for me to move on and back off. I was not needed after five or six years of working that hard. [But] it was a chance for me in my life to rebalance, [overcome my] workaholism. . . . I chose not to take on other projects for about three months.

Gary has continued in her commitment to the Women's Foundation in particular and the women's funds movement in general. She is now the director of the Managing Inherited Wealth program (still a special project of the Women's Foundation); beginning in 1988, she and an assistant have been paid a yearly $10,000 stipend for their work. Although since mid-1988, Gary has chosen to play no formal fundraising role with the Women's Foundation, it is estimated that she has influenced the redistribution and direction of more than $4 million to the foundation and other organizations for social change.

The Women's Foundation in San Francisco has been able to raise funds without depending wholly on the contributions of rich women. In an effort to insure diversity and representation within the women's community, the foundation has tried to treat all women equally. It has provided no special incentives to its wealthy donors. In Gary's case, its leaders were unwilling to fully enfranchise, and thus alienated, someone whose name throughout the country was closely associated with the organization and with the women's funding movement.

AMONG THE NEWEST WOMEN'S FUNDS[12]

I learned about the Women's Foundation when I was invited to a tea at the governor's mansion. I knew what it was about, went, and was very impressed with what I heard.

I immediately wanted to be a part of the Women's Foundation because I had been a part of the group that started the Women's Bank in Denver. . . . I knew it was going to be a success.
—JAN WHITING, a white, founding donor and board member, Women's Foundation of Colorado, 1988

The biggest struggle I see is getting the two groups (rich and poor women) together. There's this real push that the foundation not be another set of "do-gooders" who are going to come out and save us, because we don't want to be saved by them.
—BRENDA LYLE, an Afro-American, founder of the San Juan Family Learning Center, Boulder, Colorado[13]

The counterpart to the San Francisco women's fund is exemplified by one of the newest such organizations, the Women's Foundation of Colorado. I was associated with the Colorado foundation during its formative stages, from March through August 1987, first as a consultant and then as executive director. I resigned after six months over "unresolved differences in management philosophy" with some members of the board.

The Women's Foundation of Colorado is less oriented to diversity, systematic social change, and empowerment for women in greatest need than its predecessor and namesake in San Francisco. This is because of both a more conservative political climate in Colorado and the preferences of its founders. Initially, the Women's Foundation of Colorado concentrated its fundraising efforts among women of wealth and high-ranking professionals in the state. As a partial result, the sub-agenda of empowering affluent women is almost as strong at this foundation as the goal of distributing funds to programs for women in need.

One of the largest donors to the Women's Foundation of Colorado is Jan Whiting, a divorced fifty-eight-year-old millionaire. "I am almost nine years out of a marriage. I was married for thirty years. I have three grown children and two grandchildren." She had careers as both a teacher and a nurse. As a young woman from a modest background, she supported her husband through law school; he became a partner in Denver's largest law firm and later made a fortune serving as president of three different oil and gas companies. Whiting said:

> During my [married] lifetime I was very active in all sorts of political, charitable, and cultural organizations. Monetarily, at that time, I didn't do anything on my own. My husband pretty well called the shots as to what we gave to, as far as charities went. The institutions that I was particularly interested in got pretty short shrift. In fact, the main money went to the cultural things that he was interested in.

She and several other generous contributors were deeply hurt by divorces. Their work with the Women's Foundation has been one of the ways that they seek to find a new, independent identity. Whiting said:

> It has only been since I have been divorced and in control of a reasonable amount of money of my own that I have been able to indulge myself, you might say, in giving to the types of charities that I want to give to.

She was keenly interested in women's groups, "particularly after the women's lib movement. . . . I have given my major money to organizations who come in behind women and children's needs. I think women and children are in terrible straits right now, vis-à-vis the last eight years of the Reagan administration.''

I myself heard about the Women's Foundation of Colorado for the first time in January 1987. I was acquainted with the Women's Foundation in San Francisco and with several other democratically managed women's funds around the country, and I admired their work tremendously. I sent a letter expressing my interest in working with the new foundation. Within a week, Fern Portnoy, then the executive director of the Piton Foundation, one of the largest grant-makers in Colorado, telephoned me. She and I had known each other on a professional basis for several years. As chair of the search committee she was inviting me to interview for a full-time position as executive director of the Women's Foundation of Colorado.

I read all of the foundation's understandably scanty materials. According to the press release announcing the foundation's formation: ''A group of Colorado's most influential women have raised almost two million dollars for the benefit of women and girls throughout the state.''[14] I was wary of the two-board structure that had been established—a donor board and community board were to operate (following the initial model of the Vanguard Public Foundation), although grants were to be made by the two boards together.[15] But I approved of their decision to concentrate on projects for women in the greatest need.

In mid-February, after two visits to Denver that included more social than substantive interaction between myself and members of the board, I was offered the job. This in itself should have alerted me to what was to come— but how different things look in retrospect! The board did not ask me many direct questions about my experience with or perspective on particular women's issues; they seemed much more interested in my table manners and the fact that I had written two books about foundations. However, they did engage in lengthy inquiries about my political viewpoints with my references (who disclosed the nature of these conversations to me) that included veiled attempts to determine my sexual preference.

I assumed that most of the board members were liberal feminists and that if there were a few conservatives, there might also be a few radicals. I had inquired about the board's position on certain controversial issues, and had been told that all the directors were "pro-choice" on abortion. During the second interview, at a dinner meeting, I had inquired specifically about funding of lesbian projects. (This is probably why they were checking out my sexual preference.) One board member had responded that the subject had never been discussed but that she doubted whether this was the kind of thing the foundation would get into. I stated clearly that I would not work for a women's organization that discriminated against any person or group on the basis of sexual preference. One board member supported my statement and suggested that we at the table might want to know that lesbians were already involved with the foundation (the implication was that they were contributors). A discussion ensued about the public relations implications of funding lesbian projects. Although I did not yet know any of these women well, I felt that the one woman who had spoken up would be an ally on the board, and this heartened me.

While my application was under consideration, I had been making my own investigations about the foundation, its history, and its leaders and their vision for the future. I was told by a friend that a group of Colorado women of color had protested against the composition of the original board, which had included no minority women. (Those who had interviewed me had said nothing about this, and this was a bit of a surprise to me. A Latina, Kathy Archuleta,[16] had served on the search committee panel and had asked me about my ability to relate to women of varied backgrounds. An Asian board member, Sumiko Hennessy,[17] had attended an interview luncheon.)

When I had inquired about the representativeness of the boards during the second interview dinner meeting, which was attended entirely by white women, it was Swanee Hunt who responded. (She is the daughter of Texas oil tycoon H. L. Hunt and at that time had pledged more than any other donor.) She was probably the richest woman on the founding board.[18] She had made the single largest pledge of money to the foundation and by all accounts was the moving force behind its creation. She was not the foundation's president, nor was she on the search committee, but I had been told that of all the trustees she was the one who most must approve of me before I could be hired.

Hunt explained that she had been personally contacted by this group of women of color who were "upset" and that they had come to see her at home. The "dual-board structure" had been developed in her living room at that time[19] and later accepted by the founding board. I was told that there had always been a commitment to diversity on the board, but that in the enthusiasm of initial fundraising it had been overlooked.

By the time of my appointment to the staff, five of the twelve members of the community board were women of color. These five women had indeed been elected in response to pressure by an informal network of Afro-American, Latina, Native American, and Pan-Asian women. They had come together specifically for the purpose of getting the new foundation to hear them and include the concerns of their constituencies in its planning. The other community representatives were politicians and high-ranking professionals, many of whom had been involved in the initial organization of the foundation.

An additional twenty-three wealthy white women served on the founding donors' board. Each had pledged at least $50,000 to the foundation's endowment and had thus bought herself a seat on the board. Whiting, for example, had pledged $100,000 over a five-year period.

> I very much felt, at my age, that I wanted to curtail my giving to arts organizations and other organizations where you give a certain amount each year, and then it is used up. You don't have any idea how efficiently your money has been used. I wanted to give my money to a foundation where I knew that when I was dead, it would still be doing good things for women and children. In other words, it was a living legacy that would go on after me.

Whiting serves on the development committee. "I have been actively trying to find other women who will commit equally, or in some form anyway, to the [endowment] goal of $10 million. . . . I am getting the big money. . . . I think the next development efforts will be aimed towards a smaller, or a lower-money-commitment group."

There was definitely excitement in the air about the new Women's Foundation. Hopes were high on all our parts, and sometimes expectations exceeded outcome. The budget that was Express Mailed for my review prior to my final decision about the job bore almost no relation to the reality of the foundation's financial situation. During the telephone negotiation stage, I was told that the Colorado Trust, a large foundation, was probably going to make a $1 million grant to the Women's Foundation and that I would then be able to hire a program officer to work with me on women's health issues. This grant never materialized, although that year the Colorado Trust did give the foundation a small, $24,500 planning grant that was used to put on five women's forums around the state.

In April 1987, before I was in the position full-time, I attended meetings in Atlanta, Georgia, of the National Network of Women's Funds, Women and Foundations/Corporate Philanthropy, and the Council on Foundations, along with six members of the Colorado Women's Foundation board. The first meeting was attended by the women's foundations throughout the country. In comparison to the posh surroundings of the second and third meetings, ours was held in a rundown motel on the outskirts of downtown

Atlanta. Here I discovered that the Women's Foundation of Colorado was the subject of national controversy among the other women's funds.

Jan Whiting well recalls the somewhat tumultuous events at these conferences.

> It was quite a revelation to me and everyone else [from Colorado] who went to Atlanta. . . . It was an eye-opening experience to sit in on meetings which were everything from the Rockefellers and Barbara Jordan talking, down to the little storefront women's organizations that were specifically oriented towards lesbians, and blacks, and minority women . . . their philosophies, their working actions, their stands on just about everything were completely diverse. . . .
>
> The little [women's] foundations were running on about ten thousand dollars a year in total contributions. And we came in there as the new Colorado foundation, having started out—plunk!—with a two-million-dollar endowment. We were almost looked at askance, and resented a bit, by some of the other organizations who didn't realize the kind of women that had put this together.

There was resentment that the Colorado foundation seemed to be doing so well in comparison with the many older funds that were still struggling. We already had a reputation as an elitist group. This was exacerbated by the fact that our delegation was not in accord with the rules of the Conference of the National Network of Women's Funds, which required that at least half of any delegation be women of color. Five of the seven in our group were white. We also dressed differently from the others. Almost everyone else was wearing blue jeans; we had on business suits.

Most disturbing, however, was a public comment made by Swanee Hunt that the Women's Foundation of Colorado would not fund "lesbian projects." The full board of the foundation had met officially only once before I had been hired. I had read the complete minutes of that meeting, and neither the board nor the executive committee had dealt with this issue. Thus, at that point we had no policy on the subject (although by then I was aware that there were differences of opinion among board members). Hunt had been present during the conversation on this topic at the dinner meeting referred to above. It was as if she and I had heard two different things. This was my first inkling that she thought her views were the foundation's views. This incident was to have many unpleasant ramifications.

News travels fast, and the women back in Colorado soon learned about Hunt's prejudicial statements. Unbeknownst to me, the atmosphere of the women's community was already tense. On the one hand, they were looking forward to additional sources of funds. On the other, I learned of the anger and hurt of leaders in women's organizations who felt that the foundation was not interested in their concerns or input. I was an outsider, which did not help the situation.

Although I had mostly deferred to board members during the consulting stage of our relationship, I decided to try and exercise more leadership when I took over my new job. I had numerous conversations with different trustees, but particularly with the president, Mary Lou Walters, concerning the problems of the foundation and my ideas about how to address them. Walters and I had a cordial relationship. Together we developed plans to establish priorities, review the role and function of the foundation's committees, rewrite the bylaws, and rethink our approaches and goals.

An executive committee meeting in late June during which some of these matters were taken up was particularly unpleasant and unproductive. It was followed by two days of lengthy telephone conversations during which both my leadership and that of the president were called into question by Swanee Hunt and Fern Portnoy (who had recruited me). I had been working full-time on the job for barely a month.

In my view, the foundation had financial, structural, and process problems that I was not being given the authority to address. Of particular concern to me were internal power struggles, inappropriate actions of individual wealthy board members, and the basically unclarified philosophy and goals of the foundation.

I had made statements to the press and speeches that I now began to feel were inaccurate or at least misleading. For example, I was quoted as saying, "We want this [foundation] to be for all the women of the state." In more detail, I had said:

> This organization represents a new phase of the women's movement. We want to build bridges between women of color and Anglo women, between the rich and the middle-class and the poor, between urban and rural women. We want women from every walk of life, women of every age, including teenagers, and women who would normally not get involved with these kinds of organizations. Like those who can't read or write, and the handicapped. . . .
>
> I feel confident that our vision, and the vision that the founding women of this organization had, will spread throughout the state. It's time for the women's movement to become more visible again, but visible in an inclusive way, a way that encompasses all the women of Colorado.[20]

These were my goals, but they were not necessarily those of the wealthiest, most powerful women on the board, who seemed to prefer that the foundation remain an elite club. They certainly were not looking for my leadership. A few of them resented my suggestions.

Rather than prolong this account, I offer the following action of the executive committee as evidence that my concerns were justified. On the day that the executive committee accepted my resignation, they also established a trust fund for Theodore Ansbacher Hunt, Swanee Hunt's infant son. Theodore Hunt was undoubtedly one of the wealthiest newborns in the state of Colorado. While other babies were suffering from low birth weight and malnutrition, or living with their teenage mothers in poverty, the leaders of the Women's Foundation of Colorado deemed the establishment of a trust fund for this child an appropriate gesture to their esteemed colleague. Swanee Hunt is the current (1989) president of the Women's Foundation of Colorado.

I was disillusioned by this experience, but I remain committed to the idea that women of all classes can work together toward a better life for everyone. And some good has come from the awards of the Women's Foundation of Colorado, whose funding program now centers on "economic self-sufficiency." The foundation has awarded money to such groups as Mi Casa Women's Resource Center in Denver, for nontraditional job training; the Women's Center of Larimer County, for job placement services in north-central Colorado; and the Gathering Place, a daytime shelter for homeless women, for a job counselor. In 1987 the foundation made $70,000 in grants to fifteen groups. In 1988, $122,000 was distributed to twenty-two projects for women. In 1989, they plan to give approximately twenty grants totalling $200,000. By mid-1989, the Women's Foundation of Colorado had more than nine hundred members, and most of them were not rich. More than $1.3 million in new pledges had been raised in the first half of the year, $1 million as a challenge grant from one donor. Eventually, however, those in the majority may take over the organization.

PROMOTING SOCIAL CHANGE THROUGH THE ARTS

The Kentucky Foundation for Women was created in the mid-1980s by one person, Sallie Bingham, and organized as a private foundation. Other women's funds have been established by individual women, so in that regard this foundation is not exceptional. Such funds are similar to family foundations in that they are controlled largely by the donor, but their grants go primarily to projects for women and girls. A concentration on projects in the arts and humanities makes the Kentucky Foundation for Women unique.

"It is the Foundation's firm belief that the arts can be an effective vehicle for social change, particularly for women."[21]

Their promotional materials clearly articulate the intended influence of the founder. "In determining the programs of The Kentucky Foundation for Women, Inc. the directors have been guided by the artistic interests and concerns of the donor, Sallie Bingham, a playwright and short story writer. It is Sallie Bingham's hope that her leadership may lead to greater cooperation among women and men."[22]

Apparently third-generation Bingham both understood and rebelled against some of the roles that she was allotted because of her gender and class. Her background and upbringing are typical of old money. The family fortune traced primarily to a woman, the third wife of Sallie Bingham's grandfather Robert Worth Bingham. Mary Kenan Flagler Bingham was the widow of oil and railroad tycoon Henry M. Flagler. She had no children. Her last husband, his son from a former marriage, and his grandsons were to rule over what came to be a family media empire including the *Louisville Courier Journal*.

Sallie Bingham was born as Sarah, the "eldest daughter in the patrician Bingham dynasty of Louisville, Kentucky."[23] From childhood she felt "that she lived with restrictions with which her two older brothers did not have to contend."[24] In 1986, at age forty-nine, she wrote that as the daughter in a wealthy family she was taught "to avoid all displays of pride." The fortune that distinguished her from others was not considered her own. Instead she had to follow strict, "largely unspoken" rules:

- Always set a good example.
- Do not condescend to those who have less.
- Never ask the price of anything.
- Avoid being conspicuous in any way.
  The commandments were backed by fear. Rich women are always vulnerable to criticism; we do not share the justifications of the men who actually made the money. We neither toil, nor do we spin, yet we have access to a wide range of material comforts. But here there is a delicate line. The jewels must not be too big, nor the furs too obvious.[25]

Thus, Sallie Bingham was raised in the culture of philanthropy. From the time she and her siblings "were old enough to read the plaques on the walls of almost every civic and cultural organization in town, they were aware that their parents, in the tradition of the great old publishers, put their money back into the community and especially supported the arts."[26]

By adulthood Bingham was questioning the norms that kept women in an inferior status to men. Following her graduation from Radcliffe in 1958, she published her first novel and two volumes of short stories, unusually conspicuous acts for a woman of wealth. As was expected of her, however, she married and had children. But somehow her life did not go the way she had expected.

"Because we depend for our income on . . . trusts, we know that our livelihood, literally, is at stake if we oppose our male benefactors, who are usually also our relatives. The trap closes tightly with the passage of time," wrote Bingham.

> While the 20-year-old heiress may hope, through a career, to become independent of her trusts, the 40-year-old knows that is no longer probable. And the rich woman of any age, who may appear to be unusually lucky . . . usually knows how flimsy her good fortune really is. Of course we can be reduced overnight to penury by divorce, like most other women in the United States today. But we can also be disinherited, or cut off by a corporate restructuring.
>
> Since we are raised to live well, since we often lack the self-confidence that only comes from independent work and thought, we rich women are uniquely handicapped in defending our rights.[27]

After two divorces and more than twenty years away in the Northeast, Bingham returned to Louisville with her youngest sons. She came home an acknowledged feminist, hoping to deal with "some of my basic conflicts with the family, which had not been resolved due to geographical distance."[28] At about this same time, her father asked her and other women relatives to serve on the boards of the family companies. "Barry Sr. had hoped to promote dynastic unity. Instead he put Sallie in a collision course with her brother, Barry Jr., 53, who ran the newspapers."[29]

Sallie Bingham became a director of three corporations that had been in her family for almost seventy years, including two newspapers, a television station, two radio stations, and a printing facility. The most famous of these was the *Louisville Courier Journal,* long considered one of the nation's best newspapers.

> The shift from ignorant beneficiary of trusts to attendant at quarterly directors' meetings was dramatic. I found myself sitting around large tables with men whom I did not know and who knew me only as my brother's sister or my father's daughter. At first I knew nothing about the companies, and kept silent while absorbing a few details. I soon realized that either I was going to learn enough to contribute to those meetings, or I was going to die of boredom. I chose to learn.[30]

But questions from Sallie and the other Bingham women who had been put on the boards prolonged meetings and were interpreted by Barry Bingham, Jr., as implied criticism of his management policies. In 1983, he asked his five female relatives to resign as company directors. Sallie Bingham was the only one who refused to do so.

Her share of the voting stock in the companies was not large enough to permit her to reelect herself. She decided to sell out, "to the family if possible, to outsiders if necessary," rather than remain passively invested. She and her brother could not agree on a price. She claims that because of her gender he would offer her only half of the going market value.[31]

After eighteen months of family quarrels, and "over his son's vehement objections, Barry Sr. . . . decided to sell the empire rather than see it and his family shattered by dissension." Altogether the companies brought in $400 million, $50 million of which went to Sallie Bingham and her children. She used $10 million of her share to endow the Kentucky Foundation for Women.[32]

Sallie Bingham views her rebellion and her philanthropy as advocacy on behalf of women. Through her efforts, more women artists in Kentucky will find support. Yet her decision to establish a foundation is a relatively traditional response of women who come into money. She primarily funds works of art, literature, and music produced by women, in the belief that the arts can promote social change. Private foundations, however, do not seriously alter power relations; they establish new ones. Now Bingham has the authority to determine which women artists are and are not worthy of receiving funds. Furthermore, as important as these cultural forms may be in making a better world, they are unlikely to transform structural inequality and oppression.

ANOTHER BASE OF POWER

Like the alternative funds, public women's foundations have the potential to improve conditions for women in the greatest need by providing money to organizing and social-change efforts in their behalf. These financial contributions, however, do not fully empower their recipients unless the recipients play a role in the decision-making process.

Women's foundations have gained popularity among the wealthy partially because they offer upper-class women an opportunity to exercise power—an opportunity that many of them, like their poorer sisters, have never before experienced. The desire to seize this opportunity is not in itself unjustified; women deserve as much authority and influence as men. But some of the rich women who are active in these funds exercise their power at the expense of other women. There is a danger that wealthy women may become matriarchs who simply take the place of patriarchs.

As I have argued throughout this book, elite philanthropy is not a system that ultimately empowers its recipients. Rather, it forces those who are needy, women or otherwise, to hold out their hands as supplicants. It allows the donors, even when they are feminists, to establish a new hierarchy of inequality. We can formulate alternatives, however, that would allow women of all classes and races to participate more equitably in creating a better world for themselves.

Funds like the Women's Foundation in San Francisco strive to be egalitarian and representative. Women of all means, ages, ethnicity, sexual preference, and types of ability may donate and serve. In such organizations the wealthy are not particularly privileged, even if they are able to contribute more money. These women's funds, however, must work specifically to resolve issues of class and race if they are to be effective. We need a better understanding of how sexism, racism, and classism interact.

The fact that positive change rarely comes about without some conflict has been a hard lesson for both the alternative and the women's foundations to learn. Conflict is also an attribute of the relationship between professionals in the grant-making field and the wealthy people they serve. The next chapter deals with the role of philanthropic advisers and employees of grant-making organizations. Their work can lead to more progressive, thoughtful funding, or it can simply maintain the status quo.

Chapter 10

Advisers and Professionals

Frankly, the people who work with estate planning for us are really renaissance people. They are pretty hooked into the nonprofit network. Some of them sit on foundation boards in town. So it is really just getting an idea of what the philanthropic climate is in town, and what we should be participating in. A lot of times they come to us with ideas of what we should be doing.

The wealthy hire people to advise them on their finances and their philanthropy. Dynastic clans like the Mellons, the Rockefellers, and the Weyerhaeusers have centralized family offices in which paid staff coordinate and handle these affairs.[1] Other rich people employ friends and relatives; retain consultants; use prestigious accounting, investment, and legal firms; or rely on in-house corporate counsel. Along with managing their clients' wealth and charitable giving, these advisers usually bolster their clients' egos with deferential behavior.

Advisers occasionally play a role in encouraging their clients or patrons to act equitably, ethically, and responsibly, but they are more likely to assist the wealthy in reinforcing the status quo. The advisers described here are all working directly in furthering the culture of philanthropy. Most of them simply carry out their clients' wishes. Many urge the elite to give to charity but rarely to controversial organizations. Others actually bring their clients into the philanthropic culture and teach them the appropriate behavior and the rules. Though they wield a great deal of influence, their persuasiveness is dependent on the authority and whims of their employers. Advisers and retainers walk a fine line between the role of servant and that of expert.[2]

The income and the future of advisers depend on their pleasing those whom they serve. Few would risk alienating their clients in any way. Advisers do sometimes become advocates for certain nonprofit endeavors, but unless they know that the philanthropists for whom they work are interested in social change, they rarely propose projects of this type. Normally they bring to the attention of rich clients only the kinds of organizations that they have already been supporting, thus behaving not as critics but rather as employees who maintain the philanthropic norm. Most could and some do, however, play a different role.

There are two main categories of advisers to the wealthy: professionals who provide technical assistance with maintaining wealth; and consultants or employees who offer specialized, personal services in the area of philanthropy.[3] The first group—which I have labeled the professionals or technical advisers for the sake of clarity—tend to be oriented toward the preservation of fortunes. The second—which I call philanthropic advisers[4]—facilitate the charitable uses of wealth.[5] The work of both groups is related and their duties often overlap. Some individual retainers fulfill dual roles. It is not uncommon for an effective professional technical adviser to become a family philanthropic adviser.

Wealthy philanthropists need advisers both because of the complexity of the tax laws and because of the skill and time required to investigate potential recipients of charity. Most philanthropists do not have the necessary expertise or specific knowledge to make informed decisions. Many are insecure about their own abilities. Some may employ advisers because of a lack of interest and time to oversee personally either their for-profit or nonprofit endeavors. Others devote themselves entirely to charity.

Methods of managing fortunes and philanthropy fall on a continuum from total external administration by a variety of different specialists to closely controlled multi-adviser dynastic family offices. This continuum may actually form a circle. Over generations, as dynasties break up, the heirs may again seek assistance outside the family organization. Individual situations also change over time depending on the type of assets, the size of the fortune, and the personal proclivities of the wealth-holder. Investments and divestments may be monitored directly by the rich individual or family leader. They may be overseen by an executive adviser. Retainers and their clients often work in tandem. The most common arrangement is a small family office, housing a holding company and a foundation, which is reliant on the extensive services of outside professionals. Along the continuum, dynasties may or may not be created, develop, thrive, or fail.[6]

This chapter offers background on advisers—where they come from, why they are hired. Brief information is provided on what they do and how their roles vary depending on the needs of the people they serve. The material is divided into four sections. The first covers the commonalities between retainers and philanthropists. The second concerns the work of professional technicians. In the third section case studies illustrate the duties of personal philanthropic advisers. In the conclusion, the future of the advisory role is considered.

SIMILAR SOCIAL CIRCLES, DIFFERENT ROLES

Most professional retainers and philanthropic advisers have well-established reputations and status in their own right. They move in the same social circles as the wealthy philanthropists they serve. Often, for example, they attended the same prep school or college. They may belong to the same elite clubs. They also serve on the boards of nonprofit organizations. The professionals who do the technical work are highly trained and experienced accountants, bank officers, financial planners, investment counselors, and lawyers. Philanthropic advisers are usually generalists who have had careers as technical professionals, academics, business executives, foundation personnel, fundraisers, doctors, community and union organizers, or volunteers.

The majority of retainers are extremely well-educated; they sometimes hold a combination of credentials or degrees that the rich employer may lack. Many are lawyers as well as either C.P.A.s (certified public accountants) or M.B.A.s (masters in business administration). Working for the wealthy is not the sort of thing for which one usually plans or prepares. The process of serendipity has frequently led advisers to their current positions, although similar backgrounds, ideology, and social networks with philanthropists are their entrée.

One philanthropic retainer, a former Ivy League development officer, spoke of how his primary rich client

> came from a poor background—I don't think it was as poor as mine, but certainly a poor background. He worked his way through school, as I did. [We both have] a real concern about some of the less desirable values and ethics in some of our young people, particularly in the late sixties and early seventies, going through that

period of drugs, questioning our democratic society, and what seems to be also a questioning of the work ethic. . . . We feel everything that we have gained we had to work for. It was not given to us. We are interested in providing a helping hand or support for young people who are willing to work and help themselves.

In this instance adviser and client are both politically conservative, and they have found that they have "a lot of the same basic values and interests." A younger, politically liberal philanthropic consultant also believes that "this whole business is based on trust and on a perception that we can share certain ways of doing things. To some extent that means sharing values."

Most advisers and those whom they serve endorse a common political ideology about the appropriateness of exercising private power in the nonprofit sector. For example, a Chicago attorney who represents several philanthropic families, some of whom travel great distances to see him, told us that

> wealth is private except for what government finds it necessary to tax. It has never been my view that a charitable contribution deduction is a charitable subsidization. . . . I think that the money initially belongs to the private sector, and whatever is left over is private sector money. I still tend to view this as private wealth even though there are tax considerations for salting it away in the charitable sector.

This lawyer's use of the idiomatic phrase "salting it away" is telling. Philanthropists expect to use their charitable stores, if not immediately, then later. They are not giving their money away but preserving it. The attorney's sentiments mirror those of his clients and, in addition to his expertise, make him a popular professional adviser.

Wealthy people typically recruit their retainers, although in the last twenty years philanthropic entrepreneurs have been promoting their consulting services to the rich. Professionals who are retained as consultants or are employed in legal or accounting practices generally advise several different people who have come to them through referrals. Some of these professionals may help to form a family office or foundation and eventually move into a full-time executive position in the new organization. Advisory relationships may begin on either a personal basis or a professional one, but those that last usually develop into some combination of the two. The friend becomes more of an expert, the professional more of a confidant.

As we have seen, advisers to the wealthy are often their social peers. But if not, they often want to be viewed as such. Some of the latter group have upwardly mobile aspirations and, depending on financial arrangements, may actually, over time, pass into the upper class and the culture of philanthropy.

For example, a Florida millionaire explained that his main advisers are two of his closest friends and

> both happen to be bank officers. [One] has been associated with the trust area since the late nineteen fifties. [The other] was an attorney until he discontinued his legal practice and became vice chairman of the ——— Bank Holding Company, a move that I endorsed completely.

He went on to say, "He just showed me, this afternoon, a picture taken with him and President Reagan in the cabinet room. There's just the two of them standing there shaking hands. He is getting me a copy of it. I am very proud to know him."

Just as advisers benefit from the reflected stature of the person or family whom they serve, when an employee receives recognition, the employer can feel that he or she had good judgment. There are some advisers, especially donors' friends who take on the consultant role, who may have lost former wealth and are trying to hold on to their membership in the culture of philanthropy through their association with their more fortunate fellows. Advisers rarely, however, have as much money as their bosses.

However influential philanthropic advisers may prove to be, they must defer to their bosses and must be particularly careful not to take up too much of the limelight. A case in Denver, Colorado, illustrates this point. The Piton Foundation is a donor-controlled "pass-through" fund. Oil multimillionaire Sam Gary founded the enterprise and has thereby donated millions of dollars to nonprofit groups for more than a decade. Shortly after establishing his foundation Gary hired Fern Portnoy, an educational psychologist, as executive director. Under her leadership the foundation gained a national reputation for its liberal grant-making programs.

Over the years Portnoy's personal visibility steadily increased while Gary remained in the background. She served on the prestigious boards of the Council on Foundations and the Independent Sector. On 1 October 1987, Gary took over her job. An article in the *Denver Post* reported that Portnoy's "personal profile sometimes has equalled that of the foundation itself."[7] It would seem that Portnoy may have overstepped her advisory status by overshadowing the donor. After all, ultimately advisers advise; and the wealthy decide.

THE PROFESSIONAL TECHNICIANS

> I [consult] attorneys, particularly where it comes to a question of tax deduct-
> ibility of an institution. [I consult] accountants when I'm questioning the
> marginal cost of giving excess dollars to charities toward the end of the year.
> . . . With regard to charitable contributions in my will, I first ask lawyers
> who are my estate planners what kind of general level of charitable giving
> makes sense as opposed to passing funds on to heirs.
> —Third-generation, well-known male philanthropist

Advisers provide the technical information necessary for making decisions
on financial and legal matters. The rich need help with investments; with
the formation of estate plans, trusts, and other devices for maintaining and
passing on their wealth; and with charitable contributions. Only dynastic or
other extremely rich families have the necessary range of specialists right in
their own offices. Most take their business to leading accounting, investment, and law firms. In the latter case, the relationship between the adviser
and the advised is primarily professional. Because of tax issues, accountants
and lawyers are particularly important in the philanthropic arena. A well-
known New York millionaire commented, "Well, my resources are at a level
where obviously I have professional advice. My estate is set up by tax
planning experts. My only tax shelter is my giving."

ATTORNEYS

According to both advisers and clients, lawyers are the most influential of
all professional advisers, especially with regard to the choice of estate plans
and charitable instruments.[8] This situation has been reinforced by the prolif-
eration of alternative vehicles for wealth management and philanthropy,
which has led to increasing specialization in the legal field. Tax attorneys
are consulted quite frequently because they are experts on the available legal
options. One nonprofit specialist from Washington, D.C., observed:

> There are about four hundred choices as to type of charitable organizations. . . . It
> does show what has happened to our tax system. It also demonstrates the point of
> how many different options people really have. . . . It is almost mind-boggling to
> think of the possibilities. I am not saying that it is necessarily good.

He is explaining one of the reasons that lawyers are so influential in this
area: unless trained in the law, most wealthy people could not possibly be
aware of all their options. The attorney continued: "And most of [the alter-
natives] are never presented to clients or donors."

A Midwestern lawyer commented sanguinely on the tremendous influence
that attorneys can exert when they are preparing clients' wills.

When people come into attorneys' offices to talk about estate planning in particular, they are scared to death—cause they are going to talk about dying. Nobody wants to think about dying. And they are vulnerable, almost malleable.

Though wealthy people may be malleable about the form (or legal vehicle) for their gifts, they do not generally rely on practicing attorneys to determine the amounts that will go to particular recipients.

Lawyers advise their clients about issues in tax deductibility and the structuring of charitable transactions. One attorney said: "People don't come in and say, 'I want to make a million-dollar gift. Who should I give it to?' " It is more common for the attorney to ask, "Is there somebody else you want to leave this to, besides your immediate family and including charity?" And if the lawyer does not ask the question? "I suppose there would be fewer charitable contributions made."

Some subjects explained how their attorneys directed them toward charity. "What they can do," said a Southern millionaire, "is help their clients get their toe in the water. They can do a monstrous amount to encourage people to set up foundations and so forth." He continued, "I don't think most attorneys or lawyers are all that smart. But some of them are." An elderly philanthropist remembered: "Attorneys advised me on how much of my income I'd better contribute to charity; otherwise Uncle Sam was going to take it. . . . Several times they've come to me and said, 'You have got to give away more money. The government is taking away too big a part of your income. Why don't you give it to some place where it will do some good?' "

A prominent Atlanta lawyer elaborated on the process of consultation that begins once a client has decided to make a philanthropic contribution. His description points to the fact that although they may not always recognize it, attorneys tend to guide their wealthy clients in the direction of conservative funding.

The first and easiest course is to find some established charity that is already doing what they [wealthy clients] want to do. . . . You can avoid all the difficulties and expense and time of setting up something new. . . .

Option number two is to see if an organization that is already in being can be moved in the direction that they [wealthy clients] want to go. A community foundation is a good example. If a community foundation does not already have a program in support of the local theater you can say, "We've got a guy that's interested in that. . . . Would you be willing to take that on as an area of activity? . . ."

I guess only after you explore those areas do you get around to saying, "Well, let's think about creating something new."

If the "easiest" option is to give money to an "established" charity, then new ideas and grassroots or small organizations are less likely to receive contributions. Another option the attorney presented is setting up an advised fund at a community foundation, with the donor rather than a representative distribution committee determining where the grants are to be awarded. Here again the lawyer becomes an advocate for a specific charity. Indeed, the theater example he uses illustrates his assumption that wealthy clients are apt to be interested primarily in high culture. In such ways attorneys' suggestions reinforce the status quo.

Lawyers throughout the country gave similar scenarios. A Michigan attorney who specializes in setting up estate plans said: "People come in and say, 'My primary thing is I want to pay the least amount of tax possible.' I will say, 'Fine, give everything to charity. You won't have to pay any taxes.' " He continued ironically, "They say, 'No, that isn't exactly what I meant.' So what they really mean is they want their property to go to their family, in most instances, and pay the least amount of tax."

Most lawyers stress the advisory, rather than the decisive nature of their work. A Southern attorney said:

> I start out the interview by saying, "Tell me exactly what you have in mind. Ignore the tax consequences. Ignore the mechanics. But tell me what it is you want to do." . . . Then we work backward on how to accomplish it. By asking more and more questions, I bring out what they are thinking. Sometimes they have never really thought it through before. As they answer one question, this leads to another question, until I have a pretty good idea what those people really want to do. Then I lead them toward a solution that I think will accommodate them.

The determination of the best legal alternative is based on a number of factors. According to an attorney at a leading Detroit firm: "The client has certain expectations as to how much should go to a particular charity. One client may want to give five thousand dollars a year, another may want to give a hundred thousand." In his view,

> different kinds of approaches would be appropriate. . . . Other [considerations] might be the kinds of assets involved. The client wants to give cash and the result could be very different than if the client has appreciated securities, interest in a closely held or a publicly held corporation.

Occasionally a lawyer is faced with the question: "So and so is having a foundation—why can't I?"

Some philanthropists minimize the role of their lawyers, perhaps resenting having to rely on their expertise. A Southerner claimed: "I don't like to be told by anyone what to do, so they act as 'technicians' and investigate the possibilities once I have an idea. But I don't keep up with all the tax law changes like the men do." The sister of a self-made millionaire, however, indicated that her family could not have established a foundation without legal assistance but that this was expensive. "And, see, that bothers us, because we'd rather be giving it to charity than to lawyers."

Most philanthropists know that they must use legal professionals but are still wary of them. One woman complained: "They all are not very knowledgeable. And I spoke to people, I am afraid, around the country, New York, Boston, Washington. . . . I have had bad legal advice." Naturally, however, most wealthy people must think highly of the legal advisers they choose to retain, or they would find others.

ACCOUNTANTS

Accountants[9] generally see the same elite client more frequently than an attorney would—at least four times a year, when estimated income taxes are due, and anytime there is an important financial transaction. This means that they have more opportunity than many lawyers do to influence their clients. Accountants determine exactly how much might be contributed to charity, for what tax benefits. Those with the most influence also provide specific investment and philanthropic advice. In general, however, accountants usually have less than attorneys to do with their clients' philanthropy, but this is highly variable, dependent on the individual's professional expertise and rapport with a particular client.

A few lawyers and their clients remarked on this point. A prominent Chicago attorney said, "The older I get, the more I think that accountants are more important than lawyers. When it comes to tax planning, a lot of people, including very sophisticated, very wealthy people, talk to the accountant." A wealthy Atlanta attorney supported this view.

> Accountants have gotten very aggressive. Unless the lawyer is fairly close to a client, he generally doesn't volunteer advice. Accountants do volunteer advice. . . . They are expected to, in a way. If they're representing an individual, he's counting on them to keep taxes down. So they are following his income. Lawyers don't generally ask their clients what their income is.

Accountants may either work directly for a client, work for a company or holding company associated with that person, or work for a firm that keeps the books. A close relationship, however, may develop only over time.

Professionals with training in both finance and the law are especially effective and favored by the rich in the role of personal adviser. Generally, however, accountants tend to stick to the numbers and the rules. An accountant who works in a family office noted that one could

> say to a family member that there is just so much money you can leave to your children without a substantial tax impact and thereafter most of the money's going to go to taxes. . . . So therefore it might be advisable to leave it to charity. And then it is up to the family member to decide.

If the decision is to contribute money to charity, then an attorney is usually consulted to devise the mechanism. Clearly, however, "the ultimate decision is still a family decision."

OTHER ADVISERS

Several philanthropists with whom we spoke indicated that they had started giving only after they had been asked. Few people know how to ask better than professional fundraisers. Development officers at large nonprofit institutions like universities and hospitals can be important advisers to the wealthy, although they usually do not work directly for those from whom they solicit.[10] These representatives of large institutions prefer that the donor give directly to their institution, with no restrictions. They also recognize the special need of many big contributors for control.

Most fundraisers are familiar with a range of charitable vehicles that they may suggest to potential donors. One lawyer claimed that college development officers

> are pretty sophisticated these days, and have good fundraising organizations that dispense (even though they disclaim the fact) legal advice. So they can provide (fairly well in some cases such as Harvard's) infinitely sophisticated proforms, computer projections.

A millionaire philanthropist agreed. "I will go to one of the development people, who usually is a specialized person, and get the advantages and disadvantages from their viewpoint, and then go back to the attorney. I find that good development people can be an enormous help."

Bank trust officers[11] are the only group of advisers who rate highly the charitable and estate services of banks. In the past, banks often managed the funds of wealthy individuals, and many continue to hold large trusts, especially for widows and charitable organizations. Trust officers enthusiastically promoted the services of their banks, which ranged from custodial accounts to the full investment management of assets.

Most rich philanthropists, however, said that they have become leery of using bank trust departments which, on the whole, no longer have good reputations for investment performance. One millionairess admitted that she had

> had bad experience with trusts. Usually the cause was a bank. I don't think banks are very good trustees. I don't think they look after investments in a very good way. I think some money managers are good, but you need to have an overseer to really monitor the money managers.

The "overseer" that she describes is frequently the personal adviser who runs the family office or is retained on a consulting basis.

It seems that many rich people simply do that which is easy or that which professionals suggest to them. An attorney supporting this conclusion said that "unfortunately, if they [the wealthy] go to their lawyers or accountants, they too may say, 'Here's what's easy,' simply because they may not be experts in this area." Development and trust officers, like attorneys, tend to give advice that channels donations in the direction of established, prestigious, highly endowed institutions.

PERSONAL PHILANTHROPIC ADVISERS

> [The rich] tend to turn to those who have advised them successfully as professionals all during their lives. By and large that means an attorney. . . . The attorney, in the cases I know of, is more than an attorney, he's a close family friend.
> —Nonprofit organizational consultant and adviser

Philanthropic advisers may be employed in the family or foundation office,[12] may be hired as independent consultants, or may be members of the firms that are springing up around the country for this purpose. As noted earlier, they come from a variety of backgrounds. Some are the children, grandchildren, or other relatives of first-generation millionaires.[13] Others come from old money but have lost their wealth. A specialized occupational niche has developed, although the only performance standards are those established by the people performing the job and the people for whom they work.

Personal philanthropic advisers claim that their work makes for a more professional funding process.[14] Even so, there is no course of study that teaches proper grant-making methods and little evidence that most of the special retainers actually do things any differently from philanthropists themselves. Some philanthropic advisers are given great latitude because of their knowledge of the donor's wishes and the mutual trust that has developed, but they still must cater to the desires of their bosses. In doing so, personal retainers clearly serve the interests of the upper class. Their work creates a distance between the funders and the funded, and the illusion of fairness and objectivity.

Even the most "liberal" philanthropists are leery about controversial projects. The executive director of a small- to medium-sized family foundation in the San Francisco Bay Area that has a reputation for funding programs for social change provided the example of a homosexual advocacy group that had applied for a grant.

> I wanted them [the board] to fund it and they did not. After we got through a level of uncomfortable humor and then a level of curiosity—how do they do it?— then we got down to what is right—that this is a matter of private decision.
> I never really know why we do or don't fund, but I am guessing better after several years. [With] the gay advocacy group, although I still thought it should be funded, they didn't fund it for the right reasons. The group had serious organizational problems.

In this case the adviser readily accepted the rationale of the trustees for whom he works—that problems internal to the organization precluded a grant, not that the group's kind of advocacy was too controversial. An arts group, in contrast, would rarely receive such close scrutiny from this foundation. The director now understands that he cannot successfully push gay advocacy grants through this board; if he wants to keep his job, it is unlikely that he will bring similar proposals to their attention in the future. Or, if he does, he will choose them very carefully.

The basis of the philanthropic adviser-donor relationship is typically more personal than it is professional. For example, the longtime family friend and lawyer has the job because he gets along well with the donor and is generally a respected member of the community. Advisers who work full time for only one wealthy client or family have usually had a long-standing association with them.

One executive at a small foundation explained that he was hired

> in a typically capricious way. . . . A board member kept asking me to do it. That is quite common in foundations dominated by family.

They are looking for people likely to be comfortable with them. And they are not likely to be someone that they did not know before. Professional talent is too far removed from that personal tie. Nobody came out of a competitive job search in this area. There is not one who does not have some personal connection, no matter how tenuous. . . . Even though professional people know each other quite well, the rest are trustees who are finding someone in whichever networks they move.

Although a family may have initially turned to an adviser because of his legal training, for example, he does not need to know the law in order to help choose charitable recipients. In some instances the advisory role is passed down through families. A Washington, D.C., philanthropist commented that his most helpful adviser is "my lawyer, who happens to be a childhood friend, and the son of my dad's best friend."

In many cases the adviser either is or considers himself or herself to be like a member of the family. This was frequently evidenced in our interviews by the use of personal pronouns. For example, a philanthropic adviser in one large family office was noted as saying: "I find that this family, at this moment, is creating charitable trusts rather than foundations. We—they— still have the same purposes of giving to institutions." In fact, the advisers who adopt an insider/outsider role[15] often have immense influence in the family; they are usually the top or executive retainers, coordinating the work of others.

Personal philanthropic advisers are gatekeepers and guardians of the family largess. They may help the family to clarify its goals and establish grant-making criteria. They may identify and investigate specific causes or projects and make recommendations about funding. They may also serve as brokers and intermediaries by screening applications for funding, other types of solicitation, and telephone calls. Often they represent their rich employers in the larger nonprofit community.

After advisers have been socialized at charitable meetings, they may encourage their clients to interact with other philanthropists. In this manner, although a person may always have given to charity, the adviser may bring him or her into the culture of philanthropy. An adviser in Boston explained that "there is a whole environment [in] which giving exists. . . . A single donor is much better off being connected to that giving environment than attempting to do it on his or her own."

The following case summaries touch upon the careers of five family advisers.[16] Each was selected because of an experience or work style typical of other charitable advisers. The examples are organized so that they illustrate entry at various points on the philanthropic continuum, starting with advisers having a minimal connection with philanthropy and ending with a dynastic family office. This is not to suggest that giving by the wealthy follows a prescribed, unilinear course. The rate of development along the continuum varies. Some families never form philanthropic dynasties in spite of vast fortunes.

ADVISERS TO THE SELF-MADE WEALTHY

First-generation millionaires are the key to the formation of dynasties. As founders of a family fortune they are most likely to select and groom or be groomed by philanthropic retainers. Because self-made rich people usually begin giving relatively late in life but while still heavily involved in their business endeavors, the first adviser frequently comes from within the company, or has had some other personal or professional association with the principal.[17] Advisers can sometimes arrange situations that benefit the company and its owners through philanthropic contributions. The charitable propensity of the potential donor and the persuasiveness of the adviser interact to determine where they initially fall on the philanthropic continuum.

The first case given here is illustrative of the transition from a corporate-based to a more personal philanthropy. In this and all other examples in the chapter, pseudonyms are employed to protect the confidentiality of advisers and their clients. The adviser in question, Samuel Smith,[18] is near retirement; he has been employed by a West Coast company for thirty-two years. Smith started in the company's legal department, and subsequently became its head. "I was a close adviser to [the company founder and CEO]. In fact, that was his office right through there. . . . We worked very closely together." As a friend, Smith also advised the company executive on personal matters "and worked with an outside law firm that specialized in estate planning. [We] helped put together an estate plan that included a foundation."

First-generation entrants into the culture of philanthropy appear to be unsophisticated about disguising their real funding motives; their corporate advisers unabashedly revealed their donors' desire to have control over nonprofit organizations they are funding. In this case the company founder is a heavy financial supporter of a private college that trains people to work in his particular industry—in fact creates the work force for the industry from which the family makes its money. The family exercises control over the policies of the college. Most pertinent was the disclosure by Smith that

> there was a time when the school looked like it might move away from the basic principles that motivated the [family] in supporting the school. Once they got all the money free and clear, you would lose any chance to have an effective voice.

Nonprofit organizations that do not comply with donor demands do not get funded. Smith explained:

> They could have made an outright grant to the school, but by putting it into the foundation, the trustees, who are largely other members of the. . . . family, [and] future generations are able to continue an involvement in the direction of the school. Once you have made the outright gift, they [the nonprofit organization] are very appreciative, but then they are off to something else when the money is gone. This way . . . [there is] an ongoing involvement in the program of the school.

The second case spans half a decade and represents the culmination of a one-generation philanthropic empire. The adviser, Crawford Appleton,[19] had a fifty-year relationship with his famous employer, who is now deceased. The millionaire seems to have modeled himself after Andrew Carnegie by passing limited assets on to his heirs and concentrating the bulk of his fortune in a private foundation and other nonprofit institutions.

In Appleton's area of the country, and even nationally, he is widely respected for his views on philanthropy. He was asked by his friend, the famous donor, to give up an excutive position to run the foundation. The donor was never on the board of the foundation, but Appleton indicated that he "always checked with him. . . . He had a veto. Put it that way. He [was] very, very good about recognizing the recommendations. . . . A couple of times he had strong feelings, which he expressed; we talked about it. But he pretty much avoided direct responsibility."

The philanthropist trusted his retainers because they anticipated his wishes. Appleton contended:

> He was just satisfied that what was being done was what he wanted done. There were people around him who pretty well knew what his interests were. We couldn't always follow them. . . . If we had a proposition, he would understand it, participate in the decision. But he was benevolent in that sense.

In this situation, the philanthropic adviser had tremendous admiration for his employer/friend. Theirs was a relationship based on mutual trust, with each learning from the other. Yet Appleton's use of the word *benevolent* indicates that he had a subtle understanding of the donor's prerogative.

Appleton never seriously challenged his principal's authority. An adept adviser, he managed to make a host of decisions but was always sure that the philanthropist himself got the credit. Appleton has groomed his quasi-professional successors to carry on his work at the foundation. Now that the donor is dead, these advisers will have more influence. But they still serve an elite board of trustees.

ENTREPRENEUR ADVISERS: THE NEW BUSINESS CONNECTION

Paul Story[20] is a well-known personal philanthropic adviser with several clients. Story was the vice president of a college prior to taking up full-time charitable consulting. (He had initially dealt with wealthy people through the college development office.) Since the early seventies Story has worked with foundations and donors as an adviser and staff person.

"I got to know a number of wealthy executives who were willing to let me be a kind of broker about projects that needed some money that they might want to support." Later, the widow of one of these executives invited Story to help her in administering a foundation. He claimed:

> I am successful because I do not surprise them [his clients]. I build real expectations rather than "hyping" a project. I figured out how to match project and donor without wasting time on either end. I will not recommend a project to a donor unless I know they are really interested. I will on occasion privately give them a copy of something, but I won't tell a project to write to so-and-so unless I know it's likely to be of interest. Part of this world is back-scratching.

Story acts as both an adviser and a fundraiser. He sees that many backs are scratched, including his own. Story has widely recognized influence with both donors and donees, and serves as a powerful intermediary in the culture of philanthropy.

Story described his work with a second-generation heiress in a family of immense wealth. The father, who had made the initial fortune, has a reputation for business acumen but not for philanthropy. The daughter wanted to establish her own giving program. Story indicated:

> After three or four hours she started to cry. I said, "What's the matter?" And she said, "You're the first person who even hears, who's answering my questions, or saying you don't know and you'll find out, and trying to hear what I want to do and not talk about what my father would have done."
>
> A lot of wealthy donors have that kind of experience. People who are working for them aren't really working for them. They see their job as serving the assets. Wealthy people are handicapped by an insecurity about being accepted for themselves.

Story has a talent for showing rich novices that they can develop personal power through their giving. At least initially, however, they are dependent on him to show them the way.

Story also recruits new participants and trains them in the mores of giving.

I have tried to find particularly wealthy people who were interested in philanthropy but did not have a focus. I have put a lot of time into this and have helped them tighten up their giving patterns. . . .

I have had a couple of strikeouts, after some conversation, mainly because there was no tax incentive, and also because, as is one of the many characteristics of wealthy people—especially those who haven't made the money themselves, and sometimes even if they have—they are whimsical. They worry about what are they getting into in terms of their social life. . . . Some of them will do things one or two times a year, anonymously, but do not want to do more.

I have always pretty much worked as a consultant, leaving myself enough time to do several other things I want to do, such as serving on other foundation boards.

In his consulting Story has become an advocate for and member of the culture of philanthropy. He takes on all the roles in the nonprofit sector but that of direct service provider. He is an adviser, board member, and fundraiser.[21]

The fourth advisor to whom we turn is another consultant, Sheila Reynolds,[22] who owns a three-person firm that manages the program and administration of small foundations. Reynolds finds most of her clients among the second-generation rich, especially those who have inherited a foundation. She is an example of a retainer whose primary task is to organize generational transitions.[23]

Reynolds currently has ten clients—ten foundations that make her office their home. Their letterheads carry her address and telephone number; her firm answers their phones: "From that point what we actually do for them depends on how our letter of agreement reads. We work as advisers . . . and they decide what they want to do."

Reynolds divides her work into three areas: "the day-to-day administrative operations, . . . the advising or counseling with trustees and directors, and finally, interfacing with both the potential grantees—the applicants—and the professionals who provide services to the organization, including investment counsel, legal counsel, accounting services."

Her firm is usually retained in times of perceived crisis.

That crisis tends to be the death of the founder, who until that point . . . has called the shots. . . .

So when they come to us they are in a state of high concern. . . . We are not initially looked upon as their potential managers—we are looked upon as some kind of outside manager. That is a very distant relationship. . . . We try to assure them that they can lean on us for as much help as they need. . . .

We try to point out to them that we can do it all in an orderly manner. We can make a checklist. We can develop priorities. And in the process of doing that, they then disclose what their values are and we can respond to them.

Reynolds indicated, "I think at this point you could really influence them to do almost anything, including changing program priorities. Obviously, that would be both undesirable and unethical."

Reynolds claimed that her work "is a systematic, businesslike approach to transferring their organization's management over to us." She is an innovator in what may well be the philanthropic wave of the future.

MULTI-GENERATION FAMILY ADVISERS

Personal philanthropic advisers in multigenerational family offices may also act like consultants.[24] A fourth-generation member of an Eastern dynastic family said that she, her siblings, and her cousins tended to use the family retainers "when we were younger and didn't really know what shape our interests were. . . . The older we get, the clearer we are about what we do want to give to."

Several "family offices" have changed hands in recent years, with former employees gaining ownership. One prominent adviser, Harold Bates,[25] now owns a major share of such a firm and considers the individual members of the family his clients. Although he has other clients as well, most of his business comes from this family; the Bates firm provides them with accounting, tax, charitable administration, financial planning, and estate planning services. There are forty-five staff members, the principal ones being lawyers or CPAs. Bates is both. The firm counsels two hundred individuals. Most of the non-family clients are in-laws or close friends. The firm handles 500 personal trusts. It also houses a holding company. The family members are immensely wealthy and able to pay the very high fees charged for "personal quality" service.

Before entering his current position, Bates ran one of the family's foundations. He recalled that he and other employees had two functions: "One was to be the staff of the foundation and the other one was to be philanthropic advisers to individuals." He received his salary in two checks—one from the family and one from the foundation. "It was the decision of the family, advised by their attorneys, that it was not in the spirit of the 1969 Tax Act to have the staff of the foundation fulfilling those two roles." This practice might make it look as if "the family was using foundation funds for their own personal purposes. They never did that, because they paid us separately. . . . At that time, this office was created."

Bates is the principal philanthropic adviser in the firm. "How much I do for the individual members of the family, and how I do it, depends on the interests and tendencies of the people." He continued:

> I know each family member, and what that family member's philanthropic interests are. I have, for my own use, developed guidelines for the giving and charitable interests of [each of] them. These are never published because [that makes it] very easy to change them. All they have to do is say, "I think I've given enough in this area, now I want to give to this." No board has to decide on it.

The family members are particularly sophisticated, and use all their charitable options, including several foundations.

Bates discussed the question of philanthropic control. "There are some institutions where a family member will approve of activity in this area but not in that," he said. He opposes funding in these cases.

> I have a very strong feeling that one should not demand control with giving. . . . If they [family members] attempt to control the institution, which they will do, I believe it's to the detriment of the institution.
>
> If one doesn't have confidence in the program, the management, or whatever, then don't give the money. And say, if you want to, this is why we're not giving it. But don't attempt to console them . . . because nothing consoles.

Bates had slipped into the style he would use when advising a client. His manner as he spoke was deferential, as if he were speaking to a member of the family. He noted that his suggestions are not always followed but that he tries to keep his "clients" on the straight and narrow.

Bates presented his rationale for concentrating funding in larger nonprofit organizations.

> If you give money to the [university], [for a particular project] obviously that makes it a little easier. If we give money to the museum, for use on a [particular exhibit], that is where it will go. So, the bigger, the more established, and the wealthier the institutions are, the easier it is to direct money. Directed money is different from control.

Even when philanthropists form family offices and employ retainers to investigate nonprofit groups, it is easier to fund the large, established institutions.

THE FUTURE FOR ADVISERS

A lot of people have wealth [but] have really not thought about what they are going to do with it. Until, by one happenstance or another, a college development officer, or a friend, or a trustee, or somebody who's the president of some organization comes to them and says, "You know we could really use a significant infusion of capital." That has caused a number of people to become philanthropists.
—Attorney

Thus, as in any hierarchy, the wealthy are not alone in their exercise of power; they hire highly skilled specialists with ideology and values similar to their own to help clarify and carry out their objectives. Advisers may think that they are simply undertaking "professional" work, but their activities help perpetuate, reinforce, and serve the upper class.[26]

There is no doubt that advisers have tremendous influence in the philanthropic arena. The work of technical and charitable retainers has become essential to the consolidation of family fortunes and the transition of wealth between generations. Both technical professionals and personal philanthropic advisers lead the newly rich and unsocialized inheritors into the culture of philanthropy. Attorneys and accountants point out tax advantages and recommend contributions to nonprofit organizations for the sake of deductions. Fundraisers approach the rich for donations to alma maters and community institutions. Philanthropic consultants target the wealthy as potential clients. The evidence indicates that the rich are becoming increasingly dependent on the use of advisers. And some advisers are advocates for responsible philanthropy.

But the wealthy also wish to be protected from throngs of humanity seeking their charity. Whether it is intended or unintended,[27] there is less direct contact today between the rich and the people and projects they fund. One attorney mused:

Fewer and fewer people think of charity in the sense it was maybe twenty-five or fifty years ago—of helping the poor person on the street. Charity has taken on a much different overtone. Most of the people I know who talk about charity are looking at more antiseptic and grandiose kinds of ideas as to where monies ought to be placed in society. [They] are turned off by a lot of the welfare programs. . . . Many of the grassroots kinds of charities that liberals such as myself might push them to are not the kind of thing that they want to do.

His observations have extremely important implications. The word *antiseptic* is on the mark. For many of the wealthy, charity means preventing infection or decay, maintaining a clean society. The elite are untouched in their practice of charity. Philanthropic projects are posed in scientific terms by advisers who claim that philanthropy should be based on systematic knowledge. Charity today, says the lawyer, is also less liberal, given less freely or generously. It goes to fewer grassroots organizations. It is no longer for the people. When the lawyer says that philanthropy is grandiose, he may mean that it is pompous and showy, or he may be referring to its part in a bigger, more conservative schema.

The philanthropic adviser typically functions to shield the donor from problems that he or she does not wish to face. This is precisely what many rich employers consciously desire. One well-known philanthropic consultant explained:

> Foundations and the wealthy think the rest of the world is full of wolves. They are frightened that they will be easy marks for the world outside, which is waiting to gobble them up. There is a strange amount of nervousness in this field, whether in trustees or staff.

If the wealthy and their advisers had more contact with the poor and greater knowledge of their problems through specific projects oriented toward ameliorating those problems, they might alter some of their funding priorities. In recent years, certain foundation staff have been encouraging their trustees to make site visits to prospective grantees. They have also arranged tours of deteriorating neighborhoods and shelters for the homeless. This is not the rule, however.

There is already competition among the different kinds of advisers, particularly between attorneys and personal consultants who lack legal training. Both groups could benefit from increased knowledge of funding alternatives as well as a greater consideration of ethical issues. Lawyers criticize "unqualified" consultants for giving out legal advice. Some philanthropic advisers, whose occupations are less well defined and recognized, are quick to point out the faults of the more technical advisers. One charitable consultant noted, "In my own business there is an undercurrent of concern or even resentment about attorneys as advisers in philanthropy." Another claimed: "Attorneys' interest is to protect their clients from taxation. . . . I think people get mesmerized by their lawyer." He contends that lawyers often block the philanthropic impulses of their rich clients.

Technical advisers may currently have the competitive edge, because their duties are more clearly understood and their practices more institutionalized and widespread. Philanthropic advisers, however, are catching up. The personal retainer is favored by some philanthropists because of the additional aura of privilege that such advisers confer upon them. Almost anyone can hire a lawyer, but how many people have a "personal professional"? Furthermore, the philanthropic consultant claims to be especially knowledgeable about charity, and in many cases the claim is true. These advisers can be helpful to both donors and applicants by establishing guidelines and responding to requests for information. Competition has fostered the "professionalization" of the nonprofessionals. A literature is developing in this area. Associations are cropping up. Codes of ethics are being proposed.

Another outcome of competition and specialization may be the redivision of professional turf. One wealthy donor pointed out that she has to know what she wants before she can choose a consultant to help her accomplish a particular goal. She thinks that most advisers know only about certain things and follow the lead of clients, rather than directing them. She claimed:

> If you are going to an estate planner, you say to the person, "I really want to leave a certain amount of money to charity," or "These are the groups that I want." You are paying the person two hundred and fifty dollars an hour to consult. It is pretty unlikely the person is going to say, "Well, you should not give your money away. You should burn it."

In this woman's view, the interaction is structured so that there is an inherent conflict of interest. The adviser is selling a particular service, which he or she advocates above other options. Relatively few professionals of any type are familiar enough or experienced enough with the full range of charitable alternatives.

As I have indicated, advisers to the wealthy, whether professionals or personal retainers, do not alter but rather serve the culture of philanthropy. The work they do, however, holds the potential to restructure the system. If advisers viewed their role as that of public servant, rather than servant to their clients, their approach to projects to be funded might be different. If their pay and tenure were not dependent on the whims of the rich, they could be more critical and less deferential. If they were recruited from outside the social circles of their clients, they might offer board members and families a different perspective, a new way of looking at philanthropy. If they had more assistance, they might have time to do their jobs thoroughly.

Philanthropy is more responsible when nonprofit organizations and programs are investigated, held to certain standards, and carefully evaluated. The standards, though, must not be simply the standards of the upper class and must not be applied only to certain organizations. By bringing grant-seekers, grant-makers, various intermediaries, and the affected constituencies together more often, a consensus might be reached or, at a minimum, compromises could be made. Many people have been doing this work a long time, and some are very good at it. They have developed administrative, screening, and monitoring systems for evaluating proposals, investigating organizations, and tracking grant funds. These strategies and techniques could be shared, modified, improved upon.

When advisers and nonprofit organizations are as dependent as they are on the largess of elite philanthropists, they are less likely to be farsighted, to take risks, to advocate changes. The suggestions offered in the next chapter would require a revamping of the philanthropy system. If some adjustments were made, however, philanthropy could indeed provide for advocacy, the development of new ideas and innovative projects, and the monitoring of the performance of business and government.

Chapter 11

The Restructuring of Elite Philanthropy

The philanthropy of the wealthy serves many purposes, but primarily it assists in the social reproduction of the upper class. Private contributions by the elite support institutions that sustain their culture, their education, their policy formulation, their status—in short, their interests. This is not to say that the charitable giving of the rich is unworthy, or wholly detrimental to the larger society. Funding of the arts may provide the general population with greater access to high culture. Elite schools do not serve the wealthy alone but also enroll a sizable proportion of scholarship students. A new wing at a children's hospital or money for medical research may ultimately save many lives. Corporate and foundation grants for economic development or housing can be worthwhile, especially since the government has moved away from funding in these areas. Small amounts of money to grassroots, poverty, and social-change projects are absolutely basic to their survival.

The vast majority of these nonprofit agencies, groups, organizations, programs, and institutions do good work that is essential in our society. I have not been criticizing them or their performance. The evidence, however, indicates that they have been stretched thin because of federal cutbacks. Social services have suffered more than any others, and philanthropy—elite or otherwise—has not made up the difference. At least half of all private contributions come from the upper class. As I have stressed in the preceding chapters, most of this money does not go to aid the poor, and we must ask whether the funding of the wealthy serves the public good. Is this the type of human service deployment we want in a "pluralistic" society?

Even one of the leading proponents of pluralism, the political scientist Robert A. Dahl, has argued for the necessity of redistributing wealth and income. He acknowledges that in the United States the full achievement of pluralist democracy has been curtailed; all citizens do not have the opportunity to participate effectively in organizations that have an impact on the political process. Because certain groups have greater access than others to resources, "the preferences of their members count for more than the preferences of citizens who belong to weaker organizations." The "final control over the agenda" is not shared equally. "The unequal resources that allow organizations to stabilize injustice also enable them to exercise unequal influence in determining what alternatives are seriously considered."[1] A central ingredient in a solution to the dilemmas posed by Dahl is progressive taxation and redistribution.

The difficulty, of course, is that a majority of elite philanthropists already object to what they consider excessive taxation. They view their charitable giving as an alternative to even higher taxes. In addition, they derive immense personal satisfaction from their philanthropic activities. The rich continue to view any money that was once theirs as still theirs. They think of their contributions as private money going for the public good. It thus follows, the elite earnestly professed during interviews, that they should make decisions about "their" money. In this way the upper class, rather than the majority of the population, through a political process, defines the public good. The wealthy, however, feel entitled to this prerogative. After all, are they not better qualified as leaders, especially given their superior culture and knowledge?

I have argued that the elite control, influence, or want to control the organizations they fund in significant ways. Thus an already powerful group has disproportionate authority in many nonprofit endeavors. Once again, this does not mean that rich people run all the private cultural, educational, health, and welfare organizations in the country. But they do have the strongest voices in many of the biggest, most prestigious enterprises and institutions. When the elite or the foundations they have funded deem projects to be unworthy of their time and money, these causes suffer because they must increase their efforts in order to secure smaller sums from more contributors.[2]

Furthermore, wealthy board members make decisions about the disposition of more than their "own" funds. Many nonprofit groups still take in sizable government revenue as well as smaller contributions from thousands of middle- and working-class donors. The charitable tax break for itemizers has also resulted in lost income to the State. In effect, these are not private efforts but public endeavors.

At its best, the philanthropy system provides a check against corporate or government domination or indifference. It is also inextricably linked with business and political affairs. Individual nonprofit groups can be important players in a kind of balance of power, as "independent centers of thought, action, involvement, and pressure."[3] This is the type of pluralism that we should promote. I would not do away with the system, but I strongly believe that it needs to be restructured.

At a minimum, the federal government has a basic responsibility to provide for human welfare services. Rhetoric about philanthropy and other forms of private initiative must not be a substitute for State funding. We might determine that nonprofit organizations are more effective in certain areas than government programs. But as the European experience demonstrates, for redistribution to occur the bulk of the revenue should come from the State.

In the United States, the barriers to changing policy, both public and private, concerning philanthropy are daunting, especially with regard to the upper class. The charitable deduction for the average citizen who fills out a "simple" tax form was revoked in 1986, but this was a privilege too unassailable to take away from the affluent, who itemize their deductions and have political clout. Both Reagan and Bush have sung praises to philanthropy while promising small government along with no tax increases. Privatization is ascendant; Statism is in disrepute. Charity has become a rhetorical device by which to justify this dramatic political development.

The ideology of philanthropy strikes a deeply responsive chord in the psyche of Americans, in spite of the fact that it does not do what its proponents claim it does. Most citizens have consistently spent a portion of their income to support churches and community projects—projects that they hope will improve the general quality of life. And in many cases these projects succeed. The problem is that the scale of such activities is usually quite modest. Moreover, in participating in such behavior, the majority of Americans tend to look backward to the philanthropic practices of the past rather than forward to new solutions. But historical platitudes disregard the magnitude of the social problems that we face. Good personal intentions and moral behavior cannot adequately deal with homelessness, hunger, illiteracy, morbidity, and lack of opportunity. Only State action will suffice.

Many people, however, seem to think that government is to blame for the deterioration in the quality and extent of social services. But instead of trying to improve State programs, as we did during the New Deal, we have been shifting public responsibilities back to an amorphous "private sector." Some, including President Bush, believe that philanthropy is at least part of the answer. But "a thousand points of light" are not enough. One traditional role of voluntary efforts has been to make the public and elected officials aware of problems so that the State may respond. A thousand or more beams can shine on a variety of issues, and bring attention to people's needs, but they cannot adequately sustain the programs that might provide solutions.

Earlier in this century our government made a commitment to insure that all citizens had adequate food, shelter, health care, and education. Today most of us believe that the right to the pursuit of happiness, held out as a moral ideal by the Declaration of Independence, cannot be realized unless these basic human needs are met. Some contend that the human service role must be balanced with the need for a strong military. Others believe that we must move beyond the defense of nations to a new internationalism and the protection of ecosystems. The balance between human needs and military expenditures can be struck only in the political arena.

As a nation we must reach a consensus about the basic duties of government. We would never think of providing for the military through philanthropy. For most of the nation's history there has been a political consensus about the need to provision a public armed force. In the concept of private funding of the military we immediately recognize the potential threat of dictatorship and elite control. Why are we content to ignore similar threats and problems in the area of welfare? We need to reforge a consensus about the rights of all citizens to basic human services.

Given the widespread support for charity, how might the system be reformed to serve the public interest? A variety of policy options and recommendations about elite philanthropy are outlined in the remainder of this chapter.[4] An equitable tax system would lay the foundation for such reforms. Each alternative offered is built upon the need for accountability from donors, the government, intermediaries, and nonprofit service providers, as well as the desirability of a representative process. Public awareness, educational, and organizing programs could foster the participation of more citizens in philanthropy and work against elite control. Clear guidelines and standards for foundations, other grant-makers, and nonprofit governance in general would encourage fairness. There is a way for us to continue to be partners with our own government in providing for the common good. And there are several strategies for building individual choice, without elite control, into the process.

EQUITABLE TAXATION

Taxation has been the mechanism that provides revenues for the funding of national defense, public works, and public goods. Almost all Americans these days feel that they suffer from taxation. Curiously, even the wealthy are perturbed, although it is undeniable that the real tax burden is carried disproportionately by the middle class. Within the framework of a modern capitalist system, and leaving aside for the moment the particular responsibilities of a democracy to its citizens, there appears to be no alternative to taxation short of the nationalization of industry. There has to be some source of income. A reformed system could be devised along the following lines.

NONPROFIT PUBLIC POLICY

Charitable policy is currently enacted through a tax code premised on the notion that individual philanthropy is altruistic and should be rewarded. Yet some contributions are clearly more altruistic than others and some organizations more highly geared than others toward serving the public good. Americans need to rethink the system by which nonprofit groups are categorized as tax-exempt under the rulings of the Internal Revenue Service.[5] The code could, for example, require a more representative decision and governance process within individual charities, and base their exemption status partially on these criteria. Except for due care and fiduciary responsibility, the legal requirements of most voluntary groups are extremely limited; there is little regulation of the field and almost no distinction between the services that the various tax-exempt organizations actually perform.

The main exception is the private foundation, which has been treated differently since the Tax Reform Act of 1969. This act was a specific and fairly successful attempt to limit the power exercised by the wealthy through the grant-making institutions they endow. It did not, however, apply to the individual contributions of the upper class, to the elite organizations they tend to support, or to other charitable trusts and vehicles.

Certain endeavors more clearly fill a public role than others, and they should receive a larger tax break. We do have a precedent in this regard. Those who donate to public charities, for example, receive the largest deduction, 50 percent, whereas those who create or contribute to private foundations are given only a 30 percent deduction. (This disparity represents a recognition of the basic differences in the functions and roles of these types of organizations.) In addition, an individual or family cannot have a controlling business interest in the assets that comprise the endowment of a private foundation, whereas closely held assets may be contributed to other kinds of charitable vehicles, such as support organizations.

We might want to insure that people who donate money to the organizations serving the neediest members of our society will receive the greatest tax benefits. Or, a full tax exemption might be given only if the general population is free to use the services of the agency. A related option would be to require that certain nonprofit groups meet a "public interest" or "public support" test. In order to be accorded public charity status, even grant-making organizations would have to demonstrate that they have widespread support and boards of trustees that are representative of the communities to be served. Gifts to nonprofit institutions that are exclusionary or offer services for high fees would get reduced tax breaks. In the case of private schools, for example, the number of scholarships offered might be required to equal or even exceed the number of tuition-paying students in order for the institution to be accorded a particular tax standing. People of all classes could still have the option to give to whatever nonprofit group they might choose, but the tax benefits would be based on the nature of the work done by that group.

Aside from government responsibility for the provision of basic human services, there is another strategy for fostering the wider development of a grant-making system based on the model of the alternative, community, or public foundation that has merit. These foundations have the potential to be more democratic than direct gifts or private foundations, but they need to be better financed. Greater tax incentives might encourage increased contributions. The public foundations that might be formed would not necessarily be required to have a particular political perspective, serve only one geographic region, or concentrate on a single issue area. Some might focus on the arts and culture, others on social change. The staff and representative boards or distribution committees of these local, regional, and national public foundations would review applications, visit the organizations in question, and make determinations about prospective worthy causes. Prime donors, as well as those of lesser means, could select the general area or fund to which they would like to make a sizable contribution. They would not be able to designate a specific organization as the recipient of the money, but they might be permitted to endow advised funds existing during their lifetime.[6] Contributions to alternative, community, or public foundations would merit, as they do today, full charitable tax deductions.

Potential donors would be provided with the history of these foundations' previous funding decisions and could determine whether or not in their judgment the staff and board were competent. And along with other citizens they could do work on a voluntary basis for whatever nonprofit groups they chose. Their role in an organization, however, would be based on their personal ability and merit, rather than on the size of their contribution. As always, the wealthy would be free to make direct gifts of any size to whatever organizations they might choose as long as they received substantially reduced tax advantages.

At a minimum, charitable giving could be a matter of public record for those receiving tax benefits: a form might be added to the itemized tax return requiring a full listing of all contributions over a certain amount. This portion of the return would then be treated as public information.

Summarized annual records of nonprofit agency activity could also be made available to the public and to policy makers. In such cases voluntary groups would have to keep better statistics. The extent of their funding of particular activities would be made explicit, the numbers and types of clients served would be detailed, and public policy decisions would therefore be better informed. In addition, the constituency of any particular cause would know how its funds were being raised and utilized.

INCOME TAX

Whether or not philanthropy is to be viewed as an alternative form of taxation, when people are given choice about where "their" money goes, more democratic safeguards need to be instituted. If the income tax system were equitable across classes, there would be a charitable deduction for all citizens or for none. The present system is untenable. A fair income tax system would also be effectively progressive, and corporations would pay their share. Consider the following example.

Under the current tax rate, there is a ceiling of 28 percent; multi-millionaires pay proportionally the same amount in taxes as the average dual-career family. The charitable deduction, however, allows the wealthy to save even more. A million-dollar contribution or a combination of gifts to nonprofit groups decreases by $280,000 the taxable income the donor or the donor's family (unless this is more than half of the total income). If there were no charitable deduction, the donor would be paying taxes on that $280,000. According to the same basic formula, the person or couple who makes $75,000 a year also pays 28 percent in taxes, which without other deductions is at least $21,000 in a given year. This upper-middle-class family is living on roughly $54,000 annually. Let us say that they tithe, and donate to charity a generous 10 percent, or $5,400. This reduces their tax bill by a mere $1,500. The poor person on the other hand, who usually cannot itemize deductions, has no charitable break. Yet a recent survey indicates that the least privileged members of our society actually give away proportionally more of their income than the middle-class or the wealthy.[7] Poor and middle-class individuals who do not itemize their deductions pay taxes on their total income.

Another consequence of the inequality in the tax system is that it encourages the wealthy to give large contributions which allow them to control nonprofit organizations. An obvious way to limit individual power over specific groups in particular and public policy in general would be to place an annual ceiling on gifts to any one charitable agency, as we do for contributions to national political campaigns.[8] This option would undoubtedly be unpopular with many nonprofit groups that depend heavily on large gifts, especially elite preparatory schools and universities. And the increased work of fundraising could take away from the basic goals or services of the organization. But many groups that are not supported by the wealthy already face this dilemma. Perhaps a compromise would be to allow a fully deductible contribution up to a certain amount, and to limit tax breaks over that sum. It might also be stipulated that there be no limits on contributions to public charities and foundations that meet a public-support test.

In contrast to major donations, smaller gifts do become public because they are immediately absorbed into the common fund, or in the case of single works of art, into a larger collection. It is difficult to be precise about the exact figure that would constitute a major donation, but perhaps $10,000 is a good "dividing line." Or the breakoff point might change depending on the size of the budget of the recipient group. In any event, the specifics of these recommendations would require much discussion among all who would be concerned, and resolution within the political arena.

ESTATE TAXES

As we have seen, our inheritance system perpetuates inequality and the concentration of wealth. We have a myth in this country that all people are equal at birth. But almost by definition the majority of the poor are unable to accumulate possessions that they can pass on to their children or others when they die. Middle-class individuals, if they do not end up in a nursing home, may have something, perhaps a house, for their offspring to inherit.

Only the rich bequeath charitable trust funds, seats on foundation boards, non-charitable trust funds, and vast fortunes to their children. As we have seen, their children grow up in a different world—of culture, good education, and privilege. If we in the United States were to drastically alter or even disallow the inheritance system, then our people might start off more equal at birth.[9]

Another alternative to the present system would be to eliminate loopholes like annuities, special gifts, and split-interest trusts that enable the wealthy to avoid inheritance taxation. For example, charitable lead and remainder trusts enable the wealthy to sidestep taxation by receiving assets tax-free simply because for some period of time their interest income went to charity.

We might, however, want to continue to provide incentives for direct bequests to truly charitable nonprofit organizations or public foundations. The same basic guidelines that are adopted for income tax deductions might be applied to estate plans. Wealthy individuals and others with considerable assets would pay lower or even minimum estate taxes if a bequest were made to a group that clearly met and maintained full tax-exempt status.

INNOVATIVE TAX MEASURES

According to the Institute for Public Policy and Administration in Washington, D.C., "Neighborhood Assistance Act Laws" have the potential to "generate $300 million annually at a federal tax cost of only $55 million, for nonprofits serving low- and moderate-income people." Seven states already have these laws on the books; they generally provide a 50 percent tax credit to businesses that contribute cash, in-kind services, or technical assistance to "distressed communities" or to nonprofit organizations for projects that serve such constituencies.[10]

The institute's policy researchers and its panel of advisers claim that a "federal version of these laws could strengthen the programs where they currently exist, promote their enactment in more states, and significantly increase corporate contributions to nonprofits." Various limitations might be imposed, such as a limit on the combined tax credit that all businesses or any one corporation might use annually, as well as stipulations on eligible activities and sponsors.[11]

The shortcoming of this strategy is that it hands the decision about what projects are and are not to be supported over to corporations, which are not appropriate entities for making public policy. Similar or improved incentives, however, might also be offered to individual grant-makers willing to fund a public agency that would disperse their donations and make policy decisions about projects.

ACCOUNTABILITY AND REPRESENTATIVENESS

One of the greatest shortcomings of the philanthropic system is that it operates under a cloak of privacy.[12] Charitable giving is a private affair. Individual tax forms are confidential. Nonprofit enterprises of all types are private. Board meetings are held behind closed doors. Annual reports from many types of nonprofit organizations are not required, much less made public or published. The general public has no way of knowing what hundreds of thousands of groups in this country are doing with the money that is given to them, much of it in lieu of taxes.

THE NEED FOR INFORMATION

Sound public policy cannot be formulated without accurate information and research. At least in part because of the attitude toward honoring privacy, adequate statistics about charitable giving are not compiled and maintained. We have no basic data about who contributes how much to what causes. There is scanty information in the aggregate, and certainly none by class or across all regions. The statistics presented in this book were the best available at the time. Most of them are estimates.[13] We need to lift the cloak of privacy, and this can be done only if the information is made available. As my colleague John Simon, co-chairman of Yale University's Program on Non-Profit Organizations, said of philanthropy, "It's the least understood and the least covered part of our American society."[14]

Except for this study and a few others,[15] we have almost no idea of what happens to the funds the elite disperse as part of their philanthropic activities. There is little critical research on the operation of foundations.[16] We hear about very large gifts to charity only when the donor wants us to, or when a whistle is blown because some impropriety is brought to light.

There has been more press coverage about charity in the past several years, although it is still limited largely to the leading newspapers or the society pages of papers in small towns. Several papers do have reporters whose "beat" is nonprofits and philanthropy.[17] But there is not enough truly investigative reporting. Because of its connections to business—and the fact that media owners and managers sit on nonprofit boards—philanthropy can be a surprisingly controversial area, with certain topics being almost taboo. For example, a few years ago the *Los Angeles Times* had excellent nonprofit coverage. But after reporter David Johnston exposed a United Way loan scandal, he was taken off the story and all inquiry by the paper stopped, except to report the final outcome. Johnston has since left the *Times* and taken an assignment at another paper that is unrelated to charity. Instead of being rewarded for his good work, he was reprimanded. We need hard-nosed muckraking reporting of the charity scene.

We must work at developing a system that encourages accountability at all levels. Government officials, journalists, researchers, social critics, and thus the public should have ready access to information on philanthropy. Either a governmental agency or regulated nonprofit organizations might collect and analyze statistics and make them widely available. We certainly have the requisite information-gathering, retention, retrieval, and dissemination capacity and technology. Consistency in the collection of statistics would need to be insured, but, depending on the political climate, this function could be carried out by a newly developed section of any number of existing state and federal government agencies or by a national network of nonprofit organizations.[18] There are not enough journalists covering these matters; few scholars—with policy perspectives or otherwise—studying these activities; and in most cases no way for the public to make itself heard.

REPRESENTATIVE DECISION MAKING

The concept of accountability goes well beyond releasing basic information; it extends to the decision-making process as well. Accountability could promote greater representativeness at all levels of the philanthropy system. As with government activities, if board meetings were open to interested citizens or public hearings called on a regular basis, then people in all walks of life would have a greater opportunity to participate.

At a minimum, the rich, and the nonprofit organizations to which they give, could be much more accountable to the general public concerning their activities. One way of thinking about this is to regard a charitable decision as being private only until it is made: if the donor is taking a tax deduction, the money has now become "public," and citizens have a right to know all the details surrounding the donation.

Here we must anticipate the problem of the power exerted by elite philanthropists even before they make a particular charitable decision. Take the example of the art collector. Will the collection be left to a local public museum? If so, which one? Will a new institution be created to house the collection? Who will be currying the collector's favor in advance of this decision? Will the collector's decision be based on promises made before the collection is donated? Perhaps publicly representative arts boards at the local, state, and national levels could be empowered to adjudicate decisions of this type. They might rule, for example, on what type of institution could receive the collection in order for the deduction to be allowed.

If a nonprofit organization is controlled by an elite board, it is not truly public. This does not mean that all wealthy people should be excluded from responsible positions in voluntary institutions, but rather that more representative bodies should be created and new leadership cultivated. The participation of active citizens and experts should be further encouraged. Various constituencies—people of color, the disabled, homosexuals, the poor, seniors, and women—who have not had a voice on many nonprofit boards need to be added as trustees of voluntary organizations of every variety.

Brian O'Connell, a proponent of nonprofit provision and expert on the management of voluntary organizations, has also called for more representative boards of directors. But he has issued a warning as well: that diversity—he was referring primarily to people of color, but his general points apply to all unempowered groups—will make the decision-making process different:

> If you're an average board or staff member, you will assume that "having done so much good by involvement of many minority representatives, they should be grateful and should now settle into the organization." You'll hope that this part of the struggle is behind you and that things can go on as usual. If that turns out to be the case, you will have picked the wrong minority representatives. The right ones are going to bring about some very real changes. They are going to bring a different perspective, a different determination, and a lot of questions. They are not going to blindly accept on faith the organization's existing directions, policies, and programs. No matter how frustrating you find it and no matter how impertinent you view it, be prepared for the fact that your new recruits have learned the hard way not to passively accept whitey's precedents and policies.[19]

When the disenfranchised are not being invited onto the appropriate boards or committees, they should organize to be included.

People of all classes should also have the freedom to make decisions about where their charitable funds go. For example, local, regional, and national umbrella groups of nonprofit organizations, such as those belonging to the Alliance for Choice in Giving and the National Black United Fund, were created for this purpose. Along with the Combined Federal Campaign, they were formed to protest their exclusion from such monopolies as the United Way and have been demanding inclusion in the payroll-deduction campaigns of corporations, nonprofit groups, and public employers. Payroll deduction is one of the most effective ways to raise money for charity. But employees have often been coerced to contribute to the United Way and have been unable to stipulate where they would like their money to go. Their bosses, on the other hand, have been serving on the boards and distribution committees that determine which groups will and will not be served, and how much each organization will receive.[20]

EMPLOYEES, PROFESSIONALS, AND ACCESS

Paid, trained staff or advisers from all backgrounds could also help to make philanthropy more accountable and representative. It would be possible to develop educational and credentialing programs for people who wished to enter this kind of work along the lines of what already exists for social workers. Not every practicing social worker has credentials, nor would it immediately be necessary to regulate practitioners in this manner. In certain respects the untrained generalist and organizer may bring a more creative approach to the field than the highly educated professional. Agencies and clients, however, would know that those who did have licenses or had completed a certain course of education were knowledgeable about their job duties and had an understanding of the ethics of the field.

An option for small private grant-makers is provided by such groups as Joint Foundation Support in New York, Common Counsel on the West Coast, and the Charter Fund in Denver. These efforts are less representative than the public funds, because they are still private endeavors, but they are preferable to donor-controlled, unstaffed, grant-making organizations. In each case, several foundations or funds operate out of the same offices; they share expenses and employees, who investigate proposals and make recommendations to the individual grant-makers or boards. More groups get a fair hearing when there is staff to do this work, or when trustees take an active part in the pre-grant review of organizations and in post-grant evaluation.

As I indicated in the previous chapter, philanthropic advisers and foundation employees have a great deal of influence, and in some cases, latitude. One way for them to become even more independent would be for them to form their own professional associations and unions. This could increase their credibility, provide them with a mechanism for peer review, and allow them to formulate clear ethical standards. Fundraisers, for example, already have such organizations. But the primary forums for grant-making staff are groups such as the Council on Foundations, which are based on institutional memberships and include trustees in their deliberations.[21] Advisers and staff might better serve as advocates, brokers, and risk-takers for those they fund, rather than as lackeys, guardians, and conservative functionaries of the wealthy.

Foundations and other private grant-makers best serve the public when they have clear grant-making criteria, guidelines, policies, and procedures that are publicly known. Such a situation, and actually having proposals read and projects visited, would represent a nonprofit organization's primary avenue of access to a grant. In addition, a fair process for "thorough pre-grant review without interfering in the program, subverting the mission of the provider, or imposing excessive conditions or constraints on the use of funds,'' is desirable.[22]

PHILANTHROPY AND DEMOCRACY

Robert Matthews Johnson, former executive director of the Wiebolt Foundation and staff consultant to the Chicago Community Trust as well as a community organizing institute, has recently written an impassioned plea for the distribution of more philanthropic funds to organizing efforts at the local level.

> There is one role for democracy that philanthropy can fulfill: the funding of those community arrangements that seem most likely to help people get together to find answers and make democracy work, specifically in communities where people don't have the means to fund these arrangements by themselves.[23]

An avowed pluralist, Johnson is an advocate of nonprofit efforts that promote widespread participation, which he believes increases citizens' enthusiasm about public life; competence as actors in the public arena; knowledge and understanding; and leadership development. He also thinks that active citizen participation puts public officials on the alert. This approach to empowering people can be particularly effective in poor communities.

Johnson lays out a series of strategies for accomplishing his goal, including creating a safe arena for creative discussion and interaction among people from many different communities. He favors independent local programs with an overarching, ''integrative'' agenda that involves significant numbers of people who either have communications and organizing skills or have access to technical assistance in these areas. He thinks that real change comes about only when it is initiated by those affected. I agree.

Johnson's proposed solutions are laudable in many regards, but they still leave to the elite the decision about where the money goes. This situation may conform to the desires of the rich and even to the attitudes of the cynical. But it does not allow for genuine redistribution. Nor does it transform the harsh reality that contemporary American philanthropy is a system of ''generosity'' by which the wealthy exercise social control and help themselves more than they do others.

METHODOLOGICAL APPENDIX

I have tried in this book to let wealthy philanthropists and their advisers speak for themselves by selecting the most representative, or in some cases the most articulate, quotations out of thousands of pages of interview transcripts from three different but related studies. In each research project I was a principal or co-principal investigator. The material and the general trends described here were gleaned from probing conversations with 140 millionaire philanthropists, as well as several less wealthy donors with trust funds. An additional one hundred foundation staff members and seventy personal advisers to the wealthy—managers of family offices, attorneys, and accountants—were surveyed.[1] Several people, including myself, conducted the interviews. For the sake of consistency and reliability, in the few places where aggregate personal information or statistics about study participants are reported, only the 140 verifiable millionaires are counted. I also relied upon published accounts about the wealthy and about nonprofit organizations and their activities.

We requested interviews only with those who were widely regarded as millionaires, or heirs to vast wealth, and their advisers. We relied on public sources for partial confirmation of this information. In a few instances we discovered that people whom we interviewed were not as rich as we had thought; those cases are not included in this analysis. As my own work on this project progressed, I decided to conduct additional interviews with some people who are not strictly millionaires but who have trust funds from which they contribute to charity.

Our informants told my colleagues and myself what they wanted us to hear. On the whole I assume that they believe what they said and that their actions are based on their beliefs. With only a few exceptions, and outside of my experience as executive director of the Women's Foundation of Colorado, my interaction with rich philanthropists was limited to the interviews. Our meetings were typically formal; I never engaged in social or unguarded conversation with them, and after the interview I never saw them again. Although I might have heard or read about them later, I never directly observed their behavior. Therefore, my evaluation of the effects of giving by the elite is based entirely on what can be inferred from the interviews and from the sparse published data on where charitable money goes and how it is used.

Unless I obtained permission, the personal traits of the subjects of this study are not disclosed in any detail, nor are the names of specific organizations given where this might identify a study participant. I could not, for example, report that Jane or John Doe is chair of the Metropolitan Museum of Art and sits on the board of the Yale Corporation. Even if I indicated that someone might serve on these particular boards, the astute sleuth might be able to determine that person's identity from what was said. Many of those with whom we spoke are public figures, and I have had to be careful not to repeat statements similar to those they have made in other contexts that might have received widespread attention. Therefore, unless I indicate otherwise, when I use material from the transcripts, several individuals—not just one or two—have made the same kind of comments. Wherever possible when quoting an informant, I provide at least some pertinent descriptors and, when relevant, general information about the types of nonprofits to which that person contributes.

We interviewed eighty-four men and fifty-six women of wealth. The majority are married and have children. This elite group is predominantly white and Protestant, although forty of the 140 participants are Jewish. Nearly 20 percent of the millionaires are younger than forty. Forty percent are middle-aged and an equal number are over sixty years old.

A majority of rich philanthropists live in large American cities where population and wealth are concentrated. We also sought out the economic elite in small and medium-sized towns, as well as in rural areas. As a group, these people are cosmopolitan, and several maintain at least two residences in different parts of the country or abroad. Most, however, spend a good deal of time in the areas where they grew up. The exception is the "Sunbelt"—the West, Southwest, and Southeast—where many rich people have permanently relocated.

Fewer than ten of the study participants lacked college degrees. More than half of those for whom data were available graduated from Ivy League universities. Many of the others attended elite private colleges or top-ranked state universities.

Fifty of these people (35.7 percent) are first-generation millionaires; they tended to be older and richer than the other study participants. The rest (64 percent) inherited at least some of their money.[2] Approximately forty are second-generation heirs, thirty are third-generation givers, and twenty are at least four generations removed from the original fortune.

If the Great Depression marks a dividing line between the creation of "old money" and "new money" in the United States, a vast majority (eighty-two, or 91 percent) of the inheritors in this study come from families with old money. Just over half of them (forty-four), trace their family fortune back to the early 1900s. They are in the second and third generations, but in all age ranges. In addition, thirty-eight have had wealth in their families since before 1900. Of those heirs, most are over forty years old and in the third or fourth generation. The inheritors with new money are a small group, less than forty years old, typically the children of contemporary or recently deceased self-made millionaires.

The rich have complicated financial situations. Most of them, and especially those with inherited wealth, have diversified investments in various businesses and trust funds. Precise information on the amount of money held by our study participants was not available, and asking direct questions proved fruitless. Questions about income were included in the original interview guide, but during the pretest period it became apparent that such questions jeopardized rapport with potential informants. We were told that talking about money among this group is taboo.

Manufacturing was the original source of wealth for a quarter of our subjects, followed by mining and drilling, the computer and high-technology industries, real estate, and then transportation or communication. The remaining fortunes were made in agriculture, banking and finance, construction, insurance, entertainment and the arts, and in a few cases the professions. To the best of our knowledge, no one whom we interviewed had made his or her wealth primarily from criminal activities.

If the interview was conducted in a person's home, we were able to judge the size of the house and to note whether servants were present. Sometimes we saw the grounds, and noted the model of a car or cars or the existence of tennis courts. Usually, however, our interviews were conducted in offices, over lunch at restaurants, or in elite downtown clubs.

Our interviews generally lasted an hour or so, although I vividly remember exceptions. One multimillionaire said he could give me only twenty minutes of his time, and he kept strictly to his word. He glanced at his watch when I entered his office. His answers were brief but to the point. We were interrupted by a telephone call from his wife; he timed their conversation, apparently added it to his calculations, and as he was hanging up told me how long I had left. I came out of the interview mentally catching my breath but considered it a success. He had been brusque but friendly and had not hesitated to provide specific information.

Others, in contrast, spent several hours, and in a few cases a full day, talking with me or other interviewers. Some had a smile on their face and a sparkle in their eye. Others appeared affectless, with deadpan demeanors. A few were obsessed with every possible boring detail; several were incredibly shy and halting in their manner of speech. I found the majority with whom I spoke extremely engaging.

As a final note, several methodological issues do merit brief comment. This is not meant to be either a quantitative treatise or a field manual on interview technique. In this research, and in the fields of anthropology and nonprofit studies in general, causation cannot be absolutely established. I did undertake, however, mainly as a guide for my work, a content analysis for which I counted how many times certain things were mentioned. Nevertheless, this study is not a statistically representative one, and I have limited my use of figures or cited them in footnotes. I point out when quotations are illustrative or exceptional.

Owing to a general lack of good information (statistical or otherwise) concerning how much money goes to what organizations, by whom it is donated, and in what manner it is used, there is no way to "prove" in an inferential sense that the charitable wealthy tangibly benefit more than others from elite philanthropy. But the evidence from the interviews and other accounts clearly points in that direction.

As we were to learn, one of the traits philanthropists value most is individuality. In small ways, the millionaires interviewed are probably as different from each other as they are similar to the nonphilanthropic rich or the population at large. My task, however, has been to search for generalities and patterns, to make coherent a range of attitudes and expressed behavior.

NOTES

Preface

1. Later, I would travel to Newburyport, Massachusetts, the site of the famous Yankee City studies, where I saw many houses similar to Mory's. Significantly, these were not the mansions of the upper-upper class. See W. Lloyd Warner and Paul S. Lunt, *The Social Life of a Modern Community* and *The Status System of a Modern Community*, vol. 1 and vol. 2, Yankee City Series (New Haven: Yale University Press, 1941, 1942), for a description of architecture and social class.

2. Upper-class parents base their selection of the prep school their children will attend on the family's former association with the institution and its success in "placing" graduates. Phillips Academy, for example, advertises how many alumni have gone to prestigious universities (19,000), as well as how many students were admitted to Yale (25), Brown (23), Harvard (19), Dartmouth (17), the University of Pennsylvania (16), and Georgetown (12) in any given year (1987). *The Handbook of Private Schools: An Annual Descriptive Survey of Independent Education*, 69th ed. (Boston: Porter Sargent, 1988), 63.

3. In fact, as a friend of mine is fond of saying, it is a great place to see paintings of animals and ugly people. The main reason to go is to look at the building, which was designed by Louis Kahn.

4. John William Sterling made his fortune as an attorney to the Robber Barons. His benefaction to Yale doubled the university's assets. American Council of Learned Societies, *Dictionary of American Biography*, vol. 9 (New York: Scribner's, 1936), 588–89.

5. What Nelson W. Aldrich, Jr., has aptly labeled the "class curriculum," in *Old Money: The Mythology of America's Upper Class* (New York: Knopf, 1988), 97, the "schools, colleges, clubs, museums, welfare 'charities,' and the like."

6. The P-Rade is a public parade of the graduating and reuniting classes, organized by the university. Each class wears distinctive costumes, some quite flamboyant, for this central performance of the reunion.

7. "Yale's 1988 Fiscal Year," *Yale Alumni Magazine*, October 1988, 76–77. In all probability a few people made extremely large gifts, skewing the average. In addition, "the classes of 1938 and 1963 contributed more than $4 million and $5 million, respectively."

8. See Robert Hamlett Bremner, *American Philanthropy* (Chicago: University of Chicago Press, 1960; revised, 1988), for a pioneering historical overview.

9. I was convinced of the importance of what Laura Nader called "studying up" when I read her article "Up the Anthropologist—Perspectives Gained from Studying Up," in *Reinventing Anthropology*, ed. Dell H. Hymes (New York: Pantheon, 1972), 284–311. After many years of conducting research about women, I was even more certain of the need to understand those with power and wealth. All too

often social scientists have investigated those without influence, the victims of any given situation, rather than the decision makers.

10. See the methodological appendix for details of the research on which this book is based.

11. See Teresa Jean Odendahl et al., *Working in Foundations: Career Patterns of Women and Men* (New York: Foundation Center, 1985).

12. In retrospect, it makes sense that such an endeavor would be launched at an elite institution. There are now at least nineteen such centers at public and private colleges around the country. See Anne Lowrey Bailey, "More Scholars, Colleges Taking an Interest in the Study of Philanthropy and Non-Profit Organizations," *Chronicle of Higher Education,* 21 September 1988, A34.

13. Teresa Odendahl, ed., *America's Wealthy and the Future of Foundations* (New York: Foundation Center, 1987).

Chapter 1: Culture, Generosity, and Power

1. Lester M. Salamon, James C. Musselwhite, Jr., and Carol J. De Vita, "Partners in Public Service: Government and the Nonprofit Sector in the Welfare State," *Working Papers* (Washington, D.C.: Independent Sector and the United Way Institute, 1986), 3–38. This major project examined the scope and structure of the private, nonprofit "sector" in the United States, finding that less than one-third of charitable agencies focus on a poor clientele.

2. See the methodological appendix.

3. See Nelson W. Aldrich, Jr., *Old Money: The Mythology of America's Upper Class* (New York: Knopf, 1988).

4. See Paul DiMaggio, "Nonprofit Organizations in the Production and Distribution of Culture," in *The Nonprofit Sector: A Research Handbook,* ed. Walter W. Powell (New Haven: Yale University Press, 1987), 195–220; as well as Paul DiMaggio and Michael Useem, "The Arts in Class Reproduction," in *Cultural and Economic Reproduction in Education: Essays on Class, Ideology, and the State,* ed. Michael W. Apple (London: Routledge & Kegan Paul, 1982), 181–201.

5. See Pierre Bourdieu, *Distinction: A Social Critique of the Judgement of Taste,* trans. Richard Nice (Cambridge, Mass.: Harvard University Press, 1984).

6. When C. Wright Mills, *The Power Elite* (New York: Oxford University Press, 1956), initially described the power elite, he focused on the common backgrounds and interests of leaders in finance, industry, the military, and politics. Here I extend Mills's analysis to the leaders of philanthropy. Other scholars have suggested this line of inquiry. See in particular G. William Domhoff, *The Higher Circles: The Governing Class in America* (New York: Vintage, 1970); and *Who Rules America Now? A View for the 80's* (Englewood Cliffs, N.J.: Prentice-Hall, 1983); as well as Susan A. Ostrander, *Women of the Upper Class* (Philadelphia: Temple University Press, 1984).

7. The group I describe here is not subordinate as are the subcultures analyzed by Dick Hebdige, *Subculture: The Meaning of Style* (London: Methuen, 1979). The subculture of philanthropy is rather a privileged group, one that owns and consumes "high culture." See also Herbert J. Gans, *Popular Culture and High Culture: An Analysis and Evaluation of Taste* (New York: Basic Books, 1974).

    A search of recent articles and books that deal with subculture consistently produced references to subordinate groups only. For clarity, the subculture of philanthropy might be considered a "supraculture." I wish, however, to avoid the invention of unnecessary jargon and generally use the term *culture* rather than *subculture* when referring to the people I have studied.

8. See Arlene Kaplan Daniels, *Invisible Careers: Women Civic Leaders from the Volunteer World* (Chicago: University of Chicago Press, 1988); and Ostrander, *Women of the Upper Class,* especially her chapter on the community volunteer, 111–39.

9. Robert Coles has examined many of these psychological phenomena among wealthy children in *The Privileged Ones: The Well-Off and the Rich in America* (Boston: Little, Brown, 1977).

10. See John Sedgwick, *Rich Kids* (New York: William Morrow, 1985), although this was not the first use of the term and his work refers to a group larger than the social change funders.

Notes

11. The lifestyle of William Randolph Hearst (1863–1951) is a vivid example of the "other" rich. The castle he built at San Simeon, his public egoism, and his flaunted wealth are contrary to the culture of philanthropy. See Roy Everett Littlefield III, *William Randolph Hearst: His Role in American Progressivism* (Lanham, Md.: University Press of America, 1980), for a sympathetic portrayal; and W. A. Swanberg's less positive biography, *Citizen Hearst* (New York: Scribner's, 1961).

12. See Kathleen Teltsch, "Increase in Charitable Donations in '87 Was Lowest in 12 Years," *New York Times,* 26 June 1988, 18.

13. These attributions and figures were compiled from Nathan Weber, ed., *Giving USA: The Annual Report on Philanthropy for the Year 1987* (New York: AAFRC, 1988), 29–33. A few inaccuracies in the publication were corrected following conversations with recipients and with Nathan Weber. Some additional personal information came from Benjamin Lord, ed., *America's Wealthiest People: Their Philanthropic and Nonprofit Affiliations* (Washington, D.C.: Taft Corporation, 1984).

    Over seventy-five grants of $1 million each were contributed by individuals to nonprofit organizations and public universities in 1987. The vast majority of these million-dollar donations went to education, but arts and culture were also well-represented. Four gifts went to the New York Public Library, three specified for its Performing Arts Research Center. The Fine Arts Museum of San Francisco and the Fort Lauderdale New Museum of Art were each recipients of $1 million grants. There were no public or social benefit organizations on this list of donations.

    From 1983 to 1986 even larger single private donations had been made to universities: $125 million to Louisiana State University from C. B. Pennington; $55 million to the University of Miami from James L. Knight; $50 million to Stanford University from William Hewlett; an anonymous gift of $50 million to the Cornell University Medical College; $36 million to the University of California from Marion O. Hoffman; $31 million to Northeast Louisiana University from Ella S. Johnson; $21 million to Stanford University from the Systems Development Corporation; and $20 million to the Cornell University Graduate School of Management from Samuel C. Johnson of Johnson Wax. (AAFRC *Giving USA* [New York: AAFRC], 1984, 65; 1985, 63; and 1986, 24.)

    In the health area during that same three-year period (1983–86), David and Lucile Packard contributed $20 million to the Children's Hospital at Stanford University; Arthur O. and Gullan M. Wellman, $15 million to the Massachusetts General Hospital; Natalie Guggenheim Short, $13 million to the Mount Sinai Medical Center; Milton Petrie, $10 million to the Beth Israel Medical Center; and Harold Simmons, $7.5 million over ten years to the University of Texas Health Science Center. (AAFRC, *Giving USA,* 1984, 77; 1985, 76, 100; and 1986, 24.)

    Under the category of social welfare there were no individual contributions of over a million dollars, although the Provident Mutual Life Insurance Company gave $40 million to the Urban Education Foundation of Philadelphia and the Ford Foundation awarded the bulk of all the other large grants listed. (AAFRC, *Giving USA,* 1984, 86; 1985, 86.)

14. Joan Kroc has given away $35 million since 1985, including $10 million to build a hospice in San Diego and $3 million to a shelter for the homeless. Although she is said to have personally made the funding decisions, the grants have actually come from her private foundation and thus do not technically count as individual contributions. "People, Philanthropists, Look Where Joan Kroc Is Throwing Her McNuggets," *Business Week,* 5 September 1988, 74–75.

15. Foundation Center, *Foundation Directory,* 11th ed. (New York: Foundation Center, 1987), xxii. Two record gifts were made to existing private foundations: nearly $400 million to the Knight Foundation of Ohio and $277 million from the Margaret Loock Trust to the Lynde and Harry Bradley Foundation in Wisconsin. In addition Kenneth H. Olsen gave over $117 million to his Stratford Foundation in Boston, more than doubling its former endowment. In 1986, the three trustees of the Stratford Foundation, including Olsen himself, distributed nearly $5 million. The foundation has no staff. It will continue to fund "institutions closely associated with the donor, with emphasis on colleges and universities, hospitals, and religious organizations" (p. 301).

16. Mark A. Stein, "Attorneys Get $10 Million in Charity Fight," *Los Angeles Times,* 7 September 1986, 3; and "Lawyers Get $6.3 Million in Buck Trust Fund Case," *New York Times,* 7 September 1986, 26.

17. Foundation Center, *Foundation Directory,* 11th ed., xv, 54.

18. There are, of course, exceptions to this dichotomy. Some high-status professionals straddle these roles.

For example, J. Richardson Dilworth has been a senior financial adviser to the Rockefeller family for twenty-five years. He became chairman of the Metropolitan Museum of Art in New York City in early 1984, following "his powerful predecessor," C. Douglas Dillon. According to the museum's director, Philippe de Montebello, "Dilworth comes in without Dillon's capacity for personal power plays based on wealth." From Michael Brenson, "New Met Chairman Defines Objectives: Dilworth in Control," *New York Times,* 31 January 1984, C13. Dilworth was also on the board of the Yale University Corporation. He is able to move freely in higher philanthropic circles. In 1986 he was replaced by Arthur Ochs Sulzberger as chairman of the Metropolitan Museum of Art.

19. See James C. Baughman, *Trustees, Trusteeship, and the Public Good: Issues of Accountability for Hospitals, Museums, Universities, and Libraries* (New York: Quorum, 1987).

20. This interpretation is quite similar to Frances Fox Piven and Richard A. Cloward's classic analysis of the public welfare system in the United States, *Regulating the Poor: The Functions of Public Welfare* (New York: Pantheon, 1971). Since their book was written, and especially during the Reagan administration, private charity has become an increasing but insufficient source of funding for basic human services.

21. George Thomas Kurian, *The New Book of World Rankings* (New York: Facts on File, 1984), 102. Czechoslovakia was first; Sweden, tenth; Indonesia, twentieth; and Panama, thirtieth.

22. "The State of the Union, Text: 'What Unites . . . Outweighs What Divides Us,' " *Los Angeles Times,* 26 January 1988, 17.

23. See Weber, *Giving USA,* as well as Virginia Ann Hodgkinson and Murray S. Weitzman, *Dimensions of the Independent Sector: A Statistical Profile* (Washington, D.C.: Independent Sector, 1986). In 1987 the increase in charitable donations was the lowest it had been in twelve years, owing partly to a change in the rules concerning the donation of appreciated property, and partly to the elimination of the charitable deductions during the Reagan administration for the majority of taxpayers who do not itemize deductions.

24. "Transcript of Bush Speech Accepting Presidential Nomination," *New York Times,* 19 August 1988, A14.

25. U.S. Bureau of the Census, *Statistical Abstract of the United States: 1988,* 108th ed. (Washington, D.C.: U.S. Department of Commerce, 1987), 422.

26. In particular see Richard Parker, *The Myth of the Middle Class: Notes on Affluence and Equality* (New York: Harper Colophon, 1972), for a statistical summary of inequality.

27. In 1987, homelessness around the country increased sharply, especially among low-wage workers and families with children, according to a study released on 15 December by the U.S. Conference of Mayors ("Study Sees Strain on Homeless Aid: Shelters and Food Programs Fail to Meet Needs of the Poor, U.S. Mayors Say," *New York Times,* 17 December 1987, B21). Another report, by the Neighborhood Reinvestment Corporation, predicted that "more than 18 million Americans will be homeless or on the edge of homelessness within 16 years because of an increasing number of poor people and a decreasing number of affordable housing units." See Mary Jordan, "18 Million Homeless Seen by 2003: Study Blames Erosion of Low-Income Housing, Increase in Poor," *Washington Post,* 3 June 1987, A8.

28. Awareness of "the other America" was raised by Michael Harrington, *The Other America: Poverty in the United States* (New York: Penguin, 1962; with a new afterword, 1984), the popular press, and President Lyndon Johnson's War on Poverty. But many authors since have blamed the poor for their plight and been critical of the social programs developed to address poverty. See, for example, Charles Murray, *Losing Ground—American Social Policy, 1950–1980* (New York: Basic Books, 1984).

In 1986, more than 32.4 million people in the United States lived below the official poverty level, and another 11 million were desperately poor but made slightly too much money to meet the strict government poverty criteria. In 1975, just over 12 percent of Americans were living below the poverty level. In the 1960s and throughout the 1970s official statistics indicate that poverty was declining, but by 1980 it had risen again to 13 percent. Nearly 14 percent of Americans were poor in 1986. (U.S. Bureau of the Census, *Statistical Abstract of the United States,* 433.)

Although there is renewed interest in wealth-holding, the bulk of research on the rich, their money, and the distribution of wealth was undertaken in the 1960s. The best notable exceptions are Coles, *The Privileged Ones;* Domhoff, *Who Rules America Now?* (although this is an update of his work *Who Rules America?* [Englewood Cliffs, N.J.: Prentice-Hall, 1967] and *Higher Circles*);

Notes

Frank Levy, *Dollars and Dreams: The Changing American Income Distribution* (New York: Russell Sage Foundation, 1987); and Ostrander, *Women of the Upper Class.* See also Michael Patrick Allen, *The Founding Fortunes: A New Anatomy of the Super-Rich Families in America* (New York: Dutton, 1987); Waldemar A. Nielsen, *The Golden Donors: A New Anatomy of the Great Foundations* (New York: Dutton, 1985); and Vance Packard, *The Ultra Rich: How Much Is Too Much?* (Boston: Little, Brown, 1989).

29. This term was coined by Ferdinand Lundberg, *The Rich and the Super-Rich: A Study in the Power of Money Today* (New York: Lyle Stuart, 1968).

30. Federal Reserve Board data, from a press release of the Congress of the United States, Joint Economic Committee, 21 August 1986, with summary statistics and revised figures on top wealth-holders.

31. Ibid.

32. From various sources I have been able to determine that the number of millionaires in this country appears to be growing, but this is at least partially an artifact of inflation. According to *Forbes* magazine, there were 180,000 millionaires in 1976 and between 350,000 and 500,000 in 1981 (10 October 1983, 8). In the winter of 1984–85, Marvin Schwartz, a Treasury researcher, released "Preliminary Estimates of Personal Wealth, 1982: Composition of Assets," *Statistics of Income (SOI) Bulletin* (Department of the Treasury, Internal Revenue Service) 4, no. 3 (1984–85): 1–17. Schwartz writes: "Despite the fact there was only a slight change in the concentration of wealth, a large increase in the number of millionaires has occurred. Nearly 410,000 top wealthholders had net worth of $1 million or more in 1982." A much higher figure is cited by Levy, *Dollars and Dreams,* 20, who notes that "there are about 900,000 households . . . with assets over $1 million." His source is the U.S. Bureau of the Census, "Household Wealth and Asset Ownership: 1984," *Household Economic Studies,* series P-70, no. 7 (Washington, D.C.: U.S. Government Printing Office, 1986). These last figures are probably high because they include the value of homes that have appreciated tremendously.

33. Federal Reserve Board data. Over the course of this century, the super-rich have always controlled at least a quarter of the nation's wealth. See Domhoff, *Who Rules America Now?* and Lundberg, *The Rich and the Super-Rich,* for overviews of studies on wealth distribution, as well as the detailed research of Gabriel Kolko, *Wealth and Power in America: An Analysis of Social Class and Income Distribution* (New York: Praeger, 1962); Robert J. Lampman, *The Share of Top Wealth-Holders in National Wealth, 1922–56* (Princeton: Princeton University Press, 1962); Dorothy S. Projector and Gertrude S. Weiss, *Survey of Financial Characteristics of Consumers* (Washington, D.C.: Board of Governors of the Federal Reserve System, 1966); James D. Smith and Stephen D. Franklin, "The Concentration of Personal Wealth, 1922–1969," *American Economic Review* 64, no. 2 (May 1974): 162–67; and James D. Smith, "An Estimate of Income of the Very Rich," in *Papers in Quantitative Economics,* ed. James P. Quirk (Lawrence, Kan.: University of Kansas Press, 1968).

    Much of what we do know about asset-holding has been derived through the "estate multiplier method," a statistical technique wherein federal estate tax returns from the recently deceased are used to estimate wealth among the living population. See James D. Smith, "The Concentration of Personal Wealth in America, 1969," in *The Review of Income and Wealth,* series 20, no. 2 (June 1974): 148–80, for a technical explanation.

34. See Barry Bluestone and Bennett Harrison, "The Growth of Low-Wage Employment: 1963–1986," paper presented at the annual meeting of the American Economics Association, 28–30 December 1987; and Bennett Harrison and Barry Bluestone, "Labour Market Analysis and Employment Planning," working paper no. 17 (International Labour Office: Geneva, October 1987), and *The Great U-Turn: Corporate Restructuring and the Polarizing of America* (New York: Basic Books, 1988).

35. Hodgkinson and Weitzman, *Dimensions of the Independent Sector,* 16.

36. See John G. Simon, "The Tax Treatment of Nonprofit Organizations: A Review of Federal and State Policies," in *The Nonprofit Sector: A Research Handbook,* ed. Walter W. Powell (New Haven: Yale University Press, 1987), 67–98.

37. See Lester M. Salamon, "Partners in Public Service: The Scope and Theory of Government-Nonprofit Relations," in ibid., 99–117. The quotation is on page 101; the full reference for the internal citation is Lester M. Salamon and Alan J. Abramson, *The Federal Budget and the Nonprofit Sector* (Washington, D.C.: The Urban Institute Press, 1982). The data on indirect government support through tax deductions are on page 102.

38. If the revenues lost to the federal and state treasuries because of tax-deductible charitable contributions are included, this figure would be much higher.
39. Hodgkinson and Weitzman, *Dimensions of the Independent Sector,* 4.
40. Salamon, Musselwhite, and De Vita, "Partners in Public Service," 25, table 7.
41. Alan J. Abramson and Lester M. Salamon, *The Nonprofit Sector and the New Federal Budget* (Washington, D.C.: The Urban Institute Press, 1986), xvi.
42. Ibid., xvii.
43. Laura M. Heuchan, "A Survey of Nonprofit Charitable Organizations," in *Working Papers* (Washington, D.C.: Independent Sector and United Way Institute, 1986), 319–44.
44. There are no empirical data on support to different types of nonprofit organizations broken down by the income or wealth of the givers. If funding to religious organizations is discounted, it appears through extrapolation that the most financial support from the elite goes to private higher education, followed by health, then the arts and culture. Human or welfare services accounted for only 10.5 percent of all private contributions. See Weber, *Giving USA,* 1988; and Hodgkinson and Weitzman, *Dimensions of the Independent Sector.*

    Altogether, the 140 wealthy study participants referred to their interest in a specific institution or category of giving the following number of times: education, including private and public institutions, 185 times; the arts and culture, including museums and performing groups of all types, 160; human services, 140; foundations, both community and private, 105; health and religion, 50 each. These are not "significant" findings in the sense in which statisticians use the term. They point, rather, to trends. The figures are rounded off. Study participants rarely told us how much they gave to different endeavors; this information had to be gleaned from published records.
45. See Baughman, *Trustees, Trusteeship, and the Public Good.*
46. Weber, *Giving USA,* 1988.
47. Leonard Silk and Mark Silk, *The American Establishment* (New York: Basic Books, 1980), 9. See also 19, 122.
48. See Susan A. Ostrander and Stuart Langton, eds., *Shifting the Debate: Public/Private Sector Relations in the Modern Welfare State* (New Brunswick, N.J.: Transaction, 1987); and Jon Van Til, *Mapping the Third Sector: Voluntarism in a Changing Economy* (New York: Foundation Center, 1988).
49. Hodgkinson and Weitzman, *Dimensions of the Independent Sector,* inside jacket. The Independent Sector is the leading lobby on behalf of nonprofits.
50. Brian O'Connell, *Effective Leadership in Voluntary Organizations* (New York: Walker, 1981), xv.
51. Ibid., xxi.
52. See AAFRC, *Giving USA,* 1987, 58.
53. Daniels, *Invisible Careers,* makes these distinctions.

Chapter 2: Giving and Volunteering

1. Although the rich offer varying, highly personal motives for giving, I evaluate their most typical reasons and look for hidden meanings. Like all of us, the wealthy are highly adept at denial, rationalization, self-justification, and subtle evasion, but they also have important insights that helped me to draw some of my conclusions. My analysis here focuses on the common themes and the role that institutions, especially those supported by philanthropists, play in the lives of the charitable wealthy.
2. Two-thirds of the study participants had inherited their wealth. See the methodological appendix.
3. The idea of higher circles, rather than a more rigid upper-class structure, was popularized by G. William Domhoff, *The Higher Circles: The Governing Class in America* (New York: Vintage, 1970). My use of this terminology combines the notion of a class system as conceptualized by Karl Marx in *Capital: A Critique of Political Economy,* vol. 3. (New York: International Publishers, 1967), chap. 52, with the idea of intersecting social circles proposed by Georg Simmel, *Conflict and the Web of Group-Affiliations,* trans. Kurt H. Wolff and Reinhard Bendix (New York: Free Press, 1955). However,

Notes

according to my interpretation, for this subgroup, culture is as important as class. Robert Coles put it well in *The Privileged Ones: The Well-Off and the Rich in America* (Boston: Little, Brown, 1977), 362: "The issue is 'class'; but the issue is not only 'class.'"

4. For a compelling and subtle interpretation of this fact, see Nelson W. Aldrich, Jr., *Old Money: The Mythology of America's Upper Class* (New York: Knopf, 1988).

5. See Eric Gelman, with Nikki Finke Greenberg in Forth Worth, Daniel Shapiro in Houston, Penelope Wang in New York, Peter McAlevey in Los Angeles, and Christopher Ma in Washington, "The Bass Dynasty," *Newsweek,* 19 November 1984, 72–78.

6. *Forbes,* "The Richest People in America," 24 October 1988, 158, 172, 184.

7. Gelman et al., "The Bass Dynasty," 72.

8. Michael Patrick Allen, *The Founding Fortunes: A New Anatomy of the Super-Rich Families in America* (New York: Dutton, 1987), 313.

9. Foundation Library Center, *Foundation Directory,* 1st ed. (New York: Russell Sage Foundation, 1960), 631, lists 31 December 1958 assets of $6,551 and grants of $82,500.

10. Foundation Library Center, *Foundation Directory,* 2nd ed. (New York: Russell Sage Foundation, 1964), 793.

11. Foundation Center, *Foundation Directory,* 11th ed. (New York: Foundation Center, 1987), xv, 735. A smaller foundation, the Sid Richardson Memorial Fund, was created in 1965 as a scholarship fund for the direct descendants and spouses of company employees.

12. Kathleen Stauder, "Profile: How the Bass Brothers Do Their Deals," *Fortune,* 17 September 1984, 146.

13. Ibid.

14. Ibid.

15. Ibid., 148.

16. Benjamin Lord, ed., *America's Wealthiest People: Philanthropic and Nonprofit Affiliations* (Washington, D.C.: Taft, 1984), 3. Several calls to Dallas yielded no information on Boy's Inc. A receptionist at the Boys Clubs of America had heard of the organization but did not know what they did. See also Foundation Center, *Foundation Directory,* 11th ed., 1987, for information on the Tandy Foundation.

17. Julia Reed, "The Bass Brothers Fish in New Waters," *U.S. News and World Report,* 9 February 1987, 48–49.

18. "The Richest People in America," *Forbes,* 172; and "Disney Stock in Bass Divorce," *New York Times,* 9 November 1988, D19.

19. See John Taylor, "Party Place: The High Life at the Gilded Metropolitan Museum," *New York,* 9 January 1989, 20.

20. Gelman et al., "The Bass Dynasty," 78. Together, Lee and Ramona Bass sit on the National Advisory Board of the Whitney Museum of American Art.

21. *Forbes,* "The Richest People in America," 172.

22. Ibid., 184.

23. Ibid., 158.

24. Barbara Gamarekian, "Wealth and Influence: Does Texas Billionaire Aim to Be Power Broker?" *New York Times,* 15 September 1988, A8. According to Tom Furlong, "Popejoy to Become a Bass Partner, Quit American S&L Post," *Los Angeles Times,* 16 December 1988, CC1, 3, the sale was not yet final. "Bass is the publicity-shy investor from Texas who plans to buy insolvent American Savings before year-end."

25. Ibid.

26. Reilly was President Bush's first appointee to head the Environmental Protection Agency. "Washington Talk," *New York Times,* 6 January 1989, B5.

27. Gamarekian, "Wealth and Influence," A8.

28. *Forbes,* "The Richest People in America," 172.

29. Reed, "The Bass Brothers Fish in New Waters," 49.

30. Gelman et al., "The Bass Dynasty," 78.

31. Stauder, "Profile," 148.

32. Ibid.

33. Service on art museum boards and acquisition committees may also help big art collectors increase the value of their collections.
34. "Trump: Symbol of a Gaudy, Impatient Time," *New York Times,* 31 January 1988, H32. See also Art Buchwald, "A Chump for Trump," *Washington Post,* 29 September 1988, B1; and "The Richest People in America," *Forbes,* 26 October 1988, 174.
35. Coles, *The Privileged Ones,* 22.
36. Ibid., 15.
37. Again, a comparison with William Randolph Hearst is instructive. Recall that in the classic movie based on Hearst's life, Orson Welles's *Citizen Kane,* opulence with no objective but self-gratification became a theme for anomie, betrayal, and despair.
38. For an appraisal of income and wealth inequality in this country, refer to Michael Harrington, *The Other America: Poverty in the United States* (New York: Penguin, 1962; with a new afterword, 1984); and Richard Parker, *The Myth of the Middle Class: Notes on Affluence and Equality* (New York: Harper Colophon, 1972).
39. George G. Kirstein, *The Rich: Are They Different?* (Boston: Houghton Mifflin, 1968), 11, also pointed out that many of the wealthy do not consider themselves rich, perhaps because there are always others who have "more."
40. Gelman et al., "The Bass Dynasty," 72.
41. Allen, *The Founding Fortunes,* 27: "Other corporate rich families that have demonstrated a similar obsession with secrecy include the Lillys, Pews, Kelbergs, and Basses. As a result, some of the wealthiest families in America have achieved almost complete anonymity, despite the fact that they exercise enormous power as a result of their control over many major corporations and philanthropic foundations."
42. Nathan Weber, ed., *Giving USA: The Annual Report on Philanthropy for the Year 1987* (New York: AAFRC, 1988), compiled from pp. 29–33.
43. Until quite recently expensive art work was contributed frequently by the wealthy as well. However, according to "Museums Gifts Drop, Tax Reform Blamed," in *Donor Briefing* (Evanston, Ill.: Business Publishers, Inc.) 4, no. 6, (15 March 1989): 1, "Museum administrators across the country are reporting drops as high as 50 percent in . . . art gifts valued at $25,000 or more, believed to be due to restrictions provided in the Tax Reform Act of 1984. . . . High-income donors may only deduct the purchase price of gifts to charitable institutions and not the appreciated value."
44. Under current federal tax law endowed private foundations are levied a 2 percent excise tax on income derived from investments and must meet an annual minimum payout requirement of 5 percent of the market value of their assets. In addition, they are subject to rules governing the administration of investments, operating expenditures, public reporting, and grant-making activities. Pass-through foundations are not taxed, and donors receive the same deductions they would for direct contributions.
45. There are nearly 25,000 private foundations in the United States. Only about one-fifth, however, have over a million dollars in assets. We know more about these large grant-making organizations, which together hold approximately $90 billion in assets and distribute $3 billion a year to other nonprofits. The remaining 20,000 foundations are usually "charitable checkbooks" for donors and their families.
46. Council on Foundations, *1985 Community Foundations Survey* (Washington, D.C.: Council on Foundations, 1985).
47. The administration of investments at community foundations is handled by financial officers or trustee banks. Donors may be required to follow a broad program or geographical guidelines established by the foundation's board of directors. By law, community foundations must have representative boards of directors, but their governing bodies tend to be composed of local elites and professionals. Contributions to and through community foundations do not lead to as much name recognition or status for the wealthy as do direct giving and private foundation donations.
48. Charitable lead, remainder, and other split-interest trusts allow the wealthy to give and preserve assets that may later be passed on to heirs.
49. George Cooper's decade-old article "A Voluntary Tax? New Perspectives on Sophisticated Estate Tax Avoidance," *Columbia Law Review* 77, no. 2 (March 1977): 161–247, demonstrates how it is possible for the wealthy, with the assistance of knowledgeable attorneys and estate-planning professionals, to

pay minimal amounts of estate tax. This situation remains much the same today; the 1982 Marital Deduction Act allows entire estates to go to spouses tax-free.

50. "$17-Million Trust to Aid UC Irvine and Arts Groups," *Los Angeles Times,* 1 December 1988, I41.

51. Beneficiaries of the endowment of a support organization must be specified, but amounts given may vary from year to year. Because it is possible to change the list of nonprofit agencies receiving funds, a support organization may operate in a manner similar to that of a foundation. Unlike foundations, "excess business holdings"—that is, controlling interests in a closely held business—may constitute the endowment of a support organization.

52. C. Wright Mills, *The Power Elite* (New York: Oxford University Press, 1956), also referred to this, as did Coles, *The Privileged Ones,* 370, who explained that when wealthy children spoke openly about money it alarmed their parents.

53. During the course of this research, I observed cars of almost every make parked outside rich people's homes. I rode with wealthy men and women in automobiles as different as a chauffeured limousine, a Mercedes sedan, a Datsun sports car, a four-wheel-drive Jeep, and a dilapidated, junk-filled domestic station wagon. An elderly woman travelled in a limousine, a middle-aged man in the Datsun Z-car (he was allowed his midlife crisis but was still being modest by not driving a Porsche); the Jeep was functional for the mountainous region where the owner lived; and the station wagon belonged to a rich kid.

54. In 1988 all models of both Cadillac and Volvo cost at least $15,000; Volvos can actually be slightly more expensive, up to $40,000. The top price of a Cadillac was $35,000.

55. Kathleen Teltsch, "The Cousins: The Fourth Generation of Rockefellers," *New York Times Magazine,* 30 December 1984, 12.

56. Sometimes mansions are called "cottages," another denial of wealth.

57. Coles, *The Privileged Ones,* evaluates the way in which privileged children are taught that they are different from "others." He starts with the richness of their material world: "Everything, it seems, contributes to a child's sense of place, privacy, property, stability. And beyond too there are others, waiting in readiness to serve, to work, to make things as easy as possible" (p. 16).

58. See Leonard Burr, "Dropouts Make Good," *Forbes,* 26 October 1987, 77.

59. See E. Digby Baltzell, *Philadelphia Gentlemen: The Making of a National Upper Class* (New York: Free Press, 1958); Peter W. Cookson, Jr., and Caroline Hodges Persell, *Preparing for Power: America's Elite Boarding Schools* (New York: Basic Books, 1985); G. William Domhoff, *Who Rules America Now? A View for the 80's* (Englewood Cliffs, N.J.: Prentice-Hall, 1983), 24–28; and Michael Useem, *The Inner Circle: Large Corporations and the Rise of Business Political Activity in the U.S. and U.K.* (New York: Oxford University Press, 1984), 67–68.

60. Tuition at these institutions is notoriously high, although scholarships and loans are offered on the basis of need and merit. In 1986–87, total charges at all the Ivy League schools (excepting Cornell), plus Stanford and MIT, were within $250 of $16,000. A 1986 internal Princeton study, for example, indicated that "Princeton students come disproportionately from higher-income families."

61. Mills, *The Power Elite,* 67, was the first social scientist to analyze systematically the importance of elite higher education. He also considered eating clubs, fraternities, and sororities, as well as secret societies: "In the upper social classes, it does not by itself mean much merely to have a degree from an Ivy League college. That is assumed: the point is not Harvard, but which Harvard? By Harvard, one means Porcellian, Fly, or A.D.: by Yale, one means Zeta Psi or Fence or Delta Kappa Epsilon: by Princeton, Cottage, Tiger, Cap and Gown, or Ivy."

62. According to Elizabeth T. Boris, "Creation and Growth: A Survey of Private Foundations," in *America's Wealthy and the Future of Foundations,* ed. Teresa Odendahl (New York: Foundation Center, 1987), 76: "An intriguing finding is that women established a greater proportion of the foundations founded after 1970 than before. The proportion of foundations created by women rose from 20 percent to 48 percent, though more of those formed after 1970 had less than $5 million in assets."

63. See also Arlene Kaplan Daniels, *Invisible Careers: Women Civic Leaders from the Volunteer World* (Chicago: University of Chicago Press, 1988); and Susan A. Ostrander, *Women of the Upper Class* (Philadelphia: Temple University Press, 1984).

64. See Sharon Churcher, "Making It By Doing Good: Nouvelle Society Ladies Win Peer Approval Working for 'the Arts and Diseases,'" *New York Times Magazine,* 3 July 1988, 16, 33–34. Some of

these newly rich women will bring their families into the culture of philanthropy; others will not. For example, this article features a photograph of "Blain Trump, accompanied by publicist Lewis Ufland . . . at a fund-raising gala in April for the American Ballet Theatre at the Metropolitan Opera House." Because she and her husband do not follow the proper, subdued lifestyle, it is unlikely that they will be accepted. Churcher confirms, "There are still a few quiet rich, some of them self-made. To mark the 70th birthday last year of the collector and pharmaceuticals tycoon Mortimer D. Sackler, his wife staged one of the most opulent banquets that the Metropolitan Museum has ever seen. The couple, who had just endowed a gallery at the Met, did not tell the press."

65. Ibid., 34.

66. Melissa Middleton, "Nonprofit Boards of Directors: Beyond the Governance Function," in *The Nonprofit Sector: A Research Handbook,* ed. Walter W. Powell (New Haven: Yale University Press, 1987), 146.

67. For studies of corporate interlocks see Beth Mintz and Michael Schwartz, *The Power Structure of American Business* (Chicago: University of Chicago Press, 1985); as well as Mark S. Mizruchi and Michael Schwartz, eds., *Intercorporate Relations: The Structural Analysis of Business* (New York: Cambridge University Press, 1987); Michael Schwartz, ed., *The Structure of Power in America: The Corporate Elite as a Ruling Class* (New York: Holmes & Meier, 1987); and Useem, *The Inner Circle.* Similar statistical studies of nonprofit board membership interlocks would be extremely revealing.

68. Sociologists Paul DiMaggio and Michael Useem, "The Arts in Class Reproduction," in *Cultural and Economic Reproduction in Education: Essays on Class, Ideology, and the State,* ed. Michael W. Apple (London: Routledge & Kegan Paul, 1982), 191–95, make a distinction between elite and corporate boards of high arts organizations: "Elite boards, as class-based status groups, are most concerned with the screening function of high culture, and thus exclusivity, while corporate boards are most concerned with the legitimating functions of the arts and arts patronage." They cite two examples of high arts organizations, the Philadelphia Orchestra and the Seattle Opera, where "brash new money" or "labor constituencies" wanted a voice on the board, or where directors objected to the manager's attempts to "counteract opera's 'snobbish' public image." In both instances the trustee decisions were ultimately economically irrational, in that more funds might have been generated for the organizations' operations if exclusive policies had changed. DiMaggio and Useem also argue, however, that the recent rise in corporate and public subsidies of the high arts, as well as the growth of professional arts management, will lead to less upper-class domination.

69. Excerpted from a speech by Pablo Eisenberg to the annual meeting of trustees of the Northern California Grantmakers on 8 March 1988. "Probably nothing is so frustrating and infuriating to donees as the double standard, by which many nontraditional organizations are judged much more rigorously according to higher standards than some of their more traditional or establishment counterparts."

70. See Jeremy Boissevain, *Friends of Friends: Networks, Manipulators, and Coalitions* (New York, St. Martin's, 1974), for an excellent example of this type of network analysis. If elites have what Boissevain calls "centrality and multiplex relations," they are in a strategic position to hold and exercise power.

If it were feasible, it would be fascinating as well as revealing to do similar research among wealthy philanthropists. The problems of obtaining permission for "participant observation," as well as asking informants to divulge information about friends and peers, would be problematic but not insurmountable.

71. Brian O'Reilly, "The Computer Kings: A Quartet of High-Tech Pioneers," *Fortune,* 12 October 1987, 149.

72. The concept of exchange systems is prevalent in social science (and particularly anthropological) literature extending back to Bronislaw Malinowski's classic 1922 study, *Argonauts of the Western Pacific: An Account of Native Enterprise and Adventure in the Archipelagoes of Melanesian New Guinea* (New York: Dutton, 1961), which described the *kula* ring of northwestern Melanesia. The *kula* was a complex system of trade, ceremonial exchange, entertainment, and magic. The economic aspect of these transactions was hidden and not readily admitted to by participants.

Exchange analysis is equally applicable to large modern societies. A general framework of this type was established by sociologist Peter Michael Blau, *Exchange and Power in Social Life* (New York: Wiley, 1964); as well as George Casper Homans, "Human Behavior as Exchange," *American Journal of Sociology* 63, no. 3 (May 1958): 597–606; and *Social Behaviour: Its Elementary Forms* (New York:

Notes

Harcourt, Brace & World, 1961; revised, 1974). Exchange is a useful way of broadly describing and understanding the social relations of philanthropy.

73. Another part of the answer may be found in tax law. All public charities (except educational institutions) must meet a "public support test" by demonstrating that the "general public" provides it with financial resources or is "supportive" of its activities. Endowment income and large gifts from only a few donors can jeopardize this status. The public support test encourages the types of exchange and reciprocity to which I refer.

   According to Tracy Daniel Connors, ed., *The Nonprofit Organization Handbook* (New York: McGraw-Hill, 1980), 1–47, "Organizations exempt under Section 509(a)(1), 509(a)(2), or 509(a)(3) are public charities. . . . 'Public charity' requirements are not the same for each type of organization. . . . Each Section 501(a)(3) organization that is applying for exemption as a 'public charity' or that is presently exempt must know the operational needs of each category. As an illustration, Sections 509(a)(1) and (a)(2) both require that public support be more than 33⅓ percent of the total support. However, Section 509(a)(1) also permits an organization to qualify if its public support is as low as 10 percent of the total support. In such case, the 501(c)(3) organization should also include one or more of the following:/ 1. Be organized and operated to attract new and additional public or governmental support/ 2. Have a representative governing body/ 3. Make its facilities or services available to the general public."

74. The woman quoted was exceptionally candid. The rich may not consciously expect a return on their charitable investments, but they are pleased enough when it occurs, and this reinforces their behavior.

75. Gift giving is the most elemental and culturally widespread aspect of exchange. It reinforces and symbolizes the existence of mutual interdependence between individuals and groups, in both an economic and social manner. Unequal exchanges may lead to hierarchical power relations. The giver is in a good position to ask for or demand something back in the future. Relatively equal exchanges demonstrate comparability in economic and social standing. Although charitable gifts may go directly to nonprofit organizations, the giving establishes status positions and indirectly obligates others with wealth. Philanthropy exemplifies a complex institutionalization of gift giving, and sometimes commerce, for both economic and social purposes. See Marcel Mauss, *The Gift: Forms and Functions of Exchange in Archaic Societies* (New York: Norton, 1967).

76. The youngest and oldest philanthropists often made the most revealing statements. The young may not have known any better, and the elderly may not have cared.

77. DiMaggio and Useem, "The Arts in Class Reproduction." This type of analysis is not new but is not usually applied to technologically complex societies such as the United States. Apparently we can believe it of others but not of ourselves. For an exotic example, see anthropologist Frank Cancian's *Economics and Prestige in a Maya Community: The Religious Cargo System in Zinacantan* (Stanford: Stanford University Press, 1965), which evaluates the functions of a contemporary religious "cargo system" practiced in the township of Zinacantan in southern Mexico. Indian leaders host religious ceremonial festivals that require large expenditures of personal resources as well as the extensive help of friends, relatives, and paid experts. "The cargo system is crucial to the continued existence of Zinacantan as an Indian community, a community separate and distinct from its Latino environment. Among the functions of the cargo system are: definition of the limits of community membership, reinforcement of commitment to common values, reduction of potential conflict, and support of traditional kinship patterns" (p. 133). In this case, however, the people of Zinacantan have relatively little power outside their own group.

78. Philip Baloun plans these types of events for the wealthy. He has noted, however: "I'm not a peer of my clients. . . . I'm not in the league where I can afford to go to one of my $1,000-a-plate dinners." "(In Style) The Life of the Party," *New York,* 9 January 1989, 14.

Chapter 3: The Political Economy of Philanthropy

1. Recent scholarship has called the concept of three sectors, as well as the independence of such, into question. See, for example, Susan A. Ostrander and Stuart Langton, eds., *Shifting the Debate: Public/*

Private Sector Relations in the Modern Welfare State (New Brunswick, N.J.: Transaction, 1987); and Lester M. Salamon, "The Voluntary Sector and the Future of the Welfare State," *Nonprofit and Voluntary Sector Quarterly* 18, no. 1, (Spring 1989): 11–24.

2. See Virginia Ann Hodgkinson and Murray S. Weitzman, *Dimensions of the Independent Sector: A Statistical Profile* (Washington, D.C.: Independent Sector, 1986); and Lester M. Salamon, "Partners in Public Service: The Scope and Theory of Government-Nonprofit Relations," in *The Nonprofit Sector: A Research Handbook*, ed. Walter W. Powell (New Haven: Yale University Press, 1987), 99–117.

3. The U.S. Constitution is predicated on the notion of limited and competing powers. In a related manner, the wealthy may view their giving as a check on government, where the masses can wield some power.

4. Robert B. Reich, *Tales of a New America* (New York: Times Books, 1987), 222. "Political culture in America—as it always has been and will be, as it is anywhere else—is permeated by myth. Mythology is an indispensable conceptual shorthand, the means by which we comprehend, come to terms with, and talk about complicated social realities" (p. 235).

5. See Frances Fox Piven and Richard A. Cloward, *The New Class War: Reagan's Attack on the Welfare State and Its Consequences* (New York: Pantheon, 1982), 74.

6. Ibid., 84.

7. Ibid., 80.

8. See Peter Dobkin Hall, "The Invention of the Nonprofit Sector" (unpublished manuscript), as well as his "Business Giving and Social Investment in the United States," in *Philanthropic Giving: Studies in Venture and Variety,* ed. Richard Magat (New York: Oxford University Press, 1989) for a historical explanation and analysis of the influence of Andrew Carnegie on present-day philanthropic ideology. Robert B. Reich, *Tales of a New America,* 21–22, also touches on this idea in his discussion of the recent rise of conservatism. He proposes that the latest "parable presents an intricate blend of dissenting Protestant theology and social Darwinism."

9. See Paul F. Boller, Jr., *American Thought in Transition: The Impact of Evolutionary Naturalism, 1865–1900* (Chicago: Rand McNally, 1973), especially pp. 49–60, for an explanation of the roots of social Darwinism.

10. Reich, *Tales of a New America*, 235.

11. A survey conducted by the Gallup Organization lends support to my findings. Over 88 percent of those with more than $100,000 in annual income agreed that "charities play a significant role in our society." Of this group, 32.5 percent strongly agreed with the statement (the highest rate of all income groups). *Giving and Volunteering in the United States: Findings of a National Survey,* analyzed by Virginia A. Hodgkinson and Murray S. Weitzman (Washington, D.C.: Independent Sector, 1988), 61.

12. Reich, *Tales of a New America,* 101, explores similar themes in his call for new American cultural myths. He suggests that "it is becoming less clear who 'we' are anyway. 'American' corporations build factories abroad from which they ship goods to destinations around the globe. Foreign corporations establish operations here, employing American workers. 'American' banks readily lend abroad. . . . Who is 'us'? Who is 'them'?"

13. An extreme case of nationalistic or ethnocentric thinking was exhibited by a wealthy American woman who made a blatantly anti-monarchist statement. "What is really funny was that party for the Queen of England when she was here. I could not believe the Prince of Wales. Here he had all these millions, and it is almost like play money. . . . But, if they could translate that into something. There are so many needs to fill." It is ironic that this woman, who has millions herself, and quite possibly was invited to such a party, is explicitly criticizing British tradition without commenting on the conspicuous consumption of Americans. Perhaps some wealthy people feel that having a record of personal charitable giving excuses such behavior, even if in others. Or perhaps certain of the elite in the United States envy the status of aristocracy, which they can never attain.

14. Hodgkinson and Weitzman, *Giving and Volunteering*, 6.

15. Nathan Weber, ed., *Giving USA: The Annual Report on Philanthropy for the Year 1987* (New York: AAFRC, 1988), 26–27. These figures do not include the contributions of non-itemizers, who received no charitable deduction. Under the 1986 Tax Reform Act, one must have at least $5,000 in deductions in order to itemize.

A survey conducted by the Gallup Organization indicates that poor people contributed to charity a higher percentage of their lower household income than the wealthy. The organizations to which these contributions were made were not categorized by the income of donors, although we know that over half of all giving goes to religion (see Hodgkinson and Weitzman, *Giving and Volunteering*, 6). As generous or numerous as the poor may be, however, their total contributions do not match those of the rich.

16. Weber, *Giving USA*, 1988, 8, 61. Corporate giving had been increasing for two decades, but the state of the economy and "frenetic reconfiguration of U.S. industry" contributed to the leveling off of charitable donations by business.

17. Ibid., 39–41. In 1987, 70 percent of the bequests over $1 million went to education.

18. Ibid., 43.

19. Ibid., 8.

20. I took out $500 million to account for corporate giving programs that the wealthy do not control, such as employee matching programs.

21. I subtracted $1 billion in bequests that may have come from people of more modest means.

22. See Michael Patrick Allen, *The Founding Fortunes: A New Anatomy of the Super-Rich Families in America* (New York: Dutton, 1987); Beth Mintz and Michael Schwartz, *The Power Structure of American Business* (Chicago: The University of Chicago Press, 1985); and Michael Schwartz, ed., *The Structure of Power in America: The Corporate Elite as a Ruling Class* (New York: Holmes & Meier, 1987).

23. According to Arthur H. White and John Bartolomeo, *Corporate Giving: The Views of Chief Executive Officers of Major American Corporations* (Washington, D.C.: Council on Foundations, 1982), 45, the CEO "is the key to the character and extent of a corporation's philanthropic efforts."

24. See Joseph Galaskiewicz, *Social Organization of an Urban Grants Economy: A Study of Business Philanthropy and Nonprofit Organizations* (Orlando, Fla.: Academic Press, 1985); as well as Hall, "Business Giving and Social Investment," for a historical treatment of corporate philanthropy.

25. Weber, *Giving USA*, 1988, 43–44. These figures should be interpreted with care. The survey reports on only about a third of the funding in the foundation field. The grant-making patterns of nearly 21,000 family foundations are not included.

   Foundations made 138 grants over one million dollars each in 1987. More than half of them went to education. The largest single award, $50 million, was made by the Lillian B. Disney Foundation to the Los Angeles Music Center. Social service and welfare grants tended to be much smaller. The largest, $5.2 million, went from the Buck Trust to the Buck Center on Aging. The Ford Foundation awarded the Center for Community Change $2.85 million. The McKnight Foundation gave Planned Parenthood of Minnesota $2.5 million (pp. 52–57).

   Foundations have funded social movements, but they tend to do so only after some of the changes being fought for have already taken hold. See J. Craig Jenkins, "Foundation Funding of Progressive Social Movements," in *The Grantseekers Guide*, 2nd ed., ed. Jill Shellow (Mt. Kisco, N.Y.: Moyer Bell, 1985), and his "Social Movement Philanthropy and American Democracy," February 1988 (typescript).

26. See Teresa Odendahl, "Foundations and the Nonprofit Sector," in *America's Wealthy and the Future of Foundations* (New York: Foundation Center, 1987), 36–39.

27. Weber, *Giving USA*, 1988, 43.

28. J. Peter Williamson, "Inflation and the Foundation Payout Rate," *Foundation News* (March/April 1981), 18–24, and his "What's Reasonable? Investment Expectations and the Foundation Payout Rate," *Foundation News* (January/February, 1976): 13–18, has shown that over a thirty-year period the average annual income from foundation investments was only 3.5 percent. Thus many foundations must delve into capital to fulfill the payout requirement. See also Lester M. Salamon and Kenneth P. Voytek, *Managing Foundation Assets: An Analysis of Foundation Investment and Payout Procedure and Performance* (New York: Foundation Center, 1989).

29. Since 1984 noncash donations of "company products, land and equipment have accounted for about one-fifth of all corporate giving. . . . 'Among the 25 largest corporate donors, noncash contributions represented over 30 percent of their total giving.' " (Weber, *Giving USA*, 1988, 63.)

30. By training students to use their products they also create a ready-made market.

31. Most of the large oil companies, for example, are heavy funders of college and university programs

and research in the earth sciences, engineering, and geology. In this way they help educate their future workforce and encourage the development of new technology.

32. White and Bartolomeo, *Corporate Giving,* 7. ''In the eyes of CEO's, philanthropy is, at best, a small supplement to government-sponsored social programs and, at worst, has the potential for being regarded as a stand-in for those programs.

   ''Thus, the vast majority state that their giving efforts are motivated by a mixture of self-help and helping others. . . . Seven in ten are seeking to help the needy in the communities in which their company has plants/locations. . . . Two out of three emphasize the goals of improving local communities in order to benefit their own employees. . . . Two-thirds hope to improve the ''public opinion climate'' in which they do business. . . . About a third hope to improve the company's corporate image through their giving programs. . . . About a quarter expect their efforts to enhance their ability to recruit quality employees.

   ''Moreover, self-interested goals are especially important to CEO's of *Fortune* 1300 companies, which account for the lion's share of cash contributions'' (pp. 12–13).

   In 1987, at least twenty-seven gifts of over a million dollars each were made by corporations to nonprofit organizations. The two largest contributions were $40 million from RJR Nabisco, Inc., for an office building at Wake Forest University, and $35 million from the Prudential Insurance Company to the Prudential Foundation. There were only two large human service grants directly from businesses. The K Mart Corporation gave $12 million worth of clothing to Food for the Hungry, Inc., and MTV donated $3 million of free air time to Rock Against Drugs. Nineteen of the grants went to private and public universities (Weber, *Giving USA,* 1988, 67–68).

33. In a 1985 survey with 280 companies responding, 184 reported ''corporate assistance expenditures'' that were not taken as charitable deductions amounting to a total of $230 million. But many corporations are still not tracking such expenditures fully. It will be several years before accurate estimates can be provided of the full worth of such expenditures.'' (AAFRC, *Giving USA: Estimates of Philanthropic Giving in 1986 and the Trends They Show* [New York: AAFRC, 1987], 55–56.)

34. See E. B. Knauft, ''The Management of Corporate Giving Programs,'' working paper no. 114 (Yale University Program on Non-Profit Organizations, 1986); and ''Profiles of Effective Corporate Giving Programs'' (Washington D.C.: Independent Sector, 1985), as well as White and Bartolomeo, *Corporate Giving.*

35. The only real difference is in the markets reached by the public networks and the commercial ones. When the Mobil and Exxon oil companies advertise on public TV they are trying to reach elite opinionmakers. See Paul DiMaggio and Michael Useem, ''The Arts in Class Reproduction,'' in Michael W. Apple, ed., *Cultural and Economic Reproduction in Education: Essays on Class, Ideology, and the State* (London: Routledge & Kegan Paul, 1982), for a discussion of the legitimizing role of high arts funding.

36. See, for example, John Maynard Keynes, *The General Theory of Employment, Interest, and Money* (London: Macmillan, 1936).

37. Certain nonprofit organizations are limited by law in the amount of political advocacy they can undertake. Some get around the regulations by calling what might otherwise be considered lobbying ''educational activities.'' A donor receives a charitable deduction only if the agency maintains its tax deductible status.

38. Paul Houston, ''Big Cash Gifts to Parties Skirt Election Laws,'' *Los Angeles Times,* 3 October 1988, sec. I, p. 1.

39. See Robert K. Landers, ''Think Tanks: The New Partisans?'' Editorial Research Reports, *Congressional Quarterly* 1, no. 23 (20 June 1986); as well as Leonard Silk and Mark Silk, *The American Establishment* (New York: Basic Books, 1980), 153–225; James A. Smith, *The Policy Elite* (New York: Free Press, forthcoming); and Roger M. Williams, ''Capital Clout,'' *Foundation News* (July/August 1989): 14–19.

40. Charles L. Heatherly, *Mandate for Leadership: Policy Management in a Conservative Administration* (Washington, D.C.: The Heritage Foundation, 1980).

41. Smith, *The Policy Elite.*

42. Not many significant think tanks are clearly left-wing. The Institute for Policy Studies in Washington, D.C., is the most successful but has never had direct links with any administration. The World Policy Institute in New York (concerned with alternative national security policy) has been around under the

Notes

name Institute for World Order for many years, and the Christic Institute (which works on alternative foreign policy in the hemisphere) is a recent arrival.

43. See in particular Michael B. Katz, *In the Shadow of the Poorhouse: A Social History of Welfare in America* (New York: Basic Books, 1986), especially p. 274–91. Additional references include: Alan J. Abramson and Lester M. Salamon, *The Nonprofit Sector and the New Federal Budget* (Washington, D.C.: The Urban Institute Press, 1986); J. Larry Brown and H. F. Pizer, *Living Hungry in America* (New York: Macmillan, 1987); and Victor W. Sidel and Ruth Sidel, *A Healthy State: An International Perspective on the Crisis in United States Medical Care* (New York: Pantheon, 1983).

44. Salamon, "Partners in Public Service."

45. Ibid., 102. Salamon estimated that in 1980 total federal spending in the social services was $7.7 billion. Of that, $4 billion went to nonprofit organizations, constituting 52 percent of federal support in that area (see his table 6.1). "In other words, nonprofits deliver a larger share of publicly funded services in these fields than do government agencies."

46. Abramson and Salamon, *The Nonprofit Sector,* 20–21.

47. Katz, *In the Shadow of the Poorhouse,* 280.

48. Ibid., 285–86.

49. For example, in 1987, Fannie Mae (formerly called the Federal National Mortgage Association, a publicly owned corporation traded on the New York Stock Exchange) contributed $28 million to New York state and New York City to build 1,000 low-income housing units. (Weber, *Giving USA,* 1988, 67.)

50. For example, the National Gallery of Art in Washington, D.C., was a special project of Andrew Mellon, then secretary of the treasury. He, his heirs, and other wealthy people contributed millions of dollars and works of art to the National Gallery, and under an arrangement negotiated by Mellon, the federal government pays its operating costs. Similarly, the Metropolitan Museum of Art in New York is supported both by the city and by philanthropy.

51. See Neil Gilbert, *Capitalism and the Welfare State: Dilemmas of Social Benevolence* (New Haven: Yale University Press, 1983), especially part 3 on "voluntary alternatives," pages 89–187; as well as Neil Gilbert and Harry Specht, *Dimensions of Social Welfare Policy,* 2nd ed. (Englewood Cliffs, N.J.: Prentice-Hall, 1986).

52. Hodgkinson and Weitzman, *Giving and Volunteering,* 57.

53. See Abramson and Salamon, *The Nonprofit Sector;* Hodgkinson and Weitzman, *Dimensions of the Independent Sector,* 111; as well as Salamon, Musselwhite, Jr., and De Vita, "Partners in Public Service," for more details on the welfare cuts. It is important to note that, in contrast, there were only minor cuts on the so-called "defense-side" of the national budget.

54. Abramson and Salamon, *The Nonprofit Sector,* 23–24.

55. In contrast, income assistance increased by $12.3 billion, a 10 percent improvement; and health care went up $41.8 billion, or 20 percent (see ibid., 34). However, most of the growth in income assistance was in the area of housing aid. Health spending increased almost solely because of the Medicare and Medicaid programs. Smaller health services, in alcohol and drug abuse or mental health, were significantly decreased. Ibid., 35–38.

56. Because both taxes and private money pay for portions of some social service programs, it is exceedingly difficult to measure accurately the total U.S. welfare bill.

57. Hodgkinson and Weitzman, *Dimensions of the Independent Sector,* 7. The State also funds half of the budgets of civic, social, and fraternal organizations.

58. Abramson and Salamon, *The Nonprofit Sector,* 84.

59. Harold L. Wilensky, in his foreword to Ralph M. Kramer, *Voluntary Agencies in the Welfare State* (Berkeley: University of California Press, 1981), xiv–xxii, anticipated this outcome. "*Voluntarism* [is] *an ideology* justifying reliance on free markets. It is hostile to state intervention generally and to social policy in particular. It emphasizes the role of philanthropy and self-help in the solution of social problems. . . . The likely effect: to slow down welfare-state development" (p. xv).

60. AAFRC, *Giving USA,* 1987, 19–23. In 1985 the average contribution for itemizers in all income groups was $1,326, about $100 higher than the year before. Non-itemizer donations soared to a $373 average as a result of increased understanding of the Charitable Contribution Law, which allowed non-itemizers to deduct, above the line, 50 percent of their gifts to charity. The number of itemized returns

in the $30,000 to $50,000 bracket had been declining, which probably accounts for increases in their average charitable donation.

61. See Ferdinand Lundberg, *The Rich and the Super-Rich: A Study of the Power of Money Today* (New York: Lyle Stuart, 1968).

62. Gerald Auten and Gabriel Rudney, "The Variability of the Charitable Giving of the Wealthy," working paper no. 126 (Yale University Program on Non-Profit Organizations, 1987), 9.

63. Ibid., 31: "The most generous 5 percent of givers account for 43 percent of total high income giving . . . and the most generous 10 percent account for 58 percent of total giving. . . . For the $1 million and over income class, over 18 percent contributed more than 20 percent of income, accounting for nearly 60 percent of the giving in that group."

64. Ibid., 32.

65. Interviews were conducted as the new tax law was being formulated. Where relevant, bracketed dates indicate in what year a speaker made a particular remark.

66. According to Auten and Rudney, "The Variability of Charitable Giving," 12: "For taxpayers with over $1 million AGI [adjusted gross income], 59 percent of contributions were in the form of non-cash gifts. There are two probable reasons for this phenomenon: First, high-income donors are more likely to have a larger stock of wealth out of which to make property gifts. In general, previous studies have shown that the ratio of wealth to income rises with income. Second, the income tax provisions provide greater incentive to give appreciated property than to give cash. This incentive is more important for the high-income donors because of the larger gifts involved and the greater likelihood that they will have substantial appreciation in their wealthholding."

67. See Estelle James, "The Nonprofit Sector in Comparative Perspective," in *The Nonprofit Sector: A Research Handbook,* ed. Walter W. Powell (New Haven: Yale University Press, 1987), 397–415.

68. Ibid., 399.

69. Ralph M. Kramer, *Voluntary Agencies in the Welfare State* (Berkeley: University of California Press, 1981), 4.

70. "Gross spending by Dutch NPOs [nonprofit organizations] was approximately 15 percent of GNP [gross national product], 35 percent of combined spending by government plus NPOs. In contrast, in Sweden outlays by NPOs were barely 1.6 percent of GNP, only 3 percent of the combined government plus NPO total. Consistent with the aggregate figures, the private sector's share of total educational expenditures varies from 6 percent in Sweden to 61 percent in Holland. In both countries, however, education is the key activity of NPOs, constituting about 35 percent of total nonprofit production." (James, "The Nonprofit Sector in Comparative Perspective," 399.)

71. Kramer, *Voluntary Agencies in the Welfare State,* 4.

72. George Thomas Kurian, *The New Book of World Rankings* (New York: Facts on File, 1984), 97–98, 117–18, 331.

73. Kramer, *Voluntary Agencies in the Welfare State,* 4.

74. Ibid., 118.

75. Kurian, *The New Book of World Rankings.* See also Organization for Economic Co-operation and Development, *Social Expenditure, 1960–1990: Problems of Growth and Control* (Paris: OECD, 1985), 21. According to the data on the same countries in 1981, the Netherlands ranks highest at 36.1 percent of social expenditure as a share of Gross Domestic Product, followed by Sweden, 33.4 percent; West Germany, 31.5 percent; France, 29.5 percent; the United Kingdom, 23.7 percent; Canada, 21.5 percent; and the United States, 20.8 percent.

76. Although, as the label implies, most uncompensated workers in nonprofit organizations do so voluntarily, we might think about whether or not this is actually exploitation.

77. See Martin Knapp and Spyros Missiakoulis, "Inter-Sectoral Cost Comparisons: Day Care for the Elderly," *Journal of Social Policy* 11, part 3 (July 1982): 335–54. "Our results provide clear evidence to refute the oft-made assumption that voluntary services are universally cheaper than their statutory counterparts. . . . We find that voluntary-statutory cost differences are dependent upon the scale of operation. Small voluntary units certainly do enjoy a cost advantage, but larger voluntary units are unlikely to be cheaper, and are probably more expensive, than local authority units of similar scale." See also Ken Judge and Martin Knapp, "Efficiency in the Production of Welfare: The Public and

Private Sectors Compared," in *The Future of Welfare*, ed. Rudolf Klein and Michael O'Higgins (Oxford: Basil Blackwell, 1985), 131–49.

78. Kramer, *Voluntary Agencies in the Welfare State*.

Chapter 4: Dynasty and Philanthropy

1. Nelson W. Aldrich, Jr., *Old Money: The Mythology of America's Upper Class* (New York: Knopf, 1988), 30, makes the point that it is difficult to ascertain when old money begins and new money ends. "Time, the social antiquing required for New Money to become Old, is . . . elastic." He claims that even for J. P. Morgan, "time began with his children."

    The definition of *old money* is more esoteric than exoteric, but the distinction between old and new money is important because it helps determine who is inside and who is outside the culture of philanthropy. Old money is nearly synonymous with the culture, but in order to remain viable it must incorporate new money. Philanthropy does so by turning new money into old money.

2. See figure 4.1, 73.
3. See Michael Patrick Allen, *The Founding Fortunes: A New Anatomy of the Super-Rich Families in America* (New York: Dutton, 1987), especially p. 51; and David E. Koskoff, *The Mellons: The Chronicle of America's Richest Family* (New York: Crowell, 1978).
4. Allen, *The Founding Fortunes*, 360.
5. *Forbes*, "The Richest People in America," 26 October 1987, 148.
6. See Koskoff, *The Mellons*, 291.
7. Allen, *The Founding Fortunes*, 54.
8. *Forbes*, "The Richest People in America," 290.
9. Allen, *The Founding Fortunes*, 54.
10. Ibid., 55.
11. Koskoff, *The Mellons*, 358–59.
12. Allen, *The Founding Fortunes*, 55–56.
13. Koskoff, *The Mellons*, 361.
14. Foundation Center, *Foundation Directory*, 11th ed. (New York: Foundation Center, 1987), 673. Also see figure 4.2, "Selected Mellon Family Philanthropies," 78.
15. Koskoff, *The Mellons*, 362.
16. Allen, *The Founding Fortunes*, 56.
17. Koskoff, *The Mellons*, 362.
18. Foundation Center, *Foundation Directory*, 11th ed., 673.
19. *Forbes*, "The Richest People in America," 164–66.
20. Koskoff, *The Mellons*, 500. In contrast, "Nelson Rockefeller's mother had contributed $1.43 million to Rockefeller's 1968 presidential efforts, and had had to pay a bill for the gift tax of another $854,000."
21. *Forbes*, "The Richest People in America," 290.
22. Foundation Center, *Foundation Directory*, 11th ed., 664.
23. *Forbes*, "The Richest People in America," 290.
24. Benjamin Lord, ed., *America's Wealthiest People: Their Philanthropic and Nonprofit Affiliations* (Washington, D.C.: Taft Corporation, 1984), 40–41.
25. Lord, *America's Wealthiest People*, 40.
26. Koskoff, *The Mellons*, 363.
27. Ibid., 186–88, 363.
28. Allen, *The Founding Fortunes*, 56.
29. *Forbes*, "The Richest People in America," 148.
30. Lord, *America's Wealthiest People*, 40.
31. Allen, *The Founding Fortunes*, 56.
32. Foundation Center, *Foundation Directory*, 11th ed., 496–97.

33. Lord, *America's Wealthiest People*, 11.
34. *Forbes*, "The Richest People in America," 238.
35. Ibid.
36. Lord, *America's Wealthiest People*, 40.
37. Anthropologist George E. Marcus, who has been studying dynastic families in Texas, has identified and labeled the more "intimate" advisers "insider-outsiders." See "Law in the Development of Dynastic Families Among America's Business Elite: The Domestication of Capital and the Capitalization of Family," *Law and Society Review* 14, no. 4 (Summer 1980): 859–903; and "The Fiduciary Role in American Family Dynasties and Their Institutional Legacy: From the Law of Trusts to Trust in Establishment," in *Elites: Ethnographic Issues*, ed. George E. Marcus (Albuquerque: University of New Mexico Press, 1983), 221–56. He found that most families of wealth retain a primary adviser or group of advisers that "takes on generalized fiduciary functions that are similar to, but not framed by, the legal regulation of a trust instrument" (p. 222).
38. Foundation Center, *Foundation Directory*, 11th ed., xv.
39. Although mine was not a local-level study, the evidence points to Mellon family hegemony over Pittsburgh.
40. For an alternative view see John G. Simon, "Charity and Dynasty Under the Federal Tax System," *The Probate Lawyer* 5 (Summer 1978): 1–91.
41. See Teresa Odendahl and Elizabeth Boris, "Board-Staff Relations: A Delicate Balance," *Foundation News* 24, no. 3 (May/June 1983): 22–31.
42. Aldrich, *Old Money*, 31, whose pedigree allows him to lay claim to being from old money, writes: "Time or wealth, 'oldness' or richness of family—the question frequently comes up in Old Money circles as to which of these elements in people's perception of the class is the more important. To me, the answer has always been time: certainly now that time has left so little wealth in my own social portrait. Of course, there has to have been wealth. Without some intelligible, socially persuasive, and above all inheritable asset, there would be nothing for the imagination to work on, nothing to grow old. But once wealth has been there, for perception, it needn't go on being there."
43. Ibid., 97.
44. This character is based on fourteen interviews with second-generation middle-aged men. Five of them are Jewish. Four live in New York, three in the Midwest, two in California, two in Boston, and the remaining three in Connecticut, Texas, and Washington, D.C.
45. In the second generation one heir, possibly with the help of brothers or cousins, typically runs the family company. It is he who, if the founder did not do so, may decide to let the business "go public," diversify, and/or be turned over to professional managers. The family leader's vision for the future is particularly important at this stage, when often a family office and charitable vehicles are created. If the family is philanthropic, second-generation descendants like David Stein, who are not directing or working in the business, are probably active in the culture of philanthropy.
46. This composite is based on seven middle-aged women from around the country who are in the third generation of family wealth. Three of them come from the South, two live on the Northeastern seaboard, one is from Ohio, and the other hails from Texas. Six are currently married and all have children.
47. See John W. Nason, *Trustees and the Future of Foundations* (New York: Council on Foundations), 1977; and Teresa Jean Odendahl, Elizabeth Trocolli Boris, and Arlene Kaplan Daniels, *Working in Foundations: Career Patterns of Women and Men* (New York: Foundation Center, 1985).
48. This composite is based on seven interviews with men over sixty years old. Two are from Texas, two from California, and three from the Eastern seaboard.
49. Luke 6:38.
50. Marcus, "The Fiduciary Role in American Family Dynasties," 223.
51. This composite is based on six women from across the United States. All are younger than forty, have inherited wealth, and are at least four generations removed from the original fortune.

Chapter 5: Lady Bountiful

1. See Heidi I. Hartmann, "The Unhappy Marriage of Marxism and Feminism," *Capital and Class: Towards a More Progressive Union* 8 (Summer 1979): 1–33. In addition, Joan R. Acker has argued in

Notes

"Women and Stratification: A Review of Recent Literature," *Contemporary Sociology* 9, no. 1 (January 1980): 26, "that class, which we take to be sex neutral, is actually a concept built on understanding of the socioeconomic world as lived by men."

2. See Arlene Kaplan Daniels, *Invisible Careers: Women Civic Leaders from the Volunteer World* (Chicago: University of Chicago Press, 1988); and Susan A. Ostrander, *Women of the Upper Class* (Philadelphia: Temple University Press, 1984).

3. To be a woman is to be "other" than a man. This distinction is so pervasive that the division of labor according to gender is a fundamental organizing principle in all societies. In her brilliant examination of the status of women, Simone de Beauvoir, *The Second Sex* (New York: Vintage, 1974), developed this concept. See also Margaret Mead, *Male and Female: A Study of the Sexes in a Changing World* (New York: William Morrow, 1949); Michelle Rosaldo and Louise Lamphere, eds., *Woman, Culture, and Society* (Stanford: Stanford University Press, 1974); and Peggy Reeves Sanday, *Female Power and Male Dominance: On the Origins of Sexual Inequality* (Cambridge: Cambridge University Press, 1981). Childbirth and rearing are generally acknowledged as an original, primordial explanation for widespread gender differentiation, but they do not account for the tenacity of the cultural assignments over time.

4. The interview guide dealt specifically with charitable attitudes, motives, and giving behavior. Many of the women we interviewed chose to tell us about their family life and volunteer activities as well though we did not solicit such information. The fact that we have so much data despite our oversight confirms the importance that women of wealth place on the intersection between prescribed gender roles and philanthropy.

5. De Beauvoir, *The Second Sex*, 697; G. William Domhoff, *The Higher Circles: The Governing Class in America* (New York: Vintage, 1970), 33–56; Ostrander *Women of the Upper Class*, and her "Upper-Class Women: Class Consciousness as Conduct and Meaning," in *Power Structure Research* ed. G. William Domhoff (Beverly Hills: Sage, 1980), 73–96; and Dorothy Smith, "Women, the Family, and Corporate Capitalism," *Berkeley Journal of Sociology* 20 (1975–76), 55–90, have made these arguments before.

6. Of the elite nonprofit leaders interviewed for this research, 40 percent (56) are women; more than 71 percent (40) are inheritors; the rest (16) are in the first generation, and most of them married men with money. We interviewed more first-generation men than women. Only one woman in the interview sample had become a millionaire solely through her own work. Approximately half (20) of the second-generation philanthropists are women. In the third generation of wealth, 40 percent (12 of 30) are female, with another 40 percent (8 of 20) in the fourth generation and beyond.

The vast majority of philanthropists have been married and have children. Only 5 women (out of 56) indicated that they had never been married; 5 were widows; and 2 were separated or divorced at the time of the study. Twelve men (out of 84) had never married; 3 were separated or divorced; and 1 was a widower. Ten women and 13 men reported that they had no children.

Unlike the male philanthropists in this study, who tended to be over forty years old, the females cannot be characterized by their age. They are just as likely to be young as middle aged or elderly. Nearly twice as many women (19) as men (10) under forty years of age were interviewed. This is especially relevant since more men than women participated in the study. Just over a third of the women are younger than forty; a few more are between forty and sixty (21, or 37.5 percent of the women); and a few less (16, or 28.6 percent) are older than sixty. Only about 12 percent of the males are younger than forty; 41.6 percent (35) are between forty and sixty; and 46.4 percent (39 of the men) are over sixty.

7. See Marvin Schwartz, "Preliminary Estimates of Personal Wealth, 1982: Composition and Assets," *Statistics of Income (SOI) Bulletin* (Department of the Treasury, Internal Revenue Service) 4, no. 3 (1984–85): 2. Using the "estate multiplier technique" Schwartz estimated that "female wealthholders were approximately 39.3 percent, or 1.7 million of the 4.4 million top wealthholders in 1982." The average net worth of women with gross assets of $300,000 or more was $605,900, as compared to $519,600 for men.

8. See H. M. Hacker, "Class and Race Differences in Gender Roles," in *Gender and Sex in Society*, ed. Lucille Duberman (New York: Praeger, 1975), 139; and Ostrander, *Women of the Upper Class*.

9. Research in feminist psychology and sex roles has been developing rapidly, especially in the last fifteen years. On the whole this work attempts to demonstrate how and why a social construction of female

gender is internalized and passed from generation to generation. As in any significant area of scholarship, there is controversy. See Nancy Chodorow, "Family Structure and Feminine Personality," in Rosaldo and Lamphere, eds., *Woman, Culture, and Society,* 43–66, and *The Reproduction of Mothering: Psychoanalysis and the Sociology of Gender* (Berkeley: University of California Press, 1978); Dorothy Dinnerstein, *The Mermaid and the Minotaur: Sexual Arrangements and Human Malaise* (New York: Harper & Row, 1976); Carol Gilligan, *In a Different Voice: Psychological Theory and Women's Development* (Cambridge: Harvard University Press, 1982); Jean Baker Miller, *Toward a New Psychology of Women* (Boston: Beacon Press, 1976); and Juliet Mitchell, *Woman's Estate* (New York: Vintage, 1973), as well as her *Psychoanalysis and Feminism* (New York: Pantheon, 1974). None of these books, however, systematically evaluates the effects of class on gender role formation.

10. According to Sherry B. Ortner and Harriet Whitehead, eds., in *Sexual Meanings: The Cultural Construction of Gender and Sexuality* (Cambridge: Cambridge University Press, 1981), cross-culturally women are "defined almost entirely in relational terms," especially those relative to men. In contrast, there is a "general cultural tendency to define men in terms of status and role categories [such as *businessman*] that have little to do with men's relations to women" (p. 8).

11. See Ann R. Tickamyer, "Wealth and Power: A Comparison of Men and Women in the Property Elite," *Social Forces* 60, no. 2 (December 1981): 463–81.

12. According to psychiatrist Miller, *New Psychology of Women,* 49, women in therapy "often spend a great deal more time talking about giving than men do." Miller is presumably referring to women of all classes, and to the giving of oneself emotionally and physically rather than to the giving of money. Her argument, however, has a bearing on philanthropy.

13. This composite is based on interviews with four college-educated young women: one in the East, one in Minneapolis–St. Paul, and the other two on the West Coast. In addition, newly wealthy men mentioned that their daughters were working for them.

14. This description is based on one case, although there were other philanthropic sisters in the sample. In those other instances, however, both siblings had inherited money. Certain personal characteristics have been withheld from this vignette to insure confidentiality.

15. On this point see Arlene Kaplan Daniels, "Good Times and Good Works: The Place of Sociability in the Work of Women Volunteers" *Social Problems* 32, no. 4 (April 1985): 363–74.

In addition, J. Miller McPherson and Lynn Smith-Lovin, "Women and Weak Ties: Differences by Sex in the Size of Voluntary Organizations," *American Journal of Sociology* 87, no. 4 (January 1982): 883–904, found important differences between the types of voluntary organizations to which women and men belong. They found that men are members of large, core economic groups, whereas women are concentrated in smaller community and domestic associations, and "very strong evidence that the size differences in men's and women's organizations are related to differing positions held in the economic sector" (p. 890). McPherson and Smith-Lovin propose that women in gender-typed roles join organizations with members similar to themselves, who share and value their skills (p. 899). They also mention the selective manner in which people both join and are recruited into voluntary organizations (p. 900).

The McPherson/Smith-Lovin data do not include measures of the subjects' wealth or class. It is probable that rich women hold more prestigious positions in larger organizations, but there is evidence that even wealthy women tend to limit their activities to community organizations rather than national ones. Both Daniels, *Invisible Careers,* and Ostrander, *Women of the Upper Class,* refer primarily to their informants' work as community volunteers.

16. This raises the question of whether women and men of the upper class fulfill their parental roles in a less gendered manner. Neither spends most of the day with the children. It is generally lower-class women who do the repetitive tasks in the upper-class household. Unfortunately, my data do not provide an answer, but further inquiry in this area might shed more light on how class structures gendering.

17. This composite is based on nine young women with children throughout the United States. Three are in the second generation of wealth, three in the third, two in the fourth, and one in the first.

18. See Ostrander, *Women of the Upper Class.*

19. This composite case is based on four middle-aged women who married into money.

20. See Tickamyer, "Wealth and Power."

21. De Beauvoir, *The Second Sex,* attempted to explain why female oppression has persisted throughout history. Although a thorough summary of her analysis cannot be attempted here, several of de Beauvoir's key ideas merit repeating. "[Women] live dispersed among the males, attached through residence, housework, economic condition, and social standing to certain men—fathers and husbands" (p. xxii). Furthermore, "the bond that unites [woman] to her oppressors is not comparable to any other" (p. xxiii). Women believe they love the men to whom they are subordinate, and therefore find it difficult to blame their situation on individual loved ones. Women of wealth share the struggle for transcendence with other women. But, for most wealthy women, class solidarity seems to be more binding than gender solidarity.
22. Louis Auchincloss, "Brooke Astor," *New York,* 25 April 1988, 71.
23. Ibid.
24. Brooke Astor, *Footprints: An Autobiography* (Garden City, N.Y.: Doubleday, 1980), 323.
25. Ibid., 327.
26. Ibid., 341.
27. Ibid., 333–35.
28. Ibid., 342.
29. Ibid., 339–40.
30. Ibid.
31. Nancy F. Cott, *The Bonds of Womanhood: "Women's Sphere" in New England, 1780–1835* (New Haven: Yale University Press, 1977), 22.
32. Ibid., 68–69.

Chapter 6: First-Generation Men and Their Families

1. Anne Lowrey Bailey, "A Founder of Hewlett-Packard to Give $2-Billion of His Computer Fortune to His Foundation," *Chronicle of Higher Education,* 11 May 1988, A23; and New York Times News Service, "Charity to Get Packard Fortune: $2 Billion Gift Caps Family's Philanthropic Commitment," *San Diego Union,* 29 April 1988, A1.
2. New York Times News Service, "Charity to Get Packard Fortune."
3. The David and Lucile Packard Foundation, "Lucile Salter Packard, 1914–1987," *Annual Report* (1986): 6–7; and *Forbes,* "The Richest People in America," 26 October 1987, 116.
4. *Forbes,* "The Richest People in America," 116.
5. Benjamin Lord, ed., *America's Wealthiest People: Their Philanthropic and Nonprofit Affiliations* (Washington, D.C.: Taft Corporation, 1984), 11.
6. See for example, Kevin Roderick and Claudia Luther, "1 Democratic, 2 GOP House Seats May Be Vulnerable," *Los Angeles Times,* 9 June 1988, 3. This article reported that Packard is one of "the three biggest political powers" in California.
7. These older men with relatively new wealth made up the largest group defined by common age and gender of all those interviewed; they constitute 21 of the 50 people in the first generation of wealth. We spoke with an additional 8 women over sixty years of age, 8 middle-aged men, 6 middle-aged women, 3 young women, and 2 couples (1 middle-aged and 1 old) with new wealth.
8. Computer and high-tech fortunes accounted for 19.5 percent; manufacturing and real estate, 17.1 percent *each;* mining and drilling, 12.2 percent; retail trade, 9.8 percent; construction and finance, 7.3 percent *each;* with the wealth of less than 10 percent of the remaining first-generation philanthropists in a wide range of other categories.
9. The David and Lucile Packard Foundation, "Lucile Salter Packard," 6.
10. *Forbes,* "The Richest People in America," 116.
11. The David and Lucile Packard Foundation, "Lucile Salter Packard," 6.
12. New York Times News Service, "Charity to Get Packard Fortune," A10.
13. The David and Lucile Packard Foundation, "Lucile Salter Packard," 6–7.

14. Foundation Center, *Foundation Directory* 11th ed. (New York: Foundation Center, 1987), 61.
15. Bailey, "A Founder of Hewlett-Packard to Give $2-Billion of His Computer Fortune to His Foundation," A23–24.
16. The David and Lucile Packard Foundation, "Lucile Salter Packard," 7.
17. Ibid.
18. Bailey, "A Founder of Hewlett-Packard to Give $2-Billion," A24.
19. Ibid.
20. New York Times News Service, "Charity to Get Packard Fortune," A10.
21. This composite is based on seven self-made men over sixty years old. Three live in the Southwest, two live in the Midwest, one in the East, and one in the South.
22. This composite is based on interviews with eight first-generation male millionaires over sixty. Three come from the Midwest, two each from the East and the Southwest, and one from the Far West.
23. The precise amount varied from informant to informant. Anything over $100 million clearly fits into this category. Some would include much smaller amounts. Most informants agreed that a $5 million minimum is required to establish a foundation.
24. This vignette is based on five middle-aged men.

Chapter 7: Elite Jewish Giving

1. Milton Goldin, *Why They Give: American Jews and Their Philanthropies* (New York: Macmillan, 1976), photo caption opposite 126.
2. Cited in Stephen Birmingham's *"Our Crowd": The Great Jewish Families of New York* (New York: Harper & Row, 1967), 155.
3. Ibid., 151–66.
4. Ibid., 161–77.
5. Goldin, *Why They Give,* 40.
6. Ibid., 38–40.
7. Ibid. 40.
8. Birmingham, *"Our Crowd,"* 325.
9. Ibid., 189. Jacob Schiff is reported to have kept his daughter "busy with volunteer work and fundraising" to protect her innocence. Frieda Schiff eventually married Felix Warburg, a Frankfurter like her father, in spite of her father's early objections. Warburg was less a disappointment than Jacob Schiff expected, joining his company but also following in his philanthropic footsteps. Felix and Frieda's home later became the Jewish Museum in New York.
10. Ibid., 188–89.
11. Goldin, *Why They Give,* 40.
12. Birmingham, *"Our Crowd,"* 288; Goldin, *Why They Give,* 37, 40.
13. Goldin, *Why They Give,* 61–62. According to Goldin, "The weakness in this *noblesse oblige* was detachment from the masses they represented. *Shtadlanim* sought no public approval and were not much interested in conferring with social inferiors about the issues that faced Jews. Unity, like charity, was established from the top down by men of quality. All right-minded people knew this" (p. 43).
14. We interviewed 40 elite Jewish philanthropists of both central and eastern European descent; they composed over 28.5 percent of our total sample of wealthy people. Twenty-five were men, 13 were women, and there was one married couple. Sixteen were over sixty years of age; another 16, forty to sixty years old; and 8 were young people. Thirteen were from the Midwest, 11 from the Northeast, 8 from the Middle Atlantic region, 4 from the West, and 2 each from the South and Southwest. Finally, 15 were first-generation millionaires; 13, second-generation; 8, third-generation; and 3 at least fourth generation, with one subject omitted because of missing data.

    Statistics about Jewish wealth and philanthropy are scanty, although stereotypes abound. Social scientists run the risk of perpetuating myths in our search for trends. Still, the pattern of proportionately greater Jewish philanthropic activity and charitable generosity was apparent in the data. We did not try to recruit Jews for interviews; they were active in charitable networks in every city we visited.

15. Teresa Odendahl, "Independent Foundations and Wealthy Donors: An Overview," in *America's Wealthy and the Future of Foundations,* ed. Teresa Odendahl (New York: Foundation Center, 1987), 19.

16. The other main religious groups represented in our study were Catholics and Protestants, the latter being primarily Episcopalians and Presbyterians. There were far fewer Catholics than Jews, and generalizations about them are not possible. However, only Jews and fundamentalist Southern Protestants stressed their religious motives for giving. "It is quite possible that wealthy Protestants do not directly refer to religion because the fabric of social life in the United States is based on a Protestant ethic." (Ibid., 19.)

17. A pseudonym. Myrna Slote is a composite character. Her story is told in greater detail later in this chapter.

18. See Lewis A. Coser, *The Functions of Social Conflict* (Glencoe, Ill.: Free Press, 1956), and *Continuities in the Study of Social Conflict* (New York: Free Press, 1967); as well as Ralf Dahrendorf, "Toward a Theory of Social Conflict," in *Social Change: Sources, Patterns, and Consequences*, ed. Amitai Etzioni and Eva Etzioni (New York: Basic Books, 1973), 98–111; Emile Durkheim, *The Rules of Sociological Method,* trans. Sarah A. Solovay and John H. Mueller, ed. George E. Catlin (Glencoe, Ill.: Free Press, 1958); and Georg Simmel, *Conflict: The Web of Group-Affiliations*, trans. Kurt H. Wolff and Reinhard Bendix (New York: Free Press, 1955).

    Simmel, who inspired the more modern conflict theorists, used the classic example of caste in India to substantiate this general thesis. He argued that each separate caste maintains a group identity through contrast and conflict with others. According to Simmel, the entire social structure of India was built upon the continually changing and reinforced rivalries among castes (p. 18).

19. Goldin, *Why They Give,* 173.

20. See Philip Bernstein, *To Dwell in Unity: The Jewish Federation Movement in America Since 1960* (Philadelphia: Jewish Publication Society of America, 1983).

21. Goldin, *Why They Give.*

22. Ibid.

23. See also ibid., 1. He says they were the "forerunners of the largest, richest, most powerful Jewish community in history."

24. Ibid., 178–79.

25. Ibid.

26. This composite is based on seven individuals—three are from Chicago, one from Boston, another from Los Angeles, the sixth has retired to Palm Beach, Florida, and the last is from Washington, D.C. Each made his fortune in a different business endeavor.

27. This case is based in large part on a Jewish couple. However, material from interviews with three other married individuals of Jewish descent, a middle-aged man, and two women of second-generation wealth was used as well.

28. This vignette is based on five interviews with wealthy third-generation Jewish women under forty years old. Two live in Baltimore, one in Chicago, one in Los Angeles, and one in Washington, D.C.

Chapter 8: The Alternative Fund Movement

1. Vanguard Public Foundation (Katy Butler, Laura Bouyea, and Barbara Garza), *Robin Hood Was Right: A Guide to Giving Your Money for Social Change* (San Francisco: Vanguard Public Foundation, 1977), 37. Available through the Funding Exchange, 666 Broadway, Suite 500, New York, N.Y. 10012. (212) 529-5300.

2. We interviewed donors and staff at eight different organizations: the Chinook Fund in Denver, the

Common Capital Support Fund in Washington, D.C. (now defunct) the Crossroads Fund in Chicago, the Haymarket People's Fund in Boston, the Liberty Hill Foundation in Los Angeles, the Live Oak Fund for Change in Austin, the Fund for Southern Communities in Atlanta, and the Vanguard Public Foundation in San Francisco.

3. The name was taken from a historical incident. In 1886 several on-strike employees of the McCormick Harvester Company were killed in Haymarket Square by Chicago police while attending a rally in support of the forty-hour work week. Protests continued, with Haymarket becoming the symbol of the workers' rights cause.

4. Roger M. Williams, "All in The Family (Well, Mostly)," *Foundation News,* July/August 1984, 45. Sally Pillsbury herself is described as being "far from radical," a "mainstream Republican."

5. Vanguard Public Foundation, *A Brief History of Vanguard Public Foundation,* undated typescript provided by a board member/donor during an interview.

6. Vanguard Public Foundation, *Robin Hood Was Right,* 38.

7. Kathleen Teltsch, "Network of 'Alternative' Philanthropies Is Forming," *New York Times,* 5 July 1983, A10. According to the Funding Exchange, *Annual Report* 1987, 10–11: "Bread and Roses roots actually go back to 1971 when the Philadelphia People's Fund was founded by individuals and organizations critical of United Way's failure to respond to emerging issues and small advocacy organizations. . . . 'Change, not Charity,' the original slogan of the People's Fund, has become the slogan of the entire Funding Exchange Network."

8. Vanguard Public Foundation, *Robin Hood Was Right,* 45.

9. The alternative funds differentiate themselves from the women's foundations and peace development funds by pointing to the "single-issue" focus of those organizations, a distinction that is not altogether accurate. For example, many women's foundations have much in common with the alternative funds (see chapter 9), and they are hardly single-issue grant-makers.

10. Funding Exchange, *Annual Report;* Haymarket People's Fund brochure, and Vanguard Public Foundation, *Robin Hood Was Right,* 37–43; and personal conversations with staff members. Groups highlighted in the Haymarket brochure include Aroostook Family Farm Core, an advocate for farmers in northern Maine; Essex County Community Organization, a tenant and welfare rights group; Blacks for Empowerment; Gay and Lesbian Advocates and Defenders; and Parents for Justice.

11. Vanguard Public Foundation, *Robin Hood Was Right,* 38.

12. Ibid., 39.

13. According to the rhetoric of the Funding Exchange, giving control of grant-making to activists has been a key aspect of all these alternative funds. But their representatives admit that there is some contradiction between this philosophy and the actual accommodation of donor interests. Wealthy contributors, even those on the left, want to feel connected to what they are doing with their money. They see their progressive philanthropy, however, as personally aligning them outside their class.

14. Funding Exchange, *Annual Report.*

15. There are exceptions. Christopher Mogil and Chuck Collins are writing a book about people who have given away substantial portions of their wealth for peace and social justice. It is slated to be published by New Society Publishers in Philadelphia.

16. Vanguard Public Foundation, *Robin Hood Was Right,* 15–16.

17. Ela Walsh, "Alternative Foundations Support Social Change: Young Givers Spurn Usual Philanthropies," *Washington Post,* 25 December 1984, A1.

18. Vanguard Public Foundation, *A Brief History of Vanguard Public Foundation,* 1.

19. Vanguard Public Foundation, *Robin Hood Was Right,* 26.

20. Ibid.

21. These are the subject of chapter 9.

22. Vanguard Public Foundation, *A Brief History of Vanguard Public Foundation,* 1.

23. These contradictory words indicate that the donor was either unsure about the magnitude of the split or was trying to determine how, or in what light, to present the controversy to me.

24. The longtime donor specified: "We still have a $10,000 grant as a theoretical maximum, but our grants have been averaging more in the $3,000, $4,000 range, with like $5,000 as a high, because we are funding more and more things, which is a subject of some frustration to everyone involved with the foundation. We all, in theory, would like to make fewer grants and larger ones, that more substantially set up an organization, a more significant chunk of what they need."

Notes

25. Funding Exchange, *Annual Report*, 17, 18, 24. The McKenzie River Gathering was formed in Oregon with a $500,000 gift from Leslie Brockelbank and Charles Gray. They convened a meeting of social activists to discuss how to fund peace, human rights, and environmental causes in the Pacific Northwest. The People's Resource of Southwest Ohio followed; then the North Star Fund was established in New York City.

26. In the 1980s ten more alternative foundations—the Crossroads Fund in Chicago, the Fund for Southern Communities in Atlanta, the Live Oak Fund in Austin, the Wisconsin Community Fund in Madison, the Appalachian Community Fund in Knoxville, the Headwaters Fund in Minneapolis, the Baltimore Common Wealth, the Common Capital Support Fund (in operation only a few years), and the Chinook Fund in Denver—were formed with the assistance of the Funding Exchange. The newest affiliate group is the People's Fund in Honolulu, Hawaii. These funds were organized in various ways. For example, Crossroads had a dozen founding donors and the support of the Wieboldt Foundation, whereas the Fund for Southern Communities was started by seventeen leftist activists with only one major donor among them. Another alternative fund, which is not under the Funding Exchange umbrella, A Territorial Resource in Seattle, is run mainly by donors.

27. The name refers to the strong and unseasonable high-speed winds that blow out of the Rocky Mountains.

28. Liberty Hill, one of the earlier alternative funds, still operates with a dual-board system.

29. The alternative funding movement had gained momentum long before I began my research. As my familiarity with its analysis and approach increased, it directly influenced my thinking.

30. Some critics note that Haymarket's structure, with nine local committees, is unwieldy and that a centralized process would be more effective. Given the small amounts of money dispersed, this may be true. If more funds were available, however, truly local funding committees would theoretically be the most representative.

31. This rough estimate is based on the supposition that half of the $100 billion spent in 1988 on philanthropy came directly or indirectly from the wealthy.

Chapter 9: Wealthy "Feminist" Funders

1. Also referred to as the "new women's movement," it is generally (but somewhat arbitrarily) dated in the United States to the 1963 publication of Betty Friedan's *The Feminine Mystique* (New York: Dell).

2. According to Mirra Komarovsky, *Women in College: Shaping New Feminine Identities* (New York: Basic Books, 1985), 122, 52 percent of women in their senior year of college sympathize greatly with the women's liberation movement and think it was justified; 40 percent believe it was somewhat justified; 7 percent somewhat oppose it; and 1 percent are opposed to the women's liberation movement. In comparison, less than 20 percent of the wealthy women interviewed for this study indicated that they were sympathetic to feminism.

3. The first of these statistics comes from a Ford Foundation study, *Financial Support of Women's Programs in the 1970s* (New York, 1979). The second is drawn from the Foundation Center, *Grants for Women and Girls* (New York, 1988) and is based on 1986 figures.

4. The Ms. Foundation for Women was created in 1975. According to its literature, it is still "the *only* public, nationwide, multi-issue foundation entirely devoted to supporting self-help projects for women and girls." Other women's foundations, such as that sponsored by the American Association of University Women or the Business and Professional Women's Foundation, are national and public, but they fund research and scholarships rather than grassroots causes.

5. I have labeled these eleven people "feminist funders" to distinguish them from women funders who do not significantly contribute to women's issues. (None of the men we interviewed focused their grant-making on women's concerns.) I did not include in this group the several men and women who indicated that they support, for example, population control or even Planned Parenthood (if no other women's causes were mentioned).

6. In order to insure confidentiality to those who requested it, and because variability and small numbers preclude adequate composites, less detailed personal information is presented in this chapter.

7. Three have never been married, one reported that she was a lesbian. Three are divorced. Five have husbands. Four have children.

8. See Simone de Beauvoir, *The Second Sex* (New York: Random House, 1974), 697: "In the upper classes women are eager accomplices of their [husbands] because they stand to profit from the benefits provided. . . . [Elite] women . . . have always defended their class interests even more obstinately than have their husbands, not hesitating radically to sacrifice their independence as human beings."

9. Gary was interviewed on two occasions, first in 1985 and later in 1988. During the second session she indicated that she would not require confidentiality. Where relevant, the year in which she made her comments is indicated.

10. Kathleen Teltsch, "Network of Women Hopes to Change American Philanthropy," *New York Times,* 14 May 1986, C7.

11. As of December 1988.

12. The following material was taken from my personal notes, newspaper clippings, official minutes, and interviews.

13. Daryl Gibson, "Women's Group Sets High Goal," *Daily Camera,* 6 July 1987, 1B.

14. I have to admit that the $2 million endowment was a great attraction to me. That meant we could make grants of at least $100,000 a year, if not $200,000. Only later did I learn that the foundation actually had less than half a million dollars in its coffers. The announcement had been misleadingly based on pledges to be collected over a five-year period.

15. See chapter 8. I was familiar by then with the structure of Vanguard and other alternative funds, as well as the other women's foundations, because I had interviewed donors and staff at both.

16. She was an administrative assistant to the mayor of Denver, president of the board of the local Children's Museum, and past president of the board of the Women's Forum.

17. Dr. Hennessy is the executive director of the Asian Pacific Development Center in Denver.

18. I do not have direct knowledge of the details of her financial situation. She was mentioned in *Forbes,* "The Richest People in America," 26 October 1987, 310.

19. Swanee Hunt was quite knowledgable about the other alternative, social change, and women's funds around the country. She and her sister had formed the Hunt Alternatives Fund in 1982. As part of a network of progressive funders, she probably knew about the Vanguard structure.

20. Stephen Singular, "Women's Fund Targets $10 Million in Endowments," *Denver Post,* 12 June 1987, C1–2.

21. Kentucky Foundation for Women, *Articulating a Woman's Perspective,* a brochure received in 1988, n.d.

22. Ibid.

23. John Nielsen, "Sallie Bingham: After a Woman Is Scorned, A Publishing Family Cashes Out," *Fortune,* 5 January 1987, 93.

24. Alanna Nash, "The Woman Who Overturned an Empire," *Ms.,* June 1986, 44–46.

25. Sallie Bingham, "The Truth About Growing Up Rich," *Ms.,* June 1986, 48. She continued: "When the whole world is watching for a mistake . . . natural exuberance must be curbed. And when the child in question is a girl, the curbing is especially intense: as a sexual object, she represents the family's peculiar vulnerability to outsiders, predators—husbands. The little rich girl must learn to sit with her legs firmly crossed and her skirt prudently down at the same time she is learning to modulate both the tone of her voice and the color of her opinions. The result is paleness."

26. Nash, "The Woman Who Overturned an Empire," 45.

27. Bingham, "Biting the Hand," 32.

28. Nash, "The Woman Who Overturned an Empire," 46.

29. Nielsen, "Sallie Bingham," 93.

30. Bingham, "Biting the Hand," 32.

31. Ibid., 33.

32. Nielsen, "Sallie Bingham," 93.

Notes

Chapter 10: Advisers and Professionals

1. See Marvin G. Dunn, "The Family Office: Coordinating Mechanism of the Ruling Class," in *Power Structure Research,* ed. G. William Domhoff (Beverly Hills: Sage, 1980), 17–45, for a general analysis and specific information on the Weyerhaeuser family offices; David E. Koskoff, *The Mellons: The Chronicle of America's Richest Family* (New York: Crowell, 1978); and Carol J. Loomis, "The Rockefellers: End of a Dynasty?" as well as her sidebar, "The Ultimate Family Room," *Fortune,* 4 August 1986, 26–37.

2. It is not a semantic coincidence that the word *retainer* has several meanings: it is a title for a professional individual; the contractual arrangement/fee paid to a lawyer or an adviser for services or a claim on services; and a term applied to a person attached to or owing services to a household, especially a servant.

3. This chapter is based on conversations with seventy personal advisers to the wealthy and an additional one hundred foundation staff members.

     See Francie Ostrower, "The Role of Advisors to the Wealthy," in *America's Wealthy and the Future of Foundations,* ed. Teresa Odendahl (New York: Foundation Center, 1987), 247–66; as well as Teresa Jean Odendahl, Elizabeth Trocolli Boris, and Arlene Kaplan Daniels, *Working in Foundations: Career Patterns of Women and Men* (New York: Foundation Center, 1985).

     Wealthy study participants also spoke about their retainers, and their comments augment the discussion. Donors and advisers are fairly consistent in their portrayal of each other. Advisers were helpful in substantiating the ways in which their clients seek control of nonprofit endeavors.

4. I do not mean to imply that these particular advisers are not professional, but I wish to distinguish between the two types of advisers.

5. Several studies document the importance of attorneys and legal instruments in preserving and managing wealth, and using it for charitable purposes. See George Cooper, "A Voluntary Tax? New Perspectives on Sophisticated Estate Tax Avoidance," *Columbia Law Review* 77, no. 2 (March 1977): 161–247; George E. Marcus, "Law in the Development of Dynastic Families Among American Business Elites: The Domestication of Capital and the Capitalization of the Family," *Law and Society Review* 14, no. 4 (Summer 1980): 859–903; and "The Fiduciary Role in American Family Dynasties and Their Institutional Legacy: From the Law of Trusts to Trust in the Establishment," in *Elites: Ethnographic Issues,* ed. George E. Marcus (Albuquerque: University of New Mexico Press, 1983), 221–65.

6. Marcus, "Law in the Development of Dynastic Families," has made an important distinction between dynastic family offices, what he calls "family/business formations," and "externally administered failed dynasties." This emphasis on where the work is being done has merit but does not account for the ongoing development of and adjustment within dynasties. Marcus initially investigated dynastic families in Texas that had made their fortunes in the late nineteenth century. He devised a model to account for generational transitions. He suggested that dynasties cannot last more than four generations and seems to imply that "unfavorable" conditions (such as increased government regulation) militate against modern family dynasty formation.

7. Judith Brimberg, "Millionaire Founder Assuming Control of Piton Foundation," *Denver Post,* 30 September 1987, 1.

8. Ostrower, "The Role of Advisors to the Wealthy," 249.

9. The increasing importance of accountants in philanthropic advising was revealed in the course of interviews with subjects and with attorneys. We also discovered that many personal advisers were trained as accountants. Although as a result of these findings we interviewed several accountants with practices among the wealthy, accountants had been overlooked in our original research design. Along with attorneys, more accountants may now be specializing in nonprofit matters. More investigation of their role in philanthropy is needed.

10. Of course, the boards of most large nonprofit institutions are dominated by wealthy philanthropists so, in a sense, they do work for the rich. And some fundraisers leave such employment for positions with individual philanthropists.

11. We had intended to include in the sample as many trust officers as attorneys because of a misinformed but popularly held assumption about their importance to the elite. Our interviews revealed that although

bankers may have been more prominent philanthropic advisers in the past, today they tend to hold sway with less financially sophisticated wealthy people. We limited our interviews with them after we discovered their diminishing influence.

12. The foundation employees who are highlighted here work for family grant-making institutions rather than "independent" foundations like Ford, which no longer have family members on the board. For a description of their duties and situations, see Odendahl, Boris, and Daniels, *Working in Foundations.*

13. Only non-kin advisers are quoted in this section. Close relatives of millionaires, especially offspring who are apt to inherit the fortune, were designated as wealthy individuals rather than advisers. Some children of rich philanthropists are clearly being groomed to take over the family dynasty. Their comments appear throughout the book.

14. In the strict sociological sense philanthropic advisers are not members of a profession. There are no organizations that regulate their work. Some family retainers attend meetings of regional associations of grant-makers as well as the Council on Foundations, the National Network of Grantmakers, or the Philanthropic Roundtable. However, some of these organizations do not allow the individual funder or adviser to belong and recruit members only from such institutions as foundations. While certain philanthropic groups position themselves as professional associations, they are not credentialing bodies. Entry into this kind of employment is based largely on whom you know rather than what you know. See Odendahl, Boris and Daniels, *Working in Foundations.*

15. See Marcus, "Law in the Development of Dynastic Families" and "The Fiduciary Role in American Family Dynasties."

16. All but one of these are individual, not composite, cases. For that reason, personal description is kept at a minimum. Pseudonyms are used throughout.

17. As has been indicated, wives, daughters, and sisters also frequently take on this job.

18. A pseudonym.

19. A pseudonym.

20. A pseudonym.

21. He never mentioned any conflict of interest between these roles.

22. A pseudonym.

23. See Marcus, "Law in the Development of Dynastic Families" and "The Fiduciary Role in American Family Dynasties."

24. In order to insure confidentiality, a composite of two advisers with similar roles in family offices is used here.

25. A pseudonym of a composite character.

26. See Antonio Gramsci, *Letters from Prison,* selected and translated by Lynne Lawner (New York: Harper & Row, 1973); and *Antonio Gramsci: Selections from Political Writings, 1910–1920,* trans. and ed. Quintin Hoare (New York: International Publishers, 1977), especially his conception of organic intellectuals.

27. For a historical discussion of these ideas see Barry D. Karl and Stanley N. Katz, "Foundations and Ruling Class Elites," *Daedalus: Journal of the American Academy of Arts and Sciences* 116, no. 1 (Winter 1987): 1–40.

Chapter 11: The Restructuring of Elite Philanthropy

1. Robert A. Dahl, *Dilemmas of Pluralist Democracy: Autonomy vs. Control* (New Haven: Yale University Press, 1982), 6, 47, 83. See also John F. Manley, "Neo-Pluralism: A Class Analysis of Pluralism I and Pluralism II," *American Political Science Review* 77, no. 2 (June 1983): 369–89.

2. A recent report, Institute for Public Policy and Administration, *Part of the Solution: Innovative Approaches to Nonprofit Funding* (Washington, D.C.: Union for Experimenting Colleges and Universities, 1988), suggests addressing the problem of shrinking income by seeking alternative sources of funds for nonprofits. One of the ideas presented there will be given later in this chapter.

3. This phrase is from Pablo Eisenberg, president of the Center for Community Change and chair of the National Committee for Responsive Philanthropy, both located in Washington, D.C.

Notes

4. This book is limited to a consideration of the equity issues raised by the giving of the wealthy. A fuller public policy agenda would, of course, include recommendations about all aspects of nonprofit endeavor, including the ratio of administrative cost to service delivery or fundraising practices.

5. Henry Hansmann, "The Two Independent Sectors," *Working Papers* (Washington, D.C.: Independent Sector and United Way Institute, 1988), 15–24, has made a similar argument, especially concerning what he calls "commercial" nonprofits.

     The largest group of nonprofit organizations are classified as 501(c)(3). They constitute a wide range of religious, educational, charitable, scientific, and literary associations that are fully tax-exempt. Gifts of cash or property to these groups are deductible on income, estate, and gift taxes. Next in size are the 501(c)(4), non-charitable civic leagues, social welfare organizations, and local associations of employees. These are followed by some twenty-odd other categories for which deductions are not allowed. See Virginia Ann Hodgkinson and Murray S. Weitzman, *Dimensions of the Independent Sector: A Statistical Profile,* 2nd ed. (Washington, D.C.: Independent Sector, 1986), 17, table 1.4.

6. Community foundations are a version of this idea; they are generally organized to operate in this manner. However, to date there has not been enough research or evaluation on the effectiveness of the community foundation model. The only studies with which I am familiar were undertaken by the Council on Foundations and are largely descriptive of the field.

     Some argue that community foundations have to spend too much effort in the business of fundraising and are thus less knowledgeable about their communities. Others point out that these types of foundations must have a commitment to meet the needs of the total community. Many community foundations are run by a local power elite rather than a representative group. This, however, need not be the case.

7. Virginia A. Hodgkinson and Murray S. Weitzman, *Giving and Volunteering in the United States: Findings from a National Survey* (Washington, D.C.: Independent Sector, 1988), 1.

8. Dahl, *Dilemmas of Pluralist Democracy,* 170–71, suggested the remedy of a ceiling on contributions in the political arena.

9. It would be unrealistic to expect the wealthy to commit "class suicide" (a term I first heard used by economist Rhonda Williams) by divesting themselves of their capital. Such matters would have to be legislated.

10. Institute for Public Policy, *Part of the Solution,* 11, 41.

11. Ibid., 42–49.

12. See James C. Baughman, *Trustees, Trusteeship, and the Public Good: Issues of Accountability for Hospitals, Museums, Universities, and Libraries* (New York: Quorum, 1987), 3. He used this phrase in the same way before me.

13. Each year the American Association of Fundraising Counsel publishes *Giving USA,* an estimate of aggregate data on the charitable contributions of individuals, corporations, and foundations. Although their data have been steadily improving in quality, full information is not available to them for making their estimates. The Conference Board, Council on Foundations, Foundation Center, Independent Sector, National Center for Charitable Statistics, National Committee on Responsive Philanthropy, and other nonprofit groups also collect and publish information about and for their constituencies, but there is no central coordinating organization.

14. Quoted in Mary A. Anderson, "Covering Philanthropy: Only a Handful of Reporters Cover the 'Nonprofit America Beat' on a Full-Time Basis," *Presstime,* February 1988, 26.

15. See Paul G. Schervish and Andrew Herman, *The Study on Wealth and Philanthropy Final Report,* 1989, sponsored by the T. B. Murphy Foundation Charitable Trust, Social Welfare Research Institute, Boston College, Chestnut Hill, Mass. 02167; and their "Varieties of Philanthropic Logic Among the Wealthy," *Working Papers* (Washington, D.C.: Independent Sector and United Way Institute, 1987). Waldemar A. Nielsen is also working on a project concerning the charitable behavior of the wealthy.

16. For an exception, see Waldemar A. Nielsen, *The Golden Donors: A New Anatomy of the Great Foundations* (New York: Dutton, 1985).

17. See Anderson, "Covering Philanthropy." These include the *Chronicle of Higher Education,* the *New York Times,* the *Pittsburgh Post-Gazette,* the *Star Tribune* of Minneapolis, the *St. Paul Pioneer Press and Dispatch,* and the *Wall Street Journal.* Two minor papers are competing to serve the field—the *Nonprofit Times* and the *Chronicle of Philanthropy,* a recent spin-off of the *Chronicle of Higher Education.* The

magazine *Foundation News* is the trade journal of the Council on Foundations; the *Corporate Philanthropy Report* covers the business community.

18. At the federal level, the Department of the Treasury is an obvious possibility, although given the disrepute of the Internal Revenue Service, the president might consider establishing a Department of Charity or Philanthropy. It has been argued that this would make the "sector" less independent and bring it more under the thumb of government. My idea, however, simply recognizes existing relationships.

    Other alternatives include the Foundation Center, the Independent Sector, and the National Center for Charitable Statistics, groups that already exist and collect limited data. The Foundation Center, for example, might serve as a model for this kind of information collection and dissemination; it has national and regional offices. It makes copies of the official PF990, or annual reports, which must be filed by all foundations with the IRS, available to the public in microfiche form. And it has an extensive publishing program.

19. Brian O'Connell, *Effective Leadership in Voluntary Organizations: How to Make the Greatest Use of Citizen Service and Influence* (New York: Walker, 1981), 149.

20. Deborah Kaplan Polivy conducted two ground-breaking studies in this area. See "A Study of the Admissions Policies and Practices of Eight Local United Way Organizations," working paper no. 49 (Yale University Program on Non-Profit Organizations, May 1982); and "Increasing Giving Options in Corporate Charitable Payroll Deduction Programs: Who Benefits?" working paper no. 83 (Yale University Program on Non-Profit Organizations January 1985). She includes material on other types of employee-controlled corporate giving programs. Eleanor Brilliant is working on a book about the United Way. See also Wendy Melillo, "New Group Urges Companies to Let More Charities Take Part in Fund Raising by Payroll Deduction" and "United Way Studied Strategies to Fend Off Competitors," *Chronicle of Philanthropy*, 25 July 1989, 4–8.

21. In addition, the National Network of Grantmakers, representing the more progressive wing of organized philanthropy, and the Philanthropic Roundtable, the conservative grant-makers, as well as regional associations of grant-makers all contribute to professional development. However none of these provide systematic training or credentialing.

22. Elizabeth Boris and Teresa Odendahl, "Ethics and Philanthropy," manuscript, ed. Jon Van Til.

23. Robert Matthews Johnson, *The First Charity: How Philanthropy Can Contribute to Democracy in America* (Cabin John, Md.: Seven Locks, 1988), xvii.

Methodological Appendix

1. See Teresa Odendahl, ed., *America's Wealthy and the Future of Foundations* (New York: Foundation Center, 1987); as well as Teresa Jean Odendahl, Elizabeth Trocolli Boris, and Arlene Kaplan Daniels, *Working in Foundations: Career Patterns of Women and Men* (New York: Foundation Center, 1985).

2. Sociologist Michael Patrick Allen, *The Founding Fortunes: A New Anatomy of the Super-Rich Families in America* (New York: Dutton, 1987), 6, documented that a "clear majority" of the wealthiest Americans are inheritors. His work is based on archival research of public records. He provides an annotated directory of 160 families with at least $200 million in assets in 1986 (pp. 307–92). Allen's findings are consistent with my own, although our methods and the populations we investigated were different. He collected material on a group of the very wealthiest people in the United States, whether or not they gave to charity.

    Our results are at odds with *Forbes*, "The Richest People in America," 26 October 1987, 317, which has been compiling a list of the 400 richest people in the United States for the last several years. They have been steadily adding more self-made multimillionaires. In 1982, they noted 134 individuals in the first generation of wealth, but by 1987, that had climbed to 214, over half the list.

    Members of over 20 of the families in Allen's directory, and 20 individuals from the 1987 *Forbes* list (with some overlap) were interviewed for my research, as well as some of their advisers.

BIBLIOGRAPHY

AAFRC (American Association of Fundraising Counsel, Inc.) *Giving USA: A Compilation of Facts and Trends on American Philanthropy for the Year 1983*. New York: AAFRC, 1984.

———. *Giving USA: A Compilation of Facts and Trends on American Philanthropy for the Year 1984*. New York: AAFRC, 1985.

———. *Giving USA: A Compilation of Facts and Trends on American Philanthropy for the Year 1985*. New York: AAFRC, 1986.

———. *Giving USA: Estimates of Philanthropic Giving in 1986 and the Trends They Show*. New York: AAFRC, 1987.

Abramson, Alan J., and Lester M. Salamon. *The Nonprofit Sector and the New Federal Budget*. Washington, D.C.: The Urban Institute, 1986.

Acker, Joan R. "Women and Stratification: A Review of Recent Literature." *Contemporary Sociology* 9, no. 1 (January 1980): 25–39.

Aldrich, Nelson W., Jr. *Old Money: The Mythology of America's Upper Class*. New York: Knopf, 1988.

Allen, Michael Patrick. *The Founding Fortunes: A New Anatomy of the Super-Rich Families in America*. New York: Dutton, 1987.

American Council of Learned Societies. *Dictionary of American Biography*. Vol. 9. New York: Scribner's, 1936.

Anderson, Mary A. "Covering Philanthropy: Only a Handful of Reporters Cover the 'Nonprofit America Beat' on a Full-Time Basis." *Presstime*, February 1988, 26–28.

Arnove, Robert F., ed. *Philanthropy and Culture Imperialism: The Foundations at Home and Abroad*. Boston: G. K. Hall, 1980.

Astor, Brooke. *Footprints: An Autobiography*. Garden City, N.Y.: Doubleday, 1980.

Auchincloss, Louis. "Brooke Astor." *New York*, 25 April 1988, 71.

Auten, Gerald, and Gabriel Rudney. "The Variability of the Charitable Giving of the Wealthy." Working paper no. 126. New Haven: Yale University Program on Non-Profit Organizations, 1987.

Bailey, Anne Lowrey. "A Founder of Hewlett-Packard to Give $2-Billion of His Computer Fortune to His Foundation." *Chronicle of Higher Education*, 11 May 1988, A23.

———. "More Scholars, Colleges Taking an Interest in Study of Philanthropy and Non-Profit Organizations." *Chronicle of Higher Education*, 21 September 1988, A34–36.

Baltzell, E. Digby. *Philadelphia Gentleman: The Making of a National Upper Class*. New York: Free Press, 1958.

———. *The Protestant Establishment: Aristocracy & Caste in America*. New York: Random House, 1964.

———. *Puritan Boston and Quaker Philadelphia: Two Protestant Ethics and the Spirit of Class Authority and Leadership*. New York: Free Press, 1979.

Baughman, James C. *Trustees, Trusteeship, and the Public Good: Issues of Accountability for Hospitals, Museums, Universities, and Libraries.* New York: Quorum, 1987.

Bernstein, Philip. *To Dwell in Unity: The Jewish Federation Movement in American Since 1960.* Philadelphia: The Jewish Publication Society of America, 1983.

Bingham, Sallie, "Biting the Hand: The Break-up of the Bingham Family Empire." *Radcliffe Quarterly,* June 1986, 33.

———. "The Truth About Growing Up Rich." *Ms.,* June 1986, 48–50, 82–83.

Birmingham, Stephen. *"Our Crowd": The Great Jewish Families of New York.* New York: Harper & Row, 1967.

Blau, Peter Michael. *Exchange and Power in Social Life.* New York: Wiley, 1964.

Bluestone, Barry, and Bennett Harrison "The Growth of Low-Wage Employment: 1963–1986." Paper presented at annual meeting of the American Economics Association, Chicago, 28–30 December 1987.

Boissevain, Jeremy. *Friends of Friends: Networks, Manipulators, and Coalitions.* New York: St. Martin's, 1974.

Boller, Paul F., Jr. *American Thought in Transition: The Impact of Evolutionary Naturalism, 1865–1900.* Chicago: Rand McNally, 1973.

Boris, Elizabeth T. "Creation and Growth: A Survey of Private Foundations." In *America's Wealthy and the Future of Foundations,* edited by Teresa Odendahl, 63–126. New York: Foundation Center, 1987.

Boris, Elizabeth, and Teresa Odendahl. "Ethics and Philanthropy." In *Conflict, Consensus, and Change in Philanthropy: Confronting the Cutting Edge Issues,* edited by Jon Van Til. San Francisco, Jossey-Bass, forthcoming.

Bourdieu, Pierre. *Distinction: A Social Critique of the Judgement of Taste.* Translated by Richard Nice. Cambridge: Harvard University Press, 1984.

Bremner, Robert Hamlett. *American Philanthropy.* Chicago: University of Chicago Press, 1960; revised, 1988.

Brenson, Michael. "New Met Chairman Defines Objectives: Dilworth in Control." *New York Times,* 31 January 1984, C13.

Brimberg, Judith. "Millionaire Founder Assuming Control of Piton Foundation." *Denver Post,* 30 September 1987, 1.

Brown, J. Larry, and H. F. Pizer. *Living Hungry in America.* New York: Macmillan, 1987.

Buchwald, Art. "A Chump for Trump." *Washington Post,* 29 September 1988, B1.

Business Week. "People, Philanthropists, Look Where Joan Kroc Is Throwing Her McNuggets." 5 September 1988, 74–75.

Cancian, Frank. *Economics and Prestige in a Maya Community: The Religious Cargo System in Zinacantan.* Stanford: Stanford University Press, 1965.

Chodorow, Nancy. "Family Structure and Feminine Personality." In *Woman, Culture, and Society,* ed. Michelle Rosaldo and Louise Lamphere, 43–66. Stanford, Calif.: Stanford University Press, 1974.

———. *The Reproduction of Mothering: Psychoanalysis and the Sociology of Gender.* Berkeley: University of California Press, 1978.

Churcher, Sharon. "Making It By Doing Good: Nouvelle Society Ladies Win Peer Approval Working for 'the Arts and Diseases.' " *New York Times Magazine,* 3 July 1988, 16–18, 33.

Clotfelter, Charles T. *Federal Tax Policy and Charitable Giving.* Chicago: University of Chicago Press, 1985.

Clotfelter, Charles T., and Eugene Steuerle. "Charitable Contributions." In *How Taxes Affect Economic Behavior,* edited by Henry J. Aaron and Joseph A. Pechman, 403–36. Washington, D.C.: Brookings Institution, 1981.

Coles, Robert. *The Privileged Ones: The Well-Off and the Rich in America.* Boston: Little, Brown, 1977.

Colwell, Mary Anna Culleton. "Philanthropic Foundations and Public Policy: The Political Role of Foundations." Ph.D. diss., University of California, Berkeley, 1980.

Commission on Private Philanthropy and Public Needs. *Research Papers.* 7 vols. Washington, D. C.: Department of the Treasury, 1977.

Connors, Tracy Daniel, ed. *The Nonprofit Organization Handbook.* New York: McGraw-Hill, 1980.

Cookson, Peter W., Jr., and Caroline Hodges Persell. *Preparing for Power: America's Elite Boarding Schools.* New York: Basic Books, 1985.

Bibliography

Cooper, George. "A Voluntary Tax? New Perspectives on Sophisticated Estate Tax Avoidance." *Columbia Law Review* 77, no. 2 (March 1977): 161–247.

Coser, Lewis A. *The Functions of Social Conflict.* Glencoe, Ill.: Free Press, 1956.

———. *Continuities in the Study of Social Conflict.* New York: Free Press, 1967.

Cott, Nancy F. *The Bonds of Womanhood: "Women's Sphere" in New England, 1780–1835.* New Haven: Yale University Press, 1977.

Council on Foundations. *1985 Community Foundations Survey.* Washington, D.C.: Council on Foundations, 1985.

Dahl, Robert A. *Dilemmas of Pluralist Democracy: Autonomy vs. Control.* New Haven: Yale University Press, 1982.

Dahrendorf, Ralf. "Toward a Theory of Social Conflict." In *Social Change: Sources, Patterns, and Consequences,* edited by Amitai Etzioni and Eva Etzioni, 100–113. New York: Basic Books, 1973.

Daniels, Arlene Kaplan. "Good Times and Good Works: The Place of Sociability in the Work of Women Volunteers." *Social Problems* 32, no. 4 (April 1985): 363–74.

———. *Invisible Careers: Women Civic Leaders From the Volunteer World.* Chicago: University of Chicago Press, 1988.

The David and Lucile Packard Foundation. "Lucile Salter Packard, 1914–1987." *Annual Report* (Los Altos, Calif., 1986): 6–7.

De Beauvoir, Simone. *The Second Sex.* New York: Knopf, 1953; New York: Random House, 1974.

DiMaggio, Paul. "Nonprofit Organizations in the Production and Distribution of Culture." In *The Nonprofit Sector: A Research Handbook,* edited by Walter W. Powell, 195–220. New Haven: Yale University Press, 1987.

DiMaggio, Paul, and Michael Useem. "The Arts in Class Reproduction." In *Cultural and Economic Reproduction in Education: Essays on Class, Ideology, and the State,* edited by Michael W. Apple, 181–201. London: Routledge & Kegan Paul, 1982.

Dinnerstein, Dorothy. *The Mermaid and the Minotaur: Sexual Arrangements and Human Malaise.* New York: Harper & Row, 1976.

Domhoff, G. William. *Who Rules America?* Englewood Cliffs, N.J.: Prentice-Hall, 1967.

———. *The Higher Circles: The Governing Class in America.* New York: Vintage, 1970.

———. *Power Structure Research.* Beverly Hills, Calif.: Sage, 1980.

———. *Who Rules America Now? A View for the '80s.* Englewood Cliffs, N.J.: Prentice-Hall, 1983.

Donor Briefing. "Museum Gifts Drop, Tax Reform Blamed." Vol. 4, no. 6, 15 March 1989. Evanston, Ill: Business Publishers, Inc.

Dunn, Marvin G. "The Family Office: Coordinating Mechanism of the Ruling Class." In *Power Structure Research,* edited by G. William Domhoff, 17–45. Beverly Hills, Calif.: Sage, 1980.

Durkheim, Emile. *The Rules of Sociological Method.* 8th ed. Translated by Sarah A. Solovay and John H. Mueller. Edited by George E. Catlin. Glencoe, Ill.: Free Press, 1958.

Federal Reserve Board data. Press release of the Congress of the United States, Joint Economic Committee. 2 August 1986.

Forbes. "The Richest People in America." 26 October 1987.

Forbes. "The Richest People in America." 24 October 1988.

Ford Foundation. *Financial Support of Women's Programs in the 1970s.* New York: Ford Foundation, 1979.

Foundation Center. *Foundation Directory.* 11th ed. New York: Foundation Center, 1987.

———. *Grants for Women and Girls.* New York: Foundation Center, 1988.

Foundation Library Center. *Foundation Directory.* 1st ed. New York: Russell Sage Foundation, 1960.

———. *Foundation Directory.* 2d ed. New York: Russell Sage Foundation, 1964.

Funding Exchange. *Annual Report* 14. New York: Funding Exchange, 1987.

Friedan, Betty. *The Feminine Mystique.* New York: Dell, 1963.

Furlong, Tom. "Popejoy to Become a Bass Partner, Quit American S&L Post." *Los Angeles Times,* 16 December 1988, CC1, 3.

Galaskiewicz, Joseph. *Social Organization of an Urban Grants Economy: A Study of Business Philanthropy and Nonprofit Organizations.* Orlando, Fla.: Academic Press, 1985.

Gamarekian, Barbara. "Wealth and Influence: Does Texas Billionaire Aim to Be Power Broker?" *New York Times,* 15 September 1988, A8.

Gans, Herbert J. *Popular Culture and High Culture: An Analysis and Evaluation of Taste.* New York: Basic Books, 1974.

Gelman, Eric, with Nikki Finke Greenberg, Daniel Shapiro, Penelope Wang, Peter McAlevey, and Christopher Ma. "The Bass Dynasty." *Newsweek,* 19 November 1984, 72–78.

Gibson, Daryl. "Women's Group Sets High Goal." *Daily Camera,* 6 July 1987, 1B.

Gilbert, Neil. *Capitalism and the Welfare State: Dilemmas of Social Benevolence.* New Haven: Yale University Press, 1983.

Gilbert, Neil, and Harry Specht. *Dimensions of Social Welfare Policy.* 2d ed. Englewood Cliffs, N.J.: Prentice-Hall, 1986.

Gilligan, Carol. *In a Different Voice: Psychological Theory and Women's Development.* Cambridge: Harvard University Press, 1982.

Goldberger, Paul. "Trump: Symbol of a Gaudy, Impatient Time." *New York Times,* 31 January 1988, sec. II, H32, 35.

Goldin, Milton. *Why They Give: American Jews and Their Philanthropies.* New York: Macmillan, 1976.

Gramsci, Antonio. *Letters from Prison.* Selected and translated by Lynn Lawner. New York: Harper & Row, 1973.

———. *Antonio Gramsci: Selections from Political Writings, 1910–1920.* Trans. and ed. Quintin Hoare. New York: International Publishers, 1977.

Hacker, H. M. "Class and Race Differences in Gender Roles." In *Gender and Sex in Society,* edited by Lucille Duberman. New York: Praeger, 1975.

———. "Business Giving and Social Investment in the United States." In *Philanthropic Giving: Studies in Venture and Variety,* edited by Richard Magat. New York: Oxford University Press, 1989.

———. *The Invention of the Nonprofit Sector.* Typescript.

Hall, Peter Dobkin. *The Organization of American Culture, 1700–1900: Private Institutions, Elites, and the Origins of American Nationality.* New York: New York University Press, 1982.

———. "A Historical Overview of the Private Nonprofit Sector." In *The Nonprofit Sector: A Research Handbook,* edited by Walter W. Powell, 3–26. New Haven: Yale University Press, 1987.

———. "Business Giving and Social Investment in the United States." In *Philanthropic Giving: Studies in Venture and Variety,* edited by Richard Magat. New York: Oxford University Press, 1989.

———. *The Invention of the Nonprofit Sector.* Typescript.

The Handbook of Private Schools: An Annual Descriptive Survey of Independent Education. 69th ed. Boston: Porter Sargent, 1988.

Hansmann, Henry. "The Two Independent Sectors," In *Working Papers,* 15–24. Washington, D.C.: Independent Sector and United Way Institute, 1988.

Harrington, Michael. *The Other America: Poverty in the United States.* New York: Penguin, 1962; with an updated afterword, 1984.

Harrison, Bennett, and Barry Bluestone. "Labour Market Analysis and Employment Planning." Working paper no. 17. International Labour Office: Geneva, October 1987.

———. *The Great U-Turn: Corporate Restructuring and the Polarizing of America.* New York: Basic Books, 1988.

Hartmann, Heidi I. "The Unhappy Marriage of Marxism and Feminism." *Capital and Class: Towards A More Progressive Union* 8 (Summer 1979): 1–33.

Haymarket People's Fund. Brochure. Boston: Haymarket People's Fund.

Heatherly, Charles L., ed. *Mandate for Leadership: Policy Management in a Conservative Administration.* Washington, D.C.: The Heritage Foundation, 1981.

Hebdige, Dick. *Subculture: The Meaning of Style.* London: Methuen, 1979.

Heuchan, Laura M., "A Survey of Nonprofit Charitable Organizations." In *Working Papers,* 319–44. Washington, D.C.: Independent Sector and United Way Institute, 1986.

Hodgkinson, Virginia Ann, and Murray S. Weitzman. *Dimensions of the Independent Sector: A Statistical Profile.* 2d ed. Washington, D.C.: Independent Sector, 1986.

———. *Giving and Volunteering in the United States: Findings from a National Survey.* Washington, D.C.: Independent Sector, 1988.

The Holy Bible, Revised Standard Version, Luke 6:38.

Bibliography

Homans, George Casper. "Human Behavior as Exchange." *American Journal of Sociology* 63, no. 3 (May 1958): 535–606.

———. *Social Behavior: Its Elementary Forms.* New York: Harcourt, Brace & World, 1961, revised; 1974.

Houston, Paul. "Big Cash Gifts to Parties Skirt Election Laws." *Los Angeles Times,* 3 October 1988, sec. I, 1.

Independent Sector, *Americans Volunteer 1985.* Washington, D.C.: Independent Sector, 1986.

Institute for Public Policy and Administration. *Part of the Solution: Innovative Approaches to Nonprofit Funding.* Washington, D.C.: Union for Experimenting Colleges and Universities, 1988.

James, Estelle. "The Nonprofit Sector in Comparative Perspective." In *The Nonprofit Sector: A Research Handbook,* edited by Walter W. Powell, 397–415. New Haven: Yale University Press, 1987.

Jenkins, J. Craig. "Foundation Funding of Progressive Social Movements." In *Grantseekers Guide.* 2d ed. Edited by Jill Shellow. Mt. Kisco, N.Y.: Moyer Bell, [1985].

———. "Social Movement Philanthropy and American Democracy." Department of Sociology, Ohio State University. February 1988. Typescript.

Johnson, Robert Matthews. *The First Charity: How Philanthropy Can Contribute to Democracy in America.* Cabin John, Md.: Seven Locks, 1988.

Jordon, Mary. "18 Million Homeless Seen by 2003: Study Blames Erosion of Low-Income Housing, Increase in Poor." *Washington Post,* 3 June 1987, A8.

Judge, Ken, and Martin Knapp. "Efficiency in the Production of Welfare: The Public and Private Sectors Compared." In *The Future of Welfare,* edited by Rudolf Klein and Michael O'Higgins, 131–49. Oxford: Basil Blackwell, 1983.

Karl, Barry D., and Stanley N. Katz. "The American Private Philanthropic Foundation and the Public Sphere, 1890–1930." *Minerva* 19 (1981): 236–70.

——— "Foundations and Ruling Class Elites." *Daedalus* 116, no. 1 (Winter 1987): 1 40.

Katz, Michael B. *In the Shadow of the Poorhouse: A Social History of Welfare in America.* New York: Basic Books, 1986.

Kentucky Foundation for Women. *Articulating a Women's Perspective.* Brochure.

Keynes, John Maynard. *The General Theory of Employment, Interest, and Money.* London: Macmillan, 1936.

Kirstein, George G. *The Rich: Are They Different?* Boston: Houghton Mifflin, 1968.

Knapp, Martin. "Parallel Bars or Extension Ladder? Constraints on Long Run Supply Response of the Voluntary Sector." Discussion paper no. 401. University of Kent, Personal Social Services Research Unit, Canterbury, England, 1985.

Knapp, Martin, and Spyros Missiakoulis. "Inter-Sectoral Cost Comparisons: Day Care for the Elderly." *Journal of Social Policy* 11, part 3 (July 1982): 335–54.

Knauft, E. B. "Profiles of Effective Corporate Giving Programs." Washington, D.C.: Independent Sector, 1985.

——— "The Management of Corporate Giving Programs." Working paper no. 114. New Haven: Yale University Program on Non-Profit Organizations, 1986.

Kolko, Gabriel. *Wealth and Power in America: An Analysis of Social Class and Income Distribution.* New York: Praeger, 1962.

Komarovsky, Mirra. *Women in College: Shaping New Feminine Identities.* New York: Basic Books, 1985.

Koskoff, David, E. *The Mellons: The Chronicle of America's Richest Family.* New York: Crowell, 1978.

Kramer, Ralph M. *Voluntary Agencies in the Welfare State.* Berkeley: University of California Press, 1981.

Kurian, George Thomas. *The New Book of World Rankings.* New York: Facts on File, 1984.

Lampman, Robert J. *The Share of Top Wealth-Holders in National Wealth, 1922-1956.* Princeton: Princeton University Press, 1962.

Landers, Robert K. "Think Tanks and the New Partisans?" Editorial Research Reports, *Congressional Quarterly* 1, no. 23 (23 June 1986).

Langemann, Ellen Condliffe. *Private Power for the Public Good: A History of the Carnegie Foundation for the Advancement of Teaching.* Middletown, Conn.: Wesleyan University Press, 1983.

Leonard, Burr. "Dropouts Make Good." *Forbes,* 26 October 1987, 77.

Levy, Frank. *Dollars and Dreams: The Changing American Income Distribution.* New York: Russell Sage Foundation, 1987.

Littlefield, Roy Everett III. *William Randolph Hearst: His Role in American Progressivism.* Lanham, Md.: University Press of America, 1980.

Loomis, Carol J. "The Rockefellers: End of Dynasty?" and "The Ultimate Family Room." *Fortune,* 4 August 1986, 26–37.

Lord, Benjamin, ed. *America's Wealthiest People: Their Philanthropic and Nonprofit Affiliations.* Washington, D.C.: Taft Corporation, 1984.

Los Angeles Times. "The State of the Union, Text: 'What Unites . . . Outweighs What Divides Us.' " 26 January 1988, sec. I, 17.

———. "$17-Million Trust to Aid UC Irvine and Arts Groups." 1 December 1988, sec. I, 41.

Lundberg, Ferdinand. *The Rich and the Super-Rich: A Study of the Power of Money Today.* New York: Lyle Stuart, 1968.

McPherson, J. Miller, and Lynn Smith-Lovin. "Women and Weak Ties: Differences by Sex in the Size of Voluntary Organizations." *American Journal of Sociology* 87, no. 4 (January 1987): 883–904.

Malinowski, Bronislaw. *Argonauts of the Western Pacific: An Account of Native Enterprise and Adventure in the Archipelagoes of Melanesian New Guinea.* New York: Dutton, 1961.

Manley, John F. "Neo-Pluralism: A Class Analysis of Pluralism I and Pluralism II." *American Political Science Review* 77, no. 2 (June 1983): 369–89.

Marcus, George E. "Law in the Development of Dynastic Families Among American Business Elites: The Domestication of Capital and the Capitalization of the Family." *Law and Society Review* 14, no. 4 (Summer 1980): 859–903.

———. "The Fiduciary Role in American Family Dynasties and Their Institutional Legacy: From the Law of Trusts to Trust in the Establishment." In *Elites: Ethnographic Issues,* edited by George E. Marcus, 221–65. Albuquerque: University of New Mexico Press, 1983.

Marx, Karl. *Capital: A Critique of Political Economy.* Vol. 3. New York: International Publishers, 1967.

Mauss, Marcel. *The Gift: Forms and Functions of Exchange in Archaic Societies.* Translated by Ian Cunnison. New York: Norton, 1967.

Mead, Margaret. *Male and Female: A Study of the Sexes in a Changing World.* New York: Morrow, 1949.

Melillo, Wendy. "New Group Urges Companies to Let More Charities Take Part in Fund Raising by Payroll Deduction" and "United Way Studies Strategies to Fend Off Competitors." *Chronicle of Philanthropy,* 25 July 1989, 4–8.

Merton, Robert. *Social Theory and Social Structure.* New York: Free Press, 1968.

Metropolitan Museum of Art. *Annual Report.* New York: Metropolitan Museum of Art, 1986/87.

Middleton, Melissa. "Nonprofit Boards of Directors: Beyond the Governance Function." In *The Nonprofit Sector: A Research Handbook,* edited by Walter W. Powell, 141–53. New Haven: Yale University Press, 1987.

Miller, Jean Baker. *Toward a New Psychology of Women.* Boston: Beacon Press, 1976.

Mills, C. Wright. *The Power Elite.* New York: Oxford University Press, 1956.

Mintz, Beth, and Michael Schwartz. *The Power Structure of American Business.* Chicago: University of Chicago Press, 1985.

Mitchell, Juliet. *Psychoanalysis and Feminism.* New York: Pantheon, 1974.

———. *Women's Estate.* New York: Vintage, 1973.

Mizruchi, Mark S., and Michael Schwartz, eds. *Intercorporate Relations: The Structural Analysis of Business.* New York: Cambridge University Press, 1987.

Mogil, Christopher, and Chuck Collins. Untitled book manuscript. Philadelphia: New Society. Forthcoming.

Ms. Foundation for Women, *Campaign for a Second Decade, Building Lasting Change from the Bottom Up, Woman by Woman, Group by Group, Community by Community.* Promotional material. New York, 1988.

Murray, Charles. *Losing Ground—American Social Policy, 1950–1980.* New York: Basic Books, 1984.

Nader, Laura. "Up the Anthropologist—Perspectives Gained from Studying Up." In *Reinventing Anthropology,* edited by Dell H. Hymes. New York: Pantheon, 1972.

Nash, Alanna. "The Woman Who Overturned an Empire." *Ms.,* June 1986, 44–46.

Nason, John W. *Trustees and the Future of Foundations.* New York: Council on Foundations, 1977.

National Network of Women's Funds. "Development of Funds." Special report no. 3, Spring 1986. National Network of Women's Funds, 141 Fifth Avenue, New York, N.Y. 10010.

New York. "(In Style) The Life of the Party." 9 January 1989, 14.

Bibliography

New York Times. "Lawyers Get $6.3 Million in Buck Trust Fund Case." 7 September 1986, 26.

———. "Study Sees Strain on Homeless Aid: Shelters and Food Programs Fail to Meet Needs of the Poor, U.S. Mayors Say." 17 December 1987, B21.

———. "Trump: Symbol of a Gaudy, Impatient Time." 31 January 1988, H32.

———. Transcript of Bush speech accepting presidential nomination. 19 August 1988, 14.

———. "Disney Stock in Bass Divorce." 9 November 1988, D19.

New York Times News Service. "Charity to Get Packard Fortune: $2 Billion Caps Family's Philanthropic Commitment." San Diego Union, 29 April 1988, A1.

Nielsen, John. "Sallie Bingham: After a Woman Is Scorned, A Publishing Family Cashes Out." Fortune, 5 January 1987, 93.

Nielsen, Waldemar A. The Endangered Sector. New York: Columbia University Press, 1979.

———. The Golden Donors: A New Anatomy of the Great Foundations. New York: Dutton, 1985.

O'Connell, Brian. Effective Leadership in Voluntary Organizations. New York: Association Press, 1976.

———. The Board Member's Book: Making a Difference in Voluntary Organizations. New York: Foundation Center, 1985.

Odendahl, Teresa. "Foundations and the Nonprofit Sector." In America's Wealthy and the Future of Foundations, edited by Teresa Odendahl, 27–42. New York: Foundation Center, 1987.

———. "Independent Foundations and Wealthy Donors: An Overview." In America's Wealthy and the Future of Foundations, edited by Teresa Odendahl, 1–26. New York: Foundation Center, 1987.

———, ed. America's Wealthy and the Future of Foundations. New York: Foundation Center, 1987.

Odendahl, Teresa, and Elizabeth Boris. "Board-Staff Relations: A Delicate Balance." Foundation News 24, no. 3 (May/June 1983): 34–45.

Odendahl, Teresa Jean, Elizabeth Trocolli Boris, and Arlene Kaplan Daniels. Working in Foundations: Career Patterns of Women and Men. New York: Foundation Center, 1985.

O'Reilly, Brian. "The Computer Kings: A Quartet of High-Tech Pioneers." Fortune, 12 October 1987, 148–49.

Organization for Economic Co-operation and Development. Social Expenditure, 1960–1990: Problems of Growth and Control. Paris: OECD, 1985.

Ortner, Sherry B., and Harriet Whitehead, eds. Sexual Meanings: The Cultural Construction of Gender and Sexuality. Cambridge: Cambridge University Press, 1981.

Ostrander, Susan A. Women of the Upper Class. Philadelphia: Temple University Press, 1984.

———. "Upper-Class Women: Class Consciousness as Conduct and Meaning." In Power Structure Research, edited by G. William Domhoff, 73–96. Beverly Hills, Calif.: Sage, 1980.

Ostrander, Susan, A., and Stuart Langton, eds. Shifting the Debate: Public/Private Sector Relations in the Modern Welfare State. New Brunswick, N.J.: Transaction, 1987.

Ostrower, Francie. "The Role of Advisors to the Wealthy." In America's Wealthy and the Future of Foundations, edited by Teresa Odendahl, 247–66. New York: Foundation Center, 1987.

Packard, Vance. The Ultra Rich: How Much Is Too Much? Boston: Little, Brown, 1989.

Parker, Richard. The Myth of the Middle Class: Notes on Affluence and Equality. New York: Harper Colophon, 1972.

Piven, Frances Fox, and Richard A. Cloward. Regulating the Poor: The Functions of Public Welfare. New York: Pantheon, 1971.

———. The New Class War: Reagan's Attack on the Welfare State and Its Consequences. New York: Pantheon, 1982.

Polivy, Deborah Kaplan. "A Study of the Admissions Policies and Practices of Eight Local United Way Organizations." Working paper no. 49. New Haven: Yale University Program on Non-Profit Organizations, 1982.

———. "Increasing Giving Options in Corporate Charitable Payroll Deduction Programs: Who Benefits?" Working paper no. 83. New Haven: Yale University Program on Non-Profit Organizations, 1985.

Projector, Dorothy S., and Gertrude S. Weiss. Survey of Financial Characteristics of Consumers. Washington, DC: Board of Governors of the Federal Reserve System, 1966.

Reed, Julia. "The Bass Brothers Fish in New Waters." U.S. News and World Report, 9 February 1987, 48–49.

Reich, Robert B. Tales of a New America. New York: Times Books, 1987.

Roderick, Kevin, and Claudia Luther. "1 Democratic, 2 GOP House Seats May Be Vulnerable." *Los Angeles Times,* 9 June 1988, 3.

Rosaldo, Michelle, and Louise Lamphere, eds. *Woman, Culture, and Society.* Stanford, Calif.: Stanford University Press, 1974.

Salamon, Lester M. "Partners in Public Service: The Scope and Theory of Government-Nonprofit Relations." In *The Nonprofit Sector: A Research Handbook,* edited by Walter W. Powell, 99–117. New Haven: Yale University Press, 1987.

———. "The Voluntary Sector and the Future of the Welfare State." *Nonprofit and Voluntary Sector Quarterly* 18, no. 1 (Spring 1989): 11–24.

Salamon, Lester M., and Alan J. Abramson. *The Federal Budget and the Nonprofit Sector.* Washington, D.C.: Urban Institute Press, 1982.

Salamon, Lester M., James C. Musselwhite, Jr., and Carol J. De Vita. "Partners in Public Service: Government and the Nonprofit Sector in the Welfare State." In *Working Papers,* 3–38. Washington, D.C.: Independent Sector and United Way Institute, 1986.

Salamon, Lester M., and Kenneth P. Voytek. *Managing Foundations Assets: An Analysis of Foundation Investment and Payout Procedures and Performance.* New York: Foundation Center, 1989.

Sanday, Peggy Reeves. *Female Power and Male Dominance: On the Origins of Sexual Inequality.* Cambridge: Cambridge University Press, 1981.

Schervish, Paul, G., and Andrew Herman. *The Study on Wealth and Philanthropy Final Report.* Chestnut Hill, Mass.: T. B. Murphy Foundation Charitable Trust, Social Welfare Research Institute, Boston College, 1989.

———. "Varieties of Philanthropic Logic Among the Wealthy." In *Working Papers.* Washington D.C.: Independent Sector and United Way Institute, 1987.

Schneider, David M. *Class Differences and Sex Roles in American Kinship and Family Structure.* Englewood Cliffs, N.J.: Prentice-Hall, 1973.

Schwartz, Marvin. "Preliminary Estimates of Personal Wealth, 1982: Composition and Assets." In *Statistics of Income (SOI) Bulletin* (U.S. Department of the Treasury, Internal Revenue Service) 4, no. 3 (1984–85): 1–17.

Schwartz, Michael, ed. *The Structure of Power in America: The Corporate Elite as a Ruling Class.* New York: Holmes & Meier, 1987.

Sedgwick, John. *Rich Kids.* New York: William Morrow, 1985.

Sidel, Victor W., and Ruth Sidel. *A Healthy State: An International Perspective on the Crisis in United States Medical Care.* New York: Pantheon, 1983.

Silk, Leonard, and Mark Silk. *The American Establishment.* New York: Basic Books, 1980.

Simmel, Georg. *Conflict and The Web of Group Affiliations.* Translated by Kurt H. Wolff and Reinhard Bendix. New York: Free Press, 1955.

Simon, John G. "Charity and Dynasty Under the Federal Tax System." *The Probate Lawyer* 5 (Summer 1978): 1–91.

———. "The Tax Treatment of Nonprofit Organizations: A Review of Federal and State Policies." In *The Nonprofit Sector: A Research Handbook,* edited by Walter W. Powell, 67–98. New Haven, Conn.: Yale University Press, 1987.

Singular, Stephen. "Women's Fund Targets $10 million in Endowments." *Denver Post,* 12 June 1987, C1–2.

Sivard, Ruth Leger. *World Military and Social Expenditures.* 11th ed. Washington, D.C.: World Priorities, 1986.

Smith, Dorothy. "Women, the Family, and Corporate Capitalism." *Berkeley Journal of Sociology* 20 (1975–76): 55–90.

———. "A Sociology for Women." In *The Prism of Sex: Essays on the Sociology of Knowledge,* edited by Julia A. Sherman and Evelyn Torton Beck. Madison, Wis.: University of Wisconsin Press, 1979.

Smith, James A. *The Policy Elite.* New York: Free Press. Forthcoming.

Smith, James D. "An Estimate of Income of the Very Rich." In *Papers in Quantitative Economics,* edited by James P. Quirk, 254–61. Lawrence, Kans.: University of Kansas Press, 1968.

Bibliography

———. "The Concentration of Personal Wealth in America, 1969." *The Review of Income and Wealth.* Series 20, no. 2 (1974): 148–80.

Smith, James D., and Stephen D. Franklin. "The Concentration of Personal Wealth, 1922–1969." *American Economic Review* 64, no. 2 (1974): 162–67.

Stack, Carol. *All Our Kin: Strategies for Survival in a Black Community.* New York: Harper & Row, 1975.

Stauder, Kathleen. "Profile: How the Bass Brothers Do their Deals." *Fortune,* 17 September 1984, 144ff.

Stein, Mark A. "Attorneys Get $10 Million in Charity Fight." *Los Angeles Times,* 7 September 1986, 3.

Steuerle, Eugene. "Charitable Giving Patterns of the Wealthy." In *America's Wealthy and the Future of Foundations,* edited by Teresa Odendahl, 203–221. New York: Foundation Center, 1987.

Story, Ronald. *The Forging of an Aristocracy: Harvard and the Boston Upper Class, 1900–1970.* Middletown, Conn.: Wesleyan University Press, 1980.

Swanberg, W. A. *Citizen Hearst.* New York: Scribner's, 1961.

Taylor, John. "Party Place: The High Life at the Gilded Metropolitan Museum." *New York,* 9 January 1989, 20.

Teltsch, Kathleen. "Network of 'Alternative' Philanthropies Is Forming." *New York Times,* 5 July 1983, A10.

———. "The Cousins: The Fourth Generation of Rockefellers." *New York Times Magazine,* 30 December 1984, 12ff.

———. Network of Women Hopes to Change American Philanthropy." *New York Times,* 14 May 1986, C7.

———. "Increase in Charitable Donations in '87 Was Lowest in 12 Years." *New York Times,* 26 June 1988, 18.

Tickamyer, Ann R. "Wealth and Power: A Comparison of Men and Women in the Property Elite." *Social Forces* 60, no. 2 (December 1981): 463–81.

Useem, Michael. *The Inner Circles: Large Corporations and the Rise of Business Political Activity in the U.S. and U.K.* New York: Oxford University Press, 1984.

U.S. Bureau of the Census. "Household Wealth and Asset Ownership: 1984." *Household Economic Studies,* series P-70, no. 7. Washington, D.C.: U.S. Government Printing Office, 1986.

———. *Statistical Abstract of the United States: 1988.* 108th ed. Washington, D.C.: U.S. Department of Commerce, 1987.

Vanguard Public Foundation. *A Brief History of Vanguard Public Foundation.* San Francisco: Vanguard Public Foundation. Typescript.

Vanguard Public Foundation (Katy Butler, Laura Bouyea, and Barbara Garza). *Robin Hood Was Right: A Guide to Giving Your Money for Social Change.* San Francisco: Vanguard Public Foundation, 1977.

Van Til, Jon. "The Boundaries of the Independent Sector." In *Working Papers,* 57–66. Washington, D.C.: Independent Sector and United Way Institute, 1988.

———. *Mapping the Third Sector: Voluntarism in a Changing Economy.* New York: Foundation Center, 1988.

Walsh, Elsa. "Alternative Foundations Support Social Change: Young Givers Spurn Usual Philanthropies." *Washington Post,* 25 December 1984, A1.

Warner, W. Lloyd. *American Life: Dream and Reality.* Chicago: University of Chicago Press, 1953.

———. *The Living and the Dead: A Study of the Symbolic Life of Americans.* New Haven: Yale University Press, 1959.

Warner, W. Lloyd, and Paul S. Lunt. *The Social Life of a Modern Community.* Yankee City Series, vol. 1. New Haven: Yale University Press, 1941.

———. *The Status System of a Modern Community.* Yankee City Series, vol. 2. New Haven: Yale University Press, 1942.

Weber, Nathan, ed. *Giving USA: The Annual Report on Philanthropy for the Year 1987.* New York: American Association of Fundraising Counsel, 1988.

White, Arthur H., and John Bartolomeo. *Corporate Giving: The Views of Chief Executive Officers of Major American Corporations.* Washington, D.C.: Council on Foundations, 1982.

Wilensky, Harold L. "Foreword." In *Voluntary Agencies in the Welfare State,* by Ralph M. Karmer, xiv–xxii. Berkeley: University of California Press, 1981.

Willens, Michele. "'Rich Kids' Have a New Way to Give." *USA Today,* 21 September 1984, 1B.

Williams, Roger M. "All in the Family (Well, Mostly)." *Foundation News,* July/August 1984, 42–49.

———. "Capital Clout." *Foundation News,* July/August 1989, 14–19.

Williamson, Peter J. "What's Reasonable? Investment Expectations and the Foundation Payout Rate." *Foundation News,* January/February 1976, 13–18.

———. "Inflation and the Foundation Payout Rate." *Foundation News,* March/April 1981, 18–24.

"Yale's 1988 Fiscal Year." *Yale Alumni Magazine,* October 1988, 76–77.

Index

Abramson, Alan J., 60
Access, 244–45
Accountability, 241–45
Accountants, 217–18, 227n9
Adler, Cyrus, 139
Advisers: and accountability, 244; accountants, 217–
  18; attorneys, 214–17; bank trust officers, 218–
  19; categories of, 210; continuum of, 210; creden-
  tialing of, 244; dependency on, 89; development
  officers, 218; entrepreneur, 224–26; future for,
  227–31; multi-generation family, 89, 95, 226–27,
  268n37; need for, 210; personal philanthropic,
  210, 219–27; professional technicians, 10–11, 210,
  214–19; role of, 209–10; to self-made wealthy,
  222–24; social circles of, 211–13; of women, 111–
  12
AEI (American Enterprise Institute), 56, 119
AJC (Associated Jewish Charities), 155
Akers, John, 38
Allen, Charles, Jr., 9
Allen, Herbert, 9
Allen, Michael Patrick, 280n2
Alliance for Choice in Giving, 243
Alternative fund movement, 164; Chinook Fund,
  180–84, 275nn26,27; control of grant-making in,
  167, 176–79, 274n13; and dynasties, 98; Funding
  Exchange, 179–80; Haymarket People's Fund,
  163, 164–68, 274nn3,10, 275n30; Jewish philan-
  thropists in, 141, 153–54, 156–58; Pillsbury
  network in, 164–68; Vanguard Public Founda-
  tion, 164, 165, 168–79; viability of, 184–86; vs.
  women's foundations and peace development
  funds, 274n9
Aluminum Company of America, 72

Amalgamated Rich Folks (ARF), 172
American Association of Fundraising Counsel,
  279n13
American Enterprise Institute (AEI), 56, 119
American Express, 52
Anderson, Martin, 56, 57
Andrew W. Mellon Foundation, 75–76, 77
Anne Burnette and Charles D. Tandy Foundation,
  21
Annuities, 240
Anonymity, 26, 258n41
Appalachian Community Fund, 275n26
Apple Computer, 52
Appleton, Crawford (pseudonym), 223–24
Appreciated assets, 27, 63–64, 266n66
Archuleta, Kathy, 200, 276n16
ARF (Amalgamated Rich Folks), 172
Arts: Bass family donations to, 20, 22; benefits to
  elite of, 16; board of directors for, 258n33, 260n68;
  Brooke Astor's contributions to, 115–16; chari-
  table exchange for, 40; gaining entrée via, 33, 38,
  137; Klepper family donations to, 122, 123; Lucile
  Packard's involvement in, 119; Mellon family
  donations to, 72, 73, 75, 76, 265n50; promoting
  social change through, 204–7; size of donations
  to, 9; trust funds for, 28
Artwork, donation of, 258n43
Asset-holding, 255n33
Assets, contribution of, 27, 63–64, 266n66
Associated Jewish Charities (AJC), 155
Astor, Brooke, 114–16
Atlantic Richfield Company, 55
Attorneys, 94, 214–17, 277n5
Auchincloss, Louis, 114, 115

Auten, Gerald, 62
Authority, of women, 111–16; *see also* Control
Automobiles, 24, 29, 259*nn*53,54
Avalon Foundation, 75

Backdoor authority and control, 111–16
Balance of power, 45, 262*n*3; *see also* Control
Balls, charity, 41–42
Baltimore Common Wealth, 275*n*26
Bank trust officers, 218–19, 277*n*11
Baroody, William, Sr., 56
Bass, Anne, 22, 29, 33
Bass, Edward Perry, 19, 20, 21
Bass, Lee Marshall, 20, 21
Bass, Nancy Lee, 20
Bass, Perry Richardson, 20–21
Bass, Ramona Seeligsons, 21
Bass, Robert Muse, 20, 21–22, 29
Bass, Sid Richardson, 19, 20, 21, 22, 26, 29
Bass Brothers Enterprises, Inc., 21
Bass family, 19–23
Bass Group, Robert M., 21
Bates, Harold (pseudonym), 226–27
Bennett, Jane (pseudonym), 94–98, 103–4, 111–12,
    113, 114
Bequests: Andrew W. Mellon Foundation, 75–76,
    77; by Astors, 114–16; attorneys' influence on,
    214–15; bank trust officers and, 218–19; Buck
    Trust, 10; David and Lucile Packard Foundation,
    118–21; forms of, 27–28; to nonprofits vs. next
    generation, 126–31; Sarah Scaife Foundation, 73–
    74; size of, 49; tax reforms and, 239–40; to
    Women's Foundation, 191
Beth Israel Medical Center, 253*n*13
Bingham, Barry, Jr., 206, 207
Bingham, Barry, Sr., 206, 207
Bingham, Mary Kenan Flagler, 205
Bingham, Robert Worth, 205
Bingham, Sallie, 100, 187, 204–7, 276*n*25
Board of directors: community, 175–78, 182–83;
    control by, 35, 233–34; dual, 175–77; serving on,
    33–35, 36–37, 260*n*68
Bodyguards, 26
Boy's Incorporated, 21, 157*n*16
Bread and Roses Community Fund, 164, 274*n*7
Bronx Zoo, 116
Brookings Institution, 56
Brophy, Edra E., 28
Bruce, Ailsa Mellon, 72, 75
Bruce, David K. E., 75
Buck, Beryl, 10

Buck Center on Aging, 263*n*25
Buck Trust, 10, 263*n*25
Burnett, Nancy Packard, 120
Burnette, Anne, and Charles D. Tandy Foundation,
    21
Bush, George, 11–12, 234, 235
Business, and charity, 49–54, 263*n*16
Business expense, treating gift as, 52, 264*n*33

"Calling cards," 144, 146, 147, 151, 159
Canada, nonprofit activity in, 65
Capital, safeguarding of, 26–27
Capitalism, 44–49
Car(s), of philanthropists, 24, 29, 259*nn*53,54
Carborundum, 72
Cargo system, 261*n*77
Carnegie, Andrew, 262*n*8
Carnegie Endowment for International Peace, 56–57
Carnegie Hall, 149
Carnegie Institute, 74
Carnegie Museum, 73
Castilleja School, 119
Cause-related marketing, 52
Ceiling, for charitable contributions, 239
Center for Community Change, 263*n*25
Center for Strategic and International Studies (CSIS),
    56
Central Park Conservancy, 149
Charitable deductions, 61–63, 238–39, 262*n*15,
    265*n*60
Charitable donations: ceiling for, 239; channels for,
    27–28
Charitable exchange, 39–42, 260*n*72
Charitable lead trust, 240, 258*n*48
Charity balls, 41–42
Charter Fund, 244
Children: care of, 107, 270*n*16; foundations in social-
    ization of, 87–88, 152–53; inheritance by, 121,
    126–31, 135–36; lifestyle of privileged, 25
Children's Health Council, 120
Children's Hospital at Stanford University, 253*n*13
Chinook Fund, 180–84, 275*nn*26,27
Choate Rosemary Hall, 9, 75
Christic Institute, 265*n*42
CitiCorp, 53
Class, vs. culture, 5
Class suicide, 279*n*9
Clifford, Jonathon (pseudonym), 89–94
Clothing of philanthropists, 29
Cloward, Richard A., 46
Clubs, 8

Index

CNP (Council on National Priorities), 172, 183

Coca-Cola, 53

Coles, Robert, 25

Colorado Atomic-Agent Orange Veterans Coalition, 183

Colorado Trust, 201

Columbia University, 9

Combined Federal Campaign, 243

Common Capital Support Fund, 275n26

Common Counsel, 244

Community activists: at Chinook Fund, 182–83; at Haymarket People's Fund, 167; at Vanguard Public Foundation, 169, 176

Community board: at Chinook Fund, 182–83; at Vanguard Public Foundation, 175–78

Community foundations, 27, 123, 258n47, 279n6

Community Fund, 145

Computer companies, funding by, 52, 132–33, 263n30

Confidentiality, 241

Conover, Catherine Mellon, 76

Conover, Timothy, 76

Control: in alternative fund movement, 167, 176–79, 274n13; by board of directors, 35, 233–34; consequences of elite, 66–68; and funding, 35–36, 233; representativeness and, 242–45, 280n20; by women, 111–16, 207–8

Cornell University, 253n13

Corporate giving, 49–54, 263n16

Cott, Nancy F., 116

Council of Jewish Federations, 148

Council on Foreign Relations, 57

Council on Foundations, 119, 244, 278n14

Council on National Priorities (CNP), 172, 183

Credit card companies, fundraising by, 52–53

Crossroads Fund, 275n26

CSIS (Center for Strategic and International Studies), 56

Cult of domesticity, 116

Culture of philanthropy, 3–5; and gender, 116–17

Dahl, Robert A., 233

Daughters, unmarried, 102–5

David and Lucile Packard Foundation, 118

de Beauvoir, Simone, 269n3, 271n21, 276n8

Decision-making process, representativeness of, 242–43

Democracy, 44–49, 233, 245

Development officers, 218

Dilworth, J. Richardson, 254n18

Disney Foundation, Lillian B., 263n25

Division of labor by gender, 100–1, 269nn3,9

Dolan, Brian (pseudonym), 126–31

Dolan, Ginger (pseudonym), 126

Domesticity, cult of, 116

Double standard, for giving, 36, 260n69

Dynasties, 71–72; ambivalence, resolution, and deception in, 98–99; development and life of, 277n6; fourth-generation young woman, 94–98; the Mellons, 72–80; second-generation middle-aged man, 80–84; starting a, 121–25; third-generation elderly man, 89–94; third-generation middle-aged woman, 85–89

Education, 30–31, 251n2, 259nn60,61

Edwards, Valerie Roxanne, 191

Eisenberg, Pablo, 36, 270n3

Endowment: of foundations, 77–79; of nonprofit organizations, 126–31

Entrepreneur advisers, 224–26

Equipment, giving, 133

Estate(s), 29–30

Estate multiplier method, 255n33

Estate planning, 214–15, 216

Estate tax laws: as framework for philanthropy, 27–28, 258nn48,49; proposed reform of, 239–40; trust funds and, 122

Ethnocentrism, 47, 262n13

Exchange, charitable, 39–42, 260n72

"Expensing it out," 52, 264n33

Family advisers, 89, 95, 226–27, 268n37

Family-controlled business, 49–50

Family foundations, 27

Fannie Mae, 265n49

Farmers Insurance Group, 28

"Feminist" funders: demographics of, 188; Kentucky Foundation for Women, 204–7; need for, 187–88; network of, 189; paradox of, 188–89; power of, 207–8; vs. women funders, 275n5; Women's Foundation in San Francisco, 190–97; Women's Foundation of Colorado, 197–204, 276n14; work of, 190

Film Fund, 167

First-generation men: advisers to, 222–24; becoming old money, 137; characteristics of, 119, 271n8; David Packard, 118–21; endowment of nonprofits by, 126–31; incidence of, 280n2; Jewish, 145–49; potential recruits, 131–36; starting of dynasty by, 121–25

Flagler, Henry M., 205
Food for the Hungry, Inc., 264n32
Ford Foundation, 253n13, 263n25
Fort Worth Country Day School, 20
Foundation(s): community, 27, 123, 258n47, 279n6; endowed, 77–79; family, 27; money to establish, 130–31, 272n23; pass-through, 27, 148–49, 258n44; private, 27, 258nn44,45; role of philanthropist in, 88–89; in socialization of children, 87–88, 152–53; tax laws on, 236–37; time required by, 134–35
Foundation Center, 280n18
Foundation grants, 51, 263n25
France, nonprofit activity in, 65
Fuller, David, 168
Fund for Southern Communities, 275n26
Funding Exchange, 170, 172, 179–80, 274n13
Fundraisers, 218

Gary, Tracy DuVivier, 165, 172–73, 176, 190–97
Gary, Sam, 213
Gates, William, III, 38
Gathering Place, 204
Gay advocacy group, 220
"Gendering," 100–1, 116–17
Generational transitions, 225, 277n6
Gerbode, Philip, 168–69
Getty, Ann, 33
Gift giving, 261n75
Giving USA, 279n13
Goldin, Milton, 142
Goldwater, Barry, 56
Government, 44–49, 234–35
Grambs, Marya, 191, 192, 193
Grant making, reform of, 244–45
Grassroots activist, 182
Grassroots organizations, 36, 50–51
Gray, Charles, 275n25
Guilford Transportation, 76
Gulf Oil Company, 72, 73
Guy, Roma, 191, 192, 193

Hands Across America, 53
Hansmann, Henry, 279n5
Harriman, E. H. "Ned," 139
Havarah, 153
Haymarket People's Fund, 163, 164–68, 274nn3,10, 275n30
Headwaters Fund, 275n26

Health field, donations to, 9, 16, 253n13
Hearst, William Randolph, 253n11, 258n37
Heart Association, 41
Hennessy, Sumiko, 200, 276n17
Herbert Hoover Foundation, 119
Heritage Foundation, 56
Hewlett, William, 119, 132, 133, 134, 253n13
Hewlett-Packard Company, 52, 118, 119
High arts organizations, donations to, 38
Hill, James J., 139
Hoffman, Marion O., 253n13
Hole in the Wall Gang Camp, 10
Homosexual advocacy group, 220
Hoover Foundation, Herbert, 119
Hoover Institution, 56, 74
House(s), of philanthropists, 5–8
Household income, 12
Hunt, Swanee, 200, 202, 203, 204, 276nn18,19
Hunt, Theodore Ansbacher, 204
Hunt Alternatives Fund, 276n19

IBM, 52
Identity, of unmarried daughters, 104, 270n12
Ideology, of philanthropy, 44–49, 234
Income, household, 12
Income tax, 238–39
Independent Sector, 17, 280n18
Independent sector, *see* Nonprofit organizations
Individualism, 47
Information, need for, 241–42, 279n13, 280n18
Inheritance: incidence of, 280n2; vs. lifetime giving, 121, 126–31, 135–36
Inheritance taxes, *see* Estate tax laws
"Insider-outsiders," 221, 268n37
Institute for Policy Studies, 264n42
Institute for World Order, 265n42
International projects, funding of, 48

James, Estelle, 65
Jewish Agency for Israel, 148
Jewish Federation, 149, 151
Jewish National Fund, 146
Jewish philanthropists: background of, 140; Central vs. Eastern European, 140; conflicts and tensions in, 159–60; first-generation, 145–49; fundraising techniques of, 144; Jacob Henry Schiff, 138–40; oppression and, 142–43, 273n18; patterns of giving by, 141; proportion of, 141–42, 272n14; second-generation, 149–54; third-generation, 154–59; tradition of giving by, 138, 140–42, 143–44, 155

Index

Johnson, Ella S., 253n13
Johnson, Lady Bird, 115
Johnson, Robert Matthews, 245
Johnson, Samuel C., 253n13
Johnston, David, 241-42
Joint Foundation Support, 244
Jones, Susan (pseudonym), 104-5
Junior B'nai B'rith, 146
Junior League, 108-9

Kantor, Gerald B., 9
Kantor, Iris, 9
Katz, Michael B., 57
Kellogg, Mercedes, 21
Kennedy, Robert, 115
Kentucky Foundation for Women, 204-7
Kirstein, Lincoln, 22
Klepper, George (pseudonym), 121-25
Klepper, Helen (pseudonym), 122
Kluge, John W., 9
K Mart Corporation, 264n32
Knapp, Martin, 66
Knight, James L., 253n13
Knight Foundation, 253n15
Koppers, 72
Koskoff, David E., 73
Kramer, Ralph M., 66
Kravis, Henry R., 9
Kroc, Joan, 253n14
Kuhn, Loeb & Company, 138-39
Kula, 260n72

La Casa de las Madres, 173, 191-92
Lady bountiful, 101-2, 116-17
Landau, Nathan, 55
La Raza Legal Center, 48
Lawyers, 94, 214-17, 277n5
Leadership gift, 34
Lesbian projects, 199-200, 202
Levinson, Wendy (pseudonym), 154-59
Liberty Hill Foundation, 165, 179, 275n28
Lifestyle(s), 23-33; cars, 24, 29; charity vs. consumption in, 24-25; of children, 25; of men, 31-32; noblesse oblige, 24, 30; privacy vs. publicity, 26; residences, 25, 29-30; schooling, 30-31; of women, 32-33
Lillian B. Disney Foundation, 263n25
Live Oak Fund, 275n26
Loeb, Therese, 138

Loock Trust, Margaret, 253n15
Los Angeles Music Center, 263n25
Louisiana State University, 253n13
Lyle, Brenda, 197
Lynde and Harry Bradley Foundation, 253n15

Managing Inherited Wealth program, 193, 197
Mansions, 29-30
Margaret Loock Trust, 253n15
Marin Community Foundation, 10
Marsh, Evelyn (pseudonym), 109-11
Massachusetts General Hospital, 253n13
Matching gift, 140, 144, 159
May, Cordelia Scaife, 74, 76
Mayer, Joseph (pseudonym), 145-49
McGuire, Ruth M., 191
McKenzie River Gathering, 275n25
McKnight Foundation, 263n25
Media coverage, 241-42, 279n17
Medical Coalition for the Rights of Women, 48
Mellon, Andrew W., 72, 265n50
Mellon, Constance Barber, 75
Mellon, Paul W., x, 9, 72, 75
Mellon, Richard B., 72
Mellon, Richard King, 72, 73
Mellon, Richard Prosser, 74-75, 77
Mellon, Seward Prosser, 74, 75, 76, 77
Mellon, Thomas, 72
Mellon, Timothy, 76, 77
Mellon and Sons, Richard K., 74, 76
Mellon family dynasty, 72-80
Mellon Family Foundation, R. K., 75
Mellon Foundation, Andrew W., 75-76, 77
Mellon Foundation, Richard King, 75, 76-77
Mellon Institute, 73
Mellon National Bank, 72, 73, 74
Men: first-generation, 118-37; second-generation middle-aged, 80-84; third-generation elderly, 89-94
Metropolitan Museum of Art, 9, 115-16, 254n18
Mi Casa Women's Resource Center, 204
Middle-aged philanthropists: second-generation Jewish couple, 149-54; second-generation man, 80-84, 268n45; third-generation woman, 85-89
Milbury, Cassandra King Mellon, 75
Millionaires, number of, 13, 255n32
Miss Porter's School, 75
Mitchell, Christina (pseudonym), 131-32
Mitchell, James (pseudonym), 131-36
Money: old vs. new, 71, 137, 267n1, 268n42; talking about, 28, 259n52

Montefiore Hospital, 140
Monterey Bay Aquarium, 119–20
Morgan, J. P., 139
Mory's, *ix*
Mothers, 107–9
Mount Sinai Medical Center, 253*n*13
Ms. Foundation for Women, 188, 275*n*4
MTV, 264*n*32
Multi-generation family advisers, 89, 95, 226–27, 268*n*37

Nabisco, RJR, 264*n*32
National Black United Fund, 243
National Center for Charitable Statistics, 280*n*18
National Community Funds, 179
National Gallery of Art, 72, 75, 76, 265*n*50
Nationalism, 48, 262*n*13
National Jewish Resource Center, 153
National Network of Grantmakers, 278*n*14, 280*n*21
National Network of Women's Funds, 173
National Organization for Women (NOW), 188
Neighborhood Assistance Act Laws, 240
Neighborhood groups, 50–51
Netherlands, nonprofit activity in, 65, 266*n*70
Networks, philanthropic, 37–38, 39–42, 260*n*70
New Israel Fund, 153
Newman, Paul, 10
New money, 71, 137, 267*n*1
Newspaper coverage, 241–42, 279*n*17
New York, 151
New York City Ballet, 22
New York Community Trust, 153
New York Philharmonic, 149
New York Public Library, 116, 253*n*13
Nixon, Richard, 74
Noblesse oblige, 8–9; and lifestyle, 24, 30; vs. *shtadlanim*, 272*n*13; in third-generation elderly man, 89–94; training children in, 103
Noncash gifts, 63–64, 266*n*66
Nonprofit organizations, 16–17; benefits to elite of, 16, 23; board of directors of, 34–35, 37, 242–43; business contributions to, 49–54; charitable exchange in, 39; charity balls for, 41–42; choice of recipients in, 3–4, 23, 256*n*44; control of, 15, 17, 36, 222–23; cost of, 66, 266*n*77; directed money to, 227; effectiveness of, 66; endowment of, 126–31; in foreign countries, 64–66, 266*n*70; government and, 14–15, 57–60, 265*n*59; grassroots organizations, 17–18, 36, 50–51; joined by women, 270*n*15; middle class, 17; national organization for, 17, 280*n*18; overhead of, 125; political ide-

ology and, 47; and power elite, 4; recruitment for, 37–38; size of donations to, 9–10, 253*n*13; tax laws and, 14, 64–66; tax reform and, 236–38, 279*n*5; trustees of, 34–35
Northeast Louisiana University, 253*n*13
North Star Fund, 179, 180, 275*n*25
NOW (National Organization for Women), 188

Obey, David R., 13
O'Connell, Brian, 17, 243
Offices, of philanthropists, 8
Ohio State University, 39–40
Oil companies, funding by, 263*n*31
"Old boy network," 38
Old Dominion Foundation, 75
Old money, 71, 137, 267*n*1, 268*n*42
Olsen, Kenneth H., 253*n*15
Orange County Performing Arts Center, 28
Orr, Susan Packard, 121

Pacific Change, 168
Packard, David, 118–21, 132, 133, 134, 253*n*13
Packard, Julia E., 120
Packard, Lucile, 118–20, 253*n*13
Packard Foundation, David and Lucile, 118
Pass-through foundations, 27, 148–49, 258*n*44
Paternalism, 91, 130, 140
Payroll deduction, 243, 280*n*20
Pennington, C. B., 253*n*13
People's Fund, 275*n*26
People's Resource of Southwest Ohio, 275*n*25
Personal philanthropic advisers, 210, 219–27, 278*n*14
Personal Social Services Research Unit, 66
Petrie, Milton, 253*n*13
Philadelphia Orchestra, 260*n*68
Philadelphia People's Fund, 274*n*7
Philanthropic advisers, 210, 219–27, 278*n*14
Philanthropic donations, in 1987, 9–10, 253*n*13
Philanthropic Roundtable, 278*n*14, 280*n*21
Philanthropy system, 14–18
Phillips Academy, *x*, 251*n*2
Pillsbury, George, 163, 164, 165, 168, 172
Pillsbury, Sally, 164
Pillsbury, Sarah, 165
Piton Foundation, 199, 213
Pittsburgh Coal, 73
Piven, Frances Fox, 46
Planned Parenthood, 150, 263*n*25
Pluralism, 233–34

Index

Policy research institutes, 56–57, 264n42
Politics, 54–61; of Jewish philanthropists, 141, 152
Polivy, Deborah Kaplan, 280n20
Porter's School, Miss, 75
Portnoy, Fern, 199, 203, 213
Poverty, in America, 12–13, 254n28
Power, balance of, 45, 262n3; see also Control
Power elite, 4, 252n6
P-Rade, x, 251n6
Prep schools, 30–31, 251n2
Presbyterian Hospital, 9
Presidential campaigns, 55
Press coverage, 241–42, 279n17
Privacy, 26, 241, 258n41
Private charity, 11
Private foundations, 27, 258nn44,45
Professional advisers, 10–11, 210, 214–19
Property rights, 46
Provident Mutual Life Insurance Company, 253n13
Proyecto de Poder Trabajador Agricola, 183
Prudential Foundation, 264n32
Prudential Insurance Company, 264n32
Public charities, 236–37, 261n73
Publicity, 26
Public-private initiatives, 58
Public support test, 237, 261n73
Pueblans for Justice and Peace in Central America, 183
Pullman, 72

Radius Institute, 153
Rafferty, Max, 74
Reagan, Ronald, 11, 56, 74, 234
Recruitment, to philanthropy, 33–38
Red-lining, 50–51
Reform, in philanthropy, 232–36; of accountability and representativeness, 241–45; of democratic distribution of funds, 245; of tax policy, 236–40, 279n5
Reich, Robert B., 46 47
Reilly, William K., 22n26
Religion, and giving, 141, 273n16; see also Jewish philanthropists
Remainder trusts, 240, 258n48
Representativeness, 242–45, 280n20
Residences, of philanthropists, 25, 29–30
Responsibility, see Noblesse oblige
Retainers, 277n2
Reynolds, Sheila (pseudonym), 225–26
Richard King Mellon Foundation, 75, 76–77
Richard K. Mellon and Sons, 74, 76

Richards, Pamela (pseudonym), 105–7
Richardson, Sid Williams, 20
Richardson Foundation, Sid W., 20
Richardson Memorial Fund, Sid, 257n11
"Rich kids," 7
RJR Nabisco, 264n32
R. K. Mellon Family Foundation, 75
Robert M. Bass Group, 21
Rock Against Drugs, 264n32
Rockefeller, John D., III, 16, 40, 115
Rockefeller, Nelson, 267n20
Rudney, Gabriel, 62

Sachem Fund, 76
Sackler, Mortimer D., 260n64
Salamon, Lester M., 14–15, 57, 60
Salgo, Nicolas, 55
Salt Lake Citizens' Congress (SLCC), 50–51
San Francisco Symphony, 119
Sarah Scaife Foundation, 73–74, 77
Scaife, Alan, 73
Scaife, Richard M., 74, 76
Scaife, Sarah Mellon, 72, 73–74
Scaife Foundation, Sarah, 73–74, 77
Schiff, Frieda, 140, 272n9
Schiff, Jacob Henry, 138–40, 144
School(s): Bass family donations to, 20; charitable exchange for, 39–40; for children of elite, 30–31, 251n2, 259n60; clubs at, ix–x, 259n61; corporate contributions to, 263n31, 264n32; Mellon family donations to, 73, 75; Packards' donations to, 118–19; school functions and donations to, x; size of donations to, xi, 9, 16, 253n13; trust funds for, 28
Scott Paper Company, 53
Seattle Opera, 260n68
Second-generation philanthropists: middle-aged Jewish couple, 149–54; middle-aged man, 80–84, 268n45
Self-made millionaires, see First-generation men
Sexism, 100–1, 269nn3,9
Short, Natalie Guggenheim, 253n13
Shtadlanim, 139, 272n13
Sid Richardson Memorial Fund, 257n11
Sid W. Richardson Foundation, 20
Simmons, Harold, 253n13
Simon, John, 241
SLCC (Salt Lake Citizens' Congress), 50–51
Slote, Benjamin (pseudonym), 149–54
Slote, Myrna (pseudonym), 142, 143, 149–54
Smith, James A., 56

Smith, Samuel (pseudonym), 222–23
Social change, through the arts, 204–7
Social-change funders, 7, 168, 274*n*15
Social circles, 256*n*3
Social Darwinism, 46
Socialism, 45
Social welfare programs: government and, 57–60; size of contributions to, 9–10, 253*n*13; tax laws and, 64–66
Solicitation, of funds, 37–38
Split-interest trusts, 240, 258*n*48
Stanford University, 118–19, 253*n*13
Statistics, 241–42, 279*n*13, 280*n*18
Statue of Liberty, 52
Stein, David (pseudonym), 80–84
Steinem, Gloria, 187
Sterling, John William, 251*n*4
Stockton, Caroline (pseudonym), 85–89, 102, 112, 113, 114
Story, Paul (pseudonym), 224–25
Stratford Foundation, 253*n*15
Subculture, 5, 252*n*7
Super-rich, 12–13
Support organizations, 259*n*51
Sutphen, Judy, 166
Sweden, nonprofit activity in, 65, 266*n*70
Systems Development Corporation, 253*n*13

Tandy Foundation, Charles D., 21
Tax attorneys, 214
Tax laws, 61–66; charitable deductions, 61–63, 238–39, 262*n*15, 265*n*60; estate, 27–28, 122, 239–40, 258*nn*48,49; income, 238–39; on nonprofit organizations, 236–38, 279*n*5; proposed reform of, 233, 236–40; public support test, 237, 261*n*73; and redistribution of wealth, 64–66; Tax Reform Act, 63–64; trust funds and, 122, 124
Tax Reform Act (TRA) (1986), 63–64
Tax status, 14
Technical advisers, 10–11, 210, 214–19
Territorial Resource, A, 275*n*26
"Think tanks," 56–57, 264*n*42
Third-generation philanthropists: elderly man, 89–94; middle-aged woman, 85–89; young Jewish woman, 154–59
"Third sector," *see* Nonprofit organizations
Tithing, 139
Todd, Alice (pseudonym), 108–9, 113
Toomer, Barbara, 51
TRA (Tax Reform Act) (1986), 63–64
Trump, Blain, 260*n*64

Trump, Donald, 24
Trustees, 34
Trust funds, 10, 27–28, 122, 124
Tzedakah, 143, 144, 146

United Israel Appeal, 148
United Jewish Appeal (UJA), 142, 143, 150, 151
United Kingdom, nonprofit activity in, 65
United Way, 133, 145, 241, 243, 280*n*20
Universities: for children of elite, 31, 259*n*60; donations to, 9, 16, 253*n*13
University of California, 28, 253*n*13
University of Miami, 253*n*13
University of Pittsburgh, 73
University of Texas Health Science Center, 253*n*13
Urban Education Foundation of Philadelphia, 253*n*13

Vanguard Public Foundation: Amalgamated Rich Folks and new woman donor to, 172–73; community board at, 175–78; contributions to, 169–70; decade-long transition in, 173–77; donor board at, 176–77; early years of, 171–72, establishment of, 164, 168–69; founding member of, 170–71; George Pillsbury and, 164, 165; longtime donor to, 170; paid staff at, 175; size of grants at, 274*n*24; unresolved class conflicts in, 177–79
Voluntary agencies, *see* Nonprofit organizations
Volunteerism: control and, 17–18; of mothers, 108–9; politics of, 66, 266*n*76

Wagner, Robert, 115
Wake Forest University, 264*n*32
Walters, Mary Lou, 203
Warburg, Felix, 272*n*9
Wealth, distribution of, 11–13, 245
Welfare states, 45, 48
Wellman, Arthur O., 253*n*13
Wellman, Gullan M., 253*n*13
West Germany, nonprofit activity in, 65
Whiting, Jan, 197, 198–99, 201, 202
Whitney, John Hay, x
Wieboldt Foundation, 275*n*26
Williams, Rhonda, 279*n*9
Wisconsin Community Fund, 275*n*26
Wives, 109–11
Wolf Trap Foundation for the Performing Arts, 119

Index

Women: control by, 111–16, 207–8; and division of labor, 100–1, 269nn3,9; foundations created by, 259n62; fourth-generation young, 94–98; lifestyle of philanthropic, 32–33; in paying jobs, 108–9; and philanthropic culture, 116–17; status of, 102, 206, 270n10; third-generation Jewish, 154–59; third-generation middle-aged, 85–89; typical "lady bountiful," 101–2, 269n6; unmarried daughters and sisters, 102–7; volunteering by, 108–9, 270n15; wives and mothers, 107–11

Women Managing Wealth, 194

Women's Building, 173

Women's Center of Larimer County, 204

Women's Foundation in San Francisco, 165, 170, 173, 190–97

Women's Foundation of Colorado, 197–204, 276n14

Women's movement, see "Feminist" funders

World Policy Institute, 264n42

Yahudim, 139, 140

Yale-Harvard game, x

Yale University, ix–xi, 73, 75

Yidn, 140

Young Men's Hebrew Association (YMHA), 140

Young Men's Jewish Council, 147

Young women philanthropists: fourth-generation, 94–98; third-generation Jewish, 154–59

Young Women's Hebrew Association, 140